On the Arab-Jew, Palestine

On the Arab-Jew, Palestine, and Other Displacements

Selected Writings

Ella Shohat

www.plutobooks.com

First published 2017 by Pluto Press
345 Archway Road, London N6 5AA

www.plutobooks.com

Cover art:
Steve Sabella
38 Days of Re-Collection, 2014
27.4 × 47.8 cm
B&W white film negative
(generated from a digital image)
printed with b&w photo emulsion spread on color paint fragments collected from
Jerusalem's Old City house walls.
Margherita Berloni Collection

Middle East Studies / Cultural Studies / American Studies / Postcolonial Studies

British Library Cataloguing in Publication Data
A catalogue record for this book is available from the British Library

ISBN   978 0 7453 9950 8   Hardback
ISBN   978 0 7453 9949 2   Paperback
ISBN   978 1 7868 0047 3   PDF eBook
ISBN   978 1 7868 0049 7   Kindle eBook
ISBN   978 1 7868 0048 0   EPUB eBook

In Memory of Naeim Khlaschi Giladi and Tikva Amal Levi

Contents

PART IV: MUSLIMS, JEWS, AND DIASPORIC READINGS

List of Illustrations

Acknowledgements

I am profoundly grateful to Commissioning Editor David Shulman at Pluto Press for initiating this project five years ago and for his enthusiastic and active role in shaping this collection throughout its various phases. The team at the Press, especially Robert Webb, Melanie Patrick, Emily Orford, has provided indispensable help, and has been patient despite setbacks on my end. Some of the pieces included in this book are the result of stimulating dialogues taking place over the years. I wish to express my warmest appreciation to my different collaborators—co-authors, interviewers, and interviewees—who readily consented to publish our shared texts in this book, namely: Evelyn Alsultany, Layla Al-Zubaidi, Regine Basha, Manuela Boatcă, Sérgio Costa, Yerach Gover, Christian Höller, Rashid Khalidi, Richard Porton, Michael Rakowitz, Rasha Salti, Robert Stam, and the *Jadaliyya* team. Special thanks go to the editors at the "Culture" and the "New Texts Out Now" sections, Sinan Antoon and Anthony Alessandrini, as well as Ibtisam Azem, Bassam Haddad, and Sherene Seikaly.

I wish to thank the various editors of the journals, books, and Internet sites for kindly granting permission to reprint the pieces included here. The long list of names and original sources is respectively credited at the bottom of the first page of each text throughout the book. But I would like to distinctly note the following colleagues at the journals: *Middle East Report* (MERIP), especially Joe Stork and Chris Toensing; the *Journal of Palestine Studies*, especially Joseph Massad and Linda Butler; and *Social Text*, which was the home for many of my writings and collaborations since the 1980s, including with Patrick Deer, Brent Edwards, Stefano Harney, Anne McClintock, Timothy Mitchell, Fred Moten, Aamir Mufti, Gyan Prakash, Bruce Robbins, and Andrew Ross. I wish to pay tribute to the memory of editorial members: the late Randy Martin, Juan Flores, Neil Smith, and José Muñoz.

This book project required a major effort of converting scanned publications into Word. (Some of the texts included here were actually written before the age of the word processor.) The digitizing was made possible in part thanks to Tisch School of the Arts Dean's Faculty Grant at New York University. I would like to warmly thank Allyson Green for her support. The process of preparing the manuscript for print was greatly facilitated by the assistance received from various colleagues, students, and staff at NYU. I am immensely grateful to Sally Weathers for her dedication and generosity, as she did thorough and invaluable work on the many diverse tasks associated with the project over the past two years. The process was technically cumbersome due to inevitable mistakes occurring during the conversion of the scanned materials to Word. In the last stage of copyediting, the manuscript greatly benefited from the unfailing commitment and superb and meticulous work of Jennifer Shutek. I am also appreciative of the work performed over the past few years by the research assistants in the Culture and Representation track at the department of Middle Eastern and Islamic Studies, especially Shimrit Lee for her painstaking proofreading of the digitized text; and my thanks as well to Ilker Hepkaner and Jennifer Varela. And my colleagues in the track, Asli Igsiz and Helga Tawil-Souri, have made the collaboration all the more meaningful. I wish to express as well my sincere indebtedness to Kathy Engel as well as to Emily Brown from the Art and Public Policy department, NYU, for their reliably warm support on so many levels.

To visual artist Steve Sabella, who graciously agreed to have his evocative artwork "38 Days of Re-Collection" (2014) on the book cover, I extend my deep gratitude. I would also like to acknowledge the Margherita Berloni Collection. The discussion of the image now forms part of the book's preface. To my friend Lynne Jackson, filmmaker and Cinema studies scholar, my (retroactive) appreciation for insisting on taking my photos (including the one selected by Pluto Press for this back cover) when hosted by the San Francisco Jewish Film Festival in 1992.

For their support, whether bearing on this project directly or indirectly, I would like to express my deep appreciation to the following colleagues and friends: Nahla Abdo, Inbal Abergil, Ammiel Alcalay, Emma Alpert, Ilana Bakal, Guy Burak, Sami Chetrit, Nick Denes, Ghassan Fawzi, Salha Bracha Gur, Samir Jamal al-Din, Mervat Hatem, Shaista Husain, Zaineb Istrabadi, Lena Jayyusi, Rachel Jones, Dalia Kandiyoti, Caren Kaplan, Jennifer Kelly, Sana Odeh, Ori Kleiner, Ivone Margulies, Rachel Yona-Michael, Dorit Naaman, Yigal Nizri, Yvette Raby, Jacqueline Rose, Mariam Said, Viola Shafik, Ruth Tsoffar, Mariam Wissam, Anna-E. Younes, Joyce Zonana, and, also, the late Eli Hamo. Finally, to Robert Stam, as always, my boundless appreciation for enthusiastically embracing the burdens and pleasures of this word-world voyage together.

Introduction

While "the question of Palestine" has been passionately debated over the past century, what could be called "the question of the Arab-Jew" has only recently come into the glare of the journalistic, artistic, and academic spotlight. Yet in many ways, the two questions are intimately entangled, even if that entanglement has been mobilized for very divergent, even conflicting, political ends. One debate involves the question of when the entanglement began. Was it with the 1948 war, or with the arrival of Zionism in Palestine, or with colonial incursions into Arab spaces, or even earlier with the emergence of Islam in the Arabian Peninsula and its subsequent domination across various regions? To what extent can Muslim/Jewish relations in the past be read out allegorically in order to make analogies with Israeli/Arab tensions in the present?

A number of narrative grids have been deployed to account for this shared Muslim-Jewish history. One narrative takes for granted a *longue durée* history of quotidian Jewish-Muslim cohabitation and shared cultural practices from the Easternmost part of the Arab world (the *Mashriq*) to the Westernmost part (the *Maghrib*). This narrative portrays the Arab/Muslim world as plural both in ethnicity and religion, even when questioning the unequal place assigned to "*ahl al-kitab*," the followers of the other "religions of the book," i.e. the Torah and the Christian Bible. Another, diametrically opposed narrative assumes a situation of millennial persecution of Jews within the Arab/Muslim world, and the *dhimmi* status as one of endless humiliation and subjugation. The creation of Israel, within this narrative, forms the telos-point of the redemptive "ingathering" of oppressed Jews. Within this view, the history of Sephardis/Middle Eastern Jews is largely subsumed into the story of a uniquely "Jewish experience" modeled on the paradigmatic example of European anti-Semitism, now projected onto a very different Muslim world. The Israeli/Palestinian conflict is assimilated into the narrative of perennial Arab hostility to Jews and a trace-the-dot history of pogrom-like episodes. There is very little room in this "pogromatic" discourse for examining the entangled implications of Zionism, Palestine, and Israel for "the question of the Arab-Jew."

It is against this backdrop that I opted instead for a relational network approach that took into account imperial history, partition remappings, and post/colonial dislocations. My work attempted to demystify the ethnocentric self-idealizations typical of the dominant narrative, without a) prettifying the Jewish experience in Muslim/Arab spaces, or b) glorifying Arab nationalism, or c) idealizing Arab Jews/Mizrahim themselves, some of whom played a very ambiguous role in this convoluted story. Taken together, the texts included in this book tried to make a case for re-membering a world at once culturally Arab and religiously Jewish. Today, thankfully, a more critical strain of thought advanced by researchers from various disciplines and backgrounds does address these issues in relation to one another. And although the scars of partition inevitably still haunt the debate, cross-border rethinking now offers a more complex account of the cultural production of Jews within Muslim spaces.

Narrating the multifaceted cultural imbrication between Jews and Muslims in the *longue durée* is especially germane given the historical shift in the meaning of the very terms "Arab," "Jew," and "Arab-Jew." The shift transpired, even prior to the emergence of Zionism, in the wake of colonial modernity, with its discursive correlatives in the form of racialized tropes, Orientalist fantasies, and Eurocentric epistemologies. Against this backdrop, the conceptual schism between "the Arab" and "the Jew," or alternatively between "the Muslim" and "the Jew," can be traced back to the imperialized Middle East and North Africa. With the Enlightenment and its corollary, the Euro-Jewish *Haskala*, and later with Zionism, the Orientalist schema "whitened" the (Western) Jew, as the old schema began to be projected exclusively toward "the other" Semitic figure—"the Arab." The Arab-Jew, I have suggested, came to occupy an ambivalent position within the Orientalist splitting of the Semitic figure. Divide-and-rule imperial policies, furthermore, enunciated a new racialized grammar for the Muslim/Jewish religious cultural matrix that had existed for over a millennium.

The 1870 Crémieux Decree, for example, granted French citizenship to indigenous Jews in colonized Algeria but not to their Muslim neighbors. Thus even before the arrival of Zionism and the establishment of the State of Israel, indigenous Jews in colonized Algeria had already been officially endowed with an ambiguous status that generated resentment on the part of Muslim-Algerians and disorientation on the part of the Jewish-Algerians themselves. Granted French citizenship and partially incorporated into the Enlightenment-colonial project, some Algerian Jews ended up identifying with the French, while others identified with the Algerians, at times even taking up arms with the nationalist movement. Others in the *Maghrib*, such as the Jewish-Tunisian Albert Memmi, began by diagnosing the twinned pathologies of the "mind of the colonizer" and "the mind of the colonized" within an anti-colonial spirit, but ended up seeing the necessity of Jewish nationalism. In the context of the early 1970s, Qaddafi's call for the Arab Jews to return to their countries of origin was met with Memmi's vehement rejection of the possibility of such a return, and ultimately suggested a kind of burial of the very ontology of the Arab-Jew. Over a century of French domination of the *Maghrib* resulted in a Jewish/Muslim divide and physical displacement into *l'Hexagone*. Put differently, the colonizing mission of Enlightenment universalism gave way to seeking refuge in France's particularist form of supposedly race-blind republicanism.

With colonialism, European Jews also advanced their own version of the *mission civilisatrice* in relation to their co-religionists in "the backwaters of the world." The modern schooling system of the *Alliance Israélite Universelle*, for example, attempted to displace indigenous Jewish methods of teaching, creating, and the transgenerational passing on of cultural practices. Religious/cultural artifacts also came under the usual colonial "rescue" rubric, for example, the centuries-long Arab-Jewish textual corpus—known as the *Geniza*—stretching from the Indian ocean to the Atlantic. The initiative of Dr. Solomon Schechter to remove the documents from Ben 'Ezra Cairo synagogue to Cambridge University took place under Egypt's colonial authority of Lord Cromer. The dislocation reflected an increasingly dramatic Arab/Jewish split by which modern European Jews came to speak on behalf of all Jews, powerfully shaping Eurocentric representation of "Jewish History and Culture." The physical dislocation of the corpus of documents anticipated, as it were, the demographic diasporization of the living bodies of the Arab Jews themselves in the wake of the Arab/Israeli conflict. Locating the split long before the actual partition and the establishment of Israel, with the colonial incursions into Muslim spaces, highlights the ways in which the colonial/modernity project triggered novel tensions and divisions. These antecedent fissures, prior to the emergence of Zionism, what could be regarded as the micro ruptures before the macro Rupture, foreshadowed the massive post-1948 dislocation of Arab Jews.

The initial fissures of this *ruptures-before-the-Rupture* resulted in the first serious splitting of "the Arab" and "the Jew," a splitting that became more pronounced, as we know, with the unfolding translation of the Zionist idea into a political reality. Already the fall of the Ottoman Empire triggered massive dislocations and redefinitions of identity. After World War II, with decolonization and partitions, the process intensified, and life shifted for many communities, with population transfers that resulted in numerous transmutations of identity. The facts-on-the-ground *Yishuv* settlements, the 1917 Balfour Declaration, the U.N. resolution to partition Palestine, and the establishment of the state of Israel implemented a novel nationalist lexicon of Jews and Arabs. If Palestinians paid the price of Europe's industrialized slaughter of Jews, Arab Jews woke up to a new world order that could not accommodate their simultaneous Jewishness and Arabness. The anticipatory Orientalist split was to fully materialize only with colonial partition and its corollary of dispossession and dispersal of Palestinians largely to

Arab zones, as well as its concomitant dislocation of Arab Jews largely to Israel. Some (such as post-1948 Palestinians repeatedly moved from camp to camp) have been shorn of citizenship for decades; while others (like the Arab Jews) have partaken of forms of citizenship that have not been hospitable to the complexities of their cultural identity.

These traumatic displacements have shaped new national and ethnic/racial identities where officially stamped classifications did not necessarily correspond to cultural affiliation and political identification. Emotional belonging has existed in tension with identity cards and travel documents such as passports and *laissez-passers*, or with the lack of such papers altogether. Against this backdrop, "Arab" and "Jew," I suggested, came to form mutually exclusive categories, with "the Arab-Jew" becoming an ontological oxymoron and an epistemological subversion. The notions of "Palestine" and "the Arab-Jew," in this sense, stand not simply for historical facts, and for their contestations, but rather for a critical prism. Just as all communities, traditions, and identities may be said to be "invented," the idea of "the Arab-Jew" here provides a post-partition figure through which to critique segregationist narratives while also opening up imaginative potentialities.

* * *

When discussed together in the public sphere, the dislocations of Palestinians and Arab Jews are usually deployed against each other, in the combat over the monopoly on historical suffering. Addressing both—the cross-border movements of Palestinians, on the one hand, and of Arab Jews on the other—involves more than a simple exercise of comparison. Both the linking and the de-linking of the Nakba (catastrophe) and the *tasqit* (referring to the revocation of the citizenship of Iraqi Jews) have been marshalled for radically divergent purposes. The diverse and significantly distinct grids that guide the historical reading of these dislocations have serious legal, political, and cultural implications. The more common way of linking the two questions has taken the form of the "population exchange" rhetoric, which has attempted to assuage Israeli responsibility for "the Palestinian Exodus" by pairing it with the presumably equivalent case of "the Exodus of Jews from Arab countries." In its updated version, in a kind of "narrative envy" usually projected onto Palestinians, each argument used to criticize Palestinian dislocation is echoed with a similar argument and phrasing with regards to Arab Jews. The tragedy of "the Palestinian refugees" is answered with the tragedy of "the forgotten refugees from Arab countries;" "the expulsion of Palestinians" is cancelled out by "the expulsion of Jews from Arab countries;" "the transfer" and "ethnic cleansing" of Palestinians is correlated with "the transfer" and "ethnic cleansing" of Jews from Arab countries; and even "the Palestinian Nakba" is retroactively matched with a "Nakba of Jews from Arab countries."

Some versions of the "population exchange" rhetoric embed the assumption of Muslims as perennial persecutors of Jews, absorbing the history of Jews in Arab/Muslim countries into a "pogromized" Jewish History. In its most tendentious forms, this rhetoric incorporates the Arab-Jewish experience into the Shoah, now projected onto a Muslim space that did not produce, or even propose, a Final Solution. We see an example of this tendentiousness in the campaign to include the 1941 *farhud* attacks on Jews in Iraq in the U.S. Holocaust Memorial Museum. One can denounce the violence of the *farhud* without instrumentalizing it to forge a discourse of eternal Muslim anti-Semitism. One could provide, as some historians have indeed done, more intricate political contexts that engendered the vulnerable position of Arab Jews within Arab spaces. More critical forms of discourse and scholarship have delineated the complex positioning of ethnic and religious minority-communities throughout the region, taking on board such issues as: the colonial divide-and-conquer tactics and strategies that actively endangered various "minorities" including Arab Jews; the implementation of Zionism as an exclusivist project toward the Arabs of/in Palestine; the hostile rhetoric of some forms of Arab nationalism that deemed all Jews Zionists; the massive arrival of desperate Palestinian refugees in Arab countries; and the various "on the ground" activities, some violently provocative, to dislodge Iraqi, Egyptian, or Moroccan Jews from their homelands. Without engaging the consequences of nationalism for Arab Jews, the recent campaign for "justice for the forgotten Jewish refugees from Arab countries" silences the violent dispossession of Palestinians summed up in the word Nakba, as if one event annulled the ethical-political implications of the other.

The cross-border movements of the Palestinians and those of the Arab Jews are different in nature, manifested in the very question of naming. Departing in various waves, largely from the late 1940s to the 1960s, Arab Jews left their respective countries at different times (from Yemen, largely in 1949, from Iraq, 1950–51, from Egypt, 1956, etc.), each of which reflected divergent circumstances. Some Jews departed early on, while others remained for decades afterward. Given the anomalies of the situation of a community trapped between two nationalisms—Arab and Jewish—it is not a coincidence that many of the terms used to designate the displacement seem simplistic and problematic. Nationalist paradigms hardly capture the complexity of this historical moment of rupture for Arab Jews. Many of the terms—'aliya (ascendancy), *yetzia* (exit), immigration, emigration, exodus, exile, expulsion, transfer, population-exchange, and refugees—seem

5

in one respect or another inadequate or incongruous. The very proliferation of terms (as elaborated in my "Rupture and Return" in *Taboo Memories, Diasporic Voices*) points to the ambiguities. In the case of the Palestinians, the forced mass exodus easily corresponds to the notion of "refugees," since they never wished to evacuate Palestine and have maintained the desire to return, or at least a desire to have the "right" to return. In the case of Arab Jews the question of will, desire, and agency—as invoked for example in the memoirs of Arab Jews—remains highly ambiguous and overdetermined.

The historically related yet distinct instances of Arab-Jewish and Palestinian dislocations form one of the main concerns of this book. The two displacements are not equivalent or symmetrical or identical, yet they are closely related. First, they are connected metonymically, i.e. causally and spatially, in that a) there were Arab Jews in Palestine—Palestinian Jews—prior to partition who were impacted by Zionism and its shaping of Jewishness as a national identity; b) the '48 dislocation of Palestinians and that of the post-'48 Arab Jews, however different, took place in roughly the same historical period; c) both events were ultimately the consequences of the partition of Palestine and the establishment of Israel; d) to some extent, both in concrete and in symbolic terms, the displaced Arab Jews to Israel ended up in the place and the space (and were sometimes literally placed in the actual homes) of Palestinians displaced by Israel; and e) in some instances, Palestinian refugees in Arab countries were placed in Arab-Jewish buildings, although most ended up in refugee camps.

The induced diasporization of the Palestinians was linked to the project of the diasporization/ingathering of Arab Jews, at times even performed in collaboration with opportunistic Arab regimes who also benefited in different ways from the departure of Jews. Culturally Arab and religiously Jewish, Arab Jews were caught up in the contradictory currents of British and French colonialism, Zionism, and Arab nationalism. Even Jews who participated in various Arab anti-colonial and nationalist movements, who saw themselves primarily as Iraqis, Egyptians, or Moroccans, had to confront a dramatically changed landscape with the unfolding events in Palestine. The reconceptualization of Jewishness as a national identity had profound implications for Arab Jews. The Orientalist splitting of the Semite was now compounded by a nationalist splitting. The meaning of the phrase "Arab-Jew" was transformed from being a taken-for-granted marker of religious (Jewish) and cultural (Arab) affiliation into a vexed question mark within competing nationalisms, each perceiving the "Arab-Jew" as "in excess." In a different fashion, the two nationalisms came to view one side of the hyphen suspiciously. In the Arab world "the Jew" became out of bounds, while in the Jewish state, "the Arab;" hence, the "Arab-Jew," or "the Jewish-Arab," inevitably came to seem an ontological impossibility.

From the outset, the utopian *altneuland* vision rendered the Palestinians superfluous and irrelevant to the project of the Jewish "Return into History." In fact, the Herzelian idea of dislodgment and resettlement was first applied to Eastern European Jews, the *Ostjuden*. As a modern cure for an enduring pathology (anti-Semitism), the movement away from Europe to another site (be it Uganda, or Palestine) was meant to remedy the Jewish predicament. An approach that links the dislocations engendered by the restoration-of-the-Jews project in the lives of all those impacted by it was deemed therefore necessary. To re-inscribe the Palestinian and the Arab-Jew as the subjects of their own histories mandates the replacing of a single national History with a constellation of inter-connected histories, in the plural. This approach requires articulating together the various exiles produced by the modern transplanting of populations in accord with newly drawn maps. Against this backdrop, claiming a false equivalence between the mass exoduses of Palestinians and Arab Jews reproduces the same nationalist Arab-versus-Jew splitting, which had been stirring regional turmoil from the very outset.

Such quarantining maps have perpetuated rigid, sometimes literally concrete, borders and the persistence of the Arab/Jewish emotional divide; whence "the rejection of the Arab-Jew" within many Jewish institutions and publications. Pronouncing an incorrigible Arab or Muslim anti-Semitism, furthermore, all too conveniently places the burden of the Palestinian/ Israeli conflict on the Palestinians themselves. In the era of post-9/11, of the War on Terror, spreading Islamophobia, as well as of ISIS-led destruction, the campaign on behalf of "Jewish refugees from Arab lands" has gained some momentum in the public sphere. Yet, against the backdrop of the Arab-Spring turned Arab-Winter, of bloody repressions, and of sheer decimation of Iraq and Syria that has led to the current refugee crisis, "the forgotten refugees" project turns a blind-eye to other dislocations. Current violence in the Middle East often turns the departure of Arab Jews into proof of the essentialist argument that one "can't trust the Muslims" (an updated version of "can't trust the Arabs.") The many legitimate claims of Arab Jews become problematic when ignoring the complex circumstances that ejected the Arab Jews; when such claims are utilized to nullify Palestinian claims; and when oblivious to current devastations causing the exodus from the Middle East to Europe.

The "Jewish-refugees-from-Arab-countries" discourse enacts an identical role to that of the persecuted European Jews, whose experience of pogroms and the Shoah was somehow presumed to refute Palestinian arguments. In the contemporary arena, the Jewish-refugees-from-Arab-lands topos is redeployed both as a denial of Palestinian refugees' claims and as a proof of Muslim anti-Semitism. The "forgotten refugees" account, in other words, is told as a story of mutually exclusive traumas, figured as a competition for victim-status, with winners and losers, rather than as a compassionate narrative for many groups: for Jews enduring Judeo-phobia in Europe, for dispossessed Palestinians, for dislocated Arab Jews, for Muslims suffering Islamophobia, and for the victims of the ongoing devastation in the Middle East. The conversation included here, "Bodies and Borders," discusses the historical echoes between the experiences of Jews and Muslims within Europe, between the past anti-Semitism and contemporary Islamophobia.

The two questions central to this book are also intertwined metaphorically, in terms of comparing two different forms of loss, dispossession, and departure from homes and longstanding homelands. The two forms of traumatic out-of-placeness have to be articulated in relation to each other, bypassing competing nationalist narcissisms. The challenge has been to compare the two without equating them; to relationalize and transnationalize the comparison itself. In this sense, "the Arab-Jew" and "Palestine" function as tropes not only for loss of time/place and the absence left in their wake, but also for struggles to persist and remain amidst the absurdities of disappearing, or disappeared, worlds. Both the "Arab-Jew" and "Palestine" come to form tropes of dis/placement. The respective exiling of both communities gave way to the shock of arrival. And the black and white photos of dislocated Arab Jews in tents echo images of Palestinian refugees in a kind of a haunting specularity. By simultaneously linking, de-linking, and re-linking the two events, it is possible to highlight "linked analogies" without ever suggesting that the two dislocations were identical or equivalent.

*   *   *

Over the decades, Palestinians, for their part, have tended to see the Mizrahi/Arab-Jewish issue with a certain skepticism. The critique has been expressed not only outside, *fil-kharij* (in articles by Joseph Massad, for example) but also "*fil-dakhil*" (inside Israel), where Palestinians are officially defined simply as "Arab Israelis." Observing Mizrahi ambivalence toward their own Arabness/Middle Easternness, Palestinians have witnessed Mizrahi integration into the security apparatus. Indeed, the same Arab Jew who might embrace the Arab in him or herself, or laud a common Muslim and Jewish past, may also, in the current polarized situation, fear or reject the present-day Arab (Palestinian) in Israel. In a recent satiric music-video entitled "To Be an Arab" (2015), musician Jowan Safadi gives voice to the Palestinian perspective on the Mizrahi who displays Jewish nationalist symbols and chants death to Arabs, precisely because he knows all too well how hard it is to be a poor Arab/Black in a place ruled by rich Jewish/Whites.

8

Performed in Mizrahi-accented Hebrew, the music video saves Arabic for the climactic finale. It stages the seductive charm of a symbolic choreography in which "the local Arab" (the Palestinian) and "the imported Arab" (the Mizrahi) joyfully dance together in a kind of un/conscious Arab/Jewish affinity. The hint of a utopian opening is instantly cut short, however, when the word "Palestine" is uttered, ending with a bodily stand-still underlined by a freeze-frame. Such a satirical representation, even if in an upside-down manner, reveals the ongoing chasm separating "the Jew" and "the Arab" in which the Arab-Jew has been molded as a Jew in the nationalist sense of the word.

Over the years, I was trying to offer a partial genealogy for the ambivalent Mizrahi positioning as occupying the actantial slot of both dominated and dominators; simultaneously disempowered as "Orientals" or "Blacks" vis-à-vis "White" Euro-Israelis and empowered as Jews in a Jewish state vis-à-vis Palestinians. In a sense, Mizrahim are both embedded in and in excess of nation-state identity formulations. Even the newly fashionable "Arab-Jew" figure reaches its limits when it confronts the national checkpoint. The recent Mizrahi renaissance, and the present-day cultural currency of "the Arab-Jew," has led to vital personal voyages of self-discovery, to the embrace of one's cultural roots, and to productive recovery projects involving language/dialects, cuisine, music, literature, cinema, and visual culture. Given the history of rendering certain memories taboo, the very possibility of any nostalgia for an Arab cultural past becomes publically meaningful. In some versions of these cultural practices, however, the Arab-Jew, while tolerated or even celebrated, usually exists in the past tense, "back then" and "over there" when living in Arab countries. Affectionately evoking the "good Arabs," in Morocco for example, such discourses at times presume a distinct contrast to "the bad Arabs" "right here," i.e. the Palestinians. Nostalgia for the Arab past in this sense becomes a denegation and displacement of the neighboring (Palestinian) Arab.

These celebratory activities at times come accompanied not simply by hegemonic institutional denial and rejection but also by appropriation and co-optation. The nationalist anxiety around "the Arab-Jew" as an in-between and border-scrambling figure has more recently led to a containment strategy, including in recovery programs for the culture of Arab Jews. In some contemporary Jewish studies projects, a very specific "Arab-Jew" is now permitted to exist—but safely enclosed in the past, in the Arab world. Even as the Arabness of Arab Jews is enthusiastically reclaimed, the institutional apparatus continues to regulate who and how that Arabness can be enunciated. (If some of the criteria for Arabness—for example participation in Arab national modernity, or mastery of proper *fusha* Arabic, or living in Arab countries—had been applied to Arabs of Muslim or

Christian backgrounds, or to their ethnically hyphenated descendants—they too would probably have failed the Arabness test; however, *their* (non-Jewish) Arabness would not come into question.) Performed in the name of historical accuracy, the academic version of the rejection of "the Arab-Jew" forecloses any possibility of a present-day "Arabness" especially for the displaced descendants of Arab Jews. Even while scholars explore the poetic productivity of the border metaphor for the literary imagination, these temporal/spatial delimitations ironically continue to legitimate rigid national borders.

This new taboo, erected around definitional prohibitions, around any present-day Arab-Jewishness, places the scholar of the history, culture, and literature of Arabic-speaking Jews within the salvage-paradigm of the authentic Arab Jew, while actively guarding against any current re/claiming of Arabness by Jews. Such a "corrective" approach that presumes to move beyond the passé Zionist/anti-Zionist/post-Zionist debate, and which passes for academic neutrality and scholarly complexity, remains itself embedded in the national Arab/Jew split. Even while studying "Diaspora Jews" of Arab countries, the tacit rejection of present-day re/claiming of Arab-Jewish identity is ultimately anti-diasporic in thrust. A project that began as a cross-border vision, in other words, now also bumps up against the impasse of the Arab-versus-Jew as a nationalist line not to be crossed, thus restricting the imaginative potentialities of the Arab-Jew outside of Arab/Muslim spaces.

The fact and the trope of "the Arab-Jew," however, are at once past and present. The Arabness of Jews was for over a millennium the taken-for-granted designation for people whose religion was Jewish but whose culture was Arabic, without the two seen as a contradiction. (My recent work on "The Question of Judeo-Arabic," for example, highlights the self-designation of the language deployed by Jewish liturgical texts as *Arabic*—and not as "*Judeo*-Arabic"—even when written in Arabic-in-Hebrew letters.) In the present, the term "Arab-Jew" does not necessarily refer to the fact of self-designation since some Jews of Arab backgrounds might identify with the term, while others—for various reasons, including (self)rejection of the Arab in the Arab-Jew—might not. Rather, it refers to a project that attempts to move beyond the current impasse and the myth of eternal enmity. Like the shared plural space that was Palestine, the Arab-Jew is a reminder/remainder of the plurality within the Arab world more generally. Both "Palestine" and "the Arab-Jew" in this sense are not only tropes of loss and mourning but also figures of inclusivity. Even in the face of present calamity, the concepts evoke the memory of a shared past while also pointing to a possible future of re/conciliation.

* * *

In many ways, *On the Arab-Jew, Palestine, and Other Displacements* reflects an ongoing search for an alternative conceptual framework for thinking about "the Middle East." At the time, the aim was to unpack the ways that the Zionist master narrative represented the Arab Jews on a continuum with the Orientalist representation of the land of Palestine and Arab/Muslim spaces more broadly. This master narrative, at once colonial and national, I argued, was anomalous and even schizophrenic in combining a redemptive nationalist narrative vis-à-vis European anti-Semitic oppression with a colonialist narrative vis-à-vis Arab culture and Palestine. The "East" was at once sacralized as the site of Jewish origins and envisioned as a frontier outpost for the "West." The "West," meanwhile, was also viewed ambivalently, both as the historic crime scene of anti-Semitism and as an object of desire, an authoritative norm to be internalized and emulated in/by the East. Jewish nationalism saw the "return" to historical time and a reterritorialized space, on the one hand, and the "rupture" from the "Diaspora" on the other, as two parts of a single equation. (The presumed entrance into History through the nation-state—as if Jews all over the world, or for that matter any community, were not already living self-consciously in history—echoed Hegel's *The Philosophy of History* and the idea that peoples without nation-states, like Jews and Africans, were living "outside of History.") The Return, however, generated inconsistencies, contradictions, and ambivalences in the hegemonic scholarship, especially with regards to the Arabness of Jews. It is therefore not a coincidence that the present-day campaign for justice for Jews from Arab countries also oscillates with regard to the notion of the homeland of Jews. The same discourse that calls the departing Jews "refugees"—which would conventionally suggest an exodus from one's indigenous land—also hails their "return" to their true homeland—*Eretz Israel*, which would imply that they are not refugees but "returnees."

Taken together, the texts in this book destabilize the conventional dichotomous historical, geographical, and cultural framing that posited Arab-versus-Jew and East-versus-West. This framing has also at times been reproduced in nationalist Mizrahi discourse; and, albeit from a very different perspective, by a certain nationalist Arab discourse. At the time of the writing of many of the texts included here—especially throughout the 1980s and the 1990s—the Sephardi/Mizrahi issue was a marginal subject, exoticized at best and silenced at worst. Deploying class paradigms, Marxist analysts at that time formed the main group ready to seriously and critically engage the Sephardi/Mizrahi issue. And despite my appreciation for their efforts, I was searching for alternative paradigms and a different language with which to capture our predicament. Those who came to be known later as "the New Historians," meanwhile, focused largely on the partition and its aftermath, calling attention to the tragic human costs of 1948 Nakba. But that very important work ignored the story-within-the-story of the historical, economic, discursive, and political ties between the dispossession of Palestinians and the dislocation of Arab Jews. Speaking in political terms, Arab Jews were deemed irrelevant to the examination of Middle Eastern history and to the imagination of a future peace.

While progressive in the sense of conducting painstaking research that confirmed much of the Palestinian narrative about the Nakba, revisionist Israeli history of the partition and its aftermath did not engage the political and legal repercussions of these historical events for Arab Jews. Yet with the arrival of Zionism in the region, the Balfour Declaration, the various clashes in Palestine, and the establishment of the state of Israel, Arab Jews came to be increasingly affected by this history. The changing landscape of Palestine was also changing Arab terrain. And although inseparable from other prior Arab-Jewish ruptures within the colonized Arab/Muslim world, the Palestinian predicament loomed over Jews in Arab spaces. The Arab Jew came to be "a problem." Caught between the pincer-like pressures of Zionism and Arab nationalism, Arab Jews faced a seismic rupture that continues to produce its after-shocks. Today, in a strange circular effect, the idiom of "Jewish-refugees-from-Arab-countries" comes to taunt the Palestinians.

Revisionist history, it seemed to me, was itself premised on the dichotomous national postulation of Jew-versus-Arab. And although its focus differed from the historical studies of the Jews in Arab/Muslim lands (regarded as merely in the past), and from the sociology and anthropology of Mizrahis in Israel (regarded merely in the present), the revisionist history actually shared the same assumption of internal (Jewish) and external (Arab) division. Yet, a critical narrative in the wake of both Jewish and Arab nationalism had, in my view, to entail the dismantling of a number of master narratives. As a cultural studies scholar I was examining some of the foundational premises and substratal axioms of Zionist discourse, and the ways that colonialist, Orientalist, and Eurocentric discourses had shaped the notions of "the Jew," "the Arab," and "the Arab-Jew." Tracing the dislocation of Arab Jews back to the arrival of colonialism in Arab-Muslim spaces, and especially to their moment of arrival in Israel, the texts explored the "erasure of the hyphen" that rendered the "Arab-Jew" an oxymoronic figure. I found it necessary, in other words to interrogate neat historical and geographical boundaries, as well as to go beyond pervasive nationalist teleologies so as to portray an intricate landscape of belonging.

Rather than posit the Arab Jew and the Palestinian as competing for a hearing within an over-policed representational space, one can illuminate inter-related dislocations, without erasing one at the expense of another. Critical projects, in my view, required interrupting the static categories of "the Arab" and "the Jew," so as to allow for multiple voices and projects and desires, positing instead a dense web of relationalities. The texts therefore attempted to disentangle the complexities of the Arab-Jewish/Mizrahi question by unsettling the conceptual borders erected by more than a century of Zionist discourse, with its tacitly tendentious binarisms of savagery-versus-civilization, tradition-versus-modernity, East-versus-West, and Arab-versus-Jew. If hegemonic scholarship positioned Arab-Jews/Mizrahis within the restrictive parameters of what was constructed as "Jewish History" and "Israeli geography," the work included here argued against an isolationist drawing of history, geography, and culture. Such an argument was hardly restricted to the past in Arab/Muslim spaces. The Israelization of Arab Jews/ Sephardis /Middle Eastern Jews itself required a cross-border vision. A newly formed subcategory—the Mizrahim—was "invented" within the larger process of the Zionist invention of the "Jewish nation," and yet this new category also disturbed and unsettled the Eurocentric framework.

This "unsettling" also formed part of my participation in various activist groups. The speech, "Breaking the Silence," for example, was given in conjunction with two other speeches by Mira Eliezer and Tikva Levi, who headed the organization HILA–For Equality in Education (known for fighting against racism in the education system, whether on behalf of Mizrahim, Ethiopians, or Palestinians-in-Israel). At the plenary panel of the Women's Conference (1994), we ended up announcing our decision to separate from the Women's organization. Yet, that move was less about separation per se than about protesting the Orientalist attitudes of Ashkenazi-Israeli feminists, with their lack of inclusivity and lack of under-standing of intersectional analysis (a subject examined in "Mizrahi Feminism: The Politics of Gender, Race, and Multiculturalism," written in conjunction with my work on the book *Talking Visions: Multicultural Feminism in a Transnational Age*). For us, our Arab culture was present and relevant to our desire to form a space where Euro-Israelis, Palestinians, and Mizrahim could work together. Following the split, we established the Mizrahi feminist forum (also referred to as the Mizrahi Women Forum), along with women of various backgrounds. The members of the leftist Alternative Information Center and editors of *News from Within* (Tikva Honig-Parnass and Ronit Chacham) participated in the Mizrahi feminist forum (which prepared the ground for the First Mizrahi Women's Conference in 1996). *News from Within* subsequently published our speeches, various articles and special issues on the Mizrahim, thus taking on board race and gender-based oppressions—topics that had not been foregrounded up to that time.

The work included in this volume cumulatively traces the possible contours of an Arab-Jewish/Mizrahi epistemology, one that would transcend nationalist teleology as well as the narrow disciplinary frameworks that place the Palestinian question as "outside" Israel and the Mizrahi question as "inside." When seen as an "internal" Jewish-Israeli issue, the Mizrahi subject had been conventionally defined as relevant to the study of Israel but not of Palestine and the Arab world. Instead of this "cutting off" of Mizrahis from their cross-border cultural affiliations, the study of Mizrahim, I suggested, could be envisioned on a continuum with and in relation to the larger Arab/Muslim cultural geography and to the Palestinian question. Arab-Jewish/Sephardi/Mizrahi history could also be reconceptualized in relation to multiple identity formations. This book reflects this perspective on transcending the internal/external conceptual maps, assuming that the question of Arab-Jews/ Mizrahim/ Sephardim cannot be "partitioned off" as merely an Israeli issue despite the invention of the Mizrahim within Israel. The advent of a new, syncretic Mizrahi identity, as a product both of Israel's assimilationist policy and of resistance to it, has led to creative expressions and negotiations of past-in-the-present in the second and third generations of Mizrahis. The transdisciplinary field of Mizrahi studies emerges from within an exciting new wave of renovation in music, cinemas, literature, and visual culture. The thriving critical scholarship on Arab Jews/ Mizrahis challenges traditional Euro-Israeli narratives. In its more critical versions, Mizrahis articulate their history in relation to Palestinian history and, more broadly, in relation to the question of Arab culture. A diasporic polycentric perspective, then, situates post-partition Arab-Jewish/Mizrahi history within a constellation of multidirectional and palimpsestic and porous cross-border movements.

* * *

Over the years, I have been exploring these kinds of cross-border narratives and perspectives through what could be called "diasporic readings." One set of readings has revolved around the historical links and discursive parallels between the Middle East and the Americas. In the 1980s, I began touching on the analogies between Zionist discourse on Palestine and American colonial discourse on Native America. *Israeli Cinema: East/West and the Politics of Representation* (1989) pointed to the comparable representations of "the Indian" in the Western genre and of "the Arab" in the Zionist "pioneer cinema," dating back to the turn of the twentieth century. The recurrent "images of encirclement" that showed the Arabs, Indian-like, menacing the Zionist pioneers, mobilized spectators' identification with the besieged defending civilization against a savagery presumably emerging out of nowhere. (The indigenous condition shared by Palestinians and Native Americans within settler-colonial style "frontier" space has drawn increasing scholarly attention in the field of American Studies.) My work also addressed a related analogy between the representation of blacks in the U.S. and "the blacks" of Israel—the Sephardim/Mizrahim/Arab Jews— as becomes manifest within diverse genres such as comedies, melodramas, and war films. The Israeli racialization of "the Arab" was symbolically split along national lines, one reminiscent of "the Indian" and the other of "the black" of Euro-American discourse. Indeed, the resistant discourse of the Israeli "Black Panthers" was inspired by a sense of affinity with the African-American movement, a subject partly examined in the various essays included in this book.

In an attempt to chart new maps of cross-border perspectives, the work further argued for making this triangular analogy of "the white/red/black" between the Middle East and the Americas. Both *Unthinking Eurocentrism* and related-overlapping essays written in the early 1990s ("Rethinking Jews and Muslims: Quincentennial Reflections"—included here—and "Staging the Quincentenary: The Middle East and the Americas"; as well as "Columbus, Palestine, and Arab-Jews: Toward a Relational Approach to Community Identity"), highlighted the historical entanglements going back to 1492 between the Middle East and the Americas. These texts elaborated on the trilateral analogy in terms of the discursive resemblances between "the two 1492s," that is, the expulsions of Jews and Muslims from al-Andalus on the one hand, and the so-called "discovery of America" on the other. Iberia's demonizing images and "cleansing of the blood" (*limpieza de sangre)* tropes with regards to Jews and Muslims "traveled" to the Americas and were applied to indigenous and Afro-diasporic people. This argument stands in contrast to: a) the contemporary version of Orientalism that has separated "the Jew" from "the Muslim" within the public sphere; and b) the common delinking of the *Reconquista* and the *Conquista*—the two 1492s. The extension of a ready-made ideological apparatus that crossed the Atlantic could be viewed as the beginning point for Orientalism in the Occident.

As a writer and a teacher I have myself had the privilege of partici- pating in a rich transnational dialogue. I have especially appreciated the circulation and translation of my work into Arabic, appearing over the decades in publications in Jerusalem as well as in Cairo, Beirut, Damascus, and more recently in Baghdad. In this kind of writer/reader dialogue, there is a virtual encounter across linguistic geographies but which in this case evokes a time before "the Rupture," and with the could-have-beens of history. While I have often learned about these translations by chance, others formed part of a conscious ongoing dialogue. One such instance took place when I presented "Columbus, Palestine, and Arab Jews" at a 1994 conference dedicated to Edward Said at the Center for Research in Philosophy and Literature at Warwick University, where Said responded to the various papers. The literary critic Subhi Hadidi, who attended the conference, translated it into Arabic, and Mahmoud Darwish published it in his edited journal, *Al-Karmel* ("Kulumbus, Filastin, wa-alYahud al'Arab: Nahwa Muqarabah 'alaqiyyah li-hawiyyat alMajmu'ah"). The text incorporated Darwish's 1992 poem on al-Andalus, "Eleven Stars over al-Andalus," accentuating the recurrent trope of *al-kamanjat* (violins) weeping over the abandoned places, and over a disappearing epoch. (Interestingly, I met Darwish in Toledo Spain, at the memorable 1989 gathering between Palestinians and Sephardic/Arab-Jewish intellectuals which took place in the historical center of translation and the symbolic site of *convivencia*—a subject to which I will return here.)

That text tried to illuminate various past and present analogical elegies of forced departure: the departing Arabs from al-Andalus and from Palestine, but also the departing Arab Jews in the wake of the partition of Palestine. More recently, I discussed other instances of cross-border identifications as seen in Darwish's later poem, "The Speech of the Red Indian," as part of a Web-Based Documentary Project initiated by the filmmaker Eyal Sivan, entitled "Montage Interdit" (2012). The project archives and analyzes Jean-Luc Godard's anti-colonial cinematic themes. In Godard's *Notre Musique* (2004), set in Sarajevo, another historical site of Christian-Jewish-Muslim *convivencia*, Darwish's poem gives voice to the colonized Native American as living a situation not unlike that of the dispossessed Palestinians, a poetic encounter which is recapitulated in the actual presence in the film of both Darwish and Native American elders. The reverberations between the presumably divergent lives of Indigenous Americans, Muslims and Jews further highlight the haunting resemblances and subterranean affinities between past and present. (In *Unthinking Eurocentrism* Robert Stam and I began to elaborate these analogies and amplified them through the notion of "the red/black/white Atlantic" in our recent book *Race in Translation*.)

Some of the essays on cultural politics included here reflect another dimension of the global circulation of images/sounds and ideas. Since the 1980s, my work has addressed the trope of the exotic in cultural representation. While *Israeli Cinema* looked into the analogies between Hollywood and Israeli cinematic representations of "the Orient," essays such as "Gender in Hollywood's Orient" (1990)—included here—along with "Gender and the Culture of Empire" (1991), and "American Orientalism" (1997) studied Orientalism within the larger context of Eurocentrism. This work placed in relation the representations of diverse imperialized geographies, while also highlighting the intellectual and aesthetic trajectory from "Third Worldist cinema" to "post-Third Worldist" cultural practices (here discussed in "The Cinema of Displacement"). The essays on cultural politics included here also approach "the Middle East" in terms of cross-border imaginaries—how the region has been imagined elsewhere, and how the region itself has imagined its own "elsewheres." Every nation could be read as trans-nation; each region is crossed by other regions.

The essays from "Egypt: Cinema and Revolution" to "The Cinema of Displacement," register a spectrum of images and sounds across borders and their impact on identifications. Within the geographies of spectatorship, for example, the Middle East and Latin America have long since intersected within popular culture. The rumba, the tango, the bolero, and samba have all made their mark on Egyptian musicals from its inception. And similarly, the presence of belly-dancing in Brazilian or Mexican popular culture are not to be underestimated. Such cultural "displacements" reveal ambivalent imaginaries, at times mediated via French, British, and American popular culture, often dating back to the Orient of the Imperial Expositions. In the case of Brazil, for example, an ambivalent mode of Orientalism enchanted by harems and veils but which also is part of a syncretic mixing throughout the Americas. (Much of this research material and conceptualization now form part of the 2013 book, *Between the Middle East and the Americas*, co-edited by Evelyn Alsultany and myself, and which are also visited here in the conversations on "Anti-Americanism," "Diasporic Thinking," and on "Bodies and Borders.") Today, one finds exciting dialogical cross-regional musical fusions, partly impacted by the dislocations of Middle Easterners to the Americas. Such fusions can be seen as revealing deeper subterranean cultural syncretism across the Middle East and the displaced Iberia of the Americas.

Various essays included here touch on the complex relationship between Orientalism and Occidentalism. Asking exactly when Orientalism begins, one may locate its antecedents already prior to the post-Enlightenment period of the late 18th and early 19th centuries and the grand European empires. I resituate Orientalism in relation to Columbus' "discovery" of the Americas in 1492. Orientalism was constituted in the Americas, I suggest, even before it was applied to the Middle East, part of a histor-ically triangulated relationality between the Middle East, Europe, and the Americas. Columbus in this sense could be referred to as the "first Orientalist." Pre-existing Iberian phobias and stereotypes about Jews and Muslims boarded on the boats to the Americas—in a trajectory across the Sephardi-Moorish Atlantic—long before the latter-day flowerings of the British and French empires, and long before the massive emigration of Middle Eastern peoples into the Americas. Dialoguing with coloniality/

modernity and Luso-Tropical thinkers, as well as with Said and postcolonial studies, I point to what might be called "the Sephardi-Moorish unconscious of the Americas" as another path for exploring Orientalism and Occidentalism. At the 2008 plenary of the Middle East Studies Association, dedicated to the thirtieth anniversary of Said's *Orientalism*, my presentation—included here—highlighted the need for examining Orientalism within multiple geographies, outside of the assumed geography of "the Orient." This conceptual framing of discussing not merely "the Middle Eastern diaspora" but moving into "diasporic readings" of "the Orient" informs the sections on Middle Eastern and American cultures not simply in terms of demographics and the moving bodies, but as exemplifying diasporic readings, as a form of cross-border thinking.

*   *   *

Written over a period of 35 years, the texts in *On the Arab-Jew, Palestine, and Other Displacements* critique the intellectual and methodological "separation fence" that has segregated struggles, stories, and possibilities. The essays were also written from within the field of cultural studies as well as from within what later came to be called postcolonial and transnational studies, exemplifying the methodologies of these transdisciplines. At the time of the writing of the early essays and *Israeli Cinema*, Palestine and Israel were usually studied within the established methods of history and political science, but not within the cultural studies analytical framework. (Even when the subject at hand may overlap with cultural studies, the anthropologists or historians who study "culture" usually deploy different research skills and analytical methods.) Within Middle Eastern studies, especially in the 1970s and 1980s, Marxist analysis provided the critical edge by challenging the recruitment of scholarship in the service of imperial policies. At the same time, traditional Marxists tended to be suspicious of the post-Marxist field of cultural studies, largely because the category "culture" was seen as dwelling in the fuzzy realm of "superstructure." As a post-Marxist field, cultural studies, meanwhile, challenged this reductionist approach. While also seeing the critical study of culture as deeply embedded in material-political process, cultural studies turned instead to notions of hegemony (*à la* Gramsci) and to more diffused micro-political forms of power (*à la* Foucault). More broadly, cultural studies critiques "culturalism" (with emphasis on the "ism") as an essentialist projection of geographies and histories. It is invested instead in cultural politics conceived from within an intellectual paradigm where "culture" and "politics" are mutually constitutive, shaped in and through each other.

Middle Eastern studies has existed under the regime of separate disciplines, neatly defined as history, anthropology, literature, political science, etc. Given its relative youth and its transdisciplinary nature, cultural studies has had to fight for legitimacy within Middle Eastern studies as a field with a long institutional history. Cultural studies analysis with its emphasis on the problem of representation and mediation, has been invested in a reading method which co-implicates cultural and political critiques. The texts included here exemplify this approach, most obviously when discussing cinema and the media as sites through which to address the cultural politics of the Middle East. "On the Margins of Middle Eastern Studies," meanwhile, explicitly delves into the place of "cultural studies" within "Middle Eastern studies." Seeing Said's seminal *Orientalism* as a cultural studies work, the essay examines the book's circulation and reception as exemplifying the responses in circles sympathetic to the book's political critique but not to its method of discourse and institutional analysis. The position of cultural studies in Middle Eastern studies, in contrast with other area studies, has long been misunderstood and resisted by a variety of ideological forces and disciplinary guardians, but thankfully its methods have now been taken on board, resulting in new and exciting research.

What cultural studies, and the allied fields of postcolonial, transnational, indigenous, and diasporic studies, have made possible is to illuminate the relationalities often obscured by traditional academic formations. By focusing on the politics of culture in its transnational incarnations, cultural studies can help us challenge "here" and "there" thinking, transcending ghettoized regional mappings by highlighting what could be called "inter-area studies" perspectives. Such an approach is also germane to the study of Israel, Palestine, and Arab Jews/Mizrahim (explicitly discussed in the 2010 postscript of *Israeli Cinema*, as well as in the introduction to *Palestine in a Transnational Context*, coedited with Timothy Mitchell and Gyan Prakash, 2003). Some of the work reflects my ongoing concern with conceptual frameworks and the cross-regional flow of people, ideas, and images. The essay included here "Rethinking Jews and Muslims" examines the representation of Jewish-Muslim history in and around the Middle East, but also points to the implications of this representation for the Americas (a topic further developed in *Taboo Memories, Diasporic Voices*). In this work "1492" is reconceived to illuminate the affinities between the exiles of Jews and Muslims, along with the diverse dislocations of other "others"—such as indigenous people of the Americas and Africans—a theme to which I also return in the "Postscript to Frantz Fanon's *The Wretched of the Earth*."

Some of the texts reflect on diasporic reading and inter-area studies. "On the Margins of Middle Eastern Studies" also situates "Orientalism" in relation to the concept of "Occidentalism" (a work I continued in "The

Sephardi-Moorish Atlantic" in *Between the Middle East and the Americas*). Exploring the implications of Orientalism and Occidentalism for trans-national knowledge production, this work renarrates the genealogy of Orientalism. In contrast to a postcolonial studies emphasis on the grand 19th-century European empires, we can emphasize "1492" as a cataclysmic moment that illuminates the intertwined *Reconquista* discourse about Muslims and Jews and the *Conquista* imaginary of the colonized *indigene* and the enslaved African. Alongside the question of when Orientalism *began*, then, is the question of where Orientalism *went*. In contradistinc-tion to the Occidentalism thesis, this perspective envisions Orientalism as already constitutive of the Americas, deeply embedded in Occiden-talism itself, and vice versa. Some of the texts concerning diasporization from the Middle East form part of this perspective that "displaces" the "Orient," as it were, from its bounded Middle East cartography, and from its post-Enlightenment temporality, into cross-oceanic ebbs and flows. The prism of "the Moorish-Sephardi un/conscious" of the Americas reveals a deep ambivalence toward "the Orient," informed by simultaneous denial and desire.

For those of us engaged in the ongoing project of deconstructing the essentialist paradigms undergirding knowledge production about "the Middle East" (or about any other geography) the critical dissection of Orientalism seems to be an unfinished task. Some of the texts here explore the tense political atmosphere in which critical dialogue was taking place. In fact, Middle Eastern studies departments and the Middle East Studies Association have themselves been subjected to a panoptical gaze. Scholars critical of Orientalist rhetoric and policy have been "campus watched." In one version of the story, the present-day critics of Orientalism are caricatured as a corrupting influence that marks the beginning of a downward spiral for the field of Middle Eastern studies. One key issue for cultural studies has also been the critical examination of academic institutions, and the ways in which they are managed and regulated. And especially since 9/11, an old/new Orientalist impulse—this time in the form of a virulent Islamopho-bia—has targeted the academic freedom of the so-called "tenured radicals." But the ongoing backlash suggests that even tenure hardly offers a safe haven for the critics of "imperial reason." Yet, as the eulogy here for Said reminds us, it is important to remember courage in the face of attack and value the willingness to inhabit the ever-uncomfortable space of the worldly yet "out-of-place" intellectual.

The "us-versus-them" discourse—whether pronounced by Western neo-Orientalists or by Islamic fundamentalists—continues to obscure the co-implication of cultures, histories and geographies. Together the essays gathered here hopefully blur the dividing lines between "inside" and "outside" and thus contribute to a transtextual and transdisciplinary prism through which to explore entangled ideas and debates usually approached in isolation. Despite the various contexts and issues treated in this book, they are all addressed within a broader decolonizing perspective of the "unthinking" of Eurocentrism and Orientalism. Engaging the historical and philosophical issues around Arab Jews/Sephardim/Mizrahim, Palestine, Israel, and the Middle East more broadly, the selection offers an overall trajectory from anticolonial critique to diasporic readings, striving to transcend essentialist nationalist paradigms. The texts hopefully evoke the *longue durée* relationship between Jews and Muslims, critiquing the way this history has usually been represented in the public sphere. While the positing of a singular "Jewish History" (with a capital H), as suggested earlier, has been seminal for the Jewish nationalist narrative, the work here argues for the plural—"Jewish histories." And while "Jewish Diaspora" (with a capital D) has been perceived as originary and unique, I have tried to narrate multiple diasporas, scattered across various geographies.

Nationalism in the service of colonialism could be defined as regressive, while at the same time nationalism could be seen as progressive when used in the fight against oppression, especially given the lack of power symmetry between the nationalism of colonial powers and the nationalism of anti-colonial movements. But the critique of colonialism and imperialism can avoid the pitfalls of essentialist ethno-nationalism even when—understandably—used as weapons of the weak. It is one thing to critique colonialism; it is another to (re)produce monolithic nationalism, which has often ended up excluding, oppressing, and displacing communities within the post-independence nation-state. And to an extent, the story of Arab Jews at least partly has to be read against this backdrop as well. Given dislocation from Arab cultural geographies in the wake of both colonial and national practices, in other words, collective forms of belonging are thus inevitably transnational and trans-regional. Yet, the persistence of essentialist and reductionist ethnonationalism has affected every realm, including scholarly definitions and academic projects. But the effort to destabilize fixed categories, highlight cultural syncretism, diasporize the notion of "national culture," and generally transnationalize the discussion is, thankfully, growing. In this sense the critique of Orientalism has become relevant not only for Middle Eastern studies but for American studies and the various ethnic studies as well.

One encouraging development is the burgeoning trend of transdisciplinary work emerging from the interstitial regions of the various area studies. Such cross-regional grids can account for the haunting connectivities between diverse cultural geographies. The study of cross-border movements through "inter-area studies" de-territorializes regions as stable objects of study, and offers new angles on the ongoing critique of the frozen fixity of East-versus-West and North-versus-South, in work that audaciously challenges the notion that the critique of Orientalism has become *"passé."* Many of the essays included here echo *Taboo Memories, Diasporic Voices* and the introduction to *Talking Visions,* and raise questions about studying "the Middle East" as simply "over there," separating it from "the Middle East" in the Americas, "right here;" especially since we know that displaced communities shuttle frequently between "there" and "here." A decolonizing grid allows us to map cultural terrain, stretching and broadening notions of belonging. A cross-regional, transnational, relational, and diasporic reading, in sum, does not merely focus on migratory demographics, or merely follow a population from its originary base into new geographical zones. Rather, it aspires to take the "diasporic turn" seriously by thinking all regions, including the Middle East/North Africa, in a manner that sees cultural geographies as densely co-implicated and traversed by a multi-directional circulation of ideas and tropes.

*   *   *

This project came into existence thanks to the initiative of Pluto Press editor David Shulman, whose encouragement and enthusiasm have nourished and guided it since its inception five years ago. The task of assembling texts from the early 1980s up through the past decade, while also taking into account the inevitable political and intellectual transformations, along with the significant time-distance travelled by the author/person, raised a number of dilemmas. We tried to choose texts that would still resonate for present-day readers. For an author, it is an ambivalent exercise to look back at texts written by a much younger self, not necessarily because of some major shift in one's own perspective as much as of an awareness of changed ways of formulating those perspectives. It triggered the urge to take out the proverbial pen and rewrite. (The early pieces were written literally with a pen but this introduction via word processor, making this collection an inadvertent witness to technological change.) At the same time, I realized that such a collection could provide a useful documenting of the trajectory of a debate.

Published in various contexts and in different countries and languages, many of the texts here appeared originally in alternative journals, some now defunct. Over the years, I have been contacted by members of a younger generation of students and professors, as well as by general readers, inquiring about essays that are not easily available, especially for readers unaffiliated with educational institutions. Facilitating their accessibility, this Pluto Press collection hosts texts—some previously unpublished—drawn from diverse sources and belonging to divergent genres, notably essays, reviews, lectures, speeches, testimonies, interviews, conversations, and memoir pieces. As a result of an uneven publication history, and given that the texts appeared in widely varying contexts and across many years, some repetitions were inevitable. Therefore, we deleted some sections from some of the texts, as indicated by ellipses. Elsewhere, we made very slight alterations to the original texts in order to avoid redundancy. At times, however, some overlap was necessary in order to retain the logic of an argument in the respective texts. In a few instances, we made minor modifications for the sake of fluency, especially when the writing or conversations were not initially in English. Some of the images, meanwhile, did not appear in the original publications (but at times in their Hebrew or Arabic translations), and were inserted here, while others were omitted as irrelevant for this publication.

While bringing together a variety of texts, *On the Arab-Jew, Palestine, and Other Displacements* focuses throughout on issues having to do with the politics of culture in and around the Middle East. The book is organized thematically around four sections, namely "The Question of the Arab-Jew," "Between Palestine and Israel," "Cultural Politics of the Middle East," and "Muslims, Jews, and Diasporic Readings." Each section is arranged chronologically in terms of the date of publication, and each comprises diverse genres of texts. Despite their different foci, the sections echo related concerns. Many of the texts included here evoke for me memories and stories about the circumstances of their writing and reception—stories that may shed light on the fraught climate in which the issues were engaged. Here I will touch only on a few instances.

"Sephardim in Israel: Zionism from the Standpoint of its Jewish Victims" (1988), for example, formed part of a *Social Text* special double issue dedicated to "Colonial Discourse." Although most of the essays in the issue did not focus on the Middle East, I thought it was important to address the place of Middle Eastern/North African Jews in relation to the colonial debate. The special issue itself, I should add, ended up by shaping a dramatic shift in editorial orientation, that went from privileging class analysis to the engagement of multiple forms of stratification and subjugation. The emphasis on the word "discourse," meanwhile, signaled a new approach that took on board not only the materiality of history but also language, representation, and mediation. As younger members of the collective board of *Social Text*, we thought a shift in the journal's direction was crucial for opening up to a broad spectrum of critical perspectives. The title of this essay alluded to the title of another *Social Text* essay by Edward Said, "Zionism from the Standpoint of its Victims," published earlier (1979) in the very first issue of the journal at a time when the left was fractured over Israel/Palestine. As the eulogy lecture here suggests, the response to the Said essay in the following issue reflected anxieties within U.S. leftist circles about giving voice to a Palestinian perspective. A number of texts included in this book touch on the reasons for the anxiety as well as on the general ideological bewilderment in the face of Israel/Palestine. Some address the vitriolic backlash against Palestinian claims and against critical Jews of all backgrounds, a backlash that continues to impede open and honest conversation.

During this same period, the critique of colonial discourse in the academe was largely performed under the rubric of "Third World studies," which later morphed into what came to be called postcolonial studies. Indeed, when I was writing these early texts the term "post-colonial" was used only in the literal meaning of independence and the formal end of colonialism. It was not used in the later sense of a field of studies. American Third Worldist circles and publications, meanwhile, were more concerned with Latin America, Africa, and East Asia rather than with the Middle East. Those sympathetic to Palestinians, meanwhile, were usually not concerned with Arab Jews. While some critiqued Zionism from a pro-Palestinian stance, few chose to scrutinize the negative consequences for Arab Jews both of Zionism, on the one hand, and of Arab regimes on the other. And few articulated the two issues—of the Palestinians and the Arab Jews—within the same conceptual framework. Yet there were occasional efforts by Middle Eastern leftists to examine these issues together. A highly unusual encounter between Palestinians and a wide spectrum of the Mizrahis/Arab Jews, for example, took place in 1989 in Toledo, Spain. The aim of the meeting, which included researcher Abbas Shiblak and poet Mahmoud Darwish, was to facilitate "a dialogue for Arab-Israeli peace" on the basis of a new kind of *convivencia*. (That encounter is the focus of the essay "A Voyage to Toledo: Twenty-Five Years After the 'Jews of the Orient and Palestinians' Meeting.") Together with a changed academic landscape, this cross-community framework finally gained a hearing, and even a positive reception, within what came to be called postcolonial studies, including within some corners of Jewish/Hebrew/Israel studies.

Mainstream Jewish institutions and publications, for their part, were hostile to any Jewish support for Palestinian perspectives, especially when voiced by Sephardim/Mizrahim. Name-calling and character assassination of critics became all too pervasive. In the journal *Commentary*, for example, Edward Said was denounced by Edward Alexander as a "Professor of Terror" (August 1, 1989). Said's defenders, like Yerach Gover, Bruce Robbins, and myself, were compared, in Alexander's response to our letter to the editor, to "dogs" and "butchers" of prose. In words dripping with sarcasm, Alexander wrote that Said: "awarded high marks to Ella Shohat for her pseudo-scholarly acrobatics. Indeed, he ranks her study of 'Zionism from the Standpoint of Its Jewish Victims' (1988) on a par with the works of Noam Chomsky and Israel Shahak." Continuing the canine metaphor, Alexander spoke of my "beggarlike gratitude for the miserable bones of condescension thrown to hungry Jews in Said's scandalous book *The Question of Palestine.*" This kind of antagonism was directed toward critical intellectuals generally, including Euro-Israeli intellectuals; and since that time has only intensified, including in new forms in Internet space. (Back then, I addressed this type of condemnation in "Antinomies of Exile: Said at the Frontiers of National Narrations," included in *The Edward Said Reader* edited by Michael Sprinker, 1993.)

My 1989 book *Israeli Cinema: East/West and the Politics of Representation*, which dealt with Zionist discourse and the imaging of the land and its peoples, generated sulfurous public debates in Israel, especially in the academy. Included here also is a *Jadaliyya* interview about *Israeli Cinema*, which took place in conjunction with the 2010 publication of the Second Edition, and which addresses some of the key issues in the book and the surrounding controversy (partly also addressed in the postscript of the Second Edition). The documentary about exiled Jewish-Iraqi leftists, entitled *Forget Baghdad: Arabs and Jews – the Iraqi Connection* (directed by the Iraqi-Swiss Samir), cites a 1992 talk show on Israeli national TV—the only channel that existed in the country at the time—in which the host tried to refute my claims that there was structural racism toward Mizrahim. When he turned to the audience to ask them on live TV if they agreed that there was racism, he was very surprised to hear the majority defiantly respond: "yes!" (*Forget Baghdad* is discussed here in a conversation with curator Rasha Salti revolving around the question of "landscapes of belonging").

Other essays included in *On the Arab-Jew, Palestine, and Other Displacements* reflect on the history of the arrival of postcolonial studies in the Middle East, and the various histories of translation—here examined in relation to Frantz Fanon's 1961 seminal book *The Wretched of the Earth.* In 2006, the book was belatedly published in Hebrew translation for the first time, thanks to the initiative of Babel Press, where I served as scientific advisor. I also wrote the postscript specifically for the occasion of publication in Hebrew. The Hebrew book included the original preface by Jean Paul Sartre (1961), alongside translations from the 2002 La Découverte French edition of *Les Damnés de la Terre*: a preface by the Jewish-Algerian-French Alice Cherki, one of the psychiatrists who worked with Fanon, and author of *Portrait de Frantz Fanon*, as well as a postface by Mohammed Harbi, a historian of Algeria who himself fought in the war for independence. The translation project received the support of Fanon's daughter Mireille Mendès-France, who also read the postscript included here. Although the postscript drew from my general work on Fanon (for example the essay "Post-Fanon and the Colonial: A Situational Diagnosis" in *Taboo Memories, Diasporic Voices*), it was mainly addressed to the Hebrew reader and therefore highlighted the relevance of Fanon's work to the Middle East.

The Hebrew postscript to *The Wretched of the Earth* examines a rather unusual gap in the history of translation of Fanon, coming decades after the various Third Worldist manifesto books that shook the world. The politics of translation strongly impacted the "travel" of postcolonial theory to Israel. Within the field of Israeli postcolonial studies, Homi Bhabha's work on hybridity, translated into Hebrew beginning in the mid-1990s, was then fashionable and was being privileged over the work of Fanon and Said, which was being caricatured as binarist and *passé*. In Israel, most intellectuals at that time were only beginning to be aware of the foundational anti-colonial texts that formed a necessary background for understanding the postcolonial texts, and thus encountered the two bodies of texts as it were "out of sequence," resulting in a "post" without a "past." (I addressed this anomalous intellectual trajectory more fully in another essay, entitled "The 'Postcolonial' in Translation: Reading Edward Said between English and Hebrew" in *Taboo Memories, Diasporic Voices*.) Fanon's texts themselves, meanwhile, are the product of the in-betweenness of multiple geographies and linguistic currents, at once Caribbean, French, and North African. Addressing various contexts—including the English, French, Arabic, and Hebrew—the postscript highlights the question of ethnic/racial relationality in Fanon, seeing "the Black," "the Jew," and "the Arab" as analogically linked and mutually allegorizing figures. Examining Fanon's construction of Blackness, Jewishness, and Arabness, the postscript touches on the politics of translation in both the literal and the metaphorical sense of moving between identities, geographies, and discourses.

In this book, the various texts on memory, meanwhile, represent an effort to reconstruct tales of re-membering out of the fragments left in the wake of several displacements. The texts travel, as it were, not only between different continents but also between different genres of writing. In these texts the reader may encounter a shifting in pronouns, between the "I," "we," and "they" used in a kind of a poetic license to move in-between various discourses and points-of-view on the very same historical subject—the Arab-Jew. Many of the "personal" texts here explore the role played by the receiving geography in legitimizing certain categories of identification and delegitimizing others. "'Coming to America': Reflections on Hair and Memory Loss"—included here—examines how the U.S. fashions dislocated subjects who have already been displaced in other contexts (as seen, for instance, in my own experience of growing up as an Iraqi in Israel), and whose U.S. experience then confronts them with the border patrols of New World naming. By placing my familial journey (Iraq, Israel, the U.S.) vis-à-vis that of the artist Lynne Yamamoto (Japan, Hawai'i, mainland U.S.), the essay composes a kind of relationally comparative dialogue between geographies and histories that are usually kept separate. This strategy illustrates the theoretical argument put forward throughout my work for discussing cultures in-relation rather than as neatly fenced-off areas of expertise.

Such texts go beyond the predicament engendered by the single hyphen in the master narrative of immigration to America. This fixed narrative of the nation-state, and its concomitant nationalist ideology, dictate which country on the list of multiply-hyphenated identities is to be privileged and granted credence, and which are made invisible or even censored. Here "Coming to America" and "Arab Jews, Diasporas, and Multicultural Feminism" analyzes the case of Arab Jews, a community that had already been displaced within the context of Asia and Africa prior to its arrival in the U.S. The reception of Middle Easterners in the U.S. promoted discrepant narratives of dislocation where some hyphenated identities, a Moroccan-Israeli-American for example would be viewed as "Israeli" while a Moroccan-French-American would be viewed as "Arab," thus implicitly narrating identities along the lines of Arab-versus-Jew. Reading the partly autobiographical "Coming to America" against the backdrop of my scholarly work, which challenged the academic reception of the term "postcolonialism" ("Notes on the 'Post-Colonial'") as well as critiqued the hegemonic narrative of "feminism" (*Talking Visions*), facilitates a reexamination of the relationship between the institutional reception of critical ideas and that of the critics voicing them. These memoirish pieces here highlight the role of cross-border reception in determining not only how texts are received but also how writers/ intellectuals are constructed as subjects/objects by academic, cultural, and political institutions.

* * *

The reception of my work on the Arab Jew and Palestine has taken many forms, from reviews to polemics to personal communications. The conversations, the letters, and e-mails I have received over the years have given me a vivid sense of the very diverse and sometimes polarized reactions to this kind of work. On the one hand, I have received very warm responses from a wide array of readers, including from sympathetic Jews and Muslims, Israelis and Palestinians, as well as individuals from minority communities from the Middle East and elsewhere. In a kind of analogical "structure of feeling," some wrote that they lived in similar situations and were moved reading about the experiences of Arab Jews. In contrast, colleagues and institutions have exerted pressure against the referencing of my work and my presence on panels. Some institutions demanded to see the final version of my text before approving the use of archival materials, as occurred in conjunction with the preparation of my then forthcoming essay "Rethinking Jews and Muslims" for the *Middle East Report* (Middle East Research and Information Project) as part of its special 1992 issue, entitled "1492 + 500." In an unusual instance, MERIP, which often received documents from various archives, including the Pentagon, was denied access to photographs documenting Sephardi history. In its preface to the issue, the MERIP editors introduced my essay with the following parenthetical note:

> In preparing this essay for publication, we solicited accompanying photos from the Yeshiva University Museum in New York. The museum staff kindly forwarded several photos from a current exhibition, *The Sephardic Journey, 1492–1992*. Subsequently, however, higher authorities in the museum told us that we could not use the photos unless they could read the article first. When we declined, the museum administrator formally withdrew permission. We regret that this university museum's commitment to freedom of expression apparently evaporates when it comes to critical discussion of Sephardi Jews and Arabs.

In another case, at the beginning of the "first Gulf War," a *Village Voice* section editor ("Female Trouble") invited me to contribute a piece on my personal perspective on the war. The article, "Reflections of an Arab Jew," was ready to go to print when the general editor decided that the piece was "not relevant" for the section, nor, for that matter, for the weekly more generally. The essay was eventually published almost simultaneously in the journals *Movement Research* and *Emergences*. But I did receive a payment from the *Village Voice*. The stub indicated the type of payment as "kill fee"— the sum one receives for writing articles not ultimately published—which appeared in its abbreviated form as "kill." And it also indicated the subject of the unpublished article as "Arab Jew." The formulation had an unintentionally ironic, even ominous ring; it said, simply: "Kill Arab Jew."

Around the same time, the Palestinian filmmaker Elia Suleiman was working on *Homage by Assassination* (1992), which reflexively focused on a Palestinian filmmaker during the "First Gulf War," while he was in his NY apartment and his family was in Nazareth, just as Iraqi Scuds were falling on Israel. Elia incorporated a few segments from my essay into the film in the form of a faxed-letter. He recorded my reading of the slightly adopted text to the screen. As the character of "Elia Suleiman" (played by himself) is seen receiving the fax from the character of "Ella Habiba Shohat," my voice-over is heard reading the letter, which begins with the then circulating Iraqi-Israeli joke at the time that the Scuds were falling on the city of Ramat Gan in Israel, also known as Ramat-Baghdad due to its large Iraqi-Jewish population. The joke: The Scud fell on Ramat Gan because it smelled the *'amba* (mango pickle associated with Iraqis, evoked also in the conversation "Don't Choke on History.") The essay included here, "The Cinema of Displacement: Gender, Nation, and Diaspora," discusses Suleiman's film in more detail.

The ironies were compounded when some years later I presented these reflections, along with additional memories and stories, at a 1997 conference in Basel, organized as an alternative to the centennial events around the first Zionist Congress. The warm reception to my talk about Arab Jews, including from the Lebanese novelist Elias Khoury, was meaningful in a context in which the topic was generally not in the foreground, and at times felt out-of-place. Sometime later, Khoury brought up the idea of inviting a few Arab Jews as part of a conference to be dedicated to the fiftieth anniversary of the Nakba in Beirut. The list of invitees included Abraham Serfaty, Shimon Ballas, Selim Nassib, Simone Bitton, Ammiel Alcalay, and myself, but ultimately we could not participate due to vicious attacks on Khoury by some in the Lebanese press, who accused the organizers of "collaborating with Jews." (The essay here, "The Invention of the Mizrahim," cites this case as a vivid example of the aporias of nationalism.) Since our safety was at stake, we did not participate, but to acknowledge our absence, the organizers left our seats empty and voiced our words. The curator, Rasha Salti, read my text "Reflections of an Arab Jew." (And some of these Arab-Jewish tales were movingly evoked in passages in Khoury's novel *Gate of the Sun*.)

We continued these "virtual" rendezvous at a public symposium taking place in Beirut in 2009, fittingly entitled "Anywhere but Now: Landscapes of Belonging in the Eastern Mediterranean." The symposium opened with the screening of the documentary *Forget Baghdad: Arabs and Jews – the Iraqi Connection*, by the filmmaker Samir (of Muslim-Iraqi and Christian-Swiss background), which focused on Jewish-Iraqi Communist writers who reluctantly ended up in Israel by force of circumstance rather than ideological choice. The film was followed by a Live Satellite Broadcast, which consisted of two Beirut/NY conversations on the subject of Arab Jews—one with the Jewish-Iraqi journalist Naeim Giladi (former spokesperson for the Israeli Black Panthers) and the other (included here) with myself. The conversations were conducted by Layla Al-Zubaidi and Rasha Salti. In contrast with the scripted accusations of "collaboration with Jews" a decade earlier, this time an event on/with Arab Jews was greeted with enthusiasm and eagerness to engage with the Arab-Jewish question. Generating vibrant discussion with the audience, this event was considered "groundbreaking," reportedly eliciting intensely positive responses to this moment of encounter. The very fact of staging such a public dialogue "enacted" a transcendence of the long-held taboo against engaging with the lives, memories, and perspectives of Arab Jews.

In the post-9/11 era the landscape has changed and the Middle East has come to dominate U.S. news. Some of my analyses of mass-media representations of war in the Middle East and terrorism triggered attempts to censor, or at least censure, my work. In the immediate aftermath of 9/11 I was asked to present at a teach-in at New York University. My text, "Reflections on September 11," which was subsequently posted on the site of the Hagop Kevorkian Center for Near Eastern Studies, was denounced in a congressional hearing as part of a concerted attack on Title VI of the Higher Education Act, the federal program funding area studies and Middle Eastern language programs in American Universities. In an article entitled "The Ideology Police" (*The Village Voice*, February 25–March 2, 2004), the journalist Alisa Solomon courageously exposed this monitoring of area studies by Homeland Security. Solomon criticized the House Testimony of Stanley Kurtz from the Hoover Institution and the *National Review*, which resulted in the House voting to establish an advisory board to check on the activities of the international studies centers. Solomon rebutted the neo-conservative attacks and their tactics of "exaggerations, distortions, and downright falsehood." Citing my own words, Solomon showed that the critics had taken my words out of context to create a misleading image of a pro-bin Ladenist argument when in fact I had forcefully condemned his actions and propaganda as "the demonizing discourse of a zealot, one that turns all Jews, Christians, and Muslims who do not share his interpretations into infidels worthy of death;" and when I had actually argued that history of imperial policies does not transform terrorists into legitimate avengers of crimes. "Terrorist crimes," I wrote, "do not avenge other crimes; they simply add more crimes."

* * *

Displacement as metonym (in the sense of actual movement from place to place) and as metaphor (in the sense of comparable displacements) forms a binding thread that runs through *On the Arab-Jew, Palestine, and Other Displacements*. For this reason, I found Steve Sabella's "38 Days of Re-Collection" (2014) to suggestively convey the thrust of this book, and selected it for the cover. The basic material of Sabella's Re-Collection" series—B & W photo emulsion spread on swashes of color paint scraped from the interior walls of houses in Jerusalem's Old City—strangely parallels this book project itself, also composed of fragments gathered from several decades of work and now "housed" in this collection. The stand-alone materiality of the piece, literally extracted from a wall, conveys a layered history through palpable layers of paint. The scraped paint with its several strata of color, forms a literal palimpsest, testifying as it were to the various hands that had painted each one. The turquoise in particular evokes the greenish shades of the wall paint color commonly preferred by indigenous communities of the region (whether Muslims, Christians, or Jews) to protect against the evil spirits. Scraping thus becomes both an act of excavation of the buried substrata of forgotten lives, as well as a means to visualize again intermingled lives.

At the same time, the colors (the turquoise, the brown, and the beige), in conjunction with the jagged shape of the fragment, generate a strong impression of a map. As objects of visual representation, maps are premised on some correspondence to the "real" of land and sea and so forth. Yet the shape of the "map," in this instance, portrays a country nowhere to be found. Here the map becomes a signifier without a referent, a simulacrum of simulacra, a token of powerlessness and the arbitrary nature of maps. In a kind of premonition about the overpowering force of maps, the scraped fragment evokes both roots and routes. The partially discernible colors of the fragment re-present the adorned walls that wrapped generations of the living in a modicum of continuing at-home-ness. Sabella's artwork in this sense inhabits at once the present (the actual paint-piece) and the past (the inter-generational layers of paint). Similarly, the superimposition of the image of the kitchen—the window and hanging pots and pans and even a decorative cat figure—on the scraped paint suggests quotidian domesticity. The kitchen becomes the privileged site of food preparation both as digestive necessity and culinary tradition, while also redolent of sensuous delights and communal rituals. But in contrast to the materiality of the scraped paint, the black and white kitchen has the immateriality of a superimposed image, thus forming a simultaneous presence-absence that inscribes a quotidian life haunted by a ghostly past.

The black and white kitchen image in this sense evokes all that was left behind in the lives of those displaced, wandering across land and sea. The kitchen superimposed on the "map" also suggestively turns routes into a form of rootedness, as the dishes are passed on and forge home-ness even in-transit. At the same time, the paint fragment and the black and white kitchen together register a vision of scattered lives, while underscoring a possible state of exile even when literally at home. The artwork suggests a displacement of a place and particularly of Jerusalem as "a city exiled," in Sabella's words, "from itself." The black and white image, furthermore, is reminiscent of archival footage—of the photos and films associated with Jerusalem dating back to the 19th century. And this archive, which today is circulating in digital space, has become a visual testimony to a Palestinian existence prior to the "settling in" of a new order. The fragment object is a remainder but also a reminder of the kitchen's nourishing role, that of preserving and transmitting sentient life.

By literally interweaving two spaces—paint extracted from one house and the image of the kitchen of another—Sabella's artwork itself condenses and displaces, precisely the processes that psychoanalytic theorists find typical of the "dream work." In this sense, the artwork captures the desire for at-homeness for those experiencing alienation, fragmentation, and estrangement. The same paint-fragment that facilitates the coming-into-existence of the (memory) of the kitchen, is now transposed into a hospitable space of creativity. "Re-collected" memories come to form aesthetic objects, now resignified as "art" in their new home. Old paint from walls is recycled to generate new forms of beauty, expressive of a desire to escape a claustrophobic situation. The out-of-place fragment now becomes an *aide-memoire* for Jerusalem, an object that has literally crossed from the Middle East into Europe, and in this sense it is reminiscent both of the displaced artist himself and of diasporized communities in general. Physically dislocated from Jerusalem, shorn of its functional beauty, the fragmented paint/ kitchen now reflexively bears witness to exile, carrying unspoken tales of border-crossing.

Today, the word "displacement" conjures up news of the obliteration of cities, towns, and villages, as refugee camps make old refugees new refugees all over again. Camps in the Middle East, camps in Europe; past dislocations resonate with the present, simultaneously foreshadowing and reflecting back. Displacements become each other's ghosts. The memory of life projected on the wall is now superimposed on the ghost of the home, the kitchen, the quotidian—that is no longer. The series interweaves various lives, as each paint-fragment is taken from a different place, and as each black and white image represents another fragment of a home— tiles, floors, etc. In this sense, the various fragments fused together enact an imaginary threshold encounter of the living and the dead, of those who remain and those who have departed, thus blurring the boundaries between times and places. Off-balance, the photographed artwork on the book cover, furthermore, provokes a sense of disorientation, or perhaps, reorientation, in the viewer/the reader. In its metaphorical dimensions, "displacement" is, after all, a way of seeing, reading, listening, and re-membering.

The "displacements" of the book's title refer most obviously to the two major displaced communities—the Arab Jews and the Palestinians—which co-habit, as it were, the title itself. But the word "displacements" also evokes other historical dislocations in the wake both of European anti-Semitism and of colonial lines-in-the-sand. Nationalist revolutions in the Middle East, meanwhile, engendered their own demographic dislocations both within and outside regions while also "displacing" previous senses of belonging. The texts here reverberate with some of the other connotations of the word "displacement." An argument in support of displaced Palestinians, for example, is answered, in a displacement as a decoy discourse, with a bad faith *riposte* about displaced Arab Jews. In a different instance, among some on the Arab side, meanwhile, the condition of the Arab Jews is treated with a kind of defensive skepticism.

The notions of "the diasporic" and "displacement," in sum, offer a prism through which nation-states can be viewed in terms of their own expulsions, repressions, and denegations. Within colonized or dominated spaces, those who remain are "out of place." The material landscape itself also undergoes wounding displacements—of destroyed houses, uprooted trees, sliced pieces of land. And the environment itself is displaced through language, exiled through renaming. The concept of "displacement," in its many meanings, suggests a method of reading as a way of "unsettling" the settled political landscape. "Dis/placement" can also, paradoxically, become a trope for multiple belongings—a posture that accepts the fact of departure, and the holding-on to the memory of the evacuated place, but also the reality of disjointed emotional attachments to various places. Varied forms of out-of-placeness, furthermore, can become a new kind of place, opening up the possibility of multi-perspectival awareness, and, hopefully of compassionate inter-community identifications. As examples of Benjamin's "revolutionary nostalgia," the concepts of "the Arab-Jew" and "Palestine" conjure up a relatively convivial past in order to envision a shared future in Israel/ Palestine—a future of renewed *convivencia, taʿayush, shutafut kiyumit*. Imagining the contours of such a space is of vital significance *precisely* because in the present impasse imagining those contours seems so terribly difficult.

PART I

The Question of the Arab-Jew

I

Sephardim in Israel: Zionism from the Standpoint of its Jewish Victims

Alternative critical discourse concerning Israel and Zionism has until now largely focused on the Jewish/Arab conflict, viewing Israel as a constituted State, allied with the West against the East, whose very foundation was premised on the denial of the Orient and of the legitimate rights of the Palestinian people. I would like to extend the terms of the debate beyond earlier dichotomies (East-versus-West, Arab-versus-Jew, Palestinian-versus-Israeli) to incorporate an issue elided by previous formulations, to wit, the presence of a mediating entity, that of the Arab or Oriental Jews, those Sephardi Jews coming largely from the Arab and Muslim countries. A more complete analysis, I will argue, must consider the negative consequences of Zionism not only for the Palestinian people but also for the Sephardi Jews who now form the majority of the Jewish population in Israel. For Zionism does not only undertake to speak for Palestine and the Palestinians, thus "blocking" all Palestinian self-representation, it also presumes to speak for Oriental Jews. The Zionist denial of the Arab-Muslim and Palestinian East, then, has as its corollary the denial of the Jewish "Mizrahim" (the "Eastern Ones") who, like the Palestinians but by more subtle and less obviously brutal mechanisms, have *also* been stripped of the right of self-representation. Within Israel, and on the stage of world opinion, the hegemonic voice of Israel has almost invariably been that of European Jews, the Ashkenazim, while the Sephardi voice has been largely muffled or silenced.

Zionism claims to be a liberation movement for *all* Jews, and Zionist ideologists have spared no effort in their attempt to make the two terms "Jewish" and "Zionist" virtually synonymous. In fact, however, Zionism has been primarily a liberation movement for European Jews (and that, as we know, problematically) and more precisely for that tiny minority of European Jews actually settled in Israel. Although Zionism claims to

Published in *Social Text* as the opening essay for the special double issue on "Colonial Discourse," 19/20 (Fall 1988).

37

provide a homeland for *all* Jews, that homeland was not offered to all with the same largesse. Sephardi Jews were first brought to Israel for specific European-Zionist reasons, and once there they were systematically discriminated against by a Zionism which deployed its energies and material resources differentially, to the consistent advantage of European Jews and to the consistent detriment of Oriental Jews. In this essay, I would like to delineate the situation of structural oppression experienced by Sephardi Jews in Israel, to briefly trace the historical origins of that oppression, and to propose a symptomatic analysis of the discourses—historiographic, sociological, political, and journalistic—which sublimate, mask, and perpetuate that oppression.

Superimposed on the East/West problematic will be another issue, related but hardly identical, namely that of the relation between the "First" and the "Third" Worlds. Although Israel is not a Third World country by any simple or conventional definition, it does have affinities and structural analogies to the Third World, analogies which often go unrecognized even, and perhaps especially, within Israel itself. In what sense, then, can Israel, despite the views of its official spokespersons, be seen as partaking in "Third Worldness?" First, in purely demographic terms, a majority of the Israeli population can be seen as Third World or at least as originating in the Third World. The Palestinians make up about 20 percent of the population while the Sephardim, the majority of whom come, within very recent memory, from countries such as Morocco, Algeria, Egypt, Iraq, Iran, and India—countries generally regarded as forming part of the Third World—constitute another 50 percent of the population, thus giving us a total of about 70 percent of the population as Third World or Third World-derived (and almost 90 percent if one includes the West Bank and Gaza). European hegemony in Israel, in this sense, is the product of a distinct numerical minority, a minority in whose interest it is to downplay Israel's "Easternness" as well as its "Third Worldness."

Within Israel, European Jews constitute a First World elite dominating not only the Palestinians but also the Oriental Jews. The Sephardim, as a Jewish Third World people, form a semi-colonized nation-within-a-nation. My analysis here is indebted to anticolonialist discourse generally (Frantz Fanon, Aimé Césaire) and specifically to Edward Said's indispensable contribution to that discourse, his genealogical critique of Orientalism as the discursive formation by which European culture was able to manage—and even produce—the Orient during the post-Enlightenment period.[1] The Orientalist attitude posits the Orient as a constellation of traits, assigning generalized values to real or imaginary differences, largely to the advantage of the West and to the disadvantage of the East, so as to justify the former's privileges and aggressions. Orientalism tends to maintain a "flexible positional superiority" (Abdel-Malek, Said), which puts the Westerner in a whole series of possible relations with the Oriental, but without the Westerner ever losing the relative upper hand. My essay concerns, then, the process by which one pole of the East/West dichotomy is produced and reproduced as rational, developed, superior and humane, and the other as aberrant, underdeveloped, and inferior, but in this case as it affects Oriental Jews.

The Zionist Master Narrative

The view of the Sephardim as oppressed Third World people goes directly against the grain of the dominant discourse within Israel and disseminated by the Western media outside of Israel. According to that discourse, European Zionism "saved" Sephardi Jews from the harsh rule of their Arab "captors." It took them out of "primitive conditions" of poverty and superstition and ushered them gently into a modern Western society characterized by tolerance, democracy, and "humane values," values with which they were but vaguely and erratically familiar due to the "Levantine environments" from which they came. Within Israel, of course, they have suffered from the problem of "the gap," not simply the gap between their standard of living and that of European Jews, but also in terms of the problem of their "incomplete integration" into Israeli liberalism and prosperity. They are handicapped, supposedly, by their Oriental, illiterate, despotic, sexist, and generally pre-modern formation in their lands of origin, as well as by their propensity for generating large families. Fortunately, however, the political establishment, the welfare institutions, and the educational system have done all in their power to "reduce this gap" by initiating the Oriental Jews into the ways of a civilized, modern society. Fortunately as well, inter-marriage is proceeding apace and the Sephardim have won new appreciation for their "traditional cultural values," for their folkloric music, their rich cuisine, and warm hospitality. A serious problem persists, however. Due to their inadequate education and "lack of experience with democracy," the Jews of Asia and Africa tend to be extremely conservative, even reactionary, and religiously fanatic, in contrast to the liberal, secular, and educated European Jews. Anti-socialist, they form the base of support for the right-wing parties. Given their "cruel experience in Arab lands," furthermore, they tend to be "Arab-haters," and in this sense they have been an "obstacle to peace," preventing the efforts of the "Peace Camp" to make a "reasonable settlement" with the Arabs.

I will speak in a moment of the fundamental falsity of this discourse, but I would like first to speak of its wide dissemination, for this discourse is shared by Right and "Left," and it has its early and late versions as well as its religious and secular variants. An ideology that blames the Sephardim (and their Third World countries of origin) has been elaborated by the Israeli elite, and expressed by politicians, social scientists, educators, writers, and the mass-media. This ideology orchestrates an interlocking series of prejudicial discourses possessing clear colonialist overtones. It is not surprising, in this context, to find the Sephardim compared, by the elite, to other "lower" colonized peoples. Reporting on the Sephardim in a 1949 article, during the mass-immigration from Arab and Muslim countries, the journalist Arye Gelblum wrote:

> This is immigration of a race we have not yet known in the country .... We are dealing with people whose primitivism is at a peak, whose level of knowledge is one of virtually absolute ignorance, and worse, who have little talent for understanding anything intellectual. Generally, they are only slightly better than the general level of the Arabs, Negroes, and Berbers in the same regions. In any case, they are at an even lower level than what we knew with regard to the former Arabs of *Eretz Israel* .... These Jews also lack roots in Judaism, as they are totally subordinated to the play of savage and primitive instincts .... As with the Africans you will find card games for money, drunkenness, and prostitution. Most of them have serious eye, skin and sexual diseases, without mentioning robberies and thefts. Chronic laziness and hatred for work, there is nothing safe about this asocial element .... Aliyat Hanoar [the official organization dealing with immigrant youths] refuses to receive Moroccan children and the *kibbutzim* will not hear of their absorption among them.[2]

Sympathetically citing the friendly advice of a French diplomat and sociologist, the conclusion of the article makes clear the colonial parallel operative in Ashkenazi attitudes towards Sephardim. Basing his comments on the French experience with its African colonies, the diplomat warns:

> You are making in Israel the same fatal mistake we French made .... You open your gates too wide to Africans ... the immigration of a certain kind of human material will debase you and make you a Levantine state, and then your fate will be sealed. You will deteriorate and be lost.[3]

Lest one imagine this discourse to be the product of the delirium of an isolated retrograde journalist, we have only to quote then Prime Minister David Ben-Gurion, who described the Sephardi immigrants as lacking even "the most elementary knowledge" and "without a trace of Jewish or human education."[4] Ben-Gurion repeatedly expressed contempt for the culture of the Oriental Jews: "We do not want Israelis to become Arabs. We are in duty bound to fight against the spirit of the Levant, which corrupts individuals and societies, and preserve the authentic Jewish values as they crystallized in the Diaspora."[5] Over the years, Israeli leaders constantly reinforced and legitimized these prejudices, which encompassed both Arabs and Oriental Jews. For Abba Eban, the "object should be to infuse [the Sephardim] with an Occidental spirit, rather than allow them to drag us into an unnatural Orientalism."[6] Or again: "One of the great apprehensions which afflict us ... is the danger that the predominance of immigrants of Oriental origin force Israel to equalize its cultural level with that of the neighboring world."[7] Golda Meir projected the Sephardim, in typical colonialist fashion, as coming from another, less developed time, for her, the 16th century (and for others, a vaguely defined "Middle Ages"): "Shall we be able," she asked, "to elevate these immigrants to a suitable level of civilization?"[8] Ben-Gurion, who called the Moroccan Jews "savages" at a session of a Knesset Committee, and who compared Sephardim, pejoratively (and revealingly), to the Blacks brought to the U.S. as slaves, at times went so far as to question the spiritual capacity and even the Jewishness of the Sephardim.[9] In an article entitled "The Glory of Israel," published in the Government's Annual, the Prime Minister lamented that "the divine presence has disappeared from the Oriental Jewish ethnic groups," while praising European Jews for having "led our people in both quantitative and qualitative terms."[10] Zionist writings and speeches frequently advance the historiographically suspect idea that Jews of the Orient, prior to their "ingathering" into Israel, were somehow "outside of" history, thus ironically echoing 19th-century assessments, such as those of Hegel, that Jews, like Blacks, lived outside of the progress of Western civilization. European Zionists in this sense resemble Fanon's colonizer who always "makes history," whose life is "an epoch," "an Odyssey" against which the natives form an "almost inorganic background."

Again in the early 1950s, some of Israel's most celebrated intellectuals from the Hebrew University in Jerusalem wrote essays addressing the "ethnic problem." "We have to recognize," wrote Karl Frankenstein, "the primitive mentality of many of the immigrants from backward countries," suggesting that this mentality might be profitably compared to "the primitive expression of children, the retarded, or the mentally disturbed." Another scholar, Yosef Gross, saw the immigrants as suffering from "mental regression" and a "lack of development of the ego." The extended symposium concerning the "Sephardi problem" was framed as a debate concerning the "essence of primitivism." Only a strong infusion of European cultural values, the scholars concluded, would rescue the Arab Jews from their "backwardness."[11] And in 1964, Kalman Katznelson published his frankly racist book *The Ashkenazi Revolution*, where he protested the dangerous admission into

Israel of large numbers of Oriental Jews, and where he argued the essential, irreversible genetic inferiority of the Sephardim, fearing the tainting of the Ashkenazi race by mixed-marriage and calling for the Ashkenazim to protect their interests in the face of a burgeoning Sephardi majority.

Such attitudes have not disappeared; they are still prevalent, expressed by European Jews of the most diverse political orientations. The "liberal" Shulamit Aloni, head of the Citizen's Rights Party and a member of the Knesset, in 1983 denounced Sephardi demonstrators as "barbarous tribal forces" that were "driven like a flock with tom-toms" and chanting like "a savage tribe."[12] The implicit trope comparing Sephardim to Black Africans recalls, ironically, one of the favored topics of European anti-Semitism, that of the "Black Jew." (In European-Jewish conversations, Sephardim are sometimes referred to as "*schwartze chayes*" or "black animals.") Meanwhile, Amnon Dankner, a columnist for the "liberal" daily *Haaretz* that was favored by Ashkenazi intellectuals and known for its presumably high journalistic standards, excoriated Sephardi traits as linked to an Islamic culture clearly inferior to the Western culture "we are trying to adopt here." Presenting himself as the anguished victim of an alleged official "tolerance," the journalist bemoans his forced co-habitation with Oriental sub-humans:

This war [between Ashkenazim and Sephardim] is not going to be between brothers, not because there is not going to be war but because it won't be between brothers. Because if I am a partner in this war, which is imposed on me, I refuse to name the other side as my "brother." These are not my brothers, these are not my sisters, leave me alone, I have no sister .... They put the sticky blanket of the love of Israel over my head, and they ask me to be considerate of the cultural deficiencies of the authentic feelings of discrimination ... they put me in the same cage with a hysterical baboon, and they tell me "OK, now you are together, so begin the dialogue." And I have no choice; the baboon is against me, and the guard is against me, and the prophets of the love of Israel stand aside and wink at me with a wise eye and tell me: "Speak to him nicely. Throw him a banana. After all, you people are brothers..."[13]

Once again we are reminded of Fanon's colonizer, unable to speak of the colonized without resorting to the bestiary, the colonizer whose terms are zoological terms.

The racist discourse concerning Oriental Jews is not always so over-wrought or violent, however; elsewhere it takes a "humane" and relatively "benign" form. Read, for example, Dr. Dvora and Rabbi Menachem Hacohen's *One People: The Story of the Eastern Jews*, an "affectionate" text thoroughly imbued with Eurocentric prejudice.[14] In his introduction,

Abba Eban speaks of the "exotic quality" of Jewish communities "on the outer margins of the Jewish world." The text proper, and its accompanying photographs, convey a clear ideological agenda. The stress throughout is on "traditional garb," "charming folkways," on pre-modern "craftsmanship," on cobblers and coppersmiths, on women "weaving on primitive looms." We learn of a "shortage of textbooks in Yemen," and the photographic evidence shows only sacred writings on the *ktuba* or on Torah cases, never secular writing. Repeatedly, we are reminded that some North African Jews inhabited caves—intellectuals such as Albert Memmi and Jacques Derrida apparently escaped this condition—and an entire chapter is devoted to "The Jewish Cave-Dwellers."

The actual historical record, however, shows that Oriental Jews were overwhelmingly urban. There is, of course, no intrinsic merit in being urban or even any intrinsic fault in living in "cave-like dwellings." What is striking, on the part of the commentator, is a kind of "desire for primitivism," a miserabilism which feels compelled to paint the Sephardi Jews as innocent of technology and modernity. The pictures of Oriental misery are then contrasted with the luminous faces of the Orientals in Israel itself, learning to read and mastering the modern technology of tractors and combines. The book forms part of a broader national export industry of Sephardi "folklore," an industry which circulates (the often expropriated) goods—dresses, jewelry, liturgical objects, books, photos, and films—among Western Jewish institutions eager for Jewish exotica. In this sense, the Israeli Ashkenazi glosses the enigma of the Eastern Jews for the West—a pattern common as well in academic studies. Ora Gloria Jacob-Arzooni's *The Israeli Film: Social and Cultural Influences 1912–1973*, for example, describes Israel's "exotic" Sephardi community as having been plagued by "almost unknown tropical diseases"—the geography here is somewhat fanciful—and "virtually destitute." The North African Jews, we are told—in language which surprises so long after the demise of the Third Reich—were hardly "racially pure" and among them one finds "witchcraft and other superstitions far removed from any Judaic law."[15] We are reminded of Fanon's ironic account of the colonialist description of the natives: "torpid creatures, wasted by fevers, obsessed by ancestral customs."

The Theft of History

An essential feature of colonialism is the distortion and even the denial of the history of the colonized. The projection of Sephardi Jews as coming from backward rural societies lacking all contact with technological civilization is at best a simplistic caricature and at worst a complete misrepresentation. Metropolises such as Alexandria, Baghdad, and Istanbul, in the period of Sephardi emigration, were hardly the desolate backwaters without electricity or automobiles implied by the official Zionist account, nor were these lands somehow miraculously cut off from the universal dynamism of historical processes. Yet Sephardi and Palestinian children, in Israeli schools, are condemned to study a history of the world that privileges the achievements of the West, while effacing the civilizations of the East. The political dynamics of the Middle East, furthermore, are presented only in relation to the fecundating influence of Zionism on the pre-existing desert. The Zionist master narrative has little place for either Palestinians or Sephardim, but while Palestinians possess a clear counter narrative, the Sephardi story is a fractured one, embedded in both Jewish and Arab history. Distinguishing the "evil" East (the Muslim Arab) from the "good" East (the Jewish Arab), Israel has taken upon itself to "cleanse" the Sephardim of their Arabness and redeem them from their "primal sin" of belonging to the Orient. Israeli historiography absorbs the Jews of Asia and Africa into the monolithic official memory of European Jews. Sephardi students learn virtually nothing of value about their particular history as Jews in the Orient. Much as Senegalese and Vietnamese children learned that their "ancestors the Gauls had blue eyes and blond hair," Sephardi children are inculcated with the historical memory of "our ancestors, the residents of the *shtetls* of Poland and Russia," as well as with a pride in the Zionist Founding Fathers for establishing pioneer outposts in a savage area. Jewish History is conceived as primordially European, and the silence of historical texts concerning the Sephardim forms a genteel way of hiding the discomfiting presence of an Oriental "other," here subsumed under a European-Jewish "We."

From the perspective of official Zionism, Jews from Arab and Muslim countries appear on the world stage only when they are seen on the map of the Hebrew state, just as the modern history of Palestine is seen as beginning with the Zionist renewal of the Biblical mandate. Modern Sephardi history, in this sense, is presumed to begin with the coming of Sephardi Jews to Israel, and more precisely with the "Magic Carpet" or "Ali Baba" operations (the latter refers to the bringing to Israel of the Jews of Iraq in 1950 and '51, while the former refers to that of Yemenite Jews in 1949 and '50). The names themselves, borrowed from *A Thousand and One Nights*, evoke Orientalist attitudes by foregrounding the naïve religiosity and the technological backwardness of the Sephardim, for whom modern airplanes were "magic carpets" transporting them to the Promised Land. The Zionist gloss on the Exodus allegory, then, emphasized the "Egyptian" slavery (Egypt here being a synecdoche for all the Arab lands) and the beneficent death of the (Sephardi) "desert generation." European Zionism took on the patriarchal role in the Jewish Oral tradition of Fathers passing to Sons the experiences of their peoples ("*ve-higadeta le-binkha ba-yom ha-hu ...*"). And the stories of the Zionist Pater drowned out those of the Sephardi fathers (mothers) whose tales thus became unavailable to the younger generation.

Filtered out by a Eurocentric grid, Zionist discourse presents culture as the monopoly of the West, denuding the peoples of Asia and Africa, including Jewish peoples, of all cultural expression. The rich culture of Jews from Arab and Muslim countries is scarcely studied in Israeli schools and academic institutions. While Yiddish is prized and officially subsidized, Ladino and other Sephardi dialects are neglected—"Those who do not speak Yiddish," Golda Meir once said, "are not Jews." Yiddish, through an ironic turn of history, became for Sephardim the language of the oppressor, a coded speech linked to privilege.[16] While the works of Sholem Aleichem, Y. D. Berkowitz, Mendele Mocher Sforim are examined in great detail, the works of Anwar Shaul, Murad Michael, and Salman Darwish are ignored, and when Sephardi figures are discussed, their Arabness is downplayed. Maimonides, Yehuda Halevi, and Ibn Gabirol are viewed as the product of a decontextualized Jewish tradition, or of Spain, i.e. of Europe, rather than of what even the Orientalist Bernard Lewis recognizes as the "Judeo-Islamic symbiosis." Everything conspires to cultivate the impression that Sephardi culture prior to Zionism was static and passive and, like the fallow land of Palestine, lying in wait for the impregnating infusion of European dynamism. Although Zionist historiography concerning Sephardim consists of a morbidly selective "tracing the dots" from pogrom to pogrom (often separated by centuries) as part of a picture of a life of relentless oppression and humiliation, in fact the Sephardim lived, on the whole, quite comfortably within Arab-Muslim society. Sephardi history can simply not be discussed in European-Jewish terminology; even the word "pogrom" derives from and is reflective of the specificities of the European-Jewish experience.

At the same time, we should not idealize the Jewish-Muslim relationship as idyllic. While it is true that Zionist propaganda exaggerated the negative aspects of the Jewish situation in Muslim countries, and while the situation of these Jews over 15 centuries was undeniably better than in the Christian countries, the fact remains that the status of *dhimmi* applied to both Jews and Christians as "tolerated" and "protected" minorities was intrinsically inegalitarian. But this fact, as Maxime Rodinson points out, was quite explicable within the sociological and historical conditions of the time, and not as the product of a pathological European-style anti-Semitism.[17] The Sephardi communities, while retaining a strong collective identity, were generally well integrated and indigenous to their countries of origin, forming an inseparable part of their social and cultural life. Thoroughly Arabized in their traditions, the Iraqi Jews, for example, used Arabic even in their hymns and religious ceremonies. The liberal and secular trends of the 20th century engendered an even stronger association of Iraqi Jews and Arab culture allowing Jews to achieve a prominent place in public and cultural life. Jewish writers, poets, and scholars played a vital role in Arab culture, translating, for example, books from other languages into Arabic. Jews distinguished themselves in Iraqi Arabic-speaking theater, in music, as singers, composers, and players of traditional instruments. In Egypt, Syria, Lebanon, Iraq, and Tunisia, Jews became members of legislatures, of municipal councils, of the judiciary, and even occupied high economic positions; in the 1920s, the finance minister of Iraq was Sassoon Heskel, and in Egypt, Yusuf Qattawi—more elevated positions, ironically, than those usually achieved by Sephardim within the Jewish state.

The Lure of Zion

Zionist historiography presents the emigration of Arab Jews as the result of a long history of anti-Semitism, as well as of religious devotion, while Zionist activists from the Arab-Jewish communities stress the importance of Zionist ideological commitment as a motivation for the exodus. Both versions neglect crucial elements: the Zionist economic interest in bringing Sephardim to Palestine/Israel, the financial interest of specific Arab regimes in their departure, historical developments in the wake of the Arab/Israeli conflict, as well as the fundamental connection between the destiny of the Arab Jews and that of the Palestinians. Arab historians, as Abbas Shiblak points out in *The Lure of Zion*, have also underestimated the extent to which the policies of Arab governments in encouraging Jews to leave were self-defeating and ironically helpful to the Zionist cause and harmful both to Arab Jews and Palestinians.[18]

It is first important to remember that Sephardim, who had lived in the Middle East and North Africa for millennia (often even before the Arab conquest), were simply not eager to settle in Palestine and had to be "lured" to Zion. Despite the Messianic mystique of the Land of Zion, which formed an integral part of Sephardi religious culture, they did not share the European-Zionist desire to "end the Diaspora" by creating an independent state peopled by a new archetype of Jew. Sephardim had always been in contact with the "Promised Land," but this contact formed a "natural" part of a general circulation within the countries of the Ottoman Empire. Up through the 1930s, it was not uncommon for Sephardim to make purely religious pilgrimages or business trips to Palestine, at times with the help of Jewish-owned transportation companies. (Although the Zionist geographical mindset projected the Sephardi lands of origin as "remote and distant," in fact they were, obviously, closer to *Eretz Israel* than are Poland, Russia, and Germany.)

Before the Shoah and the foundation of Israel, Zionism had been a minority movement among world Jewry. The majority of Sephardi Jews were either indifferent or at times even hostile to the Zionist project. The Iraqi-Jewish leadership, for example, co-operated with the Iraqi government to stop Zionist activity in Iraq; the Chief Rabbi of Iraq even published an "Open Letter" in 1929 denouncing Zionism and the Balfour Declaration.[19] In Palestine, some of the leaders of the local (Sephardi) Jewish community made formal protests against Zionist plans. In 1920, they signed an anti-Zionist petition organized by Palestinian Arabs, and in 1923 some Palestinian Jews met in a synagogue to denounce Ashkenazi-Zionist rule. Some even cheered the Muslim-Christian Committee and its leader Musa Kazim al-Husseini, an event which the National Jewish Committee managed to prevent from being published in the newspapers.[20] Zionism, in this period, created wrenching ideological dilemmas for the Palestinian Jewish, Muslim, and Christian communities alike. The national Arab movement in Palestine and Syria carefully distinguished, in the early phases, between the Zionist immigrants and the local Jewish inhabitants (largely Sephardim) "who live peacefully among the Arabs."[21] The first petition of protest against Zionism by the Jerusalem Arabs stated in November of 1918: "We want to live ... in equality with our Israelite brothers, longstanding natives of this country; their rights are our rights and their duties are our duties."[22] The all-Syrian convention of July 1919, attended by a Sephardi representative, even claimed to represent all Arab Syrians, Muslims, Christians, and Jews. The manifesto of the first Palestinian convention in February 1919 also insisted on the local Jewish versus Zionist distinction, and even in March 1920, during the massive demonstrations against the Balfour declaration, the Nazareth-area petition spoke out only against Zionist immigration and not against Jews in general: "The Jews are people of our country who have been living with us before the occupation, they are our brothers, people of our country, and all the Jews of the world are our brothers."[23]

At the same time, there were real ambivalences and fears on the part of both Arab Jews and Arab Muslims and Christians. While some Muslim and Christian Arabs rigorously maintained the Zionist/Jewish distinction, others were less cautious. In Nazareth, the Palestinian Anglican priest of Nazareth deployed theological arguments against "the Jews" in general, while "Arab mobs," both in 1920 and again in 1929, did not distinguish between Zionist targets per se and the traditional communities quite uninvolved in the Zionist project.[24] Zionism, then, brought a painful binarism into the formerly peaceful relationship between the two communities. The Sephardi Jew was prodded to choose between an anti-Zionist "Arabness" and a pro-Zionist "Jewishness." For the first time in Sephardi history, Arabness and Jewishness were posited as antonyms. The situation led the Palestinian

Arabs, meanwhile, to see all Jews as at least potential Zionists. With the pressure of waves of Ashkenazi-Zionist immigration and the swelling power of its institutions, the Jewish/Zionist distinction was becoming more and more precarious, much to the advantage of European Zionism. Had the Arab nationalist movement maintained this distinction, as even the Zionist historian Yehoshua Porath has recognized, it would have had a significant chance to enlist Sephardi support in the anti-Zionist cause.

Outside of Palestine, meanwhile, it was not an easy task for Zionism to uproot the Arab-Jewish communities. In Iraq, for example, despite the Balfour Declaration in 1917, despite the tensions generated by Palestinian/Zionist clashes in Palestine, despite Zionist propaganda among Sephardi Jews in Arab-Muslim lands, despite the historically atypical attacks on Iraqi Jews in 1941 (attacks inseparable from the geopolitical conflicts of the time), and even after the proclamation of Israeli statehood, most Arab Jews were not Zionist and remained reluctant to emigrate. Even subsequent to the foundation of the State, the Jewish community in Iraq was constructing new schools and founding new enterprises, clear evidence of an institutionalized intention to stay. When the Iraqi government announced in 1950 that any Jews who wanted to leave were free to do so contingent upon relinquishing their citizenship and property, and set a time limit for the exodus, only a few families applied for exit permits. Since the carrot was insufficient, therefore, a stick was necessary. A Jewish underground cell, commanded by secret agents sent from Israel, planted bombs in Jewish centers so as to create hysteria among Iraqi Jews and thus catalyze a mass exodus to Israel.[25] In one case, on January 14, 1951, a bomb was thrown into the courtyard of the Mas'ouda Shemtob synagogue in Baghdad, at a time when hundreds were gathered.[26] Four people, including a boy of 12, were killed and a score were wounded.[27] These actions appear to have been the product of a collusion between two groups—Israeli Zionists (including a small group of Iraqi Zionists), and factions in the Iraqi government (largely the British-oriented ruler Nuri al-Said) who were pressured by the international Zionist-led campaign of denunciation and who had an immediate financial interest in the expulsion of the Iraqi Jews. Caught in the vice of Iraqi government/Zionist collaboration, the Sephardi community panicked and was virtually forced to leave. What its proponents themselves called "cruel Zionism"—namely the idea that Zionists had to use violent means to dislodge Jews from Exile—had achieved its ends.

The same historical process that dispossessed Palestinians of their property, lands, and national-political rights was linked to the process that dispossessed Sephardim of their property, lands, and rootedness in Arab countries (and within Israel itself, of their history and culture). This overall process has been cynically idealized in Israel's diplomatic pronouncements as a kind

Figure 1   Photo and original Israel Government Press Office caption: "Inside the Airplane, Flying from Yemen, a Moment after Landing in Lod, October 1949"

of "spontaneous population exchange," and a justification for expelling Palestinians, but the symmetry is factitious, for the so-called "Return from Exile" of the Arab Jews was far from spontaneous, and in any case cannot be equated with the condition of the Palestinians, who have been exiled from their homeland and wish to return there. In Israel itself, as the Palestinians were being forced to leave, the Sephardim underwent a complementary trauma, a kind of image in negative, as it were, of the Palestinian experience. The vulnerable new immigrants were ordered around by arrogant officials, who called them "human dust," and crowded them into *maabarot* (transit camps), i.e. tents and dwellings hastily constructed out of corrugated tin. Many were stripped of their "unpronounceable" Arab, Persian, and Turkish names, and outfitted with "Jewish" names by God-like Israeli bureaucrats. The process by which millennial pride and collective self-confidence and creativity were to be destroyed was inaugurated here. This was a kind of Sephardi "middle passage," where the appearance of a voluntary "return from exile" masked a subtle series of coercions. But while Palestinians have been authorized to foster the collective militancy of nostalgia in exile (be it under an Israeli, Syrian, or Kuwaiti passport, or on the basis of a *laissez-passer*), Sephardim have been forced by their no-exit situation to repress their communal nostalgia. The pervasive notion of "one people" reunited in their ancient homeland actively deauthorizes any affectionate memory of life before the State of Israel.

Figure 2   Photo and original Israel Government Press Office caption: "Bureaucrats of the Jewish Agency Register the *Olim* Naqqash and Albert who Arrived from Tunisia Boarded on Negba Ship, July 6, 1950"

"Hebrew Work:" Myth and Reality

The Zionist "ingathering from the four corners of the earth" was never the beneficent enterprise portrayed by official discourse. From the early days of Zionism Sephardim were perceived as a source of cheap labor that had to be maneuvered into emigrating to Palestine. The economic structure that oppresses Sephardim in Israel was set in place in the early days of the *Yishuv* (pre-state Zionist settlement in Palestine). Among the orienting principles of the dominant Socialist Zionism, for example, were the twin notions of *'avoda 'ivrit* (Hebrew work) and *'avoda 'atzmit* (self-labor), suggesting that a person, and a community, should earn from their own and not from hired labor, an idea whose origins trace back to the *Haskala* or 18th-century Hebrew Enlightenment. Many Jewish thinkers, writers, and poets, such as Mapu, Brenner, Borochov, Gordon, and Katzenelson, highlighted the necessity of transforming Diaspora Jews through "productive labor," especially agricultural labor. Such thinkers advanced *'avoda 'ivrit* as a necessary pre-condition for Jewish recuperation. The policy and practice of *'avoda 'ivrit* deeply affected the historically positive self-image of the Hebrew pioneers, and later that of Israel, as involved in a non-colonial enterprise, which, unlike colonialist Europe, did not exploit the "natives" and was, therefore, perceived as morally superior in its aspirations.

In its actual historical implications, however, 'avoda 'ivrit had tragic consequences, engendering political tensions not only between Arabs and Jews, but also between Sephardim and Ashkenazim as well as between Sephardim and Palestinians. At first, the European Jewish settlers tried to compete with Arab workers for jobs offered by previously settled Jewish employers; "Hebrew work" then meant in reality the boycotting of Arab work. The immigrants' demands for relatively high salaries precluded their employment, however, thus leading to the emigration of a substantial proportion. At a time when even the poorest of Russian Jews were heading toward the Americas, it was difficult to convince European Jews to come to Palestine. It was only after the failure of Ashkenazi immigration that the Zionist institutions decided to bring Sephardim. Yaakov Tahon from the Eretz Israel Office wrote in 1908 about this problem of "Hebrew workers." After detailing the economic and psychological obstacles to the goal of 'avoda 'ivrit as well as the dangers posed by employing masses of Arabs, he proposed, along with other official Zionists, the importation of Sephardim to "replace" the Arab agricultural workers. Since "it is doubtful whether the Ashkenazi Jews are talented for work other than in the city," he argued, "there is a place for the Jews of the Orient, and particularly for the Yemenites and Persians, in the profession of agriculture." Like the Arabs, Tahon goes on, they "are satisfied with very little" and "in this sense they can compete with them."[28] Similarly, in 1910, Shmuel Yavnieli published in *Ha-Poel Ha-Tzair* (*The Young Worker*, the official Organ of the Zionist Party of the Workers in Eretz Israel, later part of the Labor Party), a two-part article entitled "The Renaissance of Work and the Jews of the Orient" in which he called for an Oriental-Jewish solution to the "problem" of the Arab workers. *Ha-Zvi* newspaper gave expression to this increasingly disseminated position:

This is the simple, natural worker capable of doing any kind of work, without shame, without philosophy, and also without poetry. And Mr. Marx is of course absent both from his pocket and from his mind. It is not my contention that the Yemenite element should remain in its present state, that is, in its barbarian, wild present state ... the Yemenite of today still exists at the same backward level as the *fellahin* ... they [the Yemenites] can take the place of the Arabs.[29]

Zionist historiographers have recycled these colonialist myths, applied both to Arabs and Arab Jews, as a means for justifying the class-positioning into which Sephardim were projected. Yemeni workers have been presented as "merely workers," socially "primeval matter," while Ashkenazi workers as "creative" and "idealists, able to be devoted to the ideal, to create new molds and new content of life."[30]

Regarded by European Zionists as capable of competing with Arabs but refractory to more lofty socialist and nationalist ideals, the Sephardim seemed ideal imported laborers. Thus the concept of "natural workers" with "minimal needs," exploited by such figures as Ben-Gurion and Arthur Ruppin, came to play a crucial ideological role, a concept subtextually linked to color; to quote Ruppin: "Recognizable in them [Yemeni Jews] is the touch of Arab blood, and they have a very dark color."[31] The Sephardim offered the further advantage of generally being Ottoman subjects, and thus, unlike most Ashkenazim, did not have legal difficulties in entering the country, partially thanks to Jewish (Sephardi) representation in the Ottoman Parliament.[32]

Tempted by the idea of recruiting "Jews in the form of Arabs," Zionist strategists agreed to act on "the Sephardi option." The bald economic-political interest motivating this selective "ingathering" is clearly discernible in emissary Yavnieli's letters from Yemen, where he states his intention of selecting only "young and healthy people" for immigration.[33] His reports about potential Yemenite laborers go into great detail about the physical characteristics of the different Yemenite regional groups, describing the Jews of Dal'a, for example, as "healthy" with "strong legs," in contrast to the Jews of Ka'ataba with their "shrunken faces and skinny hands."[34] These policies of a quasi-eugenic selection were repeated during the 1950s in Morocco, where young men were chosen for *aliya* on the basis of physical and gymnastic tests.

Often deluding Sephardim about realities in the "land of milk and honey," Zionist emissaries engineered the immigration of over 10,000 Sephardim (largely Yemenis) before World War I. They were put to work mainly as agricultural day laborers in extremely harsh conditions to which, despite Zionist mythology, they were decidedly not accustomed. Yemeni families were crowded together in stables, pastures, windowless cellars (for which they had to pay), or simply obliged to live in the fields. Unsanitary conditions and malnutrition caused widespread disease and death, especially of infants. The Zionist Association employers and the Ashkenazi landowners and their overseers treated the Yemeni Jews brutally, at times abusing even the women and children, who labored over ten hours a day.[35] The ethnic division of labor, in this early stage of Zionism, had as its corollary the sexual division of labor. Tahon wrote in 1907 of the advantages of having Yemenite families living permanently in the settlements, so that "we could also have women and adolescent girls work in the households instead of the Arab women who now work at high salaries as servants in almost every family of the colonists."[36] Indeed, the "fortunate" women and girls worked as maids, while the rest worked in the fields. Economic and political exploitation went hand in hand with habitual European feelings of superiority. Any treatment accorded to the Sephardim was thought to be legitimate, since they were bereft, it was assumed, of all culture, history, or material achievement. Sephardim were excluded, furthermore, from the socialist benefits accorded European workers.[37] Labor Zionism, through the General Federation of Labor (Histadrut), managed to prevent Yemenis from owning land or joining cooperatives, thus limiting them to the role of wage-earners. As with the Arab workers, the dominant "socialist" ideology within Zionism thus provided no guarantee against ethnocentrism. While presenting Palestine as an empty land to be transformed by Jewish labor, the Founding Fathers presented Sephardim as passive vessels to be shaped by the revivifying spirit of Promethean Zionism.

Figure 3   Yemeni Workers in Kinneret Kibbutz, 1912

At the same time, the European Zionists were not enthralled by the prospect of "tainting" the settlements in Palestine with an infusion of Sephardi Jews. The very idea was opposed at the first Zionist Congress.[38] In their texts and congresses, European Zionists consistently addressed their remarks to Ashkenazi Jews and to the colonizing empires which might provide support for a national homeland; the visionary dreams of a Zionist Jewish state were not designed for the Sephardim. But the actual realization of the Zionist project in Palestine, with its concomitant aggressive attitude toward all the local peoples, brought with it the possibility of the exploitation of Sephardi Jews as part of an economic and political base. The strategy of promoting a Jewish majority in Palestine in order to create a Jewish national homeland entailed at first the purchase and later the expropriation of Arab land. The policy—favored by the *Zionut Ma'asit* ("Practical Zionism")—of creating de facto Jewish occupation of Arab land, formed a crucial element in Zionist claims on Palestine. Some Zionists were afraid that Arab workers on Jewish lands might someday declare that "the land belongs to those who work it," whence the need for Jewish (Sephardi) workers. This skewed version of *'avoda 'ivrit* generated a long-term structural competition between Arab workers and the majoritarian group of Jewish (Sephardi) workers, now reduced to the status of a subproletariat.

It was only after the failure of European immigration—even in the post-Holocaust era most European Jews chose to emigrate elsewhere—that the Zionist establishment decided to bring Sephardi immigrants *en masse*. The European Zionist rescue phantasy concerning the Jews of the Orient, in sum, masked the need to rescue *itself* from possible economic and political collapse. In the 1950s, similarly, Zionist officials continued to show ambivalence about the mass importation of Sephardi Jews. But once again, demographic and economic necessities—settling the country with Jews, securing the borders, and having laborers to work and soldiers to fight—forced the European Zionist hand. Given this subtext, it is instructive to read the sanitized versions promoted even by those most directly involved in the exploitation of Sephardi labor. Yavnieli's famous *shlihut* (Zionist emissary promoting *aliya*) to Yemen, for example, has always been idealized by Zionist texts. The gap between the "private" and the more public discourse is particularly striking in the case of Yavnieli himself, whose letters to Zionist institutions stress the search for cheap labor but whose memoirs present his activity in quasi-religious language, as bringing "to our brothers *Bnei-Israel* [Sons of Israel], far away in the land of Yemen, tidings from *Eretz Israel*, the good tidings of Renaissance, of the Land and of Work."[39]

The Dialectics of Dependency

These problems, present in embryonic form in the time of the pre-state era, came to their bitter "fruition" after the establishment of Israel, but were now explained away by a more sophisticated set of rationalizations and idealizations. Israel's rapid economic development during the 1950s and 1960s was achieved on the basis of a systematically unequal distribution of advantages. The socio-economic structure was thus formed contrary to the egalitarian myths characterizing Israel's self-representation until the last decade. The discriminatory decisions of Israeli officials against Sephardim began even before Sephardi arrival in Israel and were consciously premised on the assumption that the Ashkenazim, as the self-declared "salt of the earth," deserved better conditions and "special privileges."[40]

In contrast with Ashkenazi immigrants, Sephardim were treated inhumanely already in the camps constructed by the Zionists in their lands of origin as well as during transit. A Jewish Agency report on a camp in Algiers speaks of a situation in which "more than fifty people were living in a room of four or five square meters."[41] A doctor working in a Marseilles transit camp for North African-Jewish immigrants notes that, as a result of the bad housing and the recent decline in nutrition, children have died, adding: "I can't understand why in all the European countries the immigrants are provided with clothes while the North African immigrants are provided with nothing."[42] When information about anti-Sephardi discrimination in Israel filtered back to North Africa, there occurred a decline in immigration. Some left the transit camps in order to return to Morocco, while others, to quote a Jewish Agency emissary, had virtually "to be taken aboard the ships by force."[43] In Yemen, the voyage across the desert, exacerbated by the inhuman conditions in the Zionist transit camps, led to hunger, disease, and massive death, resulting in a brutal kind of "natural selection." Worrying about the burden of caring for sick Yemenites, Jewish Agency members were reassured by their colleague Yitzhak Rafael (Nationalist Religious Party) that "there is no need to fear the arrival of a large number of chronically ill, as they have to walk by foot for about two weeks. The gravely ill will not be able to walk."[44]

Figure 4 Photo and original Israel Government Press Office caption: "A Yemeni Family Walking in the Desert toward the Joint Camp near Aden, November 1, 1949"

The European-Jewish scorn for Eastern-Jewish lives and sensibilities—at times projected onto the Sephardim by Ashkenazi Orientalizing "experts" who claimed that death for Sephardim was a "common and natural thing"— was evident as well in the notorious incident of "the kidnapped children of Yemen."[45] Traumatized by the reality of life in Israel, some Sephardim, most of them Yemenis, fell prey to a ring of unscrupulous doctors, nurses, and social workers who provided some 600 Yemeni babies for adoption by childless Ashkenazi couples (some of them outside of Israel), while telling the natural parents that the children had died. The conspiracy was extensive enough to include the systematic issuance of fraudulent death certificates for the adopted children and to ensure that over several decades Sephardi demands for investigation were silenced and information was hidden and manipulated by government bureaus.[46] On June 30, 1986, the Public Committee for the Discovery of the Missing Yemenite Children held a massive protest rally. The rally, like many Sephardi protests and demonstrations, was almost completely ignored by the media, but a few months later Israeli television produced a documentary on the subject, blaming the bureaucratic chaos of the period for unfortunate "rumors," and perpetuating the myth of Sephardi parents as careless breeders with little sense of responsibility towards their own children.

Ethnic discrimination against Sephardim began with their initial settling. Upon arrival in Israel the various Sephardi communities, despite their will to stay together, were dispersed across the country. Families were separated, old communities disintegrated, and traditional leaders were shorn of their positions. Oriental Jews were largely settled in *maabarot*, remote villages, agricultural settlements, and in city neighborhoods some of which had only recently been emptied of Palestinians. As the absorption facilities became exhausted, the settlement authorities constructed *ayarot pituah* (Development Towns) largely in rural areas and frontier regions, which became, predictably, the object of Arab attack. The declared policy was to "strengthen the borders," implying a strengthening not only against Arab military attacks but also against any attempt by Palestinian refugees to return to their homeland. Although Israeli propaganda lauded the better-protected Ashkenazi *kibbutzim* for their courage in living on the frontiers, in fact their small number (about 3 percent of the Jewish population, and half that if one considers only border settlements) hardly enabled them to secure long borders, while the settlement of the more numerous Sephardim on the borders did ensure a certain security. Sephardi border settlements lacked, furthermore, the strong infrastructure of military protection provided to Ashkenazi settlements, thus leading to Sephardi loss of life. The ethnic segregation which tends to characterize Israeli housing also dates from this period. While Ashkenazim tend to live in the more prosperous northern zones, Sephardim are concentrated in the less wealthy southern zones. Despite this quasi-segregation, the two communities are generally linked in a relation of dependency, whereby the poor neighborhoods serve the privileged neighborhoods, a relational structure that mirrors that between the "socialist" *kibbutzim* and the neighboring Development Towns.

Figure 5   Photo and original Israel Government Press Office caption: "The Haddad Family from Iraq in Tira *maabara* in the 1950s"

In cases where Sephardim were moved into pre-existing housing—and in Israel pre-existing housing means Palestinian housing—the Sephardim often ended up living in precarious conditions because the Orientalist attitudes of the Israeli authorities found it normal to crowd many Sephardi families into the same house, on the assumption that they were "accustomed" to such conditions. These poor Sephardi neighborhoods were then systematically discriminated against in terms of infrastructural needs, educational and cultural advantages, and political self-representation. Later, when some of these neighborhoods became obstacles to urban gentrification, the Sephardim were forced, against their will and despite violent demonstrations, to other "modern" poor neighborhoods. In Jaffa, for example, the authorities, after the removal of the Sephardim, renovated the very same houses that they had refused to renovate for their Sephardi dwellers, thus facilitating the transition by which sections of "Oriental" Jaffa became a "bohemian" touristic locale dotted with art galleries. More recently, the Sephardi neighborhood of Musrara in Jerusalem has been undergoing a similar process. Now that the neighborhood is no longer near the pre-1967 border, the authorities have been trying to remove its Sephardi residents and force them to relocate to settlements on the West Bank, again under the pretense of improving their material conditions. The pattern is clear and systematic. The areas forcibly vacated by the Sephardim soon become the object of major investments leading to Ashkenazi gentrification, where the elite enjoy living within a "Mediterranean" *mise-en-scène* but without the inconvenience of a Palestinian or Sephardi presence, while the newly adopted Sephardi neighborhoods become decapitalized slums.

As a cheap, mobile, and manipulable labor force, Sephardim were indispensable to the economic development of the state of Israel. Given the need for mass housing in the 1950s, many Sephardim became ill-paid construction workers. The high profits generated by the cheap labor led to the rapid expansion of construction firms, managed or owned by Ashkenazim. Recruited especially into the mechanized and non-skilled sectors of agricultural production within large-scale government projects, Sephardim provided much of the labor force for settling the land. In the case of agricultural settlements, they received fewer and poorer lands than the various Ashkenazi settlements such as the *kibbutzim* and much less adequate means of production, resulting in lower production, lower income, and gradually the economic collapse of many of the Sephardi settlements.[47] After agricultural development and construction work reached a saturation point in the late 1950s and early 1960s, the government acted to industrialize the country and Sephardi workers once again were crucial to Israel's rapid development. A large section of the Sephardim came to form, in this period, an industrial proletariat. (In recent years, the monthly wage of production-line workers in textile factories has hovered around $150–200, roughly equivalent to that earned by many Third World workers.[48]) In fact Israel's appeals for foreign (largely Jewish) investment were partially based on the "attraction" of local cheap labor. The low wages of workers led to a widening gap between the upper and lower salary ranges in the industry. Development Towns, essential to industrial production, became virtual "company towns" in which a single factory became the major single provider of employment for a whole town, whose future became inextricably linked to the future of the company.[49]

While the system relegated Sephardim to a future-less bottom, it propelled Ashkenazim up the social scale, creating mobility in management, marketing, banking, and technical jobs. Recent published documents reveal the extent to which discrimination was a calculated policy that knowingly privileged the European immigrants, at times creating anomalous situations in which educated Sephardim became unskilled laborers, while much less educated Ashkenazim came to occupy high administrative positions.[50] Unlike the classical paradigm where immigration is linked to a desire for individual, familial, and community improvement, in Israel this process,

Figure 6   Photo and original Israel Government Press Office caption: "A Group of New *Olim* from Morocco in Mitzpe Ramon, April 1964"

for Sephardim, was largely reversed. What for Ashkenazi immigrants from Russia or Poland was a social *aliya* (literally "ascent") was for Sephardi immigrants from Iraq or Egypt a *yerida* (a "descent"). What was for persecuted Ashkenazi minorities a certain solution and a quasi-redemption of a culture, was for Sephardim the complete annihilation of a cultural heritage, a loss of identity, and a social and economic degradation.

The Façade of Egalitarianism

These discriminatory policies were executed under the aegis of the Labor Party and its affiliates, whose empire included a tentacular set of institutions, the most important of which was the Histadrut. The Histadrut controls the agricultural sector, the *kibbutzim*, and the largest labor unions in the industrial sector. With its own industries, marketing cooperatives, transportation systems, financial institutions, and social-service network, it exercises immense power. (Solleh Boneh, a Histadrut construction company, for example, could easily "freeze out" private builders from the Likud Party.) As a kind of caricature of trade-unionism, the Histadrut, despite its professed Socialist ideology, generally wields its vast power for the benefit of the elite, consistently favoring Ashkenazim for white-collar management positions, and Sephardim for blue-collar skilled and unskilled labor, leaving the latter most vulnerable in situations where factories are closed or workers are laid off. The same relational structure of oppression operates in the process whereby regional factories (even government-owned regional factories)

59

tend to be managed by the largely Ashkenazi *kibbutzim* while the workers are largely Sephardi or Palestinian. The dominant institutions, and the "socialist-"Zionist elite generally, then, virtually forced the Sephardim into underdevelopment, all quite contrary both to Ashkenazi denials that such processes have been taking place and contrary to the claims that those processes were unconscious and uncalculated.

The dominant Socialist-Humanist discourse in Israel hides this negative dialectic of wealth and poverty behind a mystifying façade of egalitarianism. The Histadrut and the Labor party, claiming to represent the workers, monopolize socialist language. Their May Day celebrations, the flying of red flags alongside the blue and white, and their speeches in the name of the "working class," mask the fact that the Labor network really represents only the interests of the Ashkenazi elite, whose members nevertheless still refer to themselves nostalgically as *Eretz Israel ha-'Ovedet* (Working Eretz Israel). The Sephardim and the Palestinians, the majority of workers in Israel, have been represented by special Histadrut departments called, respectively, the "Oriental Department" and the "Minority Department." (The Histadrut is not preoccupied, it goes without saying, with the economic exploitation of West Bank and Gaza Strip workers.) The manipulation of syndicalist language and the co-optation of Socialist slogans have thus served as a smokescreen for oppression. As a consequence, Sephardi militants have had to confront a kind of visceral aversion, on the part of lower-class Sephardim, to the very word "socialist," associated, for them, with oppression rather than liberation.

Figure 7   Photo and original Israel Government Press Office caption: "New *Olim* Standing in Line to Register, June 1949"

Although the official melioristic discourse suggests a gradual lessening of the gap between Sephardim and Ashkenazim, in fact the inequalities are more glaring now than they were two generations ago.[51] The system continues to reproduce itself, for example, in the differential treatment accorded to present-day European immigrants versus that accorded to veteran Oriental settlers. While second-generation Sephardim stagnate in substandard housing in poor neighborhoods, newly arrived Russian immigrants (with the exception of the Sephardi Georgians) are settled by the government into comfortable housing in central areas. (I do not examine here the discrimination suffered by the Ethiopian Falashas, now undergoing what the Sephardim experienced in the 1950s, supplemented by the added humiliation of religious harassment.) Indeed, the ethnic allegiances of the establishment become especially clear with regard to immigration policy. While supposedly promoting universal *aliya* and the end to the Diaspora, the establishment, given its (unnamed) fear of a Sephardi demographic advantage, energetically promotes immigration by Soviet Jews—a majority of whom would prefer to go elsewhere—while dragging its feet in response to the Falashas who desperately want to go and whose very lives have been endangered.

The largely segregated and unequal educational system in Israel also reproduces the ethnic division of labor through a tracking system which consistently orients Ashkenazi pupils toward prestigious white-collar positions requiring a strong academic preparation while pointing Sephardi pupils toward low-status blue-collar jobs. Ashkenazim have double the representation in white-collar occupations. The schools in Ashkenazi neighborhoods have better facilities, better teachers, and higher status. Ashkenazim have on average three more years of schooling than Sephardim. Their attendance rate in academic high school is 2.4 times as high, and it is five times as high in universities.[52] Most Oriental children, furthermore, study in schools designated by the Ministry of Education as schools for the "*te'unei tipuaḥ*" (literally, "those in need of nurture," or "culturally deprived"), a designation premised on the equation of cultural difference with inferiority. The educational system functions, as Shlomo Swirski puts it, as "a huge labelling mechanism that has, among other things, the effect of lowering the achievement and expectations of Oriental children and their parents."[53]

On whatever level—immigration policy, urban development, labor policy, government subsidies—we find the same pattern of a discrimination that touches even the details of daily life. The government, for example, subsidizes certain basic dietary staples, one of them being European-style bread; the pita favored as a staple by both Sephardim and Palestinians, meanwhile, is not subsidized. These discriminatory processes, which were shaped in the earliest period of Zionism, are reproduced every day and on

Figure 8   Photo and original Israel Government Press Office caption: "Textile Factory in Ofakim, November 1975"

every level, reaching into the very interstices of the Israeli social system. As a result, the Sephardim, despite their majority status, are under-represented in the national centers of power—in the Government, in the Knesset, in the higher echelons of the military, in the diplomatic corps, in the media, and in the academic world—and they are over-represented in the marginal, stigmatized regions of professional and social life.

The dominant sociological accounts of Israel's "ethnic problem" attribute the inferior status of Oriental Jews not to the class nature of Israeli society but rather to their origins in "pre-modern," "culturally backward" societies. Borrowing heavily from the intellectual arsenal of American "Functionalist" studies of development and modernization, Shumuel Eisenstadt and his many social-scientist disciples gave ideological subterfuge the aura of scientific rationality. The influential role of this "modernization" theory derives from its perfect match with the needs of the establishment. Eisenstadt borrows from American Structural Functionalism (Talcott Parsons) its teleological view of a "progress" which takes us from "traditional" societies, with their less complex social structures, to "modernization" and "development." Since the Israeli social formation was seen as that entity collectively created during the *Yishuv* period, the immigrants were perceived as integrating themselves into the pre-existing dynamic whole of a modern society patterned on the Western model. The underlying premise of Zionism, the "Ingathering of the Exiles," was thus translated into the sociological jargon of Structural

Functionalism. The "absorption" (*klita*) of Sephardi immigrants into Israeli society entailed the acceptance of the established consensus of the "host" society and the abandonment of "pre-modern" traditions. While European immigrants required only "absorption," the immigrants from Africa and Asia required "absorption through modernization." For the Eisenstadt tradition, the Oriental Jews had to undergo a process of "desocialization"—that is, erasure of their cultural heritage—and of "resocialization"—that is, assimilation to the Ashkenazi way of life. Thus cultural difference was posited as the cause of maladjustment. (The theory would have trouble explaining why other Sephardim, coming from the same "pre-modern" countries, at times from the very same families, suffered no particular maladjustment in such "postmodern" metropolises as Paris, London, New York, and Montreal.) At times the victim is even "blamed for blaming" an oppressive system. Here is sociologist Yosef Ben-David: "In such cases ethnic difficulties will render yet more acute the immigration crisis .... The immigrant will tend to rationalize the failure by putting the blame openly or implicitly on ethnic discrimination."[54]

The Ashkenazim, however, hid behind the flattening term "Israeli society," an entity presumed to embody the values of modernity, industry, science, and democracy. As Swirski points out, this presentation camouflaged the actual historical processes by obscuring a number of facts: first, that the Ashkenazim, not unlike the Sephardim, had also come from countries on the periphery of the world capitalist system, countries which entered the process of industrialization and technological-scientific development roughly at the same time as the Sephardi countries of origin; second, that a peripheral Yishuv society had *also* not reached a level of development comparable to that of the societies of the "center;" and third, that Ashkenazi "modernity" was made possible thanks to the labor force provided by Oriental mass immigration.[55] The ethnic basis of this process, furthermore, is often elided even by most Marxist analysts who speak generically of "Jewish workers," a simplification roughly parallel to speaking of the exploitation of "American" workers in Southern cotton plantations.

The Ordeals of Civility

The Oriental Jew clearly represents a problematic entity for European hegemony in Israel. Although Zionism collapses the Sephardim and the Ashkenazim into the single category of "one people," at the same time the Sephardi's Oriental "difference" threatens the European ideal-ego that phantasizes Israel as a prolongation of Europe "in" the Middle East, but not "of" it. Ben-Gurion, we may recall, formulated his visionary utopia for Israel as that of a "Switzerland of the Middle East," while Herzl called for a

Western-style capitalist-democratic miniature state, to be made possible by the grace of imperial patrons such as Britain or even Germany. The leitmotif of Zionist texts is the cry to form a "normal civilized nation," without the myriad "distortions" and forms of pariahdom typical of the Diaspora. (Zionist revulsion toward *shtetl* "abnormalities," as some commentators have pointed out, is often strangely reminiscent of the very anti-Semitism it presumably so abhors.) The *Ostjuden*, perennially marginalized by Europe, realized their desire of becoming Europe, ironically, in the Middle East, this time on the back of their own "*Ostjuden*," the Eastern Jews. Having passed through their own "ordeal of civility," as the "Blacks" of Europe, they now imposed their civilizing tests on their own "Blacks."[56]

The paradox of secular Zionism is that it attempted to "end a Diaspora," during which Jews suffered intensely in the West and presumably had their

Figure 9   Photo and original Israel Government Press Office caption: "A Mother and her Two Children from Kurdistan-Iraq Arrive from a Flight from Teheran, May 1951"

heart in the East—a feeling encapsulated in the almost daily repetition of the phrase "next year in Jerusalem"—only to found a state whose ideological and geopolitical orientation has been almost exclusively turned toward the West. It is in this same context that we must understand the oppression of Sephardim not only as Middle Eastern people but also as embodying, for the *sabra*-Zionist mind, what it erroneously perceived as a reminiscence of an "inferior" *shtetl* Jewishness. (This attitude was at times expressed toward Ashkenazi newcomers as well.) The immigrants from the Third World, and especially from Arab-Muslim countries, provoked "anti-Jewish" feelings in the secularly oriented *sabra* culture both because of the implicitly threatening idea of the heterogeneity of Jewish cultures and because of the discomforting amalgam of "Jewishness" with what was perceived as "backwardness." This latter combination was seen as a malignancy to be eradicated: an ideological impulse manifested in the measures taken to strip Sephardi Jews of their heritage: religious Yemenis shorn of their sidelocks, children virtually forced into Euro-Zionist schools, and so forth. The openness toward Western culture, then, must be understood within the relational context of a menacing heteroglossia, as a reaction against the vestiges of *shtetl* culture as well as against a projected penetration of "alien" Oriental Jews. The Sephardi cultural difference was especially disturbing to a secular Zionism whose claims for representing a single Jewish people were premised not only on common religious background but also on common nationality. The strong cultural and historical links that Sephardim shared with the Arab/Muslim world, stronger in many respects than those they shared with the Ashkenazim, threatened the conception of a homogeneous nation akin to those on which European nationalist movements were based.

Those Sephardim who came under the control of Ashkenazi religious authorities, meanwhile, were obliged to send their children to Ashkenazi religious schools, where they learned the "correct" Ashkenazi forms of practicing Judaism, including Yiddish-accented praying, liturgical-gestural norms, and sartorial codes favoring the dark colors of centuries-ago Poland. Some Oriental Jews, then, were forced into the Orthodox mold. The caricatural portrayal of Sephardim as religious fanatics, when not the product of *mauvaise foi*, is linked to a Eurocentric confusion between religiousness and Orthodoxy. In fact, however, the wrenching *déchirement* of the secular/orthodox split, so characteristic of the European-Jewish experience, has been historically quite alien to Sephardi culture. Among Sephardim, Jewishness has generally been lived in an atmosphere of flexibility and tolerance, downplaying both abstract laws and rabbinical hierarchy. It is not uncommon, among Sephardim, to find coexisting within the same family diverse ways of being Jewish without this diversity-entailing conflict. In Israel, the clash which pits secular against orthodox Jews largely divides

Ashkenazim rather than Sephardim, the majority of whom, whether religious or secular, feel repelled by the rigidity of both camps, as well as mindful of the ways both camps have oppressed them, albeit in different ways.

As an integral part of the topography, language, culture, and history of the Middle East, Sephardim were necessarily close to those who were posited as the common enemy for all Jews—the Arabs. Fearing an encroachment of the East upon the West, the establishment repressed the Middle Easternness of Sephardim as part of an attempt to separate and create hostility between the two groups. Arabness and Orientalness were consistently stigmatized as evils to be uprooted. For the Arab Jew, existence under Zionism has meant a profound and visceral schizophrenia, mingling stubborn self-pride with an imposed self-rejection, typical products of a situation of colonial ambivalence. The ideological dilemmas of Sephardim derive from the contradictions inherent in a situation where they are urged to see Judaism and Zionism as synonyms and Jewishness and Arabness as antonyms (for the first time in their history), when in fact they are both Arab and Jewish, and less historically, materially, and emotionally invested in Zionist ideology than the Ashkenazim.

Sephardim in Israel were made to feel ashamed of their dark olive skin, of their guttural language, of the winding quartertones of their music, and even of their traditions of hospitality. Children, trying desperately to conform to an elusive *sabra* norm, were made to feel ashamed of their parents and their Arab countries of origin. At times "the Semitic" physiognomies of the Sephardim led to situations in which they were mistaken for Palestinians and therefore arrested or beaten. Since Arabness led only to rejection, many Sephardim internalized the Western perspective and turned into self-hating Sephardim. Thus not only did the "West" come to represent the "East," but also, in a classic play of colonial specularity, the East came to view itself through the West's distorting mirror. Indeed, if it is true, as Malcolm X said, that the White man's worst crime was to make the Black man hate himself, the establishment in Israel has much to answer for. In fact, Arab-hatred, when it occurs among Oriental Jews, is almost always a disguised form of self-hatred. As research from 1978 indicates, Sephardi respect for Arabs rises with their own self-esteem.[57] Sephardi hostility to Arabs, to the extent that it does exist, is very much "made in Israel."[58] Oriental Jews had to be taught to see the Arabs, and themselves, as "Other." The kind of *selbsthass* that sometimes marked the post-Enlightenment Ashkenazi community had never been part of Sephardi existence in the Muslim world; for the Sephardim, *selbsthass* (of themselves as Orientals) had to be "learned" from the Ashkenazim, who themselves had "learned" self-hatred at the feet and among the ranks of the Europeans. Here too we are confronted with problematic antonyms, in this case the opposing words "Zionism" and "anti-Semitism." (But that subject merits separate discussion.)

The Demonization of Sephardim

The "divide and conquer" approach to Sephardi/Palestinian relations, as we have seen, operated through turning Sephardim into the most accessible targets for Arab attacks as well as through the deformation of the ideal of "Hebrew Work." But the everyday power mechanisms in Israeli society also foster concrete economic pressures that generate tension between the two communities. Those Sephardim who continue to constitute the majority of the Jewish blue-collar workers are constantly placed in competition with the Palestinians for jobs and salaries, a situation which allows the elite to exploit both groups more or less at will. The considerable government expenditures for West Bank settlements, similarly, prod some Sephardim to move there for economic reasons—rather than the ideological reasons that motivate many Ashkenazi settlers—and thus provoke Palestinians. Finally, because of the segregation between the two groups, Sephardim and Palestinians in Israel tend to learn about each other through the Ashkenazi-dominated media, with little direct contact. Thus the Sephardim learn to see the Palestinians as "terrorists," while the Palestinians learn to see the Sephardim as "Kahanist fanatics," a situation which hardly facilitates mutual understanding and recognition.

Although liberal Left discourse in Israel has in recent years taken a small step toward recognizing the "Palestinian entity," it continues to hermetically seal off the Sephardi issue as an "internal social problem" to be solved once peace is achieved. Just as this discourse elides the historical origins of the Palestinian struggle and thus nostalgically looks back to an imagined prelapsarian past of "beautiful Israel" so it also elides the historical origins of Sephardi resentment and thus constructs the myth of "reactionaries." One problem is compartmentalized as "political" and "foreign" and the other as "social" and "internal"; the mutual implication of the two issues and their common relation to Ashkenazi domination is ignored. In fact, the Sephardi movement constitutes a more immediate threat to Ashkenazi privilege and status than the abstract, perpetually deferred, future solution to the Palestinian question. Whereas the "Palestinian problem" can still be presented as the inevitable clash of two nationalities, acknowledgment of the exploitation and deculturalization of Sephardim in a putatively egalitarian Jewish state implies the indictment of the Israeli system itself as incorrigibly oppressive toward all peoples of the Orient.

Peace Now leaders such as General Mordechai Bar-On attribute the lack of Sephardi enthusiasm for Peace Now to "strong rightist tendencies" and "excited loyalty to the personal leadership of Menachem Begin," symptomatic of their "natural and traditional tendency ... to follow a charismatic leader" all compounded with a "deep-rooted distrust in the Arabs."[59] The Sephardi "Other" is portrayed as uncritical, instinctual, and, in accordance with Oriental-despotic traditions, easily manipulated by patriarchal demagogues. The Sephardim, when not ignored by the Israeli "Left," appear only to be scapegoated for everything that is wrong with Israel: "they" have destroyed beautiful Israel; "they" are turning Israel into a right-wing anti-democratic state; "they" support the occupation; "they" are an obstacle to peace. These prejudices are then disseminated by Israeli "leftists" in international conferences, lectures, and publications. The caricatural presentation of Sephardim is a way of enjoying a self-celebratory We-of-the-liberal-West image before international public opinion, at a time when Israel has undeniably lost its "progressive" allure and past unquestioned status, while continuing to enjoy, in Israel itself, a comfortable position as an integral part of the establishment. This facile scapegoating of Sephardim for a situation generated by Ashkenazi Zionists elides the reality of significant Sephardi pro-Palestinian activities as well as the lack of Sephardi access to the media and the consequent inability to counter such charges, which are then taken seriously by Palestinians and public opinion around the world. The demonization of Sephardim also has the advantage of placing the elite protestors in the narcissistic posture of perpetual seekers of peace who must bear the hostility of the government, the right wing, the Sephardim, and recalcitrant Palestinians. This martyrdom of the "shoot-and-cry" public relations Left contributes almost nothing to peace, but it does create the optical illusion of a viable oppositional peace force. Even the progressive forces in the Peace Camp that support a Palestinian state alongside Israel seldom abandon the idea of a Jewish Western state whose subtext inevitably is the ethnic and class oppression of Sephardim. Within such a context, it is hardly surprising that the membership of Peace Now is almost exclusively Ashkenazi, with almost no Sephardi, or for that matter Palestinian, participation.

Sephardi hostility toward Peace Now, rather than being discussed in class and ethnic terms, is conveniently displaced by Ashkenazi liberals onto the decoy-issue of a presumed general Sephardi animosity toward Arabs. This formulation ignores a number of crucial points. First, anti-Arabism forms an integral part of Zionist practice and ideology; Sephardim should not be scapegoated for what the Ashkenazi establishment itself has promoted. Secondly, Ashkenazim form the leadership of the right-wing parties and many Ashkenazim vote for these parties. (Polls taken during the 1981 elections showed that 36 percent of foreign-born Ashkenazim and 45 percent of Israeli-born Ashkenazim opted for Likud.[60] Sephardim, for their part, have also voted for Labor and other liberal parties, including the Communist Party.) In fact, however, the relatively high Sephardi vote for Likud has almost nothing to do with the latter's policies towards the Arabs; it is, rather, a minimal and even misplaced expression of Sephardi revolt against decades of Labor oppression. Since Sephardim cannot really represent themselves within the Israeli political system, a vote for the opposition, even though it is itself part of the ruling class, becomes a way, as some Sephardi militants put it, to "strengthen the hyena in order to weaken the bear." Some independent leftist Sephardi activists viewed Likud, for example, as "an overnight shelter" where Oriental Jews could find temporary refuge while beginning to forge a powerful Sephardi revolt. The difference between Likud and Labor with regard to the Palestinians, in any case, has not been one of practice but rather one of discourse, one aggressive-nationalist and the other humanist-liberal. The difference between the two parties with regard to Sephardim, similarly, is less one of policy than one of a contrast between populist appeals (Likud) and elitist condescension (Labor).

From Kahane to the communists, the ideologies of the Israeli parties— from non-Zionist religious Orthodoxy dating back to Eastern-European anti-Zionist opposition, through religious nationalism which foregrounds the "holiness of the land" (a religious variant on a common topos of European nationalism), to the dominant secular-humanist Zionism based on European Enlightenment ideals—"translate" on a political register the various Jewish-European identity dilemmas. Founded, led, and controlled by Ashkenazim, these parties are the locus of struggle over the sharing of power among the various Ashkenazi groups. Within this structure there is little place for Sephardi aspirations. The Jewish-Sephardi majority has been politically marginalized, in other words, in a Jewish state, and in what is ritually and erroneously referred to as the "only democracy in the Middle East." The historical reasons for this marginalization are complex and can hardly be detailed here, but they include the following: the historical legacy of the Ashkenazi domination of the institutional party apparati prior to the arrival *en masse* of the Sephardim; the inertia of a hierarchical top-down structure that leaves little room for major shifts in direction; the delegitimization of the traditional Sephardi leadership; objectively harsh conditions, in the 1950s and 1960s, which left little time and energy for political and communal re-organization; and the repression as well as the co-optation of Sephardi revolts.

Political manipulation of Sephardi immigrants began virtually on their arrival, and at times even before, when Israeli party recruiters competed for Sephardi allegiance in the Oriental countries of origin. In Israel, the immigrants were met in the airports not only by the officials in charge of arrival procedures but also by representatives of the various parties, who parceled out the Sephardim along the existing political spectrum. In the *maabarot,* as in Palestinian villages, the government controlled the populace through the intermediary of "notables" authorized to dispense favors in exchange for votes. At the time of the foundation of the State, there was some discussion of having a token Sephardi among the first twelve Cabinet Members, and considerable energy was expended on finding a sufficiently insignificant post. ("The Sephardi minister," said David Remez of the Labor party, "cannot have any grandiose pretensions.")[61] At the same time, the Ashkenazi institutional apparatus has always claimed to represent the interests of *all* Jewish people, including Sephardim, as demonstrated by the proliferation of "Oriental Departments." Unlike Palestinians, Sephardim were never denied official access to any Israeli institutions, and they were allowed, even encouraged, to find refuge in existing organizations. Class resentments could thus be exorcised through "socialist" organizations, while traditional Jewish activities could be entertained through religious institutions.

Signs of Sephardi Rebellion

Despite these obstacles, Sephardi revolt and resistance has been constant. Already in the transit camps there were *Lehem-'Avoda* (bread and jobs) demonstrations. David Horowitz, then General Director of the Ministry of Finance, during a political consultation with Ben-Gurion, described the Sephardi population in the camps as "rebellious" and the situation as "incendiary" and "dynamite."[62] Another major revolt against misery and discrimination began in Haifa, in the neighborhood of Wadi Salib, in 1959. Israeli authorities suppressed the rebellion with military and police terror. The Labor Party (*Mapai*) furthermore tried to undermine the political organization that emerged from the riots by obliging slum residents to join the Party if they hoped for a job. Another large-scale rebellion broke out again in the 1970s, when the Israeli Black Panthers called for the destruction of the regime and for the legitimate rights of all the oppressed without regard for religion, origin, or nationality. This alarmed the establishment, and the movement's leaders were arrested and placed under administrative detention. At that moment, the Black Panthers launched demonstrations that shook the entire country. In a demonstration that has since become famous (May 1971), tens of thousands, in response to police repression, went into the streets and threw Molotov cocktails against police and government targets. The same evening, 170 activists were arrested, 35 were hospitalized, and more than 70 policemen and officers were wounded. Taking their name from the American movement, the Black Panther revolt was led by the children of immigrants, some of them "delinquents" who had passed through rehabilitation centers or prisons. Gradually becoming aware of the political nature of their "inferiority," they sabotaged the myth of the "melting pot" by showing that there are in Jewish Israel not one but two peoples. They often used the term *dfukim ve-sh'horim* (screwed and blacks) to express the ethnic/class positioning of Sephardim and viewed the American Black revolt as a source of inspiration. (The choice of the name "Black Panthers" also ironically reverses the Ashkenazi reference to Sephardim as "black animals.") More recently in December 1982, riots broke out in response to the police murder of an Oriental slum resident whose only crime was to build an "illegal extension" to his overcrowded house.

Figure 10 Above: A Black Panther organization poster; Below: Black Panther leaders, Charlie Bitton and Sa'adia Marciano, record an announcement

The establishment, meanwhile, has consistently tried to explain away all manifestations of Sephardi revolt. The "bread and jobs" demonstrations in the transit camps were dismissed as the result of the agitational work of leftist Iraqi immigrants; the demonstrations of Wadi Salib and the Black Panthers were the expression of "violence-prone Moroccans;" individual acts of resistance were the symptoms of "neurosis" or "maladjustment." Golda Meir, Prime Minister during the Black Panther revolts, complained maternalistically that "they are not nice." Demonstrators were described in the press and in academic studies as lumpenproletarian deviants. The various movements were caricatured in the media as "ethnic organizing" and an attempt to "divide the nation." Class and ethnic antagonism were often suppressed in the name of a supposedly imminent "national security" disaster. In any case, all attempts at independent Sephardi political activity have faced the carrot-and-stick counter measures of the establishment, measures which range on a spectrum from symbolic gestures toward token "change" channeled via the welfare infrastructure, through systematic co-optation of Sephardi activists (offering jobs and privilege is a major source of power in a small centralized country) to harassment, character assassination, imprisonment, torture and, at times, pressures to leave the country.

The orchestrated attacks on Sephardi independent political activities—including by the "Left"—were executed in the name of "national unity" in the face of the Arab threat. The assumption throughout was that the dominant parties were *not* "ethnic"—the very word, here as often, reflects a marginalizing strategy premised on the implicit contrast of "norm" and "other"—when in fact the existing Israeli institutions were *already* ethnically based according to countries of origin. This reality was masked by a linguistic façade which made the Ashkenazim "Israelis," and the Sephardim *"Bnei 'Edot ha-Mizrah"* or "Sons of the Oriental ethnic communities." The plural here "covered" the fact of the Sephardi numerical superiority, emphasizing plurality of origin, in contrast with a presumed pre-existing (Ashkenazi) Israeli unity, and disguised the fact that the Sephardim, whatever their country of origin, have come in Israel to form a collective entity based both on cultural affinities and the shared experience of oppression. Like many other ethnically-based dominating groups, the Israeli Ashkenazim have a kind of *pudeur* about being named; they rarely refer to themselves, or their power, as Ashkenazi; they do not see themselves as an ethnic group (partially because "Ashkenazi" evokes the "unflattering" memory of *shtetl* Jews). The Sephardim, however, do not share this *pudeur*. Sephardim, whatever their superficial political allegiance, often refer to the "Ashkenazi state", "the Ashkenazi newspapers," "the Ashkenazi television," "the Ashkenazi parties," "the Ashkenazi court," and at times even "the Ashkenazi army."

The overwhelming majority of army deserters are to be found in the Sephardi community, particularly among the very lower classes whose behavior reveals a reluctance to "give anything to this Ashkenazi state," and this in a society whose very structure sends the subliminal message: "Fight the Arabs and then we will accept you." A recent editorial in a Sephardi-neighborhood newspaper, entitled "Forty Years of the Ashkenazi State," summed up Sephardi feelings after four decades of statehood:

> This is the 40th year of independence for the Ashkenazi state called Israel, but who is going to celebrate? Our Oriental brothers who sit in jails? Our prostitute sisters from Tel Baruch? Our sons in schools, will they be celebrating the decline in the level of education? Will we celebrate the Ashkenazi theater of Kishon's *Sallah*? Or the rising fanaticism in our society? The flight from peace? The Oriental music broadcast only in the ghettoes of the media? The unemployment in development towns? It seems, that the Orientals have no reason to celebrate. The joy and light is only for the Ashkenazim, and for the glory of the Ashkenazi state.[63]

Although effaced or overshadowed by the Israeli/Arab, conflict, and despite official harassment, Sephardi resistance is always present, going through transformations, changing organizational forms. Despite the attempts to engender hostility between Sephardim and Palestinians, there have always been Sephardi activities in favor of justice for the Palestinians. Many members of the older Sephardi generation, both inside and outside of Israel, were eager to serve as a bridge of peace to the Arabs and to the Palestinians, but their efforts were consistently refused or undercut by the Establishment.[64] The Black Panthers, seeing themselves as a "natural bridge" for peace, called in the 1970s for a "real dialogue" with the Palestinians, who are "an integral part of the political landscape of the Middle East" and whose "representatives must be allowed to take part in all meetings and discussions which seek a solution to the conflict."[65] The Panthers were also among the first Israeli groups to meet with the PLO. In the 1980s, movements such as East for Peace and the Oriental Front in Israel and Perspectives Judéo-Arabes in France—the names themselves point to the shedding of self-shame and the utopia of integration into the political and cultural East—have called for an independent Palestinian state led by the PLO. The Oriental Front stresses that Sephardim are not Zionists in the conventional sense, but rather "in the Biblical meaning of 'Zion,' of a Jewish life in the birthplace of the Jewish people." They stress as well the "debt of respect to Arab countries that gave [us] protection during centuries" and the strong Sephardi "love and respect for Arab culture," since "there is no alienation between the Arab existence and the Oriental [Jewish] one."[66]

Figure 11   A Black Panther demonstration in Jerusalem

Epilogue

In many respects, European Zionism has been an immense confidence trick played on Sephardim, a cultural massacre of immense proportions, an attempt, partially successful, to wipe out, in a generation or two, millennia of rooted Oriental civilization, unified even in its diversity. My argument here, I hasten to clarify, is not an essentialist one. I am not positing a new binarism of eternal hostility between Ashkenazim and Sephardim. In many countries and situations, the two groups, despite cultural and religious differences, have co-existed in relative peace; it is only in Israel that they exist in a relation of dependency and oppression. (In any case, only 10 percent of Ashkenazi Jews are in Israel.) Obviously Ashkenazi Jews have been the prime victims of the most violent kinds of European anti-Semitism, a fact that makes it more delicate to articulate not only a pro-Palestinian point of view but also a pro-Sephardi point of view. A Sephardi critique is expected to be suppressed in the name of the menaced "unity of the Jewish people" in the post-Holocaust era (as if within all unities, especially those of recent construction, there were not also differences and dissonances). My argument is also not a moralistic or characterological one, positing a Manichean schematism contrasting good Oriental Jews with evil Ashkenazi oppressors. My argument is structural, an attempt to account theoretically for the "structure of feeling," the deep current of rage against the Israeli

74

establishment that unites most Sephardim independent of their declared party affiliation. My argument is situational and analytical; it claims that the Israeli socio-political formation continually generates the underdevelopment of the Oriental Jews.

A specter haunts European Zionism, the specter that all of its victims— Palestinians, Sephardim (as well as critical Ashkenazim, in and outside Israel, stigmatized as "self-hating" malcontents)—will perceive the linked analogies between their oppressions. To conjure away this specter, the Zionist establishment in Israel has done everything in its power: the fomenting of war and the cult of "national security;" the simplistic portrayal of Palestinian resistance as "terrorism;" the fostering of situations which catalyze Sephardi/ Palestinian tension; the caricaturing of Sephardim as "Arab-haters" and "religious fanatics;" the promotion, through the educational system and the media, of "Arab-hatred" and Sephardi self-rejection; and the repression or co-optation of all those who might promote a Palestinian–Sephardi alliance. I in no way mean to equate Palestinian and Sephardi suffering— obviously Palestinians are those most egregiously wronged by Zionism—or to compare the long lists of crimes against both. The point is one of affinity and analogy rather than perfect identity of interests or experience. I am not asking Palestinians to feel sorry for the Sephardi soldiers who might be among those shooting at them. It is not Sephardim, obviously, who are being killed, time after time, in the streets of Gaza or in the refugee camps of Lebanon. What is at stake, in any case, is not a competition for sympathy but a search for alternatives. Till now both Palestinians and Sephardim have been the objects and not the subjects of Zionist ideology and policies, and till now they have been played against each other. But it was not the Sephardim who made the crucial decisions leading to the brutal displacement and oppression of the Palestinians—even if the Sephardim were enlisted as cannon fodder after the fact—just as it was not the Palestinians who uprooted, exploited, and humiliated the Sephardim.

The present regime in Israel inherited from Europe a strong aversion to respecting the right of self-determination of non-European peoples, whence the quaint vestigial, out-of-step quality of its discourse, its atavistic talk of the "civilized nations" and "the civilized world." As much as it is impossible to imagine peace between Israel and the Arabs without recognizing and affirming the historical rights of the Palestinian people, so must a real peace not overlook the collective rights of Oriental Jews. It would be short-sighted to negotiate only with those in power or embraced by it, dismissing the subjection of Jews from Arab and Muslim countries as an "internal Jewish" problem—a position that would be analogous to taking the Zionist attitude that the Palestinian question is an "internal"

Arab problem. I am not suggesting, obviously, that all Sephardim would ascribe to my analysis, although most would endorse much of its thrust. I am suggesting, rather, that only such an analysis can account for the complexities of the present situation and the depth and extent of Sephardi rage. My analysis hopes, finally, to open up a long-range perspective that might aid in a larger effort to move beyond the present intolerable impasse.

2

Dislocated Identities:
Reflections of an Arab Jew

When issues of racial and colonial discourse are discussed in the U.S., people of Middle Eastern and North African origin are often excluded. This piece is written with the intent of opening up multicultural debates, going beyond the U.S. census's simplistic categorization of Middle Eastern peoples as "whites." It's also written with the intent of multiculturalizing American notions of Jewishness. Provoked by the Gulf War, my personal narrative questions the Eurocentric opposition of Arab and Jew, particularly the denial of Arab-Jewish (Sephardi) voices both in the Middle Eastern and American contexts.

*   *   *

I am an Arab Jew. Or, more specifically, an Iraqi-Israeli woman living, writing, and teaching in the U.S. Most members of my family were born and raised in Baghdad, and now live in Iraq, Israel, the U.S., the U.K., and the Netherlands. When my grandmother first encountered Israeli society in the 1950s, she was convinced that the people who looked, spoke, and ate so differently, the European Jews, were actually European Christians. Jewishness for her generation was inextricably associated with Middle Easternness. My grandmother, who still lives in Israel and still communicates largely in Arabic, had to be taught to speak of "us" as Jews and "them" as Arabs. For Middle Easterners, the operating distinction had always been "Muslim," "Jew," "Christian," not Arab versus Jew. The assumption was that "Arabness" referred to a common shared culture and language, albeit with religious differences.

Americans are often amazed to discover the existentially nauseating or charmingly exotic possibilities of such a syncretic identity. I recall a

---

Published in *Movement Research: Performance Journal*, no. 5 (Fall–Winter, 1992), and, under the title "Reflections of an Arab Jew," in *Emergences* 3/4 (Fall 1992). Segments of this text were incorporated into Elia Suleiman's film *Homage by Assassination* (1992).

well-established colleague who despite my elaborate lessons on the history of Arab Jews still had trouble understanding that I was not a tragic anomaly, the daughter of an Arab (Palestinian) and an Israeli (European Jew). Living in North America makes it even more difficult to communicate that we are Jews and yet entitled to our Middle Eastern difference. And that we are Arabs and yet entitled to our religious difference, like Arab Christians and Arab Muslims. It was precisely the policing of cultural borders in Israel that led some of us to escape into the metropolises of syncretic identities. Yet, in an American context, we face again a hegemony that allows us to narrate only a single Jewish memory: that is, a European one. For those of us who don't hide our Middle Easternness under one Jewish "we," it becomes tougher and tougher to exist in an American context hostile to the very notion of Easternness.

As an Arab Jew, I am often obliged to explain the "mysteries" of this oxymoronic entity. That we have spoken Arabic, not Yiddish; that for millennia our cultural creativity, secular and religious, had been largely articulated in Arabic (Maimonides being one of the few intellectuals to "make it" into the consciousness of the West); and that even the most religious of our communities in the Middle East and North Africa never expressed themselves in Yiddish-accented Hebrew prayers, nor did they practice liturgical-gestural norms and sartorial codes favoring the dark colors of centuries-ago Poland. Middle Eastern Jewish women similarly never wore wigs: their hair covers, if worn, consisted of different variations on regional clothing (and in the wake of British and French imperialism, many wore Western-style clothes). If you go to our synagogues, even in New York, Montreal, Paris, or London, you'll be amazed to hear the winding quartertones of our music, which the uninitiated might imagine to be coming from a mosque.

Now that the three cultural topographies that compose my ruptured and dislocated history—Iraq, Israel, and the U.S.—have been involved in a war, it is crucial to say that we exist. Some of us refuse to dissolve so as to facilitate "neat" national and ethnic divisions. My anxiety and pain during a Scud attack on Israel, where some of my family lives, did not cancel out my fear and anguish for the victims of the bombardment of Iraq, where I also have relatives.

But war is the friend of binarisms, leaving little place for complex identities. The Gulf War intensified a pressure already familiar to the Arab-Jewish Diaspora in the wake of the Israeli/Arab conflict: a pressure to choose between being a Jew and being an Arab. For our families, who have lived in Mesopotamia since at least the Babylonian Exile, who have been Arabized for millennia, and who were abruptly dislodged to Israel 40 years ago, to be suddenly forced to assume a homogenous European-Jewish identity based on experiences in Russia, Poland, and Germany, was an exercise in self-devastation. To be a European or an American Jew has hardly been perceived as a contradiction, but to be an Arab Jew has been seen as a kind of logical paradox, even an ontological subversion. This binarism has led many Oriental Jews (our name in Israel referring to our common Asian and African countries of origin) to a profound and visceral schizophrenia, since for the first time in our history Arabness and Jewishness have been imposed as antonyms.

Figure 12   The Iraqi-issued *laissez-passer* of Aziza and Sasson, the author's parents

Intellectual discourse in the West highlights a Judeo-Christian tradition, yet rarely acknowledges the Judeo-Muslim culture of the Middle East, of North Africa, or of pre-Expulsion Spain (1492) and of the European parts of the Ottoman Empire. The Jewish experience in the Muslim world has often been portrayed as an unending nightmare of oppression and humiliation. Although I in no way want to idealize that experience—there were occasional tensions, discriminations, even violence—on the whole, we lived quite comfortably within Muslim societies. Despite George Bush's facile equation of Hussein and Hitler, for Jews in the Muslim world there was no equivalent to the Holocaust. In the case of the Inquisition (1492), both Jews and Muslims were the victims of Christian zealotry. Our history simply cannot be discussed in European Jewish terminology. As Iraqi Jews, while retaining a communal identity, we were generally well-integrated and indigenous to the country, forming an inseparable part of its social and cultural life. Thoroughly Arabized, we used Arabic even in hymns and religious ceremonies. The liberal and secular trends of the 20th century engendered an even stronger association of Iraqi Jews and Arab culture, which brought Jews into an extremely active role in public and cultural life. Prominent Jewish writers, poets, and scholars played a vital role in Arab culture, distinguishing themselves in Arabic-speaking theater, and in music, as singers, composers, and players of traditional instruments. In Egypt, Morocco, Syria, Lebanon, Iraq, and Tunisia, Jews became members of legislatures, of municipal councils, of the judiciary, and even occupied high economic positions. (The finance minister of Iraq in the 1920s was Sassoon Heskel, and in Egypt, Yusuf Qattawi—higher positions, ironically, than those our community has generally achieved within the Jewish state.)

The same historical process that dispossessed Palestinians of their property, lands, and national-political rights, was linked to the dispossession, suffered by Middle Eastern and North African Jews, of their property, lands, and rootedness in Muslim countries. As refugees, or mass immigrants (depending on one's political perspective), we were forced to leave everything behind and give up our Iraqi passports. The same process also affected our uprootedness or ambiguous positioning within Israel itself. In Israel we have been systematically discriminated against by institutions that deployed their energies and material resources to the consistent advantage of European Jews and to the consistent disadvantage of Oriental Jews. Even our physiognomies betray us, leading to internalized colonialism or physical misperception. Sephardi-Oriental women often dye their dark hair blond, while the men have more than once been arrested or beaten when mistaken for Palestinians. What for Ashkenazi immigrants from Russia and Poland was a social *aliya* (literally "ascent") was for Oriental Sephardi Jews a *yerida* ("descent").

Stripped of our history, we have been forced by our no-exit situation to repress our collective nostalgia, at least within the public sphere. The pervasive notion of "one people" reunited in their ancient homeland actively deauthorizes any affectionate memory of life before Israel. We have never been allowed to mourn a trauma that the images of Iraq's destruction only intensified and crystallized for some of us. Our cultural creativity in Arabic, Hebrew, and Aramaic is hardly studied in Israeli schools, and it is becoming difficult to convince our children that we actually did exist there, and that some of us are still there in Iraq, Morocco, and Yemen.

The notion of "in-gathering from Exile" does not permit a narration of the Exile of Arab Jews in the Promised Land. My parents and grandparents,

Figure 13   The Iraqi-issued *laissez-passer* of Aziza and Sasson, the author's parents

30 or 40 years after they left Baghdad, still long for its sights and sounds. Oriental Jews in Israel are enthusiastic consumers of Jordanian, Lebanese, and Egyptian television programs and films, just as our Oriental-Arabic music is consumed in the Arab world, often without being labeled as originating in Israel. The Yemeni-Israeli singer Ofra Haza has been recognized by the Yemenis as continuing a Yemeni cultural tradition. Back in the days before the horrific bombing of Baghdad, we used to play a bittersweet game of scanning the television to spot changes in the city's urban topography. But the impossibility of ever going there once led me to contemplate an ironic inversion of the Biblical expression: "By the waters of Zion, where we sat down, and there we wept, and when we remembered Babylon."

In the U.S., watching media images of the Middle East, one gets the impression that there are only Euro-American Jews in Israel and only Muslim Arabs in the rest of the Middle East. In the media, one finds few images of Palestinian Israelis or of Iraqi, Moroccan, or Ethiopian Israelis, even though we compose the majority of the population in Israel. During the Gulf War, most Israelis interviewed by American reporters tended to be Euro-Israelis, often speaking English with an American accent. The elision was especially striking when the missiles hit Iraqi-Jewish neighborhoods in the south of Tel Aviv (television networks referred to "working-class neigh-borhoods," the equivalent of calling Harlem a working-class neighborhood, effacing its ethnic/racial cultural identity) and in Ramat Gan, a city well known for its Iraqi population, popularly nicknamed "Ramat Baghdad." (A local joke had it that the Scuds fell there because they smelled the *'amba*, an Iraqi mango pickle.) Furthermore, some Iraqi Jews living in the U.S., Britain, and Israel still have families in Iraq. The media showed images of prayers in the mosques, and even in the churches of Baghdad, but there was no reference to prayers in the synagogue of Baghdad. In the American context too, it is only the story of European Jews that is narrated, denying Arab Jews the possibility of self-representation.

As an Iraqi Jew, I cannot but notice the American media's refusal to value Iraqi life. The crippled animals in the Kuwait Zoo received more sympathetic attention than civilian victims in Iraq. The media much prefer the spectacle of the triumphant progress of Western technology to the survival of the peoples and cultures of the Middle East. The case of Arab Jews is just one of many elisions. From the outside, there is little sense of our community, and even less sense of the diversity of our political perspectives. Oriental-Sephardi peace movements, from the Black Panthers of the '70s to the more recent East for Peace and the Oriental Front in Israel, Perspectives Judéo-Arabes in France, and the New York-based World Organization of Jews from Islamic Countries, not only call for a just peace for Israelis and Palestinians, but also for the cultural, political, and economic integration of Israel/Palestine into the Middle East. And thus an end to the binarisms of war, an end to a simplistic charting of Middle Eastern identities.

3

Breaking the Silence

Good evening everyone! *Masa' el-kher*! *Ismi Ella, bas ismi el-asli Habiba.* [My name is Ella but my original name is Habiba]. *Hiyya Mira, bas isma el-asli Rima.* [Her name is Mira, but her original name is Rima.] *Wa-hiyya Tikva, bas isma el-asli Amal.* [She is Tikva, but her original name is Amal].

For those in the audience who do not speak Arabic, I began by introducing our names, followed by our original Arabic names of Habiba, Rima, and Amal. Our Hebrew names were registered on our identity cards by our parents. They did not register our Arabic names. In my case, I was named Habiba after my mother's grandmother, yet my mother did not put down this name on my identity card. After her bitter experience in Israel because of her Arab name Aziza—she knew that in a society where our names were associated with "the Arab enemy," anything related to the Middle East was considered a life-long stigma. In a society where an Arab name triggered shame and failure, it was preferable to give a *sabra*-sounding Hebrew name. Thus, our identity crisis as Mizrahi women begins already with our very names.

The core of the problem has to do with a country that sees itself as Western while denying its location in the Middle East, one with a majority population—Mizrahim and Palestinians—originating from the region. Although the matter of naming is only one small component of our oppression, it carries symbolic importance. Having been "stamped" with our *sabra* Hebrew names, we learned that it was illegitimate for us to maintain our culture, that we must erase our Middle Eastern identity in order to give birth to a *sabra*, i.e. Ashkenazi-Israeli identity. In fact, our mothers, whose names were changed by immigration clerks without so much as a second thought,

An opening speech delivered at the plenary session of the 10th Annual Women's Conference, Givat Haviva, Israel, June 16–18, 1994 (alongside speeches by Mira Eliezer and Tikva Levi—all under the same rubric: "Breaking the Silence: My Oppression as a Mizrahi Woman"), sections of which were published in Hebrew, "*Le-Hafer et ha-Shtikot,*" *HILA News,* Issue 50 (July, 1994). The English translation included here, slightly edited, is taken from the publication of the speech, "Breaking the Silence," in a Special Section, "Mizrahi Oppression and Struggle," in *News from Within* (Alternative Information Center), Vol. 10, no. 8, August 1994.

themselves continued the process of self-denial that the establishment began. Having internalized the message that everything Middle Eastern is "disgusting," they assigned us names that lacked all personal resonance for them. This attempt to spare us—their daughters—from "shame" was also an attempt to open doors for survival in Israeli society, doors usually locked for anyone identified with Easternness. In short, think about the fact that a woman is made to be ashamed of something as simple and basic as her name. Her own name! *Kulata shem.* (After all it's just a name.)

We internalized the way in which we were viewed. According to the hierarchies of race and gender in Israel, Ashkenazi women enjoy a higher social status. Even if many of us here are politically active and aware of the ways in which Mizrahim are discriminated against in economic, political, and educational terms, that awareness does not necessarily release us from an emotional-mental state that denies our Middle Eastern identity. Even as politically conscious women we are not always able to liberate ourselves from Ashkenazi norms and expectations.

It was in order to dodge social traps that we ordered our mothers to be quiet and not speak Arabic, Persian, Turkish, or Hindi. That was why we pleaded with them to work on those Moroccan, Iraqi, and Yemeni accents, and start becoming real Israelis—that is, Ashkenazis. Consider the fact that we, even as little girls, assumed verbal power as censors to silence our own mothers—an obvious index of a self-shame about our marked Moroccan, Yemeni, or Persian identity. This rejection of our own culture did not exist in Morocco, Yemen, or Iran; it became a new phenomenon in our history, a true "blue and white" product.

I see the beginning of our struggle as Mizrahi feminists, first and foremost, in our attempt to cope both with our own internal self-silencing and with the external efforts to silence us as Middle Eastern women. These silencing mechanisms are ingrained in the patriarchal society in which we women live, but they also form part of the institutionalized racism directed against Mizrahim generally. Therefore, given that we are standing at this intersection of several different forms of oppression, our struggle must be waged on several fronts, including vis-à-vis those Mizrahi men who feel threatened by our feminist consciousness and vis-à-vis Ashkenazi women who feel threatened by our Mizrahi consciousness. For us, there can be no separation between these two forms of oppression, because any attempt to separate them will impede our activism as Mizrahi feminists. A serious feminist struggle must be based on an in-depth analysis that examines the links between various forms of subjugation at work in our lives as women.

Our analysis, in other words, must be sensitive to these multiple relations, situations, and contexts, because the sexism and racism directed towards Mizrahi women take on specific forms. The life of an Ashkenazi pupil in north Tel Aviv with a father who has a senior position in a business, or at the university or on the city council is not the same as that of the Mizrahi pupil in south Tel Aviv whose father is a factory worker. Her chances for social and economic achievement are very slim. Worst of all, that same pupil learns to internalize the oppression, to believe that everything associated with the East is negative, and that becoming a secretary or hairdresser is the highest possible aspiration.

In a world in which *a frenk es a chaye, a frenkina a mechaye*," (a Yiddish expression: "the Oriental man is a beast, the Oriental woman revivifies"), the Mizrahi woman is perceived as a wild sexual animal or a natural servant, a housekeeper. Although admittedly all women tend to be objectified, the stereotypes particular to our experience as Mizrahi women impact our place in this society and generate specific strains and pressures. Even if this society were to offer full equal rights for all women, we as Mizrahi women would still not be equal with Ashkenazi women as long as the media and the educational system continued to teach us that the Middle Easterner is inferior, backward, fanatical, and governed by uncontrollable impulses; and as long as the conception of history and culture here is premised on the elimination of the East.

In our homes we persist in speaking Arabic, Persian, Turkish, or Hebrew mixed with these languages. This culture continues to shape our daily lives. Yet our way of being in an Ashkenazi-dominated society stands in strong contrast with our customary way of being within the Mizrahi community, and especially when we are among Mizrahi feminists. While Ashkenazi women enjoy some continuity between their public and private cultures, we, as Mizrahi women, have to carefully negotiate a fractured existence between different and conflicting cultural worlds.

At the insistence of Mizrahi feminists during the last Annual Women's Conference (in 1993), there did occur a drastic change. We managed to achieve at least an agreement on the principle of equal representation. Yet the real feminist struggle and fruitful cooperation between women of different backgrounds must be worked out on the basis of an additional principle, namely that we must also discuss and struggle together against racism and colonialism. In this sense, every insistence that there be a single form of feminism is an attempt to silence us, an attempt to dictate to us what is important or not important in our lives, and which form our struggle should take. This insistence urges us to conform to an Ashkenazi feminist model. While our Mizrahi identity is under attack, the identity of Ashkenazi women is taken for granted and remains as the unquestioned norm.

Through our discourse of Mizrahi feminism as through our struggle, we are striving to come to terms with the question of our identity, and to overcome our own self-silencing as well as the attempts by others to silence us. Our way of coping involves speaking out by addressing our history, our culture, and our social conditions, while also attempting to create a Mizrahi feminist identity that would form part of a broader multicultural feminism. That is our way of breaking the silence.

Figure 14 On the plenary panel, just before announcing the Mizrahi split from the Women's Movement, Givat Haviva, June 18, 1994 (from left to right: Mira Eliezer, Ella Shohat, Tikva Levi)

4

Mizrahi Feminism: The Politics of Gender, Race, and Multiculturalism

When *News from Within* asked me to contribute an article on the upcoming first Mizrahi Women's Conference, I was absolutely delighted. As someone who had been involved in establishing the Mizrahi Feminist Forum in the wake of the fiasco at the Tenth Women's Conference in 1994, and as a moderator of a session on Mizrahi feminism at the upcoming conference, I thought it would be a wonderful occasion for us as Mizrahim to represent ourselves in terms of the background, the agenda, and the analysis of multicultural Mizrahi feminism. I also wanted to share an under-represented political vision with the magazine's international Left readership. As someone who has attempted, through writing, lecturing, and organizing, to link Mizrahi, Palestinian, and feminist concerns as part of a broad critique of Euro-Zionist discourse and practice, I have felt frustrated, over the years, with diverse Left-progressive constituencies: with the radical Ashkenazi Left and their reductionist view of the Mizrahi struggle as merely "class;" with the simplistic Palestinian dismissal of Mizrahim as "right-winger" Zionists; with Ashkenazi feminism's contemptuous approach to the problems faced by Mizrahi women as solely the result of gender/sexual oppression; and with Mizrahi men's fears that feminist Mizrahi assertiveness destroys ethnic-based organizing by caving in to an Ashkenazi agenda. (There are of course moving exceptions within every constituency.) Most progressive outlets in Israel and abroad have, for the most part, systematically and patronizingly refused to engage with the Mizrahi perspective, let alone with one that tried to bring gender into the debate.

One alliance of this kind began in 1994, when *News from Within* translated the plenary speeches, "Breaking the Silence: My Oppression as a Mizrahi Woman," given by Mira Eliezer, Tikva Levi, and myself at the

Published in English translation in *News from Within* (Alternative Information Center), vol. 12, no. 4, April 1996. Significant portions of the essay previously appeared in Hebrew, "*Likrat Feminism Rav-Tarbuti*" ("Toward a Multicultural Feminism"), in *Klaf Hazak: Feminist Lesbian Community* 12 (Summer 1994), and were based on the author's presentation at the Ninth Annual Women's Conference, Givat Haviva, Israel, May 1993.

Tenth Annual Women's Conference held in Givat Haviva (June 16–18, 1994), forwarded with a solidarity piece written by the editor, Tikva Honig-Parnass.[1] This was only the beginning of what is by now a substantial and a hopeful coalition between diverse critical voices and groups on the Left. Since then, several essays, interviews, and discussions on the subject of Sephardi-Mizrahim/Ethiopians have been published in *News from Within*, *Rou'iya Oukhra*, and *Mitzad Sheni*. Finally, I felt, there is an outlet based in Israel that allows us to speak without having to endure the tremendous censorship, character assassination, and brutal attacks that people such as I have experienced from the so-called "leftist" Euro-Israeli media, precisely for refusing to ghettoize all these concerns and struggles.[2]

It is with this renewed hope for a dialogue between diverse constituencies that I am writing about the First Mizrahi Women's Conference, "We are Here! And this is Ours!" It is also within the historical context of a specific resistance to a Euro-Israeli ideological definition of selfhood and nationhood that I want to articulate our need for a large Mizrahi women's gathering of this kind. And finally, it is within the broad context of Third World gender, race, and class struggles that I want to situate an inclusive Mizrahi feminist agenda. My hope has always been to contextualize Mizrahi feminism within racial and national Third World struggles. Similar battles over the definition of feminism have been taking place elsewhere— especially in national contexts where people of diverse origins mix and mingle every day—seen in the debates between Eurocentric versus multicultural feminists. Here, I see the U.S. and Israel, for example, not simply as "Western countries" but rather as conflictual sites shaped by colonial and racial histories.[3] My argument is that our Mizrahi desire to offer an alternative political perspective cannot be seen as limited to its Israeli/ Palestinian context, but has to be understood in conjunction with analogous multicultural feminist visions expressed by Third World women, especially those living within the context of a Eurocentric system in places such as the U.S. and Israel.

Race Matters for Feminism

In 1993, after I participated in the Ninth Women's Conference in Givat Haviva, entitled "Together Despite Differences," I returned to New York where I am currently based, in a flurry of preparation for another conference: "Cross Talk: A Multi-Cultural Feminist Symposium," which I had been organizing with the New Museum. This conference was quite unusual for a Soho gallery area,[4] where, despite U.S. media hype around multiculturalism, Eurocentric attitudes still prevail. In academic institutions, similarly, while most ethnic studies programs marginalize issues of gender and sexuality, women's studies programs privilege the research and teaching of European and Euro-American feminist history and theory, largely excluding Third World feminist perspectives (including those in the First World, such as Native-American, African-American, and Puerto-Rican). In contrast to Eurocentric events, such as the Givat Haviva women's conferences, which tend to add a few dark faces to signal open-mindedness, this NY multi-cultural feminist conference was intended to provide a space for discussing the relationships between different feminist perspectives. The goal was also to develop strategies for building alternative institutions, on a basis of creating cooperation between feminists from different racial and national groups and sexual orientations. My purpose was to celebrate the important work towards creating an anti-racist feminism, and to present it in a way that brings together feminists from different locations with activists in different fields.

Lecturing at the conference were Puerto-Rican and Native-American political activists, who organized their communities against the covert Euro-American demographic war against non-Whites. Under the smokescreen of modernization policy, state methods of family planning, for example, are actually a means of sterilizing non-White women. University lecturers and educators spoke about their attempts to change course programs in certain fields, such as history, literature, communications, law, political science, and women's studies. Within this context, they spoke of attempting to change the curriculum in order to engage with, for example, the history of Black women's struggle against a legal system informed by a racially binary imagery which animalized Black women while "pedestalizing" the virgin White woman. This imagery elides the White man's rape of Black women during slavery, while justifying the lynching of Black men for even looking at a White woman. Performers and writers at the conference gave examples of ways of critiquing exotic images assigned to Latin and Asian women, in order to create a more complex picture of their gender, sexual, and racial identities. Women from different Native-American nations (the Iroquois in New York and the Yaqui in Arizona) lectured on the attempts by their communities to strengthen their matriarchal culture against the patriarchy historically imposed on them by the Euro-American establish-ment. They reported that since the 1984 law on who is a Native American, the U.S. government has crushed progressive forces in the Native-American movement, so that children with Native-American mothers and White fathers have lost their status and rights as Native Americans. These are only a few examples of the struggles presented at the NY conference by U.S. Third World women.

The conference's guiding concept was to transcend the lip service paid by White liberalism toward the representation of non-European cultures. Whenever a person of color speaks about his/her culture, he/she is expected to do so according to a White normative framework. The emphasis at this conference, therefore, was placed on feminists who discuss the different cultural and socio-political locations from which their perspectives were articulated. The few White women who did speak at this conference had worked for years towards integrating critiques of sexism and racism; they discussed their location in the struggle as White women. Identity, therefore, was defined not simply as something into which one is born and from which all experiences stem, but also as something that is formed by the political and ideological choices that we ourselves make. In other words, to be born African American in the U.S., or Mizrahi in Israel, virtually guarantees a set of common experiences which are different from those of White or Ashkenazi men and women. However, national or ethnic membership does not necessarily ensure political consciousness or active participation in liberation struggles. By the same token, being born White or Ashkenazi must not necessarily prevent someone from freeing him/herself from a Eurocentric approach or from joining struggles which combine feminism and anti-racism.

Within the space of two weeks, I spoke on multicultural feminism in Givat Haviva and in Manhattan. And although each context demands its own analysis, I nonetheless argue that many of the subjects raised "there" are also relevant "here." Entire ideologies and discourses have been imported to Palestine/Israel over the years from Europe and the U.S., specially adapted for the "underdeveloped" population of Israel: for example, the sociological modernization theories of Eisenstadt, adopted from Parsons; the "integration" in education as an Israeli version of the U.S. response to the demands of the civil rights struggles of the 1960s; and the practice of the Zionist variant of the colonial paradigm which translated into the dispossession of Palestinians from their property and national rights, along with the colonial "population exchange" solution for the partition of Palestine, resulting in the creation of massive Arab-Jewish refugees from the Arab world. In light of this history, it seems to me imperative to learn how communities dominated by colonialism and racialized minorities in First World countries developed critical theories and alternative institutions in order to struggle for an egalitarian democratic society. On this point, I see a connection to be made between multicultural feminist ideas in the U.S. and those which can be developed in Israel, in their own specific political context. Mizrahi feminism for me therefore forms part of a global multicultural feminist project.

Toward Multicultural Feminism

What, then, is multicultural feminism? By the "culture" in "multicultural," I do not mean the conventional definition which views culture as a series of the creative achievements of one civilization or another, such as concerts, plays, museums, etc. Culture, in its broader sociological-anthropological meaning, is the sum of the diverse local and global systems shaping a certain society, its modes of living, the thoughts which inform personal and collective choices, and the explicit and implicit ideological conflicts. Multiculturalism, according to this definition, is a theory that brings to bear the multiplicity of historical perspectives, particularly on the analyses of political processes. Multiculturalism thus differs from the fig-leaf approach of liberal pluralism, presumably willing to compromise and include an African-American or Native-American, Mizrahi or Palestinian face as a demonstration of its Euro-American or Euro-Israeli tolerance. A multicultural approach contrasts with Eurocentric thinking, which places world civilizations on a hierarchal ladder with the West at the top. Within multicultural thinking there is no single cultural geography drawn at the center of the world picture so as to form an ideal to be emulated by the "backward" and "underdeveloped." Multiculturalism acknowledges and takes into account the fact that non-Western historical perspectives have been under-represented, even, as in the case of Israel, where there is majority Third World demographic representation. Multiculturalism, therefore, critiques paternalism, including the pluralistic Ashkenazi approach that presumes to do other groups a favor by giving them the stage, while simultaneously imposing a Eurocentric perspective.

While pluralism "tolerates" difference, multiculturalism analyzes and identifies the conflicts engulfing diverse communities, and begins to work from there. Multicultural feminism assumes that women from different communities face different problems resulting from distinct and even opposite institutional policies towards various ethnic/racial and national groups. As such, multicultural feminism analyzes social relationships according to a relational model, in which conflicts do not only take place simply between women and men, but also among women in accordance with other dimensions of their identities: race, ethnicity, nationality, religion, class, and sexual orientation. Women with class-racial-national privilege can be discriminated against in relation to men in their immediate class-racial-national community, but they can at the same time gain advantages at the expense of women and even men from more oppressed racial, ethnic, and national communities. Thus, mainstream feminism which uses the blanket term "women" without detailing the other aspects of their identities becomes reductionist, and in fact represents only the perspective and discourse of White or Ashkenazi women, who pose their experiences as the norm according to which all other forms of feminism must be evaluated. A heterosexual Mizrahi woman in Israel, for example, is not oppressed separately, once as a woman and once as a Mizrahi, but rather simultaneously as a Mizrahi woman. Her experiences, therefore, overlap with and differ from both those of an Ashkenazi woman and those of a heterosexual Mizrahi man, as they overlap and differ from the experiences of lesbians, including Mizrahi and Palestinian lesbians.

Multicultural feminism, therefore, requires a social analysis which places relationally all the elements of women's and men's identities as relevant to a feminist struggle, one which is actually the concentric overlapping of diverse struggles and on different levels. I am not trying to undermine the value of the struggle against "glass ceilings" or against discrimination in terms of salaries. But limiting feminism only to career does not allow us to articulate the contradictions and conflicts of interests among women. The traditional housewife labor of the Ashkenazi woman has historically been replaced by that of a working-class woman, allowing the Ashkenazi woman to develop a career and compete with the Ashkenazi man of her class. Constituting the bulk of the female working-class in Israel, Mizrahi and Palestinian women have worked outside of their houses since the early days of Zionist settlement in Palestine, and following the foundation of the state of Israel, as farm laborers, as house cleaners, as childcare workers, as secretaries, as hairdressers, as seamstresses, as textile factory workers, and as packing house workers. For them a feminist struggle that concentrates on career problems as a means of personal expression and freedom of choice is, therefore, meaningless. Ashkenazi, Mizrahi, and Palestinian women have unequal access to education, and they do not face in daily life the same media images of themselves and the same social expectations from themselves, and therefore they end up with different hopes for themselves, at a different end of the social ladder.

By the same token, institutional control over women's bodies, as in the case of abortion law, is an important subject for organizing. Yet, this struggle must be based on the understanding that institutional control over women's bodies varies according to their race, ethnicity, nationality, and sexual orientation. Given the demographic anxiety of the patriarchal Ashkenazi establishment, can anyone really believe that heterosexual Ashkenazi, Mizrahi, and Palestinian women receive the same treatment regarding encouraging birth, on the one hand, and birth control education, on the other? Similarly, male violence towards women is definitely a widespread phenomenon, but it cannot be limited to the "private" realm, focusing only on battered wives as victims of their husbands or on rape committed by misogynist men. This violence must also be viewed in a larger context and in conjunction with the practices of major state institutions. For example, the Israeli military in the occupied territories has intimidated Palestinian women from fighting for their national and women's rights by invoking the potential (or actual) punishment of "besmirching their honor." In sum, the private and the public are not mutually exclusive; they are imbricated through and in relation to each other.

Even the notion of patriarchy varies in different contexts. The stereotypical image of the powerful Mizrahi father who oppresses his daughter is more problematic than Euro-Israeli discourse suggests. A thoroughly patriarchal Mizrahi father who cannot help his daughter in the face of an education system that forces her into an underprivileged school track, or a Palestinian father who cannot defend his daughter from the degrading assault of a military occupier, demonstrate the fact that patriarchy is found not only in the home, but also in the public realm, a realm still largely dominated, primarily, by a Eurocentric Israeli system.

Such examples form part of a complex intersection between issues of gender, race, and nation, requiring a comparative and relational analysis of the location of women vis-à-vis the Ashkenazi-Zionist establishment and the hegemonic Euro-Israeli ideology. Ashkenazi *sabra* feminists, proud of their *sabra*ness, cannot expect that Mizrahi and Palestinian women will support a feminist *sabra* idea of liberation, since *sabra*ness from its very inception has formed part of a European military ideology and youth culture that admired masculinity, physical strength, and the "conquering of the desolation," while also celebrating the negation of the East (which has included both Palestinians and the Jews of Asia and Africa). In other words, the combination of feminism and *sabra*ness creates a paradox that is difficult to swallow.

Multicultural feminism claims that the context and location of women differ, and therefore require different strategies of management, struggle, and even of different forms of feminist liberation. Awareness of the contradictions and conflicts that exist among women (and men) does not have to be seen as a "deterioration" of feminism (and of the Left more generally). I do not share this fear, which seems to have gripped most of the heterosexual Ashkenazi mainstream participants at the ninth and tenth conferences at Givat Haviva. On the contrary, only an in-depth analysis of the non-homogenous nature of the feminist project can bring about a vital cooperation between diverse women (and men). Only a painful dialogue that reveals already existing conflicts of interest can allow us to form serious coalitions between different kinds of feminists and progressive forces. Coalitions, I should clarify, are not based on having privileged feminists speak out of guilt, and consequently out of their victimhood, as Ashkenazi feminists did at the ninth and tenth women's conferences. In such instances Mizrahi and Palestinian feminist perspectives are expected to be re-aligned according to the experiences and definitions of a Euro-Israeli ethnic experience and national ideology. A Mizrahi conference thus signifies precisely the refusal to collaborate with such an expectation, one that ultimately entails our Mizrahi invisibility as a community.

Conference as Allegory

Mizrahi women have hardly been part of the Israeli feminist movement. Most of our feminist work has been done within the Mizrahi arena of struggle (HILA being a case in point), just as in the 1980s we barely participated in the so-called Israeli peace movement, for we preferred to work on issues of peace in conjunction with our own struggles (the Oriental Front being a case in point). As Mizrahi feminists we have long been fed up with the so-called Israeli feminist movement, just as Mizrahi activists, in general, have been angry with the so-called Israeli "Left" as a whole. Already at the Ninth Women's Conference in Givat Haviva, the official ideology of "Together Despite Differences" proved to be flawed, precisely because togetherness could not be premised on erasing structural conflicts among women (and among men). Rather it has to involve the clarification of the sources of these conflicts, and a sorting out of the possible common grounds not for a facile "togetherness" but for a complex political alliance embracing different community histories and desires. The Tenth Women's Conference's decision to have each quarter represented (Ashkenazi, Mizrahi, Palestinian, lesbian), and speak of its oppression, was intended to address only the oppression experienced at the hands of men in "their" community. This ideology, equating very diverse realities of gender relations, did not leave room for a critique of the tensions and oppressions among women having to do with their race, class, national, and sexual affiliations. Fissures were obvious at all the conferences, partly having to do with the critique of Zionist ideology (in the tenth conference a specific panel was dedicated to the topic, moderated by Noga Dagan) but also having to do with being marginalized by Euro-Israeli cultural hegemony.

The way conferences are conceived and organized almost always forms a (usually inadvertent) allegory of a whole set of social relations. Mizrahi women, who rarely even attended the women's conferences, came in major numbers to the ninth and tenth conferences, thanks largely to the organization of HILA. In the last issue of *News from Within*, Mira Eliezer, Vera Karko, and Tikva Levi (of the Mizrahi women's conference organizing committee) detailed the abuses suffered by Mizrahi women at the hands of Ashkenazi organizers in the tenth conference.[5] The point, I would like to emphasize, is not simply that Mizrahi women are offended. The point is that such an attitude suggests that Euro-Israeli women haven't yet understood their structural position as belonging to an oppressive regime, and have not quite perceived their own "Whiteness." As White Jews, even if women, they benefit automatically from social arrangements within the state of Israel as well as from the international connections that the state apparatus facilitates for them. Living in New York, I always get to see Euro-Israeli leftists and feminist representatives of many progressive causes. How often do I get to see Mizrahim representing a Mizrahi agenda? In fact, we simply don't exist outside of Israel, despite the fact that we are the majority of the Jewish population in Israel.

The negative treatment at the tenth conference was therefore part of a broad silencing of our perspective. (It is for this reason that Mira, Tikva, and I entitled our tenth conference plenary session "Breaking the Silence.") The offensive treatment, in other words, was not an individual matter; it was structural. For we Mizrahim, who have endured the Ashkenazi treatment as "human dust," in Ben-Gurion's revealing words, the mistreatments at the conference could never just be regarded as mere accidents. Such Euro-Israeli attitudes are inflammatory precisely because they form part of a long history, one that predates our individual history, going back to our grandparents' and parents' traumatic arrival in the state of Israel, when they were poured out of trucks into the *maabarot*, the transit camps. Yet, most Euro-Israelis have not studied or acknowledged that past and its consequences for the present.

During the Ninth Women's Conference, the organizers' idea of a "cultural evening" was a performance of segments from a comic play, *My Sister-in-Law and Me*, performed by three Ashkenazi actresses. The old negative stereotypes of ignorant, vulgar, backward Mizrahim, which ultimately legitimize institutional racism, were re-enacted once again, eliciting the raucous laughter of the liberal feminists in the audience. For those who have lived with the pain of such stereotyping inscribed on our flesh since our childhood, it was an extremely painful experience. And for someone like myself, specifically, who has dedicated years to developing a scholarly critique of the politics of representation of the East-versus-West in Euro-Israeli culture, it was an unbearable moment. As soon as one of the comic segments was ended, a group of us, which included Yael Zadock, Mira Eliezer, Tikva Levi, Ronit Dagan, and myself, walked to the stage in protest, demanding an end to the stereotypical, prejudicial, and racist representation of Mizrahi women. Taking the stage, I compared the play to the old racist play/film *Sallah Shabati*, whose restaging by Habimah National Theater in 1988 already provoked major Mizrahi protests.[6] It was our way of taking center stage to express our criticism. As soon as we were done we walked out of the theater to protest not only the play itself but also the conference's organizers who, in the context of the first massive Mizrahi attendance at the women's annual conference, dared to impose such a racist play as their idea of a cultural evening. The audience immediately divided into supporters and opponents. Most Mizrahi women agreed with our intervention, and even some Ashkenazi women supported us.

Just as the politics of representation on stage was central to the politics of representation throughout the conference, so was the dance party. In both the ninth and the tenth conferences the dance party proved to be a political battle over what constitutes community pleasure. While Mizrahi and Palestinian women, along with a few Ashkenazi women, were dancing together to the sounds of Arabic and Mizrahi music, most Ashkenazi women, with few exceptions, were seeing that music as an intrusion, or at best as token music/dance to be tolerated but only for a short time. The Ashkenazi D.J. enacted a typical Euro-Israeli rejection of Arab-Mizrahi culture in a context where the majority of conference attendees were of non-European origin, in ways analogous to the marginalization of our history and culture in educational and cultural institutions, even though Mizrahim and Palestinians form the majority of the citizens of the state of Israel. And just as in the name of "culture" and "quality" the Euro-Israeli establishment has marginalized Arab-Mizrahi cultures, so the Euro-Israeli organizers denied even entertaining the possibility of democratic representation of our culture. (Similarly, the serving of—for us—indigestible Ashkenazi *kibbutz*-style bland food became a joke among us that even their food had to be shoved down our throats.) Thus the conference became an allegory of the whole experience of Mizrahim who were abruptly uprooted from their Asian and African contexts and placed, albeit in the Mediterranean of Israel, yet in a socio-political structure whose oppressive consequences are still being played out.

Zionist Discourse, Mizrahi Identity, and Imagining Alliances

The critique of Zionism cannot be separated from the critique of Eurocentrism, whereby world cultures are expected to erase their history, language, and identity in favor of a presumably superior western history, language, and identity. The definition of Israel has meant the dispossession, in very different ways, of Palestinians and Mizrahim. Given these experiences, Tikva, Mira, and myself asserted our Arab cultural difference without apology in our conference's plenary speeches, and insisted on our right to define our culture and identity for ourselves. I therefore started our panel in Arabic (in my Baghdadi dialect) by introducing the three of us with our Arabic names—Amal, Rima, and Habiba—names that were taken away from us by a system that devastated everything associated with Arabness. For we could not be Arabs and Jews at the same time within the state of Israel. We had to choose, for the first time in our history, between Jewishness and Arabness. Our speeches were also meant as a call for alliance with Palestinian women, who did relate to this shared critique of Zionism. Ironically, Palestinians found themselves at certain moments as the mediators between Ashkenazi and Mizrahi women. Although we did not need this conference to speak to Palestinians (many of us have been active on linking Mizrahi and Palestinian issues, and knew personally many of the Palestinian participants), it was important for us to make a public pronouncement on such possible affinities in a feminist context. In other words, I still see our panel as a form of doing away with the patronizing idea that Euro-Israeli feminists are somehow mediating between two groups of women oppressed by "their" men, the only acceptable narrative for mainstream Euro-Israeli feminism.

The public aggressive reception of our panel by Ashkenazi women was accompanied, however, by largely supportive gestures from Palestinian women who have also refused the rescue fantasy of Euro-Israeli patriarchal feminism: "Come to us and cry over our shoulders about what those bad Mizrahi and Palestinian men are doing to you." (For this reason precisely many international feminist conferences have featured parallel angry exchanges between Palestinian and Euro-Israeli women, who simply never took into account that Israeli occupation has anything to do with Palestinian women's oppression, and it never occurred to them that it might have a gender dimension.) Within the Mizrahi multicultural feminist perspective, as outlined earlier here, there was no way out but to break away from enslaving narratives that kept us away from issues crucial to our lives, culture, and identity.

Sometimes even compliments had an aggressive undertone. Responding to our panel, one woman approached me to ask: "It was nicely written— who wrote it for you?" And the newspaper reports on the ninth and tenth conferences were no less racist. Given the shared ethnic and class background of the Euro-Israeli organizers of the conference and of most of the female journalists, and in the context of the assertion of our identity, many of the articles about Mizrahi women were antagonistic. The articles failed to engage both the diverse issues that we raised, and the differences among the diverse Mizrahi women. In the presumably liberal paper *Ha'ir* two articles reproduced the racist Euro-Israeli argument about the Mizrahi participants.[7] Several of us wrote responses, not all of which were published. In my letter to *Ha'ir* (published in a shorter form), I suggested that the paper's Euro-Israeli feminist call for "higher standards" was in fact a refusal to recognize its own "low standards" of analysis and its own class, racial, and national privileges, deriving precisely from the existing Euro-Israeli patriarchal structures of oppression:

Miky Meltz and Orna Landaw's articles are based on the assumption that Israeli feminism has one color (white), one culture (Jewish Ashkenazi), and one sexual orientation (heterosexual). Therefore, they are amused by the idea of women's "hierarchical oppression" and are angered by the "divisiveness" that Mizrahi women, Palestinian women, and lesbians presumably create. Knowing very little about the struggle of Mizrahi women, like HILA's women, Euro-Israeli feminists participate in a racist discourse that suggests that there is a contradiction between feminism and Mizrahiness. It seems that a *schwartze* face which speaks in a Mizrahi accent cannot be feminist. As one of the three Mizrahi speakers in the plenary session where we addressed the silencing of Mizrahi feminism, I have to point to these articles as yet another attempt to silence us, and as a media attempt to dictate to us what is the "burning" feminist content and agenda. It's a shame that the reporters didn't listen better.

Predicting this Euro-Israeli feminist objection to our redefinition of what constitutes feminism, we did try to explain the "relevance" of institutionalized racism to our feminist struggle. For example, the kidnapping of Yemeni/Mizrahi children could not have occurred without the patriarchal attitude toward Mizrahi women as "swarming with children;" one or two children fewer presumably would not matter to them. It also could not have taken place without the tacit assumption that Mizrahi women formed a kind of national womb whose babies were the property of the state and its institutions.

This conference will be written up in history as an attempt to change the face of feminism in Israel. Landaw and her friends' complaints about "boredom" cannot be a criterion that will dictate our feminist discourse. In fact, *we* are bored by the simplistic Euro-Israeli analysis which reduces everything into a dichotomy of man-versus-woman, and which sees everything as beginning in the kitchen, passing through the bedroom, and ending with the bank account. In a state where there is a demographic majority for Mizrahim and Palestinians, the model proposed by Landaw is itself a "divisive" one, for it represents a minority interest and perspective, even if it is the hegemonic minority. Landaw's affected empathy and charity do not interest those of us who are fighting for a structural change, for a society where there won't be room for pointless empathy and philanthropic arrogance. Although Landaw calls for a theoretical feminist discussion, her article reflects ignorance of the academic feminist discussion of the past 20 years. As a scholar and professor who teaches multicultural feminism, I find that Landaw herself is stuck in a ragged, reductive, and obsolete feminism. A serious feminist struggle, as I argued in the speech at the Tenth Annual Women's Conference, has to be based on a deep analysis of the circumstances of women's lives, one which examines the links between diverse oppressions. Any attempt to tell us that there is one homogenous feminism is an attempt to silence us. Because it is an attempt to dictate to us what is important for our life and what is not, and what form our struggles should take.

It is not enough, in other words, to express righteous indignation about women's discrimination, without also fighting for equal distribution of resources in ways that take into account racial and national dispossessions, in the case of Israel, of Mizrahim and Palestinians. And that would also require an analysis of the relative advantages afforded to Mizrahim by the simple virtue of their being Jews in Israel, as well as a critique of the various Arab nationalisms and their historical collaboration with the dispossession of Arab Jews—all of which have led to our current crisis. Currently, furthermore, it is necessary to engage with the peace process's benefits for Israeli and Palestinian elites, in ways that have little positive economic and cultural impact on the majority of Mizrahim and Palestinians.

The same fissures that we Mizrahi activists have experienced (for example in the 1980s around the issue of peace) have repeated themselves in the context of feminism. When we established movements like East for Peace and the Oriental Front, or the New York-based NGO World Organization of Jews from Islamic Countries, it was precisely because as Mizrahim we did not see ourselves as part of a peace movement that did not take issues of class and ethnicity into account. In 1989, with the support of the Paris-based Perspectives Judéo-Arabes, we had our first meeting that was specifically designed for Sephardi Mizrahim and Palestinians at the symbolic site of Toledo, Spain. I feel that the same argument we made in Toledo about the Ashkenazi liberal-"Left" can be easily reiterated in the context of the Ashkenazi feminist movement. Almost a decade after our activism for an inclusive peace that would take into account Mizrahim and Palestinians within the state of Israel, we find ourselves making similar arguments in the context of feminism. Therefore, following the Tenth Women's Conference, we established the Forum ha-Nashim ha-Mizrahiot, out of which the organizing committee for the first Mizrahi Women's Conference emerged. Our point was to connect historical research to our experience, not only in the state of Israel, but even prior to its existence, and to discuss the research within the framework of women's experiences. (This research has also been encouraged by the new alternative school system, Kedma, for children from "the neighborhood," or the hood).

A mature feminist struggle must be created through responsible study of the histories, beliefs, and hopes of Third World women in Israel, who face a number of oppressive systems on a day-to-day basis. Politically powerful coalitions can be based only on the ability to listen and on the mutual effort to sever ourselves from exclusionary national-ethnic and gender-sexual ideologies, seeing that political identification does not have to be a direct result of the group into which one is born. Only if we analyze the complex system of links between stratifications based on sexual, national, class, religion, racial, and ethnic identities will we be able to understand the different and contradictory set of oppressions enacted on women. Only then can we propose strategies of liberation which are suited to the women (and men) in our communities.

Not all Mizrahi women share similar ideas and perspectives, certainly not around "feminism," or around such contested terrain as the "Jewish nation," "Zionism," and "Palestine." I think that we still have a long way to go in terms of a coherent Mizrahi agenda and vision that moves beyond immediate school and neighborhood issues to a full understanding of our identity in light of the history of Zionism and the Euro-Israeli state apparatus. But I also think that for those of us who devoted considerable time, thought, and work to these issues, it is important to have an occasion to speak and discuss our dilemmas within a framework in which we do not have to constantly rebuff violent attacks and hostile misrepresentations. In the tenth conference I tried to clarify to defensive Euro-Israeli feminists that the Mizrahi perspective is also inclusive of people of Ashkenazi origins, that our definition of Mizrahi feminism is not reduced merely to experience but is also about political consciousness. It is precisely for this reason that a few Euro-Israeli women are an integral part of the organizing committee of the First Mizrahi Women's Conference.

The issues to be addressed at the workshops will include: the ideology and reality of immigration in the 1950s from Mizrahi and Ashkenazi perspectives (moderated by Louise Cohen and Tikva Parnass of the conference's organizing committee); the place of Mizrahi history in the educational system (moderated by Klara Yona); coexistence between Palestinian and Mizrahi women in mixed neighborhoods (moderated by Ruty Gur); the kidnapping of Yemeni-Mizrahi children (moderated by Shoshana Madmoni); Ethiopian women's perspective on Israeli society (moderated by Rachel Malsa); expectations from ourselves and our children around motherhood (moderated by Ronit Chacham and Noga Daggan, both of the organizing committee); Mizrahi women in the media (moderated by Vicky Shiran); how as Mizrahim we should communicate with Euro-Israeli journalists (moderated by Rachel Yona); the implications of searching for a Mizrahi identity for young women (moderated by Neta Amar of the organizing committee); and past experiences which continue to accompany us today as Mizrahi women (moderated by Henriette Dahan, of the organizing committee).

I do not think that Mizrahim as a whole, and Mizrahi women more specifically, have had a chance to fully digest the traumas of displacement that have been our share in the face of the Euro-Israeli state and culture. Internalization of the imposed Euro-Zionist reading of Arab-Jewish history, and the lack of knowledge of the relevance of major struggles in the Third World for grasping Mizrahi history and identity, are in my opinion still issues to be discussed and struggled for. Of course one conference is not intended as an answer and a solution. But it is a beginning.

5

The Invention of the Mizrahim

A recent news item concerning Israel inadvertently pointed to some of the ambiguities and aporias of Mizrahi identity since the advent of Zionism. The article claimed that the Institute for Biological Research in Israel was developing a biological weapon, a kind of "designer toxin" or "ethnic bullet" tailored to attack Arabs only. (First conceived during the apartheid era in South Africa as a pigment-based weapon to be used against Blacks, it was reconfigured as an ethnic, gene-based weapon by Israel.) The report, unconfirmed but relayed in the London *Sunday Times*, mentioned in passing that the research involved Iraqi Jews.[1]

What is of interest here is the symptomatic implications of a relatively "minor" aspect of the article, the alleged choice of "Iraqi Jews," in terms of some of the paradoxes of Arab-Jewish identity in Israel. (By "Arab Jews" I refer to people of Jewish faith historically linked to the Arab-Muslim world.) On the one hand, the Israeli establishment regards Arab Jews as irremediably Arab—indeed, that Iraqi Jews were allegedly used to determine a certain toxin's effect on Arabs suggests that for genetic/biological purposes, at least, Iraqi Jews *are* Arabs. On the other hand, official Israeli/Zionist policy urges Arab Jews (or, more generally, Oriental Jews, also known as Sephardim or Mizrahim) to see their only *real* identity as Jewish. The official ideology denies the Arabness of Arab Jews, positing Arabness and Jewishness as irreconcilable opposites. For Zionism, this Arabness, the product of millennial cohabitation, is merely a diasporic stain to be "cleansed" through assimilation. Within Zionist ideology, the very term "Arab-Jew" is an oxymoron and a misnomer, a conceptual impossibility.

Published as the opening article in the *Journal of Palestine Studies*, vol. 29, no. 1 Issue 113 (Autumn 1999).

The author would like to dedicate this essay to the memory of Neelan Tiruchelvam, director of the International Center for Ethnic Studies in Colombo, Sri Lanka, member of parliament, and a leader of the Tamil United Liberation Front. A profoundly peaceful man who worked on constitutional reforms to alleviate Sri Lanka's ethnic conflict, he was targeted and killed by a suicide bomber on July 29, 1999.

Figure 15   Photo and original Israel Government Press Office caption: "70 Years Old Abraham Sallah, a Real-Estate Agent in Iraq, Undergoes Medical Examination, June 1951"

Islam, Mizrahim, and Zionist Historiography

Zionist historiography pays little attention to the history of the Jews in the Muslim world. Indeed, the Israeli establishment has tried systematically to suppress Sephardi-Mizrahi cultural memory by marginalizing this history in school curricula. Standard history books include only a few pages on the history of Islam, the Arab world, and the Judeo-Islamic "symbiosis." Little mention is made, for example, of the fact that major Sephardi texts in philosophy, linguistics, poetry, and medicine were largely written in Arabic and reflect specific Muslim influences as well as a Jewish-Arab cultural identity. When Zionist history does acknowledge what might be termed "Judeo-Islamic history," it usually organizes its narrative around a selected series of violent events, moving from pogrom to pogrom, as evidence of relentless hostility toward Jews in the Arab world, presumed to be analogous to those encountered in Europe. The notion of the unique, common victimization of all Jews everywhere and at all times, a crucial underpinning of official Israeli discourse, precludes other historical analogies and cultural metonymies, thus producing a Eurocentric reading of "Jewish History," one that hijacks the Jews of Islam from their own cultural geography and subsumes them into the history of the European-Ashkenazi *shtetl*.

Official Zionism's selective reading of Middle Eastern history makes two processes apparent: (1) the rejection of an Arab and Muslim context for Jewish institutions, identity, and history; and (2) the subordination of Arab

Jews to a "universal" Jewish experience. Zionist history texts undermine the hyphenated, syncretic culture of actually existing Jews, rendering the non-Jewish side of the hyphen nonpertinent. This unidimensional categorization, with all Jews being defined as closer to each other than to the cultures of which they have been a part, is tantamount to dismembering a community's identity.[2] And indeed, in the case of Middle Eastern Jews, the Euro-Israeli separation of the "Jewish" and "Middle Eastern" parts has ideologically facilitated the actual dismantling of the Jewish communities of the Muslim world, while pressuring the Oriental Jews in Israel to realign their identity according to Zionist Euro-Israeli paradigms. My point is not to idealize the situation of the Jews of Islam, but to suggest that Zionist

Figure 16   Photo and original Israel Government Press Office caption: "The Ingathering of the Exiles"

discourse has undermined comparative studies of Jews in the Muslim world in relation to other minorities.

The master narrative of universal Jewish victimization entailing the claim that the "Jewish nation" faces a common "historical enemy"—the Muslim Arab—requires a double-edged amnesia with regard both to Judeo-Islamic history and to the colonial partition of Palestine. False analogies between the Arabs and Nazis, a symptom of a Jewish-European nightmare projected onto the structurally distinct political dynamics of the Israeli/Palestinian conflict, have become a staple of Zionist rhetoric. In a historical context of Middle Eastern Jews experiencing within the Muslim world a history utterly distinct from that which haunted the European memories of Ashkenazi Jews, and in a context of the massacres and dispossession of the Palestinian people, the conflation of the Muslim Arab with the archetypal (European) oppressors of Jews downplays the colonial-settler history of Euro-Israel itself.

The simplistic division of Israel-as-West and Palestine-as-East also elides some core tensions within Zionist discourse itself.[3] Central to Zionism is the notion of a return to origins in the Middle East. And although Jews have often been depicted in anti-Semitic discourse as an alien "Eastern" people within the West, the paradox of Israel is that it presumed to "end a Diaspora" characterized by ritualistic nostalgia for the East, only to establish a state ideologically and geopolitically oriented almost entirely toward the West. For the roots of Zionism can be traced to the conditions of 19th- and early 20th-century Europe, not only as a reaction against anti-Semitism but also as a reaction to the rapid expansion of capitalism and of European empire building.[4] Theodor Herzl dreamt of a Western-style capitalist-democratic miniature state to be made possible by the grace of imperial powers such as Britian or Germany, while David Ben-Gurion expressed his visionary utopia of Israel as a "Switzerland of the Middle East."

The same historical process that dispossessed Palestinians of their property, lands, and national-political rights was intimately linked to the process that dispossessed Arab Jews of their property, lands, and rootedness in Arab countries, while also uprooting them conceptually from that history and culture within Israel itself. But while Palestinians have fostered the collective militancy of nostalgia in exile, Arab Jews, trapped in a no-exit situation, have been forbidden to nourish memories of having belonged to the peoples across the River Jordan, across the mountains of Lebanon, and across the Sinai desert and Suez Canal.[5] The persistent narration of a formerly scattered "one people" rejoined in their "original homeland" delegitimizes any memory of communal life prior to the State of Israel.

The fact that the "Orientals" have had closer cultural and historical links to the presumed enemy—the "Arab"—than to the

Figure 17 Photo and original Israel Government Press Office caption: "In the Tent, in the *Olim* Camp in Pardes Hanna, Seated Yossef Haim Doctori, who was a Jeweller in Kurdistan-Iraq, with Members of his Family, 1950"

Ashkenazi Jews with whom they were coaxed and coerced into shared nationhood, threatens the conception of a homogeneous nation analogous to European nations. It also threatens the Euro-Israeli self-image, which sees itself as an extension of Europe. The taboo around the Arabness of the Eastern Jews has visibly been clearly manifested in Israeli academic and media attacks on Mizrahi intellectuals who refuse to define themselves simply as Israelis and who dare to assert their Arabness in the public sphere.[6]

Fearing engulfment by the East, the Euro-Israeli establishment attempted to repress the "Middle Easternness" of Mizrahim as part of an effort to Westernize the Israeli nation and to mark clear borders of identity between Jews as Westerners and Arabs as Easterners. Arab Jews were urged to regard Judaism and Zionism as synonyms, and Jewishness and Arabness as antonyms. Thus Arab Jews were pressured to affiliate either with anti-Zionist Arabness or with pro-Zionist Jewishness. This conceptualization of East-versus-West has important implications in the age of the "peace process," since it sidesteps the fact that the majority of the population within Israel is from the Middle East—Palestinian citizens of Israel as well as Mizrahim. Peace, as it is now articulated, does not entail a true democracy in terms of adequate representation of these under-represented populations, or in terms of changing the economic, educational, and cultural stratifications within Israeli society.

The Aporias of Nationalism

In 1998, the same year as the genetic experiments referred to above, the Arab writer Elias Khoury convened a conference in Beirut on the Nakba of 1948 that included a panel on Arab-Jewish perspectives. All the Jewish participants on the panel were highly vocal critics of Zionism. While some, such as Shimon Ballas, live in Israel, others now live elsewhere—Simone Bitton lives in Paris, I live in New York. Other invited Arab Jews, such as the Moroccan Abraham Serfaty, had never been to Israel at all. Khoury's invitations continued an ongoing, if intermittent and unofficial, dialogue. Nevertheless, some Syrian-backed groups in Lebanon opposed the invitations to the point that many of the Arab Jews were either advised not to attend or themselves decided not to go for fear of their safety.[7]

Thus, in the same year that official Israel found Arab Jews to be genetically Arab, some Arabs found them—even those with strong anti-Zionist credentials—to be "insufficiently" Arab. Here we find an ironic victory for Zionism, since putatively anti-Zionist Arabs seem to have absorbed the Zionist position that all Jews must, in their heart of hearts, necessarily be Zionist. For the Arab opponents of Khoury's invitation, Arab Jews are always and everywhere genetically Jewish and ideologically Zionist, regardless of historical origins, cultural affinities, political affiliations, and even professed ideologies. Thus Arab Jews have been caught up in the crosscurrents of rival essentialist forms of nationalism.[8] As long as the political discourse, whether in Israel or in the Arab world, remains essentialist-nationalist, there is little political and scholarly place for Arab Jews or Mizrahim critical of Zionism.

With the birth of nationalism, a whole new process began. Arabness and Jewishness were formulated as nationalist concepts in historically unprecedented ways. At the height of imperialism, liberation from racial and colonial oppression could be formulated only along nationalist lines. In order to merit the end of colonial rule, Third-World nations had to be invented according to definitions supplied by the often Eurocentric ideologies of the nation as a coherent unit. The nation-state was the "logical result" of the definition of the nation as one people with one language and one culture (often including religion, even if not always declared as such) living on a demarcated land.

On a realpolitik level, this was a "reasonable" response to colonialism. Unfortunately, however, formerly colonized people have often fallen into the very same conceptual traps that oppressed them during colonialism. For the Arab-Muslim world, liberation from Europe has also marked the end of the overarching Muslim geocultural civilization in which identities and power were defined differently. The place of all protected religious minorities gradually shifted with the introduction of colonialism and nationalism. The fragile position of Assyrians in Iraq, whose identities and loyalties have been constantly tested, is eloquent in this regard. The place of Jews, similarly, was never completely secure, even if on a superficial level they were part of the great Arab nation and even if some Jews were among the leaders of the anticolonial struggle.

But what made the Arab-Jewish story more complicated than that of other minorities in the Arab-Muslim world was the gradual rise of another nationalist movement, Zionism, which asserted claims of pan-Jewishness. For some Arab Jews, tempted by the image of a place where "we" would no longer be a minority, that promise sounded liberatory. Many were exhilarated by the messianic belief that Jews had reached a new religious dispensation. Others, such as communists and some religious leaders, expressed violent opposition to Zionism. My father tells me that in the late 1930s, his high school teacher, the brother of *hakham* Sasson Khdhuri (the religious head of the Baghdadi community), reported about his visit to Palestine. Recounting the disdain he encountered from European Jews, and describing what he regarded as their "non-Jewish" ways, he warned the young students not to go to Palestine, because the "Jews there are not like us." This concept of "Jews not like us" was only dimly understood at the time, since people like my father and his classmates had had little contact with "different" (European) Jews, alien to their own Middle Eastern Jewish norms.

Zionist ideologues, for their part, had always shown an ambivalent attitude toward the Jews of the East precisely because of their non-Ashkenazi "otherness." In their texts and congresses, European Zionists consistently addressed themselves to Ashkenazi Jews and to the colonizing empires that might provide support for a national homeland, while rejecting the non-Ashkenazis as "savage" and "primitive." At the first Zionist Congress, they opposed "Levantization," the "tainting" of the settlements in Palestine with an infusion of "Levantine Jews." At the same time, however, Zionists saw the economic and political necessity of attracting and occasionally even forcing "Jews in the form of Arabs"[9] to the "land of Israel."[10] From the early days of Zionism, non-Ashkenazi Jews were seen as cheap labor that had to be maneuvered into immigrating to Palestine. Creating a Jewish national homeland required, along with the purchase and the expropriation of Arab land, the creation of a de facto Jewish population on the land— whence the need for Mizrahim. Even during the 1950s, Zionist officials showed ambivalence about the mass importation of "Levantines." But once again, demographic and economic necessity forced the Zionist hand. The rescue fantasy concerning the "Jews of the Orient," in other words, masked Zionism's own need to rescue itself from economic and political collapse. While presenting Palestine as an empty land to be transformed by Zionist enterprise, the founding fathers presented Mizrahim as passive vessels to be reshaped by the revivifying spirit of Promethean Zionism.[11]

The case of Arab-Jews, as a community on the "margins" of opposing nationalisms, also suggests that nationalism itself is never simple. The very concept is contradictory, since nationalism is inevitably the site of competing discourses, a feature that characterizes both Zionist Jewish and Arab nationalism despite the differences in their historical origins and their opposite relationships to Western colonialism and imperialism. Quite apart from the historical and ideological ambiguities of nationalism—the slippage between the original meaning of nation as racial group and its later meaning as a politically organized entity, and the oscillation between nationalism's progressive and regressive poles—nationalism changes its valence in different historical and geographic contexts. A proactive European nationalism, such as Nazi Germany's *lebensraum* ambitions against its neighbors, cannot be equated with reactive nationalisms like those in the Arab world, a case where nationalism is not directed against neighbors but against the hegemonic power of European colonialism.

But in the case of Zionism, the oppressive and liberatory poles are intermingled with an unusual density of contradiction. Zionism fought Nazi anti-Semitism at a geographical remove. It saw itself as national liberation from European anti-Semitic oppression, but at the same time it was itself responsible for the oppression of Palestinians, and, in a different way, of Arab Jews. Zionism founded one nation while destroying another nation, gathering Jews *from* the four corners of the globe while at the same time

Figure 18   Photo and original Israel Government Press Office caption: "*Maabara*, a Woman from Yemen at the Entrance to her Tent, December 1949"

dispersing Palestinians *to* the four corners of the globe. The Mizrahim were included, at least in later stages, in Zionism's national project (though in a subordinate and ambivalent position), while the Palestinians were constructed as the perennial enemy that had to be expelled, or at least disempowered, for the Jewish nation to exist.

For Palestinians, nationalism has been a means of combating the Zionist colonization of Palestine. Yet what both Jewish and Arab nationalisms have shared, in discursive terms, is the notion of a single, authentic (Jewish or Arab) nation. They both have assumed that the "national" is produced by eliminating the foreign, the contaminated, the impure, so that the nation can emerge in all its native glory. In the name of national unity, contradictions having to do with class, gender, religion, ethnicity, race, region, sexuality, language, and so forth tend to be erased or glossed over.

The rigidity of these paradigms has produced the Arab-Jewish tragedy, since neither paradigm has room for crossed and multiple identities. While Arab nationalism paid lip service to respecting the diverse ethnic and religious minorities, in fact many groups, for example Assyrians, Berbers, Copts, Kurds, Nubians, and Turkomans, have been subdued by a norm that was hegemonic and essentialist, ultimately a Sunni-Muslim-Arab notion of what a "real" Iraqi or Egyptian should be. But in the case of Jews, because of the aggressive advance of Zionism, Arab-Jewish identity was always intensely "on trial" in a way that was not true of the other minorities. All the minorities faced the insecurity engendered by marginalization, but Arab Jews had to face as well the basic question of final allegiance: were they ultimately loyal to the hegemonic threat, the "Zionist entity," or to their "local" nations of residence? Did religion outweigh nation? Did they accept the Zionist equation of religion and national allegiance—i.e., Zionism as the expression of the religious desire of all Jews? Did they ever have a choice even to reflect on this choice, or the power to make such a decision? The rigidities of these two antagonistic nationalisms inscribed Arab Jews within two very restrictive and conflicting narratives, neither of which had space for their newly invented contradiction.

The Zionist idea that Arabness and Jewishness are mutually exclusive gradually came to be shared by Arab nationalist discourse, placing Arab Jews on the horns of a terrible dilemma. The other dimension of Zionism's displacement of Palestinians was the displacement of Arab Jews from the Arab world, which took place, for the most part, without a conscious or comprehensive understanding of what was at stake and what was yet to come. Most Arab Jews, for example, could never fully foresee what the impossibility of return to their countries of origin would mean. (The official term "*aliya*"—ascent—does not capture the complexity of Arab-Jewish displacement, just as the term "immigration" does not account for the impossibility of return.)

The displacement of Arab Jews forms part of a more general process of the formation of Third-World nation-states, which often involved a double process of joining diverse ethnicities and regions previously separated under colonialism while at the same time partitioning regions and peoples within new regional definitions (such as Iraq/Kuwait) and cross-shuffling populations (India/Pakistan). I am not arguing, as Zionists often do, that what occurred was a mere "population exchange" that justifies the creation of Palestinian refugees since "we" were displaced too. But critiquing this Zionist argument should not prevent a thorough study of the wrongs done to Arab Jews.

Figure 19   Photo and original Israel Government Press Office caption: "The *Maabara* of Bat-Yam, December 1952"

What is needed, then, is a more complex analysis of the circumstances that forced the departure of Arab Jews. Such an analysis would have to take into account a number of factors: the secret collaboration between Israel and some Arab regimes (e.g., Nuri al-Said's in Iraq), with the background orchestration of the British; the impact of this direct or indirect collaboration on both Arab Jews and Palestinians, now cast into antagonistic roles on opposite sides of the political and ideological border; Zionist attempts to place a wedge between the Jewish and Muslim communities, for example by placing bombs in synagogues to generate panic on the part of Jews;[12] the Arab nationalism that failed to make a distinction between Jews and Zionists and that did little to secure a place for Jews; and Arab-Jewish misconceptions about the secular nation-state project of Zionism, which had almost nothing to do with their own religious community identity. Arab Jews left their countries of origin with mingled excitement and terror but, most importantly, full of Zionist-manipulated confusion, misunderstanding, and projections. Old-fashioned messianic religiosity was co-opted into a secular nationalist movement. At times, even Arab-Jewish Zionists (who condoned what they themselves called "cruel Zionism," the need to use violent means to dislodge Jews from Exile) failed to grasp this distinction and certainly never imagined the systematic racism that they were about to encounter in the "Jewish" state.[13]

The Arab-versus-Jew binarism has placed Arab Jews outside the Arab world and has called up some historical memories of Arab-Muslim hostility to Jews-as-Jews. The fears, anxiety, and even trauma provoked by chants of "*idhbah al-yahud*" ("slaughter the Jews") are still a burning memory for my parents' generation, who lived the anti-Zionist struggle not as Zionist occupiers in Palestine but as Iraqi Jews in Iraq and as Egyptian Jews in Egypt. And while those chants can be seen as directed at "the Zionists," one cannot overlook the way they marked the psyche of Jews in Egypt, Iraq, and Syria. At the same time, with the pressure of waves of Ashkenazi Zionist immigration, and the swelling power of its institutions, the distinction between Jews and Zionists was becoming ever more tenuous, to the benefit of European Zionism. The situation led the Palestinian Arabs to see all Jews as at least potential accomplices of Zionism. Had the Arab nationalist movement maintained the distinction between "Jew" and "Zionist," as even some Zionist historians have recognized, it might have won Arab-Jewish support for the anti-Zionist cause.[14] Thus the idea of a homogenous "Jewish Nation," even when articulated by Arabs from a presumably anti-Zionist perspective, ironically ends up reproducing the very Zionist discourses that it opposes, specifically the Zionist claim to speak on behalf of all Jews.

The Making of Mizrahi Identity

Political geographies and state borders do not always coincide with imaginary geographies,[15] whence the existence of "internal émigrés," nostalgics, rebels—that is, groups of people who share the same passport but whose relationship to the nation-state is conflictual and ambivalent. Within Israel itself, precisely because it was the state (Israel) that created the nation (Jewish), the Mizrahi belonging to the nation became a state project in which the whole educational and social apparatus was mobilized. Yet despite the efforts to transform Arab Jews into Israeli Jews, Mizrahi affiliation with Euro-Israel is complex, ambivalent, and at times skeptical, even contingent.

In a roundabout way, the Mizrahim as an "imagined community" are a Zionist invention.[16] By provoking the geographical dispersal of the Jews from the Muslim world, by placing them in a new situation on the ground, by attempting to reshape their identity as simply "Israeli," by disdaining and trying to uproot their Easternness, by discriminating against them as a group, Zionism obliged Arab Jews to redefine themselves in relation to new ideological polarities, thus provoking the aporias of an identity constituted out of its own ruins. Jews in the Muslim world always thought of themselves as "Jews," but their Jewishness was assumed as part of the Judeo-Islamic cultural fabric. With Zionism, that set of affiliations changed, resulting in a transformed semantics of belonging. But the delegitimization of Middle Eastern culture has boomeranged in the face of Euro-Israel: out of the massive encounter that has taken place between Jews from such widely separated regions as the *Maghrib* and Yemen emerged a new overarching umbrella identity, what came to be called "the Mizrahim."

The term began to be used only in the early 1990s by leftist non-Ashkenazi activists who saw previous terms such as *Bnei 'Edot ha-Mizrah* ("descendants of the oriental ethnicities") as condescending; non-European Jews were posited as "ethnicities," in contradistinction to the unmarked norm of "Ashkenaziness" or Euro-Israeli "*sabra*ness," defined simply as Israeli. "Mizrahim" also gradually replaced the term "Sephardim" (literally referring to those of Spanish origin), which was also used oppositionally up until the late 1980s. Apart from its inaccuracy, "Sephardim" can be seen as privileging links to Europe while slighting the East. The newer term "Mizrahim" (literally "Easterners" or "Orientals") references more than just origin; it evokes the specific experience of non-Ashkenazi Jews in Israel. "Mizrahim" took on some of the resistant quality of the Black/White discourse established by the Black Panther movement in the early 1970s, itself a proud reversal of the Ashkenazi racist epithet *schwartze chayes* (Yiddish for "black animals") and an allusion to the Black Liberation movement in the U.S. "Mizrahim," I would argue, condenses a number of connotations: it celebrates the Jewish past in the Eastern world; it affirms the pan-Oriental communities developed in Israel itself; and it invokes a future of revived cohabitation with the Arab-Muslim East. All these emergent collective definitions arose, as often occurs, in diacritical contrast with a newly encountered hegemonic group, in this case the Ashkenazim of Israel.

If there had been no state of Israel, my family and I would probably still be in Baghdad, living as one minority among many ethnic and religious communities (Assyrians, Chaldeans, Kurds, Shi'is, Turkomans, and so on) in a Sunni-Muslim-Arab dominant society. Or we might have become refugees from dictatorship, like so many exiled Iraqis today. But without Zionism, we would not have faced the dilemma of Arab-versus-Jew. Instead, my

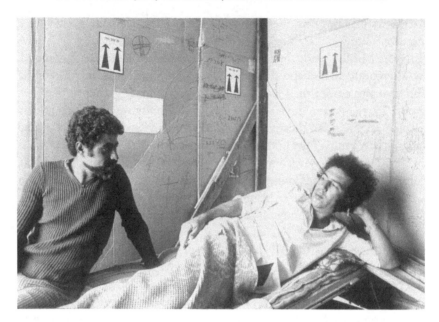

Figure 20   Photo and original Israel Government Press Office caption: "Black Panthers Dani Sa'il and Zacharia Ya'acovi in Protest Strike in Dizengoff St. Tel Aviv, October 1972"

family, refugees from Iraq, passed through Israel and ended up in the U.S., immigrants seeking refuge from, among other things, Euro-Israeli racism. For Mizrahim, Israel has not been conducive to success. Many families who led prosperous lives in Egypt, Iran, Iraq, Morocco, or Tunisia witnessed a descent in Israel, their children becoming dropouts, drug addicts, prostitutes, hustlers. While the majority of Jews in prison are of non-Ashkenazi origin, the majority at the university (students and professors) are Ashkenazi. In a short period, the identity of Arab Jews has been fractured, their life possibilities diminished, their hopes deferred.

Mizrahi identity, then, is on one level a Zionist "achievement," one that marks a departure from previous concepts of Jewishness. Although there had been a kind of regional geocultural Jewish space from the Mediterranean to the Indian Ocean, where Jews traveled and exchanged ideas, it was always within the aegis and in dialogue with the larger Islamic world,[17] a world where the Ashkenazim were on the "margins." But within that world, identities were contingently defined by hyphens. In Iraq, multiple definitions were used: "Baghdadi Jews" (in contrast with the Jews of other cities), "Babylonian Jews" (to mark historical roots in the region), "Iraqi Jews" (to mark national affiliation), and "Arab Jews" (in contradistinction to Muslim and Christian Arabs, but also when marking belonging to the greater Arab nation). Although the term "Sephardi" connoted shared liturgical traditions across Muslim spaces, "Sephardiness" was not part of the Iraqi-Jewish self-definition insofar as it referred to the Jews of Spain (*Sepharad* in Hebrew) who retained their Spanish even in Bulgaria, Egypt, Morocco, or Turkey. Zionism, however, ruptured these designations as well as the assumptions about Jewishness.

The "Arabness" of the Mizrahim not only threatened the Zionist ego-ideal fantasizing Israel as a prolongation of Europe "in" but not "of" the Middle East, it also embodied the perceived reminiscence of an "inferior" Diaspora Jewishness. (This attitude was at times expressed toward Ashkenazi newcomers as well.) The immigrants from the Third World, particularly from Arab-Muslim countries, provoked "anti-Jewish" feelings in the secularly oriented *sabra* culture both because of the threatening idea of the heterogeneity of Jewish cultures and because of the discomforting amalgam of "Jewishness" and "backwardness." The Eurocentric Israeli openness toward Western culture, then, must also be understood within the relational context of a menacing heteroglossia, as a reaction against the vestiges of *shtetl*-Diaspora culture and as a projected penetration of "alien" Levantine Jews.

Deliberate government policy favored the "modernization" of "primitive" Easterners into "civilized" Israelis. As Mizrahim arrived in Israel, violent measures were taken to strip them of their heritage: Yemenis were shorn of their sidelocks, religious artifacts were stolen by Zionist emissaries (with false promises of return), babies were kidnapped, at times literally snatched from their mothers and sold for adoption to Ashkenazim. Mizrahim under the control of Ashkenazi religious authorities, meanwhile, had to send their children to Ashkenazi Orthodox schools, where they learned the "correct" forms of practicing Judaism, including Yiddish-accented praying, liturgical-gestural norms, and centuries-old Polish sartorial codes favoring dark colors. (Here lie the partial origins of the Shas Party.) Although the Mizrahi *aliya* to Israel is described by official ideology (and sometimes seen by Mizrahim themselves) as a return "home," in fact this return, within a broader historical perspective, can be seen as a new mode of exile. For the Arab Jew, existence under Zionism has meant a profound and visceral schizophrenia, mingling stubborn self-pride with an imposed self-rejection, typical products of colonial ambivalence. The assimilative project has partially "succeeded," at least in terms of dismantling a vast civilization of the Jews of the Muslim world. And along with the trauma of geographical exile, there came another exile—from one's own self and community as one had known it.

Exile for Mizrahim can even take the form of estrangement from one's own body. Dominant media in Israel have disseminated the hegemonic

Figure 21 Photo and original Israel Government Press Office caption: "Ben-Shushan Family from Tunis, July 6, 1950"

aesthetic inherited from colonialist discourse, rendering homage to ideals of Whiteness and non-Semitic looks. The hegemony of this Eurocentric gaze explains why darker women in Israel dye their hair blonde, why Israeli TV commercials are often more suggestive of Scandinavia than of a non-European majority country, and why women undergo cosmetic surgery to look more European. (I am not suggesting that Ashkenazim are not also inferiorized by these hegemonic ideals.) The mythical norms of Eurocentric aesthetics come to inhabit the very intimacy of self-consciousness.

Mizrahim in Israel came to reject their dark or olive skin, their guttural pronunciation, their quartertone music, even their cultural practice of hospitality. Children, trying desperately to conform to an elusive Euro-Israeli *sabra* norm, were made to feel ashamed of their parents and their Arab countries of origin. At times Mizrahim were mistaken for Palestinians and arrested or beaten. Since Arabness led only to rejection, many Mizrahim became self-hating. In a classic play of colonial specularity, the East came to view itself through the West's distorting mirror. Indeed, if it is true, as Malcolm X said, that the White man's worst crime was to make the Black man hate himself, then Mizrahi internalized self-hatred means that the Israeli institutional apparatus has much to account for. (Mizrahi rejection of the Arab, in so far as it takes place, tends to be a disguised form of self-rejection.)

The present-day Mizrahi view of the Arab is very much a product of Israel. The kind of *selbsthass* that sometimes emerged among Ashkenazis in the post-Haskala era has hardly characterized Jewish existence in the Muslim world; for the Mizrahi, *selbsthass* came into existence through their new relationship with the Ashkenazim, for whom it came into existence in relation to the Christian Europeans. Thousands of Ashkenazi "wannabes" have rejected their Arab origins and mimic *sabra* Europeanized speech patterns, body language, gestures, and thinking.

Mimicry, however, forms only one dimension of the Euro-Israeli colonization of the Mizrahi mind. Occupying contradictory social and discursive spaces, Mizrahi identity, like all identities, is dynamic, mobile, less an achieved synthesis than an unstable constellation of discourses. Growing up in Israel, for Mizrahim, has involved shuttling back and forth between

Figure 22 Photo and original Israel Government Press Office caption: "Prime Minister Shimon Peres Visits Nissim Alfasi in his House in Ashdod for the Mimouna Celebrations, April 12, 1985"

conflictual cultures, split between the "private" sphere of home and neighborhood and the public sphere of Euro-Israel. Young Mizrahim made sure
that the Iraq or Morocco of home was invisible at school, work, in buses
or streets, repressing all that was culturally theirs while being induced to
emulate those who oppressed them. At the same time, they continued
family traditions, entering a space both collective and private—inaccessible
to Euro Israelis.

Meanwhile, the myth of the melting pot promoted by Euro-Israeli
ideologues was in fact taking place in the 1950s and 1960s, but not in the
ways the dominant Euro-Israeli institutions foresaw and imagined. In the
working-class neighborhoods, far from the prying eyes of the Establishment, we Mizrahim of Arab or Turkish or Iranian origin acquired new
multiplicities, the product of a new historical encounter of cultures. We
quickly learned expressions and foods from other "Oriental" countries.
While experiencing delegitimation by Euro-Israel, we were also marginally
connected to the Arab world that knew little of our new existence. In
Mizrahi neighborhoods in those years, we listened to Umm Kulthum on

Figure 23   Ya'aqub El-'Alali's CD Cover, "Fog el-Nakhel" ("Above the Palm Trees"),
autographed in Hebrew and Arabic

the radio, as well as to Arab music from our various countries of origin. The Iraqis, for example, continued to listen to Nazem Al-Ghazali, and in the age of television, especially since the 1970s, when Mizrahim *en masse* began purchasing TV sets, we viewed Arabic programs and films from within our cramped living rooms.

Hybrid identities cannot be reduced to a fixed recipe; rather, they form a changing repertory of cultural modalities. Mizrahi popular culture has clearly manifested a vibrant dialogue with Arab, Turkish, Greek, Indian, and Iranian popular cultures. Despite the separation from the Arab world, Mizrahi culture is nourished through the enthusiastic consumption of Egyptian, Jordanian, and Lebanese television programs, films, and music video performances that rupture the Euro-Israeli public sphere in a kind of subliminal transgression of a forbidden nostalgia. In fact, some Mizrahi music is produced in collaboration with Israeli Palestinians, while musical groups such as the Moroccan-Israeli Sfatayim traveled back to Morocco to produce a music video sung in Moroccan Arabic against the scenery of the cities and villages that Moroccan Jews have left behind, just as Israeli-born Iraqi singers such as Ya'aqub Nishawi, sing old and contemporary Iraqi music. This yearning for a symbolic return to "the Diaspora" results in what could be narrated as a novel reversal of the traditional phrase of "next year in Jerusalem," and a reversal of the Biblical expression that substitutes "Babylon" for "Zion:" "By the waters of Zion, where we sat down, and there we wept, when we remembered Babylon."

Reconceptualizing Identity: Toward Mizrahi Studies

What is called for, I think, is a new field of inquiry: Mizrahi studies, alongside and in relation to Palestinian studies. This field would critique and even bypass the founding premises of Orientalist representation and Eurocentric discourse. It would, at one level, critique the folklorization and exoticization of Mizrahim within Zionist discourse, its self-idealizing narrative of rescue and the concomitant demonization of Arab-Muslim culture. Such studies would interrupt the modernizing narrative in which Anthropology renders Mizrahim as living "allochronically" in another "time," in which sociology attempts to explain Mizrahi criminality, in which political science avoids the relationship between Mizrahi and Palestinian issues, and so forth. This interdisciplinary field would relocate the issues in a much wider geographical and historical perspective.

At another level, Mizrahi studies would intervene at the point of convergence of multiple communities and disciplines. Rather than demarcate neatly fenced-off areas of expertise, it would cross the geographical, historical, and disciplinary borders erected by the nationalist conceptualization of identities and Eurocentric disciplinary formations. Such an interdisciplinary framework would transcend purist notions of national identity to make room for proliferating differences within and beyond nation-states. We Arab Jews, for example, crossed a border and ended up in Israel, but our millennial "Arabness" did not thereby suddenly cease. Nor did it remain static in a previous historical incarnation. How could we change our language, our cuisine, our music, our ways of thinking overnight? Certainly, we have been changed. But to see Mizrahim as simply Israeli would be tantamount to seeing African Americans, despite their complex, conflictual, and miscegenated history, as simply American. At the same time, to expect Mizrahim to be simply Arab would be tantamount to reducing African Americans to simply African.

Figure 24   Policing a Black Panther demonstration, Jerusalem, 1971 (Photo: Shimshon Wigoder)

To address the Mizrahi case, one cannot simply proscribe an either/ or paradigm of Jewish versus Arab identity, even though it was the two opposing nationalist movements that have shaped Mizrahi identity over the last half century. And certainly the hegemonic structures and conceptual frameworks generated over the past century cannot easily be vaporized. One can no longer deal today with subaltern identities such as Mizrahim or Palestinian citizens of Israel (or the larger Middle Eastern diaspora) on the basis of purist definitions of identity that often end up becoming ahistorical and even oppressive schematizations. Given the displacement of Jews from the Arab-Muslim world and their contemporary presence largely in the "West" (Israel, France, U.K., the Americas), it is more than ever impossible to collapse a complex, layered culture into a simplistic division of East-versus-West or Arab-versus-Jew. Diasporic identities are not homogenous. Often, displacements are piled onto earlier displacements. For Arab-Jewish communities, the traumatic move to Israel came in the wake of the partition of Palestine, a process over which they had no control and in which they, like the Palestinians, were the objects and not the subjects of history, even if this objectification for Palestinians took a different, infinitely more violent form. (This is not to suggest that, once in Israel, Mizrahim have not been part of this violence against Palestinians.)

Today Mizrahim daily live the contradictions of their identity, in a visceral fashion. The accounts of the schism within Israel, which posit a clichéd Right/Left or secular/religious opposition, fail to capture the coiled confusion of Mizrahi identity in the wake of Zionism. Nor do they capture the deep roots of Mizrahi antagonism towards the Ashkenazi establishment, the variegated forms of their resistance—sometimes even unconscious, sometimes even politically misconceived, but a resistance that can be found in the crevices of a social system Mizrahim are slowly learning to master, oppose, and change. Even if this hope for change takes what seems like politically "distorted" forms, the question is how we read those forms. Such a reading must avoid the blind spots of the conventional modes of analyzing Israeli politics and society; rigid assumptions about identity do not account for complex cultural formations like the Mizrahim. What is desperately needed for critical scholars is a de-Zionized decoding of the peculiar history of Mizrahim, one closely articulated with Palestinian history.[18] Rather than segregate Palestinian and Mizrahi histories as two unrelated events, we must see their intricate links. This conceptualization does not see the Mizrahi question as simply internal to the study of Israel (as though outside of the question of Arab nationalism) or without implication for the question of Palestine. Making such links serves to "re-orient" the debate, bringing together two absolutely crucial currents of critique within a multi-perspectival analysis.

6

Remembering a Baghdad Elsewhere:
An Emotional Cartography

A widespread narrative has maintained that Israel rescued Jews from the Arab/Muslim lands, and brought them from the Diaspora to the Promised Land, thus ending a millennial Babylonian Exile. Could it be, I have asked, that this engineered Ingathering of the Exiles itself engendered new exiles that resulted in a series of traumatic ruptures? In the wake of these new diasporizations, what memories could be narrated and which were to be erased to fit the official picture of Jew-versus-Arab? Nostalgia itself, however private an enterprise, was inevitably to become an act of political enunciation, trapped in the regime of "taboo memories" and "forbidden reminiscence." For Arab/Middle Eastern Jews the remembrance of Arab/Muslim spaces has turned into a reenactment of the displacement narrative, a kind of ongoing performance of the painful nature of the rupture. Memory is now located in the definition of the dislocation itself, existing in the shadow of a terminological crisis: is the departure one of simple "immigration," or of "*aliya*," or of "refugees," or of "population exchange?"

The terminology itself, I have argued, must be used in partial and overlapping ways, "under erasure" as it were, to recount a complex, even rather anomalous, cross-border movement. In the wake of colonial partition, newly generated identities have been trapped in an imposed amnesia and the taboo on selected hyphens, hence the significance of inserting a meta-phorical hyphen linking "the Arab" and "the Jew," and "Jewishness" and "Muslimness." Although dominant cartographies, on both sides of the conflict, have tended to draw manifest boundaries between Israel and the Arab world, as well as between East and West, an alternative map can reveal glimpses of the vital possibilities of a dialogical imagination. By juxtaposing these often quarantined geographies and histories, and by interweaving

---

Published in the Culture Section of *Jadaliyya*, April 1, 2013. Based on a presentation delivered at the Memory Marathon, programmed by Hans Ulrich Obrist and Julia Peyton-Jones at the Serpentine Gallery Pavilion, venue designed by Herzog & de Meuron and Ai Weiwei, London, October 13, 2012. One section was written as "Entering Language(s): Fragments from the Memory of an Arab-Jew" for the workshop "Fear in One's Own Country: Israeli and Palestinian, Arab and Jewish Intellectuals in Dialogue," co-organized by Rafik Schami, et al., Collegium Helveticum, Zurich, May 29, 2000.

these disparate narratives, I hope to illuminate an emotional cartography of dislocation. But here, rather than rehearse my previous terminological probing, I will sketch out a disjointed map of my own journey and my familial odyssey from Iraq to Israel/Palestine to the U.S., tracing the dots that go into the making of an hyphenated identity, the pain and pleasure of hybridity within inter-generational crossings of enemy zones.

* * *

Was it inevitable that I, an Arab Jew, should end up writing in English about my lived linguistic schism between Hebrew and Arabic? As an Iraqi Jew who grew up in Israel in the 1960s, I did not enter the three languages in which I have communicated most of my life with the ease with which privileged children slide smoothly into cosmopolitanism. Only a decade had passed since my parents' hasty exodus from Iraq, with my sister in their arms and a single suitcase of belongings. For us, the name "Baghdad" did not exactly evoke the fantastic tales of Ali Baba, Aladdin, or Scheherazade, but rather a dense lived quotidian reality, even if lived outside of Iraq. Although we could not hop on the next train to Baghdad, it seemed that many of the Iraqi adults in Israel lived longing for a one-way ticket, somehow not exactly for a place, but rather to a time that shall never return. For us, the younger generation who never set foot there, Baghdad was a place in stories, but it was also our home, our neighborhood, our faces, our Arabic dialect, our accent in Hebrew, our *maqam* music, our *kubba* dishes (variety of dumplings), our *latem* grief, our *hafla* festivity, shared in the small town of Petah Tikva, or the Gate of Hope. (We were blithely unaware of how or when this 1878 Zionist settlement submerged the Palestinian village of Mlabes, even when "Arabs"—i.e., Palestinians—were passing through town to see a doctor or sell produce.) That displaced Baghdad was a secretive one, existing on the margins of the official Israeli nation and its subjugated Palestinian Arabs. And yet we were never completely alien to this epic-scale schism.

The planes that were arranged to transport Iraqi Jews to Israel uprooted millennia of life in Babylon, leading to a new diasporic existence. Overnight, we were no longer Iraqis, but Israelis; a new citizenship coupled with a strict poetic national-culture meter. The Israeli/Arab conflict formulated a new grammar of belonging where Arabness and Jewishness composed a mutually exclusive syntax, in excess of each other. Upon their arrival in Israel, my grandparents did not speak Hebrew and they never learned it until their last day. My parents, while becoming more fluent in Hebrew, persisted in speaking it with a heavy Iraqi accent, unable to erase the traces of their "*bilad al-rafidayn*" (Mesopotamia) birthplace. My father and his friends, during their first days as construction workers, communicated among themselves in Arabic but were disdainfully ordered by their Euro-Israeli boss to: "Stop speaking Arabic! We are not in an Arab country." Arabic, needless to say, was the language of the enemy. A Jew could not speak it, and a Jew could certainly not claim it as an identity marker. "In Iraq," my parents often lamented, "we were Jews. In Israel, we are Arabs."

In our own fragile and disoriented apprehension, we the children were recruited for the making of a new identity that was to clash with our parents' Iraqiness, Arabness, and Middle Easternness. At home we turned into a domesticated linguistic police force, the secret agents of Euro-Israeli hegemony. Back from school, we voiced what was expected of us: "Stop speaking Arabic!" When my grandparents took the bus with us, we wanted them to remain silent, anxious that they would forget that we were not at home, and could be heard. We virtually ordered our parents to forget that alien linguistic baggage of Iraqiness. Unknowing targets of mental coloni-zation, we were the children who were expected to delete not merely the past across the border but also the transplanted Baghdads, Cairos, or Rabats of our homes and neighborhoods. Our bodies, language, and thought were regulated to the rhythms of a disciplining, corrective, normalizing machine designed to erect us into proud Israelis.

My first public performance of the Hebrew language was hardly a textbook example of the healthy linguistic development of a child. I vividly remember my first anxious days in kindergarten, when I was less terrified about the separation from my mother than I was about Arabic words slipping into my Hebrew. Although no one had explicitly warned me, something in the social atmosphere made it clear that Arabic was a taboo language, and soon I learned to master Hebrew in the "correct" form, that is, shorn of an Iraqi accent. Unlike my father and my mother, I was becoming free from the shackles of my/their/our tongue. I was well on my way to assimilat-ing, relegating the Iraqi accent in Hebrew as well as our Arabic dialect and culture to the private space of home and family. There we could not be observed, watched, or gazed upon with silencing scorn.

Although we were on the margins of Euro-Israeli culture, as a child I felt I had a special role in the space of my own family. I acquired the role of the translator and mediator for my grandparents who could not speak or read Hebrew. They could not read the signs in the foreign streets, they could not take care of bills in Hebrew, or converse with non-Arabic speakers in the town. As a child, Hebrew gave me a sense of immense power over the adults in my community. My grandfather, Abu-Liyahu, depended on my interpreter skills to navigate the unfamiliar currents of the Hebrew-speaking world. And yet I soon learned to be ashamed of that role, not for the sake of my grandfather but because the ability to translate was a mark of the Arab side of my identity, when I just wanted to be transparent, without that dark, opaque Iraqi history, unburdened by Arabic culture. I soon learned to pretend not to speak Arabic and to speak a Europeanized Hebrew.

Standing in front of the mirror, I tried to put some order in the babble of consonants and vowels. I learned to push all the sounds to the front of the mouth as though there was a clear border dividing the deep throat where the guttural sounds of—in both Arabic and Hebrew—"ʿa," "qa," "ta," "ḥa," were made. I was very good, an excellent self-colonized subject. Gradually the sounds began crossing the interior cave of my throat through the opening of the tunnel to the front of the mouth, liberated from the chains of "the harsh" consonants. Triumphant in the ease with which all the deep sounds became lighter, I felt as though I were speaking a European language, shifting into airy sounds of "a," "ka," "ta," and even the Germanic "kha." "Hebrew is more like German, or French," I thought to myself, of which I had caught a first glimpse not from the French-speaking Moroccans in town, but from my mother. Routinely she repeated her favorite childhood French textbook dialogue—"*Joe, il fait très beau aujourd'hui; Où veux tu aller?*"—with an enthusiasm that always escaped me. The obsessive phrase from her own childhood echoed her glamorous days at Baghdad's Alliance Israélite Universelle school.

The daughter of non-literate parents, who spoke '*amiyya* (colloquial Arabic)—whether in the Baghdadi Jewish or Muslim dialects—was proudly mastering *fusha* Arabic and French, and even learning some English and Hebrew. But in my time, the French phrase was orphaned of its hopeful Baghdadi days—days in which it was still impossible to imagine my mother's eventual loss of French during her life in Israel and then in the U.S. This linguistic loss, however, was overshadowed by the persistence of Arabic, whether alongside Hebrew and/or English. The snippets of French or English at home were broken according to the master-code of Arabic, but Arabic was not broken, and persisted throughout our voyage across the Atlantic. Yet our quotidian Arabic/Hebrew bilingualism was far from reflecting a harmonious coexistence of two relative languages; it was intensely fraught, burdened by the abrasive sounds of war.

When the authorities in their diverse incarnations as teachers, social workers, or police, entered our neighborhood and home, my grandparents knew that the "honor" of the visit was hardly a sign of some reward to be vested upon our family. The anxiety level rose dramatically, especially when their sons, my uncles, would defect from the army, just for a few weeks to take a break, or would try to avoid serving in the military altogether. "Habiba," my grandmother *nana* Masʿuda would call me in the Jewish-Iraqi dialect, "*tali hon, shufi ash qa-yighdon minna*" (come here, see what they want from us), begging me to abandon the hide-and-seek games I was playing with the pigeons and chickens behind the fig tree in the backyard. My dress tainted with mud, I ran home only to find myself speaking with a military policewoman searching for my youngest uncle. The "us" and "them" was invariably clear to me. It didn't have to be spelled out. Yet, I wanted to impress the blonde woman at the door, whose proudly ironed khaki uniform made her look as though she had just stepped out of an ad in an Israeli magazine only to heroically land in our humble quarters.

"But why is *nana* so worried?" I wondered. *Nana* was far more breathless than I was after running all the way from the end of the backyard to the house's front door. *Nana*, who was always so slow and lackadaisical, went through a metamorphosis, suddenly speaking fast, like the proverbial headless chicken running in circles. "Why does *nana* want me to tell the khaki woman that she doesn't know where my uncle is? I know where he is." And, soon, I uttered the Hebrew words I thought showed respect for *nana's* *adab* (good manners), education, and hospitality. "He is at Hezqel's store. He left this morning," I said, with the confidence of an insider. "That will make *nana* calmer," I thought as I received the warmest, shiniest smile I had ever received from any khaki woman, who quickly turned away toward the central bus station, energized and reinvigorated by my useful urban topographical insights.

My speech act of hospitality was rejected by my tearful grandmother, who now froze in her spot at the entrance until one of my uncles, Naji, came. Before he said anything, I found myself running for my life far ahead of the bottle of milk that followed in my wake and was smashed to smithereens of glass floating in a white puddle. I quickly reached the backyard, frightening all the chickens and pigeons in my path and climbing to my spot in the fig tree, which proved not to be the haven I had imagined it to be. The burning memory taught me a clear lesson about the subtle but strategic difference between a translator and a traitor. Living between Arabic and Hebrew was experienced quite viscerally as a negative dialectic, except when my defenses broke down, and when, on both happy and sad occasions, I totally forgot that I was supposed to forget Arabic.

But actually, my community was not easily seduced by the linguistic cultural assimilation. Arabic was the language in which all the emotions around me were expressed. It was the language of the music I heard; of the songs we danced to; of the conversations at the Babylonian synagogue; the language in which my father washed my tears with the by-now calloused hands of a man who had never known physical labor until he arrived in Israel; the language in which my mother got good deals in the *souk*, the marketplace in Petah Tikva, a market almost exclusively inhabited by Iraqi vendors; the language in which we heard news from Arabic-speaking radio and TV; the language virtually everybody would tune in to on the radio for Umm Kulthum's monthly song from Egypt; the language in which we watched hilarious Egyptian and Syrian comedies; the language in which my grandmother would place my head in her lap and sing me an Iraqi lullaby, "*Dilelol*." Arabic was the language of the stories that my grandfather told us as he would repeat the same "*Kan ya-ma-kan, fi qadim al-zaman, wal-'aqa bna lu dekan b'souq al-midan ...*" prelude to every story, no matter what the story was, as we were munching on the *khebez*, the Iraqi pita he baked in the oven that he built with his own hands. It was the language he sought out on the big brown radio that he was so reluctant to part with, even for meals or even during war times when piercing alarms meant everyone had to run to the shelter. And when transistors were introduced into our lives, in the early 1970s, he was profoundly cheered by the invention, for now he could be liberated from the confinement of the house and walk freely, his head glued to the black speaking-box hiding his big ear, his eyes staring at the invisible space as he continued his routine of handing us *mlabes* (pastel-colored, candy-coated almonds, and, ironically, the name of the Palestinian town where we ended up).

Arabic was the language of the stories my mother told me at every lunch, often repeating the same magical story I knew by heart: "*al-ruman al-yehalhel wa-al-tufah al-yesafeq*" (the pomegranates that ululates and the apples that applaud), stories without which I refused to chew on my mother's unappetizing *bamya* (okra). It was the language my mother spoke with the Palestinian 'Amer, who carried a sack full of oranges to sell in our town, a man whose gentle smile under his moustache seemed a perfect match to my mother's ethos of "*'eb*" (shame)—both happy for a lunch break from the harsh routines when they talked about their lives. My mother, with her virtuoso shape-shifting Arabic, began her voyage into his Palestinian dialect, found in him a perfect listener for her nostalgia for Baghdad and he found in her a patient audience for his memories of a time before his village was "to disappear" with the establishment of Israel.

Arabic and Hebrew, then, were far from being neutral languages. To know Hebrew meant to be Hebrew, which, by implication, meant the erasure of anything Arabic. Thinking back on these years, it is no wonder that at a fairly young age, English became the linguistic apple of my eye. English also brought with it some affectionate memories. My father was schooled in Baghdad's Shamash high school, where matriculation exams were sanctified by an official Oxford seal. While the Iraqiness of my father was, in the lexicon of my school, a sign of backwardness, his knowledge of English, carried across borders from Iraq to Israel, promoted him to the status of a kind of village scribe in English. Suddenly, aspects of the poor man's cosmopolitanism of Iraqi history came to the rescue, a social advantage brought especially from Baghdad. In this situation, English seemed a kind of free zone immune to those painful conflicts of Hebrew and Arabic. Yet, English obviously was also not a neutral space. The U.S. post-World War II rise to global power, the 1970s Americanization of Israel, and British colonial history in Iraq and Palestine, all contributed to the English language infiltration of my young mind, unsettling the presence of both Hebrew and Arabic.

Years later, as I began reflecting on this history in English, I remember inverting the traditional Biblical verse, and instead of "weeping by the waters of Babylon," it was "by the waters of Zion that we laid down and wept when we remembered Babylon." As I began writing on "the Arab-Jew," I was hoping to inscribe a memory that would undo official national memorialization, and insert the quotidian negotiations of Arabic/Hebrew. Writing on the Arab-Jew was also an attempt to resist "the last of the Mohicans" syndrome. Perhaps my reflections on our displacement have been no more than a monument to my parents and grandparents who have lived in between hostile zones, a fragmented testimony not simply to the raw facts, but also to the labyrinthian intricacies of emotions. My words were meant to speak for a generation whose dreams were muted and mutilated by the everyday demands of hyphenated realities. Writing as an act of remembrance has helped me construct a kind of portable shrine for those taboo memories, while also framing a reluctant eulogy lest the memories completely fade away.

PART II

Between Palestine and Israel

7

The Trouble with Hanna

(with Richard Porton)

Traditionally, Hollywood's depiction of Arabs has taken the form of either fanatic, cold-blooded terrorists in films such as *Black Sunday* (1977) and *Raid on Entebbe* (1976) or exotic-sensual figures in films that include *The Sheik* (1921), *Kismet* (1944, remake 1955), *Ali Baba and the 40 Thieves* (1944) and *Lawrence of Arabia* (1962). Films with negative images, in which Arabs constitute "bad objects" within the narrative, provide easy targets for ideological analysis. But, as Robert Stam[1] has pointed out, films that present "positive images" are often intrinsically limited by their conformity to liberal shibboleths. *Lawrence of Arabia*, for example, "orientalizes the Orient," to borrow Edward Said's terminology, by constructing a romantic vision of "Arab otherness." Arabs are equated with the desert, and the only two urban sequences set in the Middle East concentrate on the British, as if the Arab world is merely a huge desert, much as Tarzan's Africa is merely a huge jungle. Topographical reductionism, among other distorted images, reflects the film's dynamic of positive portrayals whose façade of sympathy is simultaneously contrasted and counteracted by the cinematic style. Costa-Gavras's *Hanna K.* is the first Hollywood feature to deal with the Palestinian question from a sympathetic vantage point. But the film, despite its attempts to transcend its precursors, in some ways continues a negative tradition. It endeavors to negate dominant ideology concerning the Arab world, but basically still affirms Western modes of representing the Orient.

With the exception of his first feature, Costa-Gavras's work has always been noted for its passionate engagement with political controversy. Even in his earliest films, he was concerned with the disparity between "law" and justice, and attentive to the inherently repressive nature of many political systems. *Z* (1969), for example, emphasizes the restrictions on political

Published in *Film Quarterly*, vol. 38, no. 2 (Winter 1984–85). A review of the feature film *Hanna K.* (1983), produced and directed by Costa-Gavras; Script by Franco Solinas, from an original screenplay by Solinas and Costa-Gavras; and Distributed by Universal Pictures.

liberty imposed by the junta in Costa-Gavras's native Greece during the mid-1960s. *Missing* (1982), similarly, explores violations of legal due process in a country that unmistakably evokes the reality of Pinochet's Chile. Yet these controversies are always sugarcoated (and coded), and the generic gloss of the thriller or courtroom drama is always a prerequisite, fusing political sensationalism with the codes of commercial cinema. Although *Hanna K.* was hailed as a politically significant film because of its relatively compassionate treatment of the plight of the Palestinians (as well as predictably being denounced as anti-Israeli propaganda), it is "essentially unpolitical," to quote an official of the Israeli film division. This view was also echoed by American reviewers who constantly drew parallels with George Cukor's *Adam's Rib* (1949) and were understandably baffled by the film's oscillation between a saccharine romantic quadrangle and unfocussed social commentary. It is difficult to believe that this murky film was scripted by the same man who wrote Pontecorvo's *The Battle of Algiers* (1966), but the exigencies of international coproduction (with Universal Studios as a major participant) were probably responsible for the film's compromised, not to mention confusing, political and narrative orientation. Unfortunately, Costa-Gavras seems to have become, in the words of Pauline Kael, "the European Stanley Kramer." It is interesting to note that the film was produced with the full cooperation of the Israeli government, and the same official remarked: "We got favorable publicity for being liberals. Had we made problems for Costa-Gavras, the left-wing press would have had a field day."[2] This statement, unwittingly, reflects the basically reformist nature of Costa-Gavras's work. The limitations of his approach, as a paradigm for politically engaged cinema, were illuminated by a series of debates conducted during the ferment of the post-1968 period; Jean-Louis Comolli and Jean Narboni were particularly critical of films that strove for political significance but did not essentially challenge the ruling ideology, or its language and imagery.

In *Hanna K.*, the complexities of the Arab/Israeli conflict are superficially treated and undermined through stereotypical characterizations. Unlike her real-life counterparts—the famous Israeli women lawyers Lea Tsemel and Felicia Langer—Hanna lacks a fully developed political consciousness and functions within a purely individualistic and humanistic framework. Similarly, the aggressive Israeli District Attorney, Joshua Herzog (played by the Irish actor Gabriel Byrne) represents a clichéd vision of a macho *sabra* whose reactionary sentiments are meant to correspond to those of all Israelis. The specific nature of the Palestinians' political affiliations, on the other hand, is never explicitly spelled out. Isolated from any Arab social context, the principal Palestinian character, Selim Bakri, remains an enigma throughout the film. Although Arabs are present during the lengthy courtroom sequences, there is not even a hint of what personal or political affinities they might have in common. This structuring absence is somewhat reminiscent of films such as *Algiers* (1938) and *Casablanca* (1942), which virtually exclude the presence of Arabs on their own soil. The predilection for foregrounding Western characters and preoccupations led *Hanna K.* to be disparagingly referred to as "An Unmarried Woman in Israel."

In several interviews, Costa-Gavras reiterated his intention to explore the Palestinian/Israeli conflict through a woman protagonist. In this sense Hanna Kaufman, played by Jill Clayburgh, becomes the key to unveiling the effects of the Israeli legal system upon Palestinians, and the relationship of this official apparatus to questions of justice. The film, however, is almost hopelessly marred by the fact that the central role was terribly miscast. It was truly preposterous to assign this part to an actress who would seem more at home in a family drama set in the Middle West than in a "semi-engaged, single, pregnant mother" drama set in the Middle East. Her waspish persona in films such as Mazursky's *An Unmarried Woman* (1978) and Pakula's *Starting Over* (1979) is transferred to this vastly different social and political context. This miscasting raises the ideological quandary of absolutely equating the American Jew with American hegemonic culture. In happy contrast to Clayburgh's unfamiliarity with the film's milieu, Muhammad Bakri's identification with his character, Selim Bakri, even took the form of having identical surnames, a decision jointly arrived at by Costa-Gavras and Bakri himself. Paradoxically, Selim Bakri's function within the narrative is a subsidiary one, although his plight is the thematic focus of the film.

Figure 25   Muhammad Bakri and Jill Clayburgh in Costa-Gavras's *Hanna K.*, 1983

133

The films of Costa-Gavras that deal with Third World issues—*State of Siege* (1973), *Missing*, and *Hanna K.*—are focalized through a First-World protagonist. This strategy, which filters all points of view through a single, dominant perspective, raises questions concerning what the Russian literary critic Boris Uspensky terms "the norms of the text." All ideological points of view, both Palestinian and Israeli, are integrated into Hanna's perspective. The ideology of the narrator-focalizer, as Uspensky remarks, is usually understood as authoritative, and all other ideologies in the text are evaluated from this privileged position. Here Hanna's preoccupations, both romantic and legal, are incorporated into this privileged position, a contrivance that evokes the even more romanticized narrative structure of *Lawrence of Arabia.* David Lean's film emphasizes the charismatic personality of the English Lawrence whose vitality eclipses Arab political consciousness and who seems to single-handedly inspire the Arab struggle for independence. *Hanna K.,* with its sincere but superficial compassion, continues, therefore, the romantic subgenre of exotic travelogues, inevitably both ethnocentric and introspective.

The film, like other recent "Middle East thrillers" (*Circle of Deceit*, 1981, and *The Little Drummer Girl*, 1984), constructs a dynamic in which a First World protagonist invariably explains Third World oppression. This device is designed to make the film's didactic thrust palatable to a Western audience. In the courtroom sequences, for example, Hanna not only speaks for Selim but also is foregrounded within the shot, standing closer to the spectator. Dialogue and *mise-en-scène* become, therefore, essential components of her dominance within the narrative, perpetually orienting the spectator to Clayburgh's apolitical humanism. At the same time, the narrative structure allows the spectator to know only as much as Hanna knows. When Hanna follows Selim, for example, she is not cognizant (nor are the spectators) that he is planning to demonstrate to her the enormity of Palestinian suffering. The penultimate sequence in which Selim lures Hanna to an abandoned refugee camp is one more stage in the process of her ongoing education. The Western spectator's consciousness is deemed inseparable from Hanna's worldview, a process at the core of the film's underlying assumptions. In effect, the film can be seen as a *bildungsroman* that chronicles Hanna's journey from ignorance to a relative awareness of political and sexual inequalities.

Focalization is not the only device that enables Hanna K. to maintain a tone of rather schematic didacticism. The classical structure of repetition, characteristic of the *bildungsroman*, corresponds to sporadic repetitions within the film. An understanding of the film's overall structure, as well as of individual sequences, can be illuminated by the concept of narrative rhyming. The best example of this kind of rhyming sequence occurs when Hanna attempts to establish the facts concerning Selim's claim to his ancestral house. At the very beginning of the sequence, a sign identifies Kfar Rimon, a recently constructed Israeli village. The end of the sequence provides an analogical contrast to Hanna's initial encounter with the cheerful residents of Kfar Rimon. An Arab shepherd, walking near the remnants of an Arab village, cries, "This is Kafr Rumaneh." The opposition of the new houses to the village's ruins, and the opposition of the written sign of the Hebrew Kfar Rimon to the oral pronouncement of the Arabic Kafr Rumaneh, outlines the contrast between present transparency and past invisibility. This contrast is further explored within the sequence itself, which partially takes place in Selim's former house. Hanna learns to connect these two polarities with a discovery of a family photograph that corresponds to the one Selim had given her. Concurrently, a group of tourists gawk at Selim's house, and their naiveté is contrasted with Hanna's newly transformed consciousness. This contrast is reinforced through blatant visual irony, since the tour-guide scene juxtaposes a Qur'anic inscription on the gate of Selim's house with a subsequent shot of the tourists, one of whom wears a hat labelled "Welcome to Israel." The visual rhetoric of this segment reflects the antinomies of the secular and the sacred, commercialism and tradition, permanence and transience. The inscription itself ("I shall adore not that which you adore— nor will you adore that which I adore") demystifies clichéd Western notions of Islamic fanaticism.

The similarities of key events and circumstances are also apparent in the film's opening and conclusion. Already in the opening sequences, Gabriel Yared's music, replete with Arabic leitmotifs, delineates the basic terms of the conflict that will later emerge. A static shot of an Arab woman and child seated beneath a typical "Oriental house" is soon eclipsed by a pan following Israeli soldiers coming out of a doorway. Selim, suddenly, is forcibly removed from a well that has served as his hiding place. After a brief interrogation by Israeli soldiers, the owner's house is detonated. The reason for Selim's taking refuge in the well is never made completely apparent to the audience, and the question of his participation in political violence remains ambiguous, an ambiguity that continues throughout the very sequence that ends the film. The television news broadcast that announces a terrorist bombing reinforces the relationship of Selim to the recent political turmoil. The film ends as it began, with his escape from Israeli authorities, and the last shot of armed soldiers echoes the opening. Whereas classical patterns of repetition yield narrative closure, *Hanna K.*, paradoxically, employs an open-ended pattern of repetition. (Despite this façade of modernism, the film utilizes a classical shooting style and editing techniques.) Does this seem to imply that Selim's perpetual flight dooms him to being a "wandering Palestinian"?

Ironically, the "wandering Palestinian" is analogous to the traditional romantic myth of the "wandering Jew." As with many *bildungs* stories, the protagonist's quest adheres to a pattern of repetition, either circular or spiral. Hanna's literal pilgrimage from the U.S. to Israel evokes a kind of Wilhelmina Meisterin travelogue. Furthermore, the irony is doubled when one considers the fact that a straightforward political exposé ends up resembling a secular grail story, accompanied by the archetypal tropes of redemption and moral edification. The Christian theodicy in its secular version is superimposed on a primarily Jewish and Muslim Israel. Costa-Gavras's attempt to criticize a discriminatory system is, paradoxically, mirrored in his own unconscious condescension, continuing the Western heritage of objectifying the Orient. The "academic and imaginative demonology of the 'mysterious Orient'"[3] permeates, for example, sexual relationships, typified by the romanticist tendency to structure the Orient as an exotic otherness. Selim is marginalized by Hanna in a manner not unlike the traditionally Western male fetishization of Oriental women, reminiscent of Flaubert's insistent desire to omnisciently recount Salammbo's thoughts and emotions. The Oriental, whether a man or a woman, remains an enigma, never completely satisfying the desire of the romanticist-author and reader-spectator to project his/her fantasies onto an amorphous object. This contradiction is inextricable from the problems inherent in *Hanna K.* Costa-Gavras and Franco Solinas criticize Israeli policy by having Selim complain to Hanna: "They would not listen to me ... they would not hear me." The filmmakers, however, fall prey to parallel modes of hierarchical representation. Thus, they will not listen to or hear Selim, either.

This type of hierarchical representation not only inflicts itself upon the images of Palestinians, but also distorts Israeli reality through Americanized characterizations and linguistic manipulation. The same incongruous logic implies that Jill Clayburgh is an Israeli, and coincides with the rationale that the English of Hollywood scripture masquerades as "Hebrew." This garbled lingua franca characterizes Hollywood's *fata morgana* versions of the Holy Land. *Hanna K.* is unsurprisingly true to Hollywood's linguistic cannibalism, substituting English for disparate national languages. As George Steiner observes: "Intentionally or not, American English and English, by virtue of their global diffusion, are a principal agent in the destruction of natural linguistic diversity."[4] *Hanna K.* assumes a cultural universe of discourse in which the syntax and morphology of English devours Hebrew, a linguistic colonialism that ironically extends to the U.S.'s staunchest ally, Israel. The brief snippets of Arabic, meanwhile, are subtitled, creating an unequal and artificial dichotomy. Furthermore, Costa-Gavras reveals his ignorance of the linguistic realities of Israel when he suggests that Hanna, the Israeli, blithely assumes that Selim, the film's archetypal Palestinian, does not speak

Hebrew. The prevalent English dialogue, therefore, points not only to the compromised nature of this French-U.S. coproduction, but also creates an ideological homogeneity in which Israel and the West become practically indivisible.

The film, consequently, reinforces the petrified assumption that Israel and the U.S. are as inseparable as David and Jonathan. An absolute iden-tification of the two countries is reductionist in nature, and views Israel as a monolithic political entity without specific interests of its own. *Hanna K.* also ignores the schism between East and West that exists among Jews in Israel by portraying Israel as an exclusively Western entity. Forming 65 percent of the Jewish population, Oriental Jews who immigrated to Israel mainly from Arab and Muslim countries have been denied access to political power by the Ashkenazi elite. Culturally linked to the Arab world, they also form a potential source of political transformation in the area. By almost completely excluding Oriental Jews from the narrative and *mise-en-scène*, Costa-Gavras continues hegemonic patterns of representing Israel. The only presence of Oriental Jews involves a brief appearance by Hanna's maid, a marginalization reminiscent of Hollywood's traditional depiction of black characters. Ironically, even more conservative Hollywood films such as *Alice Adams* (1935) and *Gone with the Wind* (1939) tended to devote more narrative time and dialogue to blacks than the "liberal" *Hanna K.* spends on equivalent figures.

The monolithic view is perpetuated on another level when positions of both the Likud and Labor parties are fused into the character of Professor Leventhal, an acquaintance of Hanna. His diatribe recapitulates mainstream Zionist ideology, and pithily invokes the dogma shared by Ben-Gurionists as well as Beginists: "Miss Kaufman prefers tragedy. What is your alternative? Give citizenship to anyone who asks for it? Make us live as a minority in a sea of Arabs? Cram us into a new ghetto? Your family (not a bad idea to remember) also had its share in the Holocaust. Now at least we have a country, an identity, and we must defend it." In other words, the Holocaust, the official memory of Israel, is displaced into a different context. Dismissing Palestinian rights is justified in the terms of European Jewish victimization, while ignoring the vastly different experience of Jews in Arab countries. Leventhal introduces a false determinism that links European Jewish misery with an inevitable dispossession of Palestinians, thus leading the "leftist" director to exclude truly progressive positions. At the same time, the film presents the Palestinian ideology only as it is constructed by Leventhal's speech, and not through Selim, the ostensible focus of narrative attention. *Hanna K.*, ironically, provides a more succinct expression of the European-Zionist perspective than the vicissitudes of the Palestinian position it is supposedly advocating.

In a lengthy review of *Hanna K.*, Edward Said suggests that the film's "political message overrides its aesthetic problems." This artificial separation would seem to contradict Said's own subtle reflections on aesthetic questions in *Beginnings* and *The World, the Text and the Critic*, works that make explicit the relationship between textual analysis and ideological critique. Yet in his own review he praises *Hanna K.* for its positive depiction of the anguished Palestinian. As we have already observed, however, the portrayal of the Palestinian forms part of a long tradition of representing the Orient, an issue discussed brilliantly in Said's *Orientalism*. The film's significance, then, cannot be attributed to the depiction of a "noble Palestinian." In fact, if compared with *Circle of Deceit* and *The Little Drummer Girl*, which merely use the Middle East as a backdrop, *Hanna K.* emerges as creditable in its effort to "allow us to witness the Palestinian quandary as a narratable human history."[5] *The Little Drummer Girl*, for example, blurs political distinctions by emphasizing the savagery of both Israelis and Palestinians. This view assumes the superiority of the West to the "little wars" of "irrational" nations. This cynical stance is at least not shared by *Hanna K.*, which along with films such as Tawfiq Saleh's *The Dupes* (1972) and Uri Barabash's *Beyond the Walls* (1984), attempts to disinter what has been hidden from history.

8

In Defense of Mordechai Vanunu:
Nuclear Threat in the Middle East

(with Yerach Gover)

A few months ago the international media reported on the arrest of Mordechai Vanunu, an Israeli, for having given information to the *Sunday Times* of London concerning Israel's nuclear capabilities. Vanunu, now on trial, is being denounced as a traitor in Israel; yet some groups elsewhere have proposed his name for the Nobel Peace Prize. The Vanunu case has numerous implications touching on issues of nuclear proliferation, human and civil rights, and the growing militarization of Israeli society.

Mordechai Vanunu was born on October 13, 1952 in Marrakesh, Morocco, a member of a family of ten. His father, a small businessman, was relatively well off. Following the induced mass emigration of Jews from Arab and Muslim countries, Vanunu's family moved to Israel in 1963 and was settled in Beer-Sheva. On their way to Israel, the family purchased expensive rugs, carpets, an electric refrigerator, a washing machine, a record player and recording equipment, items not then widely available in Israel. Although official ideology promoted the myth of the backward and impoverished origins of Sephardim, the move to Israel represented, for most families coming from Arab and Muslim countries, a clear decline in material standards.

The Vanunus, as part of this pattern, were placed in the unexpectedly harsh conditions of a slum neighborhood in a remote town in the Negev desert. It was at that time governmental policy to settle Sephardi families away from the center of the country, along the borders, in poor and isolated regions, in so-called "development towns."

At the age of 18, Vanunu joined the military for the usual three years of compulsory service. In 1976, he was employed by Kirya le-Mehkar Gar'ini, the Negev Nuclear Research Center in Dimona. His first assignment was

Published in *Social Text*, no. 18 (Winter 1987–88).

to Makhon 2, the plutonium separation unit. Through the years he was promoted and progressively given more responsibilities and duties.

Coming from a background of relative poverty and deprivation where scarcity was presented to the immigrants as inevitable for a young nation fighting for its survival, Vanunu suddenly found himself in a sharply different environment. Here he came to perceive the misplaced priorities in the distribution of national resources, where the lower classes were being made to pay for the colossal waste of the military ambitions of the ruling class.

In 1979, Vanunu began Bachelor's studies in philosophy and geography at the Ben-Gurion University in Beer-Sheva and gradually became involved in political issues on campus, particularly the issue of discrimination against Sephardi Jews and the repression and expropriation of the Arab Palestinians. His criticism of Israeli policies has sharpened in the wake of the Lebanon war (1982). Vanunu became seriously disillusioned with his role in a nuclear enterprise and became concerned with the possibly dangerous consequences of the work being conducted in Dimona. Several times, security officials questioned him about his political activities and tried to force him to sign a statement with false confessions. In 1985 he decided to leave his work at Dimona and travel throughout Asia.

In Australia, Vanunu decided to share his information about Israel's nuclear capabilities. He contacted the *Sunday Times* of London in order to draw attention to the dangers he saw. He was interested in stimulating public debate and fostering the creation of a system of checks and balances within Israel in order to protect against aggressive actions with irreparable consequences.

Fearful for his personal security, Vanunu checked out of his London hotel and flew to Rome. There he was abducted by Israeli intelligence (Mossad) on September 30, 1986. It took 40 days for the Israeli government to admit that he was being held in an Israeli prison. He was charged with espionage, treason, and the passing of secrets to an enemy in time of war, charges which carry the maximum penalty of death. Vanunu is now being held in solitary confinement in Ashkelon prison, awaiting the closed secret trial that is to reconvene in November.

Vanunu's basic civil rights are being denied. His incoming and outgoing mail has been censored and visitations are restricted. His applications requesting religious counsel were denied, and release from solitary confinement and permission to meet with his girlfriend, Judy Zimmet, have been turned down by the courts. He is kept in a small cell with no windows and is being watched by a video camera 24 hours a day. For four months Vanunu was not allowed to leave his cell. Permission was granted only after authorities covered the fence around the yard with a canvas so no one could see him or make contact with him. He was forced to change his appearance by not being allowed to shave. When Vanunu has been called to the court, he has been transferred in a police van with windows painted and sealed. He is forced to wear a motorcycle helmet and to enter the courthouse unseen through a burlap-covered entranceway in order not to be recognized.

The events surrounding Mordechai Vanunu's abduction are being kept secret and his relatives are being threatened by Shin-Beth agents that they may face prosecution if they speak about the affair in public. His younger brother, Meir Vanunu, who has taken a major role in mobilizing world public opinion in defense of Mordechai, cannot return to Israel due to facing charges of exposing information regarding the methods of the abduction. Such information is considered "secret" in Israel and carries the penalty of 15 years in prison.

The case should be seen in light of the recent revelations about the illegal conduct of Israeli Shin-Beth officers, about their use of interrogatory torture, physical and psychological deprivation techniques, and even summary execution. Vanunu's case forms part of a broader assault on any and all opposition to or dissent from the Zionist consensus in Israel. The overwhelming majority of Israeli media and the public at large blindly accepted the accusations against Vanunu. A well-orchestrated portrayal, amounting to character assassination, permeated news and commentary, depicting him as "exhibitionist," "impotent," "homosexual," "sensationalist," "greedy," "traitor," and "mentally unbalanced." A systematic attempt has been made to delegitimize him as a human being. Furthermore, all critical discussion was narrowed to technical matters of negligence by the Israeli security institutions, which had allowed the employment of such an "unbalanced person" with "extreme leftist political views" and led to the smuggling out of "secret documents." The issue was regarded by the media as fundamentally one of Vanunu's guilt rather than one of the scandal of the illegal, and officially denied, nuclear development. To this day there has been no debate, however, about this crucial issue.

The accusation against Vanunu of exposing secret information about Israel's nuclear capabilities ignores an essential fact. Based on Israeli and international sources, it is clear that the materials provided by Vanunu were already well known to scientific and military specialists around the world.[1] Further, Vanunu is accused of committing the crime of divulging secrets to an enemy during the time of war. But Vanunu approached the *Sunday Times* of London and not the agents of enemy countries. Moreover, Israel, since its very establishment, has existed in a state of war, whether active or passive. We are confronted here with a basic question: how is it possible for a concerned Israeli citizen to express dissent in a country that claims to be a democracy?

Vanunu has repeatedly declared (through his brothers and through letters to his girlfriend) that he was motivated by his conscience and by his concern for peace in the Middle East and in the world. He insists that his act was neither an act of espionage nor a bid for financial gain, but rather an act of civil disobedience in the name of peace and justice.

WAYS TO HELP

1) *Contribute to the Mordechai Vanunu Legal Defence Fund.*
2) *Address protest telegrams to the Secretary General of the United Nations and/or to the Israeli Government through the Mordechai Vanunu Legal Defence Fund, P.O. Box 45005, Somerville, MA 02145.*
3) *Publicize this case and generate support among people, groups and legislators.*
4) *Write to Mordechai Vanunu at Ashkelon Prison, P.O. Box 17, Ashkelon, Israel.*

Figure 26 "The Mid-East: Nuclear Threat and the Vanunu Case," *Social Text*, Winter 1987/88

9

Anomalies of the National:
Representing Israel/Palestine

Critical debates around the question of "national cinema" and "national culture" have tended to avoid the "delicate" question of Israel/Palestine, perhaps betraying a feeling of discomfort in applying anti-Orientalist discourse to that region. The still-burning memory of the Holocaust as well as fears of stigmatization as "self-hating" or "anti-Semitic" malcontents, compounded by a kind of ideological bewilderment in the face of Zionism, have blocked a coherent alternative approach to the issues. In this essay I will propose a critical analysis of "Israel/Palestine" as the locus of interlinked opposing discourses ranging from "Israel" as representing the Eastern liberation of Jews from Western anti-Semitism, to Zionism as a branch of Orientalism, and "Palestine" as representing anticolonial struggle. I will examine the anomalous features of Israeli national existence as well as the attempt by Israeli filmmakers of the recent "Palestinian wave" to create a rupture with the dominant Israeli model of national identity, and finally, the recent Palestinian attempt to construct a counter-paradigm to the Zionist master narrative.

Israeli national existence (and as a consequence the encounter between it and Palestinian national existence) is anomalous. And this anomalous character is itself inseparable from the special nature of "the Jewish historical experience" as that of a dispersed, cosmopolitan, and syncretic people with an ambivalent relation to the very idea of the East. On the one hand, the "Jews of the Diaspora" have been inextricably mingled with the life of the West, yet Jews are also linked to the East. As an "ethnos" with claims to historical roots in Palestine, speaking (in Israel) a Semitic language, whose religious idiom is intimately linked with the topography of the Middle East, Jews are connected by tradition to the East, and have often been seen as an alien "Eastern" people in the West. And in the case of

Published in *Wide Angle* in a special issue on Asian Cinema, vol. 11, no. 3 (July 1989). The section on *Wedding in Galilee* is based on the article "Wedding in Galilee," published in *Middle East Report* (Middle East Research and Information Project), 154, (September–October 1988).

Sephardi/Oriental Jews—largely from Asia and North Africa—the balance shifts even further to the Eastern side of the dichotomy, for here we have a people historically and culturally rooted, in some instances for millennia, in the societies of the Orient. The paradox of Israel, however, is that it "ended a Diaspora," characterized by Jewish ritualistic nostalgia for the East, only to found a state whose ideological and geopolitical orientation has been almost exclusively toward the West. Although Jews have historically been the victims of Orientalism, Israel as a state has become the perpetrator of Orientalist attitudes and actions.[1]

The Israel/Palestine national conflict, as a result, does not fit neatly into any standard categorizations. And just as Israel partakes of both "East" and "West," it also constitutes both a "First World" and a "Third World" country. Israel can be considered "Third World" in a strangely double and even paradoxical sense; first, in terms of analogous oppressions (as Tzvetan Todorov points out, Jews formed Europe's internal "other" long before the nations in Latin America, Africa, and Asia became its external "other")[2] and secondly, in terms of Israel's structural analogies to the Third World. In purely demographic terms, an overwhelming majority of the Israeli population is Third World; Palestinians make up about 20 percent of the population in Israel proper, and Sephardi Jews, most of whom came, within very recent memory, from Third-World countries such as Iraq, Morocco, Egypt, Turkey, Iran, and India, constitute another 50 percent of the population. In political, economic and cultural terms, Palestinians and Sephardis have been marginalized and denied access to virtually all power. And if Palestinians form a captive nation, Sephardim, as a Jewish Third World people, form a semi-colonized nation-within-the-nation. In Israel, then, European Ashkenazi Jews, a distinct numerical minority, constitute a First World elite dominating both Palestinians and Oriental Jews.

Israel's anomalous character makes anticolonialist discourse at once applicable and non-applicable. On the one hand, the ideological roots of Zionism can be traced back to 19th and early 20th-century Europe, both as a reaction against anti-Semitism and as partially aligned with an expanding capitalism and European empire-building. Israel, in this sense, has clearly been allied to Western colonial and neocolonial interests; has deployed colonialist-inflected discourse; and has exercised colonialist policies toward Third-World lands and peoples. Hebrew texts portray pre-Zionist Palestine as an unproductive desert awaiting "Western" penetration and fecundation, a view explicitly embodied in the pre-state "pioneer" and post-state heroic-nationalist films of the 1950s and 1960s.[3] The question is further complicated by the socialist pretensions, and at times the achievements, of Zionism. In the nationalist discourse, the conflict between the socialist ideology of Zionism and the real praxis of Jewish domination in Palestine found "resolution" in the seductive thesis that the Arab masses, subjected to feudalism and exploited by their own countrymen, could see themselves as benefitting from the emanation of Zionist praxis. This narrative embodies the historically positive self-image of Israelis as involved in a non-colonial project and thus morally superior in their aspirations.

At the same time, Zionism cannot be simplistically equated with colonialism or imperialism. Unlike colonialism, Zionism constituted a response to millennial oppression and, in counter-distinction to the classical paradigm, metropolis and colony in this case were located in the self-same place. There was no France or Great Britain to which one might repatriate profits or to which one might return after colonial expeditions. The colonial mind-set of regarding non-European continents as "lands without people" here becomes inseparable from the Zionist concept of a Jewish people in need of land. *Eretz Israel* (the Land of Israel), furthermore, had always been the symbolic locus of Jewish cultural identity. Israel does not present the classical colonial case of European expeditions into America, Africa, and Asia since the ideology of Return to the Motherland (a view of the land as belonging to the Jews, with the Palestinians merely "guests"), in some ways constitutes a departure from traditional colonial discourse. And despite Israel's official First World orientation, Israel itself, as an emerging nation in the post-Second World War period, and as the product of a liberation struggle (whatever the consequences of that struggle for others), offers certain parallels to emerging Third World nations.

Until recently, Palestinians, for their part, have formed a kind of "structuring absence" in Israeli cinema, despite the fact that the films, at least through the 1960s, have tended to foreground the Israeli/Arab conflict. In the 1980s, Israeli cinema has attempted to create an alternative representation of the Israeli Palestinians. Since the invasion of Lebanon (1982), Israeli political films have broken with the traditional representation of the Israeli/Arab conflict by focusing more on the Palestinian, as opposed to Arab, dimension of that conflict, a shift in emphasis which parallels the emergence of an acknowledgment of a "Palestinian entity" within Left-liberal discourse as a whole. In the "Palestinian Wave" films we find not only recognition of a Palestinian entity but also a refusal of the tiny-Israel/mighty-Arabs trope, of the Manichean imagery of Arab encirclement of a besieged Israel. Rather than have *sabra* (native-born Israeli) heroes allegorize the national struggle as a whole—as in the earlier heroic-nationalist genre—the recent films have "deviant" *sabra* protagonists allegorize the films' views of the situation of the Israeli liberal Left. Instead of an axiomatic Jewish homogeneity, the recent films present fissures within Jewish Israel regarding its identity vis-à-vis a Palestinian national identity. The generic locus for the Arab/Jewish encounter, furthermore, is no longer the battlefield and the war film; instead, we discern a wide range of generic affiliations. Uri Barabash's *Beyond the Walls* (*me-Ahorei ha-Soragim*, 1984) belongs to the generic tradition of the prison film; Shimon Dotan's *The Smile of the Lamb* (*Hiukh ha-Gdi*, 1986) unfolds its narrative enigmas within the general framework of fantasy and particularly of thousand-and-one-nights folktales; and *Fellow Travellers* (*Magash ha-Kessef*, 1983) combines a thriller format with aspects of film noir.

In 1980s films, the Palestinian characters are allowed to voice their legitimate national anger, and they are granted close-ups and point-of-view shots fostering spectatorial identification. If the heroic-nationalist films constructed a classically Orientalist image of the Arab, and thus elided the question of Palestinian culture, the 1980s political films root the characters in their own terrain, thus implying the possibility of a legitimate claim on the land. Nissim Dayan's *A Very Narrow Bridge* (*Gesher Tzar Meod*, 1985), for example, features a highly symbolic image of a Palestinian fighter first seen in extreme longshot in a pastoral open space, filmed as if emerging from the land itself. A complicitous exchange of looks with roadside Palestinians underlines his status as a people's fighter. Casting, furthermore, has also been transformed. The earlier didactic nationalist films typically featured heroic *sabras*, played by Ashkenazis, fighting villainous Arabs, while Sephardi actors and characters had virtually no place at all, except in the "degraded" roles of Arabs. In virtually all the recent political films, in contrast, Palestinian actors and nonprofessionals play the Arab roles. Such casting, at times for major roles, allows for a limited, quite literal self-representation, in the form of actors representing their national identity.

Showing deep concern and involvement in the process of production with regard to their images, Israeli-Palestinian actors/actresses have actually forced radicalization of certain scenes. In *Beyond the Walls*, Muhammad Bakri effected a radicalization of a crucial point in the film. Toward the end of the film, the head of the prison attempts to break the prisoners' strike, which is directed against management violence and manipulation, by breaking the Palestinian leader, Issam (Bakri). The head of the jail brings Issam's wife, whom he has not seen for years, and his son, whom he has never even met. In the original script, Issam, with the encouragement of his fellow inmates, goes out to his wife and child. The filmmaker, Uri Barabash, expressed the following perception of the sequence:

> To me it was clear that Issam must go out with the wife and child, and that was how it was written in the script. I said that in such a human moment everyone must forget the political, social statement—there is here a human interest that stands above everything. You are a man, you

have not seen your wife for ten years, you do not know your son, you must go out; even at the price of breaking the strike.[4]

The Palestinian actor, meanwhile, perceived this moment differently, in a more political fashion. After tense discussions, Bakri suggested that the director film two takes. Barabash first shot Bakri's version in which the character Issam steps out only to tell his wife and son to go back home, a scene whose authenticity led Barabash to completely give up his original idea. And to quote Muhammad Bakri's explanation for the import of the alteration:

Throughout the rehearsals I told Uri and Beni Barabash and Eran Prize [the director and the scriptwriters] that it would work …. If I were a leader like Sirtawi [the first name of Bakri's character in the film, Issam, is a reference to PLO figure Issam Sirtawi, who was murdered], I would not have been broken, because I am a symbol. I told them that they would kill the utopia; that if I do something I do not believe in I would be a shit. I sat with my head between my hands and I could not do it. Here it was not a matter of being the fucker of the management. Here there appears a PLO leader, which in my eyes is the sole representative organization of Palestinians; and I am for PLO leadership that argues for coexistence and dialogue with Israel and the shattering of prejudices. I am indeed not a politician but an actor, but the message is important to me. The real Issam

Figure 27 Uri Barabash's *Beyond the Walls*, 1984

Sirtawi was killed because he believed in dialogue ... Issam would not break and meet with his wife and son ... [When] the cameras worked, I began walking toward my wife and son in the film. All the prisoners began to cry ... Uri [Barabash] cried, the cameraperson cried. I finished the scene and walked crying to the dressing room, because that was the story of my life that was focused in the moment.[5]

A corollary to the more self-representational casting is the incorporating of the Arabic language in the political films. The few Arabic "dialogues" in the heroic-nationalist films tended to be restricted to paralinguistic war cries, effecting the intersection of language and power as operating within asymmetrical political arrangements. The political films, in contrast, have the Palestinian characters express themselves eloquently in their own idiom. Such a mechanism forces the spectator—the films are largely aimed at Israeli and Western viewers—to meet the Palestinian characters on their linguistic turf. The Palestinian characters, furthermore, tend to be fluent in Hebrew, in contrast to the Israeli characters, who tend not to speak Arabic. Here the films do not simply imply the bilingual and even bicultural dimension of Palestinian existence in Israel, but also evoke the linguistic and social dynamics of a classical encounter between dominated people and colonizing society.[6]

Yet the ideological limitations of these films derive particularly from tensions between their surface leftism and their deep-structural liberal-conservatism. Rather than purvey a truly oppositional voice, the narratives privilege the situation and dilemmas of the Israeli "voices." The real protagonists are virtually always *sabras*, through whom the political and/or erotic interaction with Palestinians is focalized, and through whom the "norms of the text" are defined. Both on a narrative level and on the image/sound tracks, it is the "enlightened" occupier-protagonist who forms the dynamic center, who generates and focalizes the narrative, and it is he whom the camera obediently follows, even when he walks through Palestinian towns. The dialogue and *mise-en-scène* essentially relay their narrative dominance, perpetually orienting the spectator to the protagonists' peace-loving humanism.

In Shimon Dotan's episode *Souvenirs from Hebron* (*Mazkarot mi-Hevron*) in *Israel 83* (1983), similarly, the daily work of occupation performed by two young handsome *sabra* soldiers is focalized through their patrol in the *kasbah* of Hebron. The dramatic tension is structured through the subjectivization of the shots, that is, through the "filtration" of spectatorial knowledge via the soldiers. The spectator is sutured into their fear and anxiety about sudden attacks by the people of the *kasbah*; every face encountered—a child causing a watermelon to explode next to the soldiers, or a butcher sharpening his knife—is a source of terror, and every corner, alley, and upper floor is a potential place of danger. Focalizing the films through the occupier's subjectivity and fears—even of children—displaces a political issue on to a psychological register. In this sense, the film prolongs the identificatory mechanisms and even the ideology of earlier personal cinema, this time with the occupation as a backdrop for "universal" discourse, masking the historical origins of policies by foregrounding only those who carry them out, the soldiers.

In other words, even though the "Palestinian Wave" films criticize the Israeli establishment, their critical look tends to be directed more at the establishment's victimization of the Israeli protagonists than at the oppression of the Palestinians in the name of whom the protagonists are presumably fighting. Yehuda Ne'eman's *Fellow Travellers* even plays off the protagonist's victimization *against* that of the Palestinian character. The Palestinian militants are associated with violence, as opposed to the protagonist who seems to be the "real" object of the Israeli secret service rather than the Palestinians. The Palestinian intellectual who, like the Israeli, detests violence, meanwhile, is granted little narrative time. His function within the narrative is subordinated to that of the Israeli liberal, even though his plight, as a Palestinian believer in non-violence, forms the thematic focus of the film. This hierarchical representation ultimately projects the *sabra* peace activist as the real martyr caught between two violent worlds. The protagonist of Shimon Dotan's *The Smile of the Lamb* similarly represents the passive, tormented, and conflicted (anti-)hero "crucified" for his nostalgia for peace. His death, triggered by both Israeli and Palestinian extremists, evokes the fatalism of a sacrificial lamb taking all sins upon himself.

The "Palestinian Wave" films betray the symptoms of acute discomfort with the very idea of a Jewish victimizer. The Jewish people, after all, are historically unaccustomed to the role of oppressor. Jewish holidays recount tales of the oppression of Jews by a host of historical enemies, and Jewish rituals relay the collective lore of an interminable series of victimizations and near-victimizations. But Jewish History has difficulty in recounting a tale showing Jews as collective oppressors. Nothing in the historical culture of Judaism prepares its artists for such a tale. But after 1967 Israelis found themselves in the clear position of an occupying power. What were artists, primed historically to know themselves only as victims in relation to neighboring collectivities, to do? How were they to deal with the inversion of the traditional imagery of David and Goliath when Palestinian children, armed only with slings, were confronting Israeli soldiers armed to the teeth? The "political-personal" films, in this sense, convey the diverse compromises encountered in response to this challenge—compromises involving halfway confrontations, partial focalizations, and problematic displacements. A predisposition to a discourse of victimization leads to films whose narrative and cinematic codes present the *sabras* as the principal victims. The lament, therefore, is not primarily for the national oppression of the Palestinian people but rather for the *sabras'* own torment as passively innocent Isaacs, sacrificed in fear and trembling on the altar of Abrahamic (nationalist) faith.

Images of the Israel/Palestine encounter, from a different perspective, are seen in a recent Palestinian film, Michel Khleifi's *Wedding in Galilee* ('*Urs al-Jalil*, 1987).[7] The film asserts the existence of a Palestinian people possessing a national culture in the process of self-formation in various ways, including the subversion from within of traditional rituals and hierarchies in order to forge an independent political existence. Produced before the current uprising on the West Bank and in Gaza, *Wedding in Galilee* is the first major Palestinian fiction film to be made by an "insider"—that is, by an Israeli Palestinian—in this case one who left his hometown of Nazareth in 1970 and has since then lived in exile in Belgium. *Wedding in Galilee* also goes beyond the Arab/Palestinian propagandist film practice dominating not only documentaries but also the few narrative films produced on the subject. Palestinian film production, from the establishment of "Unity Cinema" in 1967 through the "Palestinian Cinema Group" in 1973 to the "Palestinian Cinema Organization," under the auspices of the PLO has always been intended as an instrument for the promotion of the Palestinian national cause and the registering of revolutionary events related to the Palestinian resistance. Virtually all production, therefore, has been devoted to news and documentary films—a situation common in societies struggling for political definition (and reminiscent, ironically, of Zionist film production in the pre-state era). The few fiction films sympathetic to the Palestinian cause— for example, *The Dupes* (*Al-Makhdu'un*, 1972), directed by the Egyptian filmmaker Tawfiq Saleh, and *Kafr Qasim* (1973), directed by the Lebanese Burhan Alawiya—were made by non-Palestinian Arabs. Alawiya's film is a recreation of a 1956 massacre of Palestinian villagers by the Israeli army, just before the halting of the joint Anglo-Franco-Israeli attack on Egypt in 1956. But whereas this film demonizes the Israelis—for example by having a Palestinian observe in the streets of Tel Aviv the sale of a presumably popular toy: a guillotine cutting off the head of an Arab in a *kafiyya*— *Wedding in Galilee* does not reduce the oppression of the Palestinian people to a Manichean schema of good Palestinians versus evil Israelis.

The story of *Wedding in Galilee* revolves around the desire of the *mukhtar* of a Palestinian village in Galilee to give his son a memorable wedding. The curfew imposed on the village by the Israeli military authorities forces the *mukhtar* to ask for the governor's permission to continue with the celebrations until nightfall. The military governor approves only on condition that he and his staff be invited to attend the ceremonies. Within this dramatic framework, the film interweaves diverse intra-Palestinian discourses. The camera in *Wedding in Galilee* is independent and attentive as it moves between diverse Palestinian perspectives, particularly that of the young radicals born under Israeli occupation, eager to take action for Palestinian liberation, and that of the older, "patient" generation. The Palestinian community, we see, is no monolith; ideological, sexual, generational, and familial tensions are brought to the narrative foreground.

As with his earlier film, *Fertile Memories* (*La Mémoire Fertile*, 1980), Michel Khleifi interweaves the history of Palestinian dispossession with the narratives of specific women within a changing Palestinian society under occupation. His films differ from most pro-Palestinian films in their refusal to separate the "internal" problems of the community from its "external" challenges. While one might object to the differential treatment of female versus male nudity in *Wedding in Galilee*, Palestinian women characters, nevertheless, possess a strong presence in Khleifi's films, in inverse proportion to their officially acknowledged place in the society he depicts; they represent both the nurture of collective memory and the insistent, daily struggle for familial and national preservation; they provide glimpses of liberation while registering the impasses of patriarchal society. The attention paid to women and children, and to the oedipalized attempts at revolt on the part of young men, was in some ways anticipatory on Khleifi's part, since the uprising on the West Bank focused attention on reversed power relations within the Palestinian community; it has been children and women who have carried out much of the uprising.

Figure 28   Michel Khleifi's *Wedding in Galilee*, 1987

Although *Wedding in Galilee* alludes to these differences, gaps, and oppositions within the Palestinian community, its main thrust is to reflect a common history and a common struggle for liberation from Israeli occupation, along with a strong sense of national cultural identity, and a rooted connection to the land and its past. Such a presentation obviously constitutes a rebuff to all the Zionist denial mechanisms, for example, Golda Meir's insistence that "the Palestinian people do not exist." In this sense, the camera's painstaking and affectionate scrutiny of rural collective ceremonies and rituals, of the people's primal love of the land and its fruits, does not remain on the level of an anthropological fascination with a Middle Eastern society but rather makes a simple political point: "We are here, and we exist." The camera's easy fluid movement from one Palestinian character to another as well as the dream-like blending of diverse voices and languages—from hallucinatory exchanges, through interior poetic monologues, through proverbs and popular rhymes to sloganistic political speech and daily slang—suggests the multi-layered richness of the society. The film, then, visually and aurally refutes the Zionist attempt to negate Palestinian existence, whether through the systematic, physical eliminations of Palestinian villages and fields, or through the verbal obfuscation of the Palestinian people under such categories as "natives" or "nomads."

While the Zionist "Prospero complex" presents vegetation and fruitfulness as the product of the Promethean gestures of European-Jewish pioneers who "make the desert bloom," *Wedding in Galilee* associates earth, crops, trees, vegetation, and abundance of food with the Palestinians. The dispossession of land by violence, meanwhile, is associated with Israelis, in the form of the mining of the Palestinian fields in order to limit their agriculture and, symbolically, their "fruitfulness." The documentation of cultural details (such as the collective preparations for the wedding, the bride's henna ceremony, the "*khamsa*" image on the wall, the villagers' oral recounting of their political narrative through singing and dancing), meanwhile, also contributes to the sense of permanence, pointing to a consciously stubborn refusal to disappear. And just as Jewish weddings ritualistically evoke the memory of Zion, so Palestinian weddings, especially in the context of occupation, become catalysts for national desire, celebrations of the memories and hopes of the community.

If *Wedding in Galilee* vividly reconstructs Palestinian lives, reaccenting them in a way very different from the Western media reductionist view of "terrorists," it also simultaneously confounds various customs and the accuracy of time and place in order to sustain the idea of a Palestinian nation. The wedding mingles Muslim and Christian customs, thus effacing religio-cultural differences. This presentation of Palestinian identity as predominantly an issue of nationality rather than of religion, on the part of a

Palestinian filmmaker of minority Christian descent, is highly significant, especially in the Israeli context where Christian Palestinians are perceived in a "better light," and where the official discourse systematically devalues Palestinian nationalism by speaking of the "diverse" "non-Jewish minorities." Although martial law for Israeli Palestinians was abolished in 1966 (only to be installed a year later in the newly occupied territories), *Wedding in Galilee* tells the story of a Palestinian village under military control in Galilee, that is, within Israel and in the present. This confounding of temporalities implies that although Palestinians within pre-1967 Israel can legally take part in the so-called Israeli democratic processes, they nevertheless experience oppression, and that even if they officially carry Israeli passports, their national identity is inseparable from that of the Palestinians on the West Bank and in Gaza. Shot in various villages, both in Galilee and in the West Bank, the film also unifies the varied topography, and to a certain extent even the architectural style, in order, again, to underline a national identity of one people. Despite being exiles on their own land and abroad, despite the Israeli attempt to linguistically and politically undermine their unity, *Wedding in Galilee* suggests the linked destinies and dreams of the various Palestinian exiles, "insiders" and "outsiders."

The narrative structure of *Wedding in Galilee* itself serves purposes of national legitimization. By focusing on a Palestinian ritual performed while surrounded by an imposed Israeli presence, the film subverts the Western media imagery of Palestinians intruding on Israeli routine. Here the central tale is Palestinian and the Israelis are merely its "visitors." This presentation undermines a Zionist master narrative which privileges the discourse of what it sees as the "original" (i.e., Jewish) inhabitants of the land versus its present-day Arab "guests." The Israeli under the Palestinian eye is above all an occupier, seen as one more foreign power coming in the wake of the Turks and British. The senile villager's monologues about the Turks constitute a lucid articulation of a history of subordinations. The character recalls the fool of Shakespeare's plays, authorized to articulate the ephemeral nature of oppression before the "king" himself.

Wedding in Galilee, then, differs dramatically from the representation of the Israeli/Palestinian encounter in the "Palestinian Wave" of films. *Wedding in Galilee* not only avoids the filmic discourse of the monadic (anti-)hero in favor of collectivity, but also shares the dream of transcending the present impasse and the sense of dead-end paranoia and claustrophobia permeating the Israeli liberal representation of the conflict. Palestinian films such as *Wedding in Galilee* and *Fertile Memories* suggest that Palestinian memory is not only alive but also fertile, capable of giving birth to new beginnings. The sequence of the Palestinian/Israeli collaborative rescue of the mare, coaxing it to freedom from a field mined by Israelis, allegorizes this vision of a dialogical future—instead of military strategies of mines and rifles, the path of gentleness and dialogue. The pastoral epilogue of the film showing the *mukhtar*'s child running in the fields and then lying down, embraced by nature, underlines this desire for harmony in a land already much stained with blood, as if closing the circle opened at the beginning of the film in which the voices of Palestinian children playing dissolve into the sounds of Israeli jets. The film's peaceful epilogue gains additional reverberations in the context of frequent media images of Palestinian children living a present-day situation that is anything but peaceful. The epilogue concerning a child of the occupation follows (in a manner of other films depicting national struggle such as Roberto Rossellini's *Rome, Open City*) the evacuation by the soldiers, implying the hope for a future life free of occupation.

Both Palestinian and Israeli national cultures, in other words, pervade each other's memories and tales. From a Palestinian standpoint, however, a dialogical future will be made possible only by an Israeli renunciation of the violence of occupation, or as a major woman character in *Wedding in Galilee* puts it provocatively to the Israeli soldier: "You will have to take off your uniform if you want to dance."

IO

Territories of the National Imagination: Intifada Observed

At a time when the Intifada's visibility in the media has been eclipsed by a war and its aftermath, it becomes especially important to recall the Palestinian dimension of the Middle Eastern entanglement—the perennial "question of Palestine." Public culture in the U.S., as Edward Said argued in 1984, provides no sanctioned narratives that could counterpoise the story of Palestinians to that of the Israelis. At the same time, one is struck by the way the Intifada erupted into the American media, destabilizing, to some extent, the Manichean representation of the Israel/Arab conflict, even reversing some of its dominant tropes—such as that of little David facing the mighty (philistine) Goliath.

Palestinian cultural production, inspired by the uprising, has even reached an American audience, albeit in relatively marginal fora. The Intifada has become the subject of poetry (Mahmoud Darwish's "Those Who Pass Between the Fleeting Words," Nizar Qabbani's "Children Bearing Rocks"), of music (the Sabreen and Rahali bands), of theater (the Jerusalem-based Palestinian theater El-Hakawati, which Joseph Papp, well-known as an anti-censorship advocate, refused to defend against political pressures, ultimately cancelling the performance for larger fora), of films (George Khleifi and Ziad Fahoum's *The Stone Throwers*, 1989), and of a series of videotapes collectively entitled "Uprising" (organized by Elia Suleiman and Dan Walworth for Artist's Space in New York). There have also been a number of panels at academic and political conferences, reflecting on Palestinian national life since the uprising, both under occupation and in exile. Nevertheless, these issues are still subjected to subtle and not so subtle forms of censorship. Private and public institutions in the U.S., responding

Published in *Transition*, no. 53 (Spring 1991). Review of: Zachary Lockman and Joel Beinin (eds.), *Intifada: The Palestinian Uprising Against Israeli Occupation* (Boston, Mass.: South End Press, 1989); David McDowall, *Palestine and Israel: The Uprising and Beyond* (London: I. B. Tauris, 1989); Don Peretz, *Intifada: The Palestinian Uprising* (Boulder, Colo.: Westview Press, 1990); and Ze'ev Schiff and Ehud Ya'ari, *Intifada: The Palestinian Uprising—Israel's Third Front* (New York: Simon & Schuster, 1989).

to vocal or "silent" pressure from funders and trustees, continue to censor Palestinian-related productions—often with convenient excuses about "unbalanced presentation." In any case, the last few years have witnessed the consolidation of the "questions of Palestine" as a legitimate issue for the North American Left.

Several recent books concerning the Intifada have been published in English, most of them in the U.S.: *Intifada: The Palestinian Uprising Against Israeli Occupation* edited by Zachary Lockman and Joel Beinin; *Intifada: The Palestinian Uprising—Israel's Third Front* by Ze'ev Schiff and Ehud Ya'ari (translated from the Hebrew), *Intifada: The Palestinian Uprising* by Don Peretz, and *Palestine and Israel: The Uprising and Beyond* by David McDowall (a British publication). These publications, which go beyond the daily media reportage of "events" and "stories" from the West Bank and Gaza Strip, reflect a noteworthy change in the debate about Palestinian national identity, even if the necessity of a Palestinian state is still not completely recognized. This change can perhaps be best summarized as a readiness to be sympathetic towards the Palestinian plight, a readiness largely produced by exposure to media images of the war in Lebanon and the Intifada. The spectator's human identification with Palestinian children armed only with slings confronting Israeli soldiers armed to the teeth is at the same time undercut by the media's superficial treatment of the uprising, which has generally elided its rootedness in the history of the Palestinian encounter with Israel. All these books contribute to filling the gap created by the dominant media coverage of the Intifada. They attempt, in different ways and to different degrees, to explicate the Intifada—for example, through a fuller survey of its international context (especially McDowall's *Palestine and Israel: The Uprising and Beyond* and Peretz's *Intifada: The Palestinian Uprising*), or through a focus on the military and diplomatic chronology of events (especially in Schiff and Ya'ari's *Intifada: The Palestinian Uprising – Israel's Third Front* and Peretz's *Intifada: The Palestinian Uprising*). By and large, these works present both Israeli and Palestinian perspectives. However, only Lockman and Beinin's *Intifada: The Palestinian Uprising Against Israeli Occupation* qualifies as a truly comprehensive, in-depth, and interdisciplinary study of the Palestinian uprising.

The Lockman and Beinin book goes beyond the conventional academic (Peretz's) and journalistic (Schiff and Ya'ari's, and McDowall's) ways of framing the subject, in which a national struggle serves as an object for analysis and study, or as an occasion for narrating a military spectacle. It is perhaps not surprising that the jackets of the Schiff and Ya'ari and Peretz books describe their work as "objective." The convention of the omniscient narrator governs most of the accounts and analyses of the Intifada, signaling a safe distance between the writer and the event covered.

Intifada: The Palestinian Uprising Against Israeli Occupation, in contrast, interweaves poetry, photography, eyewitness accounts, personal narratives, and lectures accompanied with discussions; it assembles astute political analyses and reference materials, going beyond conventional historiography. This anthology, diverse yet unified in its liberatory thrust, invites its reader to participate in writing a new history, to "become partners in the common struggle, and not onlookers or mere passive observers," as Edward Said writes in his dense and illuminating introduction. Works such as this anthology—edited, introduced, and partly written by academics whose professional vocation is not divorced from their activism—must be regarded as contemporary models for the notion of the "organic intellectual" at a historical moment when some of the academic Left seems more inclined toward scholastic disputation than any actual engagement with "crude" political matters.

The Intifada forms the site of continuity and rupture in the history of the Israeli/Palestinian conflict. On one level, as Said argues:

> there emerged a perceptible continuity between Zionist theories and actions before as well as after 1967. The occupation, for all its deliberate and programmatic humiliation of Palestinians, its bare-knuckled attempts to rob a whole people of nationhood, identity and history, its systematic assault on civil institutions and vulnerabilities, could be seen as extending the logic of earlier Zionists like Herzl, Jabotinsky and Ben-Gurion into the present.

At the same time, the Intifada marks a new phase in the media representation of the Israeli/Palestinian conflict, as well as in the political, economic, and psychological dimensions of the conflict. Schiff and Ya'ari's major argument is that the Intifada surprised Israel by opening a new, third front: "Until the uprising the Israelis knew that they must be prepared to fight on two fronts: a regular war against standing armies and both an open and secret war against terrorism. By their rebellion, however, the Palestinians opened a third front of mass, unarmed, civilian violence—a new kind of warfare for which Israel had no effective response."

The Intifada brought in its wake a feeling of national renaissance. Even Israeli Palestinians (Palestinians within Israel proper), often ignored as a factor in debates on the Israeli/Palestinian conflict, have participated in the uprising, largely through their symbolic solidarity. Despite differences of status (among Palestinian citizens of Israel, Palestinians on the occupied West Bank and the Gaza Strip, and deported and exiled Palestinians), class, region, religion (largely between Muslim and Christian), and ideology— "there exists today," as Rashid Khalidi puts it, "a strong sense of national unity, of loyalty to a unified set of symbols and concepts, and of mutual interdependence, sentiments which were lacking in 1967."

Israeli officials initially attempted to discredit the Intifada by insinuating that it was the work of outside agitators, and later blamed the international media as encouraging "Palestinian violence." As all the books suggest, however, the Intifada has gone beyond a situation in which political directives came from the Palestinian leadership in exile. Even Palestinian popular culture, one might add, has parodied the Israeli obsession with "outside agitators" through a series of Intifada-related jokes. (The amount of black humor linked to the Intifada, understandably not within the scope of the books, deserves an anthology of its own.) One joke recounts the Israeli interrogation of a seven-year-old Palestinian, aimed at finding out the identity of his "superior" who ordered him to throw stones, who turns out to be ... his four-year-old brother.

In fact, the Intifada does mark the emergence of a new, younger leadership. Although aligned with the Palestinian Liberation Organization and insistent that the PLO be the sole representative of the Palestinian people, it reflects the experiences and the perspectives of the younger generation born into occupation. This shift was displayed in the decisions of the November 1988 Palestine National Council meeting in Algiers. After decades of rejecting partition as unjust and illegitimate and of favoring a secular democratic state in all of Palestine, the PNC explicitly stated the Palestinian national movement's acceptance of the two-state solution and called for a diplomatic solution for the conflict. Apart from having an effect on the intended target, Israel, the Intifada has clearly had a symbolic impact on Palestinians themselves—on their sense of unity and leadership. Thus, on a psychological level, as Schiff and Ya'ari argue, the Palestinians showed a new measure of self-confidence, defying the Israeli strategy—as described, for example, by Yitzhak Shamir—of instilling fear of the Jews in the hearts of the Arabs. In the wake of the self-respect generated by the uprising, the PLO (as Rashid Khalidi in the Lockman and Beinin book points out) was able to downplay both the Palestine National Covenant and the old slogan of "armed struggle," neither of which is mentioned in the Palestine National Council's political statement.

Despite this remarkable shaking up of the political status quo, the Israeli government has refused any dialogue. In fact, it remained locked into old discourses and practices. Early Israeli nationalist discourse was characterized by a typical First World Promethean rescue fantasy in relation to the land and people of the Third World, epitomized in such tropes as "making the desert bloom," "fecundating the wilderness," and "enlightening the natives." This "beneficent" sense of mission has continued in the administration of the occupied territories, where policies have been conducted in the name of "improvement of the quality of life." Some of the claims of the occupation authorities, cited in the Peretz book, reveal the same Prospero complex: "Since 1967 economic life in the area [the West Bank] has been characterized by rapid growth and a very substantial increase in living standards, made possible by the interaction of economies of the areas with Israel." But the Intifada has shown that "carrot" measures could not conceal the brutality of "stick" policies. As Salim Tamari argues in the Lockman and Beinin book, Moshe Dayan has already charted the integration of the occupied territories into the body of Israel through three institutional mechanisms: infrastructure, labor, and markets. These three central modes of control constituted the foundation on which Israel built and sustained its political hegemony over the region, undergirded, of course, by Israel's monopoly of coercive force and a pervasive intelligence network.

The Schiff and Ya'ari book, *Intifada: The Palestinian Uprising–Israel's Third Front*, is most informative about the Israeli military operation and intelligence work, often seen from the angle of Israeli diplomatic and military dilemmas. Schiff and Ya'ari, as well-established Israelis, had access to information and documents from Shin Bet (the Israeli counterpart to the FBI). Adding another dimension to the accounts of the Intifada, their book relates attempted actions and unrealized plans as well as internal conflicts and contradictions in military and diplomatic circles. While the book's chronicle of events presents tactics and strategies of both Israelis and Palestinians, the focus of the book tends to be on Israel. For example, in the first chapter, "The Surprise," the imagery of encirclement subliminally drafts the reader into the besieged situation of Israeli soldiers, even if the apparent theme is the curfew and siege of Palestinians.

Although the Western media have focused on the spectacle of Israeli soldiers shooting stone-throwing Palestinian *shabab*, the real war "behind the screen" was between the consistent Israeli attempt to destroy Palestinian alternative economic and organizational structures versus the continuous Palestinian attempts to resist and sustain alternative institutional forms. If before the establishment of the state of Israel, Zionism created embryonic institutions (called in Zionist historiography "the state on the way"), "inside" and "outside" Palestinians have also created such institutions. The process started before the Intifada. In the late 1970s, for example, local institutions such as workers' unions, professional associations, municipalities, and especially universities, were developed, as Salim Tamari writes in the Lockman and Beinin collection, "to serve as institutional components of future power, so that when a Palestinian state arrives it will not arrive in a vacuum," but will have instead "an infrastructure of political and civic institutions to support it." The Intifada, however, has intensified this process of self-sufficiency. The policies of economic boycott, both of Israeli products and of employment in Israel, have fostered local production, including small-scale agriculture conducted by families in search of self-sufficiency ("victory" gardens), and the development of an "alternative economy."

Indeed, the Intifada has had far-reaching ramifications for the Palestinian people in the West Bank and Gaza, affecting most aspects of daily life and power relations in the communities; it has altered relations between country and city, between regions, generations, classes, and genders. The communiqués (*nida'*, the Arabic for "appeal") issued by the Unified National Command have addressed the diverse segments of the population, asking for different kinds of contributions and sacrifices from the working classes, from the businessmen, and the professionals: "Brother workers," reads Communiqué Number 1 reprinted in the Lockman and Beinin collection, "your abidance by the strike by not going to work and to plants is real support for the glorious uprising .... Brother businessmen and grocers, you must fully abide by the call for a comprehensive strike during the period of the strike .... Brother doctors and pharmacists, you must be on emergency status to offer assistance to those of our kinfolk who are ill."

The way that women's lives have been affected by the Intifada also varies by region and class. Women in refugee camps and villages have been more active than urban women, reflecting the central role of these communities in the uprising. As Rita Giacaman and Penny Johnson suggest in their contribution to the Lockman and Beinin collection, this constitutes a historical reversal in the orientation of the women's movement in Palestine, although it is not yet reflected in women's leadership, where decision-making still remains largely in the hands of urban middle-class women. If Palestinian national struggle has expanded the public role of women, however, the challenge they pose to the authority of men has not been without limitations, as Palestinian women well realize. "You have all heard that since the Intifada women are equal," runs one rueful Intifada joke. "They build barricades, they break barriers, they throw stones, they demonstrate, they organize local committees! But dinner is always ready at six." There is little doubt that gender relations, as much as class questions, will be battled over long after independence is won. However, to examine the achievements of Palestinian women solely in terms of gender equality, or lack thereof, is at best an exercise in bad faith. The issue of national power no less dominates their lives, even in the biological sense of the phrase; Palestinian women have suffered miscarriages caused by gas and have been subject to incarceration or to crippling, even lethal, violence.

The various authors in the Lockman and Beinin book situate the Intifada in a multi-level historical context. Rashid Khalidi's "The Palestinian People: Twenty Years After 1967," for example, provides an overview of the Palestinian struggle from the days of pan-Arabism, represented by

Nasser's aspiration to act for, and in the name of, Palestinians. Israeli official discourse, one might add, often used pan-Arabism to "prove" that there is no such thing as a distinct and separate Palestinian people. The speciousness of such an argument is obvious by a comparison with other "pan" movements, such as pan-Latin American or pan-African nationalism, where a felt sense of commonalities hardly precludes a sense of national difference and self-determination. It is also an ironic one. Official Israeli discourse promoted its claims for a Jewish state by amalgamating many differences among Jews of the world (significant differences of language, "race," history, territory) under the assumed commonalities among Jews (principally the Jewish religion, the Hebrew language as a tongue of religious observance, and the concept of a shared history in the Land of Israel before the enforced Exile of the people of Israel); yet it refused to accept the parallel logic of differences and commonalities among Arabs. What makes this refusal especially striking is the particular character of Zionist nationalism, in which the state, in many ways, created the nation, whose people had to be gathered from "the four corners of the world" and settled in a territory. The foundation of Israel as a state, unlike that of most countries, was the result of the enactment of an explicit political ideology, rather than being the product of a kind of aleatory historical accretion over centuries, a process that has been more characteristic of Palestinian nationalism.

Still, the events of 1967 marked a turning point, Rashid Khalidi argues, by encouraging Palestinian self-assertion in the face of corrupt Arab regimes. The occupied territories, no longer under Egyptian and Jordanian control, came under the responsibility of Palestinians themselves. The image and even self-image of the Palestinians as "passive refugees" was subsequently transformed, whether into the active but sinister terrorists of the Western media, or into the liberation fighters of "non-aligned" discourse. It is a historical irony that the Jewish image, after the establishment of Israel, in contrast, has been transformed in the American media from that of Diaspora victim and defenseless refugee into the heroic Israeli *sabra*, the fighter for Jewish liberation, perhaps best exemplified in Paul Newman's incarnation of the *sabra* in the film *Exodus*. But if the Jews, the "Easterners" of anti-Semitic European discourse, could be readmitted to the West via their physical rupture from Europe and "spiritual" reunion with the West (a Western-style state presumably as evidence for the Jewish metamorphosis into "normal" people), the Arab Palestinians, due to their "inherent" Easternness, could not be celebrated as either enlightened Westerners or heroic nationalist fighters. For the Palestinian version of nationalism has been formulated in the tradition of anticolonial struggles with an anti-Western thrust.

The New Jew, the Israeli, in contrast, came to be seen as an integral part of the West due to the West's identification with its Middle-Eastern representative, Israel, whose own ideologues have insisted on its Western soul despite its geographical location in the East, and despite the fact that the majority of the Jewish Israelis are not of European origins but of Asian and African origins. (The country may be located in Asia geographically, but Israel's Western self-conception is nicely exemplified by its participation in the annually televised European popular music contest, Eurovision.) In this respect, it is unfortunate that none of the books reviewed here delve into the complex impact of the Intifada on class and ethnic relation within Israel. And while Reuven Kaminer's essay in the Lockman and Beinin collection explicitly addresses the protest movement in Israel, it fails to mention the activities and movements of the Sephardi Left, which has had a different conception of peace from that of the Ashkenazi Left.

Palestinian nationalism, meanwhile, hardly internalized a "Western" superego. The liberation fighters of Palestine never spoke in terms of nationalist outposts of the West. Zionism saw itself on a 19th-century continuum of nationalist renaissance in Europe, even though the reestablishment of its state coincided with the era of Third-World nationalism; Palestinian nationalism, in contrast, defined itself in terms of that very notion of Third Worldness. Here Don Peretz's suggestion that Arab nationalism and Zionism were influenced by European nationalism fails to situate both nationalisms in relation to the Third World context, and to root the discourses of these movements in anticolonial discourses. Third World nationalisms cannot be simply defined as a mirror-image of Europe's arrangement of the world into nation-states; rather, they must be seen as a resistance to European oppression, a resistance that dates back to the first colonial encounters in America, Africa, and Asia, whose liberation took place at a historical moment when collective freedom and self-determination had been defined largely in terms of nation-states.

The Intifada, with its anticolonial overtones, and the Israeli/Palestinian conflict as a whole, touches, one might argue, on some sensitive historical nerve of "America," itself the product of a schizophrenic master narrative of a colonial-settler state interwoven with anticolonial memories. In a world filled with competing national claims, the U.S. has been subliminally more ready for Israeli nationalist discourse than for the Palestinian, in part, I would argue, because of a certain resonance of national mythology. The American hero has been celebrated as prelapsarian Adam, as a New Man emancipated from history (i.e., European history), before whom all the world and time lay available, much as the *sabra* was conceived as the antithesis of the "Old World" European Jew. The rupture with the "Old World," in both Israeli and American official discourses, was similarly premised on the absent "parent." The American Adam and the Israeli *sabra* archetypes implied not only their status as creators, blessed with the divine prerogative of naming the elements of the scene about them, but also their fundamental innocence.

The notions of an American Adam and an Israeli *sabra* elided a number of crucial facts, notably that there were other civilizations in the Promised Land; the settlers were not creating "being from nothingness." And, of course, the settlers, in both cases, had scarcely jettisoned all their Old World cultural baggage, their deeply ingrained attitudes and assumptions. Here the gendered metaphors of the "virgin land," prominent both in Israeli and American pioneer discourses, must be seen in contradistinction to the metaphor of the (European) "motherland." A "virgin" land is implicitly available for defloration and fecundation. Lacking owners, it therefore becomes the property of its "discoverers" and cultivators. Needless to say, this rhetoric of "purity" masks the dispossession of the land and its resources. A land already fecund, already producing for the indigenous peoples, and in that sense a "mother," is metaphorically projected as virgin, "untouched nature," and therefore as available and awaiting a master.

In the case of Zionist discourse, the concept of the "Return to the Motherland," however, suggests a double relation to the settled lands. This doubleness derives, in many ways, from an ambivalent relation to the "East" as the place of Jewish origins as well as the locus for implementing the "West." Israel, like the U.S., fought against British colonialism, while practicing colonial policies toward the indigenous people. (One could argue for a triangular structural analogy by which the Palestinians represent the aboriginal "Indians" of Euro-Israeli discourse, while the Sephardim constitute the "Blacks" of Israel.) The *sabra* embodied the humanitarian and liberationist project of Zionism, carrying the same banner of the "civilizing mission" that European powers unfurled during their surge into "found lands." The classic images of *sabra* pioneers, as settlers on the Middle Eastern frontiers, fighting Indian-like Arabs—along with the reverberations of the early American Biblical discourse encapsulated in such notions as "Adam," "Canaan," and "Promised Land"—made possible the sympathetic reception of Israeli nationalism in the U.S.

As recent history attests, however, the Palestinians have manifestly refused to play the role of the presumably doomed Indians of this transplanted Western. If the result has been to change, at long last, their image in the international media, it may also help serve notice to the world that another story of Palestine remains to be heard.

Exile, Diaspora, and Return:
The Inscription of Palestine
in Zionist Discourse

The emergence into academic and media prominence of Palestinian intellectuals in the U.S. has engendered vicious attacks, ranging from scholarly delegitimization through character assassination to insinuation of participating in "Palestinian terrorism." This has been particularly true since the Intifada, precisely when the Palestinian image began to acquire more sympathetic resonances. As is typical of mainstream denunciations of anticolonial critics, Palestinian intellectuals have been accused of a presumably irresponsible anger. In 1989 Edward Alexander linked Edward Said directly to terrorism in his *Commentary* article "Professor of Terror," foregrounding Said's "double career as literary scholar and ideologue of terrorism."[1] Alexander calls Said's language the "verbal equivalent of the weapons wielded by his colleagues on the Palestinian National Council." "Said," he argues, "spills ink to justify their spilling blood."[2] By "detecting" the terrorist behind the academic, Alexander forecloses any dialogue with a conflicting perspective, delegitimizing it through *ad hominem* character assassination.

Situated on the fragile borders separating cultures, nationalities, and discourses, Palestinian intellectuals in the U.S. write on the "East" in the "West" from the perspective of intimate familiarity with Western culture, and yet still as Arabs, they speak from the "margins," designated as "Third World" voices. Burdened with the weight of representing "the" Palestinian perspective, intellectuals such as Ibrahim Abu-Lughod, Edward Said, and Rashid Khalidi have attempted to transgress the Israeli national narration,

Published in Annelies Moors, Toine van Teeffelen, Sharif Kanaana, and Ilham Abu Ghazaleh (eds.), *Discourse and Palestine: Power, Text and Context* (Amsterdam, The Netherlands: Spinhuis Press, 1995), a volume based on conference at the Discourse Analysis Institute, University of Amsterdam (April 9–11, 1992). Part of this essay is based on "Antinomies of Exile: Said at the Frontiers of National Narrations," in Michael Sprinker (ed.), *Edward Said: A Critical Reader* (Oxford: Blackwell, 1992).

to break the asymmetrical representations between Israel and Palestine in the U.S., and to introduce an alternative to the Zionist master narrative within a discursive environment tainted by the symbiotic geopolitical and cultural-discursive links between Euro-America and Euro-Israel. Since Zionism has laid the ground for the national identity of the geography of Palestine, the representation of Palestine (and even the contemporary definition of "peace") is based on "coming to terms" with a Eurocentric narrative. Subsumed and elaborated by Zionism, Eurocentrism cannot be simplistically equated with any form of ethnocentrism: i.e., of a community evaluation and judgement of social conventions and rituals according to its own criteria. As an ideology of power, Eurocentrism, which diffuses its own vision of Europe as a center of world order, has historically been linked to colonial-racial practices. The project of carving space for the suppressed narrative of Palestine has thus meant a constant challenge to the Zionist discourse of national liberation.

In this essay I will place the struggle between Israel and Palestine not only within its Middle Eastern geography, but also within the context of the West. What has made possible, in the U.S., the continuous sympathetic reception of Zionist discourse and the continuous refusal of Palestine as a legitimate discourse of liberation, even in the age of photogenic handshakes? Examining the contradictions of "East" and "West" within Zionist discourse, I will argue that the very presence of Palestinians speaking from the Western diaspora has challenged Zionist self-aggrandizing ideas of Exile, Diaspora, and Return.

The Politics of Representation

What is it about the 1980s visibility of Palestinian intellectuals in the U.S. that becomes so threatening from a Zionist perspective? On one level, it is a question of the imagery of nations, of how they are represented and self-represented, particularly in the West. One thing that is striking about the last decade of Israeli-American reports on Palestinian intellectuals in the West is the preoccupation not simply with the content of Palestinian arguments, but with their style of presentation and representation; in other words the anxiety concerns the politics of style. Spokespersons such as Edward Said, Ibrahim Abu-Lughod, and James Zogby defy the stereotypical Arab look of thick elongated mustaches, hooked noses, or halting English and heavy Arabic accents; they speak within the American media's discursive norms. Edward Said, whose area of academic specialization is not Middle Eastern studies but English and comparative literature, presents an entirely mainstream appearance. Since Arabs have been consistently represented as antithetical to all things Western, the idea of a spokesperson on Palestinian Arab rights intimately aware of Western culture, living and involved in American institutions, was a new public phenomenon for Israel-centric politics of representation. Israeli journalistic accounts of Arab-American intellectuals, symptomatically, have stressed their impeccable English, as though it formed part of a manipulative scheme; if the "Americans" would be able to see the "essential truth" behind the images and sounds of their fluent English, they would not grant the Palestinian spokesperson any sympathy. Since the trope of language has been central to the ideology of civility, the "Englishness" of Arab-American intellectuals disturbs and disorients the Enlightenment binarism of Zionist discourse. Ironically, the exclusion of Jews from "civilization" in anti-Semitic and Nazi racism also had a linguistic dimension. Fluent in the German language, German Jews, in this racist view, could never really possess it since they had their own hidden tongue, the true tongue that articulates their Jewish otherness.[3] The perennial mark of exile and diaspora, bilingualism, is quite similarly raised by Zionists towards the Easterners of the American continent, the Arab-Americans, whose English, it is insinuated, masks Arab conspiracies.

These symptoms are acutely present in a long Hebrew-language article entitled "*Ashafei ha-Tikshoret*" ("The media experts," *ashafei*/experts being a pun on the Hebrew achronym for the PLO, *Ashaf*), published at the beginning of the Intifada in Israel's most widely circulated daily, *Yedioth Ahronoth*. The first page shows a large photo of Edward Said and Ibrahim Abu-Lughod after their meeting with George Schultz (the same photo was also published in a Jewish Defense League [JDL] newsletter calling them the "PLO professors"). The Hebrew article was concerned with the "conquest of the American media" by the Palestinians, focusing on the fact that among the "advocates of the PLO in the U.S. are a number of Palestinian intellectuals, polished, articulate, knowledgeable about the issues, and fluent in English. All of them speak and look like Americans..." The article verifies this observation through interviews with Israeli Orientalists:

The American media today hosts Palestinian spokespersons who look more and more like Palestinian versions of Bibi [Benjamin] Netanyahu. "They are superstars," Dr. Yossi Ulmart, an Orientalist on sabbatical in the U.S., expressed his amazement. "Impressive people, with senior academic positions, who without inhibition exploit their status in order to defend their national case..."

Eli Rekhess, an Orientalist on sabbatical in the U.S., meanwhile, speaks of their professional style: "You won't find the emotional propaganda that characterized PLO spokespersons in the past. You don't hear from them unreasonable accusations such as 'you want to destroy the Arabs.' This style has gone. Their message sounds much more moderate than the Israeli message."[4] Such anxieties, especially since the Intifada, testify to the fissures created in the Israeli monopoly over the representation of the Israeli/ Palestinian conflict. Although they occupy opposite ends of the political spectrum, Palestinian spokespersons are compared to Benjamin Netanyahu; this should not come as a surprise. Netanyahu's Eurocentric discourse (he often speaks of and in the name of the "civilized world," i.e., Israel and the West as opposed to the uncivilized Arab East) perfectly enacts the American professional manner with very little accent, presumably offering a reasonable outlook. Netanyahu represents precisely the dominant Israeli fantasy of Americanization, and reinforces the image of Israel as a Western outpost on an Eastern frontier. The knowledge of the West and the professional style of Arab-American intellectuals thus disturb the long-nurtured simplistic binarism between Jews as West and Arabs as East. It is precisely the image of efficiency and professionalism associated with the post-industrial West that alarms Israel in this battle over imagery.

The question of style, in other words, threatens the long-established paradigm of East and West with regard to the Israeli/Palestinian conflict. The issue bears on which nation belongs to the metanarrative of progress of the "civilized world," having propagandistic consequences within the American media context. This point is also sensitive for Israel's self-image (and even self-definition) in the sense that Israeli official discourse, along the typical lines of the culture of Empire, has energetically portrayed Arabs as backward. Such a representation has been especially crucial for a nation-state geographically situated in the Middle East but whose imaginary constantly revolves around the "West." Geopolitically, furthermore, Israel has "marketed" itself as suitable for Western interests in the region. During the Intifada, the official Israeli tourist ad on American television, for example, appealed to that geopolitical friendship by proclaiming "Come to Israel, come be with friends," visually emphasizing the camaraderie of an "all-American," waspish-looking family, and its counterpart in Israel, a Euro-Israeli family[5] having a great time in "modern" Tel Aviv with "old" Jaffa in the background. An Israeli tourist postcard series, entitled in English "Jaffa—Tel Aviv—Old and New," similarly visualizes the "Oriental" landscape and architecture as exotic backdrop for the region's "unique" modern state. Since Israel occupies both spatio-temporalities, Jaffa's "antiquity" is thus denuded of any Palestinian memory and contemporary Palestinian presence, while Tel Aviv is exhibited as a postmodern metropolis with presumably no relevance to the history of Palestine.

Between East and West

But the neat division of Israel as West and Palestine as East, I would argue, ignores some of the fundamental contradictions within Zionist discourse itself. Ashkenazi Jews have been inextricably mingled with European cultures, yet they also constitute an ethnos that has kept some links to a Semitic language, whose religious idiom is intimately linked with the topography of the Middle East. Jews are also connected by tradition to the East, and have often been depicted in anti-Semitic discourse as an alien "Eastern" people within the West. In the case of Sephardi Arab Jews, the account shifts even more deeply toward the Eastern side of the dichotomy since for over a millennium these communities have been historically and culturally anchored in the geography of the Arab-Muslim world. The paradox of Israel, however, is that it presumed to "end a Diaspora" typified by religious invocation of the East, only to form a nation-state ideologically and geopolitically oriented toward the West. Herzl envisioned the Jewish state as a replica of Western capitalist-democracy, to be realized by the grace of imperial benefactors such as Germany or Britain, while Ben-Gurion formulated his utopic ideal of Israel as "the Switzerland of the Middle East."

Although European Jews have historically been the victims of anti-Semitic Orientalism, Israel as a state has become the perpetrator of Orientalist attitudes and actions whose consequence has ultimately been the dispossession of Palestinians. The ideological roots of Zionism can be traced to trends in 19th- and early 20th-century Europe, not only as a reaction against anti-Semitism but also to the global spread of capitalism via European imperial ventures. Israel, in this sense, has clearly been allied to imperial interests, has deployed Eurocentric-inflected discourse, and has exercised colonialist policies toward Palestinian land and people.

The question is further complicated by the socialist pretensions, and at times the socialist achievements, of Zionism. In the nationalist-Zionist discourse, the conflict between the socialist ideology of Zionism and the real praxis of Euro-Jewish colonization in Palestine was resolved in the "redeeming idea" (Conrad) that the Arab masses, exploited by a feudal system, could only benefit from progressive Zionist modernity.[6] This formulation embeds the historical self-perception of Zionism as involved in a non-colonial project and therefore as untainted in ethical terms. Furthermore, the hegemonic socialist-humanist discourse has obscured the negative dialectics of wealth and poverty between First and Third World Jews behind a mystifying façade of egalitarianism. The Zionist mission of ending the Jewish Exile from the Promised Land was never the altruistic endeavor portrayed by official discourse, since from the first decade of the 20th century Arab Jews were perceived as a source of cheap labor which could replace the dispossessed Palestinian *fellahin.*[7] The "Jews in the form of Arabs," as they were called, were assigned the role of warding off any Palestinian claim that the land belongs to those who work it, and would also contribute to the Jewish national demographic needs. The Eurocentric projection of Middle Eastern Jews as coming to the "land of milk and honey" from desolate backwaters, from rural societies lacking all contact with scientific-technological civilization, once again deployed the Western rescue trope. Zionist discourse has cultivated the impression that Sephardi culture prior to Zionism was static and passive, and like the fallow land of Palestine, lying in wait for the impregnating infusion of European dynamism. While presenting Palestine as an empty land to be transformed by Jewish labor, the Zionist "Founding Fathers" presented Sephardim as passive vessels to be shaped by the revivifying spirit of Promethean Zionism.

The Euro-Zionist problematic relation to the question of East and West has generated a deployment of opposing paradigms that often results in hysterical responses to any questioning of Jewish Israel's "Western identity."[8] Zionism has viewed Europe as the signifier of ghettoes, persecutions, and the Holocaust, while the "Diaspora Jew" signifies an extraterritorial rootless wanderer, as though living "outside of History." Posited in gendered language as the masculine redeemer of the passive Diaspora Jew, the mythologized *sabra* simultaneously signified the destruction of the diasporic Jewish entity. The prototypical newly emerging Jew, physically strong, with blond hair and blue eyes, healthy-looking, cleansed of all "Jewish inferiority complexes," and a cultivator of the land, was conceived as an antithesis to the Zionist virtually anti-Semitic image of the "Diaspora Jew." The *sabra* figure, modeled on the Romantic ideal and largely influenced by the German *Jugend Kultur*, became a formative element in a culture in which any expression of weakness came to be disdained as "*galuti*" i.e. belonging to the Diaspora. Zionism, in other words, viewed itself as an embodiment of European nationalist ideals to be realized outside of Europe, in the East, and in relation to the pariahs of Europe, the Jews. Thus, the *sabra* was celebrated as an exemplum of eternal youth devoid of parents, as though born from spontaneous generation of nature, as, for example, in Moshe Shamir's novel *Bemo Yadav* (*In His Own Hands*), which introduces the protagonist as follows: "Elik was born from the sea." In this paradoxical idiosyncratic version of the Freudian *familienroman*, Euro-Zionist parents raised their children to see themselves as historical foundlings, worthy of more dignified, romantic, and powerful progenitors. Zionism posited itself as an extension of Europe in the Middle East, carrying its Enlightenment banner of the civilizing mission.

If the West has been viewed ambivalently as the place of oppression to be liberated from, as well as a kind of ego-ideal to be mimicked, the East has also constituted an ambivalent signifier. The East has become the locus of solace, of return to geographical origins, and reunification with Biblical history. The "Diaspora's" obsessive negation and the advocacy of the return to the homeland of Zion, which began with the *Haskalah* (European-Jewish Enlightenment), led at times to the exotic affirmation of Arab "primitiveness" as a desirable image for the Diaspora Jew. The Arab was perceived as the incarnation of "the ancient, the pre-Exiled Jews," the Semite not yet "corrupted" by exilic wanderings, and therefore on some level, paradoxically, an "authentic Jew." The projection of the Arab as preserving archaic ways, and rootedness in the land of the Bible, in contrast with the landless ghetto Jew, provoked a qualified identification with the Arab as a desired object of imitation for Zionist youth in Palestine/Israel, and as a reunification with the remnant of the free and proud ancient Hebrew.

This projection coexisted, however, with a simultaneous denial of Palestine. The role of archaeology in Israeli culture, it should be pointed out, has been crucial in the disinterring of remnants of the Biblical past of Palestine, at times enlisted in the political effort to demonstrate a historical right to the "land of Israel." In dramatic contrast to Jewish archaeology of the text, this idea of physical archaeology as demonstrating a geography of identity carries with it the obverse notion of the physical homeland as text, to be allegorically read, within Zionist hermeneutics, as a "deed to the land." And corollary to this is the notion of historical "strata" within a political geology. The deep stratum, in the literal and figurative sense, is associated with the Israeli Jews, while the surface level is associated with the Arabs, as a recent "superficial" historical element without millennial "roots." Since the Arabs are seen as "guests" in the land, their presence must be downplayed, much as the surface of the land has at times been "remodeled" to hide or bury remnants of Arab life, and Palestinian villages, in certain instances, have been replaced with Jewish ones, or completely erased. The linguistic, lexical expression of this digging into the land is the archaeology of place names. Some Arabic names of villages, it was discovered, were close to or based on the Biblical Hebrew names; in some cases, therefore, Arabic names were replaced with old-new Hebrew ones.

At the same time, throughout the century-long history of the Israeli/ Arab conflict, the representation of the Arabs has been carried out in terms of the Jewish experience in Europe with the non-Jewish "*goyim.*" The fight against the savage East has also been imagined in terms of the anti-Semitic mobs of Poland and Russia, depicting Arabs as the "new Gentile." The heroic-nationalist films of Israeli cinema, for example, celebrated the liberation from the Jewish past of oppression in Europe by demonstrating an aggressive defense of Jewish rights. That this liberation is not achieved against past oppressors but rather at the expense of the oppressed Palestinians has been largely ignored by Zionist discourse, which blurs the distinction by conveniently appealing to the more inclusive category of the "*goyim.*"

The existence of Arab Jews complicates the East/West dichotomies even further. Mizrahi (Oriental) Jews, as Middle Eastern people, had to be subjected to the European civilizing mission of Zionism and "rescued from their Arab captors." Due to demographic and economic needs, they were also incorporated into the Zionist mission to gather the Exiled Jews from "the four corners of the Earth," while also being Eurocentrically projected in terms quite similar to the imagery of the European ghetto "Diaspora Jews." Middle Eastern Jews have provoked "anti-Jewish" feelings in the secularized *sabra* culture both because of the implicitly threatening idea of the heterogeneity of Jewish cultures and because of their discomforting amalgam of "Jewishness" and what has been perceived as Middle Eastern backwardness. This latter combination was seen as a malignancy to be eradicated, an ideological impulse manifested in the measures taken to strip Sephardi Arab Jews of their Arabness and Middle Easternness.

The Arab–Jewish cultural difference was especially disturbing to a secular Zionism whose claims to representing a single Jewish people were premised not only on common religious background but also on common nationality. The strong cultural and historical links that Middle Eastern Jews shared with the Arab-Muslim world, stronger in many respects than those they shared with the European Jews, threatened the conception of a homogenous nation analogous to those advanced by European nationalist movements. As an integral part of the topography, language, culture, and history of the Middle East, Sephardim have necessarily been closer to those who were posited as the common enemy for all Jews—the Arabs. Fearing an encroachment from the East upon the West, the Israeli establishment attempted repressing the Middle Easternness of Sephardi Jews as part of an effort to Westernize the Israeli nation and to mark clear borders of identity between Jews as Westerners and Arabs as Easterners. Arabness has been systematically vilified, creating a situation where they were urged to see Judaism and Zionism as synonyms and Jewishness and Arabness as antonyms. The Arab Jews were prodded to align either with anti-Zionist Arabness or with pro-Zionist Jewishness for the first time in history.[9] Distinguishing the "evil East" (the Muslim Arab) from the "good East" (the Jewish Arab), Israel has taken upon itself to "cleanse" Arab Jews of their Arabness and redeem them from their "primal sin" of belonging to the Orient. This conceptualization of East and West has implications in this age of "peace treaty" since it avoids the inherent question of the majority of the population within Israel being from the Middle East—Israeli Palestinians and Mizrahi Oriental Jews. For peace as it is defined now does not entail a true democracy in terms of adequate representation of these populations and in terms of changing the educational, cultural, and political orientation within Israel.

History and the Discourse of Victimization

Along with these traps of "East" and "West," questions of victimization and justice still play a crucial role in the representation of Israel and Palestine. Palestinian intellectuals have had to narrate the Palestinian nation in an American context of anti-Eastern attitudes and Christian-European guilt towards European Jews. Thus Palestinian Americans have had to address not only Israeli oppression of Palestinians but also the history of European anti-Semitism. As representatives of an oppressed community, Palestinian Americans' major task has been to combat the dominant discourse of another community—the (European) Jewish—whose (self-)representation has become virtually synonymous with its history of victimization. The assertion of a Palestinian nation not simply subsumable under the category of "Arabs" has become crucial in the work of Palestinian intellectuals, for only this distinction could permit the narration of Palestinian dispossession.

The events of 1967, as a turning point in Palestinian history, encouraged Palestinian self-assertion in the face of corrupt Arab regimes. The occupied territories, no longer under Egyptian and Jordanian control, came under the responsibility of Palestinians themselves. The image and even self-image of the Palestinians as "passive refugees" was transformed into the active but sinister "terrorists" of the Western media, or from the opposite perspective, into the liberation fighters of "non-aligned" discourse. The Jewish image, meanwhile, after the establishment of Israel, gave way in the American media from that of Diaspora victim and refugee to the heroic and over-powering Israeli *sabra*, the fighter for Jewish liberation. "Israel" thus made possible the media transmogrification of the passive "Diaspora victim" into the heroic Jew, best exemplified in Paul Newman's incarnation of the Israeli in *Exodus*.[10] But if the Jews, the "Easterners" of anti-Semitic European discourse, could be re-admitted to the West via their grand act of physical rupture from Europe and "spiritual" reintegration with the West (a Western-style state serving as evidence for the Jewish metamorphosis into "normal" people), the Arab-Palestinians, due to their "inherent Easternness," could not be celebrated as enlightened Westerners, or as heroic nationalist fighters, since the Palestinian version of nationalism was formulated in the tradition of anticolonial struggles against the West. The "New Jew," the Israeli, came to be seen as an extension of the West due to Western identifi-cation with its Middle Eastern representative, Israel, whose own ideologues have insisted on its Western spirit despite its geographical location in the

East, and despite the fact that the majority of the Jewish Israelis are not of European but of Asian and African origins.

Israel has based its positive image in the West on a moral argument linking both Jewish History of victimization and the colonial ideals of enlightenment. Official Israeli representatives such as David Ben-Gurion, Golda Meir, Abba Eban, and more recently Benjamin Netanyahu, have appeared in the American media insisting on Israel as an integral part of the "civilized world," a phrase buttressed by its claim to be "the only democracy in the Middle East." Jewish and Zionist institutions in the U.S. have made great efforts to incorporate Zionist versions of Jewish History into the consciousness and conscience of American discourse. Jewishness has been equated with Zionism and "Israeliness" to the point that the two terms have become virtually synonymous. Until the late 1940s, however, Zionism was a minority movement among world Jewry. The implementation of institutions and discourses meant above all the understanding of formative experiences—diaspora, exile, and return to the motherland—as a uniquely Jewish narrative. Jewish institutions have managed in the post-Holocaust era to bring to center stage the horrible experience of European Jews. Palestinian national discourse, therefore, has threatened the central Jewish role on the privileged margins of Europe and Euro-America. Subtle and not-so-subtle forms of censorship have been directed towards any articulation of concepts such as exile, diaspora, and return used in a non-Jewish context. The Holocaust, written with a capital H, seen as uniquely Jewish, becomes de-linked from other histories of racialized genocide, for example that of Native Americans.

Within the context of the Israeli/Palestinian debate, the terms of "exile" and "return" have led some Zionist-liberal critics to accuse Palestinian intellectuals such as Edward Said of narrative envy toward Zionism. Often with little apparent knowledge of Palestinian culture, the critics ethnocentrically define that culture's national discourse as "lack," as though devoid of distinct icons, symbols, and allegories, and as though Zionism had a monopoly on the concepts of exile and return. This penchant for seeing Palestinian work as an attempt to create "imitations of Jewish stories"[11] must be viewed, I suggest, in relation to the anxiety over the growing Arab-American institutional presence in the U.S.

The question of Jewish victimization is crucial for the Zionist liberationist project. Therefore, the suggestion that a history of other victims might be told, that there might be victims of Jewish nationalism, leads to violent opposition, or in the case of liberals, to epistemological vertigo. Zionist historiography has difficulty in recounting a tale showing Jews as collective oppressor, partly since Jewish popular tradition characteristically narrates its suffering at the hands of diverse oppressors. A predisposition to a discourse of victimization leads to arguments that ultimately present the Israeli "peacenik" as the principal victim of the Israeli/Arab conflict. The Amos Ozian bewildered question throughout the 1980s, "Where is the Palestinian equivalent to Peace Now?" displaces the issue of the national oppression of the Palestinian people in favor of a narcissistic lament about the supposed absence of an interlocutor for the peace-loving Israeli liberals. Ignoring the crucial question of asymmetries of power relations between Israelis and Palestinians, the liberal-Zionist lament has focalized the *sabras'* own torment as those caught between the Israeli right wing and the Palestinians. The *sabra* liberal is represented as an innocent Isaac sacrificed on the altar of peace.

Edward Said's writings, particularly as encapsulated in such titles as "Zionism from the Standpoint of its Victims" (1979) and "Blaming the Victims" (1988),[12] touched the core of the paradoxical nature of Israeli-Jewish-Zionist identity.[13] Palestinian intellectual work in the West, furthermore, testifies to a historical irony by which the linguistic signifiers of Jewishness—exile, diaspora, wandering, homelessness—have become applicable to Palestinians themselves. Israel has very rarely had to confront "civilized" Palestinians who speak from the West, yet who deconstruct the myth of the "civilized world." The Israeli obsession with Palestinian intellectuals in the West results partly from fear of a blockage of Israel's own self-presentation in the West. Said's critique of Michael Walzer, for example, focusses precisely on this question of address: "Walzer's political and moral study is addressed to us 'in the West' and his prose is dotted with us's and our's, the net result of which is to mobilize a community of interpretation."[14]

Corollary to the issue of victimization are the concepts of Exile and Diaspora that permeate the Jewish-Zionist debates with Palestinian intellectuals. "Diaspora" and "exile" have largely been monopolized on the American intellectual scene to refer to the Jewish experience. Zionism often saw its role as a transformer of "abnormal" Jewish existence in the *gola* (Diaspora) into that of a normal nation. Its Hebrew motto was *mi-gola le-geula*, "from Diaspora to Redemption." For Zionism it was central to create a rupture with the *shtetl* Jews, and to incorporate the "extraterritorial Jews" into "History." Exile (*galut* in Hebrew) from the Promised Land, and the concomitant ingathering from "the four corners of the Earth," constitute within Zionist discourse a mark of ethno-national uniqueness. Archaeology has thus had an important ideological role, serving as scientific proof, as it were, of the right for "Jewish Return" and the refusal of Palestinian return. The explicit Palestinian evocation of the displacements experienced by Palestinians became, from a Zionist perspective, a haunting mirror-image. The imagination of the territory—the land of Israel or Palestine—involves, therefore, an attempt to recuperate identities, to construct them in relation to a Mother Land, indeed the same homeland for both national imaginations. The Palestinian narration of Palestinian people in exile (*manfa* in Arabic) from the very same "Promised Land," and the dream of return (*al-'awda*) to the very same land, raise questions about a history that simultaneously generated the ingathering of the Jewish diaspora in Israel and the exile of Palestinians to the four corners of the globe. The bombing of the Palestinian "return ship" destined to travel from Cyprus to Palestine in 1988 was an attempt to crush the intended symbolic act of return; for Zionism there is only one exodus narrative and only one return.

For a political culture that adopts a righteous stance toward the world, the very image of its own victims entails a kind of epistemological shock. The idea of Zionism from the perspective of its victims (including its Sephardi Jewish victims, as I have argued elsewhere)[15] suggests that even movements established as a response to dispossession are not necessarily immune to dispossessing others. Ronald Aronson's riposte to Edward Said's essay "Zionism from the Standpoint of its Victims" symptomatically focused on the Holocaust in order to recenter the debate on Jewish victimization.[16] This argument, however, fails to see the political uses and abuses of the Holocaust in a Middle Eastern context, where the Holocaust often becomes a rhetorical device designed to block not only Palestinian national rights but also Sephardi-Mizrahi (Oriental) self-assertion. The instant invocations of the genocide of the Jews in Europe in any context of criticism of Zionism results in silencing any criticism of the Zionist erasure of Palestine. It was thus always necessary for Zionist discourse to metaphorically and metonymically associate Arabs with Nazis, as often seen in Zionist rhetoric, including in popular films such as *Exodus* (1960) and *Raiders of the Lost Ark* (1981). Stressing the victimization of the Jews and linking Arabs with anti-Semitism has repressed the emergence of discourses sympathetic to Palestinians. Zionism, on one level the answer to Exile, has created its own exiles. And the existence of Palestinians in the West is an embodiment of that dispossession.

The blockage of Palestinian discourse in the U.S. has often concerned both the Right and Left ends of the political spectrum. It is perhaps not a coincidence that leftist academic debates around the question of "national cultures" and "Third Worldism" have tended to avoid the "delicate" question of Israel and Palestine, and that of First and Third-World Jews, betraying a feeling of discomfort with applying anticolonialist critique to that region. The haunting memory of the Holocaust, as well as the anxieties about being labelled as "self-hating" Jews or "anti-Semitic" malcontents, compounded by a kind of ideological disorientation in the face of Zionism, have blocked a coherent alternative approach to the issues, and have placed revisionist works at the razor's edge of national and racial contestations.

From the American Adam to the Israeli Sabra

To fully comprehend America's sympathetic reception of Zionist discourse and its refusal of Palestinian discourse requires an unveiling of its relation to the "New World" self-conceptualization. The Israeli/Palestinian conflict as a whole, I would argue, touches on some sensitive historical nerves within "America" itself. The Columbus narrative is linked to the Middle East in more ways than would at first appear; that narrative prepared the ground for an enthusiastic embrace of Zionist discourse within Euro-America. As a product of schizophrenic master narratives, colonial-settler state on the one hand and anticolonial republic on the other, "America" has been subliminally more attuned to the Zionist than to the Palestinian nationalist discourse. Zionist discourse contains a liberatory narrative vis-à-vis Europe that in many ways is pertinent to the Puritans. The New World of the Middle East, like the New World of America, was concerned with creating a New Man. The image of the *sabra* as a new (Jewish) man evokes the American Adam. The American hero has been celebrated as prelapsarian Adam, as a New Man emancipated from history (that is, European history) before whom all the world and time lay available, much as the *sabra* was conceived as the antithesis of the "Old World" European Jew. The rupture with the "Old World" in both Euro-Israeli and Euro-American official discourses was similarly premised on the absent "parent." The American Adam and the *sabra* masculinist archetypes implied not only their status as creators, blessed with the divine prerogative of naming the elements of the scene about them, but also their fundamental innocence.

The images of the American Adam and the Israeli *sabra*, however, obscured the existence of the other civilizations in their respective Promised Lands; that the settlers were not creating "being from nothingness," and that the settlers, in both cases, had barely discarded their Old World assumptions, their deeply ingrained Eurocentric conceptions and discourses. Hebrew texts portray pre-Zionist Palestine as an unproductive desert awaiting Western penetration and fecundation. Here the gendered trope of the "virgin land," present in both Zionist and American settler discourses, has to be considered in diacritical relation to the trope of the (European) "motherland."[17] The notion of a "virgin land" implies a readiness for acts of defloration and fecundation. Assumed to lack owners, the land could thus become the possession of its "discoverers" and cultivators. The terminology of "purity" conceals the practices of dispossession that mark the settlers' relation to the land and its resources. A land already bountiful, already producing for the indigenous communities, is metaphorically imagined as virgin, "pristine nature," and hence as inviting a master who will make the desert bloom.

In the case of Zionist discourse, the concept of "return to the motherland," however, suggests a double relation to the land, having to do with an ambivalent relation to the "East" as the place of Judaic origins as well as the locus for implementing the "West." The *sabra* embodied the humanitarian and liberationist project of Zionism, carrying the same banner of the "civilizing mission" that European powers proclaimed during their surge into "found lands." The classical images of *sabra* pioneers as settlers on the Middle Eastern frontiers, fighting Indian-like Arabs along with the echoes of the early American Biblical discourse encapsulated in such notions as "Adam," "Babylon," "(New) Canaan," and the "Promised Land," have facilitated the feeling of Israel as an extension of "us." Furthermore, both the U.S. and Israel fought against British colonialism, while also implementing colonial policies towards indigenous people. Finally, one could argue for a triangular structural analogy by which the Palestinians represent the aboriginal "Indians" of Euro-Israeli discourse, while the Sephardim/ Orientals constitute the "Blacks" of Israel. (Taking their name from the American movement, the Israeli Black Panthers of the 1970s, for example, sabotaged the myth of the "melting pot" by showing that there were in Israel not one but two Jewish peoples—one White, one Black.)

The manifest Palestinian refusal to play the assigned role of the presumably vanishing Indians of the transplanted (far-)Western narrative has testified to an alternative narrative. Sephardi Jews, along with Palestinians within Israel proper (Israeli Palestinians), compose the majority of the citizens of a state that has rigidly imposed an anti-Middle Eastern agenda. In a first-of-its-kind meeting between Sephardi Mizrahi Jews and PLO Palestinians held at the symbolic site of Toledo, Spain, in 1989, we insisted that a comprehensive peace would mean more than settling political borders, and would require the erasure of the artificial East/West cultural borders between Israel and Palestine, and thus the remapping of national and ethnic-racial identities against the deep scars of colonizing partitions.

12

The Alphabet of Dispossession

An English lesson. A glimpse into the daily practice of perseverance. A new life in-the-remaking, assembled virtually ex-nihilo somewhere in the in-between. In the tented city outside the tented classroom, women toil in the background as eager boys begin to master the sounds of a foreign language. The English words on the improvised portable blackboard—"a city," "a car"—underline the pronounced chasm between the evocative signifier and the immobile, hemmed-in existence. English mediates the modernity of a distant world. "City" and "car" seem to perform as empty signifiers, lacking an immediate referent within the confines of the camp. Do the inscribed words capture fleeting memories of the vital cities of Palestine, or conjure up new worlds yet to be discovered in the twists and turns of diasporic reroutings?

It is the fifth lesson. Some routine has been established, suggesting a reassuring semblance of normality. At the same time, routine means a troubling extension of life in transit. Each day marks a happy progress in the schooling calendar, but it also registers additional weeks, months, and years in the arithmetic of displacement. Each improvement—a blackboard, a desk, a chair—carries with it the anxiety of stabilizing a no-whereness, and the waning possibility of return. Reading is seemingly a mundane assignment written in chalk, even away from home. Yet learning to read in exile is entangled in the queasy sensation of learning to "read" exile itself.

The alphabet of dispossession spells out paradoxes. Dislocated Palestinians are handed food and medicine provided by U.N. organs, the very same U.N. whose partition plan set in motion the process leading to the dispossession. Those who claimed to be bringing modernity wrought only a shattering de-modernization. Prometheus brought not fire but ashes. The word "city" reminds us of the cities, once but no longer "of" Palestine, where standing brick and cement have given way to ruins, where residents now take shelter under makeshift cloth dwellings.

Published in Issam Nassar and Rasha Salti (eds.), *I Would Have Smiled: Photographing the Palestinian Refugee Experience* (Jerusalem: Institute of Palestine Studies, 2009).

Figure 29 "English Class Held in a Tented UNRWA Elementary School, Harash Refugee Camp, Jordan" (Photo: George Nehmeh)

Zionist discourse reads such images as a symptom of the disaster that Arabs brought upon themselves. But in another reading such images would be seen as a lesson in the fact that images can be made to lie, when they are anchored by blame-the-victim narratives. The visual archive of Palestine both documents the past and serves as evidence in the battle over the representation of partition and displacement. The moment of the English lesson in the tent is written into history, but for which historical tale will it be mobilized, and in the name of what vision?

The photograph records a Palestine away from Palestine. Refugee teachers, without schoolbooks or salaries, gathered the children and taught them in the open air. The camera captures the grammar of determination and affection. As a teacher I resonate with this distilled act of love, and as a daughter of parents dislocated in the opposite direction of that same partition, I am reminded of the loss upon our arrival from Iraq to Israel when we were herded into the tents of the *maabarot* (transit camps). We underwent an unusual situation where parents well educated in Arabic in Baghdad ended up with children less educated than they were in Hebrew, a decade later in Israel. For those Palestinians *fil-dakhil*, on the inside, Hebrew followed English as a colonizing language. But is an English lesson in the refugee camp a submission to a colonial language—that of the past British colonizer—or is it the dream of a future, the linguistic means to yet another layer of diasporic life, whether in Europe, Australia, the Americas, or elsewhere? Despite and because of its imperial status, English has granted

179

Figure 30 "A Young Girl Studying her Arabic Reader at UNRWA and UNESCO School in Ein el-Sultan Camp"

a passport outside the Hebrew/Arabic conflict. It has become a language in which official and unofficial dialogue between Palestinian and Israeli was to take place.

English was after all the language that partitioned Palestine, setting in motion disastrous consequences for Palestinian lives. English is also the language through which resolution after resolution will be reinstated attempting to undo the traumas of partition. Scattered lives, geographically discontinuous, can regain international legitimacy within the domain of English, where their remembered narrative will have a seal of approval. (Arafat, lest we forget, was obliged to "renounce terrorism" in English.) The English lesson in the tent wraps together in one blanket the melancholia of a ruptured past and the possibilities of an unknown future. Yet, the class is also filled with the enthusiasm of young hands. The dwellings have since metamorphosed but the camps continue, still breathing dreams of life

Figure 31   "Refugee School, Khan Younis"

before tents and of a less barbarous future. And the eager children, who must now be in their 50s and 60s, to which diasporic palimpsest do they belong? What mélange of languages do they speak now? Can they write the word "return" in English, and will they be allowed to inscribe it on a document of civilization?

13

On *Israeli Cinema: East/West and the Politics of Representation*
(Interview conducted by *Jadaliyya*)

Preface by Jadaliyya: When Ella Shohat's book *Israeli Cinema: East/West and the Politics of Representation* was first published in 1989, Edward Said wrote: "Shohat's *Israeli Cinema* is a tour-de-force. Not only is it theoretically sophisticated, it is also deeply rooted in the changing politics and perceptions of the Israeli predicament as they bear upon Israeli films. With brilliant humanistic insight, Shohat describes the underlying ideological myths and allegorical structures and contributes significantly to a new, enlarged understanding of the dynamics between Ashkenazi and Sephardic communities, and between them and the Palestinians." I. B. Tauris has recently published a new edition of the book, with a substantial new postscript by Shohat.

Jadaliyya: What are the central themes and concepts of *Israeli Cinema*? How do you see the place of Palestine and Palestinian filmmakers in your book?

Ella Shohat: *Israeli Cinema* offers a deconstructionist reading of Zionist discourse, dealing centrally with Israeli representations of Palestine, of Palestinians, and of Arab Jews. The book treats cinema as constitutive in the invention of the nation and looks at the myriad and proliferating Zionist representations of the land and the people in the first hundred years of cinematic production in Palestine. The book begins with a discussion of representations of the land; these include the Zionist production of emptiness in the professed endeavor to "make the desert bloom" and the exaltation of the civilizing mission evidenced in images of pioneers/*sabras* and exotic Arabs—all endemic to the settler-colonial project. Subsequent chapters deal with post-1948 didactic allegories, siege imagery, Promethean narratives, and post-1967 spectacles of war in the heroic-nationalist genre.

Published under the title, "Ella Shohat, *Israeli Cinema: East/West and the Politics of Representation*," in conjunction with I.B. Tauris's 2010 Second Edition of the 1989 book, in the "New Texts Out Now" Section, *Jadaliyya*, January 18, 2012.

A major portion of the book addresses and critiques Zionist representations of Sephardim/Mizrahim/Arab Jews, tracing issues of Orientalism, colonial rescue fantasies, and questions of dislocation and the concomitant nostalgia. In the final chapter of the book, titled "The Return of the Repressed," I looked at the then-recent Palestinian waves in Israeli cinema, in the mid-1980s. At that time, the first feature-length Palestinian film, *Wedding in Galilee*, was just being made.

Figure 32   The British Censorship Board Licencing the Yishuv's *Pai News*, Mandatory Palestine, 1933

In terms of your second question: If the original book focused on Zionist representation of Palestine, the postscript to the new edition explicitly takes up the question of Palestinian cinema over the past two decades by focusing on the struggle on the part of Palestinians for self-representation. Given the material realities of colonial-settler occupation and the diasporization of Palestine, it is important to look at Palestinian cinema within Israel, at the transnational collaborations of Palestinian filmmakers inside and outside of Israel, and at the revisionist and critical Israeli cinema, much of it collaborative and transnational, which has emerged and has offered critical perspectives on Israeli occupation.

The book and the new postscript, I believe, complicate the demarcations between Israeli and Palestinian cinema to argue that these labels are clear only to the extent that we bestow on both terms a wholesale nationalist teleology. The label "Palestinian Cinema" is assumed by diasporic Palestinian filmmakers, by filmmakers in the West Bank and Gaza, and by filmmakers born and raised within the Israeli state. The issue of naming remains centrally important. At the time of publication, the title, "Israeli Cinema" was appropriate given that the book covered Zionist cinematic production and "national cinema," and the subtitle, "East/West and the Politics of Representation," referenced the critique of this Zionist master narrative and its Eurocentrism. Since the initial publication of *Israeli Cinema*, a new cinema—both documentary and fiction—has emerged that focuses on the dislocations of Palestinians within Israel and offers historically revisionist narratives of Israel/Palestine. Moreover, since the book's initial publication, there has emerged a more visible demand by younger generations who challenge monolithic boundaries of belonging and discuss the reconceptualization of Israel as a "state of all its citizens." The new postscript looks at recent Israeli and Palestinian films that form a cinema that could be seen as a representation of all the citizens/inhabitants of the land, a cinema produced in the liminal zone between Israel and Palestine, a cinema that illustrates the imbricated relationship of Israel and Palestine in conjunction with the transnational collaborative work that demands that we interrogate what we mean by "national cinema." The discussion of Palestinian filmmakers within Israel thus inevitably traverses state borders and analyzes Israel as a state where Palestinians also live and struggle for representation.

J: What made you write this book originally, and what led to it being republished with a new and substantive postscript?

ES: The book strived to offer a coherent theoretical and critical account of the development of Israeli cinema within an East/West and Third World/ First World perspective. The manuscript was completed as a doctoral dissertation at New York University toward the end of 1986 and published virtually unaltered in 1989 by the University of Texas Press. I chose that Press precisely because of its substantial list of books on Third World literature and cinema. (Multiculturalism and postcolonial theory had not yet emerged as consolidated fields of inquiry in the Anglo-American university.) I saw my reading of Zionist discourse as relevant not only to Jewish studies, Middle Eastern studies, and cinema/media studies, but also to the thrust of the corpus of anticolonial Third Worldist literature, the field that would later morph into "postcolonial studies."

The historical scope of the text covered the emergence of the Zionist movement in the late 19th century through the mid-1980s. It was written prior to the first Intifada, in the pre-Oslo era, at a time when Israeli officials were still engaged in the mental acrobatics of denying the existence of anything called "the Palestinian people." At that time, merely enunciating the word "Palestine," or displaying images of the Israeli and Palestinian flags side-by-side, was considered unpatriotic and even treasonous by the mainstream. Meetings between Israeli citizens and Palestinian representatives were banned, and Israelis who dared cross the lines risked imprisonment. The dominant Israeli media and academia resisted any Palestinian counter-narrative, while also silencing a Sephardi/Mizrahi/Arab-Jewish perspective dissonant with the premises of the Zionist master narrative. The only "legitimate" Sephardi/Mizrahi position was to parrot the standard rhetoric of a "population exchange" between Palestinians and Jews of Arab/Muslim countries. Articulating the concept of "the Arab-Jew" apart from any triumphant nationalist teleology was taboo, and my work attempted to do precisely that: deconstruct Zionist discourse in relation to both "the question of Palestine" and (what could be called) "the question of the Arab-Jew."

The chapter-long postscript that accompanies the republication considers the film, media, and cultural production of the past two decades since the book's original publication. The discursive landscape changed dramatically in the wake of the Oslo Accords, even while the violence on the ground continued to worsen. At the same time, beginning in the mid-1990s, the Anglo-American academic debates swirling around "multiculturalism," "postnationalism," and "postcolonial theory" began to enter the academic scene in Israel. Some more critical strains of scholarly writing, notably the work that has come to be called "Post-Zionism," emerged into view. The late 1990s brought an increased receptiveness toward transgressive readings of precisely the kind that had earlier made *Israeli Cinema* such a controversial book. Collaborative intellectual projects between Israeli and Palestinian scholars became less anomalous. Some of the texts with which the book was in dialogue have since been translated into Hebrew, including Said's *Orientalism* (translated in 2000); Fanon's *Black Skin, White Masks* (2003) and *The Wretched of the Earth* (2006); and Albert Memmi's *The Colonizer and the Colonized* (2005). So the current reprint of *Israeli Cinema* appears within a somewhat transformed intellectual environment with regards to the question of Palestine in Israel as well as in the U.S.

At the same time, however, the fundamental questions—the historical and legal rights to the land, the nature of Zionism and the Palestinian struggle, the Israeli Law of Return and the Palestinian Right of Return, and the political and historical status of dislocated Arab Jews in the wake of the partition of Palestine—remain unresolved and passionately contested.

Current critical perspectives, furthermore, have also been caught up in the right-wing backlash in the wake of the second Intifada in Israel and of 9/11 in the U.S. All these contradictions haunt contemporary work on the cultural politics of Israel and Palestine. Like the original book, the postscript I have written for the new edition appears against a landscape of political impasse. Yet unlike then, this postscript was written at a time when cinematic productions about and around Israel are being disseminated globally. The postscript focusses on the mutations in the themes addressed in the original book, incorporating arguments elaborated in my subsequent publications. It also reflects on cultural practices and filmic examples pertinent to the issues raised in the book and throughout my writing, issues having to do with the critique of Eurocentrism, Orientalism, and colonial discourse.

J: What was the initial reception of the book?

ES: *Israeli Cinema* was translated and published in Hebrew in 1991 (the book was also translated into Arabic in 2000), but even before the translation into Hebrew, the arguments expressed in earlier essays and interviews in Hebrew had provoked passionate responses within and around Israel. The early attacks on the book and on "deviant" intellectuals generally at the time came largely from Euro-Israelis positioned on what was seen in Israel as the Left. The book struck a nerve, I think, because it questioned the aura of Left progressiveness, especially given the liberal-Left's historical, cultural, and familial embeddedness in the establishment. The Israeli Peace Camp generally addressed its criticism only toward that establishment, but not in dialogue with its subalterns. Its narratives often depicted peacenik protagonists besieged by both the establishment and its Arab subalterns (a depiction analyzed in the last two chapters of the book). This reading challenged a taken-for-granted sense of entitlement, including even entitlement to critique the official national his/story.

Moreover, during the early 1980s when I wrote *Israeli Cinema*, the interdisciplinary field of cultural studies was gaining momentum in the U.S. academy. While conceiving my project as part of this field, I attempted to facilitate a dialogue between cultural studies and Middle Eastern studies. At that time, cultural studies "traveled" largely along a British–American axis, while "culture" within Middle Eastern studies, when not studied by anthropology, was viewed mostly through the lens of positivist or Marxist approaches. (The endorsement of Said's *Orientalism* within anti-Orientalist Middle Eastern studies has tended to reflect a shared ideological critique, but usually not a methodological one.) Moving beyond the base/superstructure approach, and deploying poststructuralist methods, *Israeli Cinema* viewed culture and politics as intimately linked and highly contested. Rather than seeing "culture" as an afterthought of Zionist practices, I suggested that from the very early days of the Yishuv in Palestine, the diverse cultural practices of the emerging Israeli nation—language, music, dress, cuisine, landscaping, urban planning—were shaped by a discourse at once colonialist and nationalist. The dialogue between cultural studies and Middle Eastern studies that I attempted to facilitate, moreover, was explicitly anticolonial: my work was indebted to anticolonialist discourse (including the work of Fanon, Césaire, and Memmi), and specifically to Said's indispensable contribution to that critique in *Orientalism*.

In many ways, the book belonged to a historical moment characterized by a search for the analytic language appropriate for cultural production within the twinned spaces between the national and the colonial *and* a historical moment wherein Third Worldist discussions were often split around the question of Israel/Palestine. Most American academics, with the notable exceptions of a few Third Worldist leftists, were ignorant of or hostile to the Palestinian counter-narrative and entirely unaware of Sephardi/Mizrahi/Arab-Jewish perspectives. As part of the then-emerging field of "Third World literature and cinema," *Israeli Cinema* tried to draw the limits of the analogies to more paradigmatic cases of both "colonial discourse" and "national culture." Throughout, the book was developing an anticolonial critique but in relation to a national space that had rarely been seen as "Third World" in any conventional sense, but which nonetheless viewed itself in terms of national liberation. Within a comparative framework, the text highlighted the tensions and anomalies of "the colonial" and "the national" in the case of Zionist discourse. While the book was about "the national" and "national cinema," its reading was not nationalist; rather, it was concerned with dissecting the nationalist imaginary. Indeed, the text was written at a time when "nationalism" itself was beginning to be interrogated by what would later come to be called "postnationalism."

In the wake of the publication of *Israeli Cinema*, there were—along with spirited defenses of my work—*ad hominem* attacks (suggesting I could not write knowledgeably about the subject since I no longer lived in Israel), accusations that I (allegedly like Edward Said) was an inauthentic product of the Western academe, and other besmirchments of my authenticity. As for the content of the work, during the heated debate and in interviews, in my discussions of how my work examined the politics of representation in Zionist historiographical discourse and Israeli cultural practices, I insisted on the concept of the "Arab-Jew" as well as on the word "racism" rather than the more prevalent psychologizing "prejudice" or the weakly sociological "discrimination." While the book received a hostile reception from many circles, on the one hand, many critical thinkers in Israel, and especially many critics in Mizrahi and Palestinian activist and intellectual circles, on the other hand, welcomed the book. The Swiss-Iraqi filmmaker Samir also addressed the reception of *Israeli Cinema* in his 2002 film *Forget Baghdad: Arabs and Jews – the Iraqi Connection.*

Over the years, as critical perspectives have become common in academic circles, *Israeli Cinema* has been adopted as a textbook and has even been embraced by a new generation of scholars. Yet despite or even because of the impact of the work of critical scholars generally, the process of delegitimization of this kind of critical work continues both in Israel and in some quarters in the U.S. The enforcing of a very restrictive notion of Zionist correctness often has devastating consequences. In the U.S., curating any cultural events devoted to Palestinian issues usually triggers vocal complaints about "balance." At the same time, the republication of the book encounters a highly modified academic landscape, at least in terms of cracks in the hegemony of official Israeli discourse in the U.S., even while the literal landscape of Palestine/Israel has been redesigned for the worse through walls, bulldozing, settlements, and militarization.

J: What do you see as the compelling reasons the book should be re-read in today's political and intellectual climate?

ES: *Israeli Cinema* examined the shaping of national imaginary and cultural memory within a movement—Zionism—that emerged simultaneously with the cinema, and that was cognizant of film's visual force and power to shape consciousness. I argued that Zionism invented the Israeli nation partly through its literary and cinematic narrative. In this way, the book underscored the agency of cinema in narrating the nation, especially in a context where people(s) had to be brought from "the four corners of the world" in order to create the new nation-state. The cinema did not passively mirror ambient reality, but helped produce a new Jewish identity. It mobilized spectators to identify with modernization projects such as "making the desert bloom" through settlement practices, all wrapped in Messianic terminology that stressed the redemptive Return of the Diaspora to the Biblical "Land of Milk and Honey." The book traced the contours of this shaping of the nationalist historical memory through the cinema, reading films not simply as documents of fact but rather as registers of perceptions and perspectives on "reality" and even as a means to actively shape that reality through a celebratory narrative of Jewish revival.

In a larger sense, the book concerned the political uses of representation. While all representations embody political ideologies—even unconscious and implicit ones—and have real reverberations in the world, filmic representations have been especially well suited to accomplishing larger social tasks. The Palestinians have been denied the right to "self-representation." The same "blocking" of representation takes place, in a different way and by different means, with regard to the Mizrahi Jewish population within Israel.

So another key issue orienting the analysis of the book was the question of the filmic representation of the "Oriental Jews," the majority of the Jewish population in Israel, and the link between their representation and that of the "other East" of the Palestinians. The book's postscript transnational-izes the scope of what constitutes the field of Israeli cinema by addressing a diasporic cinema that has treated the contested geography of Israel/ Palestine. It also calls for seeing the cinematic space of Israel/Palestine as encompassing all the inhabitants of the land.

I think the relevance for reading and/or re-reading *Israeli Cinema* in today's political and intellectual climate lies in our ability to reflect on questions of rupture and continuity in the past two decades, both in terms of violence on the ground and in terms of the intellectual work that reflects on the current political context. The last decade witnessed a substantial modifica-tion in the realm of film, literary, and cultural studies scholarship concerned with Israel. Research on Israeli cinema/media had become a vital field of study characterized by a deeper investigation of the relation between film/ media. Moreover, Israeli and Palestinian cinemas have also become a much more visible presence on the world stage. The emergence of these films has forged a vital polyphonic space for representation and debate that one could only have hoped for in 1986. Today, both the critique of Orientalism and the dialogue with postcolonial studies have come to inform writings (in diverse languages) on Zionist discourse and Israeli culture. Scholarly writings about Israel (including *Israeli Cinema*) have been translated into Arabic, and Israel, and the work of Israeli scholars, has come to form a legitimate object of critical study for Arab writers. This transformation comes also amidst a new interest in cultural studies that has emerged in Middle Eastern studies in general. Concomitantly, the study of Israel, Palestine, and the Middle East within the framework of cultural studies has been gaining momentum in diverse academic locations. The cultural studies and intersectional approach of *Israeli Cinema* has thus found a more receptive intellectual place than when the book was initially published, but many of the questions I raised in *Israeli Cinema* remain taboo, and many of the questions concerning Israel and Palestine remain unresolved, which continues to reflect the enormity of work that still needs to be done and the enduring relevance of the book.

J: How do the book's central arguments relate to those in your other work?

ES: *Israeli Cinema* explores the cinema as a productive site of national culture and offers a deconstructionist reading of Zionism, viewing the cinema as itself participating in the "invention" of the nation. Unthinking the Eurocentric imaginary of "East-versus-West," I highlighted the

ON THE ARAB-JEW, PALESTINE, AND OTHER DISPLACEMENTS

paradoxes of an anomalous national/colonial project through a number of salient issues: the ambivalence toward the geographies of both "East" and "West"; the *sabra* figure as a negation of the "Diaspora Jew"; the iconography of the land of Israel as a denial of Palestine; the narrative role of "the good Arab" and the limits of "positive image" analysis; and the oxymoronic place allotted to Arab Jews/Mizrahim within an Orientalist historical and social discourse. *Israeli Cinema*, significantly, stresses the importance of placing the question of Eurocentrism and Zionist discourse in the same analytic frame as the Mizrahi question. Central to my work are the historical and discursive links between the representation of Palestinians and the representation of Mizrahim. My work critiques the "erasure of the hyphen" that renders the concept of the "Arab-Jew" oxymoronic, tracing the dislocation of Arab Jews not simply to their moment of arrival in Israel, but also earlier, to the advent of colonialism and later of Zionism in Arab-Muslim spaces.

In the wake of *Israeli Cinema*, I continued to outline the contours of a Mizrahi epistemology that would transcend Zionist teleology and the narrow disciplinary framework that regards the Mizrahi question as "inside" and the Arab/Palestinian question as "outside." The Mizrahi, I argued, formed an in-between figure, at once "in" in terms of privileged citizenship within the Jewish state, in contrast to the Palestinian citizens of Israel, but hardly "of" the hegemonic national culture. The new postscript written for this edition, meanwhile, examines the emergence of richly multiperspectival cultural practices that transcend earlier dichotomies through a palimpsestic and cross-border approach to Israel/Palestine. The postscript looks at the inscription of the Arab-Jewish memory of Muslim spaces, while also reflecting on the Palestinian narration of the Nakba within a revisionist cinema that actively constructs an audio-visual archive.

The methodological concerns touched on in *Israeli Cinema* are extended in my later work on the question of representation. *Israeli Cinema* was concerned with the fraught politics of national, colonial, social, and ethnic representation. The book pursued a materialist poststructuralist methodology designed to highlight issues of representation, while also investigating the question of the "real" and of "realism." The book looked at the unconscious allegories, tropes, and narrative structures as much as at the discourses and institutional politics informing the film text. Though *Israeli Cinema* was often read as a critique of the negative stereotyping of the East endemic in Israeli culture, it was in many ways a critique of a positive/negative stereotype approach by offering a relational reading of the image within broader discursive trends and narrative movements. In a subsequent work, *Unthinking Eurocentrism* (1994), Robert Stam and I developed a fuller theoretical analysis of the question of representation. A "mimetic" and "stereotypes-and-distortions" approach, we argued, entailed a number of dangers, such as essentialism, ahistoricism, and an exaggerated emphasis on "realism" and "authenticity," along with a privileging of plot and character at the expense of film language, discursive formation, and institutional politics. Such a multi-dimensional textual analysis seems all the more pertinent to the concerns of a contemporary Israeli cinema that is trying to shatter decades of stereotyping and offer ambivalent postmodern spaces for its stories and characters.

Israeli Cinema also explored what came to be called the "intersectionality" of diverse axes of social stratification, precisely those elements that fissure any nation-state and throw into question monolithically nationalist ethnographies and historiographies. Rather than separate gender from nation and race, the book deploys gender critique as part of an analysis of a masculinist national imaginary, in the heroic de-Semitization of the Euro-Israeli *sabra*, in the exoticization of Middle Eastern women, in the "feminization" of the Diaspora Semitic Jew, and in the idealized images of Western "women's equality" contrasted with Eastern patriarchy. This intersectionality can be seen, for example, in the discussion of Mizrahi representation through multiple prisms—class, gender, ethnicity, nationalism, colonialism, and Third World—rather than through the single prism of class. I pursued this work further in *Taboo Memories, Diasporic Voices* (2006), which ties together disparate essays on post/colonial discourses (including on the work of Frantz Fanon vis-à-vis the question of "the Black," "the Arab," and "the Jew," and the reception of Edward Said's work in Israel); Orientalism in American culture; the importance of gender in the cultural representation of empire; and a series of essays that treat the subject of Zionism and Palestine in conjunction with the issue of Arab Jews, all of which are deeply in dialogue with my work in *Israeli Cinema*.

More recently, my co-authored work with Robert Stam, *Race in Translation: Cultural Wars around the Postcolonial Atlantic*, to be released in May 2012, takes up many of the questions about culture and nation in a comparative look at France, Brazil, and the U.S. The book investigates the transnational travels of the "culture wars" debates and the emergence of fields like postcolonial studies and Whiteness studies in disparate geographic spaces. My postscript in *Israeli Cinema* relates to this work in terms of both texts' shared study of traveling and mutating theories and the varied reception of anticolonial intellectual work in different political contexts. Further, my work in *Israeli Cinema* relates to my recent work on the volume *The Cultural Politics of the Middle East in the Americas*, co-edited with Evelyn Alsultany and also forthcoming in 2012, which explores the dynamic presence and ambivalent and contradictory position of the Middle East within the North and South American cultural and political landscape. Like *Israeli Cinema*, this volume seeks to investigate the varying and varied political uses of representation, especially in terms of the Middle East. And, like *Israeli Cinema*, it too is profoundly interdisciplinary, reflecting on the complex relationship between American studies, ethnic studies, postcolonial studies, and disparate area studies, as they shape a complex articulation of the "Middle East" both inside and outside the Americas.

14

In Memory of Edward Said,
the Bulletproof Intellectual

How does one eulogize a passionate intellectual whose mobilizing words have energized campaigns to tell forbidden tales of abuse, humiliation, and hope? And how does one memorialize a "worldly" intellectual when the very genre of "great men" is something that the skeptic in Edward Said himself would have found suspect? At a time when many in academia fashioned a postmodern attitude of cool irony toward political engagement, Said offered a contemporary exemplar of precisely the kind of "worldly" intellectual that he described with such acuity. Here are Said's words:

> It comes ... to two images for inhabiting the academic and cultural space provided by school and university. On the one hand, we can be there in order to reign and hold sway. Here ... the academic professional is king and potentate .... The other model is considerably more mobile, more playful, although no less serious. The image of the traveler depends not on power but on motion, on a willingness to go into different worlds, use different idioms, and understand a variety of disguises, masks, and rhetorics. Travelers must suspend the claim of customary routine in order to live in new rhythms and rituals. Most of all ... the traveler crosses over, traverses territory, and abandons fixed positions, all the time.[1]

Said's intellectual dialogism, however, was often ignored or even caricatured by his opponents. Indeed, here I would like to pay tribute to the heavy price he paid for his courage. Said began to engage with Orientalism and the question of Palestine at a time when this act of narration was more or less

A lecture given at a plenary panel entitled "Edward Said Memorial Plenary" at the American Comparative Literature Association, at the University of Toronto, Canada, April 5, 2013. One section is based on the author's contribution to the introduction to "Edward Said: A Memorial Issue" (coedited with Patrick Deer and Gyan Prakash), *Social Text* 87 (Summer 2006). The Lecture was later published in expanded form as part of the "Special Commemorative Section on Edward Said," edited by Victor Li, *University of Toronto Quarterly* 83.1 (2014).

disallowed. To utter the word "Palestine" in the public sphere triggered a deep anxiety about being stigmatized as "anti-Semitic" or a "self-hating Jew." Despite his careful effort to dialogue with very diverse ideological perspectives, Said was called a Nazi by the Jewish Defense League, his office at the university was set afire, and he and his family received innumerable death threats. Yet Said consistently argued that there was no military option for either side and that only "a process of peaceful reconciliation, and justice for what the Palestinians have had to endure by way of dispossession and military occupation, would work."[2] Here are his words from "Between Worlds":

> For myself, I have been unable to live an uncommitted or suspended life: I have not hesitated to declare my affiliation with an extremely unpopular cause. On the one hand, I have always reserved the right to be critical, even when criticism conflicted with solidarity or with what others expected in the name of national loyalty. There is definite, almost palpable discomfort to such a position, especially given the irreconcilability of the two constituencies, and the two lives they have required.

* * *

A journal with which I was personally involved—*Social Text*—in a sense began its career with Said's work. In the 1979 inaugural issue, the journal published Said's groundbreaking essay "Zionism from the Standpoint of its Victims," a version of which would appear in *The Question of Palestine*.[3] The *Social Text* decision was vital for the opening-up of the debate in leftist academic circles. However, the journal ended up publishing a critical response entitled "Never Again? Zionism and the Holocaust."[4] The Marxist Ronald Aronson applauded *Social Text* for publishing Said's "moving and beautiful account," seeing its publication as witness to the "process whereby the Palestinians have finally emerged on the world stage as a people." But ultimately he cited the Holocaust as if it were an answer to the Palestinian perspective, reproducing a rather common rebuttal that failed to dialogue with a Palestinian narrative. Said's use of terms like "exile" and "return," meanwhile, led some Left critics to charge him with "narrative envy" toward Zionism, portraying Palestinian culture as lacking in icons and symbols. Some went so far as to suggest that what they called "Said's rage" derived from his awareness that Palestinians could only create "imitations of Jewish stories."

The *Social Text* decision to publish a response that marginalized the unfolding history of Palestine in the wake of Zionist settlement was indicative of the anxiety, tensions, and contradictions within the Left. At the time, the extrapolation of anticolonialist and Third Worldist analytical paradigms to the Middle East provoked heated and anguished debate in leftist circles. Although not a monolith, *Social Text*'s collective audaciously introduced a debate into the heart of the intellectual Left but also manifested a certain ambivalence toward its own decision. In the ensuing years, *Social Text* tended to shy away from addressing Zionism, Palestine, and the Middle East, at least until 1988, when a new double issue, dedicated to "Colonial Discourse," included essays on the Middle East and an interview with Said ("American Intellectuals and the Middle East Politics," conducted by Bruce Robbins)—clearly reflecting shifting editorial tendencies.[5][...]

Published a year before his 1979 *Social Text* essay, Said's book *Orientalism*,[6] a seminal text for postcolonial theory, was also published in a period when terms such as "anticolonialism," "the Third World," and "neocolonialism," were still in circulation, a decade prior to their eclipse by the term "post-colonialism." *Orientalism*, written in New York, can also be regarded as a diasporic text written by an intellectual in exile who has theorized displacement, especially through his notion of "traveling theory." [...] Seeing Said's work as a "traveling theory" requires a sense of translation and mediation, as his ideas have moved into new geographical contexts and intellectual zones. Here I would like to touch on Said's *Orientalism* and its reception, beginning briefly with its reading within non-Orientalist versions of Middle East studies and Arab-American studies; and then focusing on its reading within postcolonial studies in its Hebrew translation.

Today, the growing field of Arab-American studies, as its very name suggests, exists in relation to both ethnic studies and area studies. Indeed, Said's work has become central in the growing field of Arab-American studies (especially Arab-American cultural studies). In this sense, *Orientalism*, with its last chapter focusing on American Orientalism, can be seen as vital for transnationalizing both American studies and Middle Eastern studies, as well as for placing both fields in relation to postcolonial studies. Assumed within postcolonial/literary/cultural studies are the various structuralist and poststructuralist "turns": the linguistic turn (Saussure), the discursive turn (Bakhtin and Foucault), the cultural turn (Jameson), and more recently the affective-corporeal turn, an intertext often absent or even rejected within the conventional disciplines of Middle Eastern studies. The hybrid scholarly work of what one might call "postcolonial–Middle Eastern studies" has been largely performed on the margins of Middle Eastern studies, even in its non-Orientalist versions. Similarly, within Arab-American studies, cultural studies has formed a significant interdisciplinary approach to the study of politics. Indeed, within hybrid academic formations and transdsiciplines, *Orientalism* has generated rich and multi-faceted scholarship.

For the traditionally dominant disciplines of Middle Eastern studies such as history and anthropology, meanwhile, *Orientalism* deployed an unusual approach to the study of the region. It was therefore received with an affirmation in relation to its political critique, but with skepticism in relation to its analytical approach. The reasons for this ambivalence about Said's work within the traditional disciplines, and especially about his *Orientalism*, ultimately have less to do with his pro-Palestinian political positions than with his theoretical and methodological assumptions. Even politically sympathetic scholars sometimes portrayed Said as a deficient political scientist or historian or anthropologist. However valid from specific disciplinary perspectives, this critique sidesteps the book's central concern—the problem of representation, in terms of rhetoric, figures of speech, narrative structure, and discursive formation. Indeed, *Orientalism* could be regarded as a cultural studies book *par excellence*. The assumption that politics and culture are thoroughly imbricated forms the cornerstone of that post-Marxist field called "cultural studies" as a field that deploys Gramsci to reconfigure the base/superstructure relation within a conceptual framework where culture and politics are mutually constituted.

* * *

As a "traveling theory," Said's work proved especially problematic in relation to postcolonial studies in Hebrew. In the case of Israel, the site of the reception of Said's work is a nation-state whose very foundation engendered the massive dislocation partly responsible for Said's own exile. And when that intellectual invokes the right of return to that very same place—where a state was endowed with the power not only to authorize or deny his return, but also indirectly to oversee the arrival of his texts about displacement—then the question of that intellectual's "out-of-placeness" becomes even more fraught.

Although Said was a staunch critic of the Oslo Accords, it was ironically the Oslo era that facilitated the "voyage" of his texts into Israel. The dissemination of the intersecting Anglo-American academic debates about the diverse "posts" (postmodernism, poststructuralism, postnationalism, and postcolonialism) made possible the marriage of still another "post" with another "ism": "post-Zionism." Since the second half of the 1990s, English-language postcolonial theory has travelled into Hebrew, "landing" in a post-Zionist space and settling into a rather anomalous discursive site where the "colonial" itself had hardly been engaged. In Israel, academic and journalistic texts have fashioned a facile stagist mantra that casts Homi Bhabha as transcending and, in their words, "outclassing" Said, subverting his "hegemony." The first Hebrew introduction to the translation of Bhabha urged readers to go "beyond" the putatively binarist Said, even though *Orientalism* was not yet translated at the time of the Bhabha translation.[7]

Postcolonial theory generally, and Said's work more specifically, was thus introduced to the Hebrew reader within an intellectual vacuum in relation to both anticolonial and postcolonial writings. The classical anticolonial texts by Césaire, Fanon, Senghor, Cabral, or Retamar, for example, had not been translated into Hebrew. Fanon's *The Wretched of the Earth* was translated only in 2006, decades after most translations around the world. While Albert Memmi's books on Jewish-related questions were translated into Hebrew, his anticolonialist book *The Portrait of the Colonized* was translated only in 2005. The "going-beyond-Said" move took place in a context where the foundational anticolonial and postcolonial texts, including *Orientalism*, translated in 2000, had been little engaged. Such a translational act was not accompanied by an exploration of the broad theoretical intertext and historical context that informed Said's work and thus did not do justice to the intellectual debate.

In the U.S. context, meanwhile, the terrain for Said's *Orientalism* had been prepared, on the Left, by a long series of struggles around civil rights, decolonization, Third Worldism, Black Power, and anti-imperialism. Postcolonial theory, more broadly, emerged out of the anticolonialist moment and Third-Worldist perspective; that is at least partly what makes it "post." But in Hebrew one finds a "post" without its past. Post-Zionist postcolonial writing—and this is one reason why the analogical linkage between the two terms is problematic—comes out of an intellectual context untouched by the anticolonialist debates. In the Third World, nationalism gave way to some "course corrections" and a certain disillusionment that provided the affective backdrop for postcolonial theory—a backdrop that had hardly any equivalent in the Israeli context. In the first instance, anticolonial discourse gives way to postcolonial discourse, but in the second, it is not anti-Zionist discourse that gives way to post-Zionist discourse but rather Zionist discourse that gives way to post-Zionist discourse. It is thus the curious case of the missing history of the "anti." The intellectual "jump" into the "post" has become a magic carpet flying into the land of erasure.

One would think that the scholarly embrace of "the postcolonial" would foreground the discussion of Zionism's relation to colonialism, as articulated in Said's *The Question of Palestine*, yet analyzing Zionism through the colonial prism has remained largely taboo in the Israeli academe. One sometimes finds a kind of upside-down camera obscura discourse, even when Said's critics also oppose the occupation. Although postcolonial post-Zionists have challenged certain Zionist orthodoxies, one wonders how post is this "post" when the Palestinian desire for a right of return is repressed from the postcolonial discussion and when the relevance of the critique of the "colonial" to the account of the "Law of Return," "affirmative action," and the "Right of Return" is circumvented. The prefix "post" in "post-Zionism" erases both colonial lineages and anticolonial intellectual history with a magical stroke of the "post."

* * *

I knew Edward across two decades within the worlds of both academia and activism. My relationship with him often involved friendly teasing. He would tease me about my "barbaric" Iraqi dialect of Arabic; and I would tease him about his deafness to the beauty of the singing of the Egyptian Umm Kulthum or of the Iraqi *maqam* music with which I was raised.

In the mid-1980s the self-proclaimed "only democracy in the Middle East" decided that it was illegal for people like me to meet with people like him, since I was an Israeli citizen and he was a member of the Palestinian National Council, then listed as a terrorist organization. He was called "a professor of terror" by the journal *Commentary*, his spilling of ink said to be the equivalent of the spilling of blood. During that first Intifada period I remember strolling with him after lunch at Columbia University when I expressed concerns about the death threats he had been receiving. I made the mistake of raising the possibility of his wearing a bulletproof vest. He instantly stopped, turned to me, and, with a bemused smile, looked at me as if I were out of my mind. He gestured toward his elegant suit as if to say,

Figure 33   From left to right: Edward Said, Akeel Bilgrami, and Ella Shohat on the panel "Lessons of the Gulf War," moderated by Aamir Mufti, the Post-Colonial Studies Seminar, Columbia University, March, 1991. "Gulf War 1990 Series," Deep Dish TV, Camera and Production Simin Farkhondeh and Indu Krishnan

"Where would the vest go? How would it fit? How would it look?" His dandy-like preoccupation with his sartorial decorum trumped my concern for his life. Edward preferred simply to go on living life with all its pleasures rather than give in to fear. Anxiety and exile were to be transformed into a creative intervention.

Edward Said passed away at a moment when the task of the worldly critic was far from completed. Despite death threats, Said did not opt out. Perhaps, as an engaged intellectual, he did not have the luxury of withdrawal. Despite the doubts and self-questioning that also form part of our mandate as intellectuals, he had an inspirational capacity to dare to take bold positions in the face of danger—a capacity for which we will always be grateful.

That Said's final resting place is in Broummana, Lebanon, rather than in New York (where he lived for decades) or Jerusalem (where he was born), provides a suitably troubled allegorical note to the equally fraught voyages of his ideas across national borders. I close with his words:

> One achieves at most a provisional satisfaction, which is quickly ambushed by doubt, and a need to rewrite and redo that renders the text uninhabitable. Better that, however, than the sleep of self-satisfaction and the finality of death.[8]

I dedicate these remarks to the memory of Edward Said—the bulletproof intellectual.

15

A Voyage to Toledo: Twenty-Five Years After the "Jews of the Orient and Palestinians" Meeting

On July 3–5, 1989, an unusual gathering, which went largely unreported in the media, took place in Toledo, Spain—*Judíos orientales y palestinos. Un diálogo para la paz árabe-israelí* (Jews of the Orient and Palestinians: A Dialogue for Arab-Israeli Peace). Four years before the commencement of the Oslo Accords, the Toledo conference took place at a time when Israeli law forbade such meetings, legally defined as proscribed political contacts with Palestinian terrorist organizations. In defiance of this law, a number of meetings took place in such cities as Bucharest, Budapest, and Geneva. At that time, Israeli officials were still vocally engaged in the mental acrobatics of denying the existence of anything called "the Palestinian people." Merely enunciating the word "Palestine," or displaying images of the Israeli and Palestinian flags side-by-side, was considered unpatriotic and even treasonous. Meetings between Israeli citizens and Palestinian representatives were banned, and leftist Israelis who dared cross the lines risked harassment and imprisonment, and some were tried and penalized.

The dominant media and academia refused to consider a Palestinian perspective. The attempt to narrate Palestine was reduced to a case of "narrative envy," as though "diaspora," "exile," and "return" were exclusively Jewish concepts. During the first Intifada, for example, the American-Jewish journal *Commentary* labeled Edward Said and Ibrahim Abu Lughod "professors of terror;" their spilling of ink was compared to the spilling of blood. And an Israeli paper, *Yedioth Ahronoth*, nicknamed this new wave of Palestinian spokespersons *"Ashafei ha-Tikshoret,"* i.e., media experts, but the word *"ashaf"* (expert) also punned on the Hebrew acronym for the PLO. The American-professional style of these Palestinian intellectuals was dismissed as merely a civil mask hiding a barbaric essence. During that period, the liberal media and academia also disciplined and punished Sephardi/Mizrahi/Arab Jews who expressed alternative per-

Published in the Culture Section of *Jadaliyya*, September 30, 2014.

spectives dissonant with the premises of the Zionist master narrative. The only "legitimate" Sephardi/Mizrahi position was to parrot the standard rhetoric of "population exchange" between Palestinians and Middle Eastern Jews. Articulating the notion of the "Arab-Jew," except for a triumphant nationalist telos, was completely taboo.

Against this legal, political, and discursive backdrop, meetings between "Israelis and Palestinians" challenged the doctrine of "no dialogue with the enemy" (officially voted by the Knesset on August 6, 1986). But the Toledo conference stood out even in its remarkable self-designation as a dialogue between "Oriental Jews and Palestinians." The initiative also contradicted the Orientalist stereotype, widely promoted by Peace Now, of fanatic Mizrahi "Arab-haters" as the obstacle to peace. The presence of this caricature underlined the absence, even the silencing, of Mizrahi perspectives, as relevant to peace talks. The initiative also moved beyond the habitual division between the so-called "internal social Jewish" affairs and "external political Palestinian" matters. (Within scholarship, as I suggested at the time, academic disciplines similarly deployed a bifurcating framework, splitting off the history and culture of Middle Eastern Jews from their history and culture after their departure, conceptualized as inherently delinked.) Against the backdrop of such intellectual paradigms, and the ongoing political impasse, conjoining Palestinians and Mizrahi/Arab Jews in the same sentence spelled out new potential paradigms for the future. In the words of Toledo's Palestinian delegate, Leila Shahid: "What makes this meeting different from all the ones we have seen until now, I believe, is the presence in this room of the largest group of Oriental Jews ever to meet with the PLO delegation."

Could Arab Jews provide a path for peace between Arabs and Jews? Inside and outside Israel, the phrase "the natural bridge for peace" was mobilized by diverse Sephardi/Arab-Jewish/Mizrahi activists, a spirit that was brought to Toledo. Thoroughly believing in coexistence, the participants built on a long Sephardi history of leaders, already in Ottoman and Mandate Palestine, seeking to mediate and reach a possible solution. In his independently published 1983 book entitled *Tensions and Ethnic Discrimination in Israel*, Nahum Menahem documented the efforts by diverse Sephardi leaders—who embraced Zionism but who also acknowledged the rights of Palestinians—to reach compromise. And in the 1980s, in homage to one such figure, Eliyahu Elyashar, the Elyashar Seminary initiative was launched in conjunction with the Mizrahi leftist cultural space New Direction, in south Tel Aviv, some of whose members also attended Toledo. One of the older-generation Toledo participants, Naeim Giladi, who had also believed in the bridging idea, gradually came to the realization that peace was not truly on Israel's agenda. This realization, which he reached while working as a journalist for the *HaOlam HaZe* magazine, turned him into an anti-Zionist, a view he delineated in his 1992 self-published *Ben-Gurion's Scandals*. Although a relatively small milieu, the 1980s leftist Arab-Jewish/Mizrahi scene, whether in Israel, France, or New York, nonetheless featured varied ideological perspectives. The Toledo meeting reflected this diversity as well as the Sephardi/Mizrahi/Arab-Jewish efforts to imagine a future of coexistence.

Sponsored by the Madrid-based Foundation for the Studies of Peace and International Relations (FEPRI)—an independent academic institute with close ties to Felipe Gonzales and the Partido Socialista Obrero Español—the conference was attended by about 100 participants, coming from Europe, the Middle East, and North America. It was initiated by two Paris-based Sephardi groups, Identité et Dialogue and Perspectives Judéo-Arabes, which were themselves linked to other activists and organizations in Israel, the U.S., the U.K., and Morocco. The Jewish members of Perspectives Judéo-Arabes overlapped with Israeli groups such as East for Peace (represented, among others, by one of its founders Shlomo Elbaz) and the Oriental Front (represented by Tikva Levi and Yosef Shiloach, among others), as well as with the U.S.-based World Organization of Jews from Islamic Countries (co-founded by Naeim Giladi), an organization that participated in the U.N. NGO discussions on the question of Palestine. And these organizations themselves included activists/intellectuals historically involved with earlier movements, the Black Panthers (represented, among others, by Kokhavi Shemesh) and the Tents movement (represented by Yamin Swisa).

At the time, the Toledo group, comprised of about 40 individuals, apparently had the largest number of Jewish/Israeli participants to meet with PLO representatives. The Jewish participants in the meeting did not officially constitute a "delegation," but rather took part as "individuals," among them: Simon Levy, a leading figure in both the anticolonial movement and the Moroccan Communist party, along with André Azoulay, advisor to King Hassan II, also from Morocco; filmmaker Simone Bitton as well as past Algerian FLN (National Liberation Front) member Daniel Timsit, both from France; politician Latif Dori, poet Erez Biton, and writer Shimon Ballas, all from Israel; author Naïm Kattan from Canada; and writers Ammiel Alcalay and myself from the U.S. Also attending the conference from Israel were two Sephardi hakhams/rabbis (who were reportedly threatened with excommunication by Israel's chief Sephardi rabbi) as well as a Marxist sociologist, Shlomo Swirski, author of *Israel's Oriental Majority*, one of the few Ashkenazi participants, who had worked closely with Mizrahi activists. A few other activists for peace were members of organizations that had little to do with the Mizrahi issue, namely Women in Black and Peace Now. In sum, while the Toledo Jewish participants represented voices for dialogue and peace, they were hardly a homogenous group in terms of their political trajectories, historical positions, and philosophical views.

The Palestinian delegation, meanwhile, was largely composed of PLO members, along with a few Arab supporters from countries such as Tunisia and Egypt, and in this sense represented the Palestinian mainstream. The delegation included Abu Mazen/Mahmoud Abbas, at the time Secretary General of the PLO Executive Committee—the highest ranking member of the delegation who gave the opening speech; the renowned poet Mahmoud Darwish, who gave the concluding speech; Leila Shahid, journalist and later the Palestinian representative to France; Elias Sanbar, editor of the *Revue d'études palestiniennes*; and Abbas Shiblak, author of *The Lure of Zion: The Case of the Iraqi Jews* (a book concerning the convoluted circumstances of the departure, and to which I referred in my presentation). The Palestinians also invited a number of other Arabs to the conference, including Egyptian writer Lutfallah Suleiman; Syrian economist Fayez Malas; the Tunisian director-general of the Arab League's Paris office, Hamadi Essid; and Adel Rifaat and Baghad El-Nahdi, better known under their shared pseudonym of the Marxist Egyptian writer "Mahmoud Hussein." The Palestinian delegation also included one Jew, Ilan Halevi, the PLO representative to the Socialist International. Aspiring to create a new political landscape, some participants, on both sides, denounced the "no-meeting-with-terrorist-organizations" law as itself terrorist. During a conference break, some commented jokingly on the shared features of the participants: "It's the only such meeting where it's hard to tell who is an Arab and who is a Jew."

The Palestinians were in search of recognition for Palestinian rights in an era when the two-state solution was still unacceptable for official Israel. The Toledo meeting took place a year after the PLO proclaimed Palestine to be an independent state, and the Palestinian National Council in its Algiers meeting had accepted the two-state solution, as envisaged by UN Resolution 181 in 1947, and after, Arafat renounced terrorism. These Palestinian leaders began to seek a negotiated settlement based on Resolution 242 and Resolution 338. The conference, however, as Lelia Shahid insisted, was not about negotiation, but about dialogue. In retrospect, the two-year interval between the Toledo conference and the 1991 Madrid conference could be viewed as part of a transitional moment that culminated in the Oslo Accord. (One key difference between the largely forgotten Toledo conference and the later Madrid conference had to do with their different status; one took place under the auspices of an academic institution, and the other under the official auspices of the government.) In his Toledo speech,

Mahmoud Darwish pointed to the difference in status between the two sides participating in the dialogue. While the Oriental Jews were present as individuals who believed in peace and Palestinians' rights, the Palestinians were official representatives of the Palestinian people. He stated firmly that the Palestinians wanted to carry out this dialogue with Israel in its entirety. Addressing the Jewish participants, Darwish continued: "You are defending the conscience of the Jews." Darwish saw the Toledo conference as a step in the peace process and its Jewish participants as potential carriers of the peace message back to Israel, where they could encourage the state to simultaneously recognize Palestinian rights and thus secure a Jewish future in the Middle East.

Most of the Sephardis/Mizrahis present in Toledo, then, represented civil society. Most were not members of political parties, and certainly did not speak on behalf of Israel's government. We were activists/intellectuals outside of the centers of power. A magazine supportive of the Toledo meeting, *HaOlam HaZe*, infelicitously described our group as composed of "intellectuals and Mizrahis" as if the two categories were mutually exclusive—a formulation that triggered bitter ironic responses, but also demonstrated the vital need to speak for ourselves. In the conference, lawyer Avi Bardugo joked that the Israeli establishment could not have foreseen 40 Mizrahi intellectuals, and therefore could have not imagined a meeting of this kind. More importantly, hardly anyone addressed the Arab/Palestinian as "the enemy." Hence, in Toledo you would be hard-pressed to hear the Israeli dovish language of "making peace with the enemy," or the Peace Now quest for "a divorce between Israelis and Palestinians," to echo Amos Oz, or even the relatively more pro-Palestinian notion of "My Friend, the Enemy," the title of Uri Avneri's book.

* * *

There we were in Toledo/Tulaytulah, in the historical city of the "*tres culturas*" and "*convivencia*"—a symbolic site of Jewish, Christian, and Muslim joint creativity. In this intercultural and inter-religious learning center began the vital project of multilingual translation, including between Spanish, Arabic, and Hebrew. And several hundred years later, we, Sephardis/Arab Jews and Arabs/Palestinians, were visiting (or, for some, returning to) a centuries-long banned place for Muslims and Jews. The old city was now witnessing a new pilgrimage, not simply for a lost place, but for a lost time before the Inquisition and the Edicts of Expulsion, the forced conversions of both Jews and Muslims, and the *limpieza de sangre*—the form of state-terror fully installed in 1492. Triumphant after the fall of Granada, the Spanish unification and purification program continued until the remaining

Figure 34   *Libération's* report on the Toledo conference, July, 3–5, 1989

Muslims were completely expelled between 1609 and 1614. This trope of "al-Andalus," then, evokes not only utopia but also dystopia.

Our Spanish hosts ushered us into the old city in a special excursion that highlighted the "*tres culturas.*" We visited the Santa María la Blanca church, built sometime in the late 12th century and early 13th century as the Ibn Shushan synagogue, believed to be the oldest synagogue building still standing on European soil. Constructed under the reign of King Alfonso VIII, and designed by Muslim architects for Jewish community rituals, it embodies the *convivencia* spirit. The architectural design incorporates diverse Moorish styles, including the Almohad and the Nasrids of Granada; it displays harmonious geometric design, horseshoe arches, interior white walls, vegetal decorations. The five rows of columns crowned with arches especially recall the Mosque of Córdoba of the Moorish "Golden Age" architecture. This characteristically Moorish-style synagogue stands as a testimony to a Judeo-Arab and to a Judeo-Islamic culture. Ibn Shushan synagogue was converted into a church in the 1405 riots, impacting certain visual aspects. For example, some design alterations had the effect of blocking the original source of light, resulting in the darkness typical of cathedrals, in sharp contrast to the brightness of mosques and synagogues.

In Spain, the hybrid palimpsest of *sinagoga*-turned-*iglesia* or *mezquita*-turned-*iglesia* came to underline both harmonious coexistence and its exact opposite. The nightmare began with the 15th-century forced conversions and violent expulsions. Our Spanish Toledo guide was recounting the city's oral tales. When the Jews were forced to leave, they kept on trying to return to their homes, their gardens, their place. Those who managed to reach the city held the old keys to open the doors of their former houses, but in the end they were prevented from returning. This image of persistent attempts to return conjured up the more recent history, to wit the attempts by displaced Palestinians to cross the border and return to their former houses, to eat the fruits of the trees they watered, and sometimes to just glimpse, if only from afar, the house, the garden, the remains of the town. But in 1989, the literal and metaphorical return to al-Andalus/Sefarad concerned the expulsion and terror of the recent past embodied by 1948.

The actual—and metaphorical—keys steadfastly carried into exile by the expelled Jews and Muslims from Spain came up in our discussions, but this time the keys in question were those of the 1948 houses to which Palestinians could not return. We also invoked the keys for the homes Arab Jews left behind in Iraq, Egypt, Syria, and so forth, but in contrast to "the population exchange" discourse, we did so without erasing and negating Palestinian rights. Playwright Gabriel Bensimhon spoke of his family's departure with only two suitcases from Tefilalt, Morocco, at a time when they deeply believed—or were led to believe—that the coming of the Messiah was imminent. (Indeed, Bensimhon's play *A Moroccan King* dealt precisely with the passionate belief among some Middle Eastern Jews that the birth of Israel signified the realization of Biblical prophecy.) As they arrived in Haifa, Bensimhon's grandfather still kept the key to the Tefilalt house in his pocket. The government then settled them in "an abandoned Arab house" in Wadi Salib. The very same neighborhood was home to Abbas Shiblak's family, which hastily departed with only a box of their possessions. The box contained some pictures, identity papers, and documents, along with the house key that they held onto in the many years to come, in diverse places of exile. "Everyone lives with keys," Bensimhon exclaimed, lamenting a situation of "too many keys with too few doors."

So recent was this memory of expulsion and exile, that in Toledo one could not but stop to reflect on the wretchedly absurd turnabout of events. Indeed, the analogy between the two historical moments, between the departures of 1492 and 1948, was suggested in Darwish's *qasida* "Eleven Stars over al-Andalus," published in 1992, after what was, to my knowledge, his first visit to Spain, as part of the Palestinian delegation to Toledo, and after the PLO participation in the first official peace process initiative at the 1991 Madrid Conference, as well as on the occasion of the Quincentenary commemorations. The poem evokes the "Adam of two Edens" and losing "paradise twice," concluding with "the violins" that "weep for the Arabs leaving al-Andalus," as well as "for a time that does not return," and "for a homeland that might return." (One of the Arab-Jewish conference's organizers, Simone Bitton, later directed a documentary about Darwish, where the theme of exile and return was centrally treated.) The idea of "al-Andalus" condenses both the *convivencia* and its traumatic end, but with the difference that, in the recent historical conjuncture, the Muslims and Jews (and for that matter Arab Christians) did not carry their keys in the same geographical directions.

This recent historical trauma generated new maps of belonging. An epic-scale shift in alliances and affiliations began with divide-and-conquer colonial policies (arguably including the Crémieux Decree) and culminated with colonial partition (initiated with the Balfour Declaration). And now Palestinians are displaced and wander in exile; their homeland, in Darwish's words, has become a suitcase. And in the wake of their displacement came that of the Arab Jews, crossing the borders in the opposite direction. The dispossession of the Palestinians and the dislocation of Arab Jews, I suggested, must be viewed discursively and historically as intimately linked events, without reductively equating the two. Instead of conceiving the Arab-Jewish/Mizrahi issue merely in terms of intra-Jewish tension, Zionism must also be narrated from the perspective of Sephardi/Mizrahi/Arab Jews. (My presentation was drawn partly from my essay "Sephardim in Israel: Zionism from the Standpoint of its Jewish Victims," which dialogued with Edward Said's "Zionism from the Standpoint of its Victims," both published in *Social Text*.) In that essay, I emphasized the need to problematize the discourse of "population exchange" between Palestinians and Arab Jews, a discourse that ultimately attempted to silence Palestinian claims. While one common response to the Israeli equation of the two dislocations was to simply delink the two cases, I argued, in contrast, that they must be viewed in relation to each other. Relinking these two historically entangled issues within a complex analytical framework was actually crucial for discerning the analogies and disanalogies between them. Such a relational conceptual prism was for me foundational for any in-depth examination of the present and for the imagination of a different future.

The political partition "begat" new identity barriers: Jews could no longer be Arabs, and Arabs could no longer be Jews. In Toledo, a few of us, myself included, defined ourselves as "Arab-Jews." I pointed out that Zionism "created wrenching dilemmas for Arab Jews ... prodded to choose between anti-Zionist Arabness and a pro-Zionist Jewishness." For the first time in our history "Arabness and Jewishness were posed as antonyms." One speaker from Israel, Haim Hanegbi, who had been a member of the anti-Zionist leftist Matzpen group, asserted his family origins from Hebron/al-Khalil, seeing himself as a "Palestinian Jew." Challenging the post-1967 Rabbi Levinger return-to-Hebron settler movement, Hanegbi identified with his own grandfather, who was the last leader of Hebron's Sephardi community forced to evacuate the city during the 1929 Palestinian fighting against Zionist activities, which also included attacking and killing local Jews. Yet for Hanegbi, a return to the house in Hebron/al-Khalil could only take place when Palestinians could also return to their homes. Another participant, Anat Saragusti—who, together with *HaOlam HaZe* editor Uri Avneri and journalist Sarit Yishai, had interviewed Yasser Arafat for the first time for an Israeli paper in 1982 besieged Beirut—addressed her Sephardi/Spanish familial history: "I have a strange last name, Saragusti, and I have to spell it every time. I think that here in Spain, it is the only place I don't have to do so. My ancestors left Saragossa five hundred years ago and went directly to Palestine; and Saragossa is only a few hundred kilometers from here!" In 1989, only a few decades after the traumatic events of dispossession and dislocation, Palestinians/Arabs and Sephardis/Arab Jews could meet in Toledo, as old "neighbors" dating back to a time before borders had been erected and new passports, or *laissez-passers*, had renamed us all. We had to travel *outside* the Middle East in order to imagine living together again, side by side, *in* the Middle East.

The conference offered the thrill of breaking new ground in an old terrain. We were hosted by the Spanish, who themselves were beginning to chart new paths. As a European country, Spain was entering the international diplomatic arena (represented by Manuel Medina). But also, Spain was beginning to confront its long suppressed Muslim/Jewish history, acknowledging the traces of Arab culture. Although Muslim and Sephardi residues were everywhere—in architecture, language, ritual, music, and literature—the dominant historical narrative remained still entrenched in the values and assumptions of the *Reconquista*. The "Moros y Cristianos" set of festival rituals, celebrated in many towns and cities across Iberia—and in Latin America as well—suggest that the specter of the Moor has continued to haunt the Iberian unconscious. After all, Cervantes's magnum opus *Don Quixote* is embedded in the battles against the Moors. Not only did the author himself fight and get captured by Algerian corsairs, the reflexive novel begins with the account of the book's origins in the Toledo marketplace where worn Arabic notebooks are sold. After acquiring one manuscript, the author looks around for a Moor to translate it, testifying that it was not difficult to find a translator, including for Hebrew. The author "reports" that the Moorish translator revealed that the Arabic manuscript chronicled the "History of Don Quixote de la Mancha," composed by "an Arab historian" Cide Hamete Benengeli. And so the ludic tale of Don Quixote and Sancho Panza, the Spanish novel *par excellence*, is imbued with Iberia's Arabness.

In all these "Moros y Cristianos" reenactments, there is perhaps one consoling element—Muslims and Jews are still imagined together, against the grain of their contemporary splitting, as though from time immemorial. The Sephardi, in this sense, is always-already a Moor, and the Moor is always-already a Sephardi, a kind of a Janus-faced figure. In Toledo, we came, we witnessed the remainders, and evoked al-Andalus/Sefarad; we were no longer ghosts of Moorish/Sephardi history. Only three years before the Quincentenary, the two delegations retrieved an era that suggested that there was nothing inevitable or eternal about the "Arab-versus-Jew" polarity. In the Toledo conference, some of the Spanish speakers, along with the Iraqi Israeli David Semah, explicitly dealt with the unacknowledged Arabic heritage of Spanish culture, demonstrating the links between Arabic and Western literatures. Was our visit part of a new moment, anticipating a wave of the return of the repressed? In Toledo, we were all returning to al-Andalus, not simply to the actual historical place but to the al-Andalus as a potent trope of becoming. We were eager to write a new *convivencia* chapter for Palestine/Israel and beyond.

There, in Toledo, Palestinians and Israelis stood side-by-side witnessing the remains of the dream and the nightmare. Comparisons to 20th-century Palestine seemed inevitable, as the era of Arabs—Muslims, Christians, and Jews—living together in the Middle East gave way to a nightmarish chapter in the relationship. After the *limpieza de sangre* and the expulsion of Jews and Muslims, only *conversos* and *Moriscos* remained in Toledo, and in the aftermath of the burning of Jewish and Muslim books, the cross-cultural translation project ceased. (Indeed, this was the 16th-century Toledo of Cervantes' novel.) And yet, there we were, Jews and Muslims, hosted by the Spanish, in a kind of a historical *mea culpa*. We were embarking on an extraordinary voyage; the very act of coming together signified the possibility of becoming something else. The desire for a hopeful memory out of the "*tres culturas*" was, I believe, an example of what Walter Benjamin called "revolutionary nostalgia." (His untimely death on the Spanish border, escaping Nazi Germany, is a reminder of still another nightmare.) The idea of the use of the past for the construction of the future was expressed in Shlomo Elbaz's statement: "We didn't come to Toledo out of nostalgia for the past. We are not *passéistes*. It is because we think that in this past we will find strength ... to look into the future and go beyond the suffocating present."

My critique of the Eurocentric account of a single "Jewish History" composed of "tracing the dots from pogrom to pogrom," was inspired not only by the Spain of the *convivencia* but also by my Arab-Jewish familial history in Baghdad, including Ottoman Iraq. At the same time that the *Reconquista* was eliminating al-Andalus, many other "al-Andaluses" were flourishing throughout the Islamic world. When Queen Isabella and King Ferdinand issued the Edicts of Expulsion, it was Sultan Bayezid II, after all, who extended an immediate welcome to the expelled Jews to settle in the Ottoman Empire. The *convivencia* space that we tend to associate with Toledo, then, existed in the multiple "al-Andaluses" of Istanbul, Cairo, Teheran, Jaffa, Damascus, and so forth. However, this evocation of the *convivencia* did not negate, in my view, the importance of considering the complex issue of the protected status of minorities, including Jews, in the Muslim world. It was not a question for me of idealizing the *convivencia* but rather of avoiding an isolationist discourse that separated Jews off conceptually from other ethnic and religious communities. It was also about eschewing the reductive, relentless persecution narrative that projected the experience of European anti-Semitism onto Jewish life throughout the Muslim world. Acknowledging the difference between these histories, Ilan Halevi argued that the point is not to return to "the protected minorities status," but rather to fight for equality. Today, in Spain, these words resonate with the recent decision by Spain to grant citizenship to the expelled Sephardim but not to the Muslims, despite their linked expulsions, and despite the shared experience of masquerading religious identities common to *moriscos* and *marranos*.

* * *

The modern history and status of Middle Eastern "minorities," as well as the issue of fear and trust, were addressed by diverse speakers from different angles. The more critical Mizrahis/Arab Jews were closer in their perspectives to the Arabs/Palestinians, while others were uncomfortable with the fact that Jews, despite the shared culture, were nonetheless a minority under both Christianity and Islam. Naïm Kattan spoke of the great moments of Arab-Jewish history in periods of creativity, of "the symbiosis" of borrowing "the language of the Qu'ran to affirm the Law of Moses and sing God's praises." He reminded the audience that "we were not denied in our being by the ambient religion, nor were we rejected in our practice by the common language." As Iraqi Jews, "we did not see a contradiction between belonging to our country and to our community .... No one questioned our sense of belonging, our practices .... I learned my Jewishness and I was proud to be Arab." At the same time, Kattan asserted that "the harmony was damaged," especially since, like other minorities, "our place was unstable .... We were protected as long as we stayed in our place and among the minorities ... we were still an ethnic group whose place was unstable." This "unstable equilibrium," Kattan concluded, would require "supporting the other but in your own voice, that is the condition of peace."

Simon Levy, speaking "as a Jew from Casablanca," meanwhile, called attention to a history in which the rights of the Jewish-Moroccan community, including the rights to cultural identity, were recognized alongside those of other communities, a situation destroyed by colonialism, and by the depersonalization provoked by a Franco-centric educational system, as well as by Zionist actions, leading to the fracturing of the community and its membership in Moroccan society. In addition, Levy pointed to another key factor—"the fear and malaise created by the Israeli/Arab war." Levy evoked "the rights of Man" and "the Emancipation of Jews" advanced with the French Revolution, and emphasized that the Palestinians were deprived of these very same rights. The Palestinians, he argued, were indirect victims of the Shoah through a kind of ricochet effect. As for the remaining Jews in Morocco, Levy insisted that they often showed solidarity with the Palestinians. For example, the Casablanca synagogue around the time of the Sabra and Shatila massacre had a ceremony in honor of the Palestinian victims. Levy spoke of the occupation as "an obsolete form of colonization, completely out of synch with the present. And this colonization is also murderous. Is that the image of world Judaism we want to promote? Are we going to allow the Israeli establishment to dictate to Jewish organizations what is legitimate to say and think? ... It becomes quite clear who is practicing colonial and terrorist violence." He was concerned that now "we have to do better and faster in the interest of peace. We need to disassociate Judaism from a specific political line of the Israeli government. Judaism represents peace .... Are we going to allow this image of Judaism to be destroyed by the image that everyone sees on their TV sets?" For Levy, these actions were clearly anti-Jewish.

Daniel Timsit, a former militant with the FLN in Algeria, pleaded for more candor in the discussion so as "to open up the wounds of racism on both sides," in order to address the facts that "the Arabs disdained Jews, seeing them as arrogant and oppressive ... showing little solidarity with the Algerian struggle," while "the Jews disdained the Arabs, seeing them as inferior." Distinguishing between "legitimate nationalism and imperialist nationalism," Timsit stated: "I say as a Jew, as an Algerian, and as a French person that I have no solidarity with Israeli soldiers who kill children .... Let's stop talking about Israeli democracy ... France was democratic when it occupied Algeria; democracy coexisted with torture, murder, and concentration camps .... We have to defend the Intifada because it's a just cause."

Another speaker, Eli Baida, highlighted the "intercommunitarian coexistence" for thousands of years as in the case of Aleppo. Fear and exile of Jews from Arab countries was very much a result of the partition of Palestine. "It was after 1947 and the riots that eighty percent of the Jews left Syria, not for Israel but for Lebanon, where they joined the Palestinian refugees. Why Lebanon? Because like the Palestinians, the Syrians [Jews] hoped to go back home, that is to Syria, once the troubles were over. In this way, Palestinians and Syrian Jews shared a history, engendered by the same cause at the same time." While noting the Arab discrimination against Arab Jews in the wake of Zionism, Baida described Lebanon as the only prosperous and growing Jewish community after 1948. "Beirut became the refuge of all the Jews of the *Mashriq* who refused to leave their multi-faith, multi-community universe. Twenty-five happy years of life together, despite '56, despite '73, despite the constant Israeli aggressions against a country almost without an army."

Baida asserted that his personal story was that of a generation born and raised "in an open society, free and multi-communitarian." The Jewish community itself was multiple, ranging from left-wingers to right-wingers supportive of the phalange. After 1968, the Palestinian question became a central issue in Lebanon. "When four Jews were arrested in 1968," Baida reported, "the Lebanese universities went on strike to free the four Jews," and "in 1982, during the infamous siege of Beirut, 350 Jews refused to leave their towns, despite the effort of the Israeli army to make them leave. Three hundred and fifty Jews in Beirut experienced the Israeli siege alongside their Lebanese and Palestinian brothers." Jews were able to live there even during the seven years of the civil war. For Baida, "the multi-faith and intercommunitarian nature of Lebanon" formed "a negation, a provocative counter-model to the Jewish state." But after "the Israeli aggression," he continued, "then we knew fear, and the Jewish community dwindled down to two hundred or three hundred people in 1982 .... The end of the community came with the departure of the PLO and the emergence of the Shiite fundamentalists .... Now the goal has been achieved; the social web, the multi-faith society of Beirut has been torn, with dislocated Jews and Palestinians." Linking the fate of Palestinians and Arab Jews, Baida stated: "We have spoken here of the need for trust between Jews and Palestinians. We lived that trust from 1975 until 1982, when the PLO left. Up to then, the Jewish community was protected, supplied, and defended by all the elements of the Palestinian resistance."

André Azoulay, who to this day lives in Morocco, extended the historical issue to open up a discussion about the current fears of Israelis, rooted in a different history, the Shoah—fears that had become an obstacle to peace. Other Jewish participants, meanwhile, raised the issue of Israeli fears, asking the PLO to make further concessions, and expressed the hope that the PLO would declare that the West Bank and Gaza would constitute the final border, and renounce the Right of Return, or at least promise that the Palestinian state would be demilitarized. In this context, the Palestinians also addressed the issue of trust and fear, responding that they had condemned terrorism and accepted Resolutions 242 and 338 as a basis for negotiation, which assumed the Israeli withdrawal from the occupied territories in exchange for peace. They pointed out that they were still awaiting any such acknowledgement from the Israeli government, i.e., for Israel to recognize the rights of the Palestinian people and stop state terrorism against them in Jordan, Gaza, and Lebanon. Darwish spoke ironically of Israeli fears of the "Palestinian empire," asking "Who are you afraid of?" and asserting, "you have only yourselves to fear!" Elias Sanbar, for his part, offered both empathy and analysis of the fear: "I believe that we Palestinians know more than you imagine the panic that you have experienced, and we feel it, and we feel solidarity with the blows that you have suffered."

Figure 35   Mahmoud Darwish addressing the Toledo conference participants

Sanbar argued that in order to make progress, "the essential thing is to define your fear," which, for him, contained three elements. The first element, he explained, is the historical component, including "the barbarous and tragic crowning of the oppressive practices that culminated with Nazism in Western Europe. All that we understand as a constitutive and legitimate part of your fear." The second element is the history of Arab Jews, for which "we Palestinians are not at all responsible." He explained that "perhaps there are certain phases of your life in the heart of Arab societies that constitute bad memories. And we Palestinians have no problem with that, and no reason to deny it." And, finally the third element, for Sanbar, had to do with the fear that "in the bottom of your hearts you are aware of the harm that has been done to you by the creation of the state of Israel … you probably tell yourselves: 'After everything we have done to the Palestinians, how can we believe them when they say they want to live in harmony with us?' That is the deepest element within your panic, and I would call it panic rather than fear." Sanbar continued: "You must be thinking: 'How could people—who have been denied and displaced during forty years, considered as absent ones, even when they are physically present, humiliated, without recognition, without identity or rights—all of a sudden, become so generous as to propose a two-state solution? And how can we imagine that there would be no risk, or that we could construct a peace together?"

For Sanbar, the panic was related to a delusion about a kind of "a second disappearing" of the Palestinians, when Israelis argue that Palestinians should give up on the right to return. "For us, that demand amounts to asking us to disappear once again, not in physical terms, but as if to reassure yourselves with the idea that Palestinians should give up their very identity and become absent to themselves." However, "the right to return is established in international law, and it will be a central issue in the negotiations." Sanbar addressed specifically the Arab-Jewish/Mizrahi issue, suggesting: "I think you are waiting for us to tell you 'don't be afraid.'" You Yemeni Jews have been made absent to yourselves, to your Yemeni identity, and you Iraqi Jews have been made absent to your Iraqi identity, but you are wrong if you think that the condition for living in peace with Palestinians is for them to be absent to their own Palestinian identity." Sanbar also added: "I think the solution to your fear is in your hands. We will do a lot, for our part, to make sure you have no reason to fear, and that peace will be constructed. But you also have to do your part—and I say this in a fraternal way—to face your own fear, and not wait indefinitely for a Palestinian response. After all, we had to confront our own fears alone. I think your confronting your own fears is fundamental for the success of any peace process."

* * *

There were some moments when ideas were lost in translation. It was not so much about the common hope to arrive at a peace settlement, around which a healthy portion of the discussion revolved; many were willing to discuss the importance of bringing the Israeli government to the negotiation table, recognizing Palestinian rights, and arriving at a two-state solution. And with the more critical Mizrahis/Arab Jews, it was not even around any disagreement with the Palestinians about the interpretation of Zionism and/ or the Nakba. Rather, some of the non-meeting-of-the-minds had to do with the definition and the relevance of the Mizrahi issue to the peace process. Abu Mazen, for example, treated the Mizrahi issue as a quantitative matter of a demographic majority: "the Oriental Jews will decide if there will be war or peace." However, many Mizrahis/Arab Jews had a different understanding of this issue and its meaning not only historically but also for charting the future. Simon Levy argued against Arab criticism of Moroccan Jews, who in Levy's view had not always been understood, and were even mistreated by the Arab press. He gave two examples of meetings organized by Jewish Moroccans: first, the 1984 meeting in Rabat, attended by a group of Moroccan political leaders, from both the government and the opposition—but also by the Moroccan-Jewish Knesset deputy; and second, the 1985 Montreal meeting of the newly created World Assembly of Moroccan Jewry that included Moroccan Israelis. According to Levy, the Arab press completely missed the thrust of these invitations to Moroccan Israelis. "They didn't understand that the positions we adopted were aimed at generating links with Jewish Moroccans and their members of the Knesset, no matter what their political position, in order to create the possibility of a broad discussion that would include all the levels of the Arab-Jewish population." The point was to prevent Moroccan Israelis from "remaining under the influence of the obscurantist fanaticisms .... We happen to believe that we're having some impact thanks to this channel .... And creating links with Morocco brings with it everything that Morocco signifies in terms of lived coexistence and political courage." Levy insisted that the remaining Jewish community in Morocco is "still active and responsible, and acts with autonomy."

Other participants, meanwhile, highlighted the complex relation of Arab Jews/Mizrahis to the question of Palestine. Robin Eddi stated that he did not believe that Oriental Jews feel guilty about what was done to Palestinians "because they do not feel that they were responsible for creating the state of Israel." "What they are afraid of," Eddi argued, "is rather that peace will come at their expense, that there will be an alliance between Ashkenazis and Palestinians against them," since the Mizrahis end up "paying the price of all the money that goes to the military rather than to improving their lot." Mizrahi activists called attention to the fact that 1967 represents different things for the Ashkenazi middle class and for the Mizrahi working class. Some speakers from Israel emphasized the issue of class. For example, David Hamou, editor of the alternative Hebrew *Iton Aher*, intervened in the discussion: "As an Oriental Jew in Israel I have some questions for the Palestinians—how will the establishment of a Palestinian state affect the situation of Oriental-Jewish workers? Do the representatives here speak for the Palestinian working class? ... Will the Palestinian state be a capitalist state? The answers to these questions will show whether we can move toward a future of prosperity and peace or toward inequality and injustice for the masses in both countries." Although Arab Jews/Mizrahim agreed on the goal of a Palestinian state, they also expressed concern about the (non-Mizrahi) Israeli "Left" continuing with its racist rhetoric and oppressive economic policies.

For many Palestinians, however, the Mizrahi perspective was an "internal affair" that was up to the Israeli Jews to resolve. Some Palestinian speakers, including Abu Mazen in his opening remarks, addressed the conference participants as the carriers of the message of coexistence to Israel as a whole. The urgency of the Palestinian situation on the ground and the realpolitik agenda meant that the Mizrahi issue was in a sense becoming a burden. Evoking al-Andalus/Sefarad in the past tense and even in the future tense was one thing; but what would it mean within the current situation, where Mizrahis participate in the occupation of Palestine? The emphasis on "a common culture" also made some Palestinians uncomfortable, since it was perceived as sidestepping concretely burning matters of land, political rights, and the establishment of a Palestinian state. Certainly we understood the Palestinian sense of urgency, just as Palestinians understood our vision of peace "in" and "of" the East. But at a certain point, it became a dialogue-of-the-deaf. For the critical Arab Jews/Mizrahis, the skeptical Palestinian response to this vision seemed to echo the Euro-Israeli discourse, only from the opposite nationalist perspective. While Palestinians were stressing the official line of a two-state solution, critical Mizrahi/Arab Jews raised the issue of what the future would look like after the establishment of the two states, hoping to eliminate borders and produce a shared culture. For the Palestinians, meanwhile, this Mizrahi vision was an issue to be addressed in the future, and ultimately irrelevant when Mizrahis, as Israelis, formed part of an oppressive state apparatus in the present. The Palestinians, as Darwish put it, would eventually have to make peace not with "two different Israeli societies," but with "one Israeli society." In any case, it was clear that this specific Mizrahi perspective expressed in Toledo was unusual in the context of Israeli/Palestinian Peace meetings.

At that 1989 moment when the Spanish welcomed Jews and Muslims in an effort to renew the dialogue again, "al-Andalus/Sefarad," then, became a living site of truth and reconciliation. The Toledo meeting encapsulated the idea of "al-Andalus" not simply as an actual historical place and time, but as a trope for the *convivencia* of an imagined future. If only for these three days in the summer of 1989, Toledo witnessed once again dialogical translation. Although the Oriental-Jewish and Palestinian delegations were accommodated on different floors of the hotel, and were seated on parallel sides of the conference room separated by an aisle, dialogue was taking place both formally and informally. The hosting institute provided simultaneous translation; speeches were given in Spanish, Arabic, Hebrew, English, and French. Exchanges during breaks, meals, and excursions were carried on in varied languages depending on the interlocutors. In this three-day marathon, most members of the Palestinian delegation gave their speeches in Arabic. Arab Jews/Mizrahis, meanwhile, gave their speeches in Arabic, Hebrew, French, and English. The very diversity of the languages reflected the different trajectories and paths that have shaped Arab/Muslim spaces, in the wake of colonialism, and later of Zionism, reorganizing cultural identities and regional affiliations.

In the Toledo conference, some Arab Jews gave their speeches and spoke with the Palestinians in Arabic, and some Palestinians spoke in Hebrew in an informal setting. For the Arab Jew, Arabic was an indigenous mother tongue. For the Palestinian, Hebrew, in contrast, was the language of the occupier. Darwish (who was fluent in Hebrew) evoked in his speech the question of language, in both the literal and metaphorical senses. "Now that we are exploring our common cultural roots," Darwish asked, "I do not understand why I have to go to another language to participate in the output of our common culture." For Darwish, the Palestinians are sometimes "asked to accept the view of common Semitic origins with Israeli society," but in doing so Palestinians are "asked to discover it by looking through a different language" while also being "asked to begin from scratch in a new language." Whereas in the Arab world, the languages and dialects of the diverse minorities were marginal, in Israel, Hebrew/Arabic have existed within an occupier/occupied paradigm, even as Palestinians from Israel have mastered Hebrew. Darwish was not asking for a simple reversal of the roles of occupier and occupied but rather for undoing the occupation grammar altogether. "We are inadvertently asked," he stated, to be "either the Arabs of the Jews or the Jews of the Arabs." He thus criticized the undergirding view that only makes possible two kinds of human beings—Jews and non-Jews—and divides the world in two—the side of the Jews and the side of the Arabs. For Darwish, the answer was in *"insaniyya jadida"*—a new humanity—words that echoed for me Fanon's exhortation of a new humanism in the final pages of *The Wretched of the Earth*.

* * *

Palestinians were not unanimous on the Arab Jew/Mizrahi issue, then, just as Mizrahis were not unanimous about their relation to Zionism. Indeed, in Toledo there was a lurking tension among the diverse Arab Jews/Mizrahis about their own historical position on Zionism and about their present-day relation to Israel. The divide dates back to the arrival of Zionism in the region. While throughout the Arab/Muslim world most Jews maintained religious traditions, and did not adhere to either Zionist or anti-Zionist ideologies, some of the younger Jews educated in modern schools participated in wrenching debates about Arab nationalism, Zionism, and

Communism. In the post-World War II era and at the time of the creation of Israel, as the war in Palestine was beginning to intersect with their lives, Arab-Jewish intellectuals were increasingly involved in heated discussions about whether Zionism was a Jewish nationalist liberation movement or an oppressive settler-colonialist endeavor. In Arab countries, the Zionist underground was recruiting Jewish supporters, and actively destabilizing the leadership of traditional *hakhams* (in Iraq especially *hakham* Sasson Khdhuri) who voiced anti-Zionist sentiments, both because they feared for the Jewish community and because, philosophically, they regarded secular Zionist thought as contradicting traditional Judaism. The communist Jews, meanwhile, believed in a universal inclusive future of equality where religion and ethnicity would be obsolete in Iraq, Egypt, Morocco, etc.

In Toledo, we, the children of that generation, encountered the echoes of this historical debate. On one informal occasion, Naeim Giladi stated: "There is one thing I regret in my life—that I was an activist in the Zionist movement in Baghdad." To which Sami Michael responded: "Indeed, you should regret it! How come you all brought us Zionism to Baghdad?" And there they were: the ex-Zionist Giladi (Khlaschi), who was imprisoned, tortured, and escaped Abu-Ghraib just before his scheduled execution, illegally crossing the border to Iran, and then to Israel, and, once there, became a leader of the 1950s *maabarot* rebellions and later a spokesperson for the Black Panthers, and then moved to New York only to renounce his Israeli citizenship. And on the other side, the ex-communist Sami Michael, who also escaped from the threat of imprisonment and death, but in his case for being a communist, and who also illegally crossed the border to Iran, to the center of the Tudeh party, but, in contrast, did not believe in leaving Iraq for Israel, and yet ended up having to go there for refuge (the title of one of Michael's novels), and who, once in Israel, became an outspoken critic of racism—whether toward Mizrahis or Palestinians—and fought for citizenship rights. Although Giladi and Michael ended up leaving Iraq, Iraq did/has not left them. Michael became the president of the Society for Solidarity between the People of Israel and the People of Iraq. Giladi, meanwhile, returned to Iraq for one brief visit after 2003. As he completed his descent from the plane, as he later shared with me, he kissed the ground.

What my friend Tikva Levi and I dubbed jokingly and lovingly "the Iraqi delegation to Toledo" was revisiting the kind of arguments we heard growing up within the family and the larger displaced Jewish-Iraqi community. And as the Giladi/Michael exchange reveals, these arguments were sometimes paradoxical, considering the trajectory of the speaker: for example, bitter Iraqi-Zionists who felt deceived by Israel and its promise; Iraqi communists who felt a sense of relief to be a communist in the open in Israel; Iraqi Jews who may have celebrated the end of "the Babylonian Exile" but who simultaneously felt trapped in "Zion" and expressed an unrealistic wish to return. These conflicting sentiments within the community, within families, and sometimes within the same individual, were very much present in the world in which I grew up. Cursing and blessing Israel, or cursing and blessing Iraq, sometimes neighbored within the same thought process. But perhaps, more than anything else, the contradictory emotions, I would suggest, have to be understood as reflective of the contradictions of a world—divided between Arabs and Jews—in which Arab Jews had or felt they had little agency.

Figure 36 Members of the "Iraqi delegation" to Toledo (from left to right: Sami Michael, David Semah, Ella Shohat, Shimon Ballas, and Yosef Shiloach)

These arguments have persisted among the younger generation of Mizrahis/Arab Jews, including among those who participated in the Toledo meeting. There was no philosophical agreement over the historical meaning of Zionism for Arab Jews. But, the shared sentiment of "coming from" and "being of" the region spelled out a shared discourse that rejected racist views of Western superiority and embraced "the East," even within the—at that time—daring proposal of a two-state solution. Within this perspective, Israel needed to open up toward the East in order to envision an intertwined future of Israel and Palestine. Such was our imagined map of the future. In many ways, Arab Jews, it could be said, refused to be "the last of the Mohicans." And in the words of Serge Berdugo, who testified for Moroccan Jews currently living together with Muslims in Morocco: "We live at peace with our Muslim compatriots, sharing the same values and the same destiny. We are not the vestige of some Golden Age .... We are the active witnesses of Judeo-Arab coexistence and search for peace .... For us it's not a matter of foreign policy; it's an intimate, domestic affair." Berdugo insisted: "We will not be in peace with ourselves as long as Arab and Jewish brothers are tearing each other apart. It is also an intimate affair for us because 400,000 Israelis are Moroccan .... We understand the hopes and fears of our Muslim compatriots. And I don't think it would be pretentious to think that Muslim-Moroccans have learned from us a little bit about seeing the conflict in less dogmatic, simplistic, and Manichean ways."

This was our vision of peace that, to echo Darwish's Toledo words, was not about "closure" but about "openness." Indeed, rejecting closure and dreaming of openness for the future filled the air. Leila Shahid emphasized the Palestinian "deep conviction that co-existence based on respect of the rights of all peoples is our only common future .... Dialogue is indispensable as it alone can create the understanding and hope, and hopefully the trust and confidence without which there can be no solution worthy of the name." The dialogue at many points, then, was not "of the deaf," but mutually audible when some Palestinians envisioned that, for Oriental Jews, peace would also mean that they could go back to their "cultural roots." It seemed that the pragmatic and vital discussion about potential negotiations and resolutions took a back seat, when the conversation journeyed into rumination about the past and the vision of the future. At those moments, the Toledo meeting epitomized the meeting-of-minds.

In contrast to the dovish Euro-Israeli discourse, most of us were not seeking a "divorce," but rather an "integration" with the East, even if within the framework of the two-state solution. However impractical it may have been, our peace for the East, it could be said, was premised on a complete recasting of the relation between "East" and "West." One beautiful evening left a mark on us, embodying what is usually dismissed as "nostalgia" and "sentimental clichés." The Jewish-Moroccan-French singer and composer Sapho graciously delighted us with her singing. I would reflect back on that moment a few years later when Sapho performed Umm Kulthum's legendary song "*al-Atlal*," and when she released her album *Jardin Andalou*, that fused rock, Arabic, and Andalusian elements. While a long-time supporter of Palestinian rights, Sapho, after that visit to Toledo, began to engage with the music of the Judeo-Arab world in which she was raised. To stand up for justice in Palestine was all the more momentous when drawing on the complex memories of Sephardi/Arab Jews.

* * *

The Sephardi/Mizrahis/Arab Jews who attended Toledo showed solidarity with the Palestinian struggle against the occupation, not only crossing political boundaries but also defying the emotional wall erected between Israelis and Palestinians. The participants could be said to have subverted the false binarism of "Arab-versus-Jew." In the words of Raymond Benahim: "Peace is not just about borders;" it is also about "recognizing Palestinian memory" and going beyond "the exclusivity of Jewish memory." After Toledo, in the 1989–90 period, non-official meetings between dovish Israeli representatives and the Palestinian PLO representatives took place. Needless to say, these meetings hardly matched our vision of peace. Some years later, Ilan Halevi shared an anecdote with me about those meetings. The Israelis, he recounted, met and talked with the Palestinians, but they objected to meeting with one high-ranking PLO member—Ilan Halevi. (Apart from serving as the PLO's representative to the Socialist International, Halevi also became the PLO vice-minister of Foreign Affairs, participating in that capacity in the Madrid conference.) In one of these meetings, when the Israeli representatives still refused to speak with Halevi, the Palestinians teased them: "Now you are speaking to us, but you are refusing to meet and talk with the only *Jewish* member of our delegation? What's wrong—are you anti-Semitic?"

The rather unusual case of Ilan Halevi—a kind of a contemporary John Brown—evokes a long and troubling history of excommunication, first religious and later political, which stands in the way of dialogue and reconciliation. Within Sephardi history, the philosopher Baruch Spinosa, raised in the Portuguese-Jewish community of Amsterdam, suffered the censure of the *herem* (a word of the same root the Arabic *haram*). Considered Rationalist, his philosophical texts, seen as at odds with traditional Judaism, were denounced as "abominable heresies." Iberia's banned Sephardis in Protestant Holland, ironically, carried out an excommunication of one of their own. And to think about a different, more lethal context, in the Americas, border-crossers were viewed as insane or dangerous "race traitors" when they questioned the ambient pieties. To become "Indian," to "go native," was a punishable crime for the settler regimes, be they Spanish, Portuguese, British, or French. But in contrast, assimilation of "the natives" was blessed and celebrated as a step forward in the barbarian's entry into civilization. It was inconceivable that a White settler, by choice, could live among "the Indians" and learn anything of value (even though Europe did learn, without acknowledging it, some ideas from "the Indians"— social utopia, federation, herbal medicine, and so forth). Perhaps a possible addendum to Darwish's poem "The Speech of the Red Indian" would evoke the spirit of "the White," the renegade who became an "Indian," not so much to fight "the Whites" but rather to fight for another way of existing and coexisting.

Those who struggled to acknowledge injustice, to dialogue when dialogue was refused, are hardly the insane ones of history, but rather the future's past visionaries. Real and symbolic walls have had lethal consequences. Partition and its scarring of the land, of bodies and souls, must be rethought. In the words of one of the Toledo participants, Hisham Mustafa: "The discussion of today is the dream of a new tomorrow." The Toledo vision of a reimagined future beyond the fenced-in material and cultural borders is still, unfortunately, just a dream. In the face of current violence, blood, and impasse, the common hopes expressed there by Palestinian and Arab Jews/Mizrahis are still relevant today. In the words of Leila Shahid:

> What is peace in the Middle East if it is not a new relation to be defined between Jews and Arabs and the redefinition of the relation of the State of Israel in its environments? If we come out of these two days with some accomplishment, we would bring back to our people in the occupied territories, in the Arab world, and in Israel the hope they need to continue the long struggle for peace ahead … We have urgency today which is your urgency too … Our battle for peace is also your battle for peace.

Citing the words of one of the *hakham* (rabbi) participants, Fayez Malas affirmed that "there is no difference between blood and blood." Malas continued:

> Under this banner I came to this meeting, a call to peace and stopping of bloodshed. We all enjoyed this feeling in the past three days. Moving words and dialogue that restored our faith in humanity. Violence and killing is not our fate. This conference is to bring us back to a common discussion that has been missing. This was a step toward awakening a sleeping conscience based on fear.

Abbas Shiblak concluded with the hope that "because Toledo witnessed our Golden Age of coexistence and cooperation, Jerusalem will also witness our Golden Age of coexistence and cooperation."

Toledo, with all its limitations, nonetheless represented at that time an inspiring leap of faith. And the need and hope for a new *convivencia*, *ta'ayush*, *shutafut kiyumit* persists—one lesson perhaps worth retaining from this "voyage" back to Toledo/Tulaytulah.

PART III

Cultural Politics of the Middle East

16

Egypt: Cinema and Revolution

Like other major Third World film industries such as those of India, Mexico, and Brazil, Egyptian cinema has a long tradition (70 years) with a production often amounting to an average of 50 films a year. It has gained a central position within the Arab World, managing to break through language barriers by familiarizing other Arab countries with its particular dialect. Once Egyptian cinema became politicized it was perceived as troublesome by the colonizers in the neighboring Arab countries. The French in the *Maghrib*, for example, formed a "special department" on African problems that was "responsible for setting up a production center in Morocco whose official mission was to oppose the influence of Egyptian cinema."[1]

The political-economic realities in the colonies that substantially led to the emergence of "Third Worldism" after World War II, structured the psycho-cultural dimensions of "underdeveloped" (i.e. colonized) societies. Writing on the emergence of a "national cinema" in Egypt, therefore, necessitates examining the correspondences between the cinema and key events of political significance, especially the 1952 revolution. Despite the fact that 30 years have passed since the Free Officers movement seized power on July 23, 1952, only in recent years has it become possible to outline the revolution's repercussions for Egyptian cinema. Although some traditional genres such as the sentimental melodrama remain dominant today, another cinema has emerged, built on the foundations laid in 1952. This new cinema is characterized by an attempt to tackle the political dilemmas and social problems of contemporary Egypt. Directors such as Salah Abu-Seif, Youssef Chahine, Tawfiq Saleh, and later Ali Abd el-Khaliq, Shadi Abd-al-Salam, as well as critics such as Samir Farid, Sami al-Salamuny, Hashim al-Nahhas (members of the "New Cinema Collective") contributed to the development of a politically conscious cinema.

My purpose here will be to examine the consequences of the 1952 revolution for the orientation and structure of the film industry as well as for the films themselves. I will focus on the first decade under Gamal Abdel

Published in *Critical Arts: A Journal for Media Studies* in a special issue dedicated to "Cinema in the Third World," Vol. 2, no. 4 (1983).

Nasser's regime, which undoubtedly led to the gradual decolonization and de-Westernization of Egyptian cinema. Although filmmakers criticized the policies as well as the regime itself, especially after his death in 1970,[2] it is clear that the development of a self-conscious national cinema can be traced to the Free Officers Movement revolution of 1952.

In order to comprehend the transformations that took place in Egyptian cinema it is necessary to outline the state of the pre-revolutionary industry. As in many Third World countries, the Egyptian film industry had Europeans involved in local productions, especially in commercial cinema devoted to profits and entertainment based on the Hollywood model. It was not by chance that Egypt's film industry was called the "Hollywood of the Orient." Along with local Egyptian production companies, the Europeans—British, Greeks, Italians, and French—were active in the film industry. Their presence reflected one dimension of the political-economic regime predominant within Egyptian trade and industry. Despite the granting of formal independence in 1922, the British retained real political and economic control of Egypt until the early 1950s. The constitution of April 19, 1923 declared Egypt a sovereign, free, and independent state whose religion was Islam and whose official language was Arabic. Personal liberty was guaranteed but the liberty of the press (including the cinema) was limited "for the protection of social order." All public and military employment was restricted to nationals of the country, except where otherwise provided for by law—a reservation required to allow for the continuing role of British officials.

From the beginning the cinema played out the conflicts generated by the colonial situation, and the pro-Western orientation of the cinema persisted even when Egyptians had become part of the industry. Fearing that the audience would tire of seeing imported films, some producers, such as the Italian de Lagrane, and later the Italo-Egyptian Cinematographic Company (with the Banco di Roma as a partner), tried to produce films with local scenes to stimulate the interest of Egyptian audiences, such as Osato's *Sharaf al Badawi* (*The Bedouin's Honor*) and *al-Zuhur al-Qatila* (*Fatal Flowers*), both of 1918. These first films produced in Egypt reflected a very shallow comprehension of the religious traditions and customs of the Egyptian population. For example, *al-Zuhur al-Qatila* offended the Islamic community by garbling several phrases from the Qur'an. A more severe case occurred in 1925 when a German film company tried to produce a film entitled *The Prophet*, with Muhammad as the main character. This plan shocked the Islamic university, al-Azhar, since the Muslim religion prohibits representation of the Prophet. As a result, the film was never made.

The period between official independence and the 1952 revolution was marked by social turmoil and political struggle. The European producers and filmmakers, unconcerned with Egyptian social problems, avoided subjects that critically addressed the political situation. At the same time, however, Egyptians were gaining positions within the industry as investors and technicians. Some film companies and studios were established by Egyptians. One of the first major companies, Misr Company for Acting and Cinema, was founded in 1927 by Misr Bank; Lama Studio was established in 1936; Wahbi Studio in 1939, and so forth. However, these companies maintained the European colonial orientation, creating a "neo-colonial" cinema that paralleled the neo-colonial political situation. They produced familiar genre films, safe in terms of censorship and commercial prospects, especially the sentimental melodramas. The critic Galal El-Sharkawi summarized the plots and ethos of such films as follows:

> Love always takes pride of place, spiced with base seduction, rape, adultery, prison, murder, suicide and madness, with a background of brooding tragedy for the sympathetic victim. If we consider the 1945–46 season as an example, we find in the 23 melodramas, out of a total of 52 films: 9 girls seduced, 2 rapes, 3 suicides, 2 attempted suicides, 2 cases of madness.[3]

Arabic songs and dances were often introduced into such melodramas. In another popular form, the comedy revues, stereotypical characters frequently fell into farcical misunderstandings that sent the characters and the plot into cabarets and music halls—a pretext for the inclusion of popular songs and dances, tailored to the talents of singing stars such as Abdel Wahab, Umm Kulthum, Farid al-Atrash, Layla Murad, Nadra, Munira al-Mahdiya and others.

One exception was Kamal Selim's *al-'Azima* (*Determination,* 1939–40), which was the first realist Egyptian film to influence the later post-revolutionary filmmakers. The hero, Muhammad, is a young Egyptian who rebels against the goals of a traditional education, which encouraged careers in government service. He decides to build his own business during a period when business was dominated by foreigners. Life in the streets is presented realistically and contemporary Egyptian social problems form the source of the action. The film implicitly expresses the urban bourgeoisie's discontent with foreign intervention as well as their will to establish their independence by assuming control of trade and industry.

Egyptian censorship, which was officially instituted by the Palace and by the British Embassy in 1914 and administered by the Ministry of the Interior, heavily favored the production of traditional genre films. It forced directors to abstain from criticizing foreigners, government officials, and religious institutions. It went so far as to forbid cinematic presentation of conflicts between peasants and landowners, references to nationalist politics, and favorable portrayals of nationalist or socialist ideas either in the past or in the present. *Lashin,* made in 1938–39, offers a dramatic example of the severe code. Produced by Studio Misr, with a relatively high budget of £20,000 sterling, as a patriotic historical picture,[4] the film was suppressed because it portrayed an oppressive medieval tyrant. Censorship would not tolerate criticism of state authority or of monarchical government even at a distance of many centuries because of implicit analogies between past tyranny and the contemporary regime. Another case of censorship involved Bahiga Hafiz's *Layla Bint al-Sahra'* (*Layla, Daughter of the Desert,* 1937). The film, which dealt with the successful Arab struggle against the Persians and their brutal anti-Arab ruler, Kisra, was banned despite its big-budget production values. Thus government censors, well aware of the dangers of controversial political issues, hampered the development of an independent nationalist cinema. The tendency of profit-oriented producers was to avoid contemporary subjects close to everyday Egyptian experience precisely because they ran a greater risk of censorship.

Along with Egypt's political struggle toward complete independence came clashes over culture, often summed up as tradition-versus-modernity. While the intellectuals of Cairo's al-Azhar University, a prestigious center of Islamic thought, reacted with hostility toward the new Western ideas introduced by Egyptian writers and thinkers, Egyptians were also fascinated by European fashions and trends. Even more serious questions arose over the status of women, polygamy, and divorce. The urban bourgeoisie was selectively adopting Western values; the cinema became a venue for such desires. The cinema, besides being a means of class expression, shaped the general consciousness of the urban population.[5] With the outbreak of World War II the already strong profit orientation of Egyptian cinema was exacerbated by the *nouveaux riches* who became powerful as a result of their service to the Allies. The paradoxical situation of the colonized bourgeoisie made their aspirations somewhat schizophrenic. They resented Western domination yet also emulated Western lifestyles, technology, and power. The two major historical responses to the colonial dilemma—assimilation or revolution—were thrust upon Egyptians. But before visibly engaging in "the stage of revolution," of stripping the colonizer of his power, the urban bourgeoisie was trying to transcend the colonial situation through assimilation, by molding themselves in the colonizer's image:

> The first ambition of the colonized is to become equal to the splendid model of the colonizer who suffers from none of his deficiencies, has all rights, enjoys every possession and benefits from every prestige and to resemble him to the point of disappearing into him.[6]

In line with various anticolonial intellectuals, Gamal Abdel Nasser addressed these widespread feelings of inferiority in his book *The Philosophy of the Revolution*.[7]

The cinema at times gave indirect expression to this "inferiority complex." The traditional genres, though basically maintaining and respecting the Muslim faith, catered to the public demand for more up-to-date styles in architecture, clothes, furniture, and music. The presentation of sophisticated characters and upper-class glamor indirectly exalted European manners and implicitly belittled Arab ways. A sprinkling of casual French phrases, for example, was thought to lend an elegant air to conversation. These attitudes are not surprising when we remember that French was spoken at court and among the elite generally while Arabic tended to be reserved for insults.

The predilection for incorporating Western music, song, and dance into Egyptian films, meanwhile, reflected a Western orientation. It is important to examine this genre since singing and dancing have held a special place in Arab cinema generally and in Egyptian cinema in particular. Not a single film season passed without several musical productions and, indeed, statistics point to a predominance of musical films in certain periods. The first Egyptian talkie was a musical, *Unshudat al-Fu'ad* (*The Song of the Heart*, 1932), directed by the Italian Mario Volpi, for which the producers, the Behna Brothers, gathered a group of Egyptian stars led by the celebrated singer, Nadra.

A close examination of the structure of the music in the musical genre reveals that the Westernization had occurred even in well-established Egyptian-Arab art forms such as music. In addition to the obvious difference in vocal style between Arab and Western music, Arab music also has more tonal scales than Western music. Efforts were made by various musicians to turn popular melodies into "modern forms" influenced by European music. A striking example of this influence on Egyptian cinema is the case of the composer-singer Muhammad Abdel Wahab. In his first film, *al-Wardat al-Bayda'* (*The White Rose*, 1933–34), directed by Muhammad Karim, he introduced the new style in the art of composition. As the critic Salah Ezzedine explains, in these films the duration of each song was cut as much as three quarters without thereby losing any of its appeal. Abdel Wahab superimposed the fast rhythm of European dance music on the quartertone base of Arab music. He also used a diversity of musical instruments, with each film emphasizing a "new" instrument. Farid al-Atrash also used Western instruments, particularly the piano. The *takht*, the traditional regional ensemble (a small group of musicians, each one playing a different instrument), was seldom displayed in the films. Rather, one finds Western scoring and instrumentation with a rapid beat and light, shorter songs. Initially introduced as intermittent attractions in films, songs and dances came to form an integral part of the action. Along with belly dancing, the films introduced Western-inflected theatrical dancing. Samia Gamal, who accompanied Farid al-Atrash's songs, for example, tended to move toward a more figurative Western form.

Pre-revolutionary "feelings of inferiority," meanwhile, were present in other ways. Rather than inviting Egyptian authors to produce original scenarios, or adapting Egyptian literature to the screen, producers found an easier, and cheaper method: adaptations of Western texts, sometimes amounting to plagiarism. Western films or novels were adapted to local conditions without acknowledgement. Seif al-Din Shawkat, a Hungarian-Turkish director who settled in Egypt, was notorious for using this method. Films, plays, or novels such as *Waterloo Bridge, Camilla, Pygmalion, Les Misérables* and others appeared on Egyptian screens, usually under new titles: *Waterloo Bridge* became *Dayman fi Qalbi* (*Always in My Heart*, 1945), *Pygmalion* became *Ba'yait al-Tufah* (*The Apple Vendor*). Sometimes the same source was an inspiration for different productions, as in the case of *Camille*, which was produced four times with different casts: *Layla* with Layla Murad, *'Ahd al-Hawa* (*The Period of Love*) with Miriam Fakhr al-Din, *Sallim 'ala al-Habayib* (*Greetings to the Lovers*) with Sabah, and *'Ashq al-Ruh* (*Love of the Soul*) with Nagla Fathi. The adaptations of this period indicate not only the commercial orientation of Egyptian cinema, but also its general reluctance to use rich native sources whether from myth, theater, or literature. One of the few exceptions was the 1930 Muhammad Karim's adaptation to the screen of Muhammad Hussayn Haykal's novel, *Zaynab*. Considered the first modern Egyptian novel, *Zaynab*, which was published in 1913, deals with the psychological conflicts of a landowner torn between his love for the poor village girl, Zaynab, and his ambition to marry the daughter of a rich bourgeois family.

It was largely after the revolution that cinema turned more frequently to native sources and engaged well-known Egyptian authors as screenwriters. Political dependency, for anti-colonial critics, paralleled a "mental dependency" on a Western culture little concerned with the colonized's "national identity" on the screen; for a politically disorientated cinema there was no impetus to adapt the more committed pre-revolutionary literature. In addition, the censors considered literature less dangerous, no surprise in a country where illiteracy reached 75 percent. One celebrated example is Tawfiq al-Hakim's *'Awdat al-Ruh* (*The Soul Regained*), published in 1933. The novel, adapted for the screen by Abu-Seif only in 1969, portrayed Egyptian national identity as humiliated by British domination and suggested that it could be redeemed through the struggle of all classes against the colonialists. The pre-revolutionary cinema, meanwhile, smothered by melodramas and musicals, could offer no similar call to arms. The beginning of a revival had to await the political action of the Free Officers movement.

The revolution of 1952 which established a new era in Egypt forms part of the post-World War II decolonization of the Third World: in Indochina, France was defeated at Dien Bien Phu in 1954; the same year witnessed the beginning of the Algerian war for independence. In Iraq, the revolution of 1958 overthrew the Hashemite dynasty set up by the British. Indeed, as Fanon pointed out:

> International events, the collapse of whole sections of colonial empires and the contradictions inherent in the colonial system strengthen and uphold the native's combativity while promoting and giving support to national consciousness.[8]

The ideology of the Egyptian revolution, like that of other nationalist revolutions in the Third World, crystallized around the concept of anticolonialism. The movement's leaders, a relatively small class of petit-bourgeois nationalists, were united in their determination to win genuine political independence, modernize the economy,[9] and achieve a more equitable distribution of wealth. Agrarian reforms were undertaken, limiting agricultural landholding to 200 acres, and over one million acres were appropriated from the rich and distributed among peasant landowners. The Suez Canal and foreign property were nationalized and the educational system was made relatively more democratic.

Nasser's regime marked a turning away from Western domination and a resurgence of national Arab culture. It was this reaction against the West that shaped the cultural, social, and political discourse of Nasser's regime. The regime rejected Western culture, including Marxism, arguing that Arab nationalism could not accommodate international or atheist ideology. The exaltation of traditional cultural values, Islam, and nationalism, became the means of restoring dignity and power to Egypt. The religious dimension had already formed part of earlier definitions of "Egyptian personality." The writers Taha Hussein and Tawfiq al-Hakim defined Egypt as the synthesis of the pharaonic past, Arabic language, and Islamic religion, while the writer Mohamed Hassanein Heikal emphasized the pan-Islamic notion of "divine unity." This process of cultural rediscovery was common in countries subjected to colonial deculturization and trying to rebuild a national identity. Such transformations were illustrated in the words of Fanon:

> The passionate search for a national culture which existed before the colonial era finds its legitimate reason in the anxiety shared by native intellectuals to shrink away from that Western culture in which they all

risk being swamped. Because they realize they are in danger of losing their lives and thus becoming lost to their people, these men, hotheaded and with anger in their hearts, relentlessly determine to renew contact once more with the oldest and most precolonial springs of life of their people.[10]

Although the revolution did not produce the hoped for complete transformation, it did energize cultural activity in Egypt. Cinema became part of the initial stages of nation-building, whose ideology criticized colonial attitudes. The nationalist ideology, as conveyed by the cinema, aimed to provide the people with an interpretation of reality that claimed to transform them from traditional subjects to active citizens. Therefore, the cinema, as a vehicle of the new ideology, played the role of producing nationalist solidarity and identity.

Considering the cinema as an influential means of propagating culture and national ideas among the people, the state took important measures to reorganize the industry. The cinema was nationalized and the state had nearly complete control over the different branches of the film industry, which previously had been in private hands. Although censorship continued under Nasser's regime, its *raison d'être* was quite different. On the one hand, the regime encouraged directly political as well as historical films, on the other, it exercised a double standard since the present regime was presumed exempt from criticism. Local production had to submit scripts for approval by the Censorship Department. The censorship affected foreign productions and especially those with political implications. The Ministry of the Interior censored imported pictures with subversive ideas (such as communism), films ridiculing Muslim religion and Arab prestige, films showing Afro-Asian people as inferior, and films about Israel or Jews. And films using pro-Zionist stars and technicians such as Elizabeth Taylor, Danny Kaye, Otto Preminger, and Paul Newman, were banned.

The state established the Supreme Council for the Protection of Arts and Letters, and later in 1957 the Organization of Consolidation of Cinema was set up by the Ministry of National and Cultural Guidance, with an annual budget of Egyptian £1,500,000. Its purpose was to raise artistic and technical standards and strengthen the national film industry by encouraging the presentation of Egyptian films inside Egypt and opening new markets for distribution outside Egypt (apart from the other Arab countries). It offered investment capital and secured bank guarantees for producers, built more movie theatres throughout the country, and participated in co-productions to promote distribution. Some examples of the co-productions are *Hadath fil-Qahira* (*It Happened in Cairo*), a Hungarian-Egyptian co-production, and *'Ala Shati' al-Nil* (*On the Nile Bank*), a Japanese-Egyptian co-production. Annual awards or prizes were given for the best direction, production, and so forth. In addition, taxes were imposed on imported films in order to raise funds for native production, strengthen the distribution network, and procure the latest technology. A protectionist system of quotas was established, requiring that one week out of four be reserved for the projection of Egyptian films. These measures, together with the increase in the national production, led to a drop in imports from 431 films in 1955 to 294 in 1958. In 1959 the government established the Higher Institute of Cinema, whose purpose was to educate a new generation of filmmakers and technicians. In 1963 the Egyptian General Organization, which was a fusion of the cinema organization with that of Radio and TV, established its control over the major studios of the past, which were now state owned: Misr, Galal, Arabic, and Nahhas. The public sector in cinema, which was in fact an extension of the state control over the nationalized industry, trained in its institutions scriptwriters and offered a chance to filmmakers and actors to study abroad.

The limits of the Nasser regime, however, were soon reflected in the cinema. The revolution of 1952 was not a revolution by the people, but that of an elite acting in the name of the people. The revolution did not generate a radical political and social change through genuine redistribution of wealth or through the transfer of power from one order or class to another. Therefore, as pointed out by the Egyptian critic Qussai Samak, the cinema's public sector was not created in response to a shared desire of the people and the leadership to radically transform the dominant culture and change the state of the art and industry. It was merely a continuation of the process of bureaucratically reshaping the state sectors along the lines of what was described as "Arab socialism" in the "character of National Action." As occurred with the Egyptian state as a whole, private sector concepts continued to prevail in the cinema's public sector, although under a new organization. In other words, within the framework of the Egyptian General Organization of Cinema, the old struggle continued between the veteran producers and directors who gained their power from connections and experience in the industry, on the one hand, and the young generation struggling to produce a different kind of cinema on the other.

Despite the faults of the public sector, it played an important role in supporting the new generation, which had not had the chance to demonstrate its abilities in the pre-revolutionary period. The new filmmakers trained in the public sector were given the opportunity to work in the General Organization of Cinema, and indeed some of the new Egyptian films appeared in the late 1960s under the auspices of the public sector, such as Chahine's *al-Ard* (*The Land*), Abu Seif's *al-Qahira-Thalathin* (*Cairo 30*), Henri Barakat's *al-Haram* (*The Sin*), Hussein Kamal's *al-Bustagi* (*The Postman*), and Shadi Abd-al-Salam's *al-Mumya'* (*The Mummy—The Night of Counting the Years*).

The revolution immediately and directly influenced the themes of Egyptian films. Veterans like Badrakhan, for example, incorporated the new nationalist gospel into their films. The films of the younger filmmakers, besides criticizing the former regime, drew inspiration from contemporary events such as the Palestine War of 1948, the revolution of 1952, the nationalization of the Suez Canal and the Suez War in 1956, and the Algerian struggle for independence. (The Egyptian movement, in fact, anticipated a similar process in independent Algeria with the rise of Cinema Moudjahid, which was concerned mainly with films depicting the recent past.) The political subject-matter also generated new genres and styles. Screen criticism of the former pre-revolutionary regime emphasized social injustice, portraying the struggle of peasants exploited by landowners against the monopoly of land and markets, as in Chahine's neorealist *Sira' fil-Wadi* (*A Struggle in the Valley,* 1953), or in Ahmed Dia'-al-Din's *Ardunna al-Khadra'* (*Our Green Land,* 1956), which focuses on a love story between a peasant and his wife, recounting their struggle to save enough money to buy their land only to find that no one will sell.

This criticism of the old regime inevitably went hand in hand with praise of the new revolutionary regime, for example in Ahmad Badrakhan's *Allahu Ma'ana* (*God with Us,* 1954–55), written by the journalist and writer Ihsan Abd al-Quddus, which celebrates the Egyptian revolution and chronicles the Egyptian role in the Palestine War of 1948. The film closes on a critical note, pointing to the plight of the soldiers betrayed at the front by poor equipment and bad leadership. Izz al-Din Zulfiqar's *Rudda Qalbi* (*Give Me My Heart Back,* 1957) depicts the hard life of the Egyptian peasant before the revolution and the importance of that revolution in bringing reform, distributing land, granting opportunity and justice to the masses.

There was also an increase in patriotic anticolonial films celebrating the transformation of the people from objects of history into subjects, participating actively in history. Some examples are Husain Sidqy's *Yasqut al-Isti'mar* (*Down with Imperialism,* 1953), Henri Barakat's *Fi Baytuna Rajul* (*A Man in our House,* 1961), and Ibrahim Hilmy's *Kilo Tis'a wa-Tis'in* (*Kilometer 99,* 1955). Other films celebrated the Palestine War: Niazi Mustafa's *Samara Sina'* (*The Dark Girl of the Sinai,* 1958) and Kamal El-Sheikh's *Ard al-Salam* (*Land of Peace,* 1955). Later films depicted the Suez War of 1956, such as Niazi Mustafa's *Sajin Abu Za'bal* (*Abu Za'bal Prisoner,* 1956), Izz al-Din Zulfiqar's *Port Said* (1957) and Hasan al-Imam's *Hubb min Nar* (*Fiery Love,* 1957).

Some films presented general Arab concerns reflecting the ideology of Arab unity. Such films, promoting Arab solidarity, and portraying struggles outside Egypt, derived from Nasser's position as the symbol of radical pan-Arab nationalism and its aspiration to Arab unity. In the Third World,

Nasser had established himself as a major leader deeply committed to the anticolonial struggle, especially throughout the Arab countries and in Africa. This commitment is reflected in the portrayal of the Algerian struggle for independence in Chahine's *Jamila the Algerian* of 1958, a film that thematically anticipates Pontecorvo's *Battle of Algiers* (1966). The film concerns an Algerian girl commando, Jamila, who was tortured by the French. Chahine's long sequences of torture, suffering, and resistance became a symbol for Arab solidarity with the courageous Algerian freedom fighters.

As in other Third World countries, the desire for liberation was not simply a question of political independence but also of reasserting cultural traditions. In the face of colonial hegemony, these new attitudes towards the past, together with active and concrete involvement in the present and planning for the future, became a way of avoiding being condemned to what Memmi called the colonized's loss of memory:

> As long as he [the colonized] tolerates colonization, the only possible alternatives for the colonized are assimilation or petrification. Assimilation being refused him ... nothing is left for him but to live isolated from his age. He is driven back by colonization and, to a certain extent, lives with that situation. Planning and building his future are forbidden. He must therefore limit himself to the present, and even that present is cut off and abstract. We should add that he draws less and less from his past. The colonizer never even recognized that he had one ... the colonized seems condemned to lose his memory.[11]

Against this backdrop, one can understand the emergence of historical and religious films that celebrated the end of the "negative myth" of the colonized through reinforcement of Egyptian tradition and culture. Among the first religious films were *Bilal, Mu'azzin al-Rasul* (*Bilal, the Prophet's Mu'azzin*, 1952–53) by Ahmad al-Tukhi, and Chahine's *al-Nasir Salah al-Din* (1963), depicting Saladin as the determined leader of Muslim armies fighting against the invading crusaders. He restored Jerusalem to Islam, weakening the European position in the Near East, and improved Egypt's political and economic situation. By praising past Arab exploits, the film implicitly suggested that the Arab relationship with the European colonizers was unique in that the Arab-Muslim world had dominated certain regions of Europe, such as Iberia, and had enjoyed military victories over the West.

At the same time, the revolution also influenced artists to go beyond traditional forms. One of the noticeable tendencies was the rise of realism, reflecting a desire to explore the concrete problems of the Egyptian people. There were precedents in Egyptian literature for this kind of realism in the 1930s, when writers Taha Hussein and Tawfiq al-Hakim strengthened realism through a more colloquial Arabic; later, beginning in the 1940s, Naguib Mahfouz contributed to a realistic literature rooted in the daily experience of the Egyptian people and helped create a popular idiom based on everyday life. In the cinema, a similar move to realism occurred after 1952. Nonetheless, most of the films produced in the first decade of the revolution were marked by political naiveté, illusionism, and revolutionary romanticism, although some did explore the new alternatives created by the revolution. This realist trend in the cinema is demonstrated especially in the films of Salah Abu-Seif, who had assisted Kamal Selim in al-'Azima (Determination) as well as Youssef Chahine.

Like similar movements in Third World cinema, such as Brazil's Cinema Novo and India's New Cinema, Egyptian post-revolutionary cinema was partially inflected by Italian neorealism. The filmic portrayals of social themes drawn from Egyptian life were usually shot on location, unlike the studio-shot offerings of pre-revolutionary cinema. Songs and dances were relegated to the musicals and the traditional tendency toward melodrama was minimized. Abu-Seif's films focused on urban problems such as sexual oppression and capitalist exploitation. In his film al-Usta Hasan (Foreman Hassan, 1952), the hero, Hassan, initially rejects the alley where he grew up; his experiences in the outside world, however, convince him that he cannot abandon his own. Shot in an alley in a poverty-stricken district of Cairo, the film portrays the routine habits of the people who lived there, their speech, their manners, and their gestures. Chahine similarly showed deep concern for the ambient reality of the everyday Egyptian. His Bab a1-Hadid (Cairo Main Station, literally: Iron Gate, 1958), filmed in Cairo's railway station known as the Iron Gate, narrates the oppression and sexual frustration of a crippled newspaper vendor, Qinawi, portrayed within the framework of the harsh realities of life in the station where the workers must struggle for their livelihood and their rights.

After the revolution, more Egyptian novels were adapted to the screen and more Egyptian writers, such as Naguib Mahfouz, worked as screenwriters. Most of these adaptations relied too heavily on the literary text and created what became known as the "literary mentality of the Egyptian cinema." Hasan al-Imam's adaptation of Mahfouz's Cairo Trilogy (Thulathi-yyat al-Qahira) was one of the most notable cases in this post-revolutionary adaptation trend. At the same time, however, such adaptations indicated a new will to search for Egypt's "authentic sources" for national creativity rather than the earlier preference for Western formulae.

Changes also occurred within traditional genres such as the musical. After 1952, music became more patriotic and combative. Traditional folklore became a major source of inspiration in the process of defining the "authentic" nation. Most compositional techniques sought their inspiration in regional songs and dances. A celebrated singer-actor of this new era was Abdel Halim Hafez who, with Muhammad al-Mugi and Kamal al-Tawil as composers and Mursi Gamil 'Aziz and Salah Jahin as lyric writers, shaped this new mode of expression in the musical. The films in which Abdel Halim Hafez participated expressed the local traditions in "authentically Egyptian" songs, seen as incorporating little in the way of modernized forms.

In conclusion, the reorganization of the industry and the transformations in the films themselves contributed to the emergence of a distinctively national film culture. As a result of the 1952 revolution, the transition towards a decolonized cinema went hand in hand with the political transition. In the wake of political independence, the substantial investment in "the nation" promoted its "cultural renewal." The foundation of a dynamic and vibrant culture, in this sense, came to illustrate the intimate connection between culture and politics highlighted by Fanon in *The Wretched of the Earth:*

> The condition for its existence is therefore national liberation and the renaissance of the state …. A non-existent culture can hardly be expected to have bearing on reality, or to influence reality. The first necessity is the reestablishment of the nation in order to give life to national culture in the strictly biological sense of the phrase.[12]

17

Gender in Hollywood's Orient

From its very beginning, Western cinema has been fascinated with the mystique of the Orient. Whether in the form of pseudo-Egyptian movie palaces, Biblical spectaculars, or the fondness for "Oriental" settings, Western cinema has returned time and again to the scene of the Orient.[1] Generally these films superimposed the visual traces of civilizations as diverse as Arab, Persian, Chinese, and Indian into a single portrayal of the exotic Orient, treating cultural plurality as if it were a monolith. The Arabic language, in most of these films, exists as an indecipherable murmur, while the "real" language is European: the French of Jean Gabin in *Pepe le Moko* or the English of Bogart and Bergman in *Casablanca*.[2]

   Although Hollywood's view of the Orient has been discussed in terms of "the Arab image,"[3] there has been little discussion concerning the intersection of imperial and gender discourses. Hollywood's view of the Orient is not simply symptomatic of colonialist imagination but also a product of the (Western) male gaze. Sexual difference has been a key component in the construction of the East as Other and the West as ideal ego.

Rescue Fantasy

Consider the Western rescue fantasy, which metaphorically renders the Orient as a female saved from her own destructiveness, while also projecting a narrative of the rescue of Arab and Western women from Arab men.[4] Such an indirect apologia for colonial domination also carries religious overtones of the inferiority of a polygamous Islamic world to the Christian world as encapsulated by the monogamous couple. The contrast between Oriental "backwardness" and "irrationality," on the one hand, and Occidental "modernity" and "rationality" on the other, along with the hierarchy of identification with Western versus Arab perspective and characters, as well as the image of the menacing figure of the Arab assassin and rapist—all these structuring binarisms and tropes, taken together, subliminally enlist

Published in *Middle East Report* (Middle East Research and Information Project), no. 162 (Jan./Feb. 1990).

spectators for the West's "civilizing mission." All function as part of a cultural and geographical reductionism whose subtext is a rationale for the subordination of the East.

Gender and sexuality are significant in colonial discourse. The recurrent figure of the veiled woman in films such as *Thief in Damascus* (1952) and *Ishtar* (1987) can be seen as a metaphor for the mystery of the Orient itself, which requires a process of Western unveiling for comprehension. Veiled women in Orientalist films, paintings, and photographs ironically expose more flesh than they conceal. This process of exposing the female Other, of denuding her literally, comes to allegorize the power of Western man to possess her. She, as a metaphor for her land, becomes available for Western penetration and domination. While the Arab is associated with images of underdevelopment and backwardness (the visual motif of the desert serves as essential decor of Arab history), the colonizer, whether Lawrence of Arabia or Indiana Jones, appears as an active, productive, and creative pioneer, a masculine redeemer who conquers the feminine wilderness.

In these films, the writer-soldier T. E. Lawrence or the scientist-archaeologist Dr. Jones rescues the Orient from its own obscurantism. Colonized people, like women, here require the guidance and protection of the colonial patriarchal figure. The Madonna/whore dichotomy, applied within a colonial context, distinguishes submissive "natives" who are "warm," "giving," "noble savages" from the rebellious "barbarians" dangerous to civilization and themselves, yesterday's "assassins" and today's "terrorists." The Manichean allegory of Hollywood's cinematic Orient, in other words, does not simply depict all Arabs as "bad." Rather, it divides them according to a metaphysical clash of good and evil, depending on their historical positioning vis-à-vis the West. The threatening political assertiveness of the colonized people provokes the discourse of the dangerous, instinctual Third-World, "non-civilized" elements to be eliminated by the end of the film.

Spectatorial Initiation

Orientalist films claim to initiate the Western spectator into Arab society. Western historiography narrates European heroic penetration into the Third World through the figure of the "discoverer." The spectator, identified with the gaze of the West (whether embodied by a Western character or by a Western actor masquerading as an Oriental), comes to master, as it were, and in a remarkably telescoped period of time, the codes of a foreign culture shown as simple, stable, unselfconscious, and susceptible to facile apprehension. Any possibility of dialogue and of a dialectical representation of the East/West relation is excluded from the outset. The Orient, rendered as devoid of any active historical or narrative role, becomes—in the tradition of the distancing male regard toward women—the object of spectacle for the Western voyeuristic gaze.

In most Western films about the Orient, we accompany, quite literally, the perspective of the "discoverer"—and it is precisely this point of view that defines his historical position. A simple shift in perspective to that of the "natives" would suggest the intrusive nature of the "discovery." In such films as *Lawrence of Arabia* and *Raiders of the Lost Ark*, the camera relays the hero's dynamic movement across a passive, static space, gradually stripping the land of its enigma, as the spectator wins visual access to Oriental treasures through the eyes of the discoverer-protagonist.

In *Raiders of the Lost Ark*, the full significance of ancient archaeological objects is presumed to be understood only by the Western scientists, relegating Egyptians to the role of ignorant Arabs who happen to be sitting on a land full of historical treasures—much as they happen to "sit" on oil. The origins of archaeology as a discipline are inextricably linked to imperial expansionism. Yet Indiana Jones reproduces the colonial vision in which Western "knowledge" of ancient civilizations "rescues" the past from oblivion. This masculine rescue legitimizes denuding Egyptians of their heritage and confining it within Western metropolitan museums. *Raiders of the Lost Ark* symptomatically assumes a disjuncture between contemporary and ancient Egypt, since the space between the present and the past can "only" be bridged by the scientist, and certainly not by the ignorant Arab crowds that merely occupy the background of the film. The film, furthermore, is set in the mid-1930s, when most of the world was still under colonial power. The colonial presence in Egypt is presented as natural. The American hero liberates the ancient Hebrew ark from illegal Egyptian possession, and also from immoral Nazi control, allegorically reinforcing the American and Israeli equation of evil Nazis and their Arab cohorts.

Female Colonial Gaze

Western women characters became the delegates of the White male perspective in these films, being granted a more powerful gaze in relation not only to non-White women but also to non-White men. *Raiders* and *Sahara* (1983), for example, suggest a sexual-racial hierarchy in which the American woman is privileged cinematically and narratively over Arab male characters. In *The Sheik* (1921), which revolves around a young English-woman kidnapped by a sheikh (Rudolph Valentino) and brought to his desert camp where he holds her captive and sexually harasses her, the spectator is first introduced to the Arab world as the place of the barbarous ritual of the marriage market. At the same time, the Western woman character, largely the passive object of male gaze in Hollywood cinema, is granted in the East an active colonial gaze, insofar as she represents Western civilization. She becomes the civilizing "center" of the film.

The chromatic sexual hierarchy in these films, moreover, reflects Western racial views whereby White women/men occupy the center of the narrative. The White woman is desired by the male protagonists and antagonists. Darker women, marginalized within the narrative, appear largely as sexually hungry subalterns. While the White woman has to be lured, made captive, and virtually raped to awaken her hidden desire, the Arab/Black women are controlled by their libido. Images of Black/Arab women in "heat" versus "frigid" White women indirectly highlight the menacing figure of the Black/Arab rapist, implying the impossibility of a White rapist—and therefore mythically eliding the history of subordination of Third-World women.

Pretext for Passion

Hollywood's Orient became in some ways a pretext for eroticized images, especially from 1934 through the mid-1950s when the restrictive production code forbade depicting "scenes of passion" in all but the most puerile terms, and required that the sanctity of the institution of marriage be maintained at all times. Miscegenation, nudity, sexually suggestive dances or costumes, "excessive and lustful kissing," were prohibited; illicit sex, seduction, or rape could only be suggested, and then only if absolutely essential to the plot and if severely punished at the end.[5]

The image of the harem allowed the colonial imaginary to play out its own fantasies of sexual domination. An Oriental setting provided Hollywood filmmakers with a narrative license for exposing flesh without risking censorship; they could display the bare skin of Valentino and Douglas Fairbanks as well as that of scores of women, from Marlene Dietrich dancing with her body painted gold to Dolores Grey swaying her hips, always with the pretext of "realism." The display of rape in a "natural" despotic context continues to the present—as in Menahem Golan's *Sahara*. The Orient, much like Latin America and Africa, thus became the locus of eroticism for a puritanical society and a film industry hemmed in by a moralistic code.

The outlet for Western male heroic desire is clearly seen in *Harum Scarum* (1965), a reflexive film featuring a carnival-like Orient reminiscent of Las Vegas entertainment, itself located in the burning sands of the Nevada desert, and offering harem-like nightclubs. The film opens with Elvis Presley—attired in "Oriental" head wrap and vest—leaping off his horse to overcome two evil Arabs and free a captive woman. The triumphant rescuer sings:

I'm gonna go where desert sun is;
where the fun is;
go where the harem girls dance;
go where there's love and romance—
out on the burning sands,
in some caravan.
I'll find adventure where I can.
To say the least, go East, young man.
You'll feel like the Sheik,
so rich and grand,
with dancing girls at your command.
When paradise starts calling
into some tent I'm crawling.
I'll make love the way I plan.
Go East –
and drink and feast –
go East, young man.

The images of harems offer an "open sesame" to an unknown, alluring world whose forbidden codes are presumably desired by the instinctual primitive inhabiting all men.

The Arab man in these films plays the id to the Western man's superego. In *The Sheik*, Valentino embodies the id as long as he is known to the spectator only as Arab, but when it is revealed that he is the son of Europeans, he is transformed into a superego figure who nobly risks his life to rescue the English woman from "real" Arab rapists. The English woman, for her part,

Figure 37   Elvis Presley in Gene Nelson's
Harum Scarum, 1965

overcomes her sexual repression only in the desert, after being sexually provoked repeatedly by the Sheik. Valentino the "Latin lover" is here projected into another "exotic" space where he can act out sexual fantasies that would have been unthinkable in a contemporaneous American or European setting. *The Sheik* begins in the city—where European civilization has already "tamed" the East—but the real dramatic conflicts take place in the desert, where women are defenseless, playing off the masculine fantasy of complete control over the Western woman without any intervening code of morality.

Gender Disciplining

Similarly, in the more recent reworking of *The Sheik* and *Son of the Sheik* in *Sahara*, the male rescue fantasy and the punishment of female rebellion undergird the film. The central figure, Dale (Brooke Shields) is the feisty, race-car-driving only daughter of a 1920s car manufacturer, presented as reckless, daring, and assertive for entering the male domain of the Oriental desert and for entering the "men only" race. (She also literally disguises herself as a man, and adopts his profession and his mastery of the desert land through technology.[6]) Captured by desert tribesmen, she becomes a commodity fought over within the tribe and between tribes (the camera's fetishization of her body is the ironic reminder of the Western projection of stars' bodies as commodity). Scenes of Shields wrestling with one of her capturers invites the Western spectator not only to a national rescue operation but also to an orgiastic space. At the end, the courageous winner of the race decides on her own to return to the noble light-skinned sheik who had rescued her at the risk of his life. The woman, who could have won independence, still prefers the ancient ways of gender hierarchies.

Sahara, like earlier Orientalist films, must also be seen in the context of the threat to institutionalized power presented by the women's suffrage movements and the nascent feminist struggle. Edith Hull, the author of the novel *The Sheik* on which the film is based, expressed the view that "there can be only one head in a house. Despite modern desire for equality of sexes, I still believe that physically and morally it is better that the head should be the man."[7] The plot of her novel and of George Melfrod's film is also a Western female projection of desire for an exotic lover, for a romantic, sensual, passionate, but non-lethal play with *liebestod*, a release of the id for the bored Occidental woman.

The female spectator, the fan of Valentino, Fairbanks, or Presley, is assumed to secretly desire to be a lucky harem girl. The rescue fantasy, when literalized through rescuing a woman from a lascivious Arab, has to be seen not only as an allegory of saving the Orient from its libidinal, instinctual destructiveness, but also as a didactic allegory addressed to women at home, insinuating the dangerous nature of the uncivilized Arab man and by implication exalting the freedom Western women presumably enjoy. In *The Sheik* and *Sahara*, the woman directly rebels against the civilized tradition of marriage at the beginning of the film, calling it "captivity." The telos of her desert Odyssey is the disciplining of her fantasies of liberation and renewed appreciation for the traditional sexual order.

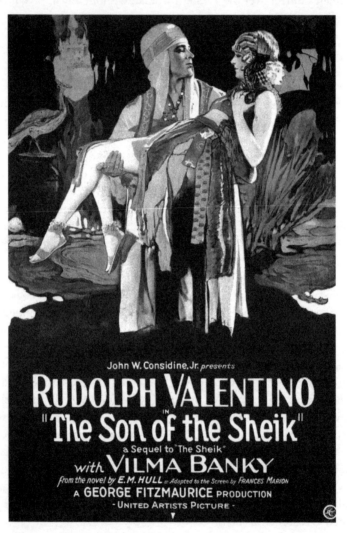

Figure 38   Poster for George Fitzmaurice's *The Son of the Sheik*, 1926

18

The Media's War

From the very inception of the Gulf Crisis, the dominant U.S. media failed to fulfill the role of independent journalism. Instead, they acted as public relations for the State Department, assimilating the language, terminology, and the assumptions of the administration, thereby undermining any critical perspectives upon the conduct of the war. Any attempt to discuss the media's coverage of the Gulf War must examine some of the ways in which it structured identification with the Pentagon's agenda, and the interests of an international elite.

Those of us who have been dealing with cultural theory and textuality know that readers or spectators find it difficult to "read against the grain" if they lack any alternative information, history, and contextualization. This is especially true since the only contextualization was provided by right-wing "experts." For example, the spectrum of "experts" interviewed on *Nightline* to discuss the Iraqi missile attacks ranged from the mainstream right to the extreme right, including: Israeli official Benjamin Netanyahu; former U.S. Secretary of State Henry Kissinger; columnist George Will; Democrat Stephen Solarz; military analyst Edward Luttwak and so forth. Edward Said, Noam Chomsky, and the political and media analysts working for alternative media organizations such as Fair and WBAI obviously did not qualify as "invitable" experts.

The media networks blatantly promote the goals of the war. Several wars were evoked in connection with the war in the Gulf, particularly Vietnam, which was presented as the negative war. The right-wing hermeneutic reading of Vietnam was that now we should fight without "one hand tied behind our back," and its media corollary was that the camera must be kept away from body bags, that reporters must be controlled, that censorship is necessary for victory. After the "victory," Vietnam was cited even more explicitly as a disease that had been overcome. Dov Zakheim attacked the Left in his article "Is the Vietnam Syndrome Dead? Happily, It's Buried

Published in *Social Text*, no. 28 (Spring 1991). A lecture delivered at a plenary session dedicated to the Gulf War, The Socialist Scholars Conference, New York, Borough of Manhattan Community College, City University of New York April, 1991.

in the Gulf."[1] In a strange generational projection, he identified with the right-leaning youth of the Reagan–Bush era to attack those 1960s activists whose "salad days" in the anti-war movement are over, simply because, according to him, the anti-war movement no longer exists.

In this war we saw American pilots penetrate the Iraqi airspace, while their airplanes ejaculated their missiles over the unresisting land. By proving its mastery of air, sea, and land in Iraq, America imagines itself cured of its trauma of (destructive) impotence whose origin lay in another Third-World country—Vietnam. But the healthy war, or the positive war paradigm—World War II—was cited more often, reflecting a deep nostalgia for the narrative of a positive war, a war more easily constructed by the dualism of good versus evil. This paradigm was used to structure an identification with "us" as opposed to "them," eliding all other narratives.

The glorification of our contemporary "allies" drew upon the positive connotations the term acquired in the context of World War II. The demonization of Saddam Hussein was particularly crucial for the positive war paradigm. CBS correspondent Allen Pizzey called Hussein "psychologically deformed" (January 24); entertainment magazines and television shows produced numerous voyeuristic projections about Hussein's putative sexual perversions, including still photos of his bunker bedroom, his harem, and stories about his tendency to kill his lovers, especially those who could testify to his failures in bed. The cover of a *National Examiner* (March 12) featured "Saddam Hussein's Bizarre Sex Life: A Recent CIA Report Reveals," with an image of Hussein the cross-dresser in a mini skirt. Geraldo's talk show (March 4) featured a series of experts' titillating descriptions of different systems of torture, all delivered up to an insatiably repelled audience. Close-ups emphasized the responses of good Americans shocked by this dark-skinned cruel leader, compared to Idi Amin, Qaddafi, Noriega, and Stalin. Hussein was nicknamed the "Butcher from Baghdad," and by Fouad Ajami, that Oriental who Orientalized the Orient, as "The Thief from Baghdad" (*New Republic*). When one of the experts on the Geraldo show inadvertently exposed the fact that Hussein learned his methods of torture from the CIA and the Mossad, Geraldo responded that he hoped it wasn't true, and went on to engage with the fascinating perversions of Hussein.

This kind of mass-mediated discourse discards political analysis in favor of melodramatic imagination of good versus evil, in which the presumed final physical and technological victory proves also the moral superiority of the victors. The TV anchors followed Bush in calling Hussein by his first name, Saddam; the series of sound associations with this pronunciation include Satan, Damn, and Sodom. (How many anchors have addressed Bush as George? And if they had addressed him as George, would it not have been with friendly cues that would make him seem an intimate member of our family, perhaps our father?) Hussein was regularly compared to Hitler, and the megalomaniac occupation of Kuwait to that of Czechoslovakia. The *New Republic* went so far as to use a *Time* cover photo of Hussein, touching up Hussein's wide moustache to make him look more like Hitler. (Those familiar with the region and with the styles of Middle Eastern moustaches know that they do not look like Hitler's.) And *Nightline*, of course, began a program with an image of Hussein targeted through a gun-sight, an image usually associated with police target practice.

In pointing to the ideological functions of these representations, I am by no means trying to recuperate the image of Saddam Hussein. To compare Hussein to Hitler, and the war in the Gulf to World War II, is to elide the fact that the Arab world, like most parts of the world (Africa, Asia, and America), has been colonized by Europe, and that this history, and the consequences of that history, are still with us. We have to remember that at the end of World War I Britain and France divided among themselves the Ottoman empire and unilaterally parceled up the region's inhabitants. These imperial powers decided where to draw lines in the sand in accordance with their own interests (in the Sykes–Picot Agreement)—installing monarchies and regimes which functioned as typical neocolonial powers collaborating with the interests of the old empires. They also made contradictory promises—for example both to Palestinians and to Zionists, in the Balfour declaration—as perhaps presently the U.S. has been taking upon itself the "burden" of its "colonial motherland" to deliver contradictory promises to different regional powers (Israel, Egypt). This crucial elision of colonial history explains why opposition to the U.S. in the Middle East could so easily be represented as the irrational, hysterical result of Islamic fanaticism. This decontextualization of events in turn helps to explain the surprise at the widespread condemnation of the bombing of Iraq, even on the part of those opposed to Hussein's regime and the invasion of Kuwait.

The analogy to Hitler reached its climax with the coverage of the Scud missiles falling over Israel and the possibility of chemical warfare. Most important were stories about Holocaust survivors now forced to confront the possibility of chemical attacks, and the fact that Hussein was armed partially by German factories. But they were always only half the story. Why was Hussein never compared to Hitler when he was armed by the U.S. and when he used chemical weapons against Iranians and Kurds? And how different was the U.S.'s use of Agent Orange and napalm during Vietnam? When TV archives provided images of the brutal consequences of chemical warfare, they used images from World War I or from the Iran–Iraq war, but never from Vietnam, where the use of chemicals continues to take its toll on both Vietnamese people and American vets.

The Hussein–Hitler analogy prolonged the historical intertext of Israeli and American imagery linking Arabs to Nazis. This link, both metonymic and metaphoric, had been a staple of didactic Israeli films (*Hill 24 Doesn't Answer, Rebels, Against the Light*) as well as of Hollywood cinema (*Ship of Fools, Exodus, Raiders of the Lost Ark*). This rhetoric has helped to delegitimize the Palestinian claims to nationhood and statehood. Hussein has thus been associated with the prospect of the extermination of the Jews. While it is true that the Scuds falling on Israel did give a certain legitimacy to this view, it remains simplistic to project the experience of Jews in Europe onto the very different context of the Middle East, where the very establishment of Israel was at least partially an exercise of power, suppressing the Palestinian counter-narrative.

The analogy implies, furthermore, a Eurocentric approach to Jewish History. In seeing Jewish History through a Euro-American Jewish perspective, the U.S. media have presented Israel simplistically as a Western country populated by European Jews. Reading and watching media images from the Middle East, one is led to believe that there are only Euro-American Jews in Israel and only Muslim Arabs in the rest of the Middle East. One finds few images of Iraqi, Moroccan, or Ethiopian Israelis, even though Oriental Arab Jews compose the majority of the Jewish population in Israel. The elision was especially striking when the missiles hit Ramat Gan, a city well known for its Iraqi population, popularly nick-named "Ramat Baghdad," and the Iraqi-Jewish neighborhoods in the south of Tel Aviv. Network reports referred to a "working class neighborhood," which is the equivalent of calling Harlem a working-class neighborhood. (The circulating joke in Israel was that the missile fell into the Iraqi neighborhoods because it smelled the '*amba*, an Iraqi mango pickle.) This ethnic elision is especially striking, since it would presumably be powerful propaganda for the U.S. and Israel to represent Hussein as attacking those who were formerly Iraqi citizens. But since Middle Eastern Jews spoil the image of Israel as a Western country, interviews were generally conducted with Israelis who spoke English with American accents, and who did not look too much like Arabs.

Above all, it is the fact of Iraq's relatively good relations with its own Jews that disrupts this narrative. What was elided was the information that Iraq, until the early 1950s, boasted a large and prosperous Jewish community. In many ways Jews in Iraq had much higher positions of authority and cultural prestige, higher economic and social status, than they and other Jews from Arab and Muslim countries were ever allowed to achieve in their 40 years in Israel. Furthermore, the emotional-cultural link to Iraq that still exists within the Iraqi-Jewish community in Israel, as well as the attempts by some of its intellectuals to serve as a "bridge" in the Arab/Israeli conflict, disappeared from the media's reports. In the experts' articles, which presumably offer a wide historical panorama for the American reader, the same syndrome persists: the discourse about perennial animosity between Jews and Arabs. Therefore, it is not surprising that during the Gulf War, the American media did not mention the 1980s contacts, or at least the rumors of contacts, that reportedly took place between three Jewish-Iraqi members of the Knesset and representatives of the Iraqi government; one of the items under discussion was Iraqi recognition of Israel and of the Camp David accords in exchange for Israeli support in the war against Iran.

The complex histories of the Middle East, the multiplicity of ethnicities, religions, and identities, are systematically elided. As a result of the war, do Americans know more about the history and culture of their allies—the Egyptians, Syrians, Kuwaitis, and Saudis? My own students seem to have only learned to read the military maps of the Middle East, at best. Colorful maps of the Middle East shown on television give an illusory sense of some overarching knowledge of the region. This political crisis led to further elaborations of the "covering the globe" trope dominant in television. On January 14, a day before the U.S. "deadline" for the Iraqi withdrawal from Kuwait, an ABC special, *A Line in the Sand*, featured Peter Jennings standing upon a colorful political map of the Middle East, as a backdrop for historical and strategic analysis. The map provided the pretext for a pedagogical tour of the recent history of the Middle East, buttressed by archival and contemporary direct-transmissions from around the Middle East, in a "covering" which was both temporal and spatial. The North American narrator literally steps on, sits on, and looks down on the map, thus striding the narrow world "like a colossus."

Commentary, typically, served to channel our empathies. Ted Koppel (ABC, January 21) said: "Aside from the Scud missile that landed in Tel Aviv earlier, it's been a quiet night in the Middle East." This was at a time when clearing weather allowed the Allies to increase their air attacks to 2,000 missions a day. Taking sides and the structuring of selective identification, cued by the anchors' intonations and facial expressions, became instrumental in disseminating the feeling of a "just war." From the onset of the war, weather reports on the Middle East employed their maps and charts to present good weather as good news, for the purpose of facilitating "sorties" (a Frenchified euphemism for carnage).

The war, presumably in the name of a victimized Arab Kuwait, has produced so much anti-Arab sentiment that most Arab grocers have taken to placing small American flags in their stores. Indian groceries followed suit, since many of them are mistaken for Arabs. (I witnessed a drunk shouting at an Indian grocer next to the Staten Island ferry that the oil in the Gulf is "ours," and the Taj Mahal too. The next day the Indian grocer had a small American flag hanging from a top shelf, and a yellow ribbon was glued to the microwave door.) Jewish Americans were also represented as more legitimate Americans than Arab Americans. Dan Rather (CBS, January 16) interviewed FBI chief William Sessions on terrorism: "If you're an American mother who happens to be of Jewish heritage ... do you send your child to school?" In the same interview, Dan Rather asked Sessions: "What should our attitude toward Americans of Arab heritage be?" Here the rhetoric of "our" includes the Jewish American, but not the Arab American.

As a result of discursive reductionism, the Jewish community has also been misrepresented by the media. Only the dominant Jewish organizations are assumed to represent "the" Jewish position, as if there were one homogenous Jewish-American position. Susan Spencer (CBS, January 19), for example, never acknowledged Jewish-American opposition to the war. She commented: "I also think from the American-Jewish community that there are going to be the same kind of calls for retaliation .... I think they're going to be absolutely united in that."

What we also saw were media reports that framed events along the lines of the war genre, thereby suturing the spectator into a familiar discourse of patriotism. News reports were introduced by logos such as "America at War," reminiscent of blockbuster movie trailers. As in ads for "soon at your local theater," we saw a montage of scenes from the war, with the major characters (the hero/villain, and the crucial images of maps and globes). The networks clearly linked themselves to the idea of the nation in a blatant self-advertisement; they appealed to the presumably patriotic sentiments through logos of popular images from the war: soldiers with guns, "the points of light" over Baghdad, camels and Bedouins in the desert. These television logos were accompanied by martial music presided over by the classical male voice-over of authority and truth in the cinema: "America's Watching ABC .... More Americans get their news from ABC than from any other source...Never is information more crucial to democracy than at times like these." These ads, which capitalize on war, promoted war and legitimized war.

Hussein as the villain, Bush as the hero, and the U.S. rescuing the victim are typical of colonial narratives. It is no accident that the metaphor of "the rape of Kuwait" appeared, in tandem with circulating rumors about actual rapes performed by Iraqis against Kuwaitis, and public statements that insinuated possible rapes of American female soldiers by Iraqi captors. (Little has been said, of course, about the sexual harassment of American female soldiers by their male colleagues.) The rescue of White or dark women from a dark rapist underlies many colonial narratives, whose conclusion is the assertion of patriarchal and imperial world order. The historical oversexualization of American Blacks and "Indians" mutated into the image of the rapacious

Arabs. The dark rapist must be punished and humiliated, supposedly in the name of the raped victim. The civilizing mission involves precisely teaching a lesson to the dark man who dared to disobey. Bush, as an imperial pedagogue, made an effort to "teach Saddam a lesson." (Perhaps this is what Bush meant when he promised to be the "Education President.") Often this order of things was sanctified by God. In the film *The Birth of a Nation*, the punishment of the Black rapist, celebrated by White supremacists, is blessed by a superimposed figure of Christ, an image echoed during the war in popular journalism. The sensationalist magazine *The Sun* (March 19) featured an exclusive report on "Desert Storm Miracle: Jesus Appears to Our Troops in the Gulf." A colorful image of Christ's appearance occupied a full page and was "anchored" with "the vision of Jesus appeared to the troops for 5 minutes when the sky was full of bright red, yellow, and orange colors." (The picture is very similar to the image at the end of *The Birth of a Nation*.) According to the magazine, Pentagon sources "refused to comment on the incident," but the soldiers themselves said, "we knew after we saw Jesus that God is on our side."

Within this scenario, another victim to be defended from the "savage" was Israel. Typically television reports used stories about specific families whose names were featured prominently—images of "rounded characters" to promote identification. We accompanied families in their sealed rooms and even learned about the psychological effects of this war on Israeli and American children. Yet how many Iraqi children, or Palestinians under curfew, received such sympathetic treatment?

Most crucial for the geopolitical narrative of rape and rescue was the low value attributed to Iraqi lives. Baghdad was seen exclusively from the air, through the gun-sights of the Allies, imagery structurally similar to that of the war movie genre and the frontier Western. Even interviews with pilots formed part of this visual heritage. You may remember the CNN close-up of a grinning pilot assuring us that "Baghdad is target rich." To top it all, CBS (March 5) reported on the atrocities committed by Iraqi soldiers on animals in the Kuwaiti zoo. The camera even zoomed in on the wounded and crippled parts of their bodies. To this day, Iraqi civilian casualties have not received anything like the sympathetic treatment accorded to the animals in the zoo.

19

The Carthage Film Festival

(with Robert Stam)

Up until the digging of the Suez Canal, Africa and Asia were one physically linked continent. The *Maghrib* (in Arabic, literally the "West") has always been a meeting place for the various cultures of sub-Saharan Africa and the Eastern part of the Arab world, the *Mashriq*. Taking place in Tunisia since 1966, the Carthage Film Festival has served as a contemporary meeting ground for the cultures of the Arab world and the diverse cultures and peoples of sub-Saharan Africa. Although the Carthage Film Festival in its beginning was inspired by Third Worldist ideology, crystallized in defiant declarations and manifestos calling for a revolutionary and anticolonial cinema, innovative in both political and esthetic terms, it has gradually evolved into a much less revolutionary forum. The festival, like the post-colonial films it now features, takes place in a context of religious tensions and class frustrations in a post-independence era dominated by global mass media and neoliberalism.

The most pronounced critique of the Third World national revolution, this time from the Left, is found in Mohamed Chouikh's *Youcef, Or the Legend of the Seventh Sleeper*, whose protagonist, Youcef, escapes from an asylum into what he believes to be Algeria in 1960, a world where the FLN is heroically battling French armies. A surreal time gap between Youcef's subjective perception and present-day Algeria becomes a satirical device for underlining the minimal progress in the life of the Algerian people since independence in 1962. Yesterday's heroes, Youcef soon learns, are today's oppressors, ready to sacrifice anyone who opposes their regime, including their old FLN comrades. Insanity no longer resides in an individual but in a social system.

Bab El-Oued City, by another key Algerian filmmaker, Merzak Allouache, also foregrounds the conflicts ripping apart the contemporary nation. Revealing the historic working-class neighborhood at the heart of Algiers

Review of Tunisia's 1994 Carthage Film/Video Festival, published in *Cineaste*, Vol. 21, No. 3, 1995.

as a microcosm of the contradictions of Algerian society, the film traces the ways in which the difficulties of daily life and the realities of social exclusion pave the way for extremist groups, and for the burgeoning urban violence. In Kamal Dehane's documentary, *Assia Djebar, Between Shadow and Sun*, contemporary Algeria is examined through the feminist reflections of the acclaimed Algerian-French writer Assia Djebar, who returns to the scenes of her childhood, reflecting on the conflictual hybridity of being brought up between the French school and the Arabic world. The film questions the future of an Algerian society undergoing an intense identity crisis.

Moufida Tlatli's award-winning Tunisian film, *The Silences of the Palace* (screened in last year's New York Film Festival), offers a gendered and class critique of Tunisia, where the hope for social transformation after independence has yet to be completely realized. The protagonist, the lower-class singer Alya—whose revolutionary lover at the time of the climactic moment of anti-French struggle had assured her that not knowing her father's identity would not matter in the new Tunisian society—is disappointed when he refuses, years later, to marry her. Instead of the symbolic birth of a nation that structures films like *The Battle of Algiers, The Silences of the Palace* dramatizes literal birth, thereby giving voice to women's struggle against colonialism from within as well as from without. Fadika Kramo-Lanchine's *Wariko Hitting the Jackpot,* from the Ivory Coast, also allegorically recounts the story of the African in search of economic and social development. The protagonist, Ali, in the course of his wanderings to find his lost lottery ticket, discovers the contrasts between country and city.

Other films focus on displacement to the West and its repercussions for issues of identity. Ali Akika's documentary, *Algeria Unveiled,* gives voice to seven Algerian intellectuals in exile in Paris. Through their narratives, the film explores Algeria's complex historical mutations over the past 300 years in relation to the more recent political tensions that have led to the current Algerian civil war. We find a more melodramatic representation of displacement in the short *Calvary,* by the Algerian Karim Bechir Traidia, in which an Algerian immigrant who tries to maintain community traditions in Amsterdam unintentionally kills his rebellious, exploitative, and aggressive son. The story of the father's acquittal by an Amsterdam court is told through the tormented flashbacks of the father himself.

Some films deploy a more reflexive approach to issues of displacement. *Babylon 2* by the Iraqi-Swiss director Samir is an autobiographical reflection on home and exile for Switzerland's native-born children of immigrants from Iraq, Jamaica, Italy, and even for German Jews, whose hybrid identities are counterposed against a normative "Swissness." Babylon no longer refers only to the filmmaker's origins in Mesopotamia/Iraq but also to the Rastafarian notion of diaspora. No wonder, in this context, that reggae and rap provide an organizing principle for a diasporic transnational culture, *Babylon 2* of the title.

Displacement is treated differently in Lebanese exile films, where the moment of return coincides with the final stages of that country's civil war. *A Story of Return*, by Jean Claude Codsi, focuses on two Lebanese war refugees who decide to return home from Paris. The film registers not only their return but also their reconciliation with the past. In Samir Habchi's *The Whirlwind*, the protagonist, on the eve of his departure for Lebanon, has a nightmare triggered by TV images of a car-bomb explosion. Back in Beirut, he finds himself implacably drawn into the pitiless logic of a war that he thought he had escaped. Jocelyne Saab's *Once Upon a Time in Beirut*, in contrast, creates a nostalgic atmosphere, as two 20-year-old women search for the memory of Beirut, their unknown city. Thanks to an old cinephile friend, they screen Beiruti films, ranging from silent newsreels and Lebanese musical comedies from the 1940s and 1950s to American Orientalist thrillers of the 1970s, on to the *engagé* cinema of the 1980s. This reflexive voyage into a celluloid Beirut becomes the key to finding out to which Beirut one is returning, and to point to the new Beirut one wishes for in the future.

In contrast with the Third Worldist phase of Arab and African cinema, with its politicized rejection of antecedent "commercial" and "colonized" cinema, the 1994 festival reflected a "postmodern" affection for early, non-revolutionary cinemas. It is often forgotten that what is now called "Third-World cinema" did not begin in the 1960s. Arab cinema, for example, long predated postcolonial independence. Some of the festival events linked this logic of return to the centennial anniversary of the cinema.

The Festival also paid homage to early Tunisian cinema, especially to one of its major pioneers, the Tunisian Jew Albert Samama-Chikli. The festival featured two of his films in which his daughter Haydée played the leading role. In *Zohra* (1922), a young woman lands on the African coast after shipwreck and is received by a Bedouin family. In *The Girl from Carthage* (1924), a young woman, in love with the *mu'azzin*, is forced to marry another man, but after the wedding she flees with the *mu'azzin*, who is ultimately killed by the husband's friends, after which the young woman commits suicide.

The most striking aspect of the festival was the first-time official presence of South Africa, reflected in the screening of the film *Friends* by Elaine Proctor, and of a jury member, South African filmmaker Chris Austin, a participation marking a new historical acceptance of the South Africa of Nelson Mandela. The politics around the Israeli/Palestinian conflict were more convoluted, however. The official invitation made to Israeli filmmakers to present their work at the festival was cancelled. Despite the beginning of economic ties between Tunisia and Israel, cultural ties are harder to

Figure 39   Haydée Chikli Tamzali, daughter of
Albert Samama Chikli, in his film *Zohra*, 1922

digest for Arab intellectuals and artists, who reportedly exerted pressure
to exclude Israel from official participation. In Tunisia, the country where
the PLO headquarters was established after its expulsion from Beirut by
the 1982 Israeli invasion, the Israeli/Palestinian issue remains sensitive. The
general director of the festival, Ahmed Baha Eddine Attia, had already been
criticized for showing some North African films in Jerusalem and Haifa
cinematheques in 1994. The disinvitation, ironically, meant that the film
Mama's Couscous, a reflexive autobiography by the Tunisian-French-Israeli
filmmaker, Serge Ankri, was not presented.

At the same time, the Jewish-Tunisian past is very present for Tunisians,
as evident in the postcards of the synagogues and the Jews of Djerba sold in
every kiosk, in the visibility of the synagogues, and in the ongoing adoration
of Habiba Msika, the Tunisian (Jewish) star of the 1920s. Apart from the
festival's homage to Albert Samama Chikli, another Tunisian film, *Testour*,
documents the typically Andalusian town of the title, focusing on the shared

customs and rituals of Andalusian Muslims and Jews who have been living together in Testour since the expulsion of Sephardi Jews and Muslims from Spain in the 15th century.

Palestinian filmmakers and actors were present, including Israeli Palestinians. When the official invitation to Israeli filmmakers was cancelled, Israeli Palestinian filmmakers, who were part of the official Israeli delegation, decided nevertheless to attend the Carthage festival as individuals. Other ironies marked the presence at the festival. Emile Habibi, one of the prominent (Israeli) Palestinian writers who recently, despite much criticism from Palestinians, accepted the Israel Prize, the official Israeli presidential award, was a member of the festival's jury. The award-winning Tunisian film, *The Swallows Never Die in Jerusalem*, illustrated this ambivalent moment in Tunisian attitudes toward the Israeli/Palestinian conflict. This well-produced and scrupulously even-handed film focuses on the harsh realities of Palestinian existence under Israeli rule, but through the eyes of an "objective" French journalist, who has to navigate between these realities and the rumors of a possible peace with Israel. Ben Gazzara plays an elderly Jew who is opposed to his daughter's "peacenik" tendencies. The film ultimately endorses a position somewhere between the PLO and the Israeli Labor Party, while condemning both Jewish settlers and Islamic fundamentalists.

The Carthage Film Festival is more than merely a showcase for art films; it also facilitates discussion about current issues. This year's festival featured debates about cinema in the age of new communication technologies such

Figure 40   Riha Behi's *The Swallows Never Die in Jerusalem*, 1994

as the "information superhighway" and pay-TV. As part of the effort to support Arab and African filmmakers, the Carthage Film Festival, in 1992, established the International Market for Audio-Visual Products (MIPAC). This year's festival also facilitated professional meetings of film archivists and film festival directors, as well as a discussion of the "Mediterranean Project." The declared purpose of the latter, in conjunction with UNESCO's charter principles of "Peace and Tolerance," was an effort by filmmakers and other artists and intellectuals to promote the cultural identity of the Mediterranean countries. It is through such gatherings, then, in addition to its film screenings, that the Carthage Film Festival continues to play an important cultural role in the region.

20

The Cinema of Displacement: Gender, Nation, and Diaspora

At a time when the *grands récits* of the West have been told and retold *ad infinitum*, when a certain postmodernism (Jean-François Lyotard) speaks of an "end" to metanarratives, and when Francis Fukuyama speaks of an "end of history," we must ask: precisely whose narrative and whose history is being declared at an "end?"[1] Hegemonic Europe may clearly have begun to deplete its strategic repertoire of stories, but Third World peoples, First World diasporic communities, women, and gays/lesbians have only begun to tell, and deconstruct, theirs.

For the "Third World," this cinematic counter-telling basically began with the post-war collapse of the European empires and the emergence of independent nation-states. In the face of Eurocentric historicizing, the Third World and its diasporas in the First World have rewritten their own histories, taken control of their own images, and spoken in their own voices, reclaiming and reaccentuating colonialism and its ramifications in the present, in a vast project of remapping and renaming. Third World feminists, for their part, have participated in these counter-narratives by insisting that colonialism and nationalism have impinged differently on men and women. All the remapping and renaming, then, has not been without fissures and contradictions.

Although relatively small in number, women in what has been termed the "Third World" already played a role as film producers and directors in the first half of the 20th century: Aziza Amir, Assia Daghir, Fatima Rushdi, Bahiga Hafiz, and Amina Rezq in Egypt; Carmen Santos and Gilda de Abreu in Brazil, Emilia Saleny in Argentina; and Adela Sequeyro,

---

Published in Hamid Dabashi (ed.), *Dreams of a Nation: On Palestinian Cinema* (London: Verso, 2006), a slightly modified version of "Framing Post-Third Worldist Culture: Gender, Nation, and Diaspora in Middle Eastern/North African Film/Video," published in *Middle Eastern Identities in Transition*, edited by Jonathan Friedlander, University of California, Los Angeles, Near East Center Colloquium Series, 1995. It was first presented in the workshop organized by the author, "The Cinema of Displacement," The Hagop Kevorkian Center for Near Eastern Studies, New York University, April 1994.

Matilda Landeta, Candida Beltran Rondon, and Eva Liminano in Mexico. However, their films, even when focusing on female protagonists, were not explicitly feminist in the sense of a declared political project to empower women in the context of both patriarchy and (neo)colonialism. In the post-independence, or post-revolution, era, women, despite their growing contribution to the diverse aspects of film production, remained less visible than men in the role of film direction. Furthermore, Third Worldist revolutionary cinemas, in places such as China, Cuba, Senegal, and Algeria, were not generally shaped by anticolonial feminist imaginary. As is the case with First World cinema, women's participation in Third World cinema has hardly been central, although their growing production over the last decade corresponds to a burgeoning worldwide movement of independent work by women, made possible by new low-cost technologies of video communication. But quite apart from this relative democratization through technology, post-independence history, with the gradual eclipse of Third Worldist nationalism, and growth of women's grassroots local organizing, also helps us understand the emergence of what I call "post-Third Worldist" feminist film and video.[2]

Post-Third Worldist Culture

Here I am interested in examining recent women's positioning[3] within (neo)colonialist and racist systems. Feminist struggles in the Third World (including those of the First World) have not been premised on a facile discourse of "global sisterhood," and have often been made within the context of anticolonial and anti-racist struggles. But the growing feminist critique of Third World nationalisms translates those many disappointed hopes for women's empowerment invested in a Third Worldist national transformation. Navigating between patriarchal nationalist excommunicating denunciations as "traitors to the nation" or "betraying the race," and Western feminism's imperial rescue fantasy of veiled and clitoridectomized women, post-Third Worldist feminists have not suddenly metamorphosed into "Western" feminists. Feminists of color have from the outset engaged in analysis and activism around the intersection of nation/race/gender. Therefore, while still resisting the ongoing (neo)colonized situation of their "nation" and/or "race," post-Third Worldist feminist cultural practices also break away from the narrative of the "nation" as a unified entity so as to articulate a contextualized history for women in specific geographies of identity. Such feminist projects, in other words, are often posited in relation to ethnic, racial, regional, and national locations.

Rather than merely "extending" a pre-existing First World feminism, as a certain Euro-"diffusionism"[4] would have it, post-Third Worldist cultural theories and practices create a more complex space for feminisms that do not abandon the specificity of community, culture, and history. To counter some of the patronizing attitudes towards (post-)Third World feminist filmmakers—the dark women who also do the "feminist thing"—it seems necessary to contextualize feminist work within national-racial discourses inscribed within multiple oppressions and resistances. Third World feminist performance histories can be understood as feminist if unearthed from the substantial resistance work these women have done within their communities and nations. Any serious discussion of feminist cinema must, therefore, engage the complex question of the "national." Third Worldist films, produced within the legal codes of the nation-state, often in (hegemonic) national languages, recycling national intertexts (literatures, oral narratives, music), projected national imaginaries. But if First World filmmakers have seemed to float "above" petty nationalist concerns, it is because they take for granted the projection of a national power that facilitates the making and the dissemination of their films. The geopolitical positioning of Third World nation-states, even in the postcolonial era, implies that Third World filmmakers cannot assume a substratum of national power.

This point about relative powerlessness is well illustrated in Youssef Chahine's film *Iskandariya Lih? (Alexandria Why?,* 1979). A semi-autobiographical film about an aspiring filmmaker haunted by Hollywood dreams, it offers an Egyptian perspective on the colonizing film culture of the U.S. Chahine's protagonist begins as a Victoria College student who adores Shakespeare's plays and Hollywood movies. The film is set in the 1940s, a critical period for the protagonist and for Egypt: Allied troops were stationed in the country then, and Axis forces threatened to invade Alexandria; although *Alexandria Why?* focuses on the would-be filmmaker, its subplots offer a multi-perspectival study of Egyptian society, describing how different classes, ethnicities, and religions—working-class communists, aristocratic Muslim homosexuals, middle-class Egyptian Jews, petit-bourgeois Catholics—react to Egyptian-Arab nationalism. The subplots stress the diversity of Egyptian experiences, yet also highlight the common rejection of European colonialism.[5] One story, for example, reaffirms the "Arabness" of Egypt's Arab Jews, through a romance subplot involving a communist of Muslim working-class background and a Jewish-Egyptian woman, daughter of a middle-class anti-Zionist communist and sister of a Zionist. Thus Chahine undoes the equation of Jews with Zionism, and with Europeanness.

Alexandria Why? weaves diverse materials—newsreels, clips from Hollywood films, staged reconstructions, Chahine's own youthful amateur film—into an ironic collage. The opening credit sequence mingles black-and-white 1940s travelogue footage of Alexandria beaches with newsreel footage of Europe at war, implementing a "peripheral" Egyptian perspective on Europe. In the following sequence, we watch a series of newsreels and Hollywood musicals along with the spectators in Alexandria. The musicals are subtitled in Arabic (Egypt was a translation center for the Middle East), while the newsreels have an Arabic voice-over suggesting a "return to sender" message from the "periphery." An anthology of musical clips featuring stars such as Helen Powell, and songs such as "I'll Build a Stairway to Paradise," are inserted into a reception context redolent of First World/Third World economic and military relations as well as of the worldwide hegemonization of the American Dream. The "Three Cheers for the Red, White, and Blue" number, for example, at once charming and intimidating in its climactic image of cannons firing at the camera (and at the Egyptian viewer, and at the spectators of *Alexandria Why?),* celebrates American power and renders explicit the nationalist subtext of First World "entertainment."

The movie-going scenes suggest a kind of obsession, a repetitive ritual of filmgoing. Meanwhile, the Egyptian musical scenes clearly mock the protagonist's Americanizing fantasies. These numbers affect a kitschy, "underdeveloped" mimicry of Hollywood production values. As Egyptian performers emulate the formula of the Hollywood-Latino musical, they also point to Hollywood's role in disseminating imagery of the Third World. One Egyptian actor, sporting poncho and sombrero, plays a mariachi-style guitar, much as an earlier sequence featured the Mexican song "Perfidia." It is Hollywood and its distribution network, we are reminded, that popularized Latin American performers such as Carmen Miranda, and dances such as the tango, rumba, and the cha-cha, among the middle classes of the Middle East and the Third World generally. The final sequences mock the power that replaced European colonial powers in Egypt after World War II: the U.S., deriding the chimera of Americanization that enthralls the protagonist, and allegorically middle-class Egyptians generally. On arriving in the musical's national homeland, the protagonist is greeted by the Statue of Liberty transformed into a laughing, toothless, decaying woman. By 1979, when *Alexandria Why?* was made, the view of the U.S. as a liberating force had given way to bitter disillusionment. The Statue of Liberty is shown via 1940s studio-style back-projection, but whereas Hollywood often exploited scenic matte-shots to show exotic locales, the Egyptian film deploys the same technique to mock the industrialized fantasies of American mass culture. The tacky papier-maché quality of Chahine's Statue of Liberty metaphorizes the factitious nature of Third World idealizations of North American freedom, particularly in the context of the postwar Middle East, where the U.S. has come to represent both an alluring model and a new imperialism supplanting European colonialisms.[6]

Figure 41   Youssef Chahine's *Alexandria Why?*, 1979

In the following, I am interested in examining the contemporary work of post-Third Worldist feminist film/video-makers in light of the ongoing critique of unequal geopolitical and racial distribution of resources and power, as a way of examining the postcolonial dynamics of rupture and continuity in relation to the antecedent Third Worldist film culture. These texts, I argue, challenge the masculinist contours of "the nation" in order to promote a feminist decolonization of national historiography. My attempt at a beginning of a post-Third Worldist narrative for recent film and video work by diverse Third World diasporic feminists is not intended as an exhaustive survey of the entire spectrum of generic practices. Highlighting works embedded at the intersection of gender and sexuality with nation and race, this essay attempts to situate such cultural practices. It looks at a moment of historical rupture and continuity when the macro-narrative of women's liberation has long since subsided, yet where sexism and heterosexism prevail, and in an age when the metanarratives of anticolonial revolution have long since been eclipsed, yet where issues of (neo)colonialism and racism persist. What then are some of the new modes of a feminist aesthetics of resistance, and in what ways do they simultaneously continue and rupture previous Third World film culture?

Third Worldist films by women filmmakers within and outside the Middle East/North Africa assumed that revolution was crucial for the empowering of women, that the revolution was integral to feminist aspirations. Sarah Maldoror's short film *Monangambe* (Mozambique, 1970) told the story of an Angolan woman's visit to her imprisoned husband, taken away by the Portuguese, while her feature film *Sambizanga* (Mozambique, 1972), based on the struggle of the MPLA in Angola, depicted a woman coming to revolutionary consciousness. Heiny Srour's documentary *Sa'at al-Tahrir* (*The Hour of Liberation*, Oman, 1973) privileges the role of women fighters as it looks at the revolutionary struggle in Oman, and *Leila wal-Dhiab* (*Leila and the Wolves*, Lebanon, 1984) focussed on the role of women in the Palestine Liberation Movement. Helena Solberg Ladd's *Nicaragua Up From the Ashes* (U.S., 1982) focalizes on the role of women in the Sandinista revolution. Sara Gomez's well-known film *De Cierta Manera* (*One Way or Another*, Cuba, 1975), often cited as part of the late 1970s and early 1980s Third Worldist debates around women's position in revolutionary movements, interweaves documentary and fiction as part of a feminist critique of the Cuban revolution.

In their search for an alternative to the dominant style of Hollywood, Third Worldist films share a certain preoccupation with First World feminist independent films, which have sought alternative images of women. The project of digging into "herstories" involved a search for new cinematic and narrative forms that challenged both the canonical documentaries and the mainstream fiction films, subverting the notion of "narrative pleasure" based on the "male gaze." As with Third Worldist cinema and with First World independent production, post-Third Worldist feminist films/videos conduct a struggle on two fronts, at once aesthetic and political, synthesizing revisionist historiography with formal innovation.

The early period of Third Worldist euphoria has since given way to the collapse of communism, the indefinite postponement of the devoutly wished "tricontinental revolution," the realization that the "wretched of the earth" are not unanimously revolutionary (nor necessarily allies to one another), the appearance of an array of Third World despots, and the recognition that international geopolitics and the global economic system have forced even the "Second World" to be incorporated into transnational capitalism. Recent years have also witnessed a terminological crisis swirling around the term "Third World" itself, now seen as an inconvenient relic of a more militant period. Some have argued that Third World theory is an open-ended ideological interpolation that papers over class oppression in all three worlds, while limiting socialism to the now nonexistent Second World.[7] Three worlds theory flattens heterogeneities, masks contradictions, and elides differences. Third World feminist critics such as Nawal el-Saadawi (Egypt), Vina Mazumdar (India), Kumari Jayawardena (Sri Lanka), Fatima Mernissi (Morocco), and Leila Gonzales (Brazil) have explored these differences and similarities in a feminist light, pointing to the gendered limitations of Third World nationalism.

Although all cultural practices are, on one level, products of specific national contexts, Third World filmmakers (men and women) have been forced to engage in the question of "the national" precisely because they lack the taken-for-granted power available to First World nation-states. At the same time, the topos of a unitary nation often camouflages the possible contradictions among different sectors of Third World society. The nation-states of the Americas, Africa, and Asia often "cover" the existence of women as well as of indigenous nations (Fourth World) within them. Moreover, the exaltation of the "national" provides no criteria for distinguishing exactly what is worth retaining in the "national tradition." A sentimental defense of patriarchal social institutions simply because they are "ours" can hardly be seen as emancipatory. Indeed, some Third World films criticize exactly such institutions: films such as *Allah Tanto* (Guinea, 1992) focus on the political repression exercised even by a pan-Africanist hero such as Sekou Toure; Kamal Dehane's *Assia Djebar: Between Shadow and Sun* (Algeria, 1994) and *Guelwaar* (Senegal, 1992) critique religious divisions; *Al-Mar'a wal-Qanun* (*The Woman and the Law,* Egypt, 1987) focuses on the legal discrimination against women; *Xala* (Senegal, 1990) criticizes polygamy; *Finzan* (Senegal, 1989) and *Fire Eyes* (Somalia/U.S., 1993) critique female genital surgeries; *Mercedes* (Egypt, 1993) satirizes class relations and the marginalization of gays; and *The Extras* (Syria, 1994) focuses on the intersection of political and sexual repression within a Third World nation.

All countries, including Third World countries, are heterogeneous, at once urban and rural, male and female, religious and secular, native and immigrant, and so forth. The view of the nation as unitary muffles the "polyphony" of social and ethnic voices within heteroglot cultures. Third World feminists especially have highlighted the ways in which the subject of the Third World nationalist revolution has been covertly posited as masculine and heterosexual. The precise nature of the national "essence" to be recuperated, furthermore, is elusive and chimerical. Some locate it in the precolonial past, or in the country's rural interior (e.g., a Palestinian village) or in a prior state of development (the pre-industrial) or in a minority religion and ethnicity (such as the Copts in Egypt or the Berbers in Algeria); each narrative of origins also has its gender implications. Recent debates have emphasized the ways in which national identity is mediated, textualized, constructed, "imagined," just as the traditions valorized by nationalism are "invented."[8] Any definition of nationality, then, must see it as partly discursive in nature, must take class, gender, and sexuality into account, must allow for racial difference and cultural heterogeneity, and must be dynamic, seeing "the nation" as an evolving, imaginary construct rather than an originary essence.

The decline of Third Worldist euphoria, which marked even feminist films such as *One Way or Another, The Hour of Liberation, Leila and the Wolves,* and *Nicaragua Up From the Ashes,* brought with it a rethinking of political, cultural, and aesthetic possibilities, as the rhetoric of revolution began to be greeted with a certain skepticism. Meanwhile, the socialist-inflected national liberation struggles of the 1960s and 1970s were harassed economically and militarily, violently discouraged from becoming revolutionary models for post-independence societies. A combination of IMF pressure, co-optation and "low-intensity warfare," as suggested earlier, have obliged even socialist regimes to make a sort of peace with transnational capitalism. Some regimes grew repressive toward those who wanted to go beyond a purely nationalist bourgeois revolution to restructure class, gender, region, and ethnic relations. As a result of external pressures and internal self-questioning, the cinema too gave expression to those mutations, as the anticolonial thrust of earlier films gradually gave way to more diversified themes and perspectives. This is not to say that artists and intellectuals became less politicized, but that cultural and political critiques have taken new and different forms. Contemporary cultural practices of post-Third World feminists intervene at a precise juncture in the history of the Third World.

A Feminist Critique of Nationalism

Largely produced by men, Third Worldist films were not generally concerned with a feminist critique of nationalist discourse. It would be a mistake to idealize the sexual politics of anticolonial Third Worldist films such as *Jamila al-Jazairiyya* (*Jamila, the Algerian*, Egypt, 1958) and the classic *La Battaglia di Algeri* (*The Battle of Algiers*, 1966), for example. On one level it is true that Algerian women are granted revolutionary agency. In one sequence, three Algerian women fighters are able to pass as Frenchwomen and consequently to pass the French checkpoints with bombs in their baskets. The French soldiers treat the Algerians with discriminatory scorn and suspicion but greet the Europeans with amiable "*bonjours*." And the soldiers' sexism leads them to misperceive the three women as French and flirtatious when in fact they are Algerian and revolutionary. *The Battle of Algiers* thus underlines the racial and sexual taboos of desire within colonial segregation. As Algerians, the women are the objects of a military as well as a sexual gaze; they are publicly desirable for the soldiers, however, only when they masquerade as French. They use their knowledge of European codes to trick the Europeans, putting their own "looks" and the soldiers "looking" (and failure to see) to revolutionary purpose. (Masquerade also serves the

Figure 42   Magda in Youssef Chahine's *Jamila, the Algerian*, 1958

Algerian male fighters who veil as Algerian women to better hide weapons.) Within the psychodynamics of oppression, the colonized woman knows the mind of the oppressor, while the converse is not true. In *The Battle of Algiers*, the women deploy this cognitive asymmetry to their own advantage, consciously manipulating ethnic, national, and gender stereotypes in the service of their struggle.

On another level, however, the women in the film largely carry out the orders of the male revolutionaries. They certainly appear heroic, but only insofar as they perform their sacrificial service for the "nation." The film does not ultimately address the two-fronted nature of their struggle within a nationalist but still patriarchal revolution.[9] In privileging the nationalist struggle, *The Battle of Algiers* elides the gender, class, and religious tensions that fissured the revolutionary process, failing to realize that, as Anne McClintock puts it, "nationalisms are from the outset constituted in gender power" and that "women who are not empowered to organize during the struggle will not be empowered to organize after the struggle."[10] The final shots of a dancing Algerian woman, waving the Algerian flag and taunting the French troops, is superimposed over the words "July 2, 1962: The

Algerian Nation is born." Here a symbolic woman carries, as it were, the allegory of the birth of the Algerian nation. But the film does not bring up the contradictions that plagued the revolution before and after victory. The nationalist representation of courage and unity relies on the image of the revolutionary woman, precisely because her figure might otherwise evoke a weak link, the fact of a fissured revolution in which unity vis-à-vis the colonizer does not preclude contradictions among the colonized.

The Third Worldist films often factored generic (and gendered) space of heroic confrontations, whether set in the streets, the *kasbah*, the mountains, or the jungle. The minimal presence of women corresponds to the place assigned to women both in the anticolonialist revolutions and within Third Worldist discourse, leaving women's home-bounded struggles unacknowledged. Women occasionally carried the bombs, as in *The Battle of Algiers*, but only in the name of "the nation." Gender contradictions were subordinated to anticolonial struggle: women were expected to "wait their turn." More often women were made to carry the "burden" of national allegory (the image of the woman dancing with the flag in *The Battle of Algiers* is an emblem of national liberation, while the image of the bride who deflowers herself in *'Urs al-Galil* (*Wedding in Galilee*, Palestine/Belgium, 1988) allegorizes the failure of an impotent patriarchy to lead toward national liberation.[11])

A recent Tunisian film, *Samt al-Qusur* (*The Silences of the Palace*, 1994) by Moufida Tlatli, a film editor who had worked on major Tunisian films of the post-independence "Cinema Jedid" (New Cinema) generation, exemplifies some of the feminist critiques of the representation of the "Nation" in the early anticolonial revolutionary films. Rather than privilege direct, violent encounters with the French, necessarily set in male-dominated spaces of battle, the film presents the 1950s Tunisian women, at the height of the national struggle, as restricted to the domestic sphere. Yet it also challenges the middle-class assumptions about the domestic sphere as belonging to the isolated wife-mother of a (heterosexual) couple. *The Silences of the Palace* focuses on working-class women, the servants of the rich pro-French Bey elite, subjugated to hopeless servitude, including at times sexual servitude, but for whom life outside the palace, without the guarantee of shelter and food, would mean the even worse misery of, for example, prostitution. Although suffering under a regime of silence in terms of what they know about the palace, the film highlights their survival as a community. As an alternative family, their emotional closeness in crisis and happiness, and their supportive involvement in decision making, shows their ways of coping with a no-exit situation. They become a non-patriarchal family within a patriarchal context. Whether through singing, while they cook once again for an opulent banquet, or through praying, as one of them heals one of their children who has fallen sick, or through dancing and eating in a joyous moment, the film represents women who did not plant bombs but whose social positioning as portrayed in the film becomes a critique of failed revolutionary hopes as seen in the postcolonial era. The information about the battles against the French is mediated through the radio and by vendors, who report on what might lead to a full, all-encompassing national transformation.

Yet this period of anticolonial struggle is framed as a recollective narrative of a woman singer, a daughter of one of the female servants, illuminating the continuous pressures exerted on women of her class. (With some exceptions, female singers/dancers have been associated in the Middle East with being just a little above the shameful occupation of prostitution.) The gendered and classed oppression she witnessed as an adolescent in colonized Tunisia led her to believe that everything would be different in an independent Tunisia. Such hopes were encouraged by the promises made by the middle-class male intellectual, a tutor for the Bey's family, who suggested that in the new Tunisia not knowing her father's name would not be a barrier to establishing a new life. Their passionate relationship in the heat of revolution, where the "new" is on the verge of being born, is undercut by the framing narrative. Her fatherless servant-history and her low status as a singer haunts her life in the post-independence era; the tutor lives with her but does not marry her, yet gives her the protection she needs as a singer. The film opens with her singing, with a sad and melancholy face, a famous Umm Kulthum song from the 1960s, *"Amal Hayati"* ("The Hope of My Life"). Umm Kulthum, an Egyptian, was the leading Arab singer of the 20th century, who thanks to her exceptional musical talent—including her deep knowledge of *fusha* (literary) Arabic—arose from her small village to become *kawkab al-sharq* (the star of the East). Her singing accompanied the Arab world in its national aspirations, and catalyzed a sense of unity throughout the Arab world, managing to transcend, at least on the cultural level, social tensions and political conflicts. She had been especially associated with the charismatic leadership of Gamal Abdel Nasser and his anti-imperial pan-Arab agenda, but the admiration, respect, and love she received have continued after her death (in 1975) to the present day. Her virtual transcendental position, however, has not been shared by many female singers and stars since.

The protagonist of *The Silences of the Palace* begins her public performance at the invitation of the masters of the palace, an invitation extended, in part, due to her singing talents but also symptomatic of the sexual harassment she begins to experience as soon as one of the masters notices that the child has turned into a young woman. The mother who manages to protect her daughter from sexual harassment is raped herself by one of the masters. On the day of the daughter's first major performance at a party in the palace, the

Figure 43   Moufida Tlatli's *The Silences of the Palace*, 1994

mother dies of excessive bleeding from medical complications caused from aborting the product of rape. In parallel scenes of the mother's screaming out of excruciating pain and the daughter's courageous crying out of the forbidden Tunisian anthem, the film ends with the mother's death and with her daughter leaving the palace for the promising outside world of young Tunisia. In post-independence Tunisia, the film implies, her situation has somewhat improved. She is no longer a servant but a singer who earns her living yet needs the protection of her boyfriend against gender-based humiliations. Next to her mother's grave, the daughter, in a voice-over, shows her awareness of some improvements in her life conditions in comparison with her mother. The daughter has gone through many abortions, despite her wish to become a mother, in order to keep her relationship with her boyfriend—the revolutionary man who does not transcend class for purposes of marriage. At the end of the film, she confesses at her mother's grave that this time she cannot let this piece of herself go. If in the opening, the words of Umm Kulthum's song *"Amal Hayati"* (Hope of my Life) relay a desire for a state of dream not to end—*"khalini, gambak, khalini/ fi hudhni albak, khalini/ u-sibni ahlam/yaret zamani ma yesahinish"* ("Keep me by your side/in your heart's embrace/and let me dream, let me/wish time will not wake me up")—the film ends with an awakening to hopes unfulfilled with the birth of the nation. Birth here is no longer allegorical as in *The Battle of Algiers*, but rather concrete, entangled in taboos and obstacles, leaving an open-ended narrative, far from the euphoric closure of "the Nation."

In contrast to the Orientalist harem imaginary, all-female spaces have been represented very differently in feminist independent cinema, largely, but not exclusively, directed by Middle Eastern women. Documentaries such as Attiat el-Abnoudi's *al-Ahlam al-Mumkiniyyaa* (*Permissible Dreams*, Egypt, 1989) and Claire Hunt and Kim Longinotto's *Hidden Faces* (U.K., 1990) examine female agency within a patriarchal context. Both films feature sequences in which Egyptian women speak together about their lives in the village, recounting in ironic terms their dreams and struggles with patriarchy. Through its critical look at the Egyptian feminist Nawal el-Saadawi, *Hidden Faces* explores the problems of women working together to create alternative institutions. Elizabeth Fernea's *The Veiled Revolution* (1982) depicts Egyptian women redefining not only the meaning of the veil but also the nature of their own sexuality. And Moroccan filmmaker Farida Benlyazid's feature film *Bab ila Sma' Maftuh* (*A Door to the Sky*, 1988) offers a positive gloss on the notion of an all-female space, counterposing Islamic feminism to Orientalist fantasies.

A Door to the Sky tells the story of a Moroccan woman, Nadia, who returns from Paris to her family home in Fez. That she arrives in Morocco dressed in punk clothing and with a punk hairstyle makes us expect an ironic tale about a Westernized Arab feeling out of place in her homeland. But instead, Nadia rediscovers Morocco and Islam, and comes to appreciate the communitarian world of her female relatives, as well as her closeness with her father. She is instructed in the faith by an older woman, Kirana, who has a flexible approach to Islam: "Everyone understands through his own mind and his own era." As Nadia awakens spiritually, she comes to see the oppressive aspects of Western society, and sees Arab-Muslim society as a possible space for fulfillment. Within the Islamic tradition of women using their wealth for social charity, she turns part of the family home into a shelter for battered women. At the same time, the film is not uncritical of the patriarchal abuses of Islam such as, for example, the laws which count women as "half-persons" and which systematically favor the male in terms of marriage and divorce. The film's aesthetic, meanwhile, favors the rhythms of contemplation and spirituality in slow camera movements that caress the contoured Arabic architecture of courtyards and fountains and soothing inner spaces. The film begins, significantly, with a dedication to a historical Muslim woman Fatima al-Fihri al-Quraysh (the 9th-century founder of one of the world's oldest universities in Fez, al-Qarawiyyin.) The filmmaker envisions an aesthetic that affirms Islamic culture, while also inscribing it with a feminist consciousness. In this way, *A Door to the Sky* offers an alternative both to the Western imaginary and to an Islamic fundamentalist representation of Muslim women. Whereas contemporary documentaries show all-female gatherings as a space for resistance to patriarchy and fundamentalism, *A Door to the Sky* uses all-female spaces to point to a liberatory project based on unearthing women's history within Islam, a history that includes female spirituality, prophecy, poetry, and intellectual creativity as well as revolt, material power, and social and political leadership.[12]

Diasporic Aesthetics

A number of recent diasporic film/video works link issues of postcolonial identity to issues of post-Third Worldist aesthetics and ideology. The Sankofa production *The Passion of Remembrance* (1986) by Maureen Blackwood and Isaac Julien thematizes post-Third Worldist discourses and fractured diasporic identity, in this case Black British identity, by staging a "polylogue" between a 1960s Black radical, as the (somewhat puritanical) voice of nationalist militancy, and the "new," more playful, voice—gays and lesbian women—all within a de-realized reflexive aesthetic. Film and video works such as Assia Djebar's *Nouba Nisa' al-Djebel Chénoua* (*The Nuba of the Women of Mount Shnua*, 1977), Lourdes Portillo's *After the Earthquake* (1979), Mona Hatoum's *Measures of Distance* (1988), Pratibha Parmar's *Khush* (1991), Trinh T. Minh-ha's *Surname Viet Given Name Nam* (1989), Prajna Paramita Parasher and Den Ellis's *Unbidden Voices* (1990), Indu Krishnan's *Knowing Her Place* (1990), Christine Chang's *Be Good My Children* (1992), and Marta N. Bautis's *Home is the Struggle* (1991) break away from earlier macro-narratives of national liberation, reenvisioning the Nation as a heteroglossic multiplicity of trajectories. While remaining anti-colonialist, these experimental films/videos call attention to the diversity of experiences within and across nations. Since colonialism had simultaneously aggregated communities fissured by glaring cultural differences and separated communities marked by equally glaring commonalities, these films suggest that nation-states were in some ways artificial and contradictory entities. The films produced in the First World, in particular, raise questions about dislocated identities in a world increasingly marked by the mobility of goods, ideas, and peoples attendant on the "multi-nationalization" of the global economy.

Third Worldists often fashioned their idea of the nation-state according to the European model, in this sense remaining complicit with a Eurocentric enlightenment narrative. And the nation-states they built often failed to deliver on their promises. In terms of race, class, gender, and sexuality in particular, many of them remained, on the whole, ethnocentric, patriarchal, bourgeois, and homophobic. At the same time, a view of Third World nationalism as the mere echo of European nationalism ignores the inter-national realpolitik that made the end of colonialism coincide with the beginning of the nation-state. The formation of Third World nation-states often involved a double process, on the one hand of joining diverse ethnicities and regions that had been separated under colonialism, and on the other, of partitioning regions in a way that forced regional redefini-tion (Iraq/Kuwait) and a cross-shuffling of populations (Pakistan, India, Israel/Palestine). Furthermore, political geographies and state borders do not always coincide with imaginary geographies, thus variously producing internal émigrés, rebels, and nostalgics—i.e., groups of people who share the same passport but whose relations to the nation-state are conflicted and ambivalent. In the postcolonial context of constant flux of peoples, affiliation with the nation-state becomes highly partial and contingent.

While most Third Worldist films assumed the fundamental coherence of national identity, with the expulsion of the colonial intruder fully completing the process of national becoming, the post-nationalist films call attention to the faultlines of gender, class, ethnicity, region, partition, migration, and exile. Many of the films explore the complex identities generated by exile—from one's own geography, from one's own history, from one's own body—within innovative narrative strategies. Fragmented cinematic forms come to homologize cultural disembodiment. Caren Kaplan's observa-tions about a reconceived "minor" literature as de-romanticizing solitude and rewriting "the connections between different parts of the self in order to make a world of possibilities out of the experience of displacement"[13] are exquisitely appropriate to two autobiographical films by Palestinians in exile, Elia Suleiman's *Homage by Assassination* (1992) and Mona Hatoum's *Measures of Distance* (1998). *Homage by Assassination* chronicles Suleiman's life in New York during the Persian Gulf War, foregrounding multiple failures of communication: a radio announcer's aborted efforts to reach the filmmaker by phone; the filmmaker's failed attempts to talk to his family in Nazareth (Israel/Palestine); his impotent look at old family photographs; and despairing answering-machine jokes about the Palestinian situation. The glorious dream of nationhood and return is here reframed as a Palestinian flag on a TV monitor, the land as a map on a wall, and the return (*'awda*) as the "return" key on the computer keyboard.

Figure 44   Elia Suleiman's *Homage by Assassination*, 1992

At one point the filmmaker receives a fax from a friend, who narrates her family history as an Arab Jew, her feelings during the bombing of Iraq and the Scud attacks on Israel, and her story of the family's displacement from Iraq, through Israel/Palestine, and then on to the U.S.[14] The communications technologies become the imperfect means by which dislocated people retain a national imaginary, while also fighting for a place in a new geography (the U.S., Britain), nation-states whose foreign policies have concretely impacted their lives. *Homage by Assassination* invokes the diverse spatialities and temporalities that mark the exilic experience. A shot of two clocks, in New York and in Nazareth, points to the double time-frame lived by the diasporic subject, a temporal doubleness underlined by an intertitle saying that the filmmaker's mother, due to the Scud attacks, is adjusting her gas mask at that very moment. The friend's letter similarly stresses the fractured space-time of being in the U.S. while identifying with both Iraq and Israel.

In *Measures of Distance*, the Palestinian video/performance artist Mona Hatoum explores the renewal of friendship between her mother and herself during a brief family reunion in Lebanon in the early 1980s. The film relates the fragmented memories of diverse generations: the mother's tales of the "used-to-be" of Palestine, Hatoum's own childhood in Lebanon, the civil war in Lebanon, and the current dispersal of the daughters in the West. (Orientalist cinema, from *The Sheik*, through *The King and I*, to *Out of*

Africa, has generally preferred showing Western travelers in the East rather than Eastern women in the West.) As images of the mother's hand-written Arabic letters to the daughter are superimposed over dissolves of the daughter's color slides of her mother in the shower, we hear an audiotape of their conversations in Arabic, along with excerpts of their letters as translated and read by the filmmaker in English.

The voice-over and script of *Measures of Distance* narrate a paradoxical state of geographic distance and emotional closeness. The textual, visual, and inter-linguistic play between Arabic and English underlines the family's serial dislocations, from Palestine to Lebanon to Britain, where Mona Hatoum has been living since 1975, gradually unfolding the dispersion of Palestinians over very diverse geographies. The foregrounded letters, photographs, and audiotapes call attention to the means by which people in exile maintain cultural identity. In the mother's voice-over, the repeated phrase "My dear Mona" evokes the diverse "measures of distance" implicit in the film's title. Meanwhile, background dialogue in Arabic, recalling their conversations about sexuality and Palestine during their reunion, recorded in the past but played in the present, parallels photos of the mother in the shower, also taken in the past but viewed in the present. The multiplication of temporalities continues in Hatoum's reading of a letter in English: to the moments of the letter's sending and its arrival is added the moment of Hatoum's voice-over translation of it for the English-speaking viewer. Each

Figure 45   Mona Hatoum's *Measures of Distance*, 1988

layer of time evokes a distance at once temporal and spatial, historical and geographical; each dialogue is situated, produced, and received in precise historical circumstances.

The linguistic play also marks the distance between mother and daughter, while their separation instantiates the fragmented existence of a nation. When relentless bombing prevents the mother from mailing her letter, the screen fades to black, suggesting an abrupt end to communication. Yet the letter eventually arrives via messenger, while the voice-over narrates the exile's difficulty in maintaining contact with one's culture(s). The negotiation of time and place is here absolutely crucial. The videomaker's voice-over reading her mother's letters in the present interferes with the dialogue recorded in the past in Lebanon. The background conversations in Arabic give a sense of present-tense immediacy, while the more predominant English voice-over speaks of the same conversation in the past tense. The Arabic-speaking viewer labors to focus on the Arabic conversation and read the Arabic scripts, while also listening to the English. If the non-Arabic speaking spectator misses some of the film's textual registers, the Arabic-speaking spectator is overwhelmed by competing images and sounds. This strategic refusal to translate Arabic is also echoed in Suleiman's *Homage by Assassination* where the director (in person) types out Arabic proverbs on a computer screen, without providing any translation. These exiled filmmakers thus cunningly provoke in the spectator the same alienation experienced by a displaced person, reminding us, through inversion, of the asymmetry in social power between exiles and their "host communities." At the same time, they catalyze a sense of community for the diasporic speech community, a strategy especially suggestive of diasporic filmmakers, who often wind up in the First World precisely because colonial/imperial power has turned them into displaced persons.

Measures of Distance also probes issues of sexuality and the female body in a kind of self-ethnography, its nostalgic rhetoric concerning less the "public sphere" of national struggle than the "private sphere" of sexuality, pregnancy, and children. The women's conversations about sexuality leave the father feeling displaced by what he dismisses as "women's nonsense." The daughter's photographs of her nude mother make him profoundly uncomfortable, as if the daughter, as the mother writes, "had trespassed on his possession." To videotape such intimate conversations is not common practice in Middle Eastern cinema, or for that matter, in any cinema. (Western audiences often ask how Hatoum won her mother's consent to use nude photographs and how she broached the subject of sexuality.) Paradoxically, the exile's distance from the Middle East authorizes the exposure of intimacy. Displacement and separation make possible a transformative return to the inner sanctum of the home; mother and daughter are together again in the space of the text.

In Western popular culture, the Arab female body, whether in the form of the veiled bare-breasted women who posed for French colonial photographers or of the Orientalist harems and belly dancers of Hollywood film, has functioned as a sign of the exotic.[15] But rather than adopt a patriarchal strategy of simply censuring female nudity, Hatoum deploys the diffusely sensuous, almost pointillist images of her naked mother to tell a more complex story with nationalist overtones. She uses diverse strategies to veil the images from voyeuristic scrutiny: already hazy images are concealed by text (fragments of the mother's correspondence, in Arabic script) and are difficult to decipher. The superimposed words in Arabic serve to "envelop" her nudity. "Barring" the body, the script metaphorizes her inaccessibility, visually undercutting the intimacy verbally expressed in other registers. The fragmented nature of existence in exile is underlined by superimposed fragmentations: fragments of letters, of dialogue, and of the mother's *corps morcelé* (rendered as isolated hands, breasts, belly). The blurred and fragmented images evoke the dispersed collectivity of the national family itself.[16] Rather than evoke the longing for an ancestral home, *Measures of Distance*, like *Homage by Assassination*, affirms the process of recreating identity in the liminal zone of exile.[17] Video layering makes it possible for Mona Hatoum to capture the fluid, multiple identities of the diasporic subject.

A discourse which is "purely" feminist or "purely" nationalist, I have tried to argue, cannot apprehend the layered, dissonant identities of diasporic or post-independence feminist subjects. The diasporic and post-Third Worldist films of the 1980s and 1990s, in this sense, do not so much reject the "nation" as interrogate its repressions and limits, passing nationalist discourse through the grids of class, gender, sexual, and diasporic identities. While often embedded in the autobiographical, they are not always narrated in the first person, nor are they "merely" personal; rather, the boundaries between the personal and communal, like the generic boundaries between documentary and fiction, are constantly blurred. The diary form, the voice-over, the personal written text, now bear witness to a collective memory of colonial violence. While early Third Worldist films documented alternative histories through archival footage, interviews, testimonials, and historical reconstructions, generally limiting their attention to the public sphere, the films of the 1980s and 1990s use the camera less as revolutionary weapon than as monitor of the gendered and sexualized realms of the personal and the domestic, seen as integral but repressed aspects of collective history. They display a certain skepticism toward metanarratives of liberation, but do not necessarily abandon the notion that emancipation is worth fighting for. But rather than fleeing from contradiction, they install doubt and crisis at the very core of the films. Rather than a grand anti-colonial metanarrative, they favor heteroglossic proliferations of difference within polygeneric narratives, seen not as embodiments of a single truth but rather as energizing political and aesthetic forms of communitarian self-construction.

2 1

Reflections on September 11

A month has passed, and we still struggle to comprehend the magnitude of the horrific carnage of September 11. These events have not only saddened and angered us; they have also left us full of questions and doubts. At a time when the dominant media and the powers that be urge us to adopt a simplistic discourse, now more than ever we, as teachers, students, artists, and activists, or simply as citizens, need to collectively respond with a complex and nuanced analysis. We need to place these unjustifiable atrocities within a wider historical perspective; we have to exercise our democratic rights, including our right to be critical.

What George Bush, our public representatives, and the dominant media have offered us is largely a Manichean discourse of false dichotomies— us against them, good against evil, democracy against tyranny, civilization against barbarism, modernity versus Islam, and Christianity versus fundamentalism.

The sheer horror of the atrocities lends a semblance of common sense to these dichotomies. Manichean narratives are tempting because they give us a false sense of moral security, wrapping us in a narcissistic cocoon, allowing us to digest the indigestible, to assimilate the unacceptable. Within this discourse, an orderly and peaceful world has been subjected to arbitrary and irrational attack, and our own regenerative violence will restore the everyday order of the world "before the fall," a prelapsarian order for which we are already nostalgic.

The desire to narrate events in this manner is an understandable response in the wake of a traumatic crisis, but it is also our responsibility to be skeptical about such ahistorical narratives. We must refuse a Hollywood war-movie script, because Schwarzenegger is not the answer. If we are to cope with what lies ahead, we must refuse to be consoled with fairy-tales.

In fact, on closer inspection, the dichotomies posited above break down. For example: good versus evil? The problem is that the good—presumably

Unpublished presentation given on a Teach-In panel moderated by Randy Martin, New York University, October 10, 2001, and posted on The Hagop Kevorkian Center for Near Eastern Studies at New York University, Fall 2001.

us—have been intimately involved with the evil—them. Bin Laden, the current incarnation of Evil, was, as we know, at one point recruited and supported by the U.S. In the 1980s, government-sponsored centers in Brooklyn recruited Muslim fundamentalists to go fight the Soviet Union in Afghanistan. At that time, bin Laden was on the good side of the Manichean divide—our government called him and his fellow *mujahidin* "freedom fighters."

In fact, since World War II, U.S. foreign policy has repeatedly used Muslim fundamentalists against both communism and progressive forms of nationalism, recruiting fundamentalist allies among the Muslim Brothers in Egypt against Nasser; using the Jamaat-i-Islami against Benazir Bhutto in Pakistan; and bin Laden against the secular communist Muhammad Najibullah in Afghanistan. At the time of the Gulf War, George Bush's father offered us a similar discourse about another incarnation of evil, Saddam Hussein, who had previously been the ally of American policy and the darling of U.S., British, and German corporations. After his fateful mistake of invading Kuwait, Hussein was transformed into a reincarnation of Hitler with the rapidity with which new enemies for "Hate Week" were fabricated in George Orwell's *1984*. Manichean discourses, then, are all too subject to these quick reversals of evaluation.

While Manichean allegories allow for righteous rage and emotional catharsis, they do not allow for complexity—for two competing evils, for example, or for lesser and greater evils—but only for absolute good against absolute evil. It is tempting to think that bin Laden's undeniable evil somehow makes his enemies good. But this too is a non sequitur. In a moment of mourning, we feel a desperate need for moral clarity. But the undeniable guilt of the terrorists, and the *absolutely* undeniable innocence of the civilian victims in the World Trade Center, does not mean that the U.S. government shares in that innocence. The U.S. government, corporate interests, multinationals, and globalization institutions have fostered injustice in many parts of the world, leading to countless deaths—through direct and indirect support for brutal dictatorships, toppling democratically elected governments, through complicity in dispossessions, famine, massacres, coups d'état, the bombings of civilians and so forth.

The discourse of "loss of innocence" is also disturbing, for it elides some primal home-based crimes committed against Native Americans, African Americans, and others. The idea that only now we have lost our innocence implies a privileged, dominant point of view. African Americans, for example, have been the victims of home-grown terror, in the form of the horrors of slavery, of lynching, and the terrorism of the Ku Klux Klan. (Indeed, we need an expanded and more precise definition of terrorism, one that also includes state terrorism and vigilante terrorism.)

The idea of an only-now-lost innocence is rooted in a deafness not only to the dynamics of U.S. history but also to the results of U.S. foreign policy in the world. Implicitly, a sense of innocence is premised on the privilege of not knowing what has been done in our name. It is one thing for citizens in an isolated island that exercises no power in the world to be ignorant of that world, but it is inexcusable for the citizens of a powerful nation-state, whose weight and pressure is felt around the world, to be ignorant of that world. Narratives of innocence simply reproduce the very kind of thinking and acting which has brought a situation of widespread resentment of the U.S., due to its unilateral and self-serving interventions around the world, resentment on which death cults like that of bin Laden can build and thrive.

In answer to the question "why do they hate us" the joke goes that they hate us because we don't even know why they hate us. There are many reasons for this ignorance—a dumbed-down schooling system, a consumerist approach to education, a corporate media that flatters Americans in the name of ratings—and it is our responsibility as teachers, scholars, and artists to combat that ignorance and the deluded narcissism of unthinking patriotism.

By the same token, the facts of the imperial policies of the U.S., of oil-driven hegemony in the Gulf, of the murderous sanctions on Iraq, of blind U.S. support for Israeli policies, do not turn the terrorists into the legitimate avengers of the crimes committed against populations in the Third World in general. Terrorist crimes do not avenge other crimes; they simply add more crimes. A fundamentalist Manichean discourse projects a righteous East pitted against a corrupt and infidel West. Bin Laden's discourse is the demonizing discourse of a zealot, one that turns all Jews, Christians, and Muslims, who do not share his interpretation, into infidels worthy of death. Even if we can understand some of the causes of resentment against the U.S., we have to affirm that terrorism should never be a means of fighting global oppression. Terrorist attacks tend to harden attitudes and legitimize repression. For example, due to September 11, the anti-globalization movement, which was gaining momentum, has been placed on the defensive.

Moreover, it is not a question of bad methods for good ends. The terrorists' long-term goal is ultimately a religious war that would universalize their truth and their distorted reading of Islam. The bin Laden/Taliban world view has posed a serious threat not only for non-Muslims around the world but also for the human rights and civil rights of Muslim citizens themselves both here and abroad. We, who have been concerned with multicultural vision and minority rights, have in the same breath to deplore not only the bin Ladenist method, but also its monological world vision and political philosophy.

The fundamentalist vision does not represent all Muslims. In fact, it is at odds with the practice of multiculturalism *avant la lettre* that has prevailed, for the most part, under the auspices of Islam. Pitting Western modernity against Eastern fundamentalist traditionalism is therefore another false binarism. This extremist strain that has nominated itself to speak on behalf of all Muslims—is actually a product of *our* own times. Current Jewish/ Arab hostility is of relatively recent date. Muslims and Jews were oppressed together during the Spanish Inquisition, and subjected together to forced conversion and expulsion. The Ottoman Empire welcomed Jews both after the Inquisition in 1492 and with the onset of the Holocaust in the late 1930s. In fact, the Holocaust took place in the modern Christian West, never in the Islamic East. Unlike the tolerant Islamic tradition that has valued Christians and Jews as protected minorities representing the "people of the book," bin Laden's discourse demonizes both Christians and Jews as infidels, creating a new tradition produced within modernity. That is why it is wrong to refer to his ideas as "Medieval," a word that is itself a Eurocentric designation for what was in Europe the so-called Dark Ages but which for Islam and for Judaism was the height of civilizational creativity.

The problem with Manichean discourse is that it produces and projects its own hated other, resulting in dangers for people of Middle Eastern, Muslim, Arab, and South Asian origins. We hear popular versions of this Manichean thinking in overheard comments in the street, for example one I heard, which went as follows: "We should nuke them, like we did with China!" Just as bin Laden makes no distinction between military and civilians, between the army general and the janitors working in the World Trade Center, our "nuker" friend confuses China and Japan, and calls for infinite slaughter on a scale that exceeds even that of bin Laden. In the same vein, the former Mayor of New York, Edward Koch, reportedly recommended that we "level the capital of any country that harbors terrorists"—an example, again, of bin Laden-style thinking, of becoming the enemy.

In conclusion, a few words about how we in educational institutions might meet some of the challenges ahead. Each one of us has also to become a media critic, stressing the role of the media in framing events, naming them, narrativizing them. Why was the response declared, almost instantly, a war and a crusade? Wars take place between nation-states, and in this sense we are not at war. Doesn't the war discourse play into bin Laden's hopes and rhetoric, since he too is calling for an all-out war between Islam and the Infidels? And why did the media designate it as only America's war, and not the struggle of an international coalition against an international problem? All of these media choices foreclose other options and forms of analysis.

We should also be aware of the role of the media in channeling emotion. The events of September 11 clearly provoked legitimate anger against the terrorists. But the media also foreclosed other forms of anger—for example anger at our government for spending billions on "defense" without actually "defending" us. Or our anger at the Pentagon and the Foreign Policy establishment for pursuing policies that put our lives in danger, in which American citizens become "collateral damage" for ill-conceived policies, presumably pursued "in our name."

We should stress the need for all of us to learn history, culture, and languages. We can use the arts and the media to offer a transnationally informed contrapuntal history, by which students would learn multiple perspectives on history—not to agree with them all but at least to understand them. Contrapuntal history would insist less on the brute facts of history, than on the various grids through which they are seen and perceived. Grids are no less important than facts. It is perhaps inevitable that the Christian fundamentalist Jerry Falwell would look at the events of September 11 and blame feminists, gays and lesbians, and the liberals. That's his Taliban-like grid. The point of contrapuntal history would be to promote awareness of the multiple perspectives on events, but always with a bass note of concern for peace, justice, and equality.

22

Anti-Americanism: The Middle East

(A Conversation with Rashid Khalidi)

Ella Shohat: As a way of beginning our conversation, I'd like to cite Samir Amin's article published in the Egyptian paper *Al-Ahram Weekly* [in Spring 2003], entitled "The American Ideology." Amin makes important criticisms of U.S. foreign policy, mostly in the mold of materialist analysis of economic and political interests. But he also offers an ahistorical account of American history, cast in culturalist and essentialist terms. For example, Amin describes U.S. neoimperialism as rooted in the Biblical, Judaic foundations of Protestantism that "facilitated the conquest of new continents by grounding its legitimacy in scriptures" and, later, extended this God-given mission "to encompass the entire globe with its predilection for apocalyptic fantasies." Consequently, he argues, "Americans have come to regard themselves as the 'chosen people,' in practice a synonym for the Nazi term Herrenvolk." American imperialism, Amin concludes, is even more brutal than its predecessors, since "most imperialists, after all, do not claim to have been invested with a divine mission."

Amin offers an exclusivist argument for U.S. behavior, rather than seeing it as part of a broader colonialist pattern in the Americas as a whole. As for his culturalist version of U.S. history, it is a reductionist and, at times, uninformed account, oblivious to the complexity of the many contradictory forces, movements, and ideologies that have shaped the U.S. state. Even the title, "The American Ideology," suggests that there is one kind of an essence to the Anglo-American spirit, and one kind of ideology.

On December 12, 2003, in conjunction with the publication of the volume *Anti-Americanism,* the author conducted the following conversation with Rashid Khalidi, Director of the Middle East Institute and Edward Said Professor of Arab Studies at Columbia University, whose books include: *Under Siege: PLO Decision-Making during the 1982 War* (Columbia, 1986) and *Palestinian Identity: The Construction of Modern National Consciousness* (Columbia, 1997). Published in the "Middle East" section of *Anti-Americanism,* coedited by Andrew Ross and Kristin Ross (New York: New York University Press, 2004).

Rashid Khalidi: I would be very wary of talking about Protestantism, even, as if it were a monolith. There are apocalyptic and eschatological aspects to some strands of Protestantism, and then there are universalist, charitable, humanistic, and anti-imperialist strands in American Protestantism. The fact that the present administration happens to have as its political base the former trend doesn't mean that it is Protestantism any more than the liberal Protestantism represented by the Council of Churches is Protestantism.

ES: Even Bush's own denomination of the Methodist Church did not line up behind him on the war! My point here is not to defend any religion but to caution that an essentialist anti-Americanism is as problematic, or as irresponsible, as essentialist Americanism. When leftist critics of U.S. foreign policy, like Amin, trace a direct line from the Salem witch trials to John Ashcroft and to the war on Iraq, they deny the U.S. its own diverse and conflicted religious history. The Quakers, after all, were the first to call for the abolition of slavery at the time of the American Revolution, and the Black Protestant churches have long played a progressive role. Most of the Protestant denominations condemned Bush's war, and their leaders were frequent speakers at anti-war demonstrations. Ultimately, the problem with this univocal account is that the extreme religious right comes to stand for the quintessence of "America."

RK: Exactly. There is something to this sense of America's manifest destiny as having been blessed by God, but that's not all of America. It doesn't represent the pioneering era when the Native-American population was destroyed, any more than it represents the first American imperial thrust across the seas into Hawai'i, the Caribbean, and the Philippines. All along, there were, and still are, countervailing forces in American history, with alternative ideologies and very real political influence. Amin's analysis typifies, in a particularly sophisticated form, one older strand of what might legitimately be called anti-Americanism. It is grounded in a Marxist critique of imperialist power and, I think you are right, tended to essentialize all policy, rather than assessing specific American policies as either imperialist or not. This view, which was once very prevalent in some parts of the Arab world, tended to look on the U.S. as evil because of an essentializing, totalizing vision of America, its essence, and its ideologies.

This viewpoint has grown much less influential over the last few decades, ironically enough, as the U.S. has become more powerful in the Middle East. Today, it represents a minuscule proportion of public opinion, even of intellectual, academic, and leftist public opinion. Those who hold the strongest anti-Americanism sentiments in the Arab world are a particular strand of Islamists. Not all Muslims, not all Islamists, not even many or most Islamists, but the people who are the inheritors of a specific historical strand of Muslim program and thought.

ES: It's not necessarily just anti-American. Due to the colonization of the region that had begun with Napoleon, it was as much anti-French, or anti-British. France and Britain had far more consequences for the daily realities of Arabs, and for the formation of their nation-states. In the Middle East, "America" was still a distant geography.

RK: It was anti-Western, but it saw the U.S. increasingly as the pre-eminent Western power. Take the example of Sayyid Qutb, who developed the thinking of Hassan al-Banna, founder of the Muslim Brotherhood in Egypt. He was a thinker of the 1960s, even of the 1950s, when America had already become a preeminent power. He also had some first-hand experience of the U.S., which I think affected him. So he and his followers—he was executed by the Egyptian regime—are one strand.

Another strand has its origins in a particularly virulent form of the old Wahabbist xenophobia. Xenophobia was an element in Wahabbist thought going back to the mid-18th century, when the movement first allied itself with the Saudi dynasty. It persisted there, but to see that strand as indicative of the whole of Wahabbism, and to see Wahabbism as all of Islam, is an extreme perversion of fact, though an increasingly common one on the part of opinion makers. There were other variants of Wahabbist thought. The fact that the xenophobes were constantly curbed by the Saudi regime indicates that there were all kinds of countervailing forces. This tendency was nowhere near as sophisticated as, say, Sayyid Qutb's followers. It was just generic xenophobia, which was then interpreted in Islamic terms when other elements of Islamic doctrine were picked up to justify it. Out of these two (and probably other) strands has grown an anti-Americanism specifically cast in Islamic terms.

These, I think, are tiny minority trends, and so I would not start any discussion of anti-Americanism in the Middle East there. Rather, I would begin by asking, what has been the primary orientation of the elites, or the major political parties, in the Arab world, over the past century and a half? For most of the region, for most of this period, these elites have been characterized by an orientation towards some form of representative government, constitutionalism, and liberal democracy. Yes, there were authoritarian trends, powerful militarist tendencies, and there was the very strong influence of a one-party system, mainly as the result of Third International communist parties. They all had a big influence on elites. But from the 1850s, some form of limitation on autocracy, some goal of representative government, and some version of liberalism were all extremely attractive ideologies for elites in the largely Arab parts of the Middle East. The

Ottoman constitutional revolution, the Iranian constitutional revolution, and efforts in Tunisia and in Egypt in the latter half of the 19th century all sought to limit the power of the ruler. The elites themselves were not always democratic, in some cases were oligarchic, and in others were extremely monopolistic in how they controlled power, but they absorbed and wielded these ideologies, which grew enormously in strength with the expansion of education in the late 19th and early 20th centuries. Consequently, by the early or mid-20th century, those liberal ideologies were very powerful throughout the Arab world.

Among the countervailing forces were the autocracies, in many cases supported externally, like the monarchy in Egypt, which was supported and operated by the British, who chose and even named the king. The colonial system, which prevented the most popular political party from controlling Egypt's politics from independence in 1922 until the revolution in 1952, was entirely dominated and controlled by the British. Democracy was foiled in Egypt not by anti-democratic Egyptian forces, nor by Islam, but by imperialism.

ES: This is the kind of paradoxical situation that populations in the Middle East, as in many countries throughout Africa and Latin America, have found themselves tangled up in. There is a bitter irony expressed in attitudes toward the discourse of democracy, when the very forces struggling to democratize have been suppressed by regimes imposed and managed by colonial or ex-colonial powers. All the talk about "bringing democracy to the Middle East" comes from powers that have stood in the way of democratizing. In fact, you can argue that this dissonance prepared the ground for the contemporary skepticism about the U.S. role in the region.

RK: The same was true in Iran, in the Ottoman Empire, and, to a lesser extent, in a number of other countries like Syria, Lebanon, Iraq. But when we look for the roots of attitudes towards the West, what's usually missing is a sense of how these elites have always been open to democratic ideas and constitutionalism.

ES: The struggle for democratization in the Middle East has often been complicated, though, by ideologies of modernization. Along with the battle for liberation from colonialism, nationalism also offered a legitimate vehicle for expressing the desire for modernity, which was identified with the "West."

RK: Precisely, and what's also missing from the general perception of the Middle East as intrinsically anti-American is the fact that for the first half of the 20th century, the Middle East was overwhelmingly pro-American.

ES: Absolutely. "America" was in many ways perceived to be somehow "outside" the violent dynamic of British and French colonialisms. Of course, this perception ignored the U.S.'s own colonial history, and also its imperial policies in places like Latin America, carried out partly under the guise of the Monroe Doctrine. But I think that, at least within the popular imagination, the distance of the U.S.—and I don't mean only geographical but also political—allowed it to remain untainted by the anticolonial sentiment throughout the first half of the 20th century.

RK: In World War I, the U.S. was seen as a possible savior from the imperial powers. From Korea and India to Morocco, and indeed all over the Third World, the U.S. was, at the time, regarded with rapture. It's no coincidence that there were national uprisings against national oppressors in Korea, India, and Egypt at the time of and after the Paris peace conference in 1919.

ES: Even later, during the Suez Canal crisis, the U.S. managed its geopolitical influence in a way that was perceived relatively favorably. Washington, via the United Nations, actually intervened to head off a war that was declared on Egypt by the Franco-Anglo-Israeli alliance.

RK: Exactly, and this continues somewhat into the second half of the 20th century. I would argue that there was a deep reservoir of pro-Americanism, a profound sympathy with American ideals, and a hope that American policy would live up to those ideals, well into the 1950s and 1960s, and partly, as you suggest, because of Suez. This wasn't simply a matter of policy; it had to do with the fact that the great colonial powers engaged in educational, missionary, and other efforts as part of an imperialist strategy for control and domination. Until the second half of the 20th century, this was not the case for the U.S.

ES: At least not to the same degree, since you could find American-based missionary activities in East Asia, sub-Saharan Africa, or Latin America, and from the 1830s onwards, in China.

RK: Yes, but in the Middle East this was certainly not the case. U.S. ideals, it was hoped, might be actuated in a way that would balance the rapaciousness of the European great powers. Of course, none of this happened. The hopes for the Fourteen Points, and Wilson's peace conference, were disappointed, and nothing much followed that would have borne out these expectations.

However, after World War II, there were specific instances where American policy did help in the removal of foreign military forces, from Libya and Iran, for example, immediately after World War I and World War II, and in the case of the former, right up to 1950, it appeared that the U.S. was helping to block the ambitions of the traditional colonial powers.

Equally in Algeria, where Washington offered support, albeit tepid, to the national liberation movement.

Things begin to change in the 1960s and 1970s, largely because of the Palestine issue. The U.S. became a much more important Middle East power and began to behave more like the other great powers. So, too, there were changes in ideology. The Ba'th Party became much more of a radical party, the Communist party assumed importance in some Arab countries, and other, more radical, nationalist parties took on explicitly anti-imperialist rhetoric. But, even in this period, I think, there was not a deep anti-Americanism in the sense of a rejection of Americans. Until the 1980s, there was very little personal or group violence against Americans in the Middle East, and American institutions were generally not attacked as such.

ES: That's true. Even during the 1967 demonstrations in front of American embassies, it was clear that the hostility was directed toward support for Israel rather than toward some American essence. Americans who traveled during this period in Tunisia or Morocco customarily spoke of people making a distinction between Washington's policies and Americans in general. Members of the U.S. Peace Corps enjoyed warm social relations with Tunisians, for example. It is important to bring up this little-written-about history, because it offers quite a contrast to the way that U.S. media today draw on traditional Orientalist narratives to explain "why they hate us." The media tend to represent anti-Americanism as some kind of deep animosity that is wholly irrational, dating back to a clash of civilizations from time immemorial. But testimonies of Americans traveling in the region offer a different picture.

RK: I think you're right, and I think you do see the change in the 1980s when the rhetoric associated with critiques of America begins to take on a religious flavor. This is partly a function of the Iranian revolution. A new strand of bitterness with American policy emerged in Iran that became quite poisonous. There was a move away from criticism of this or that American policy—from saying "the U.S. is fine but it did a bad thing in supporting the Shah" to saying, "The U.S. is bad." Not just American policy, but the U.S. as a whole.

So now we had three essentialist critiques: the Sayyid Qutb critique, which says there's nothing the U.S. can do to change its basic nature. Then the specific trend of xenophobia in Wahhabi thought, which essentially says, "Americans are bad because they are poisoning our country." And now you have a third strand, which comes with the Iranian revolution. These three merge in a new form of anti-Americanism, which is quite different from the Marxist form that is represented by the recent example of Samir Amin's article.

Yet, I still believe you can readily distinguish between that kind of visceral anti-Americanism (mainly found in minority Islamist circles growing out of these three trends) and a much broader, majority sentiment that is extremely critical of specific aspects of American policy, while at the same time having a respect, and in some cases even a love, for American values—whether these be American materialism, free-market ideology, American consumer culture, or American representative democracy and constitutionalism. For this majority, there is no intrinsic dislike of the U.S., or at least there is an appreciation of certain aspects of what America is seen as standing for.

ES: Certainly there has also been a fascinating dialogue with American popular culture. Egyptian musicals from the 1930s throughout the 1960s alluded to Hollywood musicals. In belly-dance sequences with Samya Gamal or Tahiya Carioca moving to the quartertones of Arabic music, you can find insertions of the dance forms and music rhythms of jazz, rumba, and tango, typical of the mélange of the Hollywood musical numbers. By the time of Youssef Chahine's semiautobiographical 1979 film *Iskandariya Lih?* [*Alexandria Why?*], about an aspiring young Egyptian filmmaker who entertains Hollywood dreams during World War II, you can see the shift away from that incredible fantasy that was America in an era when the Axis–Allies war took place on a land that was Egyptian. In that film, the desire for the space of hope called "America" ends with a disappointing welcome by a Statue of Liberty, pictured as a decadent, toothless woman laughing in a vulgar fashion. This highly gendered national allegory of the love–hate relationship with America reflects its context—the turbulent moment of Sadat's visit to Jerusalem, followed by the normalization of Egyptian/Israeli relations and the Camp David accords, all of which were viewed as coming at the expense of Palestine and signified deep shame for the majority of Egyptians.

RK: Yes, the cultural attraction is always combined with a harsh critique of specific policies, especially those regarding Palestine. So, too, there is always mention of U.S. support for structurally oppressive regimes, and now, of course, the policy on Iraq, both the imposition of sanctions after the Kuwait war and the policy since the recent invasion.

ES: Your point is very important, because the imaginary construct of anti-Americanism in the U.S. media and in this administration's pronouncements almost entirely glosses over the U.S. historical record of supporting undemocratic regimes throughout the world. After all, it was father Bush, during the Reagan administration, that sustained Saddam Hussein during his war with Iran, and the atrocious crimes he committed against his people were performed with the knowledge of the many functionaries who fill high offices in the current administration. U.S. media tend to underplay that famous handshake between Hussein and Rumsfeld, and when they do show this image, it is unaccompanied by any narrative that would suggest our complicity in the atrocities.

RK: In fact, as I show in my next book [called *Resurrecting Empire*], American support for the Ba'th Party started soon after the revolution of 1958 and continued almost without interruption through the 1970s, when the U.S. shifted its support to the Shah. Right after the Iranian revolution, Washington reverted to support of the Ba'th. So for the 32 years between 1958 and the invasion of Kuwait in 1990, with the exception of a few years when the U.S. supported the Shah, the U.S. was one of the foremost supporters of the Ba'th Party and its governments ....

ES: ... and of their persecution and massacre not only of Kurds and Shi'is but also of communists. We cannot forget that Iraq had the largest Communist party in the Arab world, and many of its members were tortured, killed, or forced into exile. The profile of Saddam as the bad boy who refused to listen to Washington raises serious questions not only about U.S. policy but also about how the Iraqis are represented. In spite of all the talk about making us safer by bringing democracy, many Iraqis have not forgotten that their "savior" supported, and partially funded, the expulsions and massacres.

RK: Another example was the cynical exploitation of the Kurds as a weapon against Saddam so long as it pleased the Shah. As soon as he negotiated what he wanted from the Algiers agreement, the Kurds were dropped and left to their miserable fate at the hands of the Iraqis. Admittedly, the Shah took a lead on this, but the U.S. was a disgraceful party to it.

ES: Nor should we forget that the Shah only came to power in the first place at the behest of the U.S., which engineered the coup.

RK: Finally, there is the murkiest chapter of all, which is American support for Islamist extremist (and, in some cases, Islamist terrorist) movements against secular political parties in the Arab world. This includes the CIA station in Munich, which financed and supported the Muslim Brotherhood in its war against the Ba'th regime in Syria, and Gamal Abdel Nasser's regime in Egypt, continuing through the Sadat era and Washington's use of Islamists to fight the secular, leftist tendencies. Then you have the recent history in Afghanistan. Just because Americans don't generally know about these things doesn't mean that people in the Middle East are going to forget them. When they talk about the U.S. and its policies, they're not referring to the ideal vision of the democracy-loving U.S.; they are usually talking about these backstreet, dirty, undercover operations.

ES: It's very important to speak here about popular memory as a counter-narrative to the way U.S. official discourses tend to represent anti-Americanism. These memories are clearly registered and passed on in the communities of the region, but their oral history never shows up in media reports from the region. Nonetheless, this counter-memory is crucial to the current discrepancy between what anti-Americanism means in places like the Middle East or Latin America and what it means here. I think that this discrepancy in knowledge nurtures the feeling of innocence and promotes the state of anxiety (and I am here reminded of a common Israeli trope) that "the whole world is against us."

RK: We can be even blunter. In order to cover up the fact that there are reactions to specific American policies, it's necessary for the advocates of these policies to claim purity and innocence and insist that we are hated because we are what we are. That's because they cannot ever admit to those policies, which have to be hidden or screened from the American public. The tragedy of U.S.–Middle East policy is that the U.S. has not been celebrated for its selfless devotion to democracy but rather that it has been bitterly criticized for not showing the slightest commitment to democracy, whether in Turkey, Iran, or country after country in the Arab and non-Arab Middle East, with the sole exception of Israel. And least of all in the occupied territories.

ES: Well, here we have a formal democracy, though, as we know, our president was selected in 2000. As for Israel proper—and here we are leaving aside the West Bank and Gaza—what does democracy mean for Palestinian citizens of Israel when in fact they have limited access to power and to self-representation? After all, they are systematically racialized and marginalized in a land that used to be theirs—and within the unresolved paradox of a formal democracy that is also defined as a Jewish state.

RK: There are whole issues there for non-Jewish citizens ...

ES: And Arab Jews who are also discriminated against.

RK: Nobody ever claimed that discrimination is foreign to democracy! In the U.S., we are living in a country where 50 percent of the population was disenfranchised until the second quarter of the 20th century and where all people of certain racial origins were disenfranchised until the Civil War and then officially discriminated against until the 1950s.

ES: Yes, there is a strain of anti-Americanism that forgets that many Americans are also disenfranchised by a certain idea of Americanism.

Supremacist thought is more or less foundational to colonial-settler states that dispossessed indigenous populations. But it's taboo to mention this when we are supposed to be talking about the "spread of democracy." Pragmatic amnesia is encouraged.

RK: With almost no exceptions, Washington has not exerted any effort to actually bring about constitutionalism and democracy, or respect for human rights, in most of the countries where it has influence. Perhaps you can't blame the U.S. for Iraq in a certain period, though you can say that the U.S. actively supported the Ba'th Party against the communists. But you can blame the U.S. for countries where it has had paramount influence for most of the last few decades: Saudi Arabia, Egypt, and many others.

ES: Israel, Turkey—

RK: Morocco, Tunisia, Lebanon, Jordan, and so on and so forth. Where, for example, was the U.S. when King Hussein in 1957 abrogated the only real functioning democracy in Jordanian history?

ES: We've talked about the legitimate critique of U.S. foreign policies in the region, as well as the mythification that tends to expunge from the record the U.S. interventions in the region against forces of democracy. And we've also talked about the essentialism of leftist anti-American discourses. But we also have to elaborate on the culturalist tendencies of some religious discourses, tendencies that are not uncommon in certain strands of Islam and which characterize many religions, certainly monotheist religions. To a large degree, anti-Americanism in the region now feeds off the perception of American cultural products as corrupting, even on the part of those who might otherwise espouse capitalism.

In addition, much of the tension revolves around gender questions. The veil, for example, functions as an allegory for the nation: "What kind of image or identity do we want for our country, our community?" Consequently, the veil becomes a potent symbol of the conflict between essentialized West and East alike, and in much the same way that colonialist discourse itself was grounded in an East/West binarist framework. Within this framework, a very problematic anti-Westernist discourse comes into existence where the West (as well as the East) is reduced to a monolithic entity and where the Manichean vision of good and evil is invoked on both sides of the Atlantic. Could you comment on this notion of the "corrupting influence of the West," with Israel and the U.S. as the leading bearers of that presumed corrupting influence?

RK: I think you are absolutely right; it is mainly expressed over gender. Among the extreme trends that I described earlier, the three different strands all adopt some variant of this culturalist critique because it resonates with deeply rooted revulsions that they have, especially around issues of gender.

But I think there's also a cynical and opportunistic aspect to it. You can see this in Saudi Arabia, where I think that the passion of the Saudi middle and upper classes for Western culture is something which their opponents in these Islamic trends clearly oppose, not directly, but by using it as a rhetoric with which to support their political opposition, people who want to repress public activity by women, such as driving, or the mixing of sexes. Instead of saying, "We're going to force you to do what we say" or "Our interpretation of Islam is stronger than yours," they use what they perceive to be the trump card, by saying, "These are foreign, Western things that you are trying to do. We're authentic, and you are inauthentic."

You can see the same kind of culturalist critique in Gaza and other parts of the occupied territories. Hamas is attacking its secular rivals, and the middle classes, not by saying, "This is the right Islam; here is the wrong Islam," or not only by saying that, but also by declaring, "These are perverse Israeli cultural things introduced to cause the degeneracy of our society." They are using the national banner, rather than the purely religious, to discredit their political rivals and to weaken the opposition from people of the middle classes, who are attracted to Western culture, as are, to be frank, most classes of society in most Arab countries—witness the success of Western cinema.

ES: I agree. *Rambo* was popular even among those who espoused anti-U.S. slogans during the Lebanese civil war. But I think that precisely because Islam is equated with fundamentalism, it's important to look at certain strands within Christianity and Judaism that are equally fundamentalist. Take the case of the evangelical TV station in Lebanon; it is not viewed as innocent preaching, and not just because of the historical rivalry between Christianity and Islam. Rather, its message is automatically seen as allied with U.S. regional hegemony. To what extent can we speak about opposition to these evangelical provinces in certain parts of the Middle East as tantamount to a kind of anticolonial opposition? And to what extent can such opposition be understood in religious terms?

RK: Well, it depends. In the case of Palestine, Israel, and Lebanon, it's clear that a certain evangelical trend has allied itself with Israeli expansionism, and with a right-wing view of Lebanon. This is posited in starkly Biblical terms: "We are allied with Israel, because of what we read in the Book of Revelations." It's also considered necessary that Israel should do this, that, and the other, in order for the end of days to come. At its core, that may be a profoundly anti-Semitic vision, by the way, but it doesn't stop these people from supporting Israel as it is today, or some cynical, right-wing Israeli politicians from welcoming the support.

These trends, in Lebanon, Israel, and Palestine, are very much alive, and, as a result, the opposition to them is really at the core of opposition to a certain vision of what Lebanon or Israel are. But the situation in other countries is different. For example, I do not believe that the assassination of missionaries in Yemen (or in South Lebanon, for that matter) is part of any specific resistance to American policy, or Israeli policy, or indeed to a vision of Lebanon. Rather, these actions draw on much more virulent and xenophobic forms of anti-Americanism, or anti-Westernism in general, which you see in both the Sunni and the Shi'i traditions, and they transcend differences in the Islamic worlds. While this may well be a minority trend, it is nevertheless important, certainly worth studying, and, I think, extremely dangerous. After all, we are talking about a politically shrewd minority. These are not unsophisticated people, and their manipulation of such themes is very seductive for many young people in the Arab and Islamic world.

ES: Parallel to that, here in the U.S., an extreme right wing, which is in fact a minority, is disproportionately powerful. Christian zealotry, corporate greed, and Likudnik neoconservatives form an unholy alliance that has somehow come to dominate U.S. policies toward the region.

At this point, however, I'd like us to touch on the critique of the U.S. that you find in the anti-globalization movement. Before 9/11, we were all conscious of the extraordinary activism of the "globalizers from below," who managed to coordinate an impressive opposition to the opening of the borders to global capital, and to the "closing off" of these borders to the rights of workers, immigrants, and the environment. After the attacks, the visibility of this movement suffered an immense setback, in part due to heavy filtering by media outlets. Any criticism of Bush, who stood in for the wounded America, ran the risk of being perceived as endorsing the horrific attacks. In different parts of the world, many expressed sympathy and were quick to denounce bin Laden's terrorism. But there were also others who used the occasion to rebuke "American arrogance" and who saw the attacks as "payback" for Hiroshima, Vietnam, Chile, and so on. I visited Brazil after 9/11, and, alongside the sympathy and empathy, it was not uncommon to hear the opinion that "This will teach them a lesson." Some even spoke of bin Laden as if he were a kind of Che Guevara. This was a particularly disturbing equation, in my view, because it projected the kind of anti-imperialism once characterized as Third Worldist onto a religious leader who espouses terrorism and whose anti-Americanism has very little in common with secular revolutionaries like Guevara. It is hard to imagine what an anti-globalizer from Rio would have in common with a regime that would take great pleasure in banning thong-bathing suits (*tangas*) and sambas. Just imagine burkas and beards on the beaches of Copacabana and Ipanema!

RK: Well, we don't know. Maybe that's where he's hiding.

ES: Actually, popular culture was quick to invoke such surrealistic images. During the annual carnival procession in Rio, one of the samba schools performed a dance number called "Bin Laden's Harem" in a hilarious combination of Orientalist clichés and Afro-Brazilian popular culture.

All of these sentiments which I witnessed, whether expressed in humor or anger, were pervaded by an ambivalence toward the U.S., and one could still find in them traces of a long-gone Third World solidarity. But there is something askew, to my mind, with a view that confounds the utopian hopes and goals of the tricontinental movement with the Islamic fundamentalist cause. They may both host a universalist vision, but they share little in terms of the organization of economic, social, and political life—and least of all when it comes to gender and sexuality.

But of course the anti-globalization movement is not uniform. In gatherings around the world, there are usually always demonstrators who wave the Palestinian flag because they are trying to make the link between that struggle and other forms of justice. But the Middle East is itself no less entangled in globalization policies that profit U.S.-based corporations as well as those from countries like France and Germany, which opposed the war.

RK: For a majority of people in the Middle East, the problem with the U.S. is not its ideals; it's that the U.S. is not true to them, as far as democracy, representative government, constitutionalism, and human rights are concerned. I actually think that those are very widespread values, and would even argue that the resistance to free-market capitalism and enterprise is pretty much gone among very large segments of the population. With the discrediting of the state-run economies of many of the Arab states, for instance in Egypt and Iraq, along with the parties that implemented them, the resistance— even the legitimate critiques of aspects of free-market commerce and liberalism—has diminished considerably in the Arab world. The overwhelming passion of people for certain aspects of American consumerism and material society makes me conclude that there's no profound critique of these ideas, on either the economic, the political, or the cultural level.

So, too, along with the decline of the Left, a political economy critique has diminished in the Arab world. You can still find elements of it in Turkey and Iran, but it suffered in tandem with the collapse of the Ba'th and the Communist parties, the dissolution of the Soviet Union, the destruction of Left movements and the decline of their intellectual vigor. Of all the regions in the world, anti-globalization probably has the shallowest roots in the Arab world, though I wonder if the looting and free-marketization of Iraq, which is being extensively reported in the Arab world by the ubiquitous satellite TV stations and by the press, might not rekindle that critique. After all, what is being done in Iraq is taking place on a number of levels. There's obviously military occupation, there's resistance, and there's suppression of resistance. There's also an attempt to align Iraq politically with the U.S., and it would appear also with Israel in the long run. But something more radical is happening to the Iraqi oil industry, to the health care system, to education, and to the economy generally, in the form of privatization. I was astonished to hear from someone, a friend of mine who works for the International Committee of the Red Cross, that they are actually trying to install the humongously thieving HMO system—by far the most useless element of the U.S. healthcare system—in Iraq.

ES: This is another false linkage that the Bush administration has made. In the push for free marketization, the nationalized economy, education, and health care of Saddam Hussein's dictatorship has been associated with the dependent personality of the Iraqi citizen who doesn't know what freedom is! It's reminiscent of what we used to hear about the colonized Algerian, or about the automaton Soviet citizen, just as any kind of movement in the U.S. for universal health care was once automatically labeled as communist. Iraqis, for the most part, make a healthy distinction between getting rid of their dictator and the social reorganization of the country's resources. They do not generally share the Bush–Cheney vision of a reconstructed Iraq, which entails the complete privatization of national resources.

RK: We are now going to see, among many other things, a struggle over how these two visions play out in Iraq. I believe that the nature of the Iraqi state, and the state in most of the larger Arab world, was a profoundly flawed one. I don't want to go as far as to endorse the Arab Development Report or anything like that, but to see the tragic waste of the resources that could have been invested properly over the course of three decades from the oil nationalizations and price increases in the 1970s is to see a system where the power of the state has grown without limits and where the corresponding power of civil society, the individual, and other collectives within society was diminished in the Arab world generally.

Etatism was not a good thing from that perspective, but it may now offer a basis from which to resist American free-market liberalism. Indeed, we may see it service a revived political economy critique, especially in light of the most nefarious aspects of U.S. policy in Iraq. It is clearly a violation of international law for an occupying power to give away, either to itself or to its citizens, pieces of the property of the Iraqi people. Currently, these include the oil industry and the private sector, which is going to be sold off, if they have their way, for nothing, to foreign investors. It looks like these foreign investors are going to be American, and ideally supporters of the Republican party, like Halliburton, who contribute to President Bush's campaigns. These are the people who are in a position to inherit the Iraqi people's patrimony, either by stealing it or getting it for a steal. We already saw in Russia what it all means.

23

Postscript to Frantz Fanon's
The Wretched of the Earth

The Hebrew publication of *The Wretched of the Earth*[1] comes in the wake of a powerful resurgence of interest in Frantz Fanon's work, a resurgence taking place less in Fanon's language, French, than in English.[2] A kind of posthumous wrestling over Fanon's legacy has generated lively debates about such issues as the gendered politics of the veil, Fanon's presumed therapeutic theory of violence, and the relative merits of the psychoanalytically oriented *Peau noire, masques blancs* (*Black Skin, White Masks*) book versus the revolutionary Marxism of *Les Damnés de la Terre* (*The Wretched of the Earth*). Within a post-nationalist perspective, diverse writers have scored Fanon's limitations: his occasional romanticization of violence, his idealization of the peasantry, his failure to predict religious fundamentalism, his shallow knowledge of Arab and Islamic culture, his blind spots concerning forms of oppression rooted not in nation and empire but rather in gender and sexuality.

Yet a re-reading of Fanon also reveals his extraordinary far-sightedness, making him a precursor for a number of subsequent intellectual currents. In his lapidary phrases we find the germ of many subsequent theoretical developments. Fanon can be seen as the precursor of what is variously called dependency theory and world systems theory. His claim in *The Wretched of the Earth* that "Europe is literally the creation of the Third World"— that the wealth and prosperity of an overstuffed Europe was extracted from

A Postscript to Frantz Fanon's *The Wretched of the Earth*, published in Hebrew in 2006 by Babel Press—a project initiated by Amit and Sharon Rotbard. The Postscript was translated into Hebrew by Yigal Nizri. The English text was published as "Black, Jew, Arab: Postscript to *The Wretched of the Earth*" in a special issue entitled "Being Arab: Arabism and the Politics of Recognition," edited by Christopher Wise and Paul James, *Arena Journal*, 33:4, 2009. Some sections are based on my essay "Post-Fanon and the Colonial: A Situational Diagnosis" (in *Taboo Memories, Diasporic Voices*, 2006,) initially presented at the "Finding Fanon: Critical Genealogies" conference, co-organized by Mark Nash, Isaac Julien, and Martha Gever, The Center for Media, Culture and History and The Africana Studies Program, New York University, October 11–12, 1996.

the misery and impoverishment of the Third World—anticipated in ste-
reographic, almost aphoristic, form the arguments concerning how Europe
underdeveloped Africa or how capitalism underdeveloped Black America.
It anticipated later theorists such as Walter Rodney (for Africa); Andre
Gunder Frank, James Petras, and Eduardo Galeano (for Latin America); and
Cedrick Robinson and Manning Marable (for Afro-America). Deploying
the method of materialist dialectics, Fanon eloquently reveals the sinister
underbelly of progress:

> The European opulence is literally scandalous, for it has been founded on
> slavery, it has been nourished with the blood of slaves and it comes directly
> from the soil and from the subsoil of that underdeveloped world. The
> well-being and the progress of Europe have been built up with the sweat
> and the dead bodies of negroes, Arabs, Indians, and the yellow races.[3]

Fanon subverts Europe's rescue fantasies "on behalf" of its colonized, seeing
the West itself as depending on the non-West to generate its modernity. For
Fanon, Western progress was responsible for genocide; Europe's document
of civilization, in Walter Benjamin's powerful aphorism, hid a document of
barbarism.

Fanon's anticolonialist de-centering of Europe in *The Wretched of the Earth*
can now also be seen to have both provoked and foreshadowed Jacques
Derrida's claim that European culture has been dislocated, forced to stop
casting itself as the "exclusive culture of reference."[4] In this sense, Fanon can
be seen as preparing the way for the poststructuralism of Derrida, whose
deconstruction is usually traced exclusively back to Heidegger. What Fanon
called "social therapy," similarly, can now be seen to have anticipated the
antipsychiatry of such figures as David Cooper, R. D. Laing, Gilles Deleuze,
and Felix Guattari. Although Fanon never spoke of Orientalist discourse,
similarly, his critiques of colonialist imagery provide proleptic examples
of anti-Orientalist critique *à la* Edward Said. And although Fanon has
often been caricatured as a racial hard-liner, he in fact anticipated the
anti-essentialist critique of race common in contemporary postcolonial
theory. The Black is obliged not only to be Black, but "he must be Black
in relation to the White man." The Black, as Fanon put it, is comparison.[5]

Participating in diverse intellectual dialogues and streams of thought,
including Hegelianism, Marxism, psychoanalysis, Negritude, socialism,
pan-Africanism, existentialism, and phenomenology, Fanon performed the
precocious deconstruction of what would later be called "master narratives."
Fanon can also be seen as an advance practitioner of the field of cultural
studies formed in the late 1970s. Already in the 1950s, Fanon practiced

what now goes by that rubric, taking all aspects of cultural life as legitimate objects of study. Analyzing such diverse phenomena as the veil, dance, trance, language, radio, and film as sites of social and cultural contestation, Fanon's work is profoundly interdisciplinary, drawing on psychiatry, philosophy, sociology, ethnography, history, literature, and film. In some ways, not unlike Roland Barthes's semiological readings in *Mythologies*, Fanon offers a reading of colonialist mythologies, its grammar and rhetoric, as in the case of the "Myth of the Negro."

To understand Fanon's text one has to engage diverse philosophical traditions, and note both the ways that he disrupts those narratives and the ways that he remains enmeshed within them. Fanon's work conducts an explicit conversation with Sartre on existentialism and phenomenology, with Freud and Lacan on psychoanalysis, and with Marx on historical materialism. Thus Fanon, in the fragmentary way allowed him by his short life span, both absorbed and surpassed a series of intellectual currents. He embraced psychoanalysis, but pointed to the ethnocentrism of its Oedipalism. He absorbed Marxism, but pointed to the Eurocentric limits of its class analysis. He incorporated existentialism, but pointed to the social aporia engendered by a subjectivist voluntarism, suggesting that "free will" is irrelevant for colonized people. For Fanon, Sartre's concept of "situated freedom" is itself insufficiently situated, since it fails to acknowledge the specific nature of the constraints on human freedom typical of the colonized world.

Fanon's critique is especially relevant for the intellectual debate in Israel, where for decades philosophical and literary traditions like existentialism held sway over intellectual life, yet where the discussion could have gained from the Fanonian critique. When I was a student of philosophy and literature in Israel in the late 1970s, although some of my professors were immigrants from France, my classes on existentialism made no mention of a Fanonian critique of existentialism. Discussion of fiction written by Algerian-born *Pied-Noir* Albert Camus naturalized his narrative in which Algerians form an extension of the landscape, literally denied any significant speaking role, perhaps not unlike the ways such discussions normalized the silence assigned to the speech-impaired Arab character in A. B. Yehoshua's story "In Front of the Forests," where the character becomes a vehicle for the *sabra*'s existential nausea. Fanon's project, by contrast, sets out to challenge the intellectual paradigms that would allow the colonizer to make a claim over the beginning of history. Fanon, in sum, politicized and "Third Worldized" phenomenology, turning it into a viable prism through which to look at the lived existence of the Black within White society, or of the Arab within French colonialism. What we see over and over is that Fanon takes a pre-existing discourse, and then interrogates it, often transforming its terms by bringing race and colonialism into the debate.

*   *   *

Fanon's critique of existentialism emerged against the backdrop of African national independence movements in the post-World War II era. Sartre, in his influential preface to Leopold Senghor's 1948 anthology of Negritude poetry entitled *Orphée Noir* (*Black Orpheus*), predicted the end of racism with the demise of colonialism and the advent of a true universalism, much as the same author's *Reflexions Sur la Question Juive* (*Anti-Semite and Jew*) suggested that anti-Semitism would come to an end with the dawn of socialism.[6] Within Sartre's Hegelian millenarian view, Blackness and Jewishness both functioned as the antitheses in the master–slave dialectical process. Sartre thus called for the transcendence of all particularist identities in the name of universal socialist revolution. The Sartrean model of "anti-Semite and Jew" forms a taken-for-granted matrix of analysis lurking in the background of Fanon's work. Echoing Sartre's claim that "The Jew is one whom other men consider a Jew," and that "it is the Anti-Semite who creates the Jew,"[7] Fanon too writes that it is "the racist who creates his inferior"[8] and that the "black soul is a White man's artifact."[9] Although *Anti-Semite and Jew* impacted Fanon's parallel anatomy of the generative processes of identity, for Fanon, understanding "the Black" required understanding the specificities of White racism towards Blacks. Thus, Fanon both repeats and transcends Sartre's idea of the negative dialectic between Jew and anti-Semite. In this sense, Fanon echoes Albert Memmi's critique of Sartre. For the Tunisian Jew Memmi, Sartre's Jew has no history or culture apart from that produced by the hostile otherizing of the anti-Semite. The Jew in Sartrean discourse becomes virtually an ahistorical entity, devoid of cultural specificity, and existing only in the function of the anti-Semite.

Fanon, similarly, deconstructs Sartre's view that "the Black" might constitute only a transitional stage in the inexorable march towards the universal:

> I am not a potentiality of something, I am wholly what I am. I do not have to look for the universal. No probability has any place inside me. My Negro consciousness does not hold itself out as a lack. It is its own follower.[10]

Predicated upon the denial of the Black experience, this falsely universalizing discourse, constituted, for Fanon, a symptom of intellectual subordination to imperial reason. A colorless universalism, de facto, meant Whiteness or Frenchness. This kind of universalism placed the (White French) intellectual in a position of superiority, as the spokesperson for the universal, as the omnipotent agent advancing the dialectics of history. Corporeal visibility and the history of enslavement, however, produced the particularities of being Black in the world. By situating Black neurosis and Algerian trauma within a larger race drama between Whites and Blacks, or French and Algerians, or Europeans and Africans, Fanon could address the pathologies of colonialism itself. In this way, the phenomenon of "race" could be approached at once psychoanalytically and historically, without being merely a negation or lacuna in a universalizing synthesis.[11] Fanon accepts Sartre's reversing and dismantling of the Cartesian "I think therefore I am" thesis, in other words, but he also brings to "race," as it were, the meaning of the "I am."

Throughout his work, Fanon articulates the complex entrappings of the colonizer/colonized dialectics, negotiating the colonized identity both within and beyond existentialist thought. Fanon does view the oppressed as partly a function of *le regard*, a product of projected hatreds, while he also refuses any essentialist definition of identity for the Black, the Jew, or the Arab. Yet, for Fanon, especially the Fanon of *The Wretched of the Earth*, the liberation struggle transforms the colonized, now no longer confined to the space created, constructed, and imagined by the colonizer. The emergence of anticolonial movements composed a new grammar in which the colonized spoke as subjects, substituting the paradigmatic object in the colonialist syntax. Blackness or Arabness thus could no longer be defined simply as the product of racism, an exemplum of "being for others." On one level, then, Fanon's discourse can be seen as a historicized variant of Sartre's; it aspires to break away from the negative space allotted by racism and anti-Semitism. On another level, however, Fanon conceives of Black or Arab existence in a way that transgresses Sartre's universal in that Fanon refuses to abandon the particular. Racial or ethnic specificity in Fanon's work is not eliminated, but rather transfigured. By the time of *The Wretched of the Earth*, Fanon's categories of Blackness vis-à-vis Whiteness give way to a language of national affiliations—Angolans, Algerians, Senegalese.

The subjectivity of the colonized is gained and performed through the disruption of the colonial order. Thus, in *Pour la Revolution Africaine* (*Toward the African Revolution*) Fanon writes: "It is the White man who creates the Negro. But it is the Negro who creates 'Negritude'."[12] Although never completely abandoning the hybrid psychoanalytical-phenomenological method, Fanon's *The Wretched of the Earth* is also inflected by a Marxizing phenomenological paradigm. And here we note seemingly opposite, but actually complementary perspectives. When reflecting through a psychoanalytical frame, Fanon, as we have already noted, grants agency to the White man, arguing that the White creates the Black man. But when he writes within a materialist-Marxist frame, Fanon grants agency to the Black man, arguing that the Third World creates Europe. Within both frames, however, Fanon disturbs the sheltered narcissism of Eurocentric thinking.

Written in the context of post-war Martinique and France, *Black Skin, White Masks* emphasizes the connection between European racism and anti-Semitism. Citing his philosophy professor, a native of the Antilles, Fanon writes: "Whenever you hear anyone abuse the Jews, pay attention, because he is talking about you ... an anti-Semite is inevitably anti-Negro."[13] Fanon's recollection resonates against the backdrop of the genocide of Jews only a decade earlier, during a war that also placed Senegalese, Tunisian, Ghanaian, and Indian soldiers together on the front line, defending the very same civilization that had dispossessed and massacred them. It is significant that Fanon's effort to explore Black identity is articulated in relation to other "others," such as the Jews. Fanon discusses the inauthenticity and alienation of the Black, who, like the Jew, possesses an emotional life split in two and who is in search of "a dream of universal brotherhood in a world that rejects him."[14] The attempts by the Jew or by the Black to assimilate into an anti-Semitic or racist society lead only to the pathologies of self-hatred and inferiority complexes. But Fanon also goes beyond the Black–Jewish analogy, attempting to sketch the specificities of anti-Black racism in contradistinction to the (European) Jewish experience of anti-Semitism.

For Fanon then, analogies of oppression between Jews and Blacks also come with dis-analogies. Victimization, furthermore, does not guarantee solidarity or identification, and may even result in a rolling series of hateful transferences among the oppressed themselves. In speaking of a racist Jew, Fanon writes that: "He is a Jew, he has a 'millennial experience of anti-Semitism, and yet he is racist."[15] Fanon's attention to a "racist Jew" in a period following the Jewish Holocaust may seem oxymoronic. But it also anticipates the later fissures in the alliances among the oppressed and offers a discursive foreshadowing of the latter-day tensions between Blacks and Jews, in the U.S., for example. Yet, Fanon's very mention of a racist Jew stresses the importance of locating racism's specificities, asking us to reflect on the parallel and distinct forms of racism among minorities in comparison with that of "normal" White Christian racism. Fanon's text anticipates the gradual entry—however tenuous and contradictory—of the Jew into the terrain of Whiteness (along with Europeanness) in the post-World War II era, simultaneously with Israel becoming part of the West. Here one may find in Fanon's text the germ of still another contemporary field—Whiteness studies—and more specifically the study of the progressive whitening of the Jew.

Fanon occasionally suggests a negative chain of community relationalities: "The Frenchman does not like the Jew, who does not like the Arab, who does not like the Negro."[16] But he blames the negativity on French divide-and-conquer policies. Through opportunistic flattery, as Fanon suggests, the French colonizer tells the Jew: "You are not the same class as the Arab because you are really White and because you have Einstein and Bergson."[17] (This discourse is echoed in Israel, especially among Ashkenazim, who flaunt their presumed Western superiority vis-à-vis Mizrahim, and toward the Arab East generally.) Fanon insightfully locates the whitening of the Jew within a negative dialectic vis-à-vis the colonized Arab, just as Arab anti-Jewishness is reinforced when the "Arab is told: 'If you are poor, it is because the Jew has bled you and taken everything from you'." The Negro, meanwhile, Fanon writes, "is told: 'You are the best soldiers in the French Empire; the Arabs think that they are better than you, but they are wrong'."[18] Fanon recognized the chromatic racial hierarchy that placed the (Christian) French on top, followed by assimilated European Jews, then by assimilated Algerian Arabs, and especially assimilated Algerian Jews, and at the bottom unassimilated Arabs and Berbers.

Fanon offers a path for "reading" communities as a conjunctural shaping of comparisons. As Fanon moves into the revolutionary fluid context of North Africa his text begins to address more historically specific notions of communities. By the time of *The Wretched of the Earth*, Fanon supplements the Black–Jewish axis of *Black Skin, White Masks* with the Arab–Black axis. In his book *L'an V de la révolution algérienne* (*A Dying Colonialism*), Fanon's "Jew" also becomes specific, of a particular context ("Algeria's Jews"),[19] and touches on a more mobile notion of ethnic, racial, national and religious identity. He even briefly refers to the unsettling situation of minorities caught in colonialism's Manichean divisions. The colonizer's instrumental contrast of "bad Arab" versus "good Kabyl" paralleled the construction of "bad Muslim/good Jew" in Algeria. Thus, citing the case of the Constantine Jews, Fanon writes:

One of the most pernicious maneuvers of colonialism in Algeria was and remains the division between Jews and Moslems ... Jews have been in Algeria for more than two thousand years; they are thus an integral part of the Algerian people .... Moslems and Jews, children of the same earth, must not fall into the trap of provocation. Rather, they must make a common front against it, not letting themselves be duped by those who, not long ago, were offhandedly contemplating the total extermination of the Jews as a salutary step in the evolution of humanity.[20]

* * *

Rather than cast a split between Fanon's early book *Black Skin, White Masks* and his later *The Wretched of the Earth*, as often occurs, we must see them on a continuum. Both books must be seen as part of his larger project of humanizing the enslaved, the oppressed, the colonized, and even the colonizer. Fanon's revolutionary work of "restructuring the world"[21] is intertwined with an epistemological project of creating what he calls a "new humanism."[22] The universalism of the old humanism, like the scientific objectivity of Western rationalism, according to Fanon, is directed against the colonized.[23] He calls for the colonized to "leave this Europe, where they are never done talking of Man, yet murder men everywhere they find them, at the corner of every one of their streets, in all the corners of the globe."[24] His poetic prose slices open the paradoxes inherent in Europe's humanist discourse and its narrative of progress. The revised universalism of this new humanism promises to redeem the colonized, and thus, in Fanon's words, allow them to "rise above this absurd drama that others have staged ... to reach out to the universal."[25] Thus for Fanon, "the Negro is aiming for the Universal ... the Negro is universalizing himself."[26]

Fanon's humanization project is also seen in his approach to psychoanalysis and psychiatry, detailed in the last part of *The Wretched of the Earth*. In Fanon's time, the dominant models of psychoanalysis were premised on a universalist construction of the psyche, eliding various social permutations. Normative psychoanalysis extrapolated to the world at large, to put it somewhat crudely, the neuroses of the Viennese bourgeoisie. Fanon's writing and practice, meanwhile, gradually began to engage with the cultural specificity of his patients. Freud's Eurocentric analysis of the unconscious (for example in *Totem and Taboo*) aligned it with primitivism, invoking analogies between the individual id and uncivilized tribes. Fanon's approach, in contrast, was uninterested in a "universal" Oedipus complex.

Fanon grounds the Freudian drama in culture and history. Already in *Black Skin, White Masks* Fanon coined the term "situational neurosis"[27] to unmask, as it were, the social alienation triggered by the white mask worn on a black face, to which he responded with his situational analysis. This was a strategy further developed and theorized in North Africa. In collaboration with his colleague Jacques Azoulay, Fanon attempted to "diagnose" the false universalism of standard French psychiatric methods. For the two authors, institutional therapy formed part of a colonial assimilationist policy. Conscious of the importance of linguistic and cultural difference within this process, Fanon was invested in the real and symbolic context of mental illness, in ways that anticipate the later work of the "anti-psychiatry" movement. Fanon was acutely aware of the limitations of his own practice in the psychiatric ward in Algiers, especially of his lack of command of Berber or Arabic. (Fanon began studying Arabic but never achieved fluency, and therefore had to rely on interpreters.) Within the French ward system, as with the colonial system as a whole, questions of language and power had devastating repercussions for the psyche although they were never deemed relevant to the therapeutic process.

As with a Freudian-Lacanian discourse, language would seem always already in the realm of the symbolic, and thus could not presumably be touched by the gravity of history. Yet, the very presence of an interpreter, for example, carried a specific weight for Algerians, for whom the French language embodied French power, obliging the colonized, whether in the courthouse, in prison, in school or in the mental institution, to meet the colonizer on the latter's linguistic turf. (The analogies between the realities of the institutional tensions involving Hebrew and Arabic in Israel are alarmingly familiar.) And although the Frenchified Algerian elite could join the colonizer in a linguistic rendezvous, the encounter was trapped in an absurd theatre of polite mimicry performed against the din of machine-guns. Healing tortured and traumatized Algerians was necessarily inscribed on the act of translation in a situation where the doctor's native tongue tended to be French and the patient's Arabic—all in a situation, ironically, where the French language was itself a factor in the colonial production of pathologies.

Situating their method, Fanon and his colleagues, especially the Jewish-Algerian Jacques Azoulay and the Corsican-Algerian Charles Geronimi, critiqued their own earlier psychiatric practice of administrating French therapies to Algerian patients. Largely developed for French women, who constituted the majority of patients in French wards and hospitals, such therapies, they argued, were simply inappropriate for Algerian patients. Occupational therapies using music or games had all been modeled on French cultural norms, provoking Fanon to bring local Arab musicians into the ward. In order to endow psychoanalysis with cultural content, furthermore, Fanon studied Arab-African approaches to insanity—approaches in which the insane were viewed as possessed by *jinns*—as well as the healing role played by the *taleb* or the *marabout*. Adopting a dialectical approach, Fanon and Azoulay tried to synthesize local practices with European psychiatric treatment, thus anticipating what would later be called "integrative medicine." Although Fanon was not fluent in Arabic or deeply conversant in Algerian cultural codes, in other words, he was searching for a therapeutic practice attuned to cultural difference.[28] Fanon and Azoulay came to realize that they had been the unconscious "carriers" of the French assimilationist model within the mental institution itself. But within this asymmetrical situation, Fanon at least tried to unravel the fictitious universalism of psychoanalysis and psychiatry by dialogizing theory and practice.[29]

At this point, I wish to locate my own textual dialogue with Fanon, drawing the traces of his work in my own writing. In the Israel of the 1960s and 1970s, it was common to speak about the discrimination we suffered as Sephardim. Apart from identifying with the Black Panthers, my reading of Fanon, as part of my study of colonialism and racism in the early 1980s in New York, helped me articulate the Mizrahi question in a different way. Fanon provided me with the conceptual apparatus with which to view the Mizrahi experience as part of a negative process in which the rejection of the Arab "out there" was linked to the rejection of the Arab "within us." That insight allowed me to formulate such notions as "Mizrahi self-hatred" and "cultural schizophrenia" as analogous to the minoritarian experience of Blacks or Jews vis-à-vis Europe. It was more via Fanon than via Freud that my work deployed psychoanalytical terms such as "internalization," "projection," and "displacement" to account for the Mizrahi self-hatred developed after our encounter with Eurocentric Israel. Important critical analysis on the Mizrahim existed at the time, but it had largely been performed within Marxist, class-based paradigms.[30] While valid on its own terms, such a framework, I thought, still needed to address the Eurocentrism of the Zionist project as an oppressive shaping-force of culture and identity.

I ultimately viewed my task as one of placing Zionism on the couch,[31] dissecting its inferiority/superiority complexes with regard to both "East" and "West." I saw its pathological obsession with mimicking the "West," and its (self-)rejection of the Diaspora *Ostjuden* as intimately linked to the disdain for Jews from another East, the Mizrahim. For the first time in our long history, we Jews from Islamic/Arab countries, not unlike Fanon's Blacks, began to manifest a split consciousness, and feel the schizophrenia of being at once Arabs and Jews. In that period of the early 1980s, I began to share my enthusiasm for Fanon with Mizrahi leftist circles, lecturing on his relevance in places like Kivun Hadash, in South Tel Aviv's Skhunat haTikava. Anticolonial thinkers such as Fanon were crucial for me in artic- ulating a Mizrahi critique beyond the Jewish nationalist boundaries within which the question had usually been addressed and framed. Such a Mizrahi critique, in other words, had to be written on a continuum with and in relation to the larger Arab and Palestinian question, in contrast to the deeply rooted logic of the Mizrahi issue as "an internal" problem and the question of Palestine as an "external" matter.

* * *

Fanon articulates liberation not merely within the material realm of political struggle but also within an epistemological project that envisions a refurbished and truly universal humanism. And that underlying utopian project (and not violence as is commonly assumed) imbues Fanon's writing with a transformative, even cathartic, power. In this new universalism lies both the passionate force of Fanon's writings and, to an extent, its dissonances and aporias. The "victims of progress" thesis of Fanon's text inevitably raises the question of whether Fanon's "new humanism" looks back to a pre-colonial past before European contamination, or forward to a future utopia. What are the implications of Fanon's demystifying of Europe's false universalizations for the very idea of universalism itself? Does Fanon only dissect, or completely reject, or perhaps rethink Europe's humanism?

Fanon's negotiation of the question of temporality—and here we touch on another of Fanon's dialogues, this time with Negritude and Marxism— often makes him sound more like Marx than Senghor. Although Fanon applauded certain features of the Negritude intellectual movement, he also denounced its originary, nostalgic, and binarist pitting of African emotion against European reason. At the same time, *Black Skin, White Masks* had already referred to Marx's *The Eighteenth Brumaire*, written as a response to Bonaparte's 1851 coup. Fanon especially addressed Marx's insistence, in relation to the French 1848 Revolution, that the social revolution cannot— and here Fanon cites Marx—"draw its poetry from the past, but only from the future" and that it had to "strip itself of all its superstitions concerning the past." Fanon adds that the "discovery of the existence of a Negro civilization in the 15th century confers no patent of humanity on me. Like it or not, the past can in no way guide me in the present moment."[32] In *The Wretched of the Earth* Fanon conceptualizes the relations between past and future in a similar fashion:

> I admit that all the proofs of a wonderful Songhai civilization will not change the fact that today the Songhais are underfed and illiterate, thrown between sky and water with empty heads and empty eyes.[33]

Fanon's anticolonial poetics betray little nostalgia for an Eden-like precolonial past. In his remarks on national culture, Fanon alludes to the passion with which "native intellectuals defend their pre-colonial past," offering an insight into their investment in this idealized version of the past.

In the Israeli context, the Mizrahi desire for *hahzarat ha-'atara le-yoshna*, of bringing back past glory, would have come under criticism from a Fanonian perspective, identifying the sweeping embrace of past culture as the "second stage" in the development of the Mizrahi intellectual after exhausting the "first stage" of full cultural assimilation. From a Fanonian point of view, the discovery voyage for Mizrahi roots would have been perceived as the antithesis to assimilation, as a necessary stage in the trajectory towards the desired synthesis. Fanon indeed identifies with the need of the colonized intellectual to restore the African past, since the colonized psyche, unlike that of the European intellectual, "is not conveniently sheltered behind a French or a German culture which has given full proof of its existence and which is uncontested."[34] Fanon, in other words, empathizes with the colonized intellectual's need to rehabilitate the African past, but he is uninterested in an intellectual project of archaeological recuperation.

Fanon was not a partisan of Negritude, nor can he be seen as anticipating an Afrocentric search for an originary past:[35]

> In no way should I dedicate myself to the revival of an unjustly unrecognized Negro civilization. I will not make myself the man of any past. I do not want to exalt the past at the expense of my present and of my future. It is not because the Indo-Chinese has discovered a culture of his own that he is in revolt. It is because "quite simply" it was, in more than one way, becoming impossible for him to breathe.[36]

In fact, Negritude can be seen as a positive inversion of philosophical postulations such as Hegel's that Africa did not participate in historical movement and progression, and that its "Spirit" was "still involved in the conditions of mere nature."[37] Fanon's critique of what I would call the hermeneutics of the ancient can be similarly addressed to diverse contemporaneous racialized intellectuals, for example, Jewish thinkers in France—Edmond Fleg, Emmanuel Levinas, and Éliane Amado Lévy-Valensi—who, while critiquing the modern Christian West in its own language, were trying to redeem the place of Jews in the West by demonstrating the contribution of Judaism to universal culture. Intellectual discussions were often linked to Jewish revival via Zionism. Fanon's revolutionary project, meanwhile, sought a new third stage, a synthetic space that was neither derivative nor reactive. Just as Fanon critiques those who "throw [themselves] greedily upon Western culture,"[38] he also critiques those who fixate on the past: "The colonized man who writes for his people ought to use the past with the intention of opening the future, an invitation to action and a basis for hope."[39]

Fanon's revolutionary hope is predicated on the eclipse of Europe as the unique site of freedom and liberty:

> Come, then, comrades, the European game has finally ended; we must find something different. We today can do everything, so long as we do not imitate Europe, so long as we are not obsessed by the desire to catch up with Europe .... Humanity is waiting for something from us other than such an imitation .... For Europe, for ourselves, and for humanity, comrades, we must turn over a new leaf, we must work out new concepts, and try to set afoot a new man.[40]

Yet Fanon's "new humanism" ultimately has to face the dilemma of whether to "mend or end" the Enlightenment's humanist project. To what extent, then, is his project revolutionary or merely reformative? Fanon evokes the concept of "humanism" to perform a rhetorical boomerang against Europe's writing the colonized out of humanity. His text, however, resonates ambiguously towards the Enlightenment. Fanon's goal of turning a new historical page is itself diacritically embedded in Enlightenment thought, in that he seems more concerned with false universalism than with universalism per se. Fanon thus speaks within the meta-narrative of universalism not in order to negate it altogether, but rather in order to negate its exclusivism.

Both the Enlightenment, and its offspring revolution, combine a compassionate generosity, on the one hand, and horrifying complicities with colonialism and enslavement, on the other. The hypocrisies highlighted by Toussaint L'Ouverture earlier during the Haitian revolution, and later by Aimé Césaire (Fanon's teacher) and by Fanon himself, cannot be viewed as mere oversights on the part of Enlightenment thought, but rather as constitutive of its Eurocentrism. The concept "all men are created equal" was foundational, simultaneously legalizing equality for some and inequality for others—that is, for the excluded, colonized, enslaved, and dispossessed. Some more consistent Enlightenment philosophers such as Diderot defended the right of the oppressed to revolt, thus anticipating later radical renegades such as Sartre and de Beauvoir.[41] More commonly, however, Enlightenment philosophers ignored the "progressive" subjugation of those who stood in Reason's way, failing to address the dark underside of the Enlightenment. Contemporaneous with Europe's rise to world power, the Enlightenment perpetuated, along with its progressive and liberatory "overside," an imperialist, diffusionist, hierarchical underside.[42]

Although race is sublimated, it is also not an afterthought or aberration from ostensibly raceless Enlightenment ideals, but rather a shaping constituent of those ideals. Enlightenment thinkers, whether explicitly or implicitly, tended to encode the dominant Eurocentric values. The exploitation of colonized slave laborers was accepted as a given by the very thinkers who proclaimed freedom to be an inalienable right. Both the American and the French revolutions, as political expressions of the Enlightenment, defined a falsely universalist set of values while posing as defending the "rights of man." Although the French model does not recognize "race" as a valid conceptual or institutional category, the Republican ideals of *liberté, egalité, fraternité* were undercut by another racializing discourse of the *Nos ancêtres les Gaulois* of the colonial history books, which taught the Martiniquans, the Algerians, the Senegalese, and the Vietnamese that "our ancestors, the Gauls, had blue eyes and blond hair." Colonialism, then, aided the global travel of the Enlightenment whose ideals would seem to contradict colonialism's *raison d'être*. Yet, paradoxically, colonialist discourse itself was premised on Enlightenment categories such as *la mission civilisatrice*.

* * *

Against this intellectual backdrop, and given Fanon's French education, it would be difficult to imagine a Fanonian project unmarked by Enlightenment discourse. In some respects, a certain Enlightenment was profoundly liberating for a certain stratum within Europe (among them the French Jews) and even outside it. But in the colonial context it came at a huge cost. Fanon was writing about the pathologies of race after having served as a soldier for Free France, in a war in which he was wounded, and during which he came to perceive the illusory nature of the universalist ideals of *La République*. Not unlike African Americans who spilled blood in the name of freedom during World War II only to find their own blood literally segregated from "White blood" in the army blood supply, Fanon discovered that he fought a war for a free France which was about as racist as Vichy France. The participation of diverse colonized soldiers fighting on behalf of the colonialist allies indirectly energized post-war movements, leading to a demand for an end to colonialism and racism, whether practiced by France, Britain, or the U.S. During the war itself, the Békés, the White Creoles born in Martinique and descendants of the settler planters, enthusiastically supported Vichy, hoping to reduce the political power of the Black mulatto middle class. This paralleled the situation in Algeria, where the Pieds Noirs, along with their campaigns against Muslim Arabs, succeeded in revoking the 70 long years of the *Décret Crémieux* stripping Algerian Jews of their voting rights and citizenship. Seen as a manifestation of the Enlightenment, the decree, however, introduced from the outset (1870), a dangerously ambivalent status for indigenous Algerian Jews vis-à-vis both the colonizer and the colonized.

Yet, despite the shadowy aspects of the Enlightenment, it still offered those victimized by colonial and patriarchal claims a conceptual vehicle for pointing out the failed universality of the regimes that excluded them, while returning to those same universal Enlightenment principles to press their own emancipatory claims. Fanonian revolutionary discourse thus opens up fissures in Europe's universalist humanism, yet is itself born of totalizing narratives and embedded in Enlightenment discourse. His critique of false universalization does not probe the deep generative matrix that resulted in what might be called the bad intellectual habit of false universalization. Moreover, the ultimate question of who, how, and what determines and regulates the "universal" remains obscure, forming a kind of a buried epistemology in Fanon's text. Fanon's anticolonial text endorses the project of the anticolonial liberation movement, yet that project itself remains within the discursive apparatus of Enlightenment universalism, the very same framework that informs the colonialist narrative.

Given the historical circumstances, Fanon's work was necessarily more involved with deconstructing the false universality of the European humanist master narrative than with actually advocating alternative narratives. Although at times Fanon cites specific traditions that might contribute to the revolution—for example, the Djammas, as model of political participation— he generally regards traditional culture as peripheral. As a modernization discourse, Marxizing Third Worldism was impatient with "tradition," seen as synonymous with underdevelopment and the retrograde. Bearing some traces of this discourse, Fanon's *The Wretched of the Earth* invested little rhetorical energy in imagining a future that would draw on diverse Arab, Kabyle, and African cultural resources. Although Fanon in his institutional practice gradually became aware of the vital role cultural specificity could play in the treatment of scarred psyches, his writing hardly engaged in a deep study of Algeria's palimpsestic Berber-Arab-Ottoman-Muslim heritage, or of its repercussions for modes of resistance or for their potential role within the proposed new humanism. Fanon's "Algeria," not unlike the "Algerian woman" of his text, consequently winds up acquiring a relatively abstract character. The nation, and the woman, in this sense appear to reproduce some of Sartre's postulations concerning the "Jew" or the "Black" as mere positions or moments within the historical dialectics, the very same discourse Fanon rejected earlier.

Such an approach allows Fanon, like Sartre, to de-essentialize national culture, seeing it contingently as bound to disappear with the eviction of colonialism; but it also thwarts a more complex analysis of the dynamic role played by North African-Algerian particularities of history and identity for what Fanon would have considered both progressive and regressive ends. Fanon's increasing appeal to the universal, like Sartre's, echoes the French

Republican ideal of universality that recognizes only the abstract French subject. (Any regional, ethnic, or religious particularities were perceived as a threat to the Republic's cohesiveness, hence the unease about the particular, seen even now in the debates over wearing the veil in public schools.) Fanon's anxiety about the role of the past within the revolutionary project, meanwhile, can be traced to the Marxist linear model of meliorism that increasingly informs his writing in Algeria and Tunisia.

The traumatic rupture brought on by colonialism would come to haunt the revolutionary project, revealing the difficulty of detaching the future from the past and the universal from the particular. Fanon's melioristic teleology leads him to underestimate the ongoing force of the pre-colonial social paradigms, a force that would be marshalled in moments of crisis, often in response, precisely, to the breakdown of the modernizing revolution. (In fact, colonialist discourse found its somewhat unlikely heir in post-independence Third Worldist modernization discourse and development policies.) Fanon unpacks Europe's narrative of rescue and progress, but in other ways refurbishes its goal of redemptive modernization. Suggesting the incongruity between Europe's Enlightenment ideal of humanism and its real-life de-humanizing of colonized people, *The Wretched of the Earth* formed an advance foray into what was to become the postmodernist critique of universalism. On one level, Fanon anticipates the postmodernist skepticism about the Enlightenment master narrative and its pretense of speaking on behalf of the universal; yet unlike the postmodernists, Fanon nourishes a utopian thought of a "total revolution,"[43] but also, interestingly, one devoid of a ready-made blueprint.

The ambiguity in Fanon concerning the Enlightenment can be traced to the key issue of whether the Enlightenment signifies a rupture in Europe's colonialist relation to its "others," or whether this relation was merely an extension of the Enlightenment. Fanon's text betrays two contradictory impulses toward the Enlightenment, precisely because the Enlightenment itself was inherently contradictory. Positive values, such as representative government, freedom and equality before the law, could not be reconciled with negative practices of colonialism, genocide, slavery, and imperialism, clearly the very antithesis of such values. The contradictions central to the Enlightenment, as simultaneously the source of racism and totalitarianism, as well as of its alternatives, thus shape Fanon's discursive oscillation. Fanon partially reproduces an Enlightenment discourse that assumes Europe as a diffusionist source of reason, science, freedom, and progress, while also seeing the Enlightenment as nothing more than the barbarity of instrumental reason and the annihilation of difference and the local in the name of the universal. This tension is perhaps inevitable in a revolutionary project that seeks an anticolonial humanist meliorism, while also dissecting colonialist humanist meliorism.

* * *

Fanon's writings, along with those of Mao Tse-Tung, Ho Chi Minh, and Che Guevara, influenced the Third Worldist tri-continental revolutionary vision of the 1960s. Written during his final year, as he was battling leukaemia, *The Wretched of the Earth* became the "Bible of Third Worldism," read far beyond its immediate context of the French-Algerian war. Translated into numerous languages, the book had a cross-continental life of its own, debated on campuses, in cafes, in the fields, or within prison cells. The book was a key reference for such diverse decolonization movements as FRELIMO in the Portuguese colony of Mozambique, the Front de Libération Quebecoise (FLQ) in Canada, the Irish Republican Army in Belfast, the Black Panthers in the U.S., the Black Consciousness movement in South Africa, and the diverse revolutionary Arab movements, not to mention the anti-racist and anti-imperialist movements within the West. Fanon's text was often read and adapted to the particular space into which it was translated, and at times with very different emphases. While for many movements in the Third World it was not the psychic violence but the physical violence of colonial armies and police that marked the discussion, for minoritarian movements such as the Black Power movement in the U.S. it was both at the same time. In other words, despite the fact that Fanon in *The Wretched of the Earth*, as we have seen, deployed Marxism without abandoning the analysis of the psyche, movements in the Third World tended to focus on Fanon's political diagnosis of the imperialist process and methods of resistance. Fanon's work, for this reason, was often mistakenly caricatured and reduced, especially by Fanon's antagonists, to a celebration of violence—an issue that would undoubtedly resonate with readers in Israel.

Fanon's *The Wretched of the Earth*, which emerged from the North African context, also traveled to diverse parts of the Middle East. In Turkey, sociologist Ismail Beşikçi helped make Fanon known, especially among Kurds. Beşikçi spent many years in prison for writing against the Turkish state's Kemalism, and for arguing that Kurds are a colonized people.[44] In Iran, meanwhile, Ali Shariati, the Sorbonne-educated Iranian sociologist of religion, considered by many the intellectual father of the Shi'i revolution against the Shah, translated *The Wretched of the Earth* into Farsi. Shariati deployed Islamic terms—for example, rendering the difference between "oppressors" and "oppressed" with the Qur'anic terms *mustakbireen* (the arrogants) and *mustadh'afeen* (the disinherited or the weakened)—despite his awareness of Fanon's anti-religious attitudes and pessimism concerning the positive contribution of religion to social change.[45]

In the Arab world, Fanon similarly has been largely known for *The Wretched of the Earth*, and several books were written on Fanon in Arabic early on. Mohammed Berrada, the Moroccan writer and translator (of among others, Barthes and Bakhtin), collaborated with Mohammed Zniber and the Algerian Francophone writer Mouloud Mammeri to write *Frantz Fanon, aw ma'arakatu al-shu'ub al-Mutakhallifah* (*Frantz Fanon, or the Struggle of Developing Countries*, published in Casablanca in 1961), focusing on the urgent issues faced by Morocco in the wake of decolonization. In 1975 Berrada also partook in a political report for his party, *Al-Itihad al-Ishtiraki* (the Socialist Union), where Fanon's thesis was criticized for emphasizing the role of the peasants at the expense of the urban marginalized. The Algerian Mohammed el-Milli, who worked with Fanon on the FLN's newspaper *Al-Moudjahid* (*The Freedom Fighter*) wrote about "Fanon and the Algerian Revolution" (published in *Al-Thaqafa* in March and May 1971), arguing that Fanon owed more to the Algerian revolution than it owed to him. In the 1960s the Egyptian leftist Hilmi Shaarawi reviewed Fanon's *The Wretched of the Earth*, while the liberal journalist Ahmad Baha al-Din wrote about Fanon, unveiling, and the sociology of the revolution.

Fanon was appreciated not only throughout the French-speaking *Maghrib* but also throughout the *Mashriq*. Although Soviet-oriented communists and orthodox Marxists found Fanon unsatisfying, *The Wretched of the Earth* became a popular reference for anti-imperialist discourse, including that of the Arab Ba'th Socialist Party.[46] In Syria, the translation (*Mu'adhabu al-ard*) by Sami Durubi and Jamal Atasi, published by al-Matba'ah al-Ta'awuniyah, including Sartre's preface, was on the required reading list for the last year of high school and the College for Teachers until the late 1970s. The translation was reprinted in diverse places in the Arab world. In Fatah training centers Fanon was studied along with books by Guevara, Giap, Debray, and Castro.[47] The Arabic translation was also available within the borders of the state of Israel, including in prison, apparently largely via the Jerusalem progressive Salah al-Din Press, whose books were widely distributed among Palestinians, including inside the Green Line area. In his memoir, *Palestinien sans patrie*, published in Hebrew by Mifras Publishing House, Abou Iyad mentions Fanon as one of his favorite writers, whose *The Wretched of the Earth* he had read several times.[48] For Palestinians in particular the analogies (and dis-analogies) between France and Israel on the one hand, and Algeria and Palestine on the other, were crucial. Fanon's emphasis on the role of the peasantry in the vanguard of the revolution seemed especially relevant to the Palestinian *fellahin*, although its thesis required some adjustments, since unlike the case of Algeria, many of the *fellahin* were already landless, dislocated, and scattered refugees.

Although Fanon carved out spaces of Black identity in relation to Jewishness and Arabness, and although he saw both anti-Jewishness and anti-Arabism as an integral part of French colonial ideology, the question of Palestine and Israel is not present in his work. Yet Fanon's life and text did not fully escape it. Fanon's work with the FLN in Algeria, forced him into exile in Tunisia, where he continued his psychiatric practice, experimenting with novel social therapeutic methods. Rival colleagues, however, tried to have Fanon dismissed by accusing him of being a Zionist undercover agent maltreating Arab patients on orders from Israel, an accusation dismissed outright by the Tunisian Minister of Health, Ben Salah.[49] Six years after Fanon's death, and in the wake of the 1967 war, Fanon's widow, Josie, insisted that the publisher omit Sartre's preface from the French reprint of *The Wretched of the Earth*. Living in post-colonial Algeria, Josie, of White French background, argued that Sartre's pro-Zionist position was pro-imperialist, and thus disqualified his preface.[50] It should be noted that Sartre and Simone de Beauvoir had been among the most vocal French leftists in support of Algerian self-determination, declaring that "*L'Algérie n'est pas la France*" (Algeria is not France), a slogan pronounced in opposition to the Pieds Noirs' "*Algérie Française*." Sartre's journal *Les Temps Modernes* offered an important platform for denouncing the rampant torture of Algerians and the daily violence generated by the colonial system. Even prior to his preface to *The Wretched of the Earth*, Sartre published a chapter from Fanon's earlier book *A Dying Colonialism*, while also protesting the seizure of other books on Algeria, such as *La Question*, written by the communist French Jew Henri Alleg who joined the Algerians, and was imprisoned and tortured. Those French who supported Algerian independence suffered retaliation in the form of blacklisting and attacks; Sartre was declared "public enemy number one" and, on July 19, 1961, a bomb exploded at the entrance hall to his apartment.[51]

Yet, in the post-1967 era, for many Arab critics Sartre abandoned his earlier commitment, and crossed to the other side by not condemning Israel's aggression. Sartre, meanwhile, argued that Israel was not part of the imperialist camp, and continued to defend Israel's actions, signing a petition describing Israel as threatened by its Arab neighbors.[52] The French writer Jean Genet, in contrast, took the opposite stance by supporting the Palestinian cause. Retrospectively, it seems that it is in this post-1967 historical moment that one can locate the beginnings of a gradual shift away from the full endorsement of Israel by French intellectuals. This is also the moment in which a number of Jewish intellectuals in the West, who were deterred by the equation of Palestine with the Third World, began to move to the right.

As a product of the post-Enlightenment, Zionism begs the question of the relevance of Fanon's discussion of colonialism and nationalism. In what ways is Fanon's critique of the colonial-settler project applicable to Zionism, which saw its role as liberating the Jewish people, and thus akin to other independence movements? And can France and Israel be seen as similar colonial-settler states, a comparison often made in Arab nationalist discourse? Depending on one's political outlook, Fanon's text might provoke a possible debate on the various analogies and dis-analogies between these histories.

Elsewhere I have argued that Zionism forms an anomalous project, narrating itself as liberatory vis-à-vis Europe even as it carries the same banner of the "civilizing mission" that the European powers proclaimed during their thrust into "found lands." Zionist discourse itself thus embodies schizophrenic master narratives: a redemptive nationalist narrative vis-à-vis Europe and anti-Semitism, and a colonialist narrative vis-à-vis the Arab people who happened to reside in the place designated as the Jewish homeland. Yet, unlike colonialism, Zionism also constituted a response to millennial oppression and, in contradistinction to the classical colonial paradigm, had no "mother country;" metropole and colony, in this case, were conceived as located in the self-same place. Zionist discourse concerning a "return to the mother land" suggests a double relation to that land, where the East is simultaneously the place of Judaic origins and the locus for implementing the West. Thus the East, associated on the one hand with backwardness and underdevelopment, is associated on the other with oasis and solace—a return to geographical origins and reunification with the Biblical past. The West, meanwhile, is also viewed ambivalently, both as the historic crime scene of anti-Semitism and as an object of desire, an authoritative norm to be emulated in the East.[53]

Within this perspective, Fanon's work, it seems to me, plays a paradoxical role. On the one hand, Jews might identify with Fanon's anti-racist and emancipatory project, for anti-Semitism is a form of racism, and Zionism saw itself as a nationalist project liberating oppressed Jews. On the other hand, Israel's colonialist relation to Palestinian people, and in a different way its racist discourse concerning Mizrahim, places it on the European side of the Fanonian equation. It is therefore not a coincidence that Fanon's ironic look at France's civilizing mission, and his anger at the ongoing torture, imprisonment, and sheer devastation, have chilling echoes when read in Israel and Palestine. It is also not a historical coincidence that the same kind of racist French sociological and medical discourses concerning the "North African syndrome," cited by Fanon in *Toward the African Revolution* during the upheavals of the 1950s and 1960s, were also cited, this time positively, by Euro-Israeli writers and intellectuals with regard to North African Jews, displaced to Israel around that time. In a well-known journalistic article, for example, the writer evoked the work of French colleagues who warned that, by opening the "gates too wide to Africans ... a certain kind of human material," Israel was making the same "fatal mistake" the French made, a mistake that will "debase" Israel, sealing its fate as "a Levantine state."[54]

* * *

The Wretched of the Earth enters Israeli intellectual space at a time when academic discourse is not about colonialism but rather postcoloniality. In contrast to translations into many other languages, Fanon was not translated into Hebrew at the height of the major debates over anticolonialism. As a result, the postcolonial theory arriving from the Anglo-American academy entered a certain post-Zionist, postcolonial world in Israel, where the "colonial" itself had hardly been thought through in any depth. Postcolonial theory was thus introduced to the Hebrew reader in an out-of-sequence manner, within an intellectual and political vacuum, as it were, not only in relation to the large corpus of postcolonial work, but more importantly in relation to anticolonial history and writings. In Israel, the anticolonial antecedents of postcolonial writings—for example, texts by Du Bois, C. L. R. James, Cabral, Césaire, Senghor, Retamar, Dorfman, Rodinson, and perhaps most importantly Fanon, have either only recently been translated or never translated into Hebrew. Albert Memmi's books on Jewish-related questions had been translated in the 1960s and 1970s, but not his classic anticolonialist texts. In his preface to the recent (1999) Hebrew translation of his 1982 *Racism,* Memmi writes:

> We cannot boast of having created morality and simultaneously dominate another people. For this reason, I always regretted that no Israeli publisher agreed to publish any of my writing on these issues, and especially the *Portrait of the Colonized* .... I am waiting hopefully for [it] also ... [to] be published in Hebrew. It will mean that the Israeli public will see itself finally as deserving to cope with the difficulties of its national existence.[55]

The Wretched of the Earth arrives, in other words, into an anachronistic context, where the talk of postcoloniality shows very little prior engagement with the foundational anticolonial texts. Relatively late essays by Homi Bhabha, for example, came into Hebrew existence not only before Said's *Orientalism,* but also before the books of the very figure that both Said and Bhabha assumed as a significant influence and interlocutor—Fanon himself. For some Israeli postcolonials who discover and ventriloquize Fanon only via Bhabha, the intellectual jump into the "post" becomes a magic carpet flying into the land of erasure, giving the impression of a faddish recycling of trends from the Anglo-American academy without a thoroughgoing engagement of the historical trajectories that shaped those trends.

In other national contexts, for example the U.S. context, the terrain for both anticolonialist and post-colonialist discourse had been prepared, on the Left, by a long series of struggles around civil rights, decolonization, Third Worldism, Black Power, and anti-imperialism. In Israel, intellectuals lived these moments quite differently. With a few exceptions, such as the Matzpen group and the Left wing of the Mizrahi Black Panthers, Israeli intellectuals did not engage in the debates about decolonization, Black Power, and Third Worldism, debates in which Fanon was pivotal. Thus, the arrival of the postcolonial in the Anglo-American academy in the late 1980s, unlike its subsequent arrival in Israel, formed part of a more coherent trajectory. In the U.S. academe, postcolonial discourse emerged after Black studies, Latino Studies, Native-American studies, and Asian-American studies had already challenged the Western canon, and in the wake of substantial institutional reforms and corrective measures like Affirmative Action—themselves the result of various anti-racist and anti-imperialist revolts dating back to the 1960s and 1970s. This moment of introducing Fanon to the Hebrew reader is perhaps an opportune and productive moment to re-evaluate Israeli intellectual history. It is instructive, for example, to remember that in the period when *The Wretched of the Earth* was stimulating activism on many campuses around the world, Israeli students were living the euphoria of the 1967 victory, with little engagement with a longer Palestinian perspective.

Postcolonial theory in the Anglo-American academy also emerged out of the anticolonialist moment and Third Worldist perspective; that is at least partly what makes it "post." Post-Zionist postcolonial writing in Israel comes out of an academic context often untouched by the history of anti-colonialist debates. Thus we find a "post" without its past. In the Third World, anticolonial nationalism gave way to some "course corrections" and a measure of disillusionment, partially due to the return of neocolonialism, and to the abuses taking place in the name of the revolution. This disillusionment with the aftermath of decolonization, which provides the affective backdrop for postcolonial theory, had no equivalent in the Israeli context. The question of exactly when the "post" in postcolonial begins had already provoked debate in English.[56] Outside Israel, anticolonial discourse gave way to postcolonial discourse, but in Israel, it is not anti-Zionist discourse that gives way to post-Zionist discourse, but rather Zionist discourse that gives way to post-Zionist discourse. But to propose moving beyond "the colonial"—as suggested by postcolonial theory–within a nation-state and in an academic space historically untouched by the Third-Worldist perspective requires that we pose the question of the (anti)colonial with even more vigor.

* * *

Translating Fanon into Hebrew also offers an apt moment to reflect on intellectual history in Israel in terms of which debates have been deemed relevant for discussion. Yet, although Fanon's birth into Hebrew is in a sense untimely, it is in other ways very much apropos. To read Fanon now is not a question of replicating that historical moment of Fanon as a revolutionary icon, but rather, through his renewed presence, to energize a deep historical understanding of the violence—physical, emotional, and epistemological—brought by colonialism. Even Fanon's weaknesses and ambiguities, some of which are alluded to in this essay, only highlight the vital necessity of an inter-generational and cross-regional rendezvous; for Fanon himself believed that "each generation must discover its mission, fulfil it or betray it, in relative opacity."[57]

Apart from his political analysis, Fanon's life as a Martiniquan who empathized with struggles not exactly his own proved no less inspirational than his texts. Might it be possible, in light of Fanon, to go beyond the corrosive self-righteousness that fixes our gaze solely on our own Jewish suffering, smashing any mirror that reveals our ugly spots? Might we be able to recompose the old, reductive, and self-pitying tune of "the-whole-world-is-against-us"? Can we see beyond the narcissistic paradigms that have blinded us to the pains of those we have marched upon on our historical path to liberation; and can we hear beyond all that which keeps us deaf to their persistent cries? Reading Fanon, hopefully with our defense mechanisms put aside, would demand a certain generosity. It would also require listening. Such a reading possesses the power to remind us that critique can be a form of tough love, whereby truth, reconciliation, and mutual existence can be more than a dream.

24

On the Margins of Middle Eastern Studies: Situating Said's *Orientalism*

The question of beginnings in relation to Edward Said's book *Orientalism*[1] can be narrated in very diverse ways, leading to a potentially productive question: when and where does the critique of *Orientalism* begin? Here at MESA, on the occasion of the thirtieth anniversary of Said's book, it would perhaps be instructive to situate the book in relation to the various geographies, histories, and fields of knowledge in which it is embedded. What are the contexts and intertexts of Said's work? How can we character-ize its undergirding conceptual paradigms and disciplinary methodologies? What about the neighboring fields that have impacted Said's work and that in turn have been impacted by that work—are they relevant to Middle Eastern studies? Since the Saidian critique of Orientalist epistemology has by now been extrapolated to diverse cultural geographies, how can we map these transnational currents in relation to the study of the Middle East? And, finally, what does a book, written by a diasporic Palestinian in the U.S., tell us about the kinds of analytical frames that might illuminate the study of that Middle East which is not simply "over there" but also "back here?"

Decolonization and the Seismic Shift

The critique of *Orientalism* forms part of a broader movement of thought that impacted social, cultural, and intellectual life worldwide, namely the larger political/epistemological crisis of the Post-War period. Although in the long view anticolonial discourse goes back to the early historical resistance to colonialism, its more immediate catalysts lie in a series of events—the Holocaust, the postwar disintegration of the European

A published lecture in *Review of Middle Eastern Studies* in a special section entitled "On *Orientalism* at Thirty," 43:1 (Summer 2009). The lecture was delivered at the Plenary Session of the annual meeting of the Middle East Studies Association, entitled, "Celebrating the Thirtieth Anniversary of Orientalism: Critiques and New Insights," organized by the Association President, Mervat Hatem, Middle East Studies Association, Washington, D.C., November 24, 2008.

empires, the "Third-World" revolutionary and minority movements in the West—that cumulatively undermined confidence in European modernity and its master narrative of Progress. Colonialist discourse was based on deeply entrenched hierarchies of race and nation, hierarchies that formed the hegemonic "common sense," and which were questioned by the diverse decolonizing projects of the period. The decolonization of the academy in this sense formed a local manifestation of a much larger transformation that Robert Stam and I have called the postwar seismic shift.

Against this backdrop, Said's book reverberated with the efforts to transform the so-called "Other" from the object into the subject of history. Within Middle Eastern studies, Said's *Orientalism* has been traced back to such precursors as Anouar Abdel-Malek, Abdul-Latif Tibawi, and Maxime Rodinson, but Said's text was also informed by the anticolonialist writings of such figures as Aimé Césaire, Frantz Fanon, and Roberto Fernandez Retamar. Although Fanon, for example, never spoke of "Orientalist discourse," his critique of the colonialist imaginary provided proleptic examples of anti-Orientalist critique. Indeed, in *Culture and Imperialism*,[2] Said's self-declared sequel to *Orientalism*, he acknowledges some of the catalytic figures in the postwar shift, especially C. L. R. James and Fanon, thus making explicit the tacit intertext of his earlier book.

These trends impacted different disciplines in different ways, leading to interrogations of their axial assumptions. The very qualifiers of emerging fields of inquiry, such as "revisionist history," "radical philosophy," or "dialogical anthropology," suggested that canonical disciplines were being rethought from new angles. The venerable discipline of "English literature," the disciplinary location of much of Said's work, began to expose the racially tinged assumptions of writers like Faulkner and Conrad, while literary studies began to debate the inclusion of texts by women, writers of color, and Third World authors.

Said's book entered into a transformed landscape. *Orientalism* was written at a very specific moment in the history of the U.S. academy, when ethnic studies, women's studies, and Third World studies were already challenging the epistemological foundations of what constituted a legitimate object of knowledge, and of who formed a legitimate subject of inquiry deserving institutional academic space. But these currents triggered a backlash, turning the university into a symbolic battleground of the culture wars. Written at the intersection of diverse forms of what Said himself called "adversarial scholarship," Said's work further consolidated what came to be the burgeoning fields of multicultural and postcolonial studies.

The critique of *Orientalism* exists in relations of partial homology to two multidisciplinary spaces, each with its own specific relation to colonialism.

It relates on the one hand to those academic formations based on geographical regions, i.e., the various "area studies," defined as "over there." And on the other hand it relates to the various "ethnic studies," defined as "over here." These two fields have had a somewhat different, in some ways even opposite, genealogy and drift. While ethnic studies initially emerged out of the bottom-up activism of communities of color, area studies initially arose out of top-down Cold War governmental geopolitical perspectives and needs. Yet both area studies and ethnic studies, despite their distinct beginnings, are shaped by the contexts of colonialism and imperialism. Area studies was formed during the overlapping historical transition from European (especially British and French) to U.S. hegemony, while ethnic studies was formed in the post-Civil Rights era, when Native Americans, African Americans, and Chicanos were theorized as "internal colonies." And, today the growing field of Arab-American studies has emerged against the backdrop of U.S. direct interventionist wars in the Middle East.

Orientalism In-Between Area Studies

Read through literal and figurative "translations," Said's *Orientalism* was subsequently extrapolated for diverse regions such as South Asia, the Balkans, and Latin America. In his book *The History of the Concept of "Latin America" in the United States*,[3] Brazilian political scientist João Feres Jr. deploys Said's anti-Orientalist grid to anatomize the writings of Samuel Huntington and Seymour Martin Lipset, which represent Latin Americans as irrational, passion-driven, pathological, unproductive, and condemned to historical immobility. Within this discourse, to cite Feres, "the Anglo-Saxon Protestant Occident constitutes the beacon of progress and human development, while Catholic Latin America is the prison which maintains its detainees frozen in the feudal past."[4] Feres usefully deploys a Saidian prism to examine the writings of certain U.S. scholars working in the service of Cold War ideology.

In the case of Huntington, I would add, while his book *The Clash of Civilizations and the Remaking of World Order* was basically set along an East–West axis, his recent book *Who Are We?* is largely set along a North-South axis.[5] If one book is premised on the irreconcilable differences between hermetically sealed-off cultures internationally, the other book is premised on the allegedly unbridgeable intra-national gap between Anglo-Americans and Latinos. Huntington's evolving work demonstrates that Eurocentrist/Orientalist discourse is not monolithic; it has regional variations, even in the work of the same thinker. While in the case of the Middle East, Huntington marshals an essentialist view of a retrograde Islamic East contrasted with the West, in the case of Latin America, he marshals a Hegelian-Weberian-derived view of a retrograde Catholic South, contrasted with the dynamic Protestant North, but in both instances the privileged pole maintains "positional superiority."

At the same time, however, Feres's implicit identification of the U.S. as the main source of Orientalism risks eliding the fact that U.S.-style Cold War Orientalism comes superimposed on pre-existing forms of Orientalism in Latin American history itself, in the sense that the Spanish had already "Orientalized" the native peoples. Columbus, in this perspective, could be considered the first Orientalist of the Americas, even in the sense of imagining himself, as his diaries indicate, to be literally in the Orient, in the land of the Great Khan, peopled with wild flora, fauna, mermaids, and cannibals. The traffic of ideas, then, is more multifaceted and multi-directional than might at first appear. While extending Said's critique of post-Enlightenment Orientalism for Latin America is certainly productive, in other respects it overlooks the ideological conquest of the Americas generally within Orientalist paradigms, where anti-Jewish and anti-Muslim Iberia played a crucial role.

Other Latin-American studies scholars, such as Walter Mignolo, have pointed out that postcolonial discourse, by concentrating on Orientalism as a discursive symptom of later forms of British and French imperialism, forgets that "Orientalism" was itself preceded by "Occidentalism."[6] Here, "Occidentalism" is not used in Ian Buruma and Avishai Margalit's[7] sense of a kind of "reverse Orientalism," but rather to refer to the European Conquest of the Americas. By the same token, however, one might also argue that Occidentalism à la Mignolo's sense was itself already informed by the proto-Orientalism of the *Reconquista*, and that the conquest of the Americas was already imbricated in anti-Semitism and anti-Islamism. The campaigns against Muslims and Jews as well as against other "agents of Satan" made available a mammoth apparatus of othering for recycling in the "new" continents. Such campaigns provided a disciplinary framework, which, after being turned against Europe's immediate or internal "Others," was then projected outward against Europe's distant or external Others. The point is not that there is an exact equivalence between Europe's representa-tions of Jews and Muslims and of the indigenous peoples of the Americas, but only that European Christian demonology pre-figured racialist colonialism. Indeed, we can even discern a partial congruency between the phantasmatic imagery projected onto the Jewish and Muslim "enemy" and onto the indigenous and Black-African "savage," all imaged to various degrees as "blood drinkers," "sorcerers," "devils," and "infidels."

The Nexus of Culture and Politics

Said's work is frequently referenced within the related fields of postcolonial and cultural studies, academic domains where "culture" is viewed as embedded in the political realm but not reducible to it. In *Orientalism*, Said analyzed texts and discourses in ways that emphasized the constitutive power of culture but which still went beyond any essentialist cultural*ism*, i.e., the tendency to reduce complex social phenomena to a monolithic and unchanging cultural essence, deployed as an all-purpose explanatory mechanism. Without completely abandoning the textual analysis inherited from literary studies, Said thus operated within the anti-culturalist and anti-essentialist assumptions that mark the field of cultural studies associated with the Birmingham School, for whom culture was not unified but rather a contested, heteroglossic, and dissensual arena.

Needless to say, the impact of Said's book on postcolonial and cultural studies is distinct from its impact on Middle Eastern studies. Meanwhile, the scholarly work performed in the in-between of these academic spaces, such as it is, exists on the margins of both spaces, with relatively little dialogue between the two. The reasons for this marginal dialogue have less to do with political positions, perhaps, than with methods and theoretical assumptions. Assumed within postcolonial/cultural studies are the various structuralist and poststructuralist "turns;" the linguistic turn (Saussure), the discursive turn (Bakhtin and Foucault), and the cultural turn (Jameson). The critique of Said as a deficient political scientist or historian, however valid from specific disciplinary perspectives, sidesteps on another level the book's concern with the problem of representation in terms of rhetoric, figures of speech, narrative structure, and discursive formation.

Within a postcolonial studies perspective, Said called attention to the ways regions and communities are figured, sequenced, narrated, and represented through an often unacknowledged set of axiomatic doxa. Said's method entails the simultaneous constitution and reading of a discursive corpus—in this case Orientalism. Surely it is legitimate to point out that Orientalist discourse is not homogenous, that it manifests historical and national specificities, and so forth. At the same time, the critical reading of a discourse remains productive precisely because beyond the "trees" of the differences from text to text and nation to nation, the reading discerns the "forest" of the discourse, exposing recurrent leitmotifs manifest across styles, genres, and historical contexts. Whatever the pitfalls of poststructuralist protocols of reading—and critics are certainly right to point them out—such readings can also illuminate dimensions that other grids might otherwise have missed.

It is thus not a coincidence that Said's work has constantly been referenced in literature, film/media, and cultural studies, precisely because his method of textual and discourse analysis reverberates with familiar methodological premises in those fields. Within Middle Eastern studies these fields of investigation have often been seen through the prism of a rather gendered tropology of "soft" and "hard" knowledges. The heated debates over Said's *Orientalism* have focused on "hard" knowledge, i.e. ideology and politics. It is as if the study of the politics of culture is viewed as marginal to the "real" debate over *Orientalism*, i.e., the ideological-political debate. But Said's critique bears precisely on the inextricable nexus between the supposedly hard power of institutions and the supposedly soft power of culture. Said's political critique, therefore, cannot be detached from his cultural critique. Indeed, the assumption that politics and culture are thoroughly imbricated forms the cornerstone of that post-Marxist field called "cultural studies" as a field which deployed Gramsci to reconfigure the base/superstructure relation within an intellectual paradigm where culture and politics are mutually constituted, in and through each other.

Diaspora, Transnationalism, and the Study of the Middle East

The last chapter of Said's book focuses on "Orientalism Now." And 30 years later, the era of transnational flows and the ongoing diasporization of Middle Eastern peoples pose a challenge to notions of reified cartographies and isolated regional units. But what analytical frameworks are available for studying these cross-border movements between regions? Can Middle East studies be rethought as an inclusive space in ways that expand the boundaries of what constitutes a legitimate object of inquiry within area studies? And how can such a reconceptualization bypass the notion of the Middle East as a fixed sign with demarcated boundaries between East and West, a notion that was the object of Said's critique?

Both area studies and ethnic studies, in their different ways, have historically reinforced the notion that Middle Eastern Americans are either "over there" or "over here," discouraging entry into scholarly frameworks that depart from the *terra firma* of regions to focus on diasporic in-betweenness. Mutually exclusive frameworks impede the study of the co-implicatedness of regions, for example of America in the Middle East and the Middle East in America. Nonetheless, there is an increasing visibility of cross-border analyses in publications, conferences, and course offerings. Post 9/11, associations such as the Modern Language Association, the Society for cinema and media studies, and the American Studies Association have all witnessed an increase in panels on Middle East-related themes. American studies and ethnic studies departments (at institutions such as the University of

Michigan, Ann Arbor, and San Francisco State University) have developed Arab-American and Muslim diasporas curricula; while some women's, gender, and sexuality studies programs have offered courses within trans-national perspectives on the Middle East. Such perspectives have also been addressed in such books as Amal Amireh and Liza Suhair Majaj's *Going Global*, Minoo Moallem's *Between Warrior Brother and Veiled Sister*, and Shouleh Vatanabadi and Mohammad Mehdi Khorrami's *Another Sea, Another Shore*;[8] as well as in various articles published in such journals as *Middle East Report* (*Middle East Research and Information Project*), *Journal of Palestine Studies, Arab Studies Journal, Critique, Journal of Middle East Women's Studies,* and the *Middle East Journal of Culture and Communication*, just to give a few examples.

The interdisciplinary space of cultural politics, arguably the scholarly genre within which Said's book was written, offers opportunities for an expanded notion of Middle Eastern studies. Increasingly, a vibrant and growing field of scholarship has taken on board such questions as the back-and-forth movements across borders of commodities and communities, and the diverse technologies that instantaneously link the globe. Such work addresses neo-Orientalism not only in relation to the Middle East per se but also *in* and *around* it; for example through work on the transnational reception of Middle Eastern literature, cinema, and artwork, and its impact on the "self-orientalizing" of Middle Eastern cultural production; on the politics of translation of novels and memoirs within gendered Orientalist paradigms; on globalized digital technologies as actively mediating and shaping of identities beyond national boundaries. Taken as an ensemble, such work analyzes cultural formations and practices as at once national and transna-tional, local and global.

This intersectionality of regions and cartographies of knowledge presents an opportunity to redraw static maps of scholarly terrain, stretching and broadening the field. The study of cross-border movements and inter-area studies approaches de-territorializes regions as stable objects of study, and offers new angles on the ongoing critique of the essentialist fixity of East-versus-West.

PART IV

Muslims, Jews, and Diasporic Readings

25

Rethinking Jews and Muslims: Quincentennial Reflections

"Your Highness completed the war against the Moors," Columbus wrote in a letter addressed to the Spanish throne, "after having chased all the Jews ... and sent me to the said regions of India in order to convert the people there to our Holy Faith."[1] In 1492 the defeat of the Muslims and the expulsion of Jews from Spain converged with the conquest of the so-called New World. The separate quincentenary commemorations in the Americas, Europe, and the Middle East, however, have seldom acknowledged the linkage between these events. Although intellectually challenging and politically inspiring, "goodbye Columbus" counter-quincentenary debates have, for the most part, followed the same easy path of separating these issues.

The reasons can be partially located in the scholarly inertia that compartmentalizes historical periods and geographical regions into neat areas of expertise, overlooking the interconnectedness of histories, geographies, and cultural identities. But they are also traceable to a general reluctance in progressive circles to chart the colonial dimensions of contemporary Euro-Israeli discourse. While the celebrations of Columbus's "discovery" have provoked lively opposition, the Eurocentric framing of the "other 1492" has been little questioned.

From Reconquista to Conquista

The Spanish-Christian war against Muslims and Jews was politically, economically, and ideologically linked to the arrival of Columbus's caravels in Española. Spain, triumphant over the Muslims, risked investment in Columbus's schemes. His voyages were largely financed by wealth

Published in *Middle East Report* (Middle East Research and Information Project), Special Issue entitled "1492 + 500," No. 178, Vol. 22, No. 5 (September-October, 1992). One portion of the essay is based on the author's presentation, "Tropes of Gender and Cartographies of 'Discovery,'" given at the "Goodbye Columbus" conference, co-organized by M. A. Jaimes, Terence Turner, and the author, The Society for the Humanities, Cornell University, April 3–4, 1992.

confiscated from Jews expelled during the Inquisition.[2] Columbus's fleet departed from the relatively unknown seaport of Palos because the shipping lanes of Cadiz and Seville were clogged with fleeing Jews. The *Reconquista*, which began in the 11th century with the fall of Toledo and continued until the fall of Granada in January 1492, was a long process. Its policies of settling Christians in the newly (re)conquered areas, as well as the gradual institutionalization of expulsions, conversions and killings of Muslims and Jews in Christian territories, prepared the grounds for subsequent similar *Conquista* practices across the Atlantic, as Columbus's letter suggests. Under the marital-political union of Ferdinand (Aragon) and Isabella (Castile), victorious Christian Spain strengthened its sense of nationhood, soon to be turned into an empire as it subjugated indigenous Americans and Africans. Discourses about Muslims and Jews during Spain's continental expansion crossed the Atlantic, arming the conquistadors with a ready-made ideology aimed at regions of India but in fact applied first toward the indigenous inhabitants of the accidentally "discovered" continent. (India's turn came with the arrival of Vasco da Gama in 1498 and the Portuguese conquest of Goa in 1510, and, of course, with the complete British takeover in the 18th century.)

The campaigns against Muslims and Jews, as well as against heretics and witches, made available an entire apparatus of racism and sexism for "recycling" in the newly raided continents. The Crusades, which helped inaugurate "Europe" by reconquering the Mediterranean area and making Europe aware of its geocultural identity, coincided with anti-Semitic pogroms. Christian Europe, on the verge of the conquest of the New World, indulged in fears of diverse "agents of Satan"—women, witches, heretics, Jews, and Muslims—but anti-Semitism formed an especially integral part of the European ideological system then projected outward against Europe's external others—the indigenous peoples of Africa and the Americas.[3] Although life in Spain before the expulsion of Jews and Muslims was characterized by a relatively peaceful coexistence between the three religious civilizations, the Spanish Inquisition, as an early exercise in European "self-purification," sought to punish and expel, or forcibly convert, Muslims and Jews. The indigenous peoples of the Americas similarly were officially protected from massacres by the throne only once they converted to Christianity.

European demonology, then, prefigured colonialist racism. We can even discern a partial congruence between the phantasmatic imagery projected onto the Jewish and Muslim "enemy" and the Black-African and indigenous-American "savage"—all imagined to various degrees as "blood drinkers," "cannibals," "sorcerers," and "devils." Writing about his voyages, Amerigo Vespucci drew on the stock of Jewish and Muslim stereotypes to characterize the savage, the infidel, the indigenous man as sexual omnivore and the indigenous woman as sexual object.[4] "The chiefe God they worship," wrote Captain John Smith in his *Map of Virginia* (1612), "is the Divell."[5]

Eurocentric historical discourse tends to paint a flattering picture of Europe during the "Age of Discovery" while denigrating the newly colonized peoples. At the time of the onset of colonialism and conquest, Europe was a rather brutal and superstitious place, dominated by a "demonological discourse."[6] Church-sponsored brutalities towards Jews and Muslims have to be seen, therefore, on the same continuum as the forced conversions of indigenous peoples of the Americas who, like the Jews and Muslims in Catholic Spain, were obliged to feign allegiance to Christianity.

Eliding Muslims

In November 1991, the ceremonial opening for a conference at the University of California at Los Angeles dedicated to the expulsion of Sephardi Jews included the screening of the film *El Santo Oficio* (*The Holy Office*, 1973). Arturo Ripstein's film features the attempt by the Holy See to spread the Inquisition into the New World. We see Sephardi Jewish *conversos* (also referred to as *marranos*) in Mexico obliged to practice Judaism in secret. At the film's finale, the *conversos*, along with heretics, witches, and indigenous infidels, are burned at the stake for their lack of faith. Those who refused to convert are burned alive; others are burned after hanging. Although the film focuses on the *conversos*, it does not isolate their persecution from that of other religious and racial oppressions practiced by the *Conquistadores* of the Americas, the heirs of the *Reconquistas* of Spain.

Ripstein's remarkable film provoked strong emotions at the screening, but its documentation of Sephardi-Jewish rituals practiced in tormenting secrecy, and its visual details of torture, rape, and massacre were not received in the spirit of the linkages I have charted here. The audience consisted largely of American-Jewish educators, scholars, and community workers eager to consume the narrative of the singular nature of the Jewish experience. As a result, the conference ignored the historical and discursive links of the Inquisition and the expulsion of Sephardi Jews to the genocide of the indigenous peoples of the Americas, to the devastation of African peoples, and also to the Christian persecution of Muslims in Spain. The elision of the Arab-Muslim part of the narrative is especially striking.

During the centuries-long *Reconquista*, not all Muslims and Jews withdrew with the Muslim forces. Those Muslims who remained after the change of rule were known as *mudéjars* ("permitted to remain," deriving from the Arabic *mudajjan*, with a suggestion of "tamed" or "domesticated"). Like those Jews who remained in Christian Spain, after a certain period of tolerance, and economic and cultural contribution to Christian Spain, they were persecuted. The Inquisition, which was institutionalized as a tool of the state in 1478, did not pass over the Muslims. In 1499, mass burning of Islamic books and forced conversions took place, and in 1502 the Muslims of Granada were given the choice of baptism or exile. In 1525–26, Muslims of other provinces were given the same choice. Thereafter the same Inquisitory measures taken against the Jewish *conversos* who were found to be secretly practicing Judaism were taken against *Moriscos* (Moors converted to Christianity) found to be practicing Islam. In 1566 there was a revival of anti-Muslim legislation, and between 1609 and 1614 came edicts of expulsion. As a result, about half a million are said to have fled to North Africa, where they maintained, as Sephardi Jews did, certain aspects of their Spanishness.

These details are well documented.[7] Yet they find little echo in events such as those taking place under the auspices of the International Jewish

Figure 46   Cover of *Middle East Report,* "1492 + 500," design by Kamal Boullata, using Andalusian text by al-Qandusi

Committee—Sefarad '92. The reasons cannot be simply attributed to a literalism—to the fact that the 1492 edict of expulsion was addressed to the Jews. The elision of comparative discussion of the Muslim and Jewish situations in Christian Spain is rooted in present-day Middle Eastern politics. The 1992 commemorations reflect present-day battles over the representations of history. Subordinated to a Eurocentric Zionist historiography, they lament yet another tragic episode in a homogenous, static Jewish History of persistent persecution.

The screening of *El Santo Oficio* at the Expulsion conference, not surprisingly, elicited such remarks as: "You think it's different today?" and "That's also what the Nazis did to us. If the Arabs could, they'd do it too!" Such comments underline the commemorations' role as a stage for demonstrating Israeli nationalism as the logical answer to such horrific events as the Inquisition. The Inquisition of Sephardi Jews is seen merely as foreshadowing the Holocaust of Ashkenazi Jews. In this paradigm, the traumas of Nazism are facilely projected onto the experiences of Jews in Muslim countries, and onto the Israeli/Palestinian conflict.[8] Arabs of today are merely one more "non-Jewish" obstacle in the Jewish trajectory.

The uniqueness and common victimization of all Jews at all times is a crucial underpinning of official Israeli ideology. The genocides of indigenous Americans and Africans are not a point of reference, while the linked persecution in Iberia of Jews and Muslims, *conversos* and *Moriscos*, is rendered irrelevant. This selective reading of Jewish history hijacks the Jews of Islam from their Judeo-Islamic history and culture, and subordinates their experience to that of the Ashkenazi-European *shtetl*, presented as a "universal" Jewish experience. In the Zionist "proof" of a single Jewish experience, there are no parallels or overlappings with other religious/ethnic communities. All Jews are by definition closer to each other than to the cultures of which they have been a part.

The Jews of Islam, and more specifically Arab-Jews, meanwhile, problematize this Eurocentric representation. Thus Zionist historiography, when it does refer to Islamic-Jewish history, consists of a morbidly selective "tracing the dots" from pogrom to pogrom. This picture of an ageless and relentless oppression and humiliation ignores the fact that, on the whole, Jews of Islam—a minority among several other religious/ethnic communities— lived relatively comfortably within Arab-Muslim society.

My point is not to idealize the situation of the Jews of Islam, but rather to suggest that, with a few exceptions, Zionist and anti-Zionist histories have either subsumed Islamic–Jewish history into Christian–Jewish history or ignored the status of Jews in the context of other minorities in Islamic societies.[9] On the occasion of the quincentenary, the Zionist perspective privileges Sephardi-Jewish relations with Christianity over those with Arab

Islam, projecting Eurocentric maps of Jews (West) and Muslims (East). The only Muslim country that receives some attention is Turkey, partly due to Sultan Bayezid II's ordering of his governors in 1492 to receive the Jews cordially. Even here the emphasis is less on Muslim–Jewish relations than on the voyages of refuge, and on Turkish (national) as opposed to Muslim (religious) shelter. Such a version plays down the fact that at the time of the expulsion there were well-established Jewish communities all over the Islamic Arab Middle East and North Africa.

Beyond Sephardi Exotica

The master narrative of universal Jewish victimization has been crucial for the Israeli "ingathering" of peoples from such diverse geographies, languages, cultures, and histories, as well as for the claim that the Jewish nation faces a common historical enemy in Muslim Arabs. Associating Arabs with Nazis (and in 1992 with the Inquisitors), projects a Jewish European nightmare onto the structurally distinct political dynamics of the Middle East. Sephardi Jews experienced an utterly different history within the Arab world than that which haunts the European memories of Ashkenazi Jews; the conflation of the Muslim-Arab with the archetypal European oppressors of Jews strategically understates Israel's colonial-settler dispossession of Palestinian people.

The simplistic equation of the histories of Ashkenazim and Sephardim (in the broad sense now of including all Jews of the Middle East and North Africa) functions to assimilate Sephardim into Ashkenazi history. The discussions of expulsion bring out the "wandering Jew" motif, though the Jews of the Middle East, for the most part, had stable, "non-wandering" lives in the Islamic world. Sephardim moved within the regions of Asia and Africa, and the Mediterranean and the Indian Ocean, not because of persecution but rather for commercial, religious, or scholarly purposes. The major displacement took place in recent years, when Sephardim were uprooted, dispossessed, and dislodged due to the collaboration between Israel and Arab governments and Western colonial powers, who termed their solution for the "question of Palestine" a "population exchange."[10] (That no one asked either the Palestinians or Arab Jews whether they wished to be exchanged is typical of other Third World histories.) Sephardim who have been able to leave Israel, often in response to institutionalized racism there, have dislocated themselves yet again, this time to the U.S., Canada, France, the U.K., or the Netherlands. Ironically, today it is to the Muslim-Arab countries of their origins that most Middle Eastern Jews cannot travel.

The quincentenary events also center on the Spanishness of Sephardi culture (largely on Ladino or Judeo-Español language and music) while marginalizing the fact that Jews in Iberia formed part of a larger Judeo-Islamic culture of North Africa and the Middle East and also of the European Balkan area of the Ottoman Empire. Major Sephardi texts in philosophy, linguistics, poetry, and medicine were written in Arabic and reflect specific Muslim influences as well as a strong sense of Judeo-Arab identity. The Jews of Iberia had come there from the Middle East—some with the Romans, others with the Muslims. When they fled Spain, over 70 percent returned to regions of the Ottoman Empire, while the rest went to Western Europe and the Americas.

The commonalities between Jews and Muslims, particularly the "Arabness" of Jews in Spain, North Africa, and the Middle East, is a thorny reminder of the Middle Eastern character of the majority of Jews in Israel today. Erasure of the Arab dimension of Sephardim is crucial from a Zionist perspective, since Israel has ended up in a paradoxical situation in which its "Orientals" had closer cultural and historical links to the presumed enemy—

Figure 47 'Izzat Sassoun Mu'allem, an Iraqi Jew, in his home in al-Diwaniyah, Iraq, 1949 (a relative of the author's friend, Naeim Khlaschi Giladi)

the "Arab"—than to the Ashkenazi Jews with whom they were coaxed into a common nationhood. The elision of Arab Jews (or Jewish Arabs), and the frequent narrow focus on Sephardi history in relation to Christian Spain, rejects an Arab and Muslim context for Middle Eastern Jewish history and identity, while unilaterally subsuming Middle Eastern Jews into a pan-Jewish historical perspective.

The Zionist establishment, since its early encounters with Palestinian (Sephardi) Jews, has systematically attempted to eradicate the "malignancies" of those other Jews—for example, by stigmatizing Sephardi-Arabized syntax and accents in Hebrew, by marginalizing Asia and Africa and Islamic-Arab and Jewish-Arab histories in school curricula, and by rendering Sephardi culture and political activities invisible in the media.

The 1992 events pose a problematic relation between past and present. The past of Sephardim is reduced to persecution, while the present is displaced into exotic traditions. Sephardi-Oriental identity is now accepted only in the form of folklore, adding spice to Euro-Israeli culture. Insensitive to questions of self-representation, quincentenary events have relied typically on Ashkenazi experts on the Jews-of-Islam, leaving the religious and folkloric aspects, such as cuisine and music, to "authentic" Sephardim. In fact, Sephardi "folklore" constitutes an Israeli national industry, which exports (often expropriated) goods (dresses, jewelry, liturgical objects) and ethnographic photos, films, and books about the charming folkways of Sephardim to Westerners eager for Jewish exotica. The occasion of the quincentenary has not prompted any rethinking of this colonial ethnographic model.

This appropriation contrasts with politically and culturally critical Sephardi-Oriental self-representation, seen in the last decade in such movements as East for Peace and the Oriental Front in Israel, Perspectives Judéo-Arabes in Paris, and the World Organization of Jews from Islamic Countries in New York. It also contrasts with the spirit of the meeting between Sephardi Jews and Palestinians held in Toledo, Spain, in 1989, where participants insisted that peace would mean more than geographical borders, and would require dismantling the artificial East/West cultural borders between Israel and the Arab world.

26

"Coming to America": Reflections on Hair and Memory Loss

In Search of Fatima

In the century-old film *Fatima*, a dark-haired woman, dressed in "exotic" fashion, with navel exposed, performs a "strange" dance in which her belly wiggles conspicuously. Her appearance triggers a number of questions. Who is this Fatima? What kind of a name does she have? What genre of dance is she performing? And what is she doing in an American film? Anthologized in the Museum of Modern Art's series of 1890s films, *Fatima* is mentioned in most scholarly books on film history. Yet the silently dancing Fatima has also elicited a curious century-old silence about her identity, the nature of her dance, and her baffling presence on the American screen. Is she a unique, sensational dancer captured accidentally by a tantalized camera? Or does her screen appearance point to a larger cultural phenomenon? And what was the context for this exotic display?

Although I have not finished my research on Fatima's identity, I pose these questions here in the hope of raising more fundamental questions about the place of non-European women in the narrative of immigration to the U.S. and in the imagination of "America." To unveil the mysteries around Fatima is, for me, a way of unfolding the entangled relationship between immigration, identity, and contemporary cultural critique. Fatima, in this sense, serves as both metonym and metaphor for the imagination of the East in the West. Her documented presence on the screen only accentuates her elision—and that of Middle Easterners as a whole—from the grand narrative of coming to America.

Indeed, cinema invented a geographically incoherent Orient, prodding this Orient into coherence through the production of visual consistency, mechanically reproduced from film to film and from genre to genre, even as cinema itself evolved and changed over a century. Orientalism was also

Published in Amal Amireh and Lisa Suhair Majaj (eds.), *Going Global: The Transnational Reception of Third World Women Writers* (New York and London: Garland, 2000).

Figure 48   Before and after censorship: Edison's *Fatima*, 1897

symptomatic of the relationship between popular culture and scientific exhibitions. Fatima, in this sense, was not conjured up like a genie from a bottle. A clear historical, cultural, and institutional context provided the ground for her appearance on the screen, which occurred as early as 1897. Writing about his encounter with the Egyptian belly dancer Kuchuk Hanem, Flaubert, for example, established an important paradigm for representing the Orient. His Oriental travels inspired his fictional description, in *Herodias*, of Salome's dance, a description that itself inspired a series of Orientalist visual representations of dangerously seductive dancers with exposed navels and draped snakes.[1] Meanwhile, travel narratives about camel riding, paintings of harems, photographs of narrow-laned bazaars, and postcards of veiled women with exposed breasts generated a greater appetite for flesh-and-blood Arab female dancers.

Belly-dancers were not invited to display their performative-choreographic talents in European and American theaters and music halls, however; rather, they were themselves displayed as freakish specimens in colonial exhibitions where the non-European "world" was reconstructed for local consumption. The "authentic" Algerian villages and Cairo streets fabricated in Paris, London, or New York, with their detailed objects (*killims, nargilas, diwans*), offered a rich *mise-en-scène* for the rituals performed by their colorfully dressed "dwellers," who were brought all the way from Egypt and Algeria and paraded before the West's bemused eyes. Sipping Turkish coffee, baking Berber bread, or Arab dancing and singing were just a few of the "rituals" that went into the staging of the Orient. Following the popularity of the French-coined "*dance du ventre*," American entrepreneurs decided to bring the novelty to U.S. expositions: The Philadelphia Columbia Exposition of 1876 featured Tunisian dancers; the 1893 Chicago "Century of Progress" exposition imported a whole Algerian village from France, including a dancer called "Little Egypt." The latter inspired the hoochie-coochie craze (with many Little Egypt imitators from Brooklyn), blending the Orientalism of "exotic dancers" into the American burlesque as well as into diverse striptease shows.

This "freakish" history was rarely featured in the account of immigration to the Land of Freedom. Take the history of immigrants from the Middle East/North Africa in the U.S. Media portrayals typically assume this to be a short history of the past few decades, one that has little impact on mainstream culture. But while it is true that the liberal 1965 Immigration Act opened some gates to Third World immigrants, the story of Middle Eastern immigrants as a group dates back to the 19th century. The majority of these immigrants, from what was then the Ottoman Empire, came from Syria/Lebanon. Although standard Arab-American historiography focuses on success stories, particularly of immigrants who took up peddling as their route to the "American Dream," many of these immigrants were in fact factory laborers, recruited to work in the U.S. during a period of labor shortage.[2] Fatima was in a sense one of the early hyphenated Arab-American performers. Indeed, the question of the hyphen is in some ways central to the ways in which immigrant identity is represented. Not all countries and regions that precede the hyphen in the U.S. are equal, nor do they carry the same burden of association. Sometimes sheer ignorance guides the reception of hyphenated culture.

In preparation for *Talking Visions*, a volume of essays and images I was working on several years ago, the artist Lynne Yamamoto sent me xeroxed reviews of her work, including a 1995 *New York Times* article, where the reviewer wrote: "Yamamoto inscribes the biography of her Chinese grandmother, a laundress, on nails hammered into the wall." The xerox sent to me included Yamamoto's handwritten correction with a red pencil: "Chinese" is crossed out to read "Japanese." How often, I wondered, had Lynne needed to correct that Asian-confusion syndrome of "they're all the same"? Of course, "we/they" are not all the same. At the same time, however, it is important to look at commonalities among the experiences of immigrant women of color, especially vis-à-vis institutionalized mapping of identities. Here I want to argue for a multi-cultural feminist reflection on the analogies that link these diverse experiences. Throughout this essay, I will be returning to these personal histories from East and West Asia; histories that culturally have apparently little to do with each other, but which, in the context of multiple displacements—in Lynne Yamamoto's case, Japan, Hawai'i, the continental U.S., and in my case, Iraq, Israel/Palestine, the U.S.—strangely echo each other. In interweaving these disparate narratives, I want to illuminate, through associative juxtapositions, the role of memory in the making of hyphenated identities. In this sense my essay "travels" not only between different continents but also between different genres of writing.

By placing my journey in relation to that of Yamamoto, I hope to create a contrapuntal dialogue between usually separate geographies and histories.

I also want to call into question the binarist approach through which immigrant narratives in the U.S. are only told vis-à-vis a White dominant norm. "Writing back" and "talking back" have indeed been important for multicultural feminists. Yet often this has meant a rotating chain of women of color confronting a dominant White culture. In the process we have tended to neglect the complex relationships among communities of color in general, and more specifically among immigrants and non-immigrants. Looking into the lives of immigrants of diverse colors challenges the limitations of a Black/White framing of identities. Although the Black/White binarism is strongly inscribed in the material and ideological structures of the U.S., it is crucial for multicultural feminists to examine the multi-lateral interplay of diverse communities, especially since the 1965 Immigration Act, which, by relatively democratizing access to the U.S., added even more "dark" layers to an already multilayered amalgam. Yet these recent waves of immigration by people of color are a result, not only of the inclusiveness of the 1965 Immigration Act, but also of U.S. imperial interventions, and of a globalized economic structure in which the U.S. has played a central and oppressive role in these dislocations.

Redrawing U.S. Cartographies of Asia and Africa

One of the central issues of crossing borders has to do with the classification and cataloging of identities. Although immigration from North Africa and the Middle East dates back to the end of the 19th century, and although this flow has increased since the 1960s, North Africans and Middle Easterners are seen as "forever foreign," only "from there." Chicano/as, to take another example, are also treated by the media as ontologically, quintessentially alien ("from there"), although many did not cross the border to the U.S.; it was the borders that moved around them. The first "illegal alien," Columbus, is celebrated as a discoverer, while indigenous Mexicans are seen as "infiltrating" a barbed border, one that in fact divides their former homeland. Native Americans, similarly, are "from here," but for many Native-American communities, such as the Cherokees, Nez Perce, and Modoc, their geographical dispersal across scattered swaths of U.S. territory "hides," as it were, their "trail of tears" as internal refugees. The implicit nationalism even of multicultural maps and grids disallows a narrative of refugees within the borders of the "Land of Freedom," nor does it account for displacements caused by devastating U.S. global politics.

Within the contemporary academic context, rigid classifications have affected the ways in which curricula are formed and institutional politics are shaped. What does it mean, for example, to be labeled "Asian-American"? While until the 1990s the field of American studies largely ignored the perspective of people of color, ethnic studies programs—the hard-won achievement of 1960s battles—were set up precisely to study the historical perspective of racialized minorities. The subject of ethnic studies has been often apportioned among communities that have been fundamental to the history of the U.S.: Native-American, African-American, Chicano/Latino-American and Asian-American. Within this generally critical field of inquiry, however, the term "Asian" came to reflect a Euro-American labeling, often undermining at least a century-old history of other marginalized Third World immigrant communities largely from South and West Asia, just as the term "African" came to ignore North Africa.

As an immigrant from the continent of Asia I have often been quite bewildered to learn that, despite Iraq and Mesopotamia being my family's geography of origins, I am not an Asian. And as someone who grew up in Israel/Palestine, and who was called Black there, I soon learned that few understand this conjunctural definition of Blackness. The "shock of arrival," to borrow Meena Alexander's phrase,[3] begins when one runs into the border patrols of New World naming. The diverse cultures of Asia are condensed into a homogenizing label that erases their difference and complexity: hence the typical conflation of Japanese with Chinese.

My family, like most Jewish-Arab families after the colonial partition of Palestine, became refugees from Iraq in the 1950s and ended up in Israel due to what was styled a "population exchange," whereby Palestinians and Jewish Arabs were massively swapped across borders. Once in Israel we became the *schwartzes* ("blacks" in Yiddish) of Euro-Israelis. Our Asianness in Israel was bureaucratically defined. In the highly centralized Israeli state, every aspect of our lives, whether at school, work, or hospital, was determined by checking that fatal box on official documents: "Of Asiatic/African origins."

In the U.S. I quickly learned that our earlier scars of partition and the traumatic memories of crossing the borders from Iraq to Israel/Palestine have little resonance, or else are simply censored. I also learned that not all hyphenated identities are permitted entry into America's official lexicon of ethnicities and races. I could see in people's faces how this corporeally inscribed hyphen, Iraq-Israel, produced a kind of classificatory vertigo, with the result that the hyphen immediately disappeared into an assimilable identity: "Ah, so you're Israeli!" Only one geography is allowed prior to embarking: this is the made-in-U.S.A. predicament of the single hyphen. Although in Israel we were not exactly "from here," in the U.S. we are only "from there." While "there" we are "immigrants from Asian and African countries," here, in the U.S., we are not; in fact, our Asianness disappears, subsumed under the dominant Eurocentric definition of Jewishness (equated with Europe) and Arabness (equated with Islam) as antonyms. Millennia of existence in Iraq are erased in the name of a mere three decades in Israel. I remember, during the Gulf War, reading a *New York Times* book-review section article in which the Euro-American Jewish reviewer suggested that something was as "rare as a synagogue in Baghdad." He was obviously unaware that Baghdad, as late as the 1950s, was about 35 percent Jewish and that it was crowded with well-attended synagogues. (And in which region does the writer imagine the "The Babylonian Talmud" was written?)

Some parts of Asia, namely West Asia (that is, the Middle East), are simply dropped out of the continent, just as Morocco, Algeria, Tunisia, Libya, and Egypt are dropped out of U.S. mental projections of Africa, leaving these immigrants to America standing on unstable ground with regards to the continents on either side of the hyphen. The predicament of the single hyphen in the U.S. reception of immigrants has to do with essentialist assumptions about identity as reducible to one country and one ethnicity or race. The master narrative of immigration is fixed within the rigid boundaries of the nation-state and its often-concomitant nationalist ideology. Thus, our historical intracontinental and watery routes within Asia come up against the *terra firma* of Eurocentric and nationalist chartings of regions and populations.

These master narratives of immigration have been fundamentally locked into the binarism of "East" and "West" as the twain that shall never meet. But the schism of East and West, so deeply ingrained in the Eurocentric accounts of American identity, is misleading in a number of ways. "East," "West," "North," and "South," after all, are relational terms, inseparable from the way we conceive history and geography. The "East" is divided into "Near," "Middle," and "Far," making Europe/the U.S. the arbiter of spatial evaluation, just as the establishment of Greenwich Mean Time produces Britain as the regulating center of temporal measurement. The neat divisions of East/West and North/South impose a double axis on a globe inhospitable to such conceptual rigidities. In a topographical sense, the terms are relative: what is east from one angle is west from another. The terminology to demarcate space implies a point-of-view: Near, Middle, Far East, but in relation to whom? The "Far" East is not far from China; nor is the "Near" East near to itself. The Near or Middle East, from a Chinese perspective, would refer to West Asia. The dominant terminology was generated by British colonial rule and shaped a whole field of scholarship, just as the formation of area studies in the U.S. began with the Department of Defense as part of the Cold War re-mapping of spheres of influence. (In fact, during this period the British term "Near East" became "Middle East.") Each region, furthermore, has its own east/west, north/south. In Arabic, the name for the region of "the *Maghrib*" that refers to North Africa derives from the word "*gharb*" (west,) indicating the westernmost part of the Arab world, in contrast to "the *Mashriq*," the eastern part. The South Seas, to the west of the U.S., are often posited as cultural East. Israel is seen as part of the West, while Turkey (much of which lies to the west of Israel), Egypt, Tunisia, and Morocco are all "Eastern." Thus, politics overdetermine cultural geography and cartographies of identity.

Since when did the vast continent of Asia shrink so incredibly that the face of the land is now superimposed onto a stereotypically "yellow" physiognomy? Even "Asian looks" can be deceiving in the American context, leading East Asians who have been here for generations to be perceived as "always foreign." And speaking accented English also marks the immigrant body as possessing a mysterious or menacing geography. Even as one's body crosses the Atlantic, the accent remains. The persistence of the accent is usually what distinguishes the Asian immigrant from the native-born Asian American in the public sphere. Being at once inside and outside places the immigrant in an ambivalent space. For people of my ancestry, being suddenly dropped off the Asian and African maps, after having these maps inscribed on us in a racist manner in Israel, perhaps brings, along with the frustration, a measure of relief at not being so easily boxed into one of the familiar corrals for "the Other." At times I am seduced by the possibility of a new, ethnically chaotic Babel here in the land that the Rastafarians also call Babylon.

The term "Asian-American," then, echoes for me with the voices, memories, and narratives associated with the very word "Asian." I oscillate between accepting U.S. racial discourses as they affect cartographies of memory and narratives of displacements, and feeling obliged to narrate them within their "Asian" contexts. But I first have to pierce the veil of secrecy enveloping the racism toward Asian (largely from the Middle East) and African Jews (largely from North Africa) in Israel, in hopes of invoking a multifaceted transnational dialogue among many racialized experiences. For what might seem "irrelevant" to American racialized identities, in fact, evokes deep historical affinities and structural analogies. If the Palestinians figure in official Euro-Israeli discourse as the "Indians," associated in colonial discourse with nomadism and savagery, Asian and African Israelis are, on some levels, the Blacks. Not coincidentally, our major movement of resistance in the 1970s was called "The Black Panthers," in homage to the American movement, while today we have adopted the name "Mizrahim" (Orientals). Despite its Orientalist lineage, this latter name carries an affirmation of our positive relation to the "East," within the context of a state that proudly proclaims its Westernness while choking off our "Eastern" cultural expression.

The Predicament of the Hyphen

The multi-layered history especially common to postcolonial displacements "exceeds" the misleadingly tidy five-part U.S. census categorization of "races." The census is in fact heterotopic, mingling issues of race (Blacks), language (Hispanics), and geography (Asians) as if they were commensurate categories. The notion of "Asian-American," for example, is often applied only to East Asians, excluding Iranians, Pakistanis, Lebanese, or others from South and West Asia (the Middle East). "African-American," similarly, does not usually denote immigrants from Africa, or Black immigrants from South America and the Caribbean. "Arab" is usually misconstrued as synonymous with Muslim, though some Arabs are Christian and others Jewish. Reductive categories like "Jew," "Arab," and "Latino/a," similarly, hide the racial variety of a chromatic spectrum that includes White, Black, Mestizo/a, and Brown. In the U.S. many communities and individuals fit only awkwardly into the single-hyphen boxes, yet bureaucratic pluralism does not allow for polysemy in the politics of color. The usual ways of talking about "minority" identities leave little room for the complexities of these categories, or for the porous borders between them.

The histories of Native Americans, African Americans, Latino/as, and Asian Americans may all have been shaped within U.S. colonialism, but the problematic nature of these categories becomes obvious when seen in relation to the parallel and inter-linked histories in the Americas. The "hyphenated American" is often assumed to sport only a single hyphen. But, in fact, the successive colonial and postcolonial displacements put considerable pressure on the already stressed and overdetermined single hyphen. Each chain of hyphens implies a complicated history of accreted identity and fragmented belonging as multiple displacements generate distinct "distillations" of immigrant identity. But often the "host" country acknowledges only one link in the chain, and which link is stamped as "real" tells us less about the immigrant than about the geopolitical imaginary of the host. Even within a multicultural feminist space, identities can be misconstrued or misrecognized.

A desire for a chimerical "authenticity" and officially inscribed "coloredness" and "sexuality" can lead to misapprehensions. A female bisexual of Indian-African origin, for example, may be pressured to conform to sexual orientation as defined by U.S. norms, and may be accused of passing herself off as African, a charge carrying an implication of opportunism.[4] Yet the history of Indian Tanzanian Americans, which differs from that of both Africans and Indians who immigrated to the U.S. directly from their respective continents, should not be shorn of its Africanness. To take another example, Jewish Moroccans who came to the U.S. after living in Israel are often labeled simply "Israelis." Whereas in the "Indian-Tanzanian-American" case what precedes the first hyphen is "frozen" to capture the essence of a dispersed identity, in the "Moroccan-Israeli-American" case it is the second term that is "frozen."

What is it about such multiple displacements on the way to the U.S. that makes the first part of the hyphenated label (Indian) essential in one case and the second part (Israeli) essential in the other? In the Indian-Tanzanian-American case, the African link becomes taboo because, in the U.S. context, "African" can only be equated with "real" Black Africans. In the case of the Moroccan-Israeli-American, Morocco is taboo because "Moroccan" is assumed to be only Arab (seen as an antonym to "Jewish") and Muslim, and because "Israeli" is associated with European Jews (when, in fact, the demographic majority of Israel is formed by relatively powerless Black Jews of Asian and African origin). Yet racial definitions, ethnic hierarchies, gender identities, and sexual belongings are situated and conjunctural, shifting and transmuting across histories and geographies; they explode and implode a unified narrative of what constitutes "racial," "national," and "sexual" identifications and affiliations.

Processed Memories

In a kind of homage, Lynne Yamamoto narrates her grandmother's life through the very act of producing the material of her *Ten in One Hour.* This installation reflexively alludes to the artist's own rate of production of the soap objects of the installation itself. Reenacting her grandmother's intensive labor, Yamamoto creates a parallel rhythm between her repetitive artistic work and her grandmother's repetitive movements of washing, wringing, hanging, folding. But this analogy also calls attention to class dissonance. While Lynne Yamamoto's images, like my texts, are currently produced and consumed within cultural institutions inseparable from late global capitalism, we, the granddaughters of diasporic domestic workers, have traveled a long road to join another class of cultural workers. Our art or cultural production places us now in a different category than that of our grandmothers and parents. In my writings, I have often felt a survivor's desire to tell again and again about the "hidden injuries" of translocated class, race, gender, and sexuality.

As I was looking into Yamamoto's work on the drudge labor of a laundress, I was wondering about our own work, hers and mine, as grand-daughters of dislocated domestic laborers. A critic and an artist, in our new class spaces we continue rinsing, cleaning, and scrubbing, as it were, the misrepresentations that surround our hyphenated identities. Our grandmothers worked as domestic servants in new countries, unfamiliar with their new cultural and linguistic terrains: Hebrew-speaking Israel for my Arabic-speaking grandmother and English-speaking Hawai'i for Lynne's Japanese-speaking grandmother. In her installations *Night Waters* and *They All Fall Down*, Yamamoto uses archival photographs of Japanese women working as domestics for *haole* (Euro-American) families in Hawai'i. *They All Fall Down* uses a continuous video loop of Yamamoto's aunt's hands polishing a silver tea bell. "The installation," writes Yamamoto, "is based on stories my aunts told me about working as domestics for *haole* families, and particular memories of how they were called in to change dishes for the next course."

If Yamamoto's grandmother left Japan as a "picture bride" on her way to Hawai'i, my *seta* (Arabic for grandmother), Gurgeia, left Baghdad as a widow, leaving behind her buried husband. My grandfather, Ya'aqub abu-Sasson, was buried in the 1930s in the Baghdadi-Jewish cemetery on Sheikh Omar Street, which in the 1960s was itself apparently buried under the new national television station; our millennia traces were thus erased. I have often thought it ironic, in light of this fact, that I became a professor of media studies, engaged in unearthing the deeper strata of the visual text.

I moved "*ila Amrika*," as my family would say in Arabic, in 1981. I did not come to America as a picture bride, but pictures of America made me come. I remember that as we were growing up, we loved watching American television series. *Hawaii Five-o* was one of our favorites. The hula dancer in the opening credit sequence seemed by far more exotic than our local belly dancers. Perhaps the hip movements of the hula dancer were familiar to us, but somehow we did not see this dance as part of the "East," for we only learned to recognize it as "American" and therefore as "Western." We were dreaming about a new world, even as our old world of the Euphrates and Tigris was a forbidden memory in the state of Israel.[5] Indeed, the global flow of American images and sounds gave me the feeling of a *terra cognita* even prior to my voyage to the island of Manhattan. Here, in the Gramercy Park apartment I was cleaning, I could emulate *seta*'s high rate of production, fighting so that my life, too, wouldn't go down the drain.

Soap to wash the dirt off the shirt. To wash the dirt off your body. Cleaning for others while being called dirty yourself. My dark friend Na'eema used to frantically scrub her "dirty skin" in a violent cleansing ritual that never reached the promised hidden layer of white skin she so painfully desired, but that only left her bleeding. In Israel we were called "dirty Iraqis." I can still hear the Hebrew words "*Erakit masriha!*" ("stinky Iraqi") shouted at me by a blond boy whose relatives in Europe might well have been themselves turned into "*sabonim*"—soaps—by the Nazis.

My *seta*, who died last year in her mid-90s, enjoyed cursing back. She washed their dirty laundry as she joyfully rolled out her Arabic obscenities. She never learned the language of *al-bidheen* (Arabic for "the Whites"). As she used several layers of *shaqsa* (Iraqi for female headwear) to wrap her dwindling graying braids, she was amused by my sister's efforts to bleach her hair, the stubborn roots refusing to fully erase their black past. And like many women of her class, my grandmother did not wash out of her dictionary the dirty words reserved for those whose houses emitted unpleasant smells in the absence of her ever-bleaching hand.

Some of Lynne Yamamoto's work features old photos of Asian laborers in Hawai'i. I wondered how many of the photos actually belong to Lynne's family album. Images of immigrant laborers and dislocated refugees often end up petrified in the colonial visual archives. A few years ago, during the Quincentenary of the Expulsion of Muslims and Jews from Spain, I was desperately looking for images of Jews in the Islamic world to accompany an essay I wrote for *Middle East Report* on the subject. The editor and I approached the Yeshiva University Museum in New York (directed by Euro-American Jews), then sponsoring a photographic exhibition on the subject. Most likely aware of my critical stance, the museum refused to lend such images without first reviewing the content of my essay, thereby barring access to my own community history. I have visited Jewish museums in the U.S. and in Israel, only to see disturbing cultural remains on display. Precious objects that belonged to our community, or to its individual members, ranging from religious artifacts to "Oriental" jewelry and dresses, are all exhibited in a way that fetishistically detaches them from their social context and cultural history within the worlds of Islam—Asia and Africa. In places such as the Gothic building of the Jewish Museum in New York, "exotic Jews" are rendered invisible in plain sight.

I flip through British collections of photos of Baghdad in an attempt to visualize my grandmother in the streets, houses, and markets, carrying her *beqcha* (bundle) on her head. These processed images have become processed memories. Could it be that my endlessly deconstructed colonial images are now invading my own familial memories? I see this kind of critical project as part of collective effort to bring to life a frozen past made captive in the colonial visual archive. We kidnap Orientalist images of "the exotic" and re-narrate them for our private/public memories. But that sense of the elusive homelands of Asia persists even after moving to a new continent.

In the aftermath of Pearl Harbor, many Japanese Americans were forced to burn precious family possessions, eliminating any links to Japan. Similarly, Jews in Iraq, Egypt, and Yemen, after the establishment of Israel, were caught in the vice of two bloody nationalisms: Arab and Jewish. While Euro-Israel, in its need to secure bodies to perform "Black labor," had an interest in creating the political climate of terror that led to our mass exodus, Arab authorities added their own share of terror by suspecting us *a priori* of being traitors. At the same time, the two governments, under the orchestration of Britain, secretly collaborated in lifting us overnight from millennia in Mesopotamia. Although Arab Jews were culturally closer to Muslim-Arabs than to the European Jews who founded the state of Israel, their identity was put on trial by both national projects. Even anti-Zionist Arab Jews ended up in Israel, for in the lethal context of a nationalist conflict, they could no longer enjoy the luxury of their hyphenated identity. My parents had to burn our photos, leaving little photographic inheritance from Iraq. As refugees, we left everything behind. I cling to the handful of photos of my family in Baghdad, the city we still cannot go back to after four decades of traumatic separation.

I used to pore over the few photos in a half-filled family album in order to discern the contours of a history, a lineage. I remember inverting the

Figure 49   The author's mother, Aziza bint-Ya'aqub wu-Mas'uda, with her relative Selman abu-Da'ud on the *sat'h* roof, Baghdad, 1947 (photo: Aziza's cousin, Moshi Haddad)

traditional Biblical verse (taken up again in the Jimmy Cliff Reggae song); instead of weeping by the waters of Babylon, it was by the waters of *Zion* that we lay down and wept when we remembered *Babylon*. Iraq, under Saddam Hussein, has featured its annual Babylonian Festival, even as devastating sanctions continue to "sanction" the death of many Iraqis. The staging of ancient "Babylon" boosts Iraqi national morale, but for displaced Iraqis, it is yesterday's Iraq that we cry over, as its images flicker across the television screen. In exile, Iraqi images, music, stories, and dishes are all digested in a kind of wake for what was lost. Wherever they go, London, New York, or Rio de Janeiro, my parents immediately reproduce the aromas of Baghdad, in their pots and in their tears, as they listen to the sounds of old Iraqi and Egyptian music frozen in time: Nazem Al-Ghazali, Salima Pasha Murad, Umm Kulthum, and Muhammad Abdel Wahab. I gave my parents a tape of a new Iraqi singer, Qathum Al-Sahir. They didn't enjoy it. Perhaps it was too painful to admit that, after their departure, life didn't stop "there." Perhaps that's why I have become obsessed with taking their photos. It is as if I wanted to fill out the half-empty albums.

Hairy Visions

In Lynne Yamamoto's *Wrung*, a long strand of artificial black hair hangs from a wringer, taken from an old-fashioned clothes washer. Displaced from their original context, seemingly unrelated objects are brought together, evoking a process, a narrative, and an action: something is being wrung. The clamp-like wringer and the disembodied hair highlight the potentially violent overtones of quotidian materials. But the very image of wringing long hair stands out with a nightmarish beauty. For one thing, the long black silky hair of Asian women has often stood as a metaphor for the fragile and docile "Orient." But here the image of the hair goes against the grain, intimating the pain and hardship of servitude, conjuring up the slow death of the female domestic laborer. The old wringer processes the hair like a meat grinder, as though devouring the woman whose body and face have been slowly consumed and worked over, as though the viewer is catching the last glimpses of her disappearance. The washing cycle evoked by Yamamoto's work becomes a synecdoche and a metaphor for the life cycle itself as experienced by a dislocated domestic laborer: arrive, marry, cook, clean, boil, scrub, wash, starch, bleach, iron, clean, hope, wash, starch, cook, boil, scrub, clean, wring, starch, fear, iron, fold, bleach, cook, iron, hope, rinse, whisper, boil … love, fear, weep, rinse, starch, fold, drown. (In Lynne Yamamoto's *Untitled*, from her installation *Wash Closet*, the narrative unfolds through a sequence of these words inscribed on heads of 280 nails, ending with "drown," a reference to Lynne's grandmother, Chiyo, who committed suicide ten months after the bombing of Pearl Harbor by drowning herself in an *ofuro*, a Japanese bathtub.) Playing the visible hair off against the invisible body, *Wrung* chronicles the bitter disappearance of an alienated Japanese laborer on the "picturesque" island of Kohala, Hawai'i.

The black and white photos taken on our roof in Baghdad gaze at me in my New York living room. My mother wears my father's suit. ("Just for the photos," she tells me smiling, blithely unaware of recent performance theories about cross-dressing.) Elegantly she projects authority, as she stands there, her long, thick and curly black hair flowing gently. She lost much of that hair after they became refugees, in an epoch of food rationing

Figure 50 The author's mother, Aziza bint-Ya'aqub wu-Mas'uda, wearing the suit of her husband Sasson, Bgahdad, 1949 (photo: Aziza's cousin, Moshi Haddad)

in the transit camps in Israel. She fell seriously ill, as the cold wind and rainy winter in the tent inflicted her with crippling rheumatoid arthritis. I often remember how I tried to reconcile these two mothers, the one in the photos in Baghdad, and the other one that I knew, the one courageously fighting economic and social degradation with a weakened, broken body.

In *Wrung*, plentiful hair is attached to no-body. The pleasure and pain of looking at this image has to do with the subliminal specter of disembodied hair. The visual archive is abundant with traumatic memories of hair loss, yet somehow we find it easy to lose the memory of such ghastly catastrophes. In recent years, interesting work has been done on fashioning hair and diasporic identity,[6] but *Wrung*'s disembodied hair has also to be placed within a different tradition. The aestheticized quality of the flowing silk hair, often appearing in the Orientalist erotic dream—evoked in films from *The World of Suzie Wong* to Peter Greenaway's *Pillowbook*—in *Wrung* becomes ominous, set in the context of a different kind of visual archive.

Figure 51   Lynne Yamamoto, "Wrung," 1992
(black and white reproduction; washer part, synthetic
hair, nails; 12 x 42 x 3 inches, photo: Larry Lame)

Disembodied hair, in this sense, evokes American frontier imagery of scalping—whether in the popular Western genre depiction of "Indian savagery," or in the critical Native-American representation of European settler cruelty. In 1744, for example, the Massachusetts General Court declared a general bounty on Indian scalps, £250; and in 1757 it was raised to £300, higher than the annual pay for many educated colonists.[7] A century later, the American West witnessed the horror of another wave of detached hair, in yet another 20th-century scientific spirit of experimentation: civilian accounts of hair loss by unsuspecting onlookers of nuclear testing in Nevada, Arizona, or farther west in the "Oriental" Pacific Islands. How can we, to paraphrase the song in the 1950s musical *South Pacific*, wash that memory right outta our hair?

I remember watching Alain Resnais's film *Hiroshima Mon Amour* for the first time: black and white images of the Hiroshima museum displaying piles of hair, remnants of the modern American annihilation of two cities in Japan. The film visually links two victims through the motif of hair: French women scapegoated for a more general collaboration with the Nazis have their hair cut at the end of the war, tonsured during the liberation in France. World War II also witnessed yet other mounted piles of hair in the concentration camps of Auschwitz, Dachau, Treblinka, and Bergen-Belsen, recycled for productive purposes. Nazi archival footage documents pyramids of watches, glasses, hair—visual evidence of the work of an "orderly regime."

Iraqi, Yemeni, and Moroccan refugees in the 1950s were welcomed to Israel with white DDT dust, to cleanse them, as the official Euro-Israeli discourse suggested, of their "tropical diseases." In the transit camps, their hair was shaved off, to rid them of lice. Children, some of them healthy, were suspected of ringworm, and were treated with massive doses of radiation. You could tell those who had been treated by the wraps covering their heads, covering the shame of hair loss. The Euro-Israeli authorities, wrapped in the aura of science, marched on us to eradicate our Asian and African underdevelopment. Decades later, as the children became adults, they had to wear wigs or hats to cover a second hair loss, this time due to radiation treatment for cancerous brain tumors, caused initially by their childhood "early treatment" for a simple skin disease that sometimes they did not actually have.

Can memory exist apart from the desire to memorialize? Perhaps our U.S. immigration narratives are no more than a monument to our parents' and grandparents' generations (some of whom performed "hairy" escapes across hostile borders); generations muted by the everyday burden of hyphenated realities, their dreams mutilated. And so we weave these narratives into our images and texts as a kind of a memorial, a portable shrine for those whom we fear have faded away. Perhaps the ethnicity of the silently dancing

Fatima is erased from the pages of the American archive. But in the various Babylons of New York, Los Angeles, and Detroit, new Fatimas vibrantly transform "Amrika."

The canonical narrative of the birth of America—in the beginning was Columbus, in the middle the American Revolution and the Civil War, and in the end the "melting pot"—has been challenged by recent immigrants pouring in, "spoiling" the already overcooked stew. The desire for a tidy closure aims at disciplining this chaotic, open-ended notion of the "American Nation." Anti-immigrant hysteria can be seen as a phobic reaction to the disquieting perception that "the nation" might not be and never has been a fixed entity, a core of whiteness to which other "colors" were added later. The colors were there from the beginning. Indeed, over many millennia (Eurocentrically called "pre-Columbian," as if an entire hemisphere had been just waiting for Columbus to arrive) it was whiteness that was the absent color. All the waves of immigration to this country have stirred up national anxiety, not only because of their obvious social implications but also because of more subtle questions about what "Americanness" is and about who belongs to the "American family."

Over the past centuries, the continually changing makeup of the U.S. has forced "us" always to rethink the "we." The idea of a unitary "American nation" benevolently receiving new waves of immigrants suggests that only the immigrants, rather than the nation itself, are being transformed; the U.S.'s openness is rarely conceived as multi-directional. "They," the new immigrants, are simply to be transformed into "us," when, in fact, the nation is transformed by each new wave washing up on its shores.[8] The new arrivals stretch, with their very bodies, the boundaries and definitions of Americanness.

27

Diasporic Thinking:
Between Babel and Babylon
(A Conversation Conducted by Christian Höller)

Preface by Christian Höller: Ella Shohat is a rare example of an intellectual whose theoretical work has developed in close relation to her personal
history and maintained an intricate connection to it throughout a huge
variety of transdisciplinary projects. Being raised in Israel by Baghdadi
parents, and speaking Arabic at home, she later moved to the U.S. to pursue
her studies, experiencing yet another dimension of being out of place, an
out-of-placeness that has been manifold. This existential factor of never
quite belonging where you are set, both personally and with respect to a
chosen discipline, informs her prolific work, which spans a large spectrum
ranging from film/media studies, literary theory, and visual culture to Middle
Eastern, Jewish, and postcolonial studies. From her early critique of Zionist
discourse as articulated through the history of Israeli cinema and through
her deconstructive analysis of Eurocentric thinking—carried out with her
frequent collaborator Robert Stam—to the reformulation of the project of
"critical polycentric multiculturalism" and "diasporic perspectives," Shohat's
intellectual orientation has always been one of dismantling existing power
structures and hierarchies. Not only does her work reveal the extent to
which today's transnationalism and multiculturalism necessitate new modes
of thinking, but it also emphasizes the complexity and sometimes contradictory nature of diasporic voices, which are seldom articulated with such
clarity and rigor.

A Conversation Conducted by Christian Höller, a member of the editoral board of
Springerin (Vienna) and professor at Geneva University. Published as "Diasporic
Thinking: Between Babel and Babylon—Ella Shohat in Conversation with Christian
Höller," in Christopher Wise and Paul James (eds.), "Being Arab: Arabism and the
Politics of Recognition,"*Arena Journal*, Nos. 33–34, 2009; and as "Between Babel and
Babylon: In Conversation with Ella Shohat" in Christian Höller (ed.), *Time Action
Vision* (JRP | Ringier & Les presses du réel, Zurich/Dijon, 2010).

Out of Babylon and into Babel

Christian Höller: A significant part of your writing is centered on concepts of displacement and exile. Can you briefly sketch how this concern came about, and especially how your own biography figures in the theoretical exploration of being out of place?

Ella Shohat: I was born into a situation of displacement: my parents were dislocated from Iraq and did not exactly find a home in Israel, a traumatic moment of rupture that, to an extent, has shaped my perspective on questions of belonging. Colonialism, on the one hand, and the rise of nationalism, on the other, have had disastrous consequences for diverse minorities. Given the violent geopolitics of the region, communities were uprooted overnight. Due to the Arab/Israeli conflict, my family was ejected from Baghdad, where our ancestors had lived for millennia. In Israel, partly because my parents' culture was that of the enemy, my family felt out of place. My parents used to say: "In Iraq we were Jews, and in Israel we are Arabs." Our Arab culture was taboo. Yet, even if we tried, we could not easily escape the mark of otherness. It was written all over our bodies, looks, accents. My parents did not dare put the Arabic name they had given me, Habiba, on my Israeli birth certificate. My grandparents continued to communicate only in Arabic for decades after their dislocation, until they passed away. For years, I was their everyday translator. I was raised among people who felt a great sense of loss because of the sudden move out of Iraq. Their powerlessness only added to their sense of alienation. But what was rather anomalous about this situation was that we were expected to define this exilic condition as a natural home and refuge. In my own writing I described this feeling by inverting the Biblical phrase: "By the waters of the Zion, we laid down and wept when we remembered Babylon." My writing in this sense attempted to give a voice to this rupture, permitting, as it were, the mourning and melancholia that were so taboo for the dislocated Arab Jews in Israel.

Being raised between Arabic and Hebrew was far from being a situation of happy bilingualism. It was a conflictual linguistic experience, where my school language was at war with my home language, which we were expected to forget and erase. This schism nourished my fantasies of an elsewhere. Israel may have been a land of many immigrants and displaced people, but it was not a multicultural democracy. It was a centralized nation-state dominated by the ideology of modernization that permitted only Eurocentric narratives of belonging. Israel was also a place where you could only take a boat or a plane in one direction—to the West—so perhaps it is no wonder that my fantasies centered on the U.S., around the English language and Anglo-American culture. Anglo-American culture became a kind of a third space for me, an imaginary homeland, which transcended my own two languages. But the phantasmatic space of "America," often associated with the Hollywood dream factory and the American Dream, was for me associated with the 1960s. It was rather ironic that I arrived in the conservative Reagan era.

CH: In what ways have traveling and moving out of the Middle East affected your experience and writing?

ES: I should first note that a visit to Europe in the mid-1970s preceded my move to New York. I was part of an art delegation funded by the Adenauer Foundation to encourage encounters between German and Israeli youth. We lived for a month in a little village, Hochspeyer, and as far as I can recall, I was the only Israeli of Iraqi origin, the only one who did not have direct European ancestry (although I was intimately exposed to European Jews through a few intermarriages in the family; my aunt married a German Jew from Berlin, who moved to Israel at the end of the war). Toward the end, all of us, Israelis and Germans, were taken to visit a not-so-well-known con-centration/labor camp, Natzweiler, in Alsace-Lorraine. Although it was not used for mass extermination, some Jews and gypsies were murdered in the gas chamber, often after serving as "anatomical specimens" for the medical school of Strasbourg University. The white porcelain surfaces and the shiny metal tools remained neatly displayed in the experiment room. And one could mentally animate the empty room with the sights and sounds of scientific torture. The organized pile of shoes, we were told had been left as it was since the day the camp was liberated. We were taken on a tour of the productive mechanisms of the system—for example, the daily showers of the Germans were fueled by the busy crematorium. These are some of the nightmarish images that were part and parcel of my growing up.

That tour of horror took place only a few years after the Munich massacre (1972), which was also lurking in the background of the Natzweiler experience. As was the rule, our delegation travelled with a 24-hour security person. We were there with the good German friends staring at the bad Germans now fixed as part of history; but it was the "bad Arab" that had long passed the threshold to occupy a permanent seat in the Israeli national consciousness. Or so we were taught to believe. As an Arab Jew, such a discourse presented a clear moral dualism of having to choose between the Jew and the Arab. But having an Iraqi memory perhaps made me uneasy, even back then, about such false options and disturbing linkages. Later, the Natzweiler experience would endow me with the confidence to resist the hideous equation between Nazis and Arabs—a connection often made in popular Israeli discourse. These are precisely the kind of associative images

I ended up discussing in my book *Israeli Cinema: East/West and the Politics of Representation.*

One central argument in my work on Zionist discourse concerned this rather paradoxical East/West imaginary. The West is viewed ambivalently, both as the primal scene of anti-Semitism and as an object of desire, an authoritative norm to be emulated in the East. It is as though the *Ostjuden* could only transform himself in the image of the West once he became a Jew in the (other, more Eastern) East; and let's not forget that the image of the New Jew, the *sabra*, was projected as a muscular body working the land, often with blond hair and blue eyes. Palestine/*Eretz Israel* was also viewed ambivalently—the East, associated on the one hand with backwardness and underdevelopment, was associated on the other hand with oasis and solace—a return to the place of origins and the Biblical past. Yet, in all these narratives, the Palestinian was superfluous, irrelevant to the project of the Jewish "return into History."[1]

Displacement and Multiple Belonging

CH: So I guess the discovery of a third space or "elsewhere" did not stop at the imaginary or intellectual level ... it became a reality.

ES: Travelling elsewhere became a mode of thinking of oneself "in" the world, not merely existing as a detached observer. I guess I gradually came to feel that being-at-home-in-the-world was less about a physical homeland than about participating in a community, a process of sharing ideas, wishes, hopes. There is a certain tension in my thought, almost opposite impulses, between a fundamental critique of the very idea of nation-state and the realpolitik that begs committed intellectuals to address its privileges and discrepancies. Does the situation of stateless refugees and dislocated laborers suggest that we fight for citizenship rights or for undoing the nation-state idea? Where would transnational capital and the ideology of productivity figure in either theory?

Even in a globalized world, where we are all connected, border crossing can be an act of self-fulfillment as much as it can be an act of desperation. Not all movements across borders are the same, and in all cases the question of "free choice" is complicated by economics, geopolitics, ideologies, et cetera. My family left Baghdad in a rush, having to renounce their citizenship (known as *al-tasqit*), forced to leave for Israel via Cyprus on a *laissez-passer* document—fearing staying in Iraq but later mourning the impossibility of return. Did they really want to leave? Did they have any say in their dislocation? Could they choose to return? This situation was quite different from my own move to New York, and yet, can it simply be said that my move was only of my own making? Was New York an over-determined space for my initial way out of the schism between Hebrew and Arabic? One could argue that my move signifies that the effort to socialize me into the idea of "Zion" as my homeland failed, and that I found myself gravitating back towards the "diaspora" experience discredited by Zionists, which in my case echoes an appropriate nominal geography—a new Babylon.

CH: In what ways was migrating to New York a liberating experience, and what did it mean to belong to America?

ES: I am not exactly sure what it means to belong to "America." It seems to me that because of the specific history of the Americas, one finds a dense space of diasporas, a palimpsest of displaced people who belong, simultaneously, to many places, and thus one can have a feeling of belonging to the Babel of America. [...] In this fragmented space of New York, I encountered various displaced people, including Iraqis. The borders separating Arab and Jew felt like they were melting since, at least on the surface, I no longer lived within a context of a state invested in the schism between the Arab and the Jew. New York, in a strange way, afforded me a breathing space, a way out of a virtually schizophrenic existence. In Israel, Sephardim/Mizrahim were called "Blacks" (*schwartzes* in Yiddish), and ended up actually reclaiming this term as a positive signifier. As a young girl I learned about the Black Panthers in the U.S., because the Israeli Black Panthers movement named itself after the American movement. I guess that, because of this history, when I arrived in New York I sensed an immediate affinity with the concerns and struggles of minorities/people of color.

At the same time, the question "Where are you from?" has never been easy for me. Which geography does the question assume—that of the nation-state, that of a regional culture, that of linguistic knowledges? [...] When I say that my family is Baghdadi, and also Jewish, it often bewilders non-Middle Easterners. [...] Given the widespread Arab-versus-Jew discourse, it has been difficult to inscribe the hyphen between the Arab and the Jew. It provoked me to write a series of critical essays on the subject, some of which explicitly address the problem of the erasure of the hyphen (*Taboo Memories, Diasporic Voices*, 2006). Over the years, I have received very moving letters from people of diverse backgrounds identifying with the story, or finding resonance with their own.

But I also experienced political harassment due to my critical stance toward Israel. My first book, *Israeli Cinema* (1989), was the subject of an attack in Israel that traveled into the American academic context. An article I wrote entitled "Sephardim in Israel: Zionism from the Standpoint of its Jewish Victims" (1988) partially dialogued with Edward Said's article entitled "Zionism from the Standpoint of its Victims" (1979). My essay assumed much of the Palestinian critique, but it also tried to deconstruct the idea of a homogeneous "Jewish History" (with a capital H). I felt that even critical discourses were, ironically, deploying inadvertently the axioms of nationalist historiography. I was hoping to create an intellectual space that would address Jewish histories in the plural, especially when the stories of Jews within Islam and Christianity are so markedly different.

The re-evaluation of Eurocentric discourses was applicable to other fields of knowledge as well. When [...] I began my graduate studies in the humanities, the dominant feminist discourse then was shaped by psychoanalysis. Within such a universalist methodology, race, class, and national stratification were a priori irrelevant. When I wrote essays like "Gender and the Culture of Empire" and "Imaging *Terra Incognita*" in the late 1980s it was in part a critique of the Eurocentric assumptions of feminist film and literary theory. My texts attempted to advance a different method for feminist reading; for example, looking for submerged ethnic/racial presence in lily-white Hollywood films; or examining discursive tropes of empire, such as Freud's concept of the "dark continent of female sexuality," which I tried to place in relation to contemporaneous archaeological and geographical discourses of empire. For this reason, I was especially fascinated by the work of Frantz Fanon, and the challenge he began to pose for the practices of psychoanalysis and psychiatry.[2]

[...]

The Trouble with Eurocentrism

CH: The critique of imperial discourse, among other things, led to the famous work you did together with Robert Stam, *Unthinking Eurocentrism* (1994). Let me first ask what the relation between Eurocentrism and Europe is?

ES: The concept of "Eurocentrism" is constantly misunderstood. Eurocentrism is not a synonym for "European." For us, it refers to Euro-derived hegemonies rooted in colonialism and imperialism. Eurocentrism is a monological way of looking at the world, one that embeds many arbitrary hierarchies. Europeans can be non-Eurocentric, and non-Europeans can be Eurocentric. It is not Eurocentric to love Proust, and to go to bed early reading *À la Recherche du Temps Perdu*—but it is Eurocentric to use Proust as a stick to beat up Zulus. It is not Eurocentric to teach the canon; it is Eurocentric not to notice that the Caribbean is "in" *The Tempest*, that Belgian colonialism is "in" *Heart of Darkness*, that the Native American is "in" the Renaissance, that debates about Haiti are "in" the French revolution, and so forth.

"Eurocentrism" is also not a synonym for "racism." The term is falsely seen as a "gotcha" accusation, as when people respond to our work with the reverse "gotcha," expressed in endless variations on the following sentence: "While criticizing Eurocentrism, aren't you still being Eurocentric when .... Aren't you still being inside the system you are criticizing?" Such formulations suggest that there is a simple binarism between the West and the Rest, when the whole thrust of our work argues for looking into the overlapping syncretisms that predate even modernity. We do not believe the world lines up easily into the bad Eurocentrics on one side and good non-Eurocentrics on the other. Identity and location do not preclude Eurocentrism. Even the "Black Jacobins" who abolished slavery in Haiti could be seen as Eurocentric. Eurocentrism is the discursive and mediatic air that we breathe. Our critique of Eurocentrism does not propose a nostalgic return to some pre-European mode of thought, nor a utopian projection of a post-European future; it is meant as a cognitive prod, a way of thinking within non-segregationist frameworks that would force critical projects into relational and multi-directional enunciations. It is a way of seeing Europe and non-Europe, coloniality and modernity, East and West, South and North, as mutually imbricated and mutually constitutive within asymmetrical relations of power.

For us, the term "Eurocentrism" points to the ideological substratum common to colonialist, imperialist, and racist discourse; a substratum that still undergirds, permeates and organizes many contemporary discourses, practices and representations—even after the formal end of colonialism. While "colonialist discourse" explicitly justifies colonialist practices, Eurocentric discourse takes for granted and "normalizes" the hierarchical power relations generated by colonialism and imperialism, without necessarily even thematizing those issues directly. We argued that Eurocentrism's links to the colonizing process are obscured within a buried epistemology. Like phallocentrism, Eurocentrism can be an implicit or unconscious way of organizing the world into systems of knowledge around Europe.

CH: In what ways, then, did you link the question of Eurocentrism to the polemic around multiculturalism?

ES: The idea of "multiculturalism" does not mean simply the fact of "many cultures." It is both a political and epistemological project. For us, the concept of multiculturalism has to be defined in relation to Eurocentrism. The caricature of multicultural scholarship as a naive celebration of the many cultures of the world […] points to the ignorance about the hundreds of scholarly books performing legal, philosophical, historical, literary, or ethnographic investigation, and complicating the taken-for-granted production of knowledge. And many such writers, including ourselves, have also criticized certain versions of multiculturalism. But having said that, we need to be aware how the attacks on multiculturalism by right-wing and some leftist intellectuals serve to reproduce Eurocentric premises and power. Ultimately, we can say that the heated debate over multiculturalism suggests that the term is a sliding signifier onto which conflicting anxieties and hopes are projected.

We proposed to see all the intellectual polemics about multiculturalism as just one skirmish in a larger conflict common to most countries in the "Black" (and we would add "the Red") Atlantic. The U.S. "tremors" are local manifestations of a much larger and longer seismic shift engendered by the "trifecta" that delegitimized the West as the "central culture of reference." We referred to the conjunction of events that dramatically reshaped conceptions of the world order, traditionally seen as moving toward a progressive telos with Europe in the lead. These events—World War II, the Holocaust, Decolonization (and the echoing minority struggles in the "internal colonies" of the U.S.)—simultaneously delegitimized European hegemony and affirmed the cultural and political rights of the non-European nations emerging from the yoke of colonialism. If the war, European fascism, and the Holocaust revealed in all their horror an "internal" sickness within Europe as a site of racism, anti-Semitism, and totalitarianism, the "Third World" independence struggles in Asia, Africa and Latin America revealed the "external" revolt of the colonized against European domination. (Again we use "European" in the broad sense to mean Euro-hegemony in the world, including in the White-dominated colonial settler-states of the Americas, and especially in the U.S.) Since then, the neocolonial constraints on independence, and the limitations of the anticolonial project itself, have become more visible.

At the same time, the aggressive "preventive war" policies of the Bush Administration have opened up a gap with a chastened and now relatively well-behaved Europe that sees itself more and more as a "not-U.S." Actually, in our new book, *Flagging Patriotism: Crises of Narcissism and Anti-Americanism* (2006), we examine these rather intricate continuities and discontinuities. We critique the abuse of the idea of patriotism for militaristic purposes by the U.S. right wing. We also score American exceptionalism and the Francophobia of the right, while also pointing out the problems with culturalist (as opposed to political) forms of anti-Americanism in Europe, Latin America and the Middle East.

Transatlantic Debates in Translation

CH: Can you tell us more about your recent work on the intellectual debates across the Atlantic?

ES: My current work with Robert Stam, for a book to be entitled *Culture Wars in Translation* [published as *Race in Translation*, 2012], will explore the various ways in which North American, Latin-American (especially Brazilian) and European (especially French) intellectuals have formulated these debates over race, multiculturalism, etc. The debates, we argue, must be seen in transnational terms, within a relational framework that transcends the confines of single national geographies. Our specific goal is to develop a historicized, poly-chronotopic and relational approach by seeing the culture wars against the broader backdrop of the history of an Atlantic World shaped by the violent "encounter" between Europe and indigenous America, by the exploitation and transplanting of African labor, and by the evolving attempts to go beyond "master-race democracy" to full, participatory, polyphonic equality.

This project concerning the traveling of the multicultural debates began as a response to a pair of short polemical articles by the French social scientists Pierre Bourdieu and Loïc Wacquant. The first of the Bourdieu/ Wacquant essays attacked what the authors called "American multi-culturalism," equating it with neo-liberalism, imperialism and U.S.-led globalization.[3] The second essay, "On the Cunning of Imperial Reason,"[4] attacked globalization and multiculturalism in general, and American writing about Brazil in particular, specifically Michael Hanchard's analysis of the black liberation movement in Brazil. Hanchard's work, the two sociologists argued, imposed U.S. racial binarist categories on the Brazilian situation, in what amounted to a "brutal ethnic intrusion." In a response essay (2001), we argued that the first essay's equation of multiculturalism with imperialism was simplistic and uninformed—the two authors seemed unaware of virtually all the relevant literature—and that the second essay misrepresented not only Hanchard's work but also the racial situation in Brazil and the state of scholarship on race both in Brazil and the U.S. We also went out of our way to explain that we were not criticizing Bourdieu's work in general, for which we have considerable respect. Rather than speaking ill of Bourdieu, we were speaking ill of his own ill-speaking about issues and projects about which he had very little knowledge—movements that, ironically, had some resonance with his own assaults on privilege and discrimination within France itself.

Our larger goal has been to forge a relational method for charting the transnational movement of ideas and debates across various cultural geographies and national borders. What often gets lost in these debates is the actual work, which thinks modernity through coloniality, and postmo-dernity through postcoloniality. This work "flies" under diverse names and rubrics—critical race theory, radical pedagogy, revisionist history, border theory, critical multiculturalism, subaltern studies, comparative diaspora studies, transnational feminism, postcolonial theory and so forth. But they all share a common element—a radically critical and transdisciplinary engagement with the legacies of colonialism, slavery, imperialism, racism, and Eurocentrism. For us, what such projects have in common is various forms and paths to destabilize the naturalized, or even unconscious, norms of Eurocentric epistemology.

CH: Are you suggesting, then, that the current "culture wars" have a long history?

ES: The term "culture wars" does evoke the contemporary public venom, but we have suggested that it would be misleading to propose a beginning that is simply within our living memory. For us, the contemporary projects inherit and transform very old struggles going back at least 500 years. The issues raised in contemporary debates were present, in germ and usually under different names, when indigenous people fought against European conquest or criticized European social systems, when Africans fought and critiqued enslavement, when blacks in the diaspora fought and critiqued and theorized racism in those societies. The debates were present in the Sepúlveda/de las Casas "*Controversia*." (Recently this was staged almost verbatim in a play by Jean-Claude Carrière,[5] and is still hauntingly relevant to the present.) The debates were present when Enlightenment philosophers talked about "freedom" and "natural goodness" and the "master/slave dialectic." They were present when French revolutionaries debated slavery in the colonies, and when American revolutionaries debated the "federal ratio." The various positions for and against conquest, slavery, racism, and imperialism have been present and "available" for a long time; contemporary debates form "revised" editions of those earlier debates, re-inflected and re-accentuated for new circumstances.

CH: How does the concept of translation figure in this cross-Atlantic debate?

ES: Some aspects of the local U.S. debates about race and multiculturalism and postcoloniality, at least in superficial terms, have circulated around parts of the world, intersecting with debates elsewhere. Although this dissemination is partly due to the global reach of the English language and of the American academy, it would be misleading to see these movements (for example as Bourdieu/Wacquant do) as simply "American" or to say that they "originated" in the U.S. and then "traveled elsewhere." The very ideas that formed so-called "American multiculturalism" had already "traveled" back and forth between the U.S. and other geographies, where they were combined and indigenized within other spaces. The "Voyages of Discovery," colonialism, slavery, U.S. imperialist policies, military interventions, expulsions, immigration and the "brain drain" brought a hybridized mix of peoples and ideas into the Anglo-American academe, so that the critique of Eurocentrism was impacted by many movements from elsewhere: by the anti-colonialist discourse of Césaire, Fanon, Ho Chi Minh, Memmi, Cabral (associated with the "Third World"), by poststructuralism (associated with France), by subaltern studies (associated with India), by hegemony theory (associated with Gramsci), by dependency theory (associated with Latin America), and by radical pedagogy (associated with Paulo Freire, in Brazil), and "*inter-cultaralidad*" (associated with indigenous America). These debates cannot be "contained," then, within rigid geographically bounded borders and terminologies; "inside" and "outside" is a false dichotomy. To put it in translinguistic terms—we argue that all cultural interlocution takes place on transnational territory.

Throughout *Culture Wars in Translation* we are concerned with the ways that cultural and ideological debates move across borders; the ways that they are translated, both literally and figuratively. We ask what anxieties and hopes are provoked by words such as "race" and "multiculturality" and "postcoloniality" in diverse national, institutional, and discursive contexts. What happens in the movement of debates from one geographical space and cultural semantics into another? We try to identify the rubrics and "keywords" that multicultural and postcolonial work performed in diverse spaces. We focus on the ways the terms themselves shift their political and epistemological valence as they "travel" or as they become "out of place." We examine how contemporary debates were anticipated by debates during the Renaissance and the Enlightenment. Intellectual arguments about cultural geographies are themselves shaped within specific sites, and the ways national comparisons and contrasts are mobilized tell us something about the premises, or the anxieties and projections that come into play.

At a moment when we tend to think of ourselves as post-Marxist, post-feminist, post-nationalist, post the post and beyond the meta, when few binarisms remain undeconstructed—except for the binarist/non-binarist binarism itself—one is surprised to find traces of old nationalisms and shared prejudices. Sometimes these prejudices create strange bedfellows, such as when European leftist intellectuals, for example, begin to sound like U.S. right-wingers. Why does the left-of-center French newspaper *Liberation*, in the mid-1990s, interview Dinesh d'Souza as the reigning expert on "multiculturalism?" What kind of "secret sharing" is going on here? What is the role of national exceptionalisms, narcissisms, disavowals? What is the role of the asymmetries of power in knowledge production and dissemination?

Disciplines, Geography, and the Rethinking of Boundaries

CH: So the project is very much geared towards revealing unrecognized narcissisms and nationalisms that seem to come back into play with a vengeance …

ES: Ideas no longer travel in caravels, they travel through cyberspace. Intellectuals no longer ride in carriages to the castles of kings, they jet-set to conferences, or "teleconference" in place. Cultural syncretism is not a new phenomenon, but with these new technologies, debates spread almost instantaneously, and knowledge is shaped within hybridized interlocutions. Intellectuals are located within nation-state(s), even if as exilic and dispossessed, even if having an uneasy relationship with "the national." What we found fascinating is the ways "the national" and even national narcissism enter leftist debates—unconsciously through the back door—of those leftist intellectuals who may be speaking on behalf of "the universal." We are interested in the denial and the anxiety that takes places in the context of the attack on the critique of Eurocentrism. Intellectuals still form part of the process by which nations see themselves as qualitatively different from and in partial opposition to other nations; they historically define themselves "with" and "against" and "through" their neighbors and victims and enemies. The "fictive we" of the nation may create injuries and wounds for some intellectuals, exactly as the "we" affirms and secures identity for others—but that process is articulated through a specular play of self and other, of mimesis and alterity.

Culture Wars in Translation reveals a partly phantasmatic encounter, often with right and left-wing versions, between various nationalisms, narcissisms, and exceptionalisms, each projecting its heroes and villains. Our project tries to call attention to the role of cultural and national narcissism in how intellectuals might invest their libidinal desire in the critique of the racism of other nations while sliding over the critique of their own. The vainglorious debates about "my society is less racist than yours" eerily echo the old "our slavery was more humane than yours" and "our colonialism is more enlightened than yours." This situation calls not only for a reflexivity about national narcissism but also for a transnational examination of the linked modes of institutional racism within diversely globalized spaces, all forming part of historically linked geographies.

CH: What role does hybridization play in a critical rethinking of traditional fields of knowledge? How does this complication of the issue of "the West versus the Rest" carry over to individual disciplines like art history?

367

ES: Within the discipline of art history, "art" has traditionally meant Western art. Artwork from Asia, Africa and the Americas is viewed as the domain of the respective "area studies," or of the field of anthropology. (Often the required languages for a Ph.D. degree in art history tend to be English, French, German and Italian; even Spanish tends to be excluded, not to mention non-European languages.) As we know, art in the West is deeply linked to the idea of the individual artist's signature and to the Museum as an institution. Art in many other parts of the world had a different kind of history; it was not segregated from everyday life or cultural practices, and formed an integral part of various cosmologies. As such, this kind of art could not be subsumed under the aura of "Art" (with a capital A) within the museum space. The term "artifact" signified objects that were inferior to "Art," and therefore were displayed in separate sections or museums—folklore or natural history. Art history, as a field, is embedded in such distinctions. This terminological distinction is classed and raced, and has its origins in Eurocentric, capitalist-colonialist modes of seeing the world. Even the very idea of the Museum has to be understood in the context of colonialism. The Museum emerges in conjunction with transporting new "exotic" objects from the "discovered" continents of the Americas, Asia, and Africa. Categorizing and classifying this wealth of new objects were ways of mastering their foreignness, and defining the West vis-à-vis the rest. The ethnographic museum, the exposition, the circus and the fair—all exhibited objects, plants, animals, and people from the colonized world. The ethno-graphic museum, such as the Musée de l'Homme in Paris or the Museum of Natural History in New York, has allotted a space for the "Other," signifying an inferior culture. In contrast, the "Art Museum" exhibited the subjecthood of the Western artist as an individual genius creator. In other words, the Museum contains in its foundation an epistemological project, with a rather ambivalent genealogy.

I have also been concerned with the stageist discourse on the sequencing of the history of the arts and aesthetics. This field is framed around a linear meta-narrative: realism leads to modernism, which leads to post-modernism, where everything else is assumed to be pale copies of European originals; where the "Rest" (the non-West) follows the cultural innovations of the West, the so-called "advanced world." This temporality is totally question-able, since realism was not an aesthetic that was dominant in most parts of the world. The avant-garde rebellion against modernism has to be seen as a local European rebellion, rather than as a universal transformation. In fact, the "West and the Rest" were never as segregated as Eurocentrism suggests. Greece, Rome, Renaissance, Enlightenment, Modernism—are seen as the highpoints of Western civilization; but they can also be understood as moments of cultural syncretism. Aesthetic ideas have always traveled in multiple directions, in parallel fashion or crisscrossing each other. Think back for example to the Moorish influence on the poetry of courtly love, or the African influence on modernist paintings, or even the impact of Asian forms like Kabuki, or Balinese theater; or Picasso's encounter with African sculpture and the kind of aesthetic innovations that arose from this encounter. Even the notion of modernist avant-garde cannot be narrativized in a vacuum without taking into account all these kinds of cross-cultural dialogues.

In my chapter "Sacred Word, Profane Image: Theologies of Adaptation" (in *Taboo Memories, Diasporic Voices*), I have elaborated on the paradoxes of mimesis when taking into account multiple geographies, especially as their encounter intensifies under the auspices of imperial culture. At the very same period when the European avant-garde was experimenting with breaking away from mimesis, colonial Western institutions were spreading institutionalized mimesis to the colonies as an artistically superior mode to the "local" aesthetics. Verism was genealogically linked to the discourse of modernization—a discourse shared by both imperialist and nationalist ideologies. As appendages to the modernization project, art schools were founded in cities like Istanbul, Alexandria, and Beirut. Artists of the "Orient" were learning to "disorient" regional aesthetics by mimicking Western styles of mimesis. Figurative art signaled a world in transition, in contrast to the largely abstract art of Islam, now rendered "traditional," an obsolescent practice that would inevitably have to be abandoned in favor of the forces of progress. Within this melioristic meta-narrative, mimesis conveyed not merely learning a mode of artistic technique, but also the process of becoming conversant with the aesthetic and cultural norms of so-called Western modernity.

In this strange rendezvous between "East" and "West," realistic aesthetics signified modernity; while non-figurative art was implicitly cast as archaic. But such an encounter generates some fascinating paradoxes. During the same period that the "Orient" was learning realism, the "Occident" was unlearning it. The ideology of political and economic modernization found its aesthetic corollary not in avant-garde modernism, but rather in realism. In the same period that the modernist avant-garde was rebelling against mimesis, opting for new modes of abstract, geometric and minimalist representation, Arab-Muslim aesthetic practices were moving toward mimesis as an integral part of modernity. The introduction of aesthetic modernization in the Middle East was done as though this geography existed in a different temporal stage of history, without links to its contemporaneous modernist experimentation with the new languages of Futurism, Surrealism and Cubism—even as, ironically, these Western movements were borrowing and dialoguing with diverse non-mimetic aesthetics. The so-called non-West has not only been cast out of the meta-narrative of art history, but also presented within a developmental discourse—seeming to always lag behind. But it is a whole other matter if we move beyond such segregationist intellectual paradigms, viewing cultures as heteroglossic, rather than hermetically sealed off from one another. In a sense, my scholarly project tries to offer a multi-perspectival approach, a kind of a "Cubist" re-reading of the multi-directional travel of aesthetic ideas.

28

Arab Jews, Diasporas, and Multicultural Feminism

(A Conversation Conducted by Evelyn Alsultany)

Preface by Evelyn Alsultany: In this interview, Ella Habiba Shohat discusses her family's multiple displacements from Iraq to Israel and to the U.S. She articulates the relevance of what she has called "the question of the Arab-Jew" to the Israeli/Palestinian conflict as well as to the Middle Eastern-American diaspora. Shohat discusses the fraught position of Arab Jews in a historical context in which "Arab-versus-Jew"became the operating framework for identities with the emergence of Zionism. In addition to discussing the dislocation from Iraq to Israel of her own family, Shohat also addresses her scholarly work on the question of Arab-Jews as part of her broader work on postcolonial displacements. She addresses her writing on multicultural feminism within her broader work on the critique of Euro-centrism—for example, the tendency of Eurocentric feminism to frame the debate within the rescue fantasy of saving brown women from brown men. Shohat concludes this interview by discussing the potential of multicultur-alism as an epistemological project for critical thinking and social change.

Evelyn Alsultany: Your writing often highlights the paradoxes of exile and home. I wanted to begin with your own Arab-Jewish background and your family's history in Iraq, Israel, and then the U.S. What was your family's experience of coming to Israel from Iraq?

Ella Shohat: Displacement marked my life from the beginning. In the early 1950s, my parents had to depart from Iraq, and went to Israel via Cyprus.

A conversation conducted by Evelyn Alsultany, Associate Professor of Arab-American studies at the department of American Culture and Director of Arab and Muslim American Studies, University of Michigan, Ann Arbor. Published in Rabab Abdulhadi, Nadine Naber, and Evelyn Alsultany (eds.), *Arab and Arab American Feminisms: Gender, Violence and Belonging* (Syracuse, N.Y.: Syracuse University Press, 2011) as a modified version of: "Dislocations: Arab Jews and Multicultural Feminism: An Interview with Ella Shohat," *MIT Electronic Journal of Middle East Studies* (MIT-EJMES), Volume 5 (Spring 2005).

My grandparents, uncles, aunts, and different members of the larger family arrived, dispersed and separately, to the point that it took a good while for them to locate each other. My parents carried only a suitcase and their baby—my sister—as they descended from the plane in the airport of Lod, in Hebrew, and, in Arabic, Lydda. Some of my relatives were sprayed with DDT because it was assumed that they were disease-ridden. The Iraqi Jews descended into a whole new world, a world that had its own lexicon and cultural repertoires, and that aggressively shaped a new collective identity, which Arab Jews were supposed to join. The first period in Israel was full of rude shocks for our family and for most families like ours. Within a few months of our arrival, the authorities at the *maabara* [transit camp] removed my sister from the baby-care center [where parents were obliged to leave their babies under the care of state workers] without my parents' knowledge and on false pretenses. In a combination of luck and help, my parents were able to locate my sister in another city, in a hospital in Haifa. But my grandmother was less fortunate. She gave birth to her last child in Israel, and was told that the baby died, and yet she was never given a body or issued with a death certificate. Later we learned that such experiences had been common, and that many babies—some say in the thousands—had been taken away by the authorities and sold for adoption. The assumption was that one group—us—was having too many children, while another group needed children and could offer a better life than the biological parents, seen as primitive breeders. Activists claim that the payments went to the state, which obviously hasn't been eager to investigate itself. The scandal, which is still a major unresolved sore point, is known as the case of the "kidnapped Yemeni and Sephardi-Mizrahi babies."

In Israel, partly because of racism and partly because theirs was the culture of the Arab enemy, my family felt out of place. My parents used to say: "In Iraq we were Jews, and in Israel we are Arabs." Our Arab culture was taboo in Israel. Yet, even if we tried, we could not easily escape the mark of otherness. It was written all over our bodies, our looks, our accents. My parents didn't dare put my Arabic name, Habiba, from my maternal grandmother who passed away soon after their arrival to Israel, on my birth certificate.

If in the Arab world the Jewishness of Arabs gradually came to be associated with Zionism, and therefore was subjected to surveillance, in Israel their Arab culture was under watchful eyes, disciplined, and punished. Ben-Gurion, the first Prime Minister of Israel, referred to Levantine Jews as "savages," and many scholars during that period wrote about the need to civilize the "backward" Sephardim and "cleanse" them of their Orientalness. The new context obliged Arab Jews to redefine themselves in relation to new ideological paradigms and an overwhelming new polarity: Arab-versus-Jew.

I was raised among people who, due to the sudden dislocation and disorientation, felt an immense sense of loss; today it would probably be diagnosed as a state of post-traumatic stress. And in many ways I think I lived and internalized my parents' and grandparents' pain. To an extent, I believe that my writing about the subject was also a mode of translation: translating their pain into words; giving voice to their sense of loss. [...]

EA: In your work you have offered a different take on what you call "the rupture."[1] For those who are unfamiliar with this history: how in your view did Arab Jews in general, and Iraqi Jews in particular, end up in Israel?

ES: The violence generated in the wake of colonial partitions (Israel–Palestine, Pakistan–India) led to the uprooting, virtually overnight, of vulnerable communities. What such abstract terms as "the Arab/Israeli conflict" and "population exchange" concretely meant for my family was the abandonment of Baghdad, Iraq, Mesopotamia, where Jews had lived and often prospered for millennia. The displacement of Iraqi Jews was not the result of a decision made simply by Arab Jews themselves, though this is how it is often narrated. Even if some Arab Jews expressed a desire to go to Israel upon its creation in 1948, the displacement for most Arab Jews was the product of complex circumstances that forced their departure. There were the efforts of the Zionist underground in Iraq to undermine the authority of traditional Jewish religious leaders, and also to place a "wedge" between the Jewish and Muslim communities in order to generate anti-Arab panic on the part of Jews.

At the same time, just because we criticize Zionism doesn't mean that we should not also take a critical look at the fragile place of minorities in the Arab world. It's not about equating Zionism and Arab nationalism. But it is about offering a complex understanding of tensions and contradictions that made such a rupture possible. In the case of Iraq, the anti-Jewish propaganda, especially as channeled through the *Istiqlal*, or Independence Party, also played a role in the insecurity and fear sensed by Iraqi Jews. As the Israeli/Palestinian conflict escalated, with the Palestinians violently scattered and dispossessed, the distinction on the ground between Jews and Zionists was gradually eroding in Arab countries. In my various essays I have examined the complexity of this issue in terms of when and where such a distinction was maintained, but also in what ways it was not always maintained. In Arab countries, as the conflict in Palestine was accelerating, Arab Jews were gradually regarded more and more as simply "the Jews," and ended up bearing the brunt of the anger about what Zionism, in the name of presumably all Jews, was doing to the Palestinians. As a result, even when the distinction between Jews and Zionists was asserted in theory, it was not always lived as such. Ultimately, the erosion of such distinctions helped provoke the dislocation of Arab Jews, ending up with negative consequences for Palestinians as well. There was a failure to actively secure the place of Jews in the Arab world in spite of what was happening in Palestine. At the time the majority of Jews in Iraq were not Zionists. The word "Zion," or "*Sion*," in our Arabic pronunciation, was thoroughly associated with traditional Biblical Jewish celebrations and lamentations, having little to do with a political nationalist project in Palestine. For the most part, Arab Jews at the time were not aware what settlements in Palestine had meant for Palestinians on the ground.

It is therefore not surprising that there were misconceptions on the part of many Arab Jews about the differences between their own religious identity and sentiments and the secular nation-state project of Zionism, which didn't have much to do with those sentiments. The Jews within Islam regarded themselves as Jews, but that Jewishness formed part of a larger Judeo-Islamic cultural fabric. Under pressure from Zionism, on the one hand, and Arab nationalism, on the other, that set of affiliations gradually changed. Arab Jews, to my mind, have come to occupy an ambivalent position vis-à-vis both movements. The explosive politics after the partition of Palestine, especially the establishment of the state of Israel and the arrival of Palestinian refugees to Arab countries, rendered Arab-Jewish existence virtually impossible. Within this new context, Iraqi or Egyptian Jews came to be viewed as almost by definition "Zionist traitors." This history is full of ironic twists. In Iraq, the persecution of communists, among them Jews who actively opposed Zionism, created a paradoxical situation in which the only viable way to stay alive or avoid imprisonment for communist Jews was to leave for Israel. Another irony: despite the pro-Palestinian posturing of Arab regimes, in practice they collaborated in what Israeli officials came to call "population exchange."

EA: What were then the Arab cultural aspects of your home, and given your own Iraqi-Israeli-American history, what is your sense of home? And to what extent does language play a role in this?

ES: As I reflect back, I think that Baghdad did not really disappear but continued to live in Israel, at home, in the neighborhoods. And today, you can even speak of a certain public renaissance among young Mizrahim, even if Arab culture is transformed and takes place within highly modified forms. But for the first decades in Israel, Arab culture for the newly arrived Jews and their children was an unofficial public culture; it was, as it were, collectively private. For my parents, it was as if time was frozen in 1940s Baghdad. My father played the *kamanja* [violin] in the *hafla*, or the family gathering. Even now, in New York, my parents listen to exactly the same songs of the Iraqis Nazem Al-Ghazali and Salima Pasha Murad or of the Egyptians Umm

Kulthum and Mohammad Abdel Wahab. They are still faithfully dedicated to daily rituals of preparing Iraqi dishes (*kubba hamez-helu, ketchri, tbeet*, and so on), even as elderly people living in their third country, the U.S. Their lack of openness to any other culture at times reflects a kind of Judeo-Baghdadi provincialism, experienced decades later and lived in several elsewheres. I read this kind of provincialism as a sign of refusal of an enforced cosmo-politanism that descended upon them. Years ago they came to visit me in Rio de Janeiro, where I was living. All they were looking for were some familiar spices and foods, and in no time we found ourselves in Rio's Middle Eastern Sahara neighborhood. Food, it seems to me, has become a kind of portable home, where the repetitive, almost ritualistic act of cooking the same old dishes becomes a way of maintaining a sense of stability in an unstable situation, a sense of home when they are no longer really at home in the world. Instead of George Steiner's "homeland as text," it's more like "homeland as cuisine." The obsessive repetition of listening to the same old music, viewing the same old films, or cooking the same old dishes, cannot be reduced to a simple melancholic nostalgia; it also represents an act of defiant survival in the face of a disappearing cultural geography.

For them, Arabic continues to be a vital language of reference, and to this day we still communicate at home largely in our Baghdadi dialect. [...]my grandparents, decades after their arrival, before they passed away, continued to speak only in the Jewish-Baghdadi dialect, never mastering Hebrew. [...] With the passing away of my parents' and my own generation, Arabic dialects are not likely to continue as a language actually spoken by Jews. And the elegy you may hear in my tone is linked to this linguistic "last of the Mohicans" feeling. [...]

In 1981, I moved to New York, where I found a place inhabited by various kinds of dislocated people. Here, belonging to multiple geographies was not out of the norm; it was almost a norm! Being "at home" for me could no longer be easily bounded by geography. Iraq was out of bounds, but at the same time, I insisted on reclaiming the part of my identity and history that was denied me: my Arabness. Therefore, my work on the notion of the "Arab-Jew" tried to offer a non-Eurocentric reading of the past, while suggesting potentialities beyond the impasses of Arab-versus-Jew. It was in New York that I could meet and befriend Iraqi Muslims and Christians. New York, in a strange way, afforded me a relief from a somewhat schizo-phrenic existence.

EA: Can you now address another dimension of your New York experience? How did your background in the Middle East affect your relationship to people of color in the U.S.? And what was the context for your scholarly work on race issues, and how is that related to your personal history?

ES: I grew up in a situation that I only later recognized as "racialized." In Israel, we were sometimes called "Blacks" (in the negative sense), and we ended up actually reclaiming this term as a positive signifier. I learned about the American Black Panthers through the Israeli Black Panthers, an activist group named after and inspired by the American movement, and which generated a storm of Sephardi-Mizrahi protest in the early 1970s. Not simply gender but race and class left dramatic marks on my life. When I was six years old, my shyness at school was understood to be a sign of "retardation" by my Ashkenazi teacher, who wanted to send me to a "special school." Although I knew the material and the answers, I was afraid to speak. A nuanced awareness of "cultural difference" was not part of my teacher's cultural repertoire or pedagogical understanding when she made her "diagnosis." But my mother fought the verdict successfully, because by that point she had become aware of what such a system of labeling and tracking meant. Later, I learned that it was a similar system that reproduced the "savage inequalities": the mechanisms, ideas, and attitudes toward minorities, especially Native Americans, Blacks, and Latinos in the U.S. This is only one example from my life, to explain that sense of identification with racialized minorities that I felt when I came to the U.S. The American academy and New York afforded me an intellectual space from which to speak, alongside others with similar experiences and projects.

But, when I am asked where I am from, I can never give a simple answer. That my family is from Baghdad, and that they are also Jews, startles many Americans. Over and over, I have to go through the same detailed explanation about my origins. If I say I'm an Arab Jew, some people assume that I'm the product of a mixed marriage. Others, of a certain ideological inclination, become apoplectic at the very idea of an Arab-Jew. In my work I have insisted on the hyphen, but the Arab-versus-Jew discourse has made it difficult for some people to comprehend that not all Arabs are Muslims, that one can be culturally Arab and religiously Jewish.[2]

In my scholarly work on the subject, I wanted to create an intellectual and institutional space that would address various Arab-Jewish and Sephardi-Mizrahi perspectives on Zionism. I felt that even critical discourses, ironically, were falling inadvertently into the paradigms of Eurocentric historiography. [...]

EA: How is your critique of the homogenizing view of "Jewish History" related to the question of Orientalism and Eurocentrism?

ES: It is very directly related, but in complex ways. On the one hand, Jews have been the victims of Orientalism and of anti-Semitism. On the other, Zionism itself has an Orientalist dimension, shaped within a sense of inferiority toward the West and superiority toward the East. Herzl's book

Altneuland manifested obsessive competitiveness with Europe, demonstrating that Jews can generate utopian modernity. Within that framework, I have attempted to disentangle the complexities of the Mizrahi question by unsettling the conceptual borders erected by more than a century of Zionist discourse, with its Eurocentric binarisms of savagery-versus-civilization, tradition-versus-modernity, East-versus-West, and Arab-versus-Jew. I have argued that Zionist discourse, in a sense, has hijacked Jews from their Judeo-Islamic cultural geography and subordinated them into the European Jewish chronicle of *shtetl* and pogrom.

Zionist discourse, it seems to me, offers a schizophrenic master narrative, not unlike America's own settler-colonial narrative, which is why so many Americans find it so easy to identify with Israel. The U.S. combines elements of anticolonialist discourse vis-à-vis British with colonialist practices toward the indigenous peoples. It's interesting in this regard to think about the common trope about America and Palestine as "virgin lands."[3] In the case of Zionist discourse, it contains a redemptive nationalist narrative vis-à-vis European anti-Semitism and a colonialist narrative vis-à-vis the Arab people portrayed as those who "happened" to reside in the place designated as the Jewish homeland and therefore presumably with no claim over the land. But I also suggested that, unlike colonialism, Zionism constituted a response to oppression in Christian Europe, and in contradistinction to the classical colonial paradigm, it did not regard itself as having a "mother country." Zionist discourse partially repeats the *terra nullius* of conquest and discovery doctrines, with the difference that Jews, if only in part and distantly, have some claim (although not an exclusive one) to indigenous roots. And just to further complicate the analogy, within Zionist discourse the "East" is simultaneously the place of Judaic origins and the locus for implementing the "West." In other words, the "East" is associated with backwardness, but also with solace, because it signifies a return to the oasis of the Biblical past. Meanwhile, the West is also viewed ambivalently. It is the historic site of the Shoah, yet it remains an object of desire, as evoked in the Founding Fathers' wish to make Israel the "Switzerland of the Middle East." The paradox of Zionist discourse, in my view, is that despite the victimization of Jews by European anti-Semitism, it ended up taking a Eurocentric path, absorbing the assumption that the "West" should be the authoritative norm to be emulated in the "East."

EA: What has been the reception of your work? Have you encountered resistance? Political harassment? If so, what forms has it taken?

ES: I should begin by saying that although the childhood and family experiences I described earlier are quite common to people of my background, I don't think that my perspective is necessarily representative of a large movement. I don't pretend to speak for all Sephardim or Mizrahim. And ironically, although in recent years I have not been terribly vocal on this topic, I continue, in large part, to be stigmatized. In Israel and the U.S. the harassment has taken different forms over the years, including public attacks (especially in the Israeli media), character assassination, words taken out of context, censorship, hate mail, blacklisting, the "uninviting" from conferences because of outside pressure, events canceled at the last minute, and so forth. In non-academic contexts, articles that had been solicited were refused, when seen by the higher-ups. (I even "earned" a few kill fees over the years.) My work has been more or less excommunicated from fields related to Jewish studies. Those of us who have taken critical positions have been the objects of harassment, years before the establishment of Campus Watch.

My first book, *Israeli Cinema: East/West and the Politics of Representation*, was the object of extremely virulent attack in Israel. Some critics tried to delegitimize my academic credentials, as if symbolically to take away my Ph.D. A number of critics suggested that I never could have gotten a Ph.D. in Israel, which was probably true, at least then, if only for reasons of academic prejudice and political views in Israel. Another critic compared Edward Said and myself to "the *kushi* [roughly the n-word] admiring the shiny buttons on the colonial general's coat." We were seen as borrowing and mimicking theories of the West that had little to do with the Middle East.[4] Panels were organized not to debate my work but to denounce it. Nor did this "banning" cease in the U.S. In both countries, whether here or there, students and scholars have told me that they were warned against citing my work. A New York Jewish institute refused to allow MERIP [Middle East Research and Information Project] to use archival images of Arab Jews for an article I was writing without their prior reading and approval. Obliged to submit to their "politically correct" requirements, we have lost the right even to use the archive concerning our own lives in order to narrate our own experiences in our own voice. Recently, a young professor in an Israeli university was told that it would hurt her academic career to include in her CV that she was a translator of my work (from English to Hebrew). The Institute for Sephardic Studies, at my previous University, in my decade of teaching there, never invited me (or my Sephardi colleagues) to speak; nor did it engage the critical perspectives associated with this kind of work. When I was introduced to the director of the Institute, upon hearing my name, she refused to shake my hand, because, she said, I had "met with Palestinians." (She was referring to my participation in the meeting between Palestinian and Sephardi intellectuals in Toledo, Spain, in 1989). This is just a small sample of incidents, but I think you get the drift. But frankly, I don't feel like a victim, and overall I am quite happy with the reception of my work; obviously, we are touching here on a broader issue of institutional politics.

To be fair and give a well-rounded picture, the field has been changing for the better as critical Arab-Jewish/Mizrahi scholars and scholars sympathetic to Mizrahi perspectives, have emerged. More recently, you can find courses that have also been inclusive of my work and of the work of other critical Arab-Jewish/Mizrahi intellectuals and activists. There are more critical Arab-Jewish/Mizrahi spaces now than existed decades ago when I began writing about this question, when also the words "Palestinian" and "Palestine" could hardly be uttered. There is a growing number of young scholars from diverse academic formations working on these issues; many more dissertations are currently being written. I find this development truly exciting. For example, Shoshana Madmoni-Gerber wrote a dissertation about the Israeli media representation of the establishment-sanctioned kidnapping of Yemeni and Mizrahi babies. And Sami Shalom Chetrit published a book about the history of the Mizrahi struggle. Also, over the years you cannot imagine how many sympathetic e-mails and letters I have received from Arabs who have fond memories of Jewish friends and neighbors from Baghdad, Cairo, Tunis, and Tangier. So, on the whole, it's decidedly a mixed bag.

EA: Your work has also dealt with the intersection of gender and race discourse, or with the imaginary of sexuality and empire. Can you elaborate more on the academic context in which you began your work on this intersection? What were you trying to accomplish in *Talking Visions*, and can you elaborate on the subtitle of the book, *Multicultural Feminism in a Transnational Age*?

ES: My academic background is in philosophy, literature, and cinema/media studies. In the humanities, when I began writing, the dominant feminist discourse then was feminist psychoanalysis. Such scholarship allowed little place for race, class, nation, and other forms of social stratification. When in the late 1980s, I wrote my first explicit critique of Eurocentric feminist approaches, it was, in part, a response to feminist literary/film Theory, with a capital T.[5] The essays proposed alternative methods for feminist analysis. For example, I looked for a submerged racial presence in all-White films, or I examined tropes of empire—for example, Freud's notion of the "dark continent of female sexuality," which I contextualized within archaeological and geographical discourses of empire.

Talking Visions tried to provide a space for many constituencies and for many discourses concerning the intersection of race, gender, nation, and sexuality. The book came out of a 1993 conference, "Cross Talk: A Multicultural Feminist Symposium," which I organized at the New Museum of Contemporary Art in New York, a museum that in many ways represented a White urban art-world space. My goal was to "color" the museum and present alternative work and vision. However, the book is not an essentialist celebration of identity and difference with a Latina contributor speaking for "the Latina woman" or a Black contributor speaking for "the Black woman." We cannot reduce any community to one representative speaking on its behalf. The book's purpose, in any case, wasn't simply to include representatives of different origins, but rather to orchestrate multiple voices and issues.

The subtitle calls attention to issues that tend to be segregated and not addressed in relation to each other: feminism in relation to both multiculturalism and transnationalism, and also transnationalism in relation to multiculturalism. It does not exalt one political concern (feminism and sexuality) over another (multiculturalism and transnationalism); rather, it highlights and reinforces the mutual embeddedness between these concerns. My hope was to tie these terms together, and thus refuse any assertion of a hierarchy within class, racial, national, sexual, and gender-based struggles. The essays taken together highlight the intersection of all these different axes of stratification. The term "multiculturalism" tends to be associated with issues of race addressed within the North American context, and too often fails to take into account transnational and cross-border perspectives. Meanwhile, "transnationalism" is associated with a debate about globalization, immigration, and displacement that is not usually associated with issues of race in the North American context. And both of these debates do not necessarily address issues of gender and sexuality. The hope, in *Talking Visions*, was to create a space for a multifaceted debate.

The subtitle also reflects my effort to go beyond the cartographic zoning of knowledges. The circulation of goods and ideas, of images and sounds, and of people is not a new phenomenon, but it has intensified over the past decades due to new technologies and new modes of capitalism. In *Talking Visions*, the assumption was that genders, sexualities, races, classes, nations, and even continents cannot be fenced off into hermetically sealed compartments. Here, I was picking up on the work that I did with Robert Stam in *Unthinking Eurocentrism*. Instead of segregating historical periods and geographical regions into neatly fenced-off areas of expertise, the goal was to highlight the multiplicity of community histories and perspectives, as well as the hybrid culture of all communities, especially in a world characterized by the "traveling" of images, sounds, goods, and people.

The notion of "multicultural feminism" for me was to take as a starting point the cultural consequences of the worldwide movement and dislocations of peoples associated with the development of "global" or "transnational" capital. National borders and disciplinary boundaries are in tension with such transnational movements. Even if the major point of reference in the book is the U.S.—since that is the context of the production of the book—the book isn't nationalist in intent and hopefully isn't provincial in scope. In fact, the introduction criticizes certain modes of multicultural and queer works that often embed an implicit U.S. nationalist agenda, just as it critiques a certain tendency in transnational and postcolonial studies in the U.S. to detach itself from issues of race within the U.S. In this sense, *Talking Visions* attempts to place diverse gendered/sexed histories and geographies in dialogical relation in terms of the tensions and overlaps that take place "within" and "between" cultures, ethnicities, and nations.

Talking Visions was a book not about women of color but about multicultural feminism as a shared political, social, and epistemological project. At the same time, I suggested that it's not a coincidence that it was largely women of color who "engendered" multicultural feminist thought, because their experiences at the intersection of oppressions have generated their pioneering work toward a different kind of knowledge. In a sense, multicultural feminism is an inclusive space, which is not to suggest that there are no contradictions. I was also hoping to articulate those contradictions. I wanted us to be more conscious of what's taking place and why it's so hard to actually do coalitionary work, since there are different interests at stake: different utopias, social desires, and political visions.

EA: How do you see feminism in this context? Can you elaborate on what you find to be the limits of feminism, particularly in the case of Middle Eastern women?

ES: It depends on how we narrate feminism. This is precisely why I find a multicultural critique of Eurocentrism quite central to feminist studies. *Talking Visions* offers a critique of the linear master narrative of how feminism began, and it is usually a very Eurocentric narrative, which imagines women fighting to empower themselves in the "West," with their ideas then spreading to the "backward" world. It's the usual diffusionist narrative. Elided in this modernizing narrative is the reality of the "other" women around the world struggling in other battles, but who have been disqualified as feminists because they have not labelled themselves as such. Take the anticolonialist movement in Algeria. How can one not understand it as a feminist struggle when Algerian women were fighting to empower themselves within the anticolonial movement? Should we not incorporate their perspective into feminist studies just because we have been using this word in a very narrow, Eurocentric sense? The anti-patriarchal, and even, at times, anti-heterosexist subversions within anticolonial struggles remain marginal to the feminist canon, because, unfortunately, one strand of feminism generally exercises the power of naming and narrativizing. The book argues that we need to redefine what we mean by feminist studies, to broaden its significations to include a variety of battles.

From the perspective of multicultural and transnational feminists, it is important to view Muslim and Arab women not simply as victims. To reduce Muslim culture to one term, "fundamentalism," for example, is to miss a more complex picture. We need to analyze questions of agency: how women fighting for social change have exercised a modicum of power. Let's take the case of clitoridectomy. We all react very strongly to this practice because it denies women's pleasure, reinforces the ideology that women are impure, excludes women from marriage if they don't practice it, and so forth. Yet many women around the world practice it and initiate one another into that practice. How do we then think of the contradictions generated from a feminist perspective? When women participate in oppressive practices, how should we react as feminists? Such dilemmas become more complicated in relation to issues having to do with human rights and international immigration. The work of transnational feminism addresses the tensions generated when women or gays apply for asylum as refugees, claiming they are suffering gender or sexual oppression, but their application is premised on reinforcing the conception of the "barbaric" nature of their culture to the sympathetic "Western ears." We should worry about activism in the West that fights to rescue Arab and African women, but does so in a way that reproduces Eurocentric discourse about the Middle East and Africa. The work of transnational feminists on the subject is therefore really crucial. Writers such as Caren Kaplan, Inderpal Grewal, Chandra Talpade Mohanty, Jacqui Alexander, and Minoo Moallem and others have contributed significantly to the illumination of such dilemmas.

The problem, in other words, is not only the practice but also what narrative we deploy to resist such practices. The challenge is to avoid narcissistic rescue fantasies, which take us back to colonial narratives; but instead of White men rescuing Brown women from Brown men, it becomes White women, or even First World women of color, rescuing Brown women from Brown men. I am reminded of the film *Around the World in Eighty Days*, where David Niven rescues an Indian princess, played by Shirley MacLaine, from *sati*, the burning of the widow. Yet today, Eurocentric feminists also occupy the traditional position of the male rescuer in colonial narratives. They play the role of the heroine in the discourse of modernization. Implicit in this rescue narrative is the assumption that the "West" is free of gender oppression. Simply discussing clitoridectomy as barbaric erases the struggles of women in Kenya or Egypt who are against such practices, and elides the complexity of African cultures, which cannot be reduced to this practice. It also erases the pathology of appearance in the West. My point is that the question for feminist studies is not simply whether we should or should not condemn a specific practice, but how to represent it, and in what context. Feminist analysis must situate practices within a complex local–global economic, social, political, and cultural context.

Another problem in the traditional feminist assumption concerning gender and colonialism is the claim that patriarchy and homophobia have existed everywhere at all times. I find such statements to be ahistorical. For instance, among some indigenous Americans there have been different traditions, which have not necessarily been homophobic, which have not necessarily been patriarchal, which have been marked by egalitarian structures, and where the question of gender identity has been very fluid. This is not romanticization. When colonizers arrived to the Americas, not only did they occupy indigenous land, they also imposed new structures that were patriarchal. The colonizers, for example, would not negotiate with indigenous women who had the right to represent their people. Native American women scholars have addressed the consequences of such impositions.

EA: In your view, does the concept of multiculturalism provide us with theoretical and political tools to problematize dichotomies, including the local–global one?

ES: First of all, "multiculturalism" is just one of many legitimate terms that evoke decolonizing and anti-racist movements. The idea of "multiculturalism" does not mean simply the fact of "many cultures;" it is, rather, a political and epistemological project. Moreover, the concept of multiculturalism has to be defined in relation to Eurocentrism and the decolonization of knowledge. I'm uncomfortable with the image of multiculturalism as just celebrating the many cultures of the world, all dancing around the maypole. For that, we can go to Disneyland. This is a caricature of the geneaology of the concept of multiculturalism. Especially in the 1990s, multiculturalism was attacked not only in the U.S. but also in Brazil and France. For example, in a widely circulated series of essays, French sociologists Pierre Bourdieu and Loïc Wacquant argued that multiculturalism was a product of Anglo-American hegemony, a tool of globalization and of American imperialism. (They seemed not to be familiar with any of the actual work.) Robert Stam and I are presently working on a book entitled *Culture Wars in Translation* [published as *Race in Translation*, 2012], examining how issues of multiculturalism, postcolonialism, race, and globalization are articulated and translated across borders. We also criticize surreptitiously nationalistic versions of multiculturalism, but having said that, we need to be aware of how the attacks on critical versions of multiculturalism and race studies by some leftist intellectuals serve not only to reinforce right-wing attacks but also to reproduce Eurocentric premises and power.[6]

Other critics of multiculturalism argue that it has nothing to do with the "real world," that it is restricted to the academy and the debates about curricular innovation. What these critics do not realize is that these curricula are designed for a large number of people, and that it does matter how students will study history, geography, anthropology, and literature! Besides, if the academy is shown to have little impact on public debates, it might be because we, critical academics, are often pushed out of the public debates in the U.S. context by a corporate culture that limits access to the media for critical scholars. And if the academy is so irrelevant, why is it so often under fire? Pedagogy is very much part of the real world!

29

Forget Baghdad: Arabs and Jews – the Iraqi Connection

(A Conversation Conducted by Rasha Salti and Layla Al-Zubaidi)

Preface by book editors, Samar Kanafani, Munira Khayyat, Rasha Salti, and Layla Al-Zubaidi: On Thursday April 2, 2009, the "Anywhere but Now" conference opened with a welcome note by Layla Al-Zubaidi, director of the Heinrich Böll Foundation, Middle East Office, and the screening of *Forget Baghdad: Arabs and Jews – the Iraqi Connection* by Samir. Naeim Giladi and Ella Shohat had been invited to attend the conference and discuss the film after its screening....Ella Shohat could not travel to Beirut due to a family emergency. Rather than resigning ourselves to accepting [this] absence... through a live satellite broadcast, Ella Shohat was able to speak with the audience in Beirut from a studio in New York.
[...]

Rasha Salti: So I am going to start by asking you a few questions and we will try to take questions from the audience afterwards. Can you tell us what the film *Forget Baghdad: Arabs and Jews – the Iraqi Connection* represents to you, how Samir came in contact with you, and what your involvement with the film was beyond appearing in it and giving the interview?

Ella Shohat: Yes, the story of meeting with Samir has an interesting dimension because before I met Samir in the flesh, I had actually seen

"Re-enactments and Transcripts" of a conversation published in *Anywhere but Now: Landscapes of Belonging in the Eastern Mediterranean* coedited by Samar Kanafani, Munira Khayyat, Rasha Salti, and Layla Al-Zubaidi (Beirut: Heinrich Böll Foundation, Middle East Office, 2012). The conversation and the Q & A with the audience, which was transcribed by Hiba Haidar, took place after the screening of Samir's *Forget Baghdad: Arabs and Jews – the Iraqi Connection* at the opening of a three-day public symposium, "Anywhere but Now," organized by the Heinrich Böll Foundation and held at the Beirut Art Center. Conducted by independent curator and writer Rasha Salti and Layla Al-Zubaidi, director of the Heinrich Böll Foundation, Middle East Office, the conversation took place between Beirut and NY via Live Satellite Broadcast (April 2, 2009).

Figure 52   From left to right: Rasha Salti and Layla Al-Zubaidi at the opening of
the public symposium "Anywhere but Now," Beirut, April 2, 2009 (photo: Hussam
Msheimish)

one of his earlier films at the Carthage Film Festival in Tunisia. The film,
Babylon 2, about minorities in Switzerland, included in part the story of
his friendship with a Swiss Jew. I was very excited to see a film that dealt
with Middle Eastern displacements which used the metaphor of Babylon
for contemporary "scattering," but I did not think much about the matter
afterwards. A few years later, I met a relative of Samir at a conference in
Basel (an alternative event on the occasion of 100 years of Zionism), and she
told me that Samir had sent his greetings and that he appreciated my work
on Iraq and on Arab Jews. I had no idea that he had read my work. We met in
London for the first time and, sure enough, he told me about his new project
and asked me to serve as an advisor, a consultant for the film. I was very
happy to be part of the project for a number of reasons. Besides appreciating
Samir as a filmmaker, feeling affinity with his aesthetics vision, I was also
very moved that someone who was not an Iraqi Jew but an Iraqi of Muslim
background, would take an interest in our story. It was rather unusual at
the time. Eventually, during the process, he invited me to be an interviewee
in the film as a representative of the younger diasporic generation, as if I
were, at least metaphorically, the "daughter" of the protagonists at the center
of the narrative. In turn, I suggested he should not hide his presence and
therefore should insert himself into the narrative as well. So, in this sense, the
film reflects our dialogue. On one level, my story does not form part of the

Figure 53 Poster for Samir's documentary *Forget Baghdad: Arabs and Jews —the Iraqi Connection*, 2002, screened at the "Anywhere but Now" opening

framework of the four protagonists—it is outside of it—and yet my own story (as well as Samir's) is nonetheless crucial for the history of rupture; it adds another dimension to the telling of exile.

RS: I am sure that there will be a lot of questions from the audience and from my colleagues on exile, diaspora, identity, and all that. I just want to focus a bit on the film for now. Did you attend any screenings and can you tell us how audiences reacted to the film?

ES: Yes, on a number of occasions Samir and I spoke in conjunction with screenings of the film. On other occasions, I traveled with the film both in and outside of the U.S., Latin America, and Europe. Over the years, I've had incredible encounters with audiences. Some people whom I have never met have written me about their response to the film. In the U.S., the responses have been varied. Some of those coming from a traditional Zionist perspective were incredibly hostile to the film, because even though the four protagonists live in Israel, they offer substantial critiques of Israeli policies in relation to Arab Jews. The film also bears witness to a younger generation of Arab Jews who have not forgotten their Arab heritage. The film's premise is very difficult for American Jews who have a hard time with people like us asserting our belonging to an Arab cultural heritage, precisely because "Arab" is always constructed in opposition to "Jew;" for them, the notion of an "Arab-Jew" is oxymoronic, strange, even surreal.

On the other hand, I've received very moving responses, particularly from Arab Americans who feel that the story of Arab Jews is partially their own story—a story of dispossession, exile, and multiple belongings and identities. Living in between spaces, they feel affinity not only with the Arab world, but also with the various places through which they have passed, while also thinking of themselves as Americans. As for those American audiences without any direct relationship to the Middle East, for the most part they show a lively curiosity about the experiences related in the film, particularly because they have never been exposed to our side of the story. To them, all Jews are from Europe and all Arabs are Muslims. The notion of Arab-Jews, or Arab-Christians, is usually very foreign to mainstream audiences in the

Figure 54 Teleconferencing between Beirut and NY—on the screen, Ella Shohat (photo: Hussam Msheimish)

U.S. On that level, I think the film and the conversations following the screenings have been quite an education for such audiences.

RS: It sounds brilliant. I just want to note that in the Arab world, it is very troubling to read the name of a filmmaker who has only a first name— Samir. I have been asked a hundred times: "Samir who?" "What is his father's name?" "What is his family name?"

ES: Well, let me say that it is true not only in the Arab world, but also in most places at this point. Nation-state bureaucracy has introduced us to a first and last name; no longer "*abu*" or "*ibn*," "*um*" or "*bint*." I think it is quite a provocative gesture on the part of Samir. By the way, his last name is Jamaladdin. He is not hiding it, but I think using the name Samir is a way of asserting his belonging to multiple places and communities, and not only to the well-respected Muslim religious background associated with his last name.

RS: Were there any screenings in the Arab world or among Iraqi communities in the diaspora, or in Palestine?

ES: Yes, there have been quite a few screenings of the film. To my knowledge, Samir has travelled with the film in the Arab world. I know that it was screened in Cairo recently and was actually reviewed in *Al-Ahram* newspaper. There was one previous screening in Beirut. The film has also been shown in Palestine, Israel, the U.K., the Netherlands, France, and Brazil, so it has had quite a number of screenings in very different places. I don't want to generalize about Arab audiences, but I can speak about my encounters with Iraqis of diverse backgrounds. Iraqis, whether in Britain, Austria, the Netherlands, or Germany, have found the film very moving. That is precisely because, after the diverse wars on and in Iraq, displacement, dislocation, dispossession, and exile have become the story of *all* Iraqis, not only of Iraqi Jews. Samir is very thoughtful and careful, too: while he focuses on the question of Iraqi Jews, he always places it in relation to the question of Palestine, even though that is not the central theme of the film. At the same time, it is the narrative of many Iraqis—in his own case, of an Iraqi of Shi'i communist background—as someone also with multiple dislocations and exiles. The rallying around the film has created a kind of emotional space where Iraqis of diverse backgrounds can mourn the loss of Iraq with poignant emotion—"*Rahet Baghdad, Rah al-Iraq*" ("Baghdad is finished, Iraq is finished"). There is an astounding melancholy. I know that atrocities have been committed in Lebanon and Palestine; people have been killed, Palestinians and Lebanese massacred. But precisely because the film represents the perspective of Iraqi Jews who do not subscribe to the dominant Israeli narrative, it has been particularly moving to Iraqis. At least this is what I have experienced in encounters with the Iraqis who have seen the film.

RS: The tragedy of Iraq is ongoing and is overwhelming, and takes on different natures. You are absolutely right. I am going to ask you one last question before I hand the microphone to the audience. You speak of dislocations and identities in exile: what have these dislocations done to you? You choose to live in New York; you're incredibly prolific; you're one of the most creative scholars to have written about Israeli cinema, and what you have written about Palestinian cinema has been groundbreaking; the same goes for your writings on gender. Now you're more interested in exploring the way the world works, global economies, and neoliberalism. The expanse of your work is riveting. Do you want to talk a bit about what the dislocations mean to you, what they have done to you? And are you just going to stay in New York?

ES: Well, thank you for the kind words. I can only say that the question of this "choice" is not exactly a choice; it is a very complicated matter. As you have seen in the film, this dislocation, especially of Jews from Iraq, is not simply a natural occurrence and it cannot be separated from the question of Palestine. The way the story of Arab Jews circulates is saddening. It is not only about Palestinians and Arab Jews being dislocated, but about the way in which the story of Arab Jews is constantly "surfaced" to suppress the rights of Palestinians. I think this is one aspect of the question i.e. the physical aspect of bodies being dislocated, of people losing their homes. But there is also another aspect of the question which is how the story of dislocation is used to justify ongoing dislocation, in this case that of Palestinians. The question of Arab Jews and Palestinians is part of a larger story of colonial partitions. The case of India and Pakistan, for instance, is telling in terms of the tragic consequences for the diverse populations in the region. Partition is not necessarily something natural—nor is it a matter of choice. Palestinians were not asked whether they would like to leave Palestine, nor were Arab Jews asked if they would like to live in Palestine. But as a result of the dispossession of Palestinians in 1948 with the Nakba, we Arab Jews were caught in a situation where we had little agency. I don't mean to equate our story with that of the Palestinians, even when making a comparison. There are no exact analogies. Quite the contrary: the question is a complex one of the nature of the departure from the Arab world. We can only say—I can say—with a great deal of sadness, that the tension, anxiety, and fear of the equation between being a Jew and being a Zionist has made our place in the Arab World an anxious one.

This is one kind of departure; the other—in my case of leaving Israel—is largely a matter of choice, a political choice, of a departure from a place which I felt robbed me of my Arab identity. I am not speaking for all Arab Jews. I wouldn't want to be perceived as representing all Arab Jews—but I am speaking for a certain community of leftist Arab Jews who feel that in many ways we were dispossessed. For me to have reclaimed my Arab identity—to claim it, to write about it, to investigate it—was not a simple task, precisely because of this context in which the notion of Jews-versus-Arabs is constantly reasserted, and precisely because I did not grow up in Iraq. Being in a place like New York has been very positive, because there are so many refugees here, exiled people who have had to leave their own places because they could not belong to one particular nation. To me, New York, despite its problems—racial discrimination against Blacks and Latinos; the profiling and harassment of Muslims—is still a place that allows people to have multiple belongings. In a strange way, it was in New York that I was able to make friendships with people of diverse backgrounds, to live with Arabs, to become a part of a Middle Eastern community of exiles, as it were.

RS: Thank you, Ella. We're going to pass the microphone to the audience. Everybody has watched the film and some people are familiar with your work. […]

Ralf Ftouni: I am from the south, from the region of Tyre. First I want to say it is really nice to have this live conversation with you from Beirut. It seems interesting to me that in the film the communists who are usually atheists are the ones that seem to be carrying on the Arab-Jewish heritage. My question to you is: do you see many people outside of the communist circles maintaining this tradition, trying to protect this heritage?

ES: Thank you. It is also my pleasure to be "virtually" in Beirut. Thank you for the question. In the film most of the participants, like Sami Michael and Shimon Ballas are actually no longer members of the Communist Party; I myself was never a member of the Communist Party. But now the notion of the "Arab-Jew" has become part of a loosely leftist vision that strives for justice and peace. The approach to the question of heritage and maintaining Arab traditions varies along a wide spectrum of diverse political positions. Claiming your heritage does not necessarily indicate where you stand politically in relation to the Israeli/Palestinian conflict or in relation to Zionism. I want to be clear about that, because it is one thing to claim one's cultural affinities and cultural heritage; exactly how to go about claiming it, within which political perspective, especially when we speak about the question of Palestine, is quite another matter. There is no unanimous approach here. So I would say that Samir's choice was to highlight Arab Jews who claim their *Arabness*, but who also have a leftist perspective. Yet I wouldn't say that we represent all Arab Jews across all political perspectives. You could say that we represent one kind of voice and one kind of perspective among Arab Jews. There are others who celebrate their Iraqi-ness or Moroccan-ness, or their Syrian-ness, etc., but that does not necessarily mean that they share our critical position with regards to Zionist history and Israeli policies.

Sarah: Hi, I am Sarah. I would like to ask you where you consider home to be?

ES: You know, you are touching on the core of the problem of what "home" is. This has been a very painful question for me, because here I am, a person who grew up in an Iraqi household in Israel, a place where I spoke Arabic at home but was schooled in Hebrew, then I moved to the U.S., and now I have been living in New York longer than I have ever lived anywhere else in the world. So you know, of course New York is the city where I feel most at home. But, again: why do I feel most at home here? Precisely because it does not insist that I belong to only one place. It allows for a multiple, hyphenated identity. So my home—in terms of emotional geography—I would say that Baghdad will always be an integral part my feeling of home; it lives in me even though I have never lived there. Certainly people like my parents continue to carry with them in New York the Baghdad of *maqam*, of Saleh and Daoud al-Kuwaity, of Salima Pasha Murad and Nazem Al-Ghazali.

But I also want to emphasize that home for me is friends and people, a community of people like Rasha, people who think and view the world in a way that does not confine belonging to a single narrow sense of ethnicity or religion or nation. So while I want to fight against injustice, I am not necessarily suggesting that I believe in purist notions of nationalism. An affinity with a given nation does not mean that one does not fight for justice more generally. In cultural terms, Iraqi culture itself contains multiple influences; just as Lebanese culture consists of multiple influences. If you remember the music in the film: it includes different genres and is drawn from diverse sources—Egyptian musicals, Iraqi music, nationalist songs, jazzistic Arabic music and so on. And the images also use multiple sources: still photographs, archival footage, newsreels, and so on. The thing I liked about the film aesthetically is that it brings together so many visual and acoustic layers, taken from different periods and places. Aesthetically, the film's very technique embodies the notion that home is not a single place in the present. Especially in the era of globalization, in the era of multiple dislocations and movements of populations, whether by choice or not, it is hard to speak of an affinity or home only in relation to one place. I think that belonging is complex, plural, and is mediated through these multiple affinities, and, for me reflects not only all the places I have lived in but also the ones passed on to me, and also the new ones I have encountered. [...]

Figure 55   Audience member at the "Anywhere but Now" event (photo: Hussam Msheimish)

Question from audience: Thank you for being with us. I wanted to ask you how much you think that racism and the singular identity and narrative used against Arab Jews in Israel is actually inherent to nationalisms?

ES: Well, this is a very interesting question. Although nationalism can be racist it is not necessarily; but it is perhaps inherently exclusionary in so far as it insists on homogeneity. It depends on what the vision of that nationalism is. Third world nationalism, meanwhile, is problematic partly because of its genealogy; after all, nationalist ideology emerged in the Third Worlds as a response, a kind of conceptual vehicle, against colonialism and the oppression and the injustice it had wrought. It is fascinating to read Frantz Fanon on the subject of Algeria. He was one of the groundbreaking intellectuals in formulating his ideas of anticolonialism and anti-racism and yet he was careful to include Jews in the discussion so as not to participate in the French divide-and-conquer strategy that has separated Muslims from Jews ever since the Crémieux Decree. Again, I don't want to idealize any version of the history of religions or ethnicities in the Middle East, but I think colonialism played an important role in the new formations of identities in ways that created nation-states and produced very problematic positions for religious and ethnic minorities. And I am saying this with a great deal of caution, because I am acutely aware of the ways in which the stories of Arab Jews, Iraqi Christians, or Egyptian Copts, are now sometimes used to produce a very racist image of Islam, as if to argue that Islam is by definition a racist ideology. That's why I'm trying to be very careful when speaking about the question of minorities in the Arab/Muslim world, because I don't want to reproduce this narrative. At the same time, I don't buy into the narrative of any rigid homogenous nationalism emerging out of anger at colonial injustice. Rigid and monologic understandings of nationalism have often had lethal consequences for minorities.

I will add one more point about the question of Arab Jews: the first book I wrote, about the history of the representation of Palestinians and of Arab Jews in Zionist discourse as reflected through the cinema, actually traces the genealogy of this kind of East/West conceptualization to Europe's racist relation to the Middle East. I wanted to show the links between the broader Orientalist interpretive model—in the way intellectuals like Anouar Abdel-Malek and Edward Said have used the term—to the specific case of Zionism's representation of "the East" and "the West" with its production of a very shallow, stereotypical, and binary image. The story of Arab Jews for me is not a separate story from the general story of the way Eurocentric discourse imagined the Middle East. In *Orientalism*, Edward Said speaks about how—in the post-enlightenment era, and especially after World War II—Orientalist discourse began gradually to split the European Jew from the Arab, and build up a general anti-Arab image of the Middle East. My argument has been that Zionism itself split the Jews according to Orientalist paradigms. It represented European Jews in ways that echo stereotypical discourses about "the Eastern European Jew," who for Zionism had to be Westernized, when later, it was Arab Jews who had to be de-Orientalized. In Zionist discourse, Arabs and Palestinians continue to be a negative element—just as generally in Orientalist discourse—but Arab Jews had to be de-Arabized to be regarded positively. Usually, the Middle East is imagined as devoid of (Arab) Jews; we appear in the Zionist rescue narrative only when Euro-Israel sees itself as saving us from our Muslim captives and oppressors, as well as from our own inferior culture. This has now become the dominant narrative. Thus, it is not simply racism per se that is the problem, but rather racism in conjunction with a settler colonial ideology, on the one hand, and with Orientalist discourse on the other. I regard the question of "the Arab-Jew" as a complex intersection that gains meaning within the context of the larger question of Zionism and Palestine, on the one hand, and of Eurocentrism and Orientalism as a whole, on the other. […]

Samar Kanafani: I am one of the organizers of this event. I would like to return to the notion of nostalgia. It is very prominent in the remembrances of the people we saw in the movie, and in the interview that Layla Al-Zubaidi did with Naeim Giladi over the phone. Can you tell us a bit about nostalgia

Figure 56   Samar Kanafani, an organizer of
"Anywhere but Now" (photo: Hussam Msheimish)

and how in some way it can be one of the constituent factors of the Arab
Jews living in exile, if you consider that memories are constructed out of the
position from where we are remembering?

ES: Nostalgia can be used for very conservative purposes, sometimes even
racist purposes. Nostalgia can also be used for more progressive ends: articulating a new version of history and identity, especially in the context of
oppression, denial, and taboo memories. So if we speak about the Israeli/
Arab wars and the question of Palestine, I have tried to write about
nostalgia in a context where Arabness was denied to people like myself.
It was Arabness that was forbidden; Arabs were the enemy. This is how I
was schooled in Israel. At the same time, at home, my culture was Arabic.
In my early work, I talked about that kind of schizophrenia, and tried to
reconstruct a different kind of memory of the Arab world. Precisely because
I did not grow up in Iraq, even now I am attacked in certain quarters and
sometimes even by Arab Jews, those with a different political perspective:
"How dare you claim that? You never lived in Iraq. You are not an Iraqi."
The question for me is how to articulate that memory, despite not growing
up in the Arab world, because I am saying that the severing, the rupture that

has happened in my family between, say, my sister who was born in Iraq and myself, had to do with the partition of Palestine and how we ended up as dislocated people. However, even though the official narrative claimed that the Arab is the enemy, we still grew up with an affectionate relationship to Arab culture at home. For me, it was important to articulate in the public sphere what up to that point had only been articulated within the private sphere. It was not just about fighting for economic and political rights; from the outset, the question of cultural rights was also important for me. And in this sense the reconstruction of memories is crucial for an alternative vision of the future. If you take another example, in the context of Israel and Palestine, the debate over *falafel* and who has the right to claim *falafel* is ultimately a symbolic debate over indigeneity. You know, there is a debate over the appropriation of the Palestinian or Lebanese food, *hummus* ...

SK: That's Lebanese.

(*Audience laughter.*)

ES: (*Laughing.*) It is not merely a question of a silly debate, it is a very-meaningful debate. It is significant because culture is not separate from the political realm. In this way, people like us who engage in cultural activism and write about culture, refuse to see culture as a realm separate from politics. In other words, what we are trying to argue for is the concept of "cultural politics." And therefore nostalgia forms an important element of how we write about the past, how we articulate the past, how we narrate this relationship of Jews and Muslims and Christians and others within that vast geo-political space of the Arab world. How we articulate this relationship is very meaningful. What you have now is a debate between those of us (like Naeim Giladi, myself, and others) who try to articulate the very specific disaster that colonialism and Zionism catalyzed for Jews and Muslims in Arab countries, and those who argue the opposite, that Jews in the Muslim world, not unlike in the Christian world, were always persecuted and therefore there is ultimately a justification for what happened to the Palestinians. So nostalgia is not just about weeping when you listen to Nazem Al-Ghazali or Umm Kulthum, which is of course an important element; but it is also about how intellectuals and cultural activists resist official narratives and institutional taboos, and generate different, complex memories of these relationships.

I will give another example—you can find it on YouTube—an Al-Jazeera reportage, I believe, called "The Last Jew of Babylon." It is about an old Iraqi man who was presumably rescued from Baghdad after the American occupation of Iraq, and taken to Israel where he was presumably liberated. But the film shows him to be quite happy in Baghdad; he arrives in Israel and becomes very lonely, depressed, and melancholy until he goes to Jaffa, where he mixes with Palestinians in a coffee house, and plays *shesh-besh* (or *tawle*). When he enters an Arab-speaking world, he no longer feels isolated and estranged. It's interesting that he even feels estranged in the world of those who are now Iraqi Israelis because of the incredible separation gap of some 50 to 60 years. Why do I bring up this example? Because upon arriving in a context that regards the Arab as the enemy, the Baghdadi Jew feels the pain of losing Iraq, not unlike the way the generation of Naeim Giladi (or of my parents) has been nostalgic for Iraq, and felt cheated out of their country. Nostalgia gains political meaning not simply because you have a hankering for smoking *nargila*, but because you are denied something which has been forecefully taken away from you, and in a context where you are not supposed to remember Iraq, and are supposed to have amnesia about your past.

Figure 57 "Anywhere but Now," organized by the Heinrich Böll Foundation, from left to right Heiko Wimmen and Rasha Salti (photo: Hussam Msheimish)

Heiko Wimmen: I would like to ask about the 60-year gap. I was in New York in 2003, which of course for Iraq was unlike any other year. I think it was April or May 2003, and I had this conversation with a young Israeli lawyer, obviously an educated person, of Iraqi origin. She was amazed by the images broadcast on television. She said, "I have seen all these pictures of Iraq now and I was surprised to see such huge cities like Baghdad, because I imagined it to be a completely agricultural place."

(*Ella laughs.*)

397

This was the daughter of Iraqi immigrants to Israel, so only one generation removed. Now we have heard all these wonderful stories about the Black Panthers and all of this. But what is left of this? I mean what else is left other than those who voted for Begin in 1977, other than those who maybe now vote for Shas? What is left of the opposition, the force that was mounted against the dominant Zionist narrative, by people who thought like you or the generation of Naeim Giladi?

ES: Thank you. Well, I think this is a very tough and very appropriate question. First, it shouldn't be surprising that Arab Jews, or the Mizrahim [children of Arab and Middle Eastern Jews], living in Israel should imagine Iraq as completely rural. One thing that we have to understand about Israel—and I can tell you that some Palestinians *fil-dakhil* also deploy these discourses—is that until 1967, you have to imagine that Palestinians *fil-dakhil* and Arab Jews, especially the younger generations, were completely disconnected from the Arab world. Israel is a highly centralized state, where education is totally controlled by the state. In fact, until 1993 there was only one TV channel, owned by the state—even if there was some Arabic programming—and the same applies to radio. So in other words, even when the government had broadcasts in Arabic, it was according to the paradigmatic political, national, and Orientalist perspective. When I was in school, we did not read anything about the Arab world. We were basically taught European history, and the very few pages dedicated to the Middle East were only about Muslim and Arab persecution of Jews, and about the Arab world's underdevelopment, primitiveness, and backwardness. To the extent that some Palestinians and Arab Jews growing up in Israel have fallen for that narrative, you can understand that children who were raised that way would buy into it.

It takes an incredible amount of resistance, and took an incredible amount of resistance, to shape alternative narratives. I would say that especially after the Oslo Accords—despite their problematic impact on Palestinians in terms of their basic rights, the right of return, etc.—there has been a visible discursive shift. Within Israel, the Oslo Accords made it possible to utter the name *filastin* [Palestine] and discussions of Palestinian rights became more legitimate, however problematic and manipulative. But still, at least as far as discourses go—as opposed to practices—it opened up the debate, also within the U.S. It also opened up the debate on Arab Jews. All of us who appear in *Forget Baghdad: Arabs and Jews – the Iraqi Connection*, with our kind of work and writing, became accustomed to being denounced. But gradually we gained some visibility, to the point that, by the late 1990s and early 2000s, the question of Arab-Jews even became fashionable among the younger generation of Arab-Jewish/Mizrahi intellectuals and activists. Now people are using the term "Arab-Jews" in previously unthinkable ways. I am talking about young people who were born in the 1980s, so really the equivalent of the grandchildren of Naeim. Culturally, it has now become a realm of *engagement*, for instance the new fusion music.

In terms of films, we find an impressive amount of production. *Forget Baghdad* was screened at the Tel Aviv Cinemathèque; 15 years ago, that would have been unthinkable. At the same time, while the question of Arab-Jews has become quite fashionable, unfortunately it is sometimes emptied of its critical meaning. Now it can be a nostalgic celebration of our special identity, but sometimes appropriated for dominant narratives. It is as though: "We are Arab Jews, but we don't talk about the question of Palestine." You hear that discourse sometimes in such statements as: "It's irrelevant, I just enjoy listening to Arabic music." In such instances, the celebration engages Arabic culture and produces new fusion music, with Moroccan tunes and Spanish tunes, but without actually engaging the political dimension. In other words, in response to your question "What is left? The Black Panthers, etc." There are some things that are left, but I will not tell you that they necessarily challenge the dominant perspective. At the same time, it's there and who knows ... As you know, with every kind of community, identity is in flux. I cannot say that this is a fixed history. People believe in certain ideologies and they also change, and this is part of an ongoing dynamic process in a conflictual zone. But given the dislocation from the Arab world and the generational gap, Arab-Jewish culture cannot be regarded as if it were still existing in the same moment of the 1960s and 1970s, or even the 1980s. [...]

MK: Hi, my name is Munira. I am a Ph.D. student at Columbia University and I had the honor of seeing you speak many times in New York in the flesh, and I've admired you for many years. My question to you: do you think there is a possibility to recuperate the place of the Jews in the Arab world, apart from the realm of the intangible, and by that I mean culture, memory, music, cooking, film, etc.? I am thinking of the physical space and the social space; I am thinking of the crumbling or already gone Jewish quarters in the Arab cities, the locked-up synagogues, the few old people languishing or hanging on to the last years of their lives, who will soon be gone. Or it is all over?

ES: Well, thank you so much, because this question is deeply moving. While I think we are in agreement here about the question of Palestine and Zionism, and that this is one dimension of the narrative .... To me, the question of the Arab-Jew and the question of what happened in the Arab world post-the-establishment-of Israel have been very difficult to engage. Of course for people like myself, the burden is always that we have been accused of being traitors, just as Palestinians *fil-dakhil* have been accused sometimes of being traitors. At the same time, we understand that what happened to us as Arab Jews, that our departure, was not exactly a choice, but was the result of a set of very complex causes, which I can expand on at a later point. But the padlocked synagogues that I have seen in Tunis and Cairo, or the cemeteries that are being taken care of in Marrakesh, those right now are the sites—very significant sites—of this battle; and represent the kind of discomfort that I think many Arabs have been feeling about Arab Jews. Who are those Arab Jews? Are they with us or against us? Then when people with more critical perspectives like Naeim and the writers you saw in the film appear on the scene, it obviously forces us to engage with the question from a different angle. I believe it is possible; I think what's happening here is a courageous, very courageous dialogue, and I thank you all for coming. Because I understand this is something that *is* possible to recuperate. We *can* think about it and talk about it, and I can share with you that a young generation of students, including Palestinians, are working on the question of Arab Jews from a critical perspective. And I think this is very important because right now the question of Arab Jews forms a symbolic battle over the fraught tale of colonialism in the region. I believe that we can open a dialogue in diverse Arab countries—without reproducing the narratives of traitors or non-traitors—to truly understand the complexities, including, truly, the question of fear (without reproducing Zionist discourse). I think it is possible.

The Iraqi-Jewish family of a very good friend of mine left Baghdad in the late 1960s. They were among those who remained after the massive departure of Jews. She herself also lived and studied in Lebanon. She did not grow up in Israel, never lived there, and never subscribed to Zionism. And yet she feels that she cannot give expression to an Arab-Jewish perspective without it being immediately understood as if she were somehow rejecting Palestinian rights or reproducing Zionist narratives. And this is not the case. We have to understand that there are several other ways in which we can open up the debate beyond the "us versus them" narrative, and I think it requires a multi-levelled understanding of what happened, as well as a really courageous look at the question of nationalism. If we're honest enough to understand that we can produce critical perspectives about certain aspects of nationalist narratives but without endorsing colonialism, Eurocentrism, imperialism, and so on, we'll see that there are many other more complex ways to engage in this conversation. So, thank you.

(Big round of applause from the audience.)

ES: *Inshallah da'iman bi-khayr* (May you always be well.)

LAZ and RS: Bye-bye.

ES: *Alf shukur, ma'a salama* (A thousand thank yous, goodbye.)

30

Bodies and Borders

(An Interview Conducted by Manuela Boatcă and Sérgio Costa)

Preface by Manuela Boatcă and Sérgio Costa: Scholar Ella Habiba Shohat has long dealt with the real and imaginary boundary lines that inform some of the most insidious conflicts of our times. She defines herself as an "Arab-Jew" of Jewish-Baghdadi background, who has made the U.S. her adopted home, where she is Professor of Cultural Studies at New York University [...] Her work unsettles and reinterprets the boundaries between "the West and the Rest," as well as between the global South and global North. We spoke with Ella Shohat in a Berlin restaurant about the politicization of culture and the culturalization of politics. Here she tackles such varied subjects as the intimate connections between Jewish and Muslim histories and culture and the debates over circumcision, Islamophobia, and anti-Semitism, always in a sensitive and empathetic manner, while still retaining analytical distance and a sharp theoretical vision.

Sérgio Costa: As you know, politics in the post-war world was dominated by the presence of nation-states, and intellectual debates were very much shaped by a feeling of national belonging. Intellectuals were, in a certain way, pressured to declare their loyalty to a single national state. Your biography and your oeuvre are very much in-between—between national belongings, between ethnic belongings, and without a fixed national position. Could you please tell us about your trajectory and how this in-between positionality has influenced your work?

Ella Shohat: After World War II, with decolonization and partitions, life shifted for many communities. There were transfers of populations, wherein one identity was transformed into another identity. A Muslim Indian became

A conversation conducted on September 22, 2012 by Manuela Boatcă, Professor of Sociology and Chair of the School of the Global Studies Program, University of Freiburg, Germany; and by Sérgio Costa, University Professor of Sociology and Director of the Institute for Latin American Studies, Freie University, Berlin. Published in the Culture Section of *Jadaliyya*, November 18, 2013.

a Pakistani. In our case, Arab Jews became Israelis. All of this happened virtually overnight. These new official identities did not reflect the feelings of the displaced people, and could not translate the contradictions on the ground. This new situation did not necessarily reflect those communities' sense of belonging. Hence, a crucial tension was generated between one's official documentation and one's emotional map of identity and sense of home and belonging. I have tried to explain this historical context in order to make sense out of our brutal rupture in the wake of partition. I grew up in Israel as a Jew, in a country that defines itself as a state for the Jews and as a Jewish state, which was presumably a solution for "the Jewish problem." But for which Jews, and a solution for what? Being schooled in Hebrew in a Jewish state required that I completely reject everything associated with my home: namely, the Arabic that we spoke at home; my Iraqi parents; my Iraqi grandparents who didn't speak a word of Hebrew. The fact is that many people in my community missed Baghdad. But in this context, Iraq and the Iraqis were the enemy of the state to which we now officially belonged. I often describe my experience as a child as one of virtual schizophrenia, where I had to simultaneously live two identities, one outside of the home and another inside the home.

In 1948, after the partition of Palestine, a huge number of Palestinians were dispossessed and became refugees. Many ended up in neighboring countries, in Syria, in Iraq, in Lebanon, in Egypt (not to mention other parts of the world). What was the impact of Palestinian dislocation on Arab Jews? The Arab Jews never suffered a holocaust in the Arab world, but the emergence of Zionism and the situation with Palestinians created intense anxiety. It was no longer possible to simply be a Jew cohabiting with Arab Christians and Arab Muslims. But while Arab Christians and Arab Muslims could maintain their identity, Arab Jews could not. Suddenly, we had to choose between a Jewishness that was equated with Israel, seen as virtually coterminous with the West and with Europeanness, versus an Arabness that was now equated with Islam and the East, and for the first time, an East without Jewishness. The conflict between Israeli Zionism and Arab nationalism generated a situation where we had no place.

SC: What role did religious practices play in relation to these identity constructions?

ES: It is often forgotten that there have always been tensions—including in Europe and the Americas—between Zionist Jews and those religious Jews who from the very beginning thought Zionism was an aberration because it was secular. They believed that the only acceptable moment to return *en masse* to the Holy Land would be with the coming of the Messiah. (Many secular Jews were also skeptical.) But, after the Holocaust, the Zionist perspective gained momentum and came to be seen as more legitimate among Jews, slowly becoming a kind of normative discourse.

It is also problematic when the history of Jews in Arab countries and in Islamic spaces is viewed as being identical to the history of Jews under Christianity—that is, as a history of relentless persecution. Today, this narrative has unfortunately become a dominant—and, I would argue, Eurocentric—mode of representing Jewish histories. Even Orientalists such as Bernard Lewis, despite the problems with many of his formulations, did recognize the existence of a "Judeo-Islamic symbiosis." The Judeo–Muslim dialogue was both cultural and theological. So, although there were certain moments in the history of Jews within Islam where discrimination, and sometimes even persecution, took place, there was also a pattern of strong cultural affinities and relatively peaceful co-habitation. In any case, Jews were not the only minority in a Middle East replete with ethnic and religious minorities; thus, our history cannot be discussed only in relation to Jews within Christian Europe, but must be discussed also in relation to the diverse minorities in the Middle East.

Manuela Boatcă: There seems to be little awareness of the location of Jews within a global perspective. In Europe and the U.S., and perhaps in other parts of the world as well, many people see Jews as always and everywhere European, a view that excludes not only Arab Jews but also Latino Jews and African Jews. Would you say that this is part of the construction of Jewishness as Whiteness? Do you think that this has something to do with the way that the Jewish Diaspora is constructed in terms of European history to the exclusion of other parts of Jewishness across the world?

ES: Yes. Because of a certain Eurocentric discourse, it has been difficult to articulate a Judaism embedded in Arab culture. With colonial domination in the Middle East and North Africa, certain institutions gained power, including Euro-Jewish institutions that were connected to colonial power, which were instrumental in our Westernization even before the arrival to Israel. For example, the Alliance Française Israelite, or the Jewish French schooling system, was established in North Africa, Lebanon, Iraq, and Turkey. As part of French enlightenment, the Alliance combined a French education with a kind of secular Jewish education, all in the French language. But this Western influence existed even before French colonial rule or outside its colonized territories, in places that were still under the Ottoman Empire before World War I. In Baghdad, the Alliance Française-Israelite continued after the fall of the Ottoman Empire, when Iraq came under British influence. French Jews saw themselves as instruments of reason and civilization and extended this view even to their co-religionists within the Islamic/Arab world. It was not only the French state that promoted this "civilizing mission;" the French Jews believed in it as well and spread it to non-Western spaces.

MB: This hegemony of the White European Jew seems to be a quite recent moment, yet the whitened European Jew is also a moment in the history of Jewishness. What do you think of that schism?

ES: I think it is fascinating because the whitening of the Jew takes place on several levels. If we go back to Iberia, with the Inquisition and the *limpieza de sangre* (the purity of blood), we see that the diabolization operated against the Jew and the Muslim together. And racist discourse, especially as it culminated in 19th-century scientific racism, categorized Jews along with Asians and Africans, for example, as inferior. Hegel's "idealist" approach in *The Philosophy of History* sees diverse peoples, especially Africans and Jews, as living "outside of History"—a highly problematic concept: how can any community be regarded as living outside of history, outside of time and place?

Zionism can thus be seen as the response, at the discursive and theoretical level, to these prejudicial discourses, an attempt to place the Jew *inside* of history. Theodor Herzl's visionary utopia *Altneuland* has the "New Jew" transforming Palestine, imagined as a backwater, into a modern, civilized space. In a way, Herzl was responding to anti-Semitic discourses about the Jew. Zionism, to my mind, can be described as an effort to whiten the Jew philosophically and even literally. The ideal of the New Jew was posited in contrast to the anti-Semitic stereotype of the *Ostjuden*: a kind of feminized, weak, wandering Jew, a *luft-mensch* pondering texts. The New Jew was to be masculine and a worker of the land, grounded in nature, no longer the cosmopolitan exiled diasporic but a Jew who has returned to his homeland. The notion of the New Jew was influenced by the *Jugendkultur*, or youth movement in German, and appeared in Hebrew novels and Zionist and (later) Israeli cinema; the hero would often be blond, blue-eyed, or at least light skinned, and of course never graced with the stereotypical hooked nose. This de-Semitization took place within the logic of Western hegemony, somewhat like the case of the Aryanization of Christ in European painting. And therefore one can argue that there has been a kind of Aryanization and whitening of the Jew as a result of the experience of anti-Semitism. Moreover, Israel was created with the idea that it would be a Western outpost—a Switzerland of the Middle East, as the phrase went—even though located in the Middle East, and even though the majority of Jews in Eastern Europe were called *Ostjuden*, and even though Israel ended up with many Jews from places like Yemen, Iraq, Syria, and Morocco. It would be hard to describe Israel, then, as simply a Western entity. And, of course, this characterization ignores the Palestinians who are citizens of Israel. Even in demographic terms, then, Israel cannot be simplistically reduced to "West," but nonetheless this equation persists.

SC: To skip to some current debates, it is quite ironic that this political investment of Jews in Westernizing themselves seems to have limits, at least in religious practices. As you know, circumcision is interpreted by some legal scholars and now by a court in Cologne, Germany, as a barbaric ritual that violates fundamental rights of children. So lawyers are using universalistic arguments in order to restrict the religious freedom of parents. Do such conflicts show a limit for this strategy of Westernization?

ES: That is an interesting question because the problem with these debates is that they fragment and fetishize one aspect of a culture, resulting in an ahistorical discourse that is insensitive to the history of colonial domination and Western hegemony. It also becomes a kind of self-righteous discourse that presents itself as acting on behalf of "the universal." The target of these discourses is obviously what has been seen as "the particular" and those "others" who need to be saved from their particularity. The circumcision debate mobilizes a similar discourse that has been used around the veil. The question is: who represents and acts on behalf of "the universal"? The particular/universal dichotomy often gets enlisted into a rescue narrative. We cannot forget how colonial discourse often represented colonialism as not simply conquering and exploiting, but also as advancing a universal civilizing mission, rescuing those barbaric people—especially, of course, their women and children—from their own horrible traditions, rituals, and culture. This idealist discourse was framed by the arrogant imperialism that saw itself as bringing light to dark places.

This is unfortunately one side of the Enlightenment. And addressing the intersection of the Enlightenment meta-narrative with colonial discourse does not mean rejecting the Enlightenment in general. The Enlightenment is a complex phenomenon featuring contradictory discourses; what is required, therefore, is to highlight its philosophical contradictions as well as its imperial dark side "on the ground." In the colonial context, the Enlightenment often meant cultural subordination and psychic devastation. So the question is, what is a "barbaric practice," and who has the right to determine what is barbaric? Who has the right to say, "I am the savior of these children?" It is not a question of being "for or against" circumcision. I come from a culture of circumcision, but I would not necessarily see myself endorsing it just because it is my tradition. Apart from the fact that there are Jews and Muslims who refuse to circumcise their children, I object to the way the movement against circumcision has relied on an Orientalist imaginary. I would be disturbed by any kind of state idolatry that would grant the nation-state the power to determine, legalize, and enter the private/

community zone of familial decisions and disallow certain cultural practices, under the assumption that "the state knows best." Also, especially in contexts of dislocation and alienation, where individuals and communities find it difficult to maintain their language, culture, and identity—as in the context of Germany, where there is little dignified place for Muslim culture(s)—a rejection of circumcision cannot *but* be interpreted as another form of cultural violence. Such a rejection is inevitably perceived as an imposition of Christian practices, values, and traditions on Muslims. Given colonial history, as well as the persistence of anti-Semitism and Islamophobia, circumcision, like the veil, becomes a highly contested signifier. Of course, some might argue that these are not Christian values but just universal secular humanistic values. But humanism can be seen as a sublimated, secularized form of Christian ideas such as providence, salvation, charity, etc. The rescue narrative concerning Muslim children assumes the cultural normativity of Christian children whose Christian background goes often unstated. Yet, all children are born into particular contexts and nation-states, as secular or religious, of a certain class or ethnicity; in other words, every child is born into a web of multiple affiliations, intersecting identities, and potential identifications.

SC: Perhaps, for example, some children are born with a Christian name …

ES: If one has a Christian name, is taken to church as a child, is shaped by certain ideologies, sometimes in a sublimated semi-secular form, one is no less particular than a Jew or a Muslim. So what makes the state the arbiter of which particulars are legitimate and which not? Why is going to a church a more legitimate practice in a supposedly secular state; why is celebrating Christmas and the story of Christ's resurrection considered acceptable? To resort to a *reductio ad absurdum,* why should children be exposed to the story of the crucifixion, of nails being hammered into the body of Christ, with all the blood and the tears? One might argue that the crucifixion story is traumatizing for children, and that children should not be exposed to it, and that fact alone would sanction state intervention. It is certainly legitimate to have a discussion about whether or not circumcision is a good idea. The debate is a healthy one, but I am concerned about granting the state, to paraphrase Max Weber, a monopoly on *religious* violence, especially when state power is wielded in a discriminatory fashion.

Moreover, it is important to recognize that there is a particular burden concerning the history of circumcision in Christian Europe in terms of the role of circumcision in terms of passing and assimilation during the Holocaust and World War II, not only in Germany but in Vichy France. If the authorities suspected someone of being Jewish but passing for a non-Jew, the authorities could check whether the person was circumcised. During

World War II, Jewish children who were sent to be adopted by non-Jewish families were warned by their biological parents to "never go to the urinal" in order not to be exposed as Jews. Given the history of circumcision as a marker of identity that could determine life and death, how could we *not* recognize that circumcision has served as an index of stigmatized religious minorities? In a contemporary context of Islamophobia—where people feel very vulnerable around the denial of their identity, about the refusal of their culture, about the persistent equation of Islam with terrorism—to my mind, any kind of policing of the practice can only be read as a kind of imposition, as assimilation, and even as a kind of cultural violence on the part of the German nation-state. Against this backdrop, violence cannot be read as solely something Muslim parents do to their children, who therefore need to be rescued by the state. The implicit focus of the circumcision debate has been on Muslims, but what would be the place of the Jew in that discourse? Would the state allow Jews to continue with the ritual but not Muslims? There is a sense that in the wake of the Holocaust, the German state has to be sensitive about offending Jews. But where do we draw the lines about related Muslim religious practices that may be regulated differentially? One is reminded of the French banning of religious insignia, where it was common knowledge that it was aimed at Muslims and not at Catholics (crucifixes, for example), or at Jews (with the *kippa*), or at Sikhs (with their turbans), or at Santeiros (with their amulets), and so forth.

MB: The debate about circumcision would also be the point where the protests of Muslim communities and Jewish communities in Germany would come together and have come together. Because, there, a politics of coalition emerged where there had long been a dividing line that emphasized the difference between Muslims and Jews.

ES: It is an irony of history, at least of recent history. Because in recent times, largely because of the Arab/Israeli conflict, there has been a construction in the public sphere of Jews and Muslims as always already enemies. In the media, journalists often appeal to the cliché that "this conflict goes back thousands of years." But historically that is false; it largely goes back to the late 19th century and the emergence of Zionism. For many centuries and even millennia, Jews and Muslims often faced Christian prejudice together. During the *Reconquista*, culminating in 1492 and the fall of Granada, the remaining Jews and Muslims were forced to either leave or convert. Perhaps the Inquisition was the first case of policing by an emerging power—a kind of embryonic nation-state formation. The policing of culinary practices and bodily rituals were part of this religious-cultural surveillance. To investigate if conversion was real, the authorities would check the penises of male babies or children. Another form of policing by the Inquisition was to enter the kitchens and search for colanders. Jewish *kashrut* (and for that matter Islamic *halal*) dietary laws require draining of the blood. In Jewish tradition the draining is performed through salting the meat and usually with a colander, allowing the blood to drip out to separate from the meat. Thus the very presence of a colander in a *converso* house was proof of Jewishness for the Inquisition. Another marker of Jewish and Muslim identity was the prohibition on eating pork. Could one speculate that the widespread practice in Spain of hanging pork in restaurants, something not found in many countries, was meant as a marker of identity? Does it go back to the *Reconquista*, where the serving of *jamón* became a distinctive marker of Christian identity vis-à-vis the Jews and the Muslims?

The two stories/histories of Jews and Muslims are often told in isolation, but in fact the two groups were subjected to the same inquisition and continued to live together within Muslim spaces. The *convivencia* of Iberia was in fact the norm within Muslim spaces even if unusual within Christian spaces. Jews were invited by the Ottoman Empire in 1492 to settle within its diverse territories. Sephardi Jews in Turkey, Bulgaria, Greece, Egypt, and Morocco, have continued to speak Spanish up until very recently. Yet the dominant view of Jewish–Muslim relations continues the false narrative about an eternal split between the Jew and the Muslim, but ironically this current debate brings to the surface the largely erased Judeo-Muslim history. In my work, I have insisted on the Judeo-Muslim hyphen, because while the Judeo-Christian hyphen implies a legitimate meta-narrative, the Judeo-Muslim hyphen has been elided. Yet, historically the Judeo-Muslim hyphen could be seen as the norm rather than the Judeo-Christian, which is a relatively recent phenomenon, going back to the Euro-Jewish Enlightenment and reinforced by Zionist Eurocentrism. Spain has recently issued a call to those who can prove Sephardi ancestry to apply for Spanish citizenship, but has not issued a similar call to Muslims who would also be able to prove their Andalusian ancestry. As with France's ban on religious insignia and Germany's circumcision debate, Spain's policy legitimizes one "Semitic" group but not another within the new European context. In this sense, a de-Orientalization of "the Jew," as it were, has taken place, but not of the "Muslim-Arab."

MB: The question of cruelty to animals was also brought into the debates about circumcision in Germany. Opponents on both sides of the issue raised arguments about the idea of pain. I think what is fascinating is that, in order to avoid the question of religion or religious practices, the issues that are raised are those of cruelty to animals, bodily harm, or things that seem not to be related to cultural practice but are rather stigmatized as criminal acts that have been written out of legitimate social practice.

ES: I think it is legitimate to bring out these questions of bodily harm and cruelty to animals. The overlapping dietary laws of Jewish *sh'hita* and Muslim *dhabiha* (ritual slaughter) insist on avoiding cruelty to the animal through detailed regulations about the kind of knife used, where it is applied, etc. There can be conversation and argument in the public sphere about whether ritual slaughter is indeed a form of cruelty to animals. Similar questions apply to circumcision: is it a form of bodily harm? It is vital to generate this conversation; but there is a difference between having this conversation and translating it into the state imposing a single point of view. Such an approach does not take on board the burdens of history, does not acknowledge the philosophical dilemmas, and does not face the ways in which prohibiting circumcision is problematic when declared in the name of a pseudo-universality.

31

Don't Choke on History:
Reflections on *Dar al Sulh*, Dubai, 2013

(A Joint Conversation with
Michael Rakowitz and Regine Basha)

Preface by Michael Rakowitz: In 2013, the Moving Museum, an itinerant institution founded and directed by Aya Mousawi and Simon Sakhai, invited me to contribute to an exhibition they were curating in Dubai. They asked me to produce a version of *Enemy Kitchen*, a 2012 project revolving around the communal preparation and eating of Iraqi food with Americans post-9/11, which had evolved to become a fully functional food truck on the streets of Chicago with Iraqi refugee cooks and U.S. veterans of the Iraq War serving as their sous-chefs (inverting the power dynamic in Iraq, as Americans now take orders from the Iraqis). The truck features the Chicago flag rendered in Iraqi colors, and serves food on paper replicas of the plates looted from Saddam Hussein's palaces in 2003.

In the context of Dubai, the project would not be able to create and/or explore the frictions and the antagonisms it was able to create in the U.S.; in the U.A.E, there are many Iraqi refugees and quite a few excellent Iraqi restaurants. And so I said to them if I was going to create a new culinary-based project that was about making something that was not there tangible and create those same kinds of frictions that were foregrounded in *Enemy Kitchen*, I would introduce Iraqi-Jewish cuisine as a way to speak about the resuscitation or this reanimation of the identity of Arab Jews as an opposition to the dominant Zionist narrative that propagandizes the erasure of Arab-Jewish culture. When they replied positively and enthusiastically to this offhanded suggestion, I suddenly realized what a crazy proposition it was.

My conception of the project began with the title. In Islam, *Dar Al Sulh*, or Domain of Conciliation, is a territory where an agreement between Muslims and non-Muslims has been made, and provides freedom of religion,

---

Unpublished joint conversation with Michael Rakowitz, artist and professor at Northwestern University, and independent curator Regine Basha. Based on a transcribed radio conversation, Creative Time Reports, New York, June 28, 2013.

autonomy, and protection. It is this agreement that applied to Jews in Iraq, and elsewhere in the Middle East. *Dar Al Sulh* would thus become the first restaurant in the Arab World to serve the cuisine of Iraqi Jews since their exodus, which began in the 1950s as a result of riots and reprisals leading up to and after the establishment of the state of Israel. Today, it is believed that less than ten members of the once 150,000-strong community remain in the entire country. *Dar Al Sulh* featured my Iraqi-Jewish grandmother's recipes, whose ingredients and combinations of flavors represent something of an endangered species, as whatever slight differences there may have been between Iraqi "Jewish" and Iraqi cooking has all but disappeared with the departed Jewish community. The dishes were served on plates and trays that originally belonged to members of this ancient community and which survived the departure from their homeland.

Jews were once Arabs, too. Their exodus from Arab lands is one that has been propagandized and mythologized by Israel, by the flawed narrative of Zionism, and by other entities in order to bolster specific cultural and political positions. *Dar Al Sulh* sought to be a time machine, traveling to a not-too-distant past that could be a better future, to reactivate a space when there was harmony, when Jews had not yet abandoned their Arab selves, before Jewish populations in the Arab world were assumed to be complicit with Zionism. The notion of conciliation was the central philosophy of *Dar Al Sulh*, meant to be reflected in the food and the conversations spoken around it.

The restaurant also hosted *Tuning Baghdad*, which provided a rich soundtrack for the dining experience. This is an ongoing project initiated by independent curator Regine Basha, who was one of my co-hosts and collaborators on *Dar Al Sulh*. *Tuning Baghdad* brings together a growing archive of rare video footage, audio clips, and historical information on Iraqi-Jewish musicians and the music scene that was displaced from Baghdad in the late 1940s and early 1950s, including Basha's father, an avid 'oud and violin player. The last generation of Iraqi-Jewish musicians who performed in Baghdad are now in their 70s and 80s, and some in their 90s; they represent an era when an unusually large number of Iraqi Jews were composing and performing Arabic music. For decades these musicians were the teachers and beloved performers of Iraq's traditional *maqams* and modern compositions on the country's National Broadcast Station.

We were also joined by another collaborator and co-host, Ella Habiba Shohat, who was teaching at the time at NYU Abu Dhabi. Ella Shohat's work has been foundational and transformative for both Regine and I. Since the 1980s, she has been writing extensively on Orientalism, postcoloniality, and diasporic cultures, while also developing critical approaches to the study of Arab Jews, focusing especially on Iraq and its diaspora.

Dar Al Sulh operated for one week, from May 1–7, 2013. It appeared and disappeared like an apparition, haunting in delicious and loving ways. Ella, Regine and I had an opportunity to sit down and reflect on our collective experience a month later in New York.

Figure 58 "Dar Al Sulh," performance piece, Traffic Gallery, Dubai, May 1–7, 2013

* * *

Michael Rakowitz: It's hard to believe that only a little while ago, we were all together in a tiny kitchen in Dubai, communicating and convening with over 50 dinner guests each night. So here we are in New York, over a month since we left and maybe we can just go from here.

Ella Shohat: Well, I want to refer to your idea and what you saw as a "crazy proposition." In many ways it is unbelievable to think back now, that over a month ago we were in Dubai speaking about Iraqi-Jewish identity, addressing the disappearance of the Judeo-Arabic culture from the Arab world. It almost seems like a fantasy, dream, a *fata morgana* .... It was one intense week in which we cooked together, hosted every night diverse people and different communities, from various professional backgrounds in such a transnational space that is Dubai and the U.A.E. And here we are, reflecting back on this experience in New York, in a city where Jewishness is a norm, but not Arab-Jewishness. Here, to be an Arab Jew is an oxymoron. There,

Arab-Jewishness is something that is historically familiar. There, to say, "I am an Arab Jew" is not by any means an absurd idea. Nonetheless, because of our long absence, our physical presence as Arab Jews there became a new kind of an anomaly.

It is sad to see that in two or three generations our disappearance, our departure from the Arab world has turned our presence there into "an event." But in any case, to experience our difference within an Arab context is quite dissimilar to experiencing this difference within an American-Jewish context. To articulate the idea of the "Arab-Jew" has triggered immense hostility, especially from the Jewish and the Israeli establishment. In the Arab world, meanwhile, the idea of the Arab-Jew is often warmly embraced. Apart from assuming the diversity of being an Arab, there was a sense of homecoming for the participants. I believe it has to do with the historical wound, that is, the psychic injury impacting not only us but also Arabs in general. Our departure left a kind of scar on the Arab body-politics. Over the years, many have shared with me their stories and feelings about our absence, or better, remembering our presence, either from personal memories or from what they heard from the older generation.

In *Dar Al Sulh*, there were guests who were speaking about their own Jewish neighbors, their Jewish friends who disappeared overnight, and how they have been missing them. Some of them were even asking: "Do you happen to know so and so? He was my neighbor in Batawin." And: "Do you happen to know what happened to him?" At the same time, there were second and third-generation guests who have never experienced their Iraqi-Jewish neighbors, but they were extremely curious, eager to absorb an untold history.

So it would seem that our visit was actually at the right place and at a ripe moment for *Dar Al Sulh*. Here we were, in the Gulf region, so close to Iraq, in a region where multiple generations of exiled Iraqis now live, ten years after the U.S.-led invasion in 2003. In this context, a discussion about the multiplicity of Iraqi identity in general, and more specifically about the history of Iraqi Jews, seemed especially relevant—even vital. At the same time, an Arab youth subculture has emerged on the Internet since the Iraq War, excavating the history of Iraq, and in search of the religious and ethnic diversity that constituted the country. As part of this nostalgia for a past Iraq, there has been a kind of resurgence of interest in the cultural contribution of Iraqi Jews and in the question of Arab-Jews in general. So it's a nostalgia, which can't be reduced to a fixation about the past, since it also suggests hope for a different future.

Regine Basha: What you are saying about the absence of Arab Jews reminds me of the project's subtitle and epigram: "Cuisine of an Absent Tribe" and

"You are eating a dying language from the plate of a ghost," both of which were displayed on the window. Instead of saying "Iraqi-Jewish cuisine," Michael referred to an absent tribe from Iraq. This addressed a potentially delicate diplomatic nature for an event defined as "Jewish"—a word that, in the context of the Arab world would have immediately been read as Israeli and Zionist. For this reason, the event was not announced as "Jewish," and was not advertised through mainstream channels. Most people found out through word of mouth.

To go back to that moment, in the industrial zone of Al Quoz, where many of the workers reside, I was surprised that so many people stood in line to enter this nondescript space that was once a warehouse. I think all of us were incredibly—I don't know if surprised is the word—but certainly overwhelmed by the people who came. Every night the numbers increased significantly, as well as the enthusiasm. And what I started to understand about that particular context for our project was that our hosting and their joining us was a familiar social act for all of us. The large family-style gathering was something that was instantly familiar to our guests—who came from various cultures—and seemed to feel very at home in this setting. Around the dinner table an unlikely group of people sat every night—Emiratis, people from the Gulf region, from Iraq, Palestine, Lebanon, Syria, Morocco, as well as expats from Europe, North America, and Latin America. It was as if they were in the home of their grandparents.

The fact that this food was coming from a very old culture seemed to resonate deeply with their own respective memories of dinners in their own homes. This connection to grandparents' culture, in the context of Dubai being so new, being so overly stylized, produced, and Westernized, provided the guests with an older Arab culture that they seemed to be missing.

Perhaps it would seem strange that Iraqi-Jewish food would trigger this feeling, but basically the dishes overlapped with many of the dishes they are already so familiar with. Some guests were beginning to wonder what made any of this food 'Iraqi-Jewish' in the first place. The conversations around the table revolved around comparing the diverse kinds of cuisines from the region, about Iranian food and Lebanese cooking, and about the shared and different ingredients. I had tremendous conversations with Iraqi food blogger Labiba Laith, about the mango pickle, the 'amba, and it just went on forever. The 'amba provided almost like the soul of each dish.

ES: Especially since each night appealed to one of the five different sensations of taste, the 'amba salad was the only repeated refrain in a menu orchestrated by Michael to trigger various sensory…

MR: Our aprons are forever stained with 'amba.

RB: Actually, a valuable part of the project was how Michael conceived of a theme for each night based on properties or flavors of the dishes. Five of them corresponded to the different taste sensations of the tongue: sweet, salty, bitter, sour, and umami. One night focused on a *light* meal and another night—the Sabbath meal featuring *tbeet* [a slowly cooked stuffed chicken dish]—was *heavy*. It felt like the connective tissue that linked all evenings. It made its way into every conversation, allowing people to speak in parallel ways about their situations, their contexts, their cultures, about what was lost. I think it's also heavy to talk about these issues, but during the dinner the heaviness was consciously one of the menu's themes. It was both delightful and very useful to have that framework.

ES: In terms of your comment about what makes it especially an Iraqi-Jewish food, I think it was crucial that our project offered an explicit meta-comment about this issue. Although we used the terms "Iraqi-Jewish cooking" and "Iraqi-Jewish food," we used them, as it were, under erasure, as though to evoke them but also to question them. In the context of Dubai, we used these terms precisely due to our recent absence from Arab spaces. But at the event we also emphasized that Iraqi-Jewish food forms part of a continuum of Iraqi and regional cooking. Some of the guests commented exactly on this issue, and it provoked an important conversation.

Not that there are no specificities to Iraqi-Jewish cuisine and culture. In fact, there are even some differences among Iraqi-Jews themselves depending on cities and towns in which they lived. Of course, there are also differences among Muslim Iraqis; there are also differences among Christian Iraqis, and so on. But nonetheless there is also much in common. I believe that the very fact that Jews disappeared from the Arab world means that the notions of "Iraqi-Jews" and "Arab-Jews" became necessary. The hyphen between "Iraqi" and "Jewish" to describe food in a sense registers a desire to go against the grain of defining this cooking as presumably unique only to Jews. But it was not at all a coincidence that in *Dar Al Sulh* the dishes were intimately familiar to the guests who felt thoroughly at home. It was therefore inevitable, for them and for us, to raise the question: "Is there such a thing as Iraqi-Jewish food?" Ultimately, our project came to be about deconstructing the idea of "Iraqi-Jewish food" as a notion completely separate from Iraqi cuisine as a whole.

To an extent, I see our project as an implicit critique of Jewish cookbooks, a genre that energetically attempts to create a cohesive space of "Jewish food" despite divergent Jewish cuisines. Jewish cookbooks make an acrobatic attempt to "homogenize" culinary customs and practices of preparing food. Such books include under one rubric a variety of geographies, which, while obeying *kashrut* dietary laws, widely differ in their flavoring and cooking

Figure 59   "Dar Al Sulh"—exterior view

methods. Polish and Yemeni dishes, Russian and Tunisian dishes, and so on, come to form one continuous culinary geography, usually separated from their contextual non-kosher cuisines. But in fact, Middle Eastern *kasher* dishes are more closely related to Middle Eastern *halal* cooking grammar than to Ashkenazi dishes which themselves have more in common with Eastern-European cuisine as a whole. In this sense, Moroccan-Jewish cuisine is intimately linked to Moroccan cuisine in general, just as Iraqi-Jewish cooking is deeply infused with the recipes, flavoring, spices, and smells of Baghdad, Mosul, and Basra. Whether implicitly or explicitly, a certain kind of a nationalist agenda has informed this delinking of Arab Jews from their larger Arab culinary geography. Placing all Jews under one cultural rubric, grouping them separately from their millennial Judeo-Islamic spaces, represents an extension of the idea of "the diversity of the Jewish nation." It also often tends to assume a Eurocentric discourse of "exotic Jews."

Around the long dinner table, the Arab participants raised doubts about the notion of "a Jewish-Iraqi cuisine" since it was virtually similar to Iraqi cuisine. And we responded that indeed Iraqi-Jewish dishes are deeply ingrained in Iraqi cooking, even if these are sometimes variations on a theme. But within the context of the Arab world, given the now unfortunate axiomatic invisibility of Arab Jews, we had to call attention to the absent-presence of Jews within Arab spaces. Our emphasis on the "Jewish" in the "Iraqi food" category also reflected our approach to actively remembering Iraq, not simply for what it was, but also for what it could become—an inclusive place. We wanted to claim and reclaim Jewishness as part of Iraq.

At the same time, we did not intend to deny a certain specificity to Jewish religious practices, just as there are specific Shi'i dishes cooked for specific holidays. Obviously our Shabbat serving of the *tbeet*, the overnight slowly cooked stuffed chicken, pointed to a specifically Iraqi-Jewish dish. But in contrast to the sweeping rubric of "Jewish cuisine," we addressed the ways this dish—its spicing, stuffing, and the stitching of the chicken—reflects the ingredients and cooking methods shared by diverse ethnic and religious communities across Iraq. Cooking protocols came to be the thread binding the discussion around the table.

I was really intrigued by the responses of the participants. Some of them completely got it, while others did not. Do you remember the comment from an older Iraqi who came especially for the Friday Shabbat dinner, eager to consume *tbeet*?

RB: Yes, I remember.

ES: He said that he enjoyed the *tbeet*, but then he pointed to his wife, who was sitting by his side, and said emphatically: "My wife cooks *tbeet* much better than this!" On the one hand, he was bragging about his wife's cooking, that ours did not measure up to. On the other hand, he was claiming an affinity to Iraqi Jews, proud of the mutual neighborly relations and of his wife's mastery of this Jewish Iraqi dish.

MR: Or he was in the doghouse …

RB: He was the same man who asked me to ask my father about a Jewish neighbor he once knew well in his youth. I was so excited that I texted my father in Los Angeles right there from the table to see if he knew the neighbor in question, describing to him the scene, the dinner project, and this Iraqi man who was sitting next to me eagerly awaiting an answer. Twenty minutes later, my father texted me back, flatly, "He's dead!" … A very typical kind of dry humor from that generation, I think. That's all my father texted and it was very difficult to relay the news to this older Iraqi guest.

ES: I also think that his comment about preferring his wife's *tbeet* over ours reflects intimacy; in his case of a Christian Iraqi who loved his Jewish neighbors, and has been missing them. The *Tbeet* around the table gained a flavor of memory.

MR: Absolutely. This dish became a memorial for departed Jewish neighbors.

ES: … a memorial for a departed community among other departed communities of Iraq, of various ethnicities and religions, and of political affiliations. In a way, even if as Iraqi Jews we may feel that we were left out of Iraq historically and culturally, this event afforded us a kind of a return to our own past. Our Arab-Jewish history may seem like it was and was not there—itself becoming a kind of a *kan ya makan*. But traveling to Dubai was a kind of voyage to a proxy Iraq. We felt that all Iraqis around the table were, like us, displaced Iraqis, together mourning our and their exile. And in this coming together, we returned, in an imaginary voyage, to *bilad al-rafidayn*.

MR: This conversation about the cultural sameness of diverse Iraqis and their food was a critical moment of the event. One of the participants, a Dubai resident and a Sunni, originally from Mosul, had his arms folded and said, irritably: "I don't get it. I don't understand. What's so Jewish about all of this? We make all these dishes! We came here for an Iraqi-Jewish meal! And this is just Iraqi!" And then his daughter, who generously joined the cooking team, whispered: "That's the point!" And he said with relief: "Oooh! So when Michael comes back we're going to open up an Iraqi restaurant together." And that's of course one of the ways of deconstructing these labels and these categories, which end up becoming a kind of tragic-comic condition.

ES: I think that for us this tragic-comic encounter was an affirming experience. Because our families were dislocated from Iraq and placed in a new context where our history and culture have been taboo, the recognition by Arabs becomes emotionally vital. It takes a lot of mental effort to rearticulate our links to what was defined as "our enemy" culture, and to claim our Arabness back. And when you go to Iraqi restaurants—such as Al Masguf in Dubai or Masguf al Baghdadi in Abu Dhabi—you immediately appreciate the fact that the served dishes are the ones we grew up eating at home. The culinary continuum was evident. Regional sameness is at least as significant as religious variation.

Some dishes in the south, in Basra, such as *fasanjoon*, are shared with Iranian/Persian cooking. In the north, in Mosul, dishes are closer to Halab/Aleppo in Syria; for instance, *kubbat halab*. Other examples of regional variation, including among Jews, can be seen in the dialects of Arabic. What is called the "Iraqi dialect" consists of diverse dialects, even among Jews. The Jews of Baghdad spoke differently than the Jews of 'Anna. And the Jewish dialect of Baghdad is actually quite similar to the general dialect of Mosul, spoken in the north not only by Jews but also by Christians and Muslims alike. These definitions cast doubt on any idea of a distinct "Judeo-Arabic language" just as they raise doubts about a distinct "Jewish cuisine." Even in different regional Arab spaces, Jews do not exactly share a cuisine—Jewish-Iraqi dishes are closer to their Muslim and Christian neighbors than, say, to Jewish-Moroccan dishes.

MR: It has also been my experience in an Iraqi restaurant in London. It was actually a Kurdish-Iraqi restaurant called *Arbil* on Edgware Road. Despite some differences, most of the dishes were recognizably the dishes I grew up with. For example, *mahshi*, which Iraqi Jews call *mhasha*—the stuffed vegetables—and the boiled rice-flour *kubba*—kubbat Mosul.

ES: It seems to me that the representation of a unified Jewish culture, and in this case a separate Iraqi-Jewish identity that is not attuned to Iraq's multiplicity, is clearly reflected in the nationalist genre of Jewish cookbooks. And our project, to my mind, was an attempt to rearticulate the complexities of our own culture, especially within the context of Iraq. The fact that there are dietary *kasher* codes religiously shared among Jews doesn't mean that we can treat these hugely varied spicing and cooking methods as a homogenous Jewish cuisine. There are dietary differences between *halal* and *kasher* food but there are also considerable commonalities—precisely what tends to be overlooked in the Jewish cookbooks. It's not only that Jews and Muslims do not eat pork, but that their cuisine belongs to the same culinary genre. And it is also about the shared culture around eating, such as the practices of hospitality, of how we invite and host, and how we address and bless our guests.

Linguistically, the diverse Iraqis there used shared "core" phrases. In *Dar Al Sulh*, each evening, we opened with the welcoming words "*Hala, hala bikum*," and the guests concluded with "*'ashtidak*" (may your hand live), to thank Michael for his delicious meals. The nightly ritual of sitting around the table, with the Iraqi *maqam* from Regine's father's parties playing in the background, tuned us all into the past of shared festivities and shared longings. The home movies of the *haflat* (parties) of Regine's parents added significantly to the feeling of being-at-home in all senses of the word.

RB: You mentioned the word tuning, and I think it is a good moment to talk about this idea of tuning. The reason why I called the website "Tuning Baghdad" was because I was struggling with the notion of nostalgia—or with sentimentalizing or romanticizing an old culture of people who are no longer in Iraq. I felt as close to Iraqi music as I did mostly because my father is a musician who learned to play the 'oud and violin in Iraq. I felt that the only way to describe their diasporic condition perhaps is through the process of tuning, as if they are continually trying to tune in to the right frequency—to hear yet again that language, that music, and one's own culture, but never quite arriving at it. So most of the home-based performances I captured for the website present this sort of attempt at tuning. It's like they are in a constant state of rehearsal.

In a way they are not arriving at any destination; they're not going to go back to Iraq. They may not even be interested. Actually, in many cases there are a lot of Iraqi Jews who feel that the Iraq they left is still with them in their home. It's a very complex condition; not everyone feels the same way about it. It's a very heterogeneous group of people living around the world and certainly, having various kinds of social relations in which they continue to speak Arabic to one another. They continue to have these dinner parties. In my family's case, they also had these all-night music parties, or *chalghi*— the footage of which *Tuning Baghdad* houses—which maybe helped them process this unsettled relation to Iraq—this kind of continual back and forth.

The quartertones used in Arabic music often sound off-key to Western ears. I mean there's a whole history of Western ethno-musicologists, for instance Edelson, who traveled in the late 1920s throughout the Middle East and recorded local musicians. He mistakenly thought that they were playing to the best of their ability and were still playing off-key.

ES: That could be called acoustic Orientalism. Just because the ethno-musicologist is unable to hear the quartertones, he is projecting it as off-key according to his normative aural range.

RB: Exactly. That's the sort of melancholic aspect about being displaced and living in a culture in which you are always going to be off-key, always tuning, never quite producing the right music, or always in a state of rehearsing; it became symbolic of their existence. The Iraqi *qanun* player, Abraham Salman, who just passed away sadly, had little access to his loving fans when he left Iraq, but continued to play Iraqi *maqams* from his living room couch for his friends in Ramat Gan.

And also just to add on to the discussion about the cuisine being not particular to Jewish culture, it's very much the same case for the music scene. I did not want to call it the "Iraqi-Jewish music scene" because I knew that "Jewish" would be read as a particular music style and in this case it's not. In fact, it's simply the musicians that happen to be Iraqi-Jewish. Many musicians, instrumentalists, and composers worked and performed on the Iraqi National Radio when it was first established in the 1930s. The orchestra was run by the brothers Sallah and Daoud Al Kuwaity, who are known very well in the Middle Eastern classical music world, from Egypt to all around the Middle East. They weren't known as "Jewish" musicians but as *Iraqi* musicians. They were composing classical Arabic music, deriving from the *maqam*—which is a very traditional scale in Arabic music. So this phenomenon was not particularly Jewish. There just happened to be a lot of musicians who were Jewish at that time. When they left, their absence was sorely felt in the culture.

In the 1930s and 1940s, Egypt was the main generator of modern Arabic music, and many of the Iraqi musicians were really trying to emulate the Egyptian greats: Umm Kulthum, Abdel Halim Hafez, and Abdel Wahab.

My father's cassette collection spans that era. So again, that kind of devotion or commitment, was almost like a musical citizenship between people of the region. It is as if they are saying, "yes we are Jews," but we can also have a deep love of Umm Kulthum—who was actually very much against Israel. This provides a very complex picture of the transition that these people went through from leaving Iraq, and in my family's case, having to go to Israel, and leaving again to Canada and then to the U.S. They brought with them all the problematic cultural baggage that they had and it couldn't fit anywhere.

MR: And when you grew up around it and the world changed the way that it did in the 60s and the 70s, and then I think about growing up in the 80s, I knew about Iraq more or less through the food, and through my grandmother and my mother speaking Arabic in the kitchen. But then, like the night-time news of the Iran/Iraq War—or the Iraq/Iran War, depending on which side you were on—it provided an opportunity to come to terms with this identity. It was actually confusing and really horrifying being introduced to Iraq only through the green-tinted night vision of CNN cameras that captured footage of the bombs falling on Baghdad during the first Gulf War.

And I came to it, I think, from the other side of not having to leave something, and saying: "Well, the Iraq we know is in our homes," you know. But to try to figure out what that Iraq is now was a whole other matter. As much as *Dar Al Sulh* was about eroding this notion of Iraqi-Jewish or even Arab-Jewish cuisine, it provided a way of declaring ourselves as Arabs. And not just for those seven nights in Dubai, but beyond, and showing it as a complicated, thorny issue for us. This event was not only about the convivial audience with whom we shared seven nights—which was wonderful and important—but also was a way of speaking truth to power. It was a way of refusing the anti-Arab stance of the Zionist Jewish establishment.

In Dubai, the event, from the first night onward, attracted some diners who normally wouldn't have revealed that they were Jews. They heard about it through word of mouth. These mostly Ashkenazi Jews, from Europe, North America, Australia, and South Africa showed up at this temporary Iraqi-Jewish restaurant and were eager to speak about their Jewish identity. One couple shared with us stories of the difficulty of practicing Jewish rituals in a place where there are very few Jews. They mentioned how they had to "secretly smuggle in" a *mohel* from South Africa to perform a *brith*, a circumcision for their son. I don't know if you recall, but we talked about it that night, after the event. The three of us felt a certain uneasiness: we understood the difficulty of declaring being a Jew in an Arab country, especially given the history of Israel/Palestine. But we also felt that some of the statements did not acknowledge this history. Such statements in this context are naively oblivious to this history and simply put forward the common perception of Jewish persecution. But in the end, after dining side by side with so many Arabs from different countries, one of them confessed, much to my delight, that he and his family finally felt that they were part of the Dubai community because they were not withholding who they were.

RB: Yeah, that's true.

MR: For me it really echoed Ella's reconceptualization of the notion of "the Arab-Jew" as not simply an anomaly but also as something that simultaneously was and could become normative. Having Jews there also pointed exactly to the false binary of Arab-versus-Jew, as you, Ella, have written about and continue to write about.

ES: I think this binarism has been very fraught for us. We have lived and coped with all these contradictions in a situation of ongoing wars, asked to choose only one identity. I see the *Dar Al Sulh* project on a continuum with the effort to bring together multiply suppressed histories of the Middle East and of its diaspora. We see ourselves within the larger picture of this diaspora, demonstrating through food, music, and words our cultural affinity that is inextricable from the region. In some sense, the project is an act of refusal to hide our cultural belonging. I see our history as collateral damage of the question of Israel/Palestine. And we are attempting to piece together the fragments and mend broken pieces. A related Arabic word to "*ṣulḥ*," of the same root, is "*iṣlaḥ*," which refers to mending, fixing, reclaiming, retrieving, piecing together.

Figure 60 "Dar Al Sulh"—interior view

The restaurant in transit displayed a kind of a *convivencia* space that we tend to associate with Spain, but actually it also existed in the many "al Andaluses" of the Arab world. As a performance piece *Dar Al Sulh* ultimately challenges the millennial persecution narrative projected onto the experience of Jews in the Muslim world. Elsewhere, I characterized this Eurocentric historical narrative as connecting the dots from pogrom to pogrom. Recently it can be seen through the effort to *Farhudize* our history, as though the 1941 moment is emblematic of the story of Jews under Islam. Yet, in general, the emergence of the Zionist movement could itself be seen as igniting trouble for Middle Eastern Jews. And in this sense, it is not that Israel rescued us, but rather it is that we were placed in an impossible position, especially since post-48 Palestinian refugees were arriving *en masse* to the Arab world. Suddenly Iraqi Jews, Egyptian Jews, Syrian Jews had to defend a Jewishness that was associated for the first time in their history not with religion but with colonial nationalism.

At the same time, certain Arab nationalists viewed all Jews as "traitors." But the majority of Middle Eastern Jews could hardly be defined as actively Zionist or anti-Zionist. The "Arab-versus-Jew" split emerged as a new dilemma, but in any case, the ideological orientation of Zionism/anti-Zionism was mainly debated by a relatively small group of young educated Iraqi Jews. The Zionist underground effort to dislocate Jews is also crucial for our efforts to tell a different tale. And yet, one also has to hold some Arab leaders and political parties accountable for their failure to distinguish between "Jewish" and "Zionist." The broiling atmosphere in the post-48 era generated much fear and anxiety. These circumstances made our dislocation inevitable.

And so in a sense we are back to Regine's point about nostalgia and romanticism; they must be understood against the backdrop of the unusual circumstances of the dislocation itself. Since it's not a simple story of immigration, and it's also not simply a story of refugees who insist on returning, as in the case of Palestinian refugees, we have to tell our story as a complex and convoluted displacement event. We are not exactly refugees and we are not exactly immigrants, and for the most part, it is a rather anomalous cross-border movement. There was also an element in which Arab Jews crossed the border with a misleading Zionist-fueled Messianic narrative—a kind of Prophetic return to the Promised Land. But that expectation was soon met with the disappointing Israeli reality on the ground, in a country that had little to do with the religious traditions of Arab Jews.

I do believe that if it weren't for the conflict, Middle Eastern Jews would have continued to move back and forth between Baghdad and Jerusalem, between Beirut and Haifa, between Alexandria and Jaffa. They didn't necessarily need the Euro-Israeli rescue to allow them to see Zion. But once they experienced Zion in Israel, they realized that it wasn't exactly the holy place of their imagination. And that was a shock! That's why I think that our contemporary conversation, including about Middle Eastern food and music, is a form of *sulha* with our own past. We are not simply romantic nostalgics. It is about rewriting our history and writing a new pathway for the future.

So I actually think that the *Dar Al Sulh* project is very meaningful because it intervenes in the public sphere in what can be addressed, i.e. the Arab-Jew. "Nostalgia" in itself can be a very problematic notion, but in a context where certain memories are forbidden, even taboo, nostalgia is an active gesture of reclaiming exactly what has been erased, denied, elided. In Dubai, we were guests who had the opportunity to invite our hosts to an imaginary space, *Dar Al Sulh*. The Iraqi dishes, like the sounds of the *maqam* in the background, evoked the memories of the participation of Jews, Muslims and Christians in producing Iraqi culture. For me, this project is about taking an active role in reshaping the ingredients of our tale.

MR: One of the things that I really loved about being in Dubai, at that particular time, was just how much construction and destruction was around us.

RB: Yes, throughout the whole city.

MR: We had a wonderful host, Rami Farook, who is the founder and the director of Traffic Gallery, along with Nina Trojanovic, who is co-director. *Dar Al Sulh* was located in a former warehouse space that now looks like the storefronts and restaurants in that same area of Al Quoz. The history of the space was rooted in the world of industrial commerce, and then—like so many art spaces around the world—became a gallery. When it became clear that we could not open up an Iraqi-Jewish restaurant in the middle of Dubai, Traffic became a *dar al sulh* for the project. It was the domain of conciliation; it enabled this temporary restaurant's existence when it would have been impossible to do it elsewhere in the city.

I should explain the title, *Dar Al Sulh*. As I just mentioned, it means domain of conciliation and it's an agreement between conflicting parties. It was historically a treaty between Muslims and non-Muslims that provided freedom of religion, tolerance, tranquility, peace, and protection. This concept informed the way Jews lived within Muslim societies.

Outside the restaurant, there was so much construction. Specifically, there were cavernous trenches where plumbing was being rerouted, and signs that warned of DEEP EXCAVATION in Arabic and English. It was the perfect readymade caption describing the somewhat psychoanalytic process in which we were all engaged at the dinners and its accompanying conversations.

I also want to address the interior of the gallery. Because we already had the recall of old Baghdad through food, music and video, it would have been redundant to hang on the wall photos of early 20th-century Iraq, as is usually the case in commercial restaurants. I just wanted blank walls. I wanted the whole place under construction. The one image we put up on the wall was a photograph of Palestinian militiamen in 1975, during the Lebanese civil war, protecting Beirut's Maghen Abraham Synagogue from attacks. For me, this image allowed me to conjure an earlier event from 1941 that wasn't photographed, of the many Muslims and Christians who protected their Jewish neighbors during the *farhud* in Iraq. That image became a way of making those narratives and those stories present.

Figure 61   On the wall of Traffic Gallery during the performance of "Dar Al Sulh"

Further connecting that photograph to our own history as Iraqi Jews is the beautiful comment that was written by a young Palestinian scholar who attended several of our dinners. She wrote: "As a Palestinian in the diaspora, I understand that our struggles are inseparable. In the long term, our liberation will be your liberation. It is our purpose as beings in this world to reclaim the history of Mizrahi Jewry as a monumental chapter in both Arab and world history. In Solidarity and Conciliation."

There was also a purposeful reanimation of plates, which were all taken out of Iraq by the Jews who departed. Only the metal ones survived the journey because they wouldn't shatter. Two of them were the serving trays from the Great Synagogue of Baghdad. It was almost like breaking the glass of a museum vitrine and bringing those implements back to the Arab world for another meal, to actually be used the way they were intended to be used, close to the place they belonged.

Figure 62 Jewish-Iraqi trays, collected by Michael Rakowitz for the "Dar Al Sulh" event

RB: I wonder if you would say something about the people who came forward to help us cook and became part of this daily cooking family? There's a young Iraqi woman in particular who helped us tremendously from Day 1. We did not know her, but she found us through the grapevine—and she was extremely enthusiastic about the project.

MR: This young woman in her 20s just walked in and said: "I've read all about this. I've watched all your lectures on YouTube and I think you're crazy and I need to work at this restaurant." She came every day at 4 o'clock after she was done with her job and would cook with us and would be there the whole night. Her boss asked her: "What are you doing these evenings?" She said: "Oh, I'm actually helping out at this Iraqi-Jewish restaurant that's opened up temporarily here in Dubai called *Dar Al Sulh.*" Her boss took her by the arm into another room and said: "I didn't know you were Jewish." She said: "I'm not, I'm Iraqi and they are Iraqi."

ES: She told us that she had never actually met a Jew before us.

MR: She drove us home the night before the last meal. She started to kind of groan a little bit and she said: "I can't believe this is almost over. What am I going to do when you guys go back? I'm going to have to hang out with all my non-Jewish friends." And of course that's lovely and funny, but I think there's something about these links to the past that are also propositions for the future.

ES: The Iraqi exiled community is highly visible in Dubai and Sharjah, but at the same time there is a sense of an ongoing sadness and melancholy, which is ultimately about the fact that they cannot really go back to Iraq. And I think this is the point, or the intersection in which our project entered the psyche of exiled Iraqis there, which is that they also miss the Iraq of the past. They have a nostalgia for an Iraq that is gone, but not necessarily because everything was great—since none of us would be outside of Iraq if that were the case—but because of the potentialities of what Iraq could have been. They tend to compare Iraq to the U.A.E. They say: "We could have been that. We also had oil." There is a certain kind of envy, I would say. They say: "Look what the U.A.E leaders have managed to do with their oil for their own citizens, for their own welfare." That's the analogy that is being generated, especially as the situation in Iraq has become beyond disastrous. So there is a sense in which exiled Iraqis have been living, contributing, and shaping the modern Gulf states, although for the most part they cannot get citizenship, even if they spend most of their life or were born there, which exacerbates the feeling of being out of place. They live in a limbo; their relation to the nation-states of the Gulf is highly ambivalent.

Figure 63 Flying from Abu Dhabi—over Iraq—to New York, May 2013 (photo: Ella Shohat)

MR: You talk about the limbo, you know, and you talk about the ambivalence of nation-states, and the one thing that we can say I think collectively and agree upon is that if we are only aiming for some kind of acknowledgement of nation-states, then we are aiming really low. The desire really is to get rid of all these terminologies and these borders and to really speak to porousness. That was one of the great things about being in the kitchen, because people felt so much freer to disagree with one another on gastronomic levels as opposed to political. They would articulate it in the kitchen: "That's not how you do it!" But then when it comes to politics it becomes something that silences the conversation more easily.

RB: I was just thinking about some of the volunteers. The young Iraqi woman we just mentioned not only came and volunteered, but also felt deeply connected to the project. As we were preparing the meal, she came to me and said: "I've also never been to Iraq." I was wondering how that was possible; after all she grew up right next door. She's in her 20s, but she made a point to tell me, that, like us, she has never been there but also, like us, she hears about it all the time.

MR: As a gift I gave her my copy of Samir's film *Forget Baghdad*, which delineates the story of Iraqi Jews and their departure, and where Ella also appears. It was a kind of closing of a circle—a film about Iraqi Jews by a diaspora Iraqi (of Muslim and Christian backgrounds). We made present this "absent tribe," to use the language that I wrote on the glass façade of the temporary restaurant.

Concluding as a chorus: We hope that some day this project will become the ghost of itself.

دار الصلح

DOMAIN OF CONCILIATION

"You are eating a dying language
from the plate of a ghost."

Notes

All translations to the English were made by the author, unless otherwise indicated. Hebrew and Arabic transliterations of names of individuals, movements, newspapers, and places follow their common designation. Lyrics and spoken phrases are usually transliterated according to their dialectical idiom rather than to the convention of *fusha* in order to render the pronunciation "audible," as it were, to the reader.

1   Sephardim in Israel: Zionism from the Standpoint of its Jewish Victims

1. Edward Said, *Orientalism* (New York: Vintage, 1978), p. 31.
2. Arye Gelblum, *Haaretz*, April 22, 1949.
3. Ibid.
4. David Ben-Gurion, *Netzah Israel (Eternal Israel)* (Tel Aviv: Ayanot, 1964), p. 34.
5. Quoted in Sammy Smooha, *Israel: Pluralism and Conflict* (Berkeley, Calif.: University of California Press, 1978), p. 88.
6. Abba Eban, *Voice of Israel* (New York, 1957), p. 76, as quoted in Smooha.
7. Smooha (1978), p. 44.
8. Ibid., pp. 88–9.
9. Quoted in Tom Segev, *1949: The First Israelis* (New York: Free Press, 1986), pp. 156–7.
10. Quoted in Tom Segev, *1949: Ha-Israelim ha-Rishonim (1949: The First Israelis)*, (Jerusalem: Domino Press, 1984), p. 156.
11. Quotations are taken from Segev (1984), p. 157.
12. Quoted in David K. Shipler, *Arab and Jew* (New York: Times Books, 1986), p. 241.
13. Amnon Dankner, "En li Ahot" ("I Have No Sister"), *Haaretz*, February 18, 1983.
14. Dr. Devora and Rabbi Menachem Hacohen, *One People: The Story of the Eastern Jews* (New York: Adama, 1986).
15. Ora Gloria Jacob Arzooni, *The Israeli Film: Social and Cultural Influences, 1912–1973* (New York: Garland Press, 1983), pp. 22, 23, 25.
16. On the various forms of encouragements given to Yiddish in Israel, see Itzhak Koren (of the World Council for Yiddish and Jewish Culture), "Letter to the Editor," *Maariv*, December 4, 1987.
17. See Maxime Rodinson, "A Few Simple Thoughts on Anti-Semitism," in *Cult, Ghetto, and State* (London: Al-Saqi, 1983).
18. See Abbas Shiblak, *The Lure of Zion* (London: Al Saqi, 1986).
19. Yosef Meir, *Me-'Ever la-Midbar (Beyond the Desert)* (Tel Aviv: Ministry of Defence, 1973), pp. 19, 20.
20. Yehoshua Porath, *Tzmihat ha-Tnu'a ha-Leumit ha-'Arvit-Falestinait, 1919–1929 (The Emergence of the Palestinian-Arab National Movement, 1919–1929)* (Tel Aviv: Am Oved, 1976), p. 49.
21. Ibid., p. 48.
22. Ibid.
23. Ibid., pp. 48–9.
24. Ibid., p. 49.

25. See *HaOlam HaZe*, April 20, 1966; *'Iton ha-Panter ha-Shahor* (*The Black Panther*) magazine, November 9, 1972; Wilbur Crane Eveland, *Ropes of Sands: America's Failure in the Middle East* (New York: Norton, 1980), pp. 48–9; Shiblak (1986); Uri Avneri, *My Friend, the Enemy* (Westport, Conn.: Lawrence Hill, 1986), pp. 133–40.
26. Segev (1984), p. 167.
27. See "Denaturalization" and "Exodus" in Shiblak (1986), pp. 78–127.
28. Quoted in Yosef Meir, *Ha-Tnu'a ha-Tzionit ve-Yehudei Teman* [*The Zionist Movement and the Jews of Yemen*] (Tel Aviv: Afikim Library,1983), p. 43.
29. Quoted in Meir (1983), p. 48.
30. See Yaakov Zerubavel, *Alei-Haim* (Tel Aviv: Y. L. Peretz, 1960), pp. 326–7.
31. Arthur Ruppin, *Pirkei Hayai Chapters of My Life* (Tel Aviv: Am Oved, 1968), part 2, p. 27.
32. Yaakov Rabinowitz, *Ha-Poel Ha-Tzair*, July 6, 1910.
33. Shmuel Yavnieli, *Masa' le-Teman* [*A Journey to Yemen*] (Tel Aviv: Ayanot, 1963), p. 106.
34. Ibid., pp. 83–90.
35. Meir (1983), pp. 97–8.
36. Quoted in Meir (1983), p. 44.
37. See Meir (1983), particularly pp. 113–21. See also Nizta Druyan, *Be-En "Marvad Qsamim"* (*And Not with a "Magic Carpet"*) (Jerusalem: Ben-Zvi Institute for the Study of Jewish Communities in the East, 1982), pp. 134–48.
38. Meir (1983), p. 58.
39. Meir (1983), p. 65.
40. Segev (1984), pp. 171–4.
41. Quoted in Segev (1986), p. 169.
42. Quoted in Segev (1984), p. 166.
43. Segev (1984), pp. 167, 328.
44. Ibid., p. 330.
45. Ibid., p. 178.
46. See Dov Levitan, "'Aliyat 'Marvad Qsamim' ke-Hemshekh Histori le-'Aliyot mi-Teman me-Az trm"b": Nituah Socio-Politi shel 'Aliyatam u-Qlitatam shel Yehudei Teman be-Israel ba-'Et ha-Hadasha" ("The 'Magic Carpet' Aliya as a Historical Continuation of Aliyas from Yemen Since 1881: A Socio-Political Analysis of the Aliya and the Absorption of the Jews of Yemen in Israel in the Modern Era"), M.A. thesis, Political Science Department, Bar Ilan University (Israel),1983; Segev (1984), pp. 185–7, 331.
47. Segev (1984), pp. 172–3.
48. Shlomo Swirski and Menachem Shoushan, *'Ayarot Pituah be-Israel* (*Development Towns in Israel*) (Haifa: Breirot, 1986), p. 7.
49. See Swirski and Shoushan (1986).
50. For citations from some of the document see Segev (1949), particularly Part II, "Between Veterans and Newcomers," pp. 93–194.
51. Yaacov Nahon, "Dfusei Hitrahvut ha-Haskala u-Mivne Hizdamnuyot ha-Ta'asuka: ha-Memad ha-'Adati" ("Patterns of Education Expansion and the Structure of Occupation Opportunities: The Ethnic Dimension"), (Jerusalem: Jerusalem Institute for the Research of Israel, 1987).
52. Smooha (1978), pp. 178–9.
53. Shlomo Swirski, "The Oriental Jews in Israel," *Dissent*, vol. 31, no. 1 (Winter 1984), p. 84.

54. Yosef Ben David, "Integration and Development," in S. N. Eisenstadt, Rivkah Bar Yosef, and Chaim Adler (eds.), *Integration and Development in Israel* (Jerusalem: Israel Universities Press, 1970), p. 374.

55. Shlomo Swirski, *Lo Nehshalim ela Menuhshalim* (*Orientals and Ashkenazim in Israel*) (Haifa: Mahbarot le-Mehkar ule-Vikoret, 1981), pp. 53–4.

56. For a discussion of the secular European-Jewish encounter with Protestant culture see John Murray Cuddihy, *The Ordeal of Civility* (Boston, Mass.: Beacon Press, 1974).

57. See Hashem Mahameed and Yosef Gottman, "Autostereotypes and Heterostereotypes of Jews and Arabs Under Various Conditions of Contact," *Israeli Journal of Psychology and Counseling in Education* (Jerusalem: Ministry of Education and Culture), no. 16 (September 1983).

58. See a recent study, *The Sephardic Community in Israel and the Peace Process* (New York: Institute for Middle East Peace and Development, CUNY, 1986), directed by Harriet Arnone and Ammiel Alcalay.

59. Mordechai Bar-On, *Shalom 'Akhshav: Li-Dyoqna shel Tnu'a* (*Peace Now: The Portrait of a Movement*) (Tel Aviv: Hakibbutz Hameuchad, 1985), pp. 89–90.

60. Swirski (1984), pp. 89–90.

61. Segev (1984), p. 174.

62. Segev (1984), p. 161.

63. Beni Zada, "40 Shana le-Medinat ha-Ashkenazim" ("40 Years for the State of Ashkenazim"), *Pa'amon*, no. 16 (December 1987).

64. Abba Eban, for example, opposed "regarding our immigrants from Oriental countries as a bridge toward our integration with Arabic-speaking world" (Smooha, 1978, p. 88).

65. Cited from a Black Panther report on a press conference held in Paris, March 1975.

66. Quotations are taken from several speeches of the Oriental Front delivered in their meeting with the PLO in Vienna, July 1986.

4 Mizrahi Feminism: The Politics of Gender, Race, and Multiculturalism

1. See *News from Within*, vol. 10, no. 8 (August 1994).

2. I am referring here to the massive Euro-Israeli (liberal) media attack on myself, following the 1991 Hebrew publication of my book *Israeli Cinema: East/West and the Politics of Representation* (Austin, TX: University of Texas Press, 1989), translated as *Ha-Kolno'a ha-Israeli: Historia ve-Ideologia* (Tel Aviv: Breirot, 1991).

3. On the East/West complexity of the gendered Israeli national imaginary, I elaborate in *Israeli Cinema*; and in "Making the Silences Speak" in *Calling the Equality Bluff*, Barbara Swirski and Marilyn Safir (eds.), Pergamon Press, 1991.

4. A New York neighborhood with many art institutions.

5. *News from Within*, vol. 12, no. 3 (March 1996).

6. The progressive list party in 1988 tried to use the argument offered in my *Israeli Cinema* Ph.D. dissertation to have a Knesset ban on the National Theater Habimah's staging of a musical version of the well-known racist film *Sallah Shabatti* (1964) which was staged for the 40th anniversary of the state of Israel. Needless to say, the attempt did not gain a majority vote in a Knesset where the Euro-Israeli discourse is common not only to the Ashkenazi Knesset majority but also to the Mizrahi representatives.

7. See reports on the tenth conference by Miki Meltz and Orna Landaw, *Ha'ir* (June, 24, 1994), and the responses written by several Mizrahi women in the following issue, not all of which were published. During the previous year as well, hostile Orientalist representations of the conference dominated. The journalist Iris Oded was one of the few exceptions who attempted in her *Hadashot* review of the ninth women's conference to give some expression to Mizrahi women's perspective: "But those who thought that Mizrahi women only came to dance and vacation, were soon disappointed. Their presence was very strong at the conference, and their non-compromising independence caused that every subject brought for discussion—health, the female body, violence against women, sexual harassment— was at a certain point diverted to the conflict between Ashkenazi and Mizrahi women" (May 24, 1993).

5   The Invention of the Mizrahim

1. Uzi Mahnaimi and Marie Colvin, "Israel Planning Ethnic Bomb as Saddam Caves in," *Sunday Times,* November 15, 1998.
2. On this concept of a relational approach to identity, see Ella Shohat and Robert Stam, *Unthinking Eurocentrism: Multiculturalism and the Media* (London: Routledge, 1994).
3. See Shohat, 1989; and Ella Shohat, "Columbus, Palestine, and Arab Jews: Toward a Relational Approach to Community Identity," in Keith Ansell Pearson, Benita Parry, and Judith Squires (eds.), *Cultural Identity and the Gravity of History: On the Work of Edward Said* (London: Lawrence & Wishart, 1997).
4. For more on the links between European capitalism and the Zionist colonization of Palestine, see Maxime Rodinson, *Israel: A Colonial Settler State?* trans. David Thorstand (New York: Monad Press, 1973).
5. While Iraqi Jews, for example, had to give up their Iraqi passports to move to Israel, the passports of Moroccan Jews "disappeared" and were recently "discovered" in the state archives.
6. Such attacks were made, for example, on Shimon Ballas after the publication of his novel *Ve-Hu Aher [And He Is an Other]* (Tel Aviv: Zmora-Bitan, 1991), as well as on myself after the Hebrew publication of *Israeli Cinema* (Tel Aviv: Breirot, 1991).
7. For a report on this controversy, see the editorial, "Lubnan: Makhatir al Tatbi' am 'Uqdat al-Yahud?" [Lebanon: The Dangers of Normalization or the Jewish complex?]; Antwan Gharib, "Al-'Aqida al-Yahudiyya Tatadamman al-Istila' 'ala Ardina" [The Jewish Creed Includes the Takeover of Our Land]; Elias Khoury, "Al-Suhyuniyya 'Unsuriyya wa-Kadhalika al-Hamla 'Alayna" [Zionism Is Racist and So Is the Attack on Us] in *Al-Wasat,* no. 326 (April 27, 1998).
8. I hasten to add that I am in no way equating Arab and Zionist nationalism. While historically Arab nationalism was framed in the Middle East/North Africa as part of a Third World anticolonial struggle, Zionism, as I have argued elsewhere, was first formulated within Europe, within a colonial context, resulting in a complex amalgam of colonial practice and liberatory desires, carried out not in relation to the European Christian oppressors of Jews but rather, in a displaced logic, on Palestinian land and against Palestinian people.
9. For Zionist arguments in favor of bringing "Jews in the form of Arabs" to strengthen the hold on Palestine, see, e.g., Yaakov Zerubavel, *Alei-Haim [Leaves of Life]* (Tel

Aviv: Y. L. Peretz Library, 1960), and Arthur Ruppin, *Pirkei Hayai* [*Chapters of My Life*] (Tel Aviv: Am Oved, 1968).

10. Yaakov Tahon from the Eretz Israel Office was one of the first Zionists to propose, in 1908, the importation of Eastern Jews to "replace" the Arab agricultural workers. And Shmuel Yavnieli, who called for an Eastern Jewish solution for the "problem of the Arab workers," wrote in *Ha-Poel Ha-Tzair* newspaper in 1910 that "The Yemenite of today still exist at the same backward level as the *fellahin*. ... They can take the place of the Arabs." Yavnieli engineered the immigration of more than 10,000 Yemeni Jews before World War I. See his memoir, *Masa' le-Teman* [*A Journey to Yemen*] (Tel Aviv: Ayanot, 1963).

11. Both Zionist and anti-Zionist historiography fail to make the links between the Zionist settlement of Palestine and the Mizrahi question. I began to address this connection in my essay, "Sephardim in Israel: Zionism from the Standpoint of its Jewish Victims," *Social Text*, nos. 19–20 (Fall 1988), pp. 1–35. See especially the section "'Hebrew Work': Myth and Reality."

12. See *HaOlam HaZe*, April 20, 1966; *Black Panther* magazine, November 9, 1972; Abbas Shiblak, *The Lure of Zion* (London: Al-Saqi Press, 1986); and G. N. Giladi, *Discord in Zion* (London: Scorpion, 1990).

13. A number of Arab-Jewish Zionist activists came to lament that they ever set foot in Israel. Naeim Giladi, a former Zionist activist in Iraq, for example, has become an anti-Zionist activist.

14. Yehoshua Porath, *The Emergence of the Palestinian-Arab National Movement 1919–1929* (Tel Aviv: Am Oved, 1976; Hebrew), p. 49.

15. Here the phrase partly alludes to Said's "imaginative geography" in *Culture and Imperialism* (New York: Knopf, 1992).

16. The phrase "imagined communities" is borrowed from Benedict Anderson, *Imagined Communities: Reflections of the Origins and Spread of Nationalism* (London: Verso, 1983).

17. For an account of travel in the region, from the Mediterranean to the Indian Ocean, see Amitav Ghosh, *In an Antique Land* (New York: Knopf, 1992).

18. For writing that tries to perform this kind of linkage, see Shohat's "Sephardim in Israel"; *Israeli Cinema*; "Taboo Memories, Diasporic Visions," 1999; Joseph Massad, "Zionism's Internal Others: Israel and the Oriental Jews," *Journal of Palestine Studies*, vol. 25, no. 4 (Summer 1996), pp. 53–68; and *News from Within*, vol. 13, no. 1 (January 1997), which is a special issue on Mizrahim and Zionism, with articles by Shiko Behar, Zvi Ben-Dor, and Sami Shalom Chetrit (published by the Alternative Information Center, Jerusalem/Bethlehem).

7 The Trouble with Hanna

1. See "Colonialism, Racism and Representation," *Screen*, vol. 24, no. 2 (March–April 1983). Also "Slow Fade to Afro: The Black Presence in Brazilian Cinema," *Film Quarterly*, vol. 36, no. 2 (Winter 1982–83).

2. Joan Borstein, *Jerusalem Post* (International Edition), November 10–12, 1983.

3. Edward W. Said, *Orientalism* (New York: Random House, 1978).

4. George Steiner, *After Babel* (Oxford and New York: Oxford University Press, 1978), p. 470.

5. Edward Said, "Hanna K.: Palestine with a Human Face," *Village Voice*, October 11, 1983.

8 In Defense of Mordechai Vanunu: Nuclear Threat in the Middle East

1. *HaOlam HaZe*, no. 2608; August 26, 1987, p. 8.

9 Anomalies of the National: Representing Israel/Palestine

1. For a broader discussion of Orientalist discourse see Edward Said, *Orientalism* (New York: Vintage, 1978).
2. See Tzvetan Todorov, *The Conquest of America*, trans. Richard Howard (New York: Harper & Row, 1984).
3. For a fuller critical account of the history of Israeli cinema see Shohat, 1989.
4. Quoted in Meir Shnitzer, "Barabash," *Hadashot*, September 26, 1984.
5. Quoted in Brurya Avidan-Brir, "'Im kol Stira Hevanti et ha-Be'aya ha-'Arvit" ("With Each Slap I Understood the Arab Problem,") *Laisha*, September 17, 1984, p. 98.
6. On the theoretical dimensions of language and power see Ella Shohat and Robert Stam, "The Cinema After Babel: Language, Difference, Power," *Screen*, vol. 26, nos. 3–4 (May–August 1985).
7. *Wedding in Galilee*, a Franco-Belgian-Palestinian co-production, has garnered various international awards such as the Cannes Film Festival International Federation of Film Critics Award (FIPRESCI, 1987), the San Sebastian Grand Prize (Gran Concha de Oro, 1987), Best Belgian Film (1988), and the Humanism Award of the Union of Belgian Critics for 1988. Extremely successful in its opening night showing at the Cairo International Film Festival, the film was also selected to open the New Directors/New Films series in New York. Fear of official Israeli co-optation, however, led the director to refuse one honor: a screening of the film at the Israeli Jerusalem Cinematheque. The film is distributed in the U.S. by Kino International.

11 Exile, Diaspora, and Return: The Inscription of Palestine in Zionist Discourse

1. Edward Alexander, "Professor of Terror," *Commentary*, vol. 88, no. 2, 1989. See also Edward Alexander, "'Professor of Terror': An Exchange/Edward Alexander and Critics," *Commentary*, vol. 88, no. 2, 1989.
2. Alexander, "Professor of Terror," *Commentary*, vol. 88, no. 2, 1989.
3. See Sander L. Gilman, *Jewish Self-Hatred: Anti-Semitism and the Hidden Language of the Jews* (Baltimore, Md. and London: Johns Hopkins University Press, 1986).
4. Arel Ginai, Tzadok Yehezkeli, and Roni Shaked, "Ashafei ha-Tikshoret," *Yedioth Ahronoth*, February 17, 1989.
5. By using the term "Euro-Israeli," I have chosen to emphasize not simply the Ashkenazi origins but more the Eurocentric intellectual framing of Israeli hegemony, as well as its network of support in the First World.
6. See for example Maxime Rodinson, *Israel, A Colonial-Settler State?* trans. David Thorstad (New York: Monad Press, 1973).
7. See Yosef Meir, *Ha-Tnu'a ha-Tzionit ve-Yehudei Teman* [*The Zionist Movement and the Jews of Yemen*] (Tel Aviv: Sifriat Afikim, 1983); G. N. Giladi, *Discord in Zion: Conflict Between Ashkenazi and Sephardi Jews in Israel* (London: Scorpion, 1990).

8. Such anxiety about the Western identity of Jewish Israel results in public attacks on Sephardim who claim their "Easternness" as their major identity. The taboo around the Arabness of Sephardi history and culture is clearly manifested in Euro-Israeli academic and media attacks on Sephardi intellectuals who assert their Arabness, seen most vividly after the publication of Shimon Ballas's *Ve-Hu Aher [And He is an Other]* (Tel Aviv: Zmora Bitan, 1991) and my own *Ha-Kolno'a ha-Israeli: Historia ve-Ideologia [Israeli Cinema: History and Ideology]* (Tel Aviv: Breirot, 1991).

9. For more on Sephardi identity in the wake of Israel, see Shohat, "Sephardim in Israel," 1988; and Ammiel Alcalay, *After Jews and Arabs: Remaking Levantine Culture* (Minneapolis, Mn.: University of Minnesota Press, 1993).

10. *Exodus* reinforces the *sabra*/Waspish cultural and geopolitical links. The casting of a virtually archetypical Anglo-American star, Paul Newman, in the role of the *sabra* undoes the largely negative connotations of the stereotypes of the Jew within the Western-Christian popular mind and equates him with the desired hero of American dreams. Newman embodies the virility of both *sabra* soldier and the American fighter, merging both into one myth, reinforced and paralleled by the close political and cultural Israeli–American links since the 1960s. The film suggests that the Israeli experience has "normalized" the Jew, so that now even the English anti-Semitic officer cannot spot him. The *sabra*-Wasp link is further reinforced on a linguistic level. While the weak Jewish immigrants to Israel generally speak Yiddish-accented English, the *sabra* hero and his heroine sister speak with the hegemonic American accent.

11. Although Mark Krupnick (in "Edward Said: Discourse and Palestinian Rage," *Tikkun*, vol. 4, no. 6, 1989, p. 23) acknowledges Palestinian national rights, he argues that Palestinian national culture, when compared with Zionism, lacks narratives and symbols. He even goes so far as to suggest that "Said's rage ... derives in part from his perception that the stories of his people have tended to be imitations of Jewish stories."

12. Edward Said, "Zionism from the Standpoint of its Victims," *Social Text*, vol. 1 (1979) and *Blaming the Victims: Spurious Scholarship and the Palestinian Question* (London and New York: Verso, 1988).

13. See also the debate in Said, "An Exchange on Edward Said and Difference," *Critical Inquiry*, no. 15, Spring 1989.

14. Arab Americans in Western media, it must be pointed out, have now begun to also use the rhetoric of "we."

15. See Shohat, "Sephardim in Israel," 1988.

16. Ronald Aronson, "Never Again? Zionism and the Holocaust," *Social Text*, vol. 3, Fall 1980.

17. For further discussion of gendered metaphors and colonial discourse, see my "Imaging Terra Incognita: The Disciplinary Gaze of Empire," *Public Culture*, vol. 3.

14   In Memory of Edward Said, the Bulletproof Intellectual

1. Edward W. Said, "Identity, Authority, and Freedom: The Potentate and the Traveler," *boundary 2*, vol. 21, no. 3 (1994), pp. 1–18.

2. Edward W. Said, "Between Worlds, "*London Review of Books*, vol. 7, May 1998, pp. 3–7.

3. Edward W. Said, "Zionism from the Standpoint of its Victims," *Social Text*, vol. 1, no. 1 (1979), pp. 7–58; *The Question of Palestine* (London: Routledge & Kegan Paul, 1980).

4. Ronald Aronson, "Never Again? Zionism and the Holocaust," *Social Text*, vol. 3, no. 3 (1980), pp. 60–1.

5. Bruce Robbins, "American Intellectuals and the Middle East Politics: Interview with Edward Said," *Social Text*, vol. 19–20 (1988), pp. 37–53. The opening essay, meanwhile, took off, as it were, from the journal's inaugural issue, alluding to Said's earlier contribution ("Zionism from the Standpoint of its Victims"): Shohat, "Sephardim in Israel," 1988.

6. Edward W. Said, *Orientalism* (New York: Random House, 1978).

7. My critique here is taken from Shohat, "Postcolonial in Translation: Reading Said between English and Hebrew," in *Taboo Memories, Diasporic Voices* (Durham, N.C.: Duke University Press, 2006).

8. Said (1979), p. 7.

16   Egypt: Cinema and Revolution

1. Hala Salmane, Simon Hartog, and David Wilson (eds.), *Algerian Cinema* (London: British Film Institute, 1976).

2. One of the most famous films critical of Nasser's regime was *The Bullet is Still in My Pocket* (1973), scripted by Ihsan Abdel Quddous and directed by Houssam el-Din Mustafa. A hero of the October War, after carrying out his duty successfully on the Canal Front, saves one bullet for the enemy at home: the man who raped his girlfriend and whom the film associates with the Arab Socialist Union.

3. Georges Sadoul, *The Cinema in the Arab Countries* (Paris: UNESCO, 1966); and specifically Galal Al-Sharkawi, "History of the UAR Cinema," p. 89.

4. Paradoxically, this Egyptian historical film was directed by a man who knew no Arabic, the German Fritz Kramp.

5. The cinema was mainly an urban medium and the *fellahin* (peasants) who formed about 65 percent of the population had little access to it.

6. Albert Memmi, *The Colonizer and the Colonized* (Boston, Mass.: Beacon Press, 1967), p. 120.

7. Gamal Abdel Nasser, *The Philosophy of the Revolution* (Cairo: GO Printing Offices, 1954).

8. Frantz Fanon, *The Wretched of the Earth* (New York: Grove Press, 1968), p. 238.

9. As G. Chaliand notes in *Revolution in the Third World* (rev. edn., London: Penguin, 1989), the Free Officers saw modernization essentially as a matter of technology, for unlike their Chinese, North Vietnamese, and Cuban counterparts, they were socially and culturally conservative, and despite occasional lip-service to "socialism," the 1952 revolution rejected class struggle or any profound social upheaval.

10. Fanon (1968), pp. 209–10.

11. Memmi (1967), pp. 102–3.

12. Fanon (1968), pp. 244–5.

17   Gender in Hollywood's Orient

1. Although American and European films share a similar Orientalist representation, my examples will be drawn largely from Hollywood. The Orientalist films

437

can be tentatively grouped into seven subgenres: 1) films concerning contemporary Westerners in the Orient: *The Sheik* (1921), *The Road to Morocco* (1942), *Casablanca* (1942), *The Man Who Knew Too Much* (1956), *Indiana Jones* (1981), *Sahara* (1983), *Ishtar* (1987); 2) films concerning "Orientals" in the first world: *Black Sunday, Back to the Future* (1985); 3) films based on ancient history, such as the diverse versions of *Cleopatra*; 4) films based on contemporary history: *Exodus* (1960), *Lawrence of Arabia* (1962); 5) films based on the *Arabian Nights*: *The Thief of Baghdad* (1924), *Oriental Dream* (1944), *Ali Baba and the Forty Thieves* (1944), *Kismet* (1955); 6) films based on the Bible: *Samson and Delilah* (1949), *The Ten Commandments* (1956); 7) films in which ancient Egypt and its mythologized enigmas serve as pretext for contemporary horror, mystery, and romance (the *Mummy* films).

2. Already in the silent era, films such as *The Dance of Fatima, The Sheik,* and *Son of the Sheik* (1926) included eroticized dances, featuring a rather improbable melange of Spanish and Indian dances combined with a touch of Arabian belly dancing. And even in *Lawrence of Arabia*, presumably sympathetic to the Arabs, we generally hear almost no Arabic, but rather English spoken in a motley of accents having little to do with Arabic.

3. See for example Laurence Michalak, "Cruel and Unusual," a special issue from the American-Arab Anti-Discrimination Committee, no. 19 (January 1988); and Jack Shaheen, *The TV Arab* (Bowling Green, Oh.: Bowling Green State University Popular Press, 1984).

4. See Edward W. Said, *Orientalism* (New York: Vintage, 1978), p. 31. "Gender Metaphors: Hollywood's Orientalist Imaginary" was the topic of my paper presented at the Middle East Studies Association Conference, University of California, Los Angeles, October 1988.

5. The Motion Picture Producers and Distributors of America, or the Hays Office, was established in 1922 but it was largely in the 1930s that it established strict "moral" regulations.

6. There is also a subtext of "camp" fantasy. The exotic space of the Orient in these films gives an outlet for a carnivalesque play of changing ethnic, national, and at times gender identities. Isabelle Adjani in *Ishtar* is dressed as an Arab male rebel. Brooke Shields is an American male racer in the Sahara desert. Rudolph Valentino (*The Sheik*), Elvis Presley (*Harum Scarum*), Peter O'Toole (*Lawrence of Arabia*), Warren Beatty and Dustin Hoffman (*Ishtar*) wear Arab disguise.

7. *Movie Weekly*, November 19, 1921.

18 The Media's War

1. Dov Zakheim, "Is the Vietnam Syndrome Dead? Happily, It's Buried in the Gulf," *New York Times*, March 4, 1991.

20 The Cinema of Displacement: Gender, Nation, and Diaspora

1. Lyotard, despite his skepticism about "metanarratives," endorsed the Persian Gulf War in 1990 in a collective manifesto published in *Libération*, thus endorsing Bush's metanarrative of a "New World Order."

2. I am proposing here the term "post-Third Worldist" to point to a move beyond the ideology of Third Worldism. Whereas the term "postcolonial" implies going beyond anticolonial nationalist theory and a movement beyond a specific point

in history, post-Third Worldism emphasizes "beyond" a certain ideology—Third World nationalism. See Ella Shohat, "Notes on the 'Post-Colonial,'" *Social Text*, vols. 31–2 (Spring 1992).

3. For more on the debate on "location" see e.g. Chandra Talpade Mohanty, "Feminist Encounters: Locating the Politics of Experience," *Copyright*, no. 1 (Fall 1987), p. 31; Michele Wallace, "The Politics of Location: Cinema/Theory/Literature/Ethnicity/Sexuality/Me," *Framework*, vol. 36 (1989), p. 53; Lata Mani, "Multiple Mediations: Feminist Scholarship in the Age of Multinational Reception," *Inscriptions*, vol. 5 (1989), p. 4; Inderpal Grewal, "Autobiographic Subjects and Diasporic Locations: *Meatless Days* and Borderlands," and Caren Kaplan, "The Politics of Location as Transnational Feminist Practice," both in Inderpal Grewal and Caren Kaplan, *Scattered Hegemonies: Postmodernity and Transnational Feminist Practice* (Minneapolis, Mn.: University of Minnesota Press, 1994).

4. See J. M. Blaut, *The Colonizer's Model of the World: Geographical Diffusionism and Eurocentric History* (New York and London: Guilford Press, 1993).

5. Chahine portrays Egyptian Jews positively, as connected to the socialists fighting for an equal and just Egyptian society, forced to evacuate Egypt fearing the Nazis' arrival, and thus migrating to Palestine/Israel. Here the film structures point-of-view so that the Egyptian Jew views the clashes between Israelis and Palestinians together with Arabs from the Arab point of view; realizing that the rights of one people are obtained at the expense of another people, he returns to Egypt. The film thus distinguishes between Arab (Sephardi) Jews and European Jews, a distinction reinforced at the end of the film through the protagonist's arrival in the U.S. and his encounter with Ashkenazi Hassidim, implicitly suggesting the distance between his Jewish-Egyptian friends (with whom he shares a similar culture) and European Jews. Such a representation, however, is rather rare in Arab fiction, resulting in the banning of the film by several Arab countries, even though it was approved by Palestinian organizations.

6. The critique of the U.S. must be seen in a context when Sadat was beginning his diplomatic negotiation with Israel, an act that was extremely unpopular in Egypt and the Arab world.

7. See Aijaz Ahmad, "Jameson's Rhetoric of Otherness and the National Allegory," *Social Text*, no. 17 (Fall 1987), pp. 3–25; and Julianne Burton, "Marginal Cinemas," *Screen*, vol. 26, nos. 3–4 (May–August 1985).

8. See Benedict Anderson, *Imagined Communities: Reflections on the Origins and Spread of Nationalism* (London: Verso, 1983); and E. J. Hobsbawm and Terence Ranger (eds.), *The Invention of Tradition* (Cambridge: Cambridge University Press, 1983).

9. Pontecorvo recently (1991) returned to Algiers to make *Gillo Pontecorvo Returns to Algiers*, a film about the evolution of Algeria during the 25 years elapsed since *The Battle of Algiers* was filmed, and focusing on topics such as fundamentalism, the subordinate status of women, and the veil.

10. Anne McClintock, "No Longer in a Future Heaven: Women and Nationalism in South Africa," *Transition*, no. 51 (1991), p. 120.

11. For more on this issue see Ella Shohat, "Wedding in Galilee," *Middle East Report*, no. 154 (Sept./Oct. 1988).

12. See Fatima Mernissi, *The Forgotten Queens of Islam*, trans. Mary Jo Lakeland (Minneapolis, Mn.: University of Minnesota Press, 1993).

13. Caren Kaplan, "Deterritorializations: The Rewriting of Home and Exile in Western Feminist Discourse," *Cultural Critique*, no. 6 (Spring 1987), p. 198.

14. The friend in question is Ella Habiba Shohat. The letter in the film is based on my essays, "Sephardim in Israel," 1988; and "Dislocated Identities: Reflections of an Arab Jew," *Movement Research*, no. 5 (Fall/Winter 1992).
15. I further elaborate on the subject in "Gender and the Culture of Empire: Toward a Feminist Ethnography of the Cinema," *Quarterly Review of Film and Video*, no. 131 (Spring 1991); and in Shohat and Stam,1994.
16. Or as the letter puts it: "This bloody war takes my daughters to the four corners of the world." The reference to the dispersion of family, as metonym and metaphor for the displacement of a people, is particularly ironic given that Zionist discourse itself has often imaged its own exiles from the four corners of the globe.
17. *Measure of Distance* in this sense goes against the tendency criticized by Hamid Naficy that turns nostalgia into a ritualized denial of history. See "The Poetics and Practice of Iranian Nostalgia in Exile," *Diaspora*, no. 3 (1992).

23 Postscript to Frantz Fanon's The Wretched of the Earth

1. Bavel Publishers, Tel Aviv, 2006.
2. This essay is a translation from the Hebrew postscript to Frantz Fanon's *Les Damnés de la Terre* [*The Wretched of the Earth*] (Bavel, 2006). My text here is based on my work on Fanon over the past two decades, discussed in *Taboo Memories, Diasporic Voices*, 2006.
3. F. Fanon, *The Wretched of the Earth* (New York: Grove Press, 1963), p. 96.
4. See J. Derrida, "Structure, Sign and Play in the Discourse of the Human Sciences," in *Writing and Difference*, trans. Alan Bass (Chicago, Ill.: University of Chicago Press, 1978), pp. 278–94. I owe this point to Robert Stam who also deals with the intellectual anticipations in Fanon's text: see Stam's "Fanon, Algeria, and the Cinema: The Politics of Identification," in Shohat and Stam (eds.), *Multiculturalism, Postcolonialism, and Transnational Media* (New Brunswick, N.J.: Rutgers University Press, 2003).
5. F. Fanon, *Black Skin, White Masks* (New York: Grove Press, 1967), p. 211. (First published in French in 1952.)
6. L. S. Sénghor (ed.), *Anthologie de la Nouvelle Poésie Nègre et Malgache de Language Française* (Paris: Presses Universitaires de France, 1948).
7. J.-P. Sartre, *Anti-Semite and Jew* (New York: Shocken, 1976), p. 143.
8. Fanon (1967), p. 93.
9. Ibid., p. 14.
10. Ibid., p. 135.
11. Ibid., pp. 160–5.
12. Fanon, *Toward the African Revolution* (New York: Grove Press, 1967), p. 29.
13. Ibid., p. 122.
14. Ibid., p. 10.
15. Ibid., p. 201.
16. Ibid., p. 103.
17. Ibid., p. 103.
18. Ibid., p. 103.
19. Fanon, *A Dying Colonialism* (New York: Grove Press, 1967), p. 155.
20. Ibid., p. 157.
21. Ibid., p. 82.
22. Ibid., p. 7.

23. Ibid., p. 77.
24. Ibid., p. 311.
25. Ibid., p. 197.
26. Ibid., p. 186.
27. Ibid., p. 60.
28. H. Ghania, "Fanon–Blida. Blida–Fanon," in *Revolution Africaine*, December 11, 1987, p. 14.
29. F. Fanon and J. Azoulay. "La Sociotherapie dans un Service d'Hommes Musulmans," *L'Information Psychiatrique*, vol. 30, 1954, pp. 349–61 (reprinted in vol. 51, 1975).
30. I have in mind especially Shlomo Swirski's significant contribution, *Lo Nehshalim, ela Menuhshalim* (Haifa: Mahbarot le-Mehkar ule-Vikoret, 1981).
31. "Putting Zionism on the psychoanalyst's couch" was actually a phrase I used in an interview that typically generated violent attacks in its wake during a period in which critical Mizrahim had hardly any hearing in the Israeli media. See interview with Dalia Karpel, *Ha'ir*, no. 472, 1989.
32. Fanon (1967), p. 223.
33. Ibid., p. 209.
34. Ibid., p. 209.
35. Fanon was not a black nationalist, although he sometimes was perceived as one by the major figures of the Black Power movement in the U.S. (for example by Stokely Carmichael and Eldridge Cleaver). Here one must also note that while the Afrocentric stream tends to focus on Ancient Egypt as the birthplace of black African culture, earlier movements such as the Rastafarian Pan-Africanism dialogued with the Zionist movement. Zionism offered a philosophical and organizational model for widely different activists and writers, like the American W. E. B. Du Bois, author of *The Souls of Black Folk*, and the Jamaican Marcus Garvey, leader of "Black Zionism," who coined the slogan "back to Africa."
36. Fanon (1967), p. 226.
37. G. W. F. Hegel wrote that, "Africa … has no movement or development to exhibit … what we properly understand by Africa, is the Unhistorical, Undeveloped, Spirit still involved in the conditions of mere nature" (*The Philosophy of History*, trans. J. Sibree, New York: Dover, 1956), p. 99.
38. Fanon (1967), p. 218.
39. Ibid., p. 232.
40. Ibid., pp. 312, 315–16.
41. Two key works that unearth Diderot's often hidden contributions to these debates are Y. Benot, *De l'Athéisme à l'Anti-Colonialisme* [*From Atheism to Anti-Colonialism*] (Paris: Parution, 1970) and M. Duchet, *Diderot et les Histoires des Deux Indes, ou l'Ecriture Fragmentaire*, Paris: Nizet, 1978).
42. Robert Stam and I elaborate on this point in the section "Antinomies of Enlightenment and Progress," in our 1994 book.
43. On the "total revolution," see Fanon (1967).
44. P. Rojhilat, "Eppur Si Muove" (Galileo Galilei), www.xs4all.nl/-tank/kurdish/litdocs/lib/besikci.html
45. J. Keppel, *Jihad: The Trial of Political Islam* (Cambridge, Mass.: Harvard University Press, 2002). See also Ali Shariati's account of his discussion with Fanon concerning their difference about religion, "Where Shall We Begin?" www.iranchamber.com/personalities/ashariati/works/where_shall_we_begin.php
46. I. L. Gendzier, *Frantz Fanon: A Critical Study* (New York: Vintage, 1974), p. 266.

47. G. Chaliand, *La Résistance Palestinienne* [*The Palestinian Resistance*] (Paris: Editions de Seuil, 1970), p. 11.
48. A. Iyad, *Palestinien sans Patrie, Entretiens avec Eric Rouleau* (Paris: Fayolle, 1978), trans. into Hebrew as *Le-Lo Moledet: Sihot 'im Eric Rouleau* by N. Peled with an introduction by M. Peled (Tel Aviv: Mifras, 1979). p. 65.
49. See P. Geismar, *Frantz Fanon* (New York: New Dial Press, 1971), pp. 139–40.
50. D. Macey, *Frantz Fanon: A Biography* (New York: Picador, 2000), pp. 467–8.
51. S. de Beauvoir, *La Force des Choses*, vol. 2 (Paris: Livre de Poche, 1971), p. 243.
52. Macey (2000), pp. 467–8.
53. I elaborated on the Zionist schizophrenic discourse in such texts as "Master Narrative/Counter Readings," in Robert Sklar and Charles Musser (eds.), *Resisting Images: Essays on Cinema and History* (Philadelphia, Pa.: Temple University Press, 1990); "Taboo Memories, Diasporic Visions: Columbus, Palestine and Arab Jews" in May Joseph and Jennifer Fink (eds.), *Performing Hybridity* (Minneapolis, Minn.: University of Minnesota Press, 1999).
54. See Arye Gelblum, "Hodesh Yamim Hayiti 'Ole Hadash" ("For a Month, I was a New Immigrant,") *Haaretz*, April 22, 1949; or the work of Hebrew University scholars such as Karl Frankenstein, whose discourse I discussed partly within a Fanonian perspective in "Sephardim in Israel," 1988.
55. Albert Memmi's books appeared in Hebrew in the following order: *Pillar of Salt* (Tel Aviv: Am Oved, 1960); *Jews and Arabs* (Tel Aviv: Sifriat HaPoalim, 1975), *The Liberation of the Jew* (Tel Aviv: Am Oved, 1976) and *Racism* (Jerusalem: Karmel, 1999). With the signing of this postscript, Memmi's book *The Colonizer and the Colonized* was published (Jerusalem: Karmel and Van Lear, 2005). This celebratory moment, however, cannot conceal the decades-long lack of interest, or sheer avoidance of dialogue with anti-colonial literature; and we must name this absence.
56. See Shohat, "Notes on the 'Post-colonial'," 1992 (in Hebrew, *Zichronot Asurim*, 2001). For a re-examination of the reception of postcolonial theory in Israel, see also "The 'Postcolonial' in Translation: Reading Said in Hebrew," *Journal of Palestine Studies*, vol. 33, no. 3, 2004, pp. 55–75.
57. Fanon (1963), p. 132.

24 On the Margins of Middle Eastern Studies: Situating Said's Orientalism

1. Edward W. Said, *Orientalism* (New York: Random House, 1978).
2. Edward W. Said, *Culture and Imperialism* (New York: Vintage, 1993).
3. João Feres, Jr., *A História do Conceito de "Latin America" nos Estados Unidos* (São Paulo: Edusc, 2005).
4. Feres (2005), p. 129.
5. Samuel P. Huntington, *The Clash of Civilizations and the Remaking of World Order* (New York: Simon & Schuster, 1996); *Who Are We? The Challenges to National Identity* (New York: Simon & Schuster, 2004).
6. See Walter D. Mignolo, *The Idea of Latin America* (Malden, Mass.: Blackwell, 2005); in our 1994 book, Robert Stam and I advanced a parallel critique of postcolonial theory, which focused on the "colonial" as beginning with the heights of the 19th-century imperial expansionism, of British and French imperialism, while tending to ignore 1492.
7. Ian Buruma and Avishai Margalit, *Occidentalism: A Short History of AntiWesternism* (London: Atlantic, 2004). See also James Carrier, *Occidentalism: Images of the West* (Oxford: Clarendon Press, 1995).

8. Amal Amireh and Liza Suhair Majaj (eds.), *Going Global* (New York: Garland, 2000); Minoo Moallem, *Between Warrior Brother and Veiled Sister* (Berkeley, Calif.: University of California Press, 2005); Shouleh Vatanabadi and Mohammad Mehdi Khorrami (eds), *Another Sea, Another Shore* (Northampton, Mass.: Interlink, 2004).

25 Rethinking Jews and Muslims: Quincentennial Reflections

1. Quoted in Jean Comby, "1492: Le Choc des Cultures et l'Evangelization du Monde," *Dossiers de l'épiscopat Français*, no. 14 (October 1990).
2. See Charles Duff, *The Truth about Columbus* (New York: Random House, 1936).
3. See Jean Delumeau, *La Peur en Occident* (Paris: Fayard, 1978) and *Le Peche et la Peur* (Paris: Fayard, 1983). See also Joshua Trachtenberg, *The Devil and the Jews: The Medieval Conception of the Jew and its Relation to Modern Anti-Semitism* (New York: Harpers, 1943). Jan Pieterse makes the more general point that the theme of civilization against barbarism was a carryover from Greek and Roman antiquity, while the theme of Christianity against pagans was the keynote of European expansion culminating in the Crusades. The Christian theme of "mission" was subsequently used with "civilization," as in the mission civilisatrice. See Jan Pieterse, *Empire and Emancipation* (London: Pluto, 1990), p. 240.
4. See Jan Carew, *Fulcrums of Change: Origins of Racism in the Americas and Other Essays* (Trenton, N.J.: Africa World Press, 1988).
5. Captain John Smith, Map of Virginia (1612), quoted in Roy Harvey Pearce, *Savagism and Civilization: A Study of the Indian and the American Mind* (Berkeley, Calif.: University of California Press,1988).
6. See Delumeau. As late as the 16th century, Martin Luther expressed his strong belief that the Turks against which Christians were struggling were not "flesh and blood beings" but rather "an army of devils" against whom only "angels" could be efficacious, using a God-is-on-our-side rhetoric subsequently invoked in diverse colonial and neocolonial military venues, most recently during the Persian Gulf War.
7. See for example W. Montgomery Watt and Pierre Cachia, *A History of Islamic Spain* (Edinburgh: Edinburgh University Press, 1977); James T. Monroe, *Hispano-Arabic Poetry* (Berkeley, Calif.: University of California Press, 1974).
8. For the analogies between Nazis and Arabs in Zionist discourse see Shohat, 1989, and "The Media's War," *Social Text*, vol. 28 (Spring 1991).
9. For such complex analysis see Ilan Halevi, *A History of the Jews: Ancient and Modern* (London: Zed Books, 1987); and Maxime Rodinson, *Cult, Ghetto, and State: The Persistence of the Jewish Question* (London: Al-Saqi, 1983).
10. For more see Abbas Shiblak, *The Lure of Zion: The Case of the Iraqi Jew* (London: Al-Saqi, 1986); G. N. Giladi, *Discord in Zion: Conflict Between Ashkenazi and Sephardi Jews in Israel* (London: Scorpion, 1990); and Ella Shohat, "Sephardim in Israel," 1988.

26 "Coming to America": Reflections on Hair and Memory Loss

1. Gustave Flaubert, *Herodias* (New York: G. P. Putnam & Sons, 1903) (trans. from *Trois Contes: Un Coeur Simple; La Legende de Saint-Julien l'Hospitalier; Herodias* (Paris: G. Charpentier, 1877)).

2. See Alixa Naff, "The Early Arab Immigrant Experience," in Ernest McCarus (ed.), *The Development of Arab-American Identity* (Ann Arbor, Mich.: University of Michigan Press, 1994), p. 26.
3. Meena Alexander, *The Shock of Arrival* (Boston, Mass.: South End Press, 1996).
4. See May Joseph, "Transatlantic Inscriptions," in Ella Shohat (ed.), *Talking Visions: Multicultural Feminism in a Transnational Age* (Cambridge, Mass.: MIT Press and New Museum, 1998), pp. 357–90.
5. See my article, "Taboo Memories, Diasporic Visions: Columbus, Palestine and Arab Jews," 1999.
6. I have in mind the works, for example, of Ayoka Chenzira, Kobena Mercer, Lisa Jones, and Lorna Simpson.
7. See, for example, Raymond William Stedman, *The Shadows of the Indian* (Norman, Okla.: University of Oklahoma Press, 1971); James Axtell, *The European and the Indian* (Oxford: Oxford University Press, 1981).
8. The discussion here of the non-finalized American Nation is based in part on "Ethnicities in Relation" in Robert Stam's and my co-written 1994 book (ch. 6, pp. 220–47). I thank Margo Machida and May Joseph for inviting me to serve as a final commentator on "New Hybridities: Immigration and Asian Arts" at New York University, June 1995, where I presented some of this material. I also thank Inderpal Grewal for sharing with me her work in progress, *Umrika*, which makes parallel arguments.

27 Diasporic Thinking: Between Babel and Babylon

1. Shohat, 1989.
2. See the chapter "Post-Fanon and the Colonial: A Situational Diagnosis," in *Taboo Memories, Diasporic Voices*, 2006.
3. Pierre Bourdieu and Loïc Wacquant, "La nouvelle vulgate planétaire," in *Le Monde Diplomatique*, May 2000, pp 6–7, http://www.monde-diplomatique.fr/2000/05/BOURDIEU/13727.
4. Pierre Bourdieu and Loïc Wacquant, "On the Cunning of Imperial Reason," in *Theory, Culture & Society*, vol. 16, no. 1 (1999), pp. 41–58.
5. Jean-Claude Carrière, *The Controversy of Valladolid*. English version by Richard Nelson. New York: Dramatist's Play Service 2005.

28 Arab Jews, Diasporas, and Multicultural Feminism

1. See e.g. Ella Shohat, "Rupture and Return: Zionist Discourse and the Study of Arab-Jews," *Social Text*, vol. 21, no. 2 (2003). Also included in Shohat, *Taboo Memories, Diasporic Voices*, 2006.
2. See e.g. Ella Shohat, "The Narrative of the Nation and the Discourse of Modernization: The Case of the Mizrahim," *Critique*, no. 10 (Spring 1997), pp. 3–38; and "Master Narrative/Counter Readings," in Robert Sklar and Charles Musser (eds.), *Resisting Images: Essays on Cinema and History* (Philadelphia, Pa.: Temple University Press, 1990), pp. 251–78.
3. On such analogies, see Ella Shohat, "Staging the Quincentenary: The Middle East and the Americas," *Third Text*, no. 21 (Winter 1992–93), pp. 95–105; and "Taboo Memories, Diasporic Visions," in May Joseph and Jennifer Fink (eds.), *Performing*

Hybridity (Minneapolis, Mn.: University of Minnesota Press, 1999), pp. 131–56. Also included in Shohat, *Taboo Memories, Diasporic Voices*, 2006.

4. For more on this topic, see Shohat, "The 'Postcolonial' in Translation: Reading Said in Hebrew," 2004. Also included in Shohat, *Taboo Memories, Diasporic Voices*, 2006.

5. Shohat, "Gender and the Culture of Empire," 1991; and "Imaging Terra Incognita: The Disciplinary Gaze of Empire," *Public Culture*, vol. 3, no. 2 (1991), pp. 41–70.

6. Ella Shohat and Robert Stam, "Traveling Multiculturalism: A Trinational Debate in Translation," in A. Loomba et al. (eds.), *Postcolonial Studies and Beyond* (Durham, N.C.: Duke University Press, 2005), pp. 293–316; and *Culture Wars in Translation* (published as *Race in Translation*), 2012.

29   *Forget Baghdad: Arabs and Jews – the Iraqi Connection*

1. Arabic for "inside," here referring to the Palestinians and Palestinian territory within the Israeli state, i.e. within those Israeli borders established in 1948.

Index

About the Book

Ella Shohat's seminal writing on the Middle East has since the 1980s been generating groundbreaking critical grids and conceptual frameworks. Collected now in a single volume, *On the Arab-Jew, Palestine, and other Displacements* gathers together some of her most influential essays, interviews, speeches, testimonies, and memoir-pieces, along with a few previously unpublished texts. A key thread in the book engages the intimate and interlocking relationships between "the question of Palestine" and "the question of the Arab-Jew." Defying the binarist Arab-versus-Jew rendering of the Israeli/Palestinian conflict, Shohat's work has dared to engage the undergirding issues swirling around Orientalism, colonialism, nationalism, and Zionism. Like the inter-communally shared space of historical Palestine, the Arab-Jew here is a reminder/remainder of the variegated multiplicity of Arab cultural geographies. Both "Palestine" and "the Arab-Jew" in this sense form not only tropes of loss but also figures for visionary cross-border possibilities

Organized thematically, the book is composed of four sections: "The Question of the Arab-Jew;" "Between Palestine and Israel;" "Cultural Politics of the Middle East;" and "Muslims, Jews, and Diasporic Readings." Despite their different emphases, the sections resonate with related inquiries. They unpack such fraught issues as: the anomalies of the national/colonial in Zionist discourse; the narrativization of Jewish pasts in Muslim spaces; the relationalities connecting *Nakba* dispossession and *Tasqit* dislocation; the traumatic scars of partition; the critical resignifications of "exile," "diaspora," and "return;" the links between the *Reconquista* and the *Conquista*; the "invention of the Mizrahim" within the larger invention of "the Jewish nation;" transgressive intersectionality in Mizrahi feminism; colonial gendered tropes and the return-of-the-gaze; Arab revolutionary discourses and the formation of national and postnational cinemas; the transnational reception of Said's *Orientalism* in the academe; the postcolonial politics of translating Fanon; the echoes within Islamophobia of the anti-Semitic imaginary; Arab-American intellectuals facing Orientalism and anti-Americanism; the emotional cartography of Baghdad; the fecund possibilities of the concept of the Arab-Jew; and the imaginative potentialities of a latter-day *convivencia* for Israel/Palestine, Iraq, and the region as a whole.

Shohat's formulations have formed part of her ongoing contribution to the decolonization of knowledge and culture. More specifically, the author's reconceptualizations have helped shape the emerging critical field of Arab-Jewish/Mizrahi studies. Her transdisciplinary approach highlights the cultural politics in and around "the Middle East" while also revealing the substratal interconnectedness of usually segregated geographies (for example those of the Arab world and the Americas). The concepts of "the diasporic" and "displacement" here offer a prism through which to view nation-states in terms of their own expulsions, repressions, and denegations. But rather than merely a demographic descriptive of movements across regions, "displacement" becomes a method of reading that "unsettles" an all-too-settled political landscape. Juxtaposing

463

texts of various styles and genres, the book's diasporic perspective touches on a cultural spectrum that includes the cinema/media, music, literature, language, archeology, cuisine, and the visual arts. *On the Arab-Jew, Palestine, and other Displacements* offers the reader a vivid sense not only of the author's intellectual trajectory but also of the history of an ongoing passionate debate.

About the Author

Ella Shohat is Professor of Cultural Studies at the departments of Art & Public Policy and Middle Eastern & Islamic Studies at New York University. Over the past decades, she has lectured and written extensively on issues having to do with Eurocentrism, Orientalism, Postcolonialism, transnationalism, and diasporic cultures. More specifically, in a series of publications, Shohat has developed critical approaches to the study of the Arab-Jew. Her books include: *Taboo Memories, Diasporic Voices* (2006); *Israeli Cinema: East/West and the Politics of Representation* (1989; Updated Second Edition with a new postscript chapter in 2010); *Le sionisme du point de vue de ses victimes juives: les juifs orientaux en Israel* (2006); *Talking Visions: Multicultural Feminism in a Transnational Age* (1998); *Dangerous Liaisons: Gender, Nation and Postcolonial Perspectives* (coedited with Anne McClintock and Aamir Mufti, 1997); *Between the Middle East and the Americas: The Cultural Politics of Diaspora* (coedited with Evelyn Alsultany, 2013, Arab-American Book Award's Honorable Mention, The Arab-American Museum); and with Robert Stam, *Unthinking Eurocentrism* (the Katherine Kovacs Singer Best Book Award, 1994; 20th Anniversary Edition with a new Afterword chapter, 2014); *Multiculturalism, Postcoloniality and Transnational Media* (2003); *Flagging Patriotism: Crises of Narcissism and Anti-Americanism* (2007); and *Race in Translation: Culture Wars Around the Postcolonial Atlantic* (2012).

Shohat coedited a number of special issues for the journal *Social Text*, including "Palestine in a Transnational Context," "Edward Said: A Memorial Issue," and "911-A Public Emergency?" Her writing has been translated into diverse languages, including: Arabic, Hebrew, French, Spanish, Portuguese, German, Polish, Turkish, and Italian. She has also served on the editorial board of several journals, including: *Social Text*; *Middle East Critique*; *Interventions: International Journal of Postcolonial Studies*; and *Middle East Journal of Culture and Communication*. Shohat is a recipient of such fellowships as Rockefeller and the Society for the Humanities at Cornell University, where she also taught at The School of Criticism and Theory. Together with Sinan Antoon, Shohat was awarded the NYU Humanities Initiative fellowship for their "Narrating Iraq: Between Nation and Diaspora." She was also awarded a Fulbright research/lectureship at the University of São Paulo, Brazil, for studying the cultural intersections between the Middle East and Latin America. Recently, Shohat has been examining "the question of the Arab-Jew" in conjunction with "the question of Judeo-Arabic."